RELIGION AND THE CONSTITUTION

ALSO BY KENT GREENAWALT

Religion and the Constitution

VOLUME 2:
ESTABLISHMENT AND FAIRNESS

Kent Greenawalt

PRINCETON UNIVERSITY PRESS

PRINCETON AND OXFORD

Copyright © 2008 by Princeton University Press
Published by Princeton University Press,
41 William Street, Princeton, New Jersey 08540
In the United Kingdom: Princeton University Press, 6 Oxford Street,
Woodstock, Oxfordshire OX20 1TW

Library of Congress Cataloging-in-Publication Data

Greenawalt, Kent, 1936–
Religion and the constitution / Kent Greenawalt
p. m.
Includes bibliographical references and index.
Contents: Vol. 1. Free exercise and fairness. Vol. 2. Establishment and fairness.
ISBN-13: 978-0-691-12583-1
1. Freedom of religion—United States. 2. Church and state—United States. I. Title
KF4783.G74 2006
342.7308′52—dc22   2005049522

British Library Cataloging-in-Publication Data is available

This book has been composed in Sabon and Helvetica Neue

Printed on acid-free paper. ∞

press.princeton.edu

Printed in the United States of America

1   3   5   7   9   10   8   6   4   2

To Carla, Claire, Isabel, Sanja, and Sebastian
WITH JOY AND HOPE

CONTENTS

PREFACE

This volume, a companion to *Free Exercise and Fairness*, addresses problems involving the establishment of religion. As with free exercise, I express strong disquiet with some major directions in which the Supreme Court is moving, but resist suggestions for a radical overhaul of our understanding of the Establishment Clause.

Since over the last decade I have worked on the topics of free exercise and nonestablishment together, the preface to the first volume covers this one as well. Thus, that preface's naming of colleagues who gave criticisms and suggestions, of research assistants who performed so ably, and academic institutions where I made presentations cover material in both volumes. Here I add only the names of persons who helped and institutions I visited after the earlier volume was complete.

Among colleagues whose assistance was focused on this volume are Robert Audi, Carl Esbeck, Robert Ferguson, Jeffrey Gordon, Ira Lupu, Michael Perry, Stephen Shiffrin, Nelson Tebbe, Robert Tuttle, and John Witte, Jr. Providing exceptionally helpful research have been Matthew Dysart, Caleb Edwards, Kerry Ann Fitzgerald, Guy Gribov, Heather Koffman, and Madhu Pocha. I profited from comments on presentations at University of California, Berkeley, School of Law, Cardozo School of Law, St. John's School of Law, Northwestern University School of Law, and West Virginia University School of Law.

As someone who still relies on the ancient method of writing longhand, I have been very fortunate to have computer drafts of chapters done by Sally Wrigley (before her death), Susannah Silvey, and Katherine Bobbitt, who, as in respect to volume 1, also provided fine editing and additional research help.

I received perceptive and extensive criticisms of my original draft from Andrew Koppelman and Stephen Shiffrin, who reviewed the manuscript for Princeton University Press.

Ian Malcolm, my substantive editor, gave this manuscript the same thoughtful attention as its predecessor, and many points are clearer than they would have been without his questions and suggestions. Ellen Foos again saw the book through to publication in a manner that made the process smooth and comfortable, and Richard Isomaki's copyediting again saved me from various errors and infelicities. The index was prepared with care by Katherine Bobbitt and Marc DeGirolami.

The citations and index reveal many of the authors from whose work I have learned. But there are many others whose ideas have influenced me over time. When I started teaching, relatively few scholars wrote about the law of church and state. The change from then until now in terms both of the number of scholars and the quality of their articles and books has been striking, and all of us who think about problems of religious liberty are the beneficiaries.

During the months after volume 1, my personal life has been enriched by the births of three grandchildren, and the book's dedication is to them and their mothers.

Some of the material in this volume's chapters has previously appeared in "How Does 'Equal Liberty' Fare in Relation to Other Approaches to the Religion Clauses?" 85 *Texas Law Review* 1217 (2007); "Moral and Religious Convictions as Categories for Special Treatment: The Exemption Strategy," 48 *William and Mary Law Review* 1605 (2007); "Common Sense about Original and Subsequent Understandings of the Religion Clauses," 8 *University of Pennsylvania Journal of Constitutional Law* 179 (2006); "Natural Law and Public Reasons," 47 *Villanova Law Review* 531 (2002); "How Persuasive Is Natural Law Theory?" 75 *Notre Dame Law Review* 1647 (2001); "Diverse Perspectives in the Religion Clauses: An Examination of Justifications and Qualifying Beliefs," 74 *Notre Dame Law Review* 1433 (1999); "Religious Law and Civil Law: Using Secular Law to Assure Observance of Practices with Religious Significance," 71 *University of Southern California Law Review* 781 (1998); "Has Religion Any Place in the Politics and Law of Liberal Democracy?" 142 *Proceedings of the American Philosophical Society* 378 (1998); "Viewpoints from Olympus," 96 *Columbia Law Review* 697 (1996); "Quo Vadis: The Status and Prospects of 'Tests' under the Religion Clauses," 1995 *Supreme Court Review* 323.

RELIGION AND THE CONSTITUTION

CHAPTER 1

Introduction

Two fundamental principles of American liberal democracy are that citizens should be able to freely practice their religion and that government should not establish any religion. This volume, the second of two devoted to an examination of these principles, concentrates on nonestablishment. The wording of the First Amendment of the federal Constitution that embodies that principle is "Congress shall make no law respecting an establishment of religion." States have their own establishment clauses, and the federal provision now applies to states and localities.

An ideal of nonestablishment relates closely to a belief in free exercise, and the fairness of treating religious practices and organizations differently from nonreligious ones figures prominently in the coverage of the two principles. As we found it necessary to consider nonestablishment concerns in volume 1, *Free Exercise and Fairness*, many chapters in this volume will bring us back to the values of free exercise and the way those values should be realized in legal standards. Nonetheless, various problems about establishment are sufficiently distinctive to warrant this separate volume As in the previous volume, we will look at legislative choices and claims of political philosophy as well as constitutional constraints.

As I have explained in more detail in the first volume, my approach to the subject is grounded on the following three premises: (1) Neither free exercise nor nonestablishment is reducible to any single value; many values count. (2) Sound constitutional approaches to the religion clauses cannot be reduced to a single formula or set of formulas, although we can identify major considerations that should guide legislators and judges. (3) The most profitable way to develop sensible approaches is from the "bottom up"—addressing discrete issues in their rich complexity and investigating conflicting values over a range of issues.

After noting some major issues, this introductory chapter comments on the scope of the federal Establishment Clause, summarizes the undisputed core of impermissible establishments of religion, analyzes the basic values that underlie nonestablishment, and briefly summarizes what follows in succeeding chapters of the book.

Some Typical Issues

Establishment Clause issues have been among the most controversial decided by the Supreme Court in the last half century. It is not hard to see why.
The American people remain dominantly religious, with over 90 percent
affirming a belief in God, and more than half regularly active in group worship. Rulings under the Establishment Clause generate greater public concern than those under the Free Exercise Clause. Free exercise claims usually
arise when legislatures or administrators have declined to make accommodations to religious minorities; most citizens care little about the acceptance
or rejection of those claims. When people claim that the government is establishing religion, they typically object to measures that favor dominant religious groups. If courts uphold these claims, they are likely to vindicate some
members of discontented minorities at the price of upsetting members of the
dominant groups. As a consequence, decisions holding government practices to be invalid establishments tend to be particularly controversial. The
Supreme Court's decisions that devotional Bible reading and prayer in public schools are unconstitutional provide striking examples.[1] These have
proved among the Court's most unpopular rulings in the last fifty years—
comparable in the negative reactions they triggered only to its invalidation
of racial segregation[2] and its creation of a constitutional right to abortion.[3]
In many communities, the great majority of parents want school prayer,
and some districts have simply continued those practices despite the Court's
determinations.[4]

The display of religious symbols and messages on public property constitutes another significant establishment issue. Most people in a community
may welcome an expression of Christian sentiment, such as a crèche at
Christmas time, on public property. They will not favor decisions forbidding
such displays. And, when the Ninth Circuit Court of Appeals upheld an
atheist father's challenge to his daughter's public school reciting "under

---

[1] *Engel v. Vitale*, 370 U.S. 421 (1962); *Abington Township v. Shempp*, 374 U.S. 203 (1963). In the
last decade, the Court has extended these rulings to graduation ceremonies, *Lee v. Weisman*, 505 U.S.
577 (1992), and organized prayer at football games, *Santa Fe Independent School Dist. v. Doe*, 530
U.S. 290 (2000).

[2] *Brown v. Board of Education*, 347 U.S. 483 (1954).

[3] *Roe v. Wade*, 410 U.S. 113 (1973).

[4] See Marjorie Silver, "Rethinking Religion and Public School Education," 15 *Quinnipiac Law
Review* 213, 215 (1995). The Court's decisions about desegregation and abortion had widespread
support, as well as opposition, among individuals and organizations. Relatively few ordinary citizens
may have regarded the prayer and Bible-reading decisions as protecting vital rights, although some
leading religious organizations approved them.

God" in the Pledge of Allegiance,[5] politicians and citizens alike expressed outrage.[6]

Of pervasive concern in establishment litigation is the degree of assistance governments may offer to religious organizations. Until recently, financial support for religious groups that supply services that nonreligious organizations also provide, such as hospitals, adoption agencies, and soup kitchens, has produced little controversy. Religious groups, often setting up independent corporations, have participated with others in the receipt of government benefits, so long as they offer their services to all comers, do not discriminate in employment, and do not use public money for religious purposes. President George W. Bush has aimed to make greater use of faith-based organizations and has sought to allow the organizations that receive government aid greater latitude to implement their particular religious perspectives as they provide public services. Aspects of this program, most notably the proposal to allow religious groups to discriminate on religious grounds in employment, have provoked intense opposition.

The establishment issue most frequently litigated in the Supreme Court has been financial aid to parochial schools. For many years, the Supreme Court was extremely restrictive about such aid; over time it has become much more permissive. The question of whether government may offer vouchers for private education, available for religious schools among others, was the focal point of that general problem up to the year 2002. The Supreme Court's approval of vouchers that yield substantial monetary aid for the schools themselves[7] has shifted attention to the status of state constitutional provisions that are more restrictive of aid.

FREE EXERCISE AND NONESTABLISHMENT

As the volume on free exercise reveals, free exercise and establishment are in tension for a number of important issues, but in fundamental respects a

---

[5] *Newdow v. Elk Grove Unified School Dist.*, 292 F.3d 597 (2002), amended opinion by original panel after rehearing en banc denied, 328 F.3d 466 (2003). The Supreme Court declined to rule on the phrase "under God" because the father, a noncustodial parent, lacked standing. *Elk Grove Unified School Dist. v. Newdow*, 542 U.S. 1 (2004). Enough justices did rule on the merits to make the Court's acceptance of "under God" seem likely in the future.

[6] Reports of reactions to the initial court of appeals decision include Charles Lane, "U.S. Court Votes to Bar Pledge of Allegiance; Use of 'God' Called Unconstitutional," *Washington Post*, June 27, 2002, and Robert Salladay and Zachary Coile, "Judge in Pledge Case Puts Brakes on Ruling; 'Under God' Uproar Prompts 3-line Order for Delay Pending Full Appeals Court Hearing," *San Francisco Chronicle*, June 28, 2002.

[7] *Zelman v. Simmons-Harris*, 536 U.S. 639 (2002).

principle of nonestablishment supports free exercise. Historically, countries with establishments of particular churches typically engaged in outright denials of religious freedom, for example prohibiting worship not in accord with the established religion and imposing disabilities on dissenters. Even if a country avoids all such penalties for outsiders, any single established church, a church recognized as the official religion of the government, may be thought to compromise religious liberty to some degree.

We can identify the core of what it meant *not* to have an established church at the time of the Bill of Rights by reference to the institutions in England against which early Americans reacted. The Anglican Church was the state's official church, and the king was its head. Parliament had adopted the basic regulations, doctrinal statements, and liturgical forms of the Anglican Church, and participated in the designation of occupants for ecclesiastical positions. The government supported the church financially. Other forms of worship were forbidden or restricted. Bishops occupied seats in the House of Lords, as a number still do. Church courts decided various matters of civil significance. Many civil offices were open only to Anglicans.[8]

An *absence* of establishment entails that no particular religion enjoys official government status. Religious groups must set their doctrines, practices, and structures of internal governance for themselves, and they do not depend on government for financial support. The government cannot announce and defend particular religious doctrines, such as the Virgin Birth. It cannot make appointments to religious offices. The political rights of citizens do not depend on their religious affiliations, and religious leaders do not, by virtue of their positions, exercise civil authority.

Although active persecution in England of Protestant dissenters, Roman Catholics, and non-Christians had ended before our Revolutionary War, non-Anglicans continued to suffer various disabilities, including ineligibility for civil office. Citizens of our founding era associated established churches with serious disadvantages for those outside the fold, and leaders who strived for disestablishment regarded that as a crucial element of religious liberty.

But suppose a government forswears all such negative treatment for non-believers—neither coerces them to conform nor subjects them to disabilities. An official religion may still diminish liberty. Those who are outside the

---

[8] Judge Michael W. McConnell, in "Establishment and Disestablishment at the Founding, Part I: Establishment of Religion," 44 *William and Mary Law Review* 2105, 2131–81 (2003), has examined six historic elements of establishment in England and the colonies, including government control of the state church, mandatory attendance at that church, prohibition of other worship, financial support, use of the church for civil functions, and bars on political participation by nonmembers. See also Thomas J. Curry, *The First Freedoms: Church and State in America to the Passage of the First Amendment* (New York: Oxford University Press, 1986).

church may be perceived as not quite full members of the citizenry, in the manner of members of the approved faith. In two more specific ways, an establishment may be thought to trespass on the religious consciences of nonadherents. First, requiring someone to contribute to the upkeep of a religion he does not support may violate his religious conscience.[9] This view faces the powerful objection that modern taxpayers inevitably contribute to various government endeavors to which they may strongly object, but perhaps there is something special about being forced to support what one believes are misguided forms of worship.[10]

Another way in which an establishment may violate free exercise concerns forced instruction. Even if one can worship as one chooses, one's conscience may be violated if one is instructed regularly in the doctrines of the established church. If state schools teach these doctrines to children, that infringes on the religious consciences of dissenting children and their parents.

Although the institution of an established church mainly raises questions about outsiders' religious liberty, members of the official church also suffer a diminution of liberty, because political officials exercise control or influence over their religion.[11]

The point is often made that countries such as England and Sweden have established churches *and* religious liberty. No doubt, a country can possess a high degree of religious liberty along with an established church,[12] but the maximum degree of religious freedom may be realized when no church is established. Nonestablishment promotes free exercise by removing government from individuals' choices about which religion to practice and by allowing all religious groups to worship and order their affairs as they deem best. Someone might respond that this judgment reflects a liberal view, as

[9] This view is urged by James Madison in his "Memorial and Remonstrance Against Religious Assessments," in Philip B. Kurland and Ralph Lerner, eds., 5 *The Founders' Constitution* 82–84 (Chicago: University of Chicago Press, 1987). Indeed, Madison thought that one should not be compelled even to give money to one's own denomination. One might conclude that what Madison says about a small tax applies only to a tax instituted for the purpose of supporting religion, *not* to use of general tax funds, but Madison certainly did not express such a narrow view.

[10] One might think that personal convictions about blasphemy or the biblical injunction not to worship other gods are relevant. Members of one faith may think that members of another are worshiping other gods or committing blasphemy. Perhaps the state should not demand that anyone indirectly support a religion he or she abhors.

[11] Anthony Trollope's 1857 novel *Barchester Towers* (London: Penguin Classics, 1987) begins with the death of a bishop whose son, the archdeacon, hopes to succeed him. The son's prospects were excellent under an outgoing government but dismal under a new government, and as his father lay close to death, the son "at last dared ask himself whether he really longed for his father's death." Id. at 3.

[12] These modern examples may be somewhat misleading, because the countries have become so pervasively secular. *Religious liberty* may flourish better when an established church loses its hold on most citizens than when it remains a vital force in a society's life.

opposed both to a conviction that governments have a responsibility to follow and promote religious truth and to a communitarian understanding that religious exercise in a particular faith warrants support as part of a national culture, a perspective one finds in some Eastern European countries. My answer is that the liberal view of free exercise is dominant in American law and culture *and* that on grounds of political philosophy, it is preferable to the idea that government should carry forward the true religion and to the sense that a national faith warrants special state privilege.

What promotes religious liberty becomes more complex and debatable when governments consider providing broad financial support to religious organizations that offer valuable secular services. Nonestablishment may be best achieved if the government declines to provide such support, but if those organizations are denied aid, that may impair the religious exercise of those who run the organizations and use their services. And if the government offers comparable services itself or finances nonreligious private organizations to do so, denying aid to religious organizations may seem acutely unfair.

We have seen in our examination of various free exercise issues that government grants of special accommodations to religious claimants may seem to establish religion over nonreligion or to establish favored religions over those who do not benefit. These concerns about establishment dominate consideration of what are constitutionally permissible and wise forms of accommodation.

In its undisputed core, nonestablishment definitely promotes the free exercise of religion, but potential conflicts with aspects of free exercise exist at the outer edges of nonestablishment. Perhaps the most crucial aspect of establishment analysis is deciding when more robust versions of nonestablishment should give way to claims of free exercise enshrined in the Constitution or embodied in legislation.

Nonestablishment Values

We can summarize the interrelated values lying behind nonestablishment of religion as the protection of religious conscience, the promotion of autonomy, the withdrawal of civil government from an area in which it is markedly incompetent, the removal of one source of corruption of religion and deflection from religious missions, the removal of one source of corruption of government, the prevention of unhealthy mingling of government and religion, the avoidance of political conflict along religious lines that could threaten social stability, and the promotion of a sense of equal dignity among citizens. I shall comment on each of these in turn, and then address directly five competing approaches to nonestablishment and equal treatment. Three initial cautions may be helpful. First, because nonestablishment of religion helps to sustain free exercise, and the first volume explores values underlying the Free Exercise Clause, my treatment of those values is briefer here than is my discussion of values that more distinctly concern nonestablishment. This is not a mark of comparative importance.

Second, from the founders' era up to the present, people have disagreed about which of these values are of greatest significance and, indeed, about whether some of the values I list should count at all for judges deciding establishment cases. Not surprisingly, when members of the Supreme Court stake out different positions on this score, the justices can have different convictions about how individual controversies should be resolved. We shall see confirmation of this truth many times over in the chapters that follow.

Third, the disagreement about which values to emphasize can take the form of differential assessments of what the adopters of the First Amendment (or people at that time) believed, or of varying distillations of what judicial decisions under the Establishment Clause up to the present suggest, or of competing normative judgments of what should count in our modern liberal democracy. These three perspectives may be mixed in judicial opinions, and one often has the sense that a justice's own normative appraisal is flying under the flag of a claim about original intent or about the combined force of precedents. When an outsider—a scholar, a lawyer, or an ordinary citizen—seeks to evaluate the work of the Supreme Court, her judgment will strongly reflect her sense of the comparative importance of underlying values. Although I do not believe one can reasonably offer a neat hierarchical ordering of these values (whether in general or for particular subjects), my appraisals throughout the book evidence my own sense of how they bear on a wide range of issues. I encourage the reader to look at the problems we shall address with a thoughtful attention to these underlying values.

Protection of Religious Conscience

Nonestablishment protects religious conscience. This is illustrated by the historical establishments of individual churches with which the Framers of the Bill of Rights were familiar. If a person is required to worship in a particular fashion, or may not worship at all in the way that she chooses, or may not worship in public in the way that she chooses, she does not enjoy freedom of religious conscience. The denial is real, though less severe, if she may worship as her convictions tell her, but suffers penalties or denials of opportunities (such as eligibility for public office) as a consequence.

We should not conceive potential restrictions or disabilities as attaching only to corporate worship. A country with an established religion might allow adherents of other faiths to worship freely but not to proselytize for converts. For persons whose religious convictions tell them they should preach "the good word" (this includes many Christians), a prohibition on proselytizing is a restriction on religious conscience. The effect on potential recipients is a bit harder to categorize. If one actively seeks to learn from adherents of various religions, a ban on proselytizing by others serves to restrict one's religious conscience. That characterization does not seem apt for the passive listener who has no thought about an alien religion until approached by missionaries. But we can say that his *autonomy* is not fully recognized if others cannot communicate their religious ideas to him. The issue of restrictions on proselytizing is a serious one within many countries, including some from Eastern Europe who wish to safeguard their traditional Orthodox Christian religions from the active missionary efforts of groups like the Church of Jesus Christ of Latter-day Saints (Mormons) and Jehovah's Witnesses.

For most people, forced exposure to another religion would violate their religious conscience. If I am allowed to worship as I please, but *must* sit through a Roman Catholic worship service twice a week, I do not enjoy full freedom of conscience. This aspect of freedom of religious conscience is plainly implicated, if students in state schools are required or pressured into participating in rituals of an established religion.

If a person is compelled by the state to contribute financially to a religion in which she does not believe, or even to a religion in which she does believe, that infringes on her religious conscience, at least if she feels that her own convictions should dictate what religion she supports and how she does so. People may or may not feel differently if what they "contribute" is general taxes, with the government allocating some general revenues to religious organizations. And whatever some people may feel, it is arguable, as the discussion in the previous section indicates, whether they have a *reasonable* claim of conscience if the money given to religious groups is for appropriate public purposes.

Finally, if one thinks that religion is essentially not the business of civil government, one who is a member of an established church over which the government has some control may regard that control as violating his religious conscience.

Promotion of Autonomy

In categorizing autonomy separately from religious conscience, I do not mean to suggest that a sharp line separates the two; indeed, freedom of conscience is one aspect of autonomy. But I conceive autonomy as involving unfettered freedom to choose among various options, whether or not an absence of freedom restricts one's exercise of his convictions. In this sense, even if every citizen is free to practice religion as she chooses, including the freedom to practice no religion, full autonomy of choice is limited if the government "stacks the deck" in favor of one religion or all religions. It can do this by formal recognition of a religion as "the religion" of the society (the Church of England), by other signs of favor, or by financial support. In this light, autonomy of choice is most fully realized if no religion is favored over others and if religious groups are treated similarly to relevantly situated nonreligious groups. (A qualification to this principle of similar treatment that becomes highly relevant in later chapters concerns the possibility that some religious groups operating social welfare programs, such as drug rehabilitation centers, may themselves threaten the autonomy of nonbelievers who participate.)

In thinking about autonomy and government endeavors, we need to recognize that the government promotes all sorts of points of view over others. When I was growing up, I was left in little doubt that Communism was highly disfavored, a conclusion supported by statutes and many other official government actions. In one sense, I was "free" to find Marxist Communism a sound political philosophy, but I would have needed to be a hardy resister of social pressure to do so. One can certainly say similar things now about explicitly racist and sexist beliefs. If we do not object to the government "tipping the scales" in favor of some political and moral views in favor of others, why should we be concerned with whatever modest interference with full autonomy might be generated by its favoring of some or all religions? Unless one thinks that the government should refrain from promoting political and moral views and ideas of the good life (by such measures as campaigns against drug use and smoking cigarettes), one needs to see religion as special in some way. A typical stance is that when a person's sense of her relationship to God (or gods) or to ultimate reality is concerned, the government should particularly refrain from attempted influence. This stance is based both on the essential nature of the questions religions address and on the government's incompetence to deal with them.

The Government's Incompetence as to Religion

People elected to government in modern liberal democracies have no special competence in respect to religion. Indeed, their needs to focus on the exigencies of modern life and to compromise their ideals in the give-and-take of politics may render them particularly unsuited to pursue deep questions of religious understanding. Add to this that they would be under a constant temptation to favor those religions that support their political programs, or are likely to aid their reelection, or both. Centuries ago, these evident disabilities may have been thought offset by the perceived need for a government to promote a coherent religious position in order for a society not to fragment. By the time of our Constitution, this perception had been largely dispelled. In modern times, we recognize that societies (at least most societies) can well survive with a wide range of religious diversity. No need for social order serves as a counter to the incapacities of government with respect to religion.

Avoidance of a Source of Corruption of Religion and Deflection from Religious Mission

If one religion is established by the government, there is a constant danger that it will be turned to serve the political purposes of the government. Two more subtle risks can go with financial support. If a particular religion is heavily subsidized by public funds, its priests or ministers may become self-satisfied and relatively passive, not needing to win a following among individual citizens. This was a danger remarked on by Adam Smith,[13] and it possibly may help to explain a relative lack of vitality among established churches in Western Europe. Another risk goes along with modern public support of church-related schools and welfare programs. As the degree of public financing increases, so also may the perception that services should be provided in a way that conforms with public objectives. If a religious organization becomes heavily dependent on state funds, it may find it nearly impossible to forgo that support, even when the conditions that are attached to funding begin to interfere with its own sense of practices that are called for by its religious mission.

---

[13] See Adam Smith, *Wealth of Nations*, bk. 5, chap. 1, pt. 3, art. 3, "Of the Expense of the Institutions For The Instruction of People of all Ages," William Playfair, ed. (London: W. Pickering, 1995).

Avoidance of a Source of Government Corruption

If an established church is, or a group of favored religions are, very powerful, political leaders may cater to the wishes of religious leaders. Of course, if one believes that a government ideally should be the servant of higher religious purposes, this would present no problem, as long as the religious leaders had both the right religious view and decent political judgment. But a general assumption about civil governments in modern diverse societies is that political rule should be basically independent of particular religious objectives. From that point of view, established religion can be a threat to sound government.

Avoidance of Unhealthy Intermingling

Nonestablishment helps religion and government to remain relatively independent. Of course, in a modern society a host of interconnections are unavoidable; but if public officials become heavily involved in the review and supervision of religious endeavors or if religious leaders end up making governmental decisions, the risks of heavy-handed interference within one domain by the other are substantial.

Avoidance of Religious Conflict That Could Threaten Social Stability

It was long thought that a critical element of political stability was the domination of one religion in a society. After the Protestant Reformation, the first measure of religious freedom was that individual rulers could select the religion for their territories, not that ordinary citizens within a territory could worship as they chose. By the American Revolution, a very different understanding had developed, namely that political orders could function very well with a diversity of religious opinions. From this perspective, certainly ours today, the avoidance of conflict along religious lines is an important objective. Inevitably, some tensions will exist between adherents of different religions who believe each other to be fundamentally misguided about ultimate truth. But the tensions are bound to increase if those adherents see themselves in a struggle for state support—financial and other—and for the levers of political power. It is difficult to say how an objective so general and vague as political stability should figure in evaluation of any proposed program, but it lies in the background as one important value underlying the ideal of nonestablishment.

Promotion of a Sense of Equal Dignity among Citizens

In addition to the concerns about autonomy and potential conflict, it is undesirable for some citizens to feel they are specially "in" because they adhere to a religion or religions that the government favors. Members of a minority (at least adults) may be firm enough in their religious convictions, or their disbelief in any positive religion, not to have a government endorsement of a dominant faith threaten their autonomy of choice, and the minority may be too small to threaten political stability; yet if the members feel like "outsiders," not fully accepted into the society, that in itself is undesirable. No one likes to feel excluded. And however people may feel, governments should not convey messages of exclusion. Except perhaps in the case of criminal punishment, the government should not aim to make citizens feel excluded, and even when its actions are not designed to exclude, if they generate feelings of exclusion without a sufficient justification, they may be seen as infringing a basic right to equal dignity.[14]

Nonestablishment and Equality

As with free exercise, people may adopt different perspectives about nonestablishment and principles of equal treatment. One position is that in our country, with its deep religious heritage, the government may favor religion in various ways, so long as it refrains from actually establishing a church (and treats religions equally). According to a second position, the basic values of disestablishment, values for religious institutions as well as government, call on the state to accord religion less than equal treatment in many matters. The first and second positions may be combined if one thinks that religion should be favored in some respects, disfavored in others. These positions make little direct reference to equality. A third position is that the basic standard for religion and nonreligion is equality—religious ideas should be treated just like any other set of ideas and no distinctions should be drawn between religious and other groups. A fourth approach is more flexible; according to it, the overall aspiration should be to some sort of equality between religious and other groups, but this may involve favoring or disfavoring religion specially in respect to various subjects. The third and fourth positions both accept equality between religion and nonreligion as a guide, but they implement the focus on equality in quite different ways. A final,

[14] I mean here to distinguish justified measures, such as fighting a necessary war or desegregating schools, that might predictably make some people (pacifists or racists) feel like outsiders.

fifth, position is that both independent principles of disestablishment *and* equality have constitutional significance; courts must sometimes decide which of these to give priority. Strongly believing that establishment law cannot be reduced to any single value, I think the fifth approach is most apt. As a similar view informed discussions in the free exercise volume, that view underpins the exploration of particular problems in the chapters that follow.

Principles of equality figure more directly and uncontroversially in the assumption that the religion clauses forbid discrimination *among* religions;[15] when the government prefers some religions over others, that establishes the favored religions and inhibits the free exercise of the disfavored ones. As chapter 3 of the first volume retells, when Minnesota adopted guidelines that exempted most religious groups from ordinary reporting standards for charitable organizations, but did not include groups such as the Unification Church, which raised more than half their money from outsiders, the Supreme Court concluded that the state could sustain the distinction among groups only upon showing that it was needed to satisfy a compelling interest.[16] Applying that test as it would in an equal protection case, the Court, with only one dissenter, declared the law to be an invalid establishment.[17]

The principle of equal treatment among religions is now widely accepted. The more controversial principle that the government should not prefer religion over nonreligion will occupy us in many of the chapters that follow.

DOES ESTABLISHMENT CLAUSE DOCTRINE REST ON A FUNDAMENTAL MISCONCEPTION?

In legal circles, one frequently hears the assertion that the development of Establishment Clause principles against the states rests on a fundamental misconception. Here is a succinct account of the most popular version of that claim.

---

[15] *Larson v. Valente*, 456 U.S. 228 (1982). Some have argued that the original idea of nonestablishment allowed approval or support of Christianity, in general, against other religious persuasions, a position expressed by Joseph Story in his famous nineteenth-century treatise. See, e.g., *Wallace v. Jaffree*, 472 U.S. 38, 104 (1985) (Rehnquist, J., dissenting). A favored position for Christianity is now indefensible in our country of increasing religious diversity, with modern immigration laws that virtually assure (by *not* now engaging in heavy favoritism of European immigrants) that this diversity will continue to grow.

[16] *Larson v. Valente*, 456 U.S. 228 (1982).

[17] The Supreme Court reached a similar conclusion on free exercise grounds when the City of Hialeah directed ordinances against the practice of animal sacrifice by one religious group. *Church of the Lukumi Babalu Aye, Inc. v. City of Hialeah*, 508 U.S. 520 (1993).

Although no state had an established church in the full sense when our Constitution was adopted, a number afforded supports to various religions. The original U.S. Constitution said nothing about established religion.[18] In providing that Congress shall "make no law respecting an establishment of religion," the First Amendment guaranteed that issues of establishment were left to states. Congress could no more terminate a state establishment than it could establish a national religion. The Supreme Court had no basis to convert this guarantee of state power into a restriction on states.

This argument rests on at least two mistakes, explored more fully in the next chapter. Even if the original language was partly a guarantee of federalism, it was not only such a guarantee. The federal government had from the beginning certain limited domains of exclusive authority, including its own internal operations, any federal military forces, federal embassies and consulates abroad, the District of Columbia (recognized in the Constitution though not yet established), and federal territories, such as the Northwest Territory. Congress could not create a full-blown established church for these domains.[19]

A second flaw in the argument that the Establishment Cause cannot limit the states is its disregard of the period between the adoption of the Bill of Rights and the Civil War. By the Civil War, all states had abandoned their established churches, and many had incorporated antiestablishment language in their own state constitutions.[20] The post–Civil War Fourteenth Amendment was designed partly to grant citizens a protection of fundamental rights against state infringements, a protection citizens previously enjoyed only against the federal government. The Supreme Court has held that the protected rights included virtually all of the rights conferred by the Bill of Rights.[21] Given the broad acceptance of the nonestablishment principle for all American governments in 1866 and the close connection between free exercise and nonestablishment, Fourteenth Amendment language protecting liberty and privileges can reasonably be thought to include the Establishment Clause.

---

[18] However, it did (and does) provide that there can be no religious test for federal offices and that federal and state officeholders can affirm rather than swear an oath of office.

[19] One might believe that Congress could have taken some actions concerning religion in federal territories that it could not take for the whole country, but, despite some uncertainty about whether the Constitution applied to the territories, Congress probably could not have created an official church within them.

[20] At present, virtually all state constitutions contain antiestablishment language, although the wording typically varies from that of the federal Constitution.

[21] Whether the adopters of the Fourteenth Amendment really meant to "incorporate" large chunks of the Bill of Rights is debated.

Thus, despite arguments to the contrary, a powerful case exists for applying the Establishment Clause to state and local governments. But even those who reject that application must see that nonestablishment principles are rooted in state constitutions. Because state judges may interpret state documents to have more or less scope than the Supreme Court gives the federal Constitution, the rule that the federal establishment guarantee applies to the states does make some practical difference, but the issue is *not* whether states should have, or are permitted to have, strong forms of religious establishments.

In the chapters that follow, I take as a given that no state should have an established religion, and I also assume, somewhat more controversially, that limits drawn from the federal Constitution should apply in the same manner to federal and state governments.

THE STRUCTURE OF THIS VOLUME

The remainder of this book is roughly organized according to subtopics. Chapters 2 through 4 constitute an extended introduction to later chapters dealing with discrete subject matters. Chapter 2 describes the history leading up to the Establishment Clause, and analyzes what was its originally understood content. The chapter also contains a much briefer account defending the view that the Fourteenth Amendment has properly been employed as a vehicle for making the restrictions of the clause applicable against the states. Chapter 3 traces the development of Supreme Court doctrine regarding the Establishment Clause, indicating the important respects in which restrictions discerned by the Supreme Court after World War II have been relaxed in recent years. Chapter 4 sets out four basic principles of nonestablishment as that has been conceived in the United States. Governments cannot aid particular religions as such or promulgate particular religious doctrines. Thus, a state may nor single out Presbyterian churches for financial aid: it may not declare that the true meaning of Christian communion is transubstantiation. Governments also may not aid religion in general as such or support religious ideas that unite a high percentage of religious believers. These principles are much more controversial, and, as we shall see, various practices are hard to square with their rigorous application. These principles are also much more insecure than those concerning aid to particular religions. They are not accepted by a number of Supreme Court justices, as well as many scholars; and one who engages in prediction must acknowledge that their survival into even the near future depends significantly on who is appointed to the Supreme Court.

Chapters 5 through 12 all, with one exception, concentrate on various expressions of ideas that are indisputably expressions by the government or may be attributed to the government. Chapter 5 focuses on religious words and symbols in public places, including crèches as parts of Christmas displays and copies of the Ten Commandments posted in government buildings or on public monuments. Chapter 6 deals with the delicate problem of what I call "mild endorsements," practices, such as "under God" in the Pledge of Allegiance that appear to enlist the government in support of religious ideas, but may be defended as not doing so at all or as not doing so in a manner sufficiently coercive to make it unconstitutional. The following three chapters are about religion in public schools: devotions, such as prayer and Bible reading; teaching about religion as contrasted to teaching the truth or falsity of religious ideas; and teaching of content that rests on religious premises, as exemplified by the issue of whether creationism or intelligent design may be taught alongside evolution. Chapter 11 treats the principle that when a government makes its facilities generally available for private groups, as when a public school permits private, voluntary clubs to use its classrooms, it cannot, given applicable principles of free speech, treat religious groups less favorably than others. Chapter 12 addresses the special problems of chaplains in the armed forces and within prisons, asking whether the religious needs of service personnel and prisoners can justify forms of support that would otherwise violate the Establishment Clause.

Chapter 10 is a kind of intermezzo. It analyzes various tests and standards Supreme Court justices have used to discern whether the Establishment Clause has been violated. I have postponed this analysis until the reader has enough of a sense of how the tests and standards are employed in actual cases to grasp the nuances that this chapter considers.

Chapters 13 and 14 concern intertwined authority of religious groups and government: first, a state's assigning what are essentially governmental decisions to religious bodies, and, second, the state's supporting religious restrictions, as with kosher enforcement laws, and the state's attempting to influence actions with religious significance, such as the religious divorce Orthodox Jewish husbands may or may not grant to their wives.

Chapters 15 to 17 are primarily about exemptions that may go to religious individuals or groups, treating them differently (and more favorably in a sense) than others who are subject to the law. This topic in many particular manifestations is a dominant concern of volume 1, on free exercise. Chapter 15 deals with the special issue of taxation, asking when various forms of tax breaks for religious organizations and individuals are permissible under the Establishment Clause, and whether the permissibility of such exemptions depends on their extension to nonreligious organizations and concerns. Chapter 16 undertakes a general inquiry about religious exemptions. Are they warranted, are they (sometimes) a matter of justice, are they (sometimes) properly seen as constitutional rights, should they, or must they, be extended beyond religious claims? The following chapter seeks to find standards to determine when exemptions that might otherwise be an acceptable accommodation to the free exercise of religion are formulated in such a way that they violate the Establishment Clause.

Chapters 18 and 19 tackle a problem of great practical importance and controversy: the appropriateness of giving government financial assistance to religious groups that undertake programs that confer substantial nonreligious benefits, operating, for example, hospitals, adoption agencies, drug treatment programs, and schools. As we shall see, the existence of such aid—even substantial aid—to many kinds of programs is widely accepted, although sharp dispute arises over the exact conditions that should attach to it. The primary area of conflict in our country's history has been over aid to schools—fueled by concern over religious indoctrination and a sense that public schools play a crucial unifying function in this society. Chapter 19 is devoted exclusively to that topic.

The last five chapters are largely theoretical, addressing religion and government in legal theory and in political theory. Chapter 20 answers skeptics who claim that we lack viable principles for adjudication under the religion clauses, and chapter 21 considers three specific proposals for interpretation of the clauses. Each of these proposals aspires to be more straightforward than the Court's own serpentine course, and at least two of the three suggest radical redirection. Chapter 22 inquires about the underlying premises one might embrace that would support the basic principles of the religion clauses, and considers whether the various premises people might accept will much affect the content of the principles as they see them. The last two chapters deal more broadly with the problem of religious convictions that underpin political judgments and argument. I there provide a summary explanation and defense of my own intermediate position about whether the politics of our liberal democracy should be grounded on "public reasons," and I explore the possible implications for constitutional law of legislators relying on religious convictions when they decide what laws to enact.

CHAPTER 2

History

This chapter reviews the history of the Establishment Clause through its possible application to the states via the Fourteenth Amendment. Volume 1 has discussed the historical background of both that clause and its companion, the Free Exercise Clause; here, we will concentrate on legal developments and political writings that particularly concern nonestablishment, and that tie nonestablishment to free exercise. The next chapter provides a sequential account of Supreme Court establishment doctrine, clarifying how later cases build on earlier cases, and designed to assist understanding of the chapters on specific topics that follow.

A Historical Understanding of "Congress Shall Make No Law Respecting an Establishment of Religion"

In Western civilization through most of the eighteenth century, governments with official religions restricted the free exercise of nonmembers. For many centuries, the Roman Catholic Church was the overarching religious institution; local governments participated in it and supported its practice. Emperors, kings, and princes chose (or influenced the choice of) local bishops.[1] Nonbelievers lacked the rights of worship and civil privileges of Roman Catholics and might be persecuted as heretics.

With the Protestant Reformation and the rise of the nation-state, the tie between ruling governments and religious orthodoxy tightened, whether the territories remained Catholic or became Protestant. The Peace of Augsburg in 1555 settled that princes or city councils (in roughly 350 distinct polities) could choose the religion for their territory. According to John Witte, civil law established "the appropriate forms of religious doctrine, liturgy, charity, and education—with religious dissenters granted the right to worship privately in their homes or to emigrate peaceably."[2]

---

[1] Within the world of Roman Catholicism, emperors and kings often struggled with popes for authority, and the balance of power shifted between them. See, e.g., Frank Lambert, *The Founding Fathers and the Place of Religion in America* 26–29 (Princeton: Princeton University Press, 2003).

[2] John Witte, *Religion and the American Constitutional Experiment* 10–11 (2d ed., Boulder, Colo., Westview Press, 2005).

When Henry VIII established the Anglican Church in England, he became the head of the church, bishops sat in the House of Lords, and Parliament formally prescribed details in the Book of Common Prayer. Only members of the Church of England were citizens, and Catholics and Protestant dissenters alike were persecuted. During the rule of Puritans, after Charles I was deposed, toleration was granted for all Protestants but not for Catholics and Jews. Restoration of royal rule brought back repression of dissenting Protestants. After James II was displaced in favor of William and Mary, however, the Toleration Act of 1689 guaranteed freedom of association to all Protestants.[3] Not until the early nineteenth century were laws against the practice of Catholicism and Judaism actually repealed.

England's American colonies differed from each other in respect to established religion. A number had an Anglican establishment. In Massachusetts, Puritans established a form of Calvinism. As in Europe, these establishments went hand in hand with restraints on free exercise.

The connection between establishment and restrictions on free exercise raises historical questions that correspond to theoretical questions we looked at in the introduction. The two crucial questions of normative political theory are (1) whether all forms of establishment, or only some, are at odds with free exercise, and (2) whether establishments that do not impinge much on free exercise do any harm. These questions have modern bite because most Western liberal democracies recognize rights of free exercise[4] but retain established churches.[5] International human rights documents guaranteeing free exercise are silent about establishment, as are the relatively new constitution of South Africa and the 1982 Charter of Rights and Freedoms in Canada.[6] Although a very substantial degree of free exercise is compatible with the existence of an established religion, one reason not to have an established religion is that more complete freedom of choice about religion is then possi-

---

[3] Although certain legal restrictions on dissenters remained, these were increasingly unenforced.

[4] However, many Western European governments have proved less open to fringe religions, such as Scientology, than has the United States. See Paul Horwitz, "Scientology in Court: A Comparative Analysis and Some Thoughts on Selected Issues in Law and Religion," 47 *DePaul Law Review* 85 (1997).

[5] The Anglican Church remains the Church of England; the Church of Scotland is Presbyterian; and the Church of Sweden is Lutheran. Italy and Spain have concordats with the Vatican that confer a special status on the Roman Catholic Church.

[6] Convention for the Protection of Human Rights and Fundamental Freedoms, Article 9, 213 U.N.T.S. 222 (1953); International Covenant on Civil and Political Rights, Article 18, 21 U.N. GAOR Supp. (No. 51) at 171; Donald L. Beschle, "Does the Establishment Clause Matter? Non-establishment Principles in the United States and Canada," 4 *University of Pennsylvania Journal of Constitutional Law* 451 (2002); David M. Brown, "Freedom from or Freedom for? Religion as a Case Study in Defining the Content of Charter Rights," 33 *University of British Columbia Law Review* 551 (2000).

ble. Other reasons mentioned in the first chapter concern ideals of demo-cratic government.[7]

The related historical inquiries concern beliefs about establishment held at the time of the Bill of Rights and the Fourteenth Amendment. Did people suppose that *any* establishment compromised religious freedom, or did they believe that some forms of establishment could coexist with robust free exer-cise? And what laws and practices would they have regarded as establishing one or more religions? Two sources of evidence are influential theoretical writings and the content of state laws during the relevant periods.

John Locke's writings were especially influential among American colo-nists; and his first Letter Concerning Toleration, published in 1689, the year after William and Mary were brought to the throne in England, is a classic in the literature on religious freedom.[8] Locke was unambiguously opposed to coercive aspects of establishment. Many of his claims seem incompatible with any form of religious establishment, but he drew back from concluding that all establishments are misconceived.[9]

Locke's three-pronged argument against coercion in respect to religion was that toleration is "agreeable to the Gospel of Jesus Christ";[10] that gov-ernment's business is limited to "procuring, preserving, and advancing . . . civil interests,"[11] the magistrate's jurisdiction not extending to "the salvation of souls";[12] and that, since the power of the government consists in outward force, it cannot compel belief.[13] Locke goes on to describe a church as a free and voluntary society.[14]

---

[7] It does not follow, of course, that countries that have had established religions for centuries should disestablish them straightaway.

[8] Reproduced in John Locke, *A Letter Concerning Toleration, in Focus*, John Horton and Susan Mendus, eds. (New York: Routledge, 1991).

[9] If one takes the text at face value, he was not opposed to some forms of establishment, but perhaps he regarded it as impolitic to take that position. See note 18, infra.

[10] Locke, note 8 supra, at 16. The "Prince of Peace . . . sent out his soldiers" to gather people into his church, not with instruments of force, "but prepared with the Gospel of peace, and with the exemplary holiness of their conversation." Id.

[11] By "civil interests" Locke means "life, liberty, health, and indolence of body; and the possession of outward things, such as money, land, houses, furniture, and the like." Id. at 17. We saw in volume 1 that Locke thought that the government need not exempt people with religious reasons for per-forming acts (such as the killing of cattle) if the government adopts a general prohibition of those acts for secular reasons.

[12] Id. at 18.

[13] Id. It is "the nature of the understanding, that it cannot be compelled to the belief of any thing by outward force"; and "true and saving religion consists in the inward persuasion of the mind."

[14] Id. at 20. Passages in Locke's Letter suggest exceptions from full religious liberty for atheists, who cannot be trusted to keep their promises, and Roman Catholics, who have allegiance to a foreign power. (England's main enemy at the time was Spain, and various Catholic countries were assisting

Locke's notion of churches as voluntary societies and his account of the proper jurisdiction of governments[15] seem to suggest that governments have no proper concern with religion, except to treat churches as they treat other voluntary societies. But Locke does not say that: "Rather, it may indeed be alleged that the magistrate may make use of arguments, and thereby draw the heterodox into the way of truth, and procure their salvation. I grant it; but this is common to him with other men. . . . Magistracy does not oblige him to put off either humanity or Christianity. But it is one thing to persuade, another to command; one thing to press with arguments, another with penalties."[16]

One might take this language as treating the magistrate or members of the magistracy as persons who in their individual capacities may express religious views in public, as well as in private company, as American presidents might talk about their religious convictions in published interviews, making clear in doing so that they are not representing the government. This is not what Locke means. He is thinking of the magistrate as the government, and the idea of the king speaking publicly in his own person but *not* for the government would not have occurred to him. Locke's apparent willingness to countenance the highest officials expressing religious positions as representatives of the government lies in some tension with the limited role he ascribes to government.

Anything *like* the Anglican establishment raises yet more serious problems. The advantages that church enjoyed gave it a strong edge over its competitors, in holding the adherence of clerics and the patronage of ordinary folk, that went far beyond the relatively innocuous idea that the magistrate may express his views, as may all other people.

Locke's main interest concerns freedom for dissenters, but what of freedom for Anglicans? They suffered an impairment of religious exercise because the monarch was automatically the head of their church and Parliament adopted the order of worship. Voluntary societies choose their own leaders and forms of government. Members of the Anglican Church lacked that option.[17]

James II [James Stuart] to regain the English throne, so it was not wholly implausible to think of some Roman Catholics within England as constituting a disloyal fifth column.) But apart from these exceptions, Locke's notion of religious liberty is expansive.

[15] This account that fits with his social contract account in John Locke, *Two Treatises of Government*, Peter Laslett, ed. (Cambridge: Cambridge University Press, 1988).

[16] Id. at 18.

[17] It might be responded that anyone may drop out of the Anglican Church and join a more voluntary religious society, but this rejoinder disregards the power of a government that owns parish churches, helps pay for Anglican worship, and approves appointments of priests. A noncompliant

Locke does not discuss these aspects of establishment, but they are impossible to justify according to his most fundamental principles. Whatever his own views may have been,[18] Locke's Letter supplied powerful arguments for a degree of nonestablishment that exceeded anything for which he argued explicitly.[19]

John Witte has suggested that one can differentiate Puritan, Evangelical, Enlightenment, and Republican perspectives on religious liberty in colonial America.[20] Over time, he writes, these views largely coalesced around five overlapping principles: liberty of (religious) conscience, free exercise of religion, religious pluralism, religious equality, and separation of church and state. Some, but not all, of the founders also wanted disestablishment of religion. Separation and disestablishment were the domain of the Establishment Clause; together with the Free Exercise Clause, it guaranteed religious equality.[21]

In modern usage, separation of church and state has come to be identified with disestablishment *or* to include disestablishment and go *beyond* it to require a more absolute noninvolvement of government with religion.[22] But to many colonists, separation of church and state referred only to a separation of function between religious leaders and government officials and did not necessarily imply disestablishment of religion. In this sense, the Massa-

---

priest may lose his livelihood, and a parishioner who drops out will give up worship at his familiar parish church.

[18] Perhaps Locke, focusing on the right of dissenters, advanced arguments that went further than the government practices he wished to condemn. Perhaps he recognized the broader implications of the arguments, but refrained from drawing them explicitly because he did not wish to offend those Anglicans who were willing to move toward a position of tolerance for dissenters. Noah Feldman indicates that Locke helped draft the original colonial charter for the Carolinas, which included an established Church of England, but that provision is said to have been added by others. *Divided by God: America's Church-State Problem—and What We Should Do about It* 31–32, 259 n. 33 (New York: Farrar, Straus and Giroux, 2005).

[19] In his *Essay Concerning Human Understanding*, Peter H. Nidditch, ed. (New York: Oxford University Press, 1979), Locke emphasizes environmental influences on the formation of belief. This should have led him to be particularly troubled by the kind of edge all these advantages of establishment would confer.

[20] Witte, note 2 supra, at 22–35.

[21] Id. at 41–61. Although some combination of free exercise and nonestablishment was designed to assure equality among religions, not everyone assumed that all religions were included. In a famous passage, Justice Story wrote that the guarantees of the two federal clauses mainly concerned Christian religions, and that preferences for Christianity over other religions were perfectly acceptable. *Wallace v. Jaffree*, 472 U.S. 38, 104 (1985) (Rehnquist, J., dissenting); Joseph Story, *Commentaries on the Constitution of the United States* 700–701 (Durham, N.C.: Carolina Academic Press, 1987) (1833).

[22] In an influential book, Philip Hamburger, *Separation of Church and State* (Cambridge: Harvard University Press, 2002), suggests that modern notions of separation are far more stringent than ideas of disestablishment. I comment critically on aspects of his theories in Kent Greenawalt, "History as Ideology: Philip Hamburger's *Separation of Church and State*," 93 *California Law Review* 367 (2005).

chusetts Bay Colony had separation of church and state, although Puritan Calvinism was effectively the established religion.[23]

Those founders who called for disestablishment meant to end anything like traditional establishments of religion, with a single state religion being imposed or favored; some also endorsed a strong separation of church from government in order, in the words of Tunis Wortman, to protect "the purity and usefulness of both."[24] "The question that remained controversial," according to Witte, "was whether more gentle and generic forms of state support for religion could be countenanced."[25]

Two points stand out in importance when one looks at state practices and constitutions. Seven of the original states still provided significant aid to one or more religions.[26] Not until a Massachusetts act of 1833 did the last of these schemes of assistance fall. No state constitution in 1789 had a clause forbidding establishment. Since these constitutions did guarantee the free exercise of religion, at least to Christians or worshipers of God, one concludes that many people did not then believe that full disestablishment was essential to protect whatever religious exercise deserved protection.[27]

A central question of historical and constitutional interpretation is how to regard the experience of Virginia preceding James Madison's leading role in drafting the Bill of Rights.[28] A popular version of constitutional history, found in major Supreme Court opinions, is that the religion clauses repre-

---

[23] In the eighteenth century, Massachusetts law provided that towns would support the dominant religion. In theory, this created the possibility that Presbyterians or some other group might become the established religion within a town, but the law worked in practice to assure that the Congregational religion, which prevailed throughout the state, was established. See Thomas J. Curry, *The First Freedoms: Church and State in America to the Passage of the First Amendment* 108–9 (New York: Oxford University Press, 1986).

[24] Quoted by Witte, note 2 supra, at 54.

[25] Id. at 59–60.

[26] It is often said that these states retained establishments, and their laws *would* count as establishments under modern Supreme Court doctrine, but whether all these forms of assistance constituted establishments, as the term was then understood, is arguable. People then, as now, disagreed about what exactly amounted to an establishment of religion.

[27] Perhaps people did not fully perceive the link between free exercise and nonestablishment, in part, because they had yet to accept even a robust inclusive version of free exercise.

[28] When one thinks about constitutional history, complicated questions arise about relevance and weight. Is history to be thrown in as one partisan argument for positions otherwise reached? Or should those who work in the law take the historical inquiry seriously? If the latter, how much, comparatively, do the judgments of drafters, members of Congress, members of state legislatures, and ordinary citizens count about what constitutional amendments mean? How much do any of these judgments count in relation to other standards of interpretation, such as modern understandings of language and principles, and prior cases? These questions will arise in various forms throughout this volume, as they did in respect to free exercise, but we need not resolve them in order to review the Virginia approach to nonestablishment.

sented a federalization of a conception widespread in the states that linked free exercise and nonestablishment. Others have argued that the Establishment Clause was entirely, or principally, a recognition of state authority, and that, in any event, many founders did not share the views of Madison and Jefferson, the prominent sponsors of Virginia's approach.[29] Nonetheless, the Virginia events loom large in the understanding of disestablishment.

After the War for Independence had ended, the Virginia legislature considered a bill that would have replaced the earlier establishment of the Anglican religion with a property tax to pay Christian clergy and keep up churches, leaving it to individual taxpayers to decide which denominations would get their contributions.[30] In response to this proposal, James Madison circulated his famous "Memorial and Remonstrance."[31]

According to Madison, religion is both an unalienable right and a duty we owe to our Creator;[32] it is exempt from the authority of society at large and its legislature. We should "take alarm at the first experiment on our liberties" because "the same authority which can force a citizen to contribute three pence . . . for the support of any one establishment, may force him to conform to any other establishment."[33] The assessment bill denied "equal freedom to those whose minds have not yet yielded to the evidence which has convinced us" and unfairly granted exemptions to Quakers and Mennonites but not to others "who think a compulsive support of their religion unnecessary and unwarrantable."[34] The bill wrongly implied that the civil magistrate may competently either judge religious truth or use religion for civil policy. Experience shows that ecclesiastical establishments undermine the purity and efficacy of religion, and are not needed to support Christianity.[35]

In contrast to Locke, Madison explicitly contended that financial and other government support of religion is not consonant with a voluntarist view of free exercise. It has long been assumed that Madison was strongly opposed to any financial support for religious institutions. That conclusion has recently been challenged by some historians whose position Justice

[29] In a dissenting opinion Justice Rehnquist, before he became chief justice, contended that in working on the religion clauses, Madison was a realistic statesman, attempting to bridge differences of view by compromise, not writing his own views into the Constitution. *Wallace v. Jaffree*, note 21 supra, at 98–99.

[30] Curry, note 23 supra, at 140–42.

[31] Id. at 143.

[32] A duty that we can discharge "only by reason and conviction, not by force and violence." James Madison, "Memorial and Remonstrance Against Religious Assessments," in Philip B. Kurland and Ralph Lerner eds., 5 *The Founders' Constitution* 82 (Chicago: University of Chicago Press, 1987).

[33] Id.

[34] Id. at 82–83.

[35] Id. at 83.

Thomas has embraced.[36] Although it is true that Madison's focus was on aid to religion as such, not aid to a variety of groups that happens to include religious organizations, his language and his stringent later view of the Establishment Clause support the more sweeping prohibition on aid.[37]

Following the legislature's rejection of the assessment bill, Virginia's General Assembly adopted a statute for religious freedom that declared: "[T]o compel a man to furnish contributions for the propagation of opinions which he disbelieves, is sinful and tyrannical; . . . even forcing him to support this or that teacher of his own religious persuasion, is depriving him of the comfortable liberty" of contributing according to his own judgment.[38] Drafted by Jefferson, the statute corresponded with Madison's views.

For Madison and Jefferson, religion should be a subject of voluntary choice. The government was not competent in matters of religion, and mixtures of government and religion tended to corrupt both. Madison's "Memorial and Remonstrance" also strikes a theme dominant among Calvinists and Evangelicals, and heavily reflected in state constitutions; namely, that people have a preeminent duty to worship God as their consciences dictate, and they cannot surrender this duty to the outside authority of the state. Therefore, the state cannot compel religious beliefs and actions. According to Noah Feldman, the idea of liberty of conscience, including a right not to be compelled to support religious teachings with which one disagrees, was the dominant theme about religion and government in the Revolutionary era and underlay both religion clauses.[39] (It is somewhat ironic that many of those asserting this point of view were quite accepting of strong pressures *within* religious groups to keep members on the right path.)

---

[36] See *Rosenberger v. Rector and Visitors of the University of Virginia*, 515 U.S. 819, 855–58 (concurring opinion) (1995). In brief, Justice Thomas argued that Madison was concerned about financial aid to religion *as* religion, that he was not opposed to neutral assistance, given to religious and nonreligious groups for a valid secular reason, even if religious groups spend their money for religious purposes. For support by historians, see Robert L. Cord, *Separation of Church and State: Historical Fact and Current Fiction* 20–23 (New York: Lambeth Press, 1982); Rodney K. Smith, "Getting Off on the Wrong Foot and Back on Again: A Reexamination of the History of the Framing of the Religion Clauses of the First Amendment and a Critique of the *Reynolds* and *Everson* Decisions," 20 *Wake Forest Law Review* 569, 590–91 (1984).

[37] Justice Souter defended this more traditional understanding in response to Justice Thomas. 515 U.S. at 869–72 (dissenting opinion).

[38] Thomas Jefferson, Virginia Statute for Religious Freedom, in *The Virginia Statute for Religious Freedom: Its Evolution and Consequences in American History*, Merrill D. Peterson and Robert C. Vaughan, eds. xvii (Cambridge, Cambridge University Press, 1988). This act also provided that "no man shall be compelled to frequent or support any religious worship . . . nor enforced, restrained, molested, or burthened in his body or goods, nor otherwise suffer on account of his religious opinions . . . or suffer any diminution of civil capacities." Id. at xviii.

[39] See Feldman, note 18 supra, at 12, 20, 27–32, 42.

This Protestant Christian view about the need to protect religious conscience is undoubtedly a powerful justification for the Free Exercise Clause. It also supports nonestablishment, a connection that is especially compelling if government is incompetent as to religion and potential mutual corruption awaits religion and government if the two mix. However, a principle of nonestablishment based dominantly on freedom of religious conscience may be less absolute than if one also regards as important other grounds for keeping church and state apart.

The Establishment Clause and Federalism

The question of how freedom of religious conscience may relate to nonestablishment bears on whether the Establishment Clause should be understood as exclusively or mainly about federalism, or as reflecting nonestablishment as a principle. The clause reads, "Congress shall make no law respecting an establishment of religion." As the language of the First Amendment indicates, it (like the rest of the Bill of Rights other than the Tenth Amendment) restricted only the federal government, not the states. A shared starting point for analysis is that states were then left free to have established religion, if they chose. The federalism argument we reviewed in chapter 1 is that people were concerned that the original Constitution would lead to federal encroachments on state authority, and that the language, "no law respecting an establishment," protected existing state establishments from federal interference every bit as much as it forbade Congress from imposing a federal church on the states.[40]

This federalism argument may be sound as far as it goes, but it definitely does not go as far as some scholars have intimated. Akhil Amar has thus summed up what he calls the jurisdictional view (which he adopts): "The original establishment clause on a close reading is not antiestablishment but pro–states' rights; it is agnostic on the substantive issue of establishment versus nonestablishment and simply calls for the issue to be decided locally."[41] This position founders on the authority of Congress over exclusive

[40] In the debates over ratification of the original Constitution, it was sometimes said that the federal government had no authority over religion, but (whether the proponents of this view realized it or not) this was an oversimplification. Even apart from federal domains, discussed below, the federal government might have signed a treaty with a Roman Catholic wartime ally guaranteeing freedom of religious exercise for its citizens. Such a measure could have interfered with a state determination to establish Protestant Christianity in some form.

[41] Akhil Reed Amar, *The Bill of Rights* 34 (New Haven: Yale University Press, 1998). See also Steven D. Smith, *Foreordained Failure: The Quest for a Constitutional Principle of Religious Freedom* 17 (New York: Oxford University Press, 1995).

federal domains, domains in which the states had no power.[42] These domains included the organization of Congress and other parts of the federal government, the operation of embassies and diplomatic missions, the regulation of federal military forces, control of the District of Columbia (once that was created),[43] and control of the federal territories. In these domains, federal laws about religion would not have interfered with any state's decisions about how to treat religion within its own borders.[44]

If the Establishment Clause was *purely* jurisdictional, Congress could have created outright religious establishments within federal domains (at least establishments that were supported by enumerated powers and did not impair the free exercise of dissenters).[45] The textual argument for a purely jurisdictional reading of the Establishment Clause is weak. Nothing in the language indicates that it is irrelevant for federal domains. The bar on laws respecting an establishment of religion evidently precludes Congress's creating an established religion in those domains.

Examination of historical arguments does not alter this strong impression from the language. We may divide historical arguments into roughly three categories. The first concerns the background of the religion clauses—including ideas about individual rights, religion, and government at the time, relations between religion and government within the separate states, and the debate over the original Constitution leading up to the Bill of Rights. The

---

[42] I develop this argument in much greater detail in Kent Greenawalt, "Common Sense about Original and Subsequent Understandings of the Religion Clauses," 8 *University of Pennsylvania Journal of Constitutional Law* 479 (2006). One might think that Professor Amar, note 41 supra, simply failed to consider federal domains, but his comment that the Establishment Clause is "agnostic on the substantive issue of establishment versus nonestablishment" seems to suggest that, so long as it was exercising an enumerated power, such as regulating military forces, the federal government could establish religion within a federal domain. Steven Smith, note 41 supra, at 28–29, specifically raises the possibility that the enactors of the religion clauses may have thought either that Congress had power similar to states over religion in federal domains *or* that they failed to consider federal domains, and he suggests that early Congresses may not have regarded themselves as bound in respect to federal areas "by any adopted constitutional principle controlling the relationship between government and religion."

[43] Although the District of Columbia did not become the seat of the federal government until 1800, the original Constitution, art. 1, § 8 (17), already provides for such a District over which Congress shall "exercise exclusive legislation." Thus, when the Bill of Rights was adopted, the existence of the District was provided for in constitutional law.

[44] I do not assume the exact scope of federal domains is clear. For example, states might have claimed that federal military forces drawn from state militias still fell within an area of state concern.

[45] Given the language of the Free Exercise Clause, and its conjunction with the Free Speech and Free Press clauses, it is very hard to argue that Congress could have prohibited free exercise (or abridged freedom of speech and of the press) in federal domains.

A theory that is at odds with my view and with the jurisdictional view is that the religion clauses removed all authority of Congress to deal with the subject of religion. See Kurt T. Lash, "Power and the Subject of Religion," 59 *Ohio State Law Journal* 1069 (1998). I discuss that view in "Common Sense," note 42 supra, but do not do so here.

second kind of historical argument relies on the drafting and adoption of the religion clauses. The third kind concerns measures adopted by Congress at around the time of the Bill of Rights—the understanding being that Congress would not lightly have passed legislation that would conflict with a constitutional mandate—as well as views of prominent figures about what the clauses accomplished.

Historical arguments about the Establishment Clause have proved more controversial than those over the Free Exercise Clause. On the one hand, we find the claim in various Supreme Court opinions beginning with *Everson v. Board of Education*[46] that the founders strongly believed in disestablishment as an aspect of religious liberty. Noah Feldman's claim that a common belief that liberty of conscience includes a right not to be forced to contribute to religion supports that view.[47] Many defenders of what we would now consider to be establishments of religion urged that various nonpreferential systems of support were not true establishments.[48] Thus, only a limited number of people in 1789 were prepared to defend what they themselves characterized as establishments. That the First Amendment would forbid Congress from moving toward establishing a religion well fit contemporary views.

What of members of Congress and state legislatures who did understand their own states to have a kind of establishment of religion of which they approved? Even they would probably have wished that the federal government not have the power to establish a religion, given the risk that such a federal establishment would not be to their liking.[49] They *might* have supposed that states did not need protection for their own supports of religion, whether establishments or not, because they assumed that the original delegated powers of Congress did not reach that subject.

Opposed to a reading of the original Establishment Clause that rendered it purely *against* establishment, not providing state establishments protection from federal interference, are a number of historical arguments. The most general of these reverts to the very reason why the First Amendment was adopted. When state conventions considered ratification of the original Constitution, anti-Federalists complained that it failed to protect individual

---

[46] 330 U.S. 1 (1947).

[47] Noah Feldman, "The Intellectual Origins of the Establishment Clause," 77 *New York University Law Review* 346 (2002); Feldman, note 18 supra, at 48–49.

[48] Feldman, note 18 supra, at 41; Thomas J. Curry, note 23 supra, at 172–91 (1986).

[49] See Douglas Laycock, "Two Problems in the Original Understanding of the Establishment Clause: Religious Exemptions and the Claim That the Clause Was Really about Federalism," paper presented to Columbia Law School Legal Theory Workshop on December 12, 2005, the relevant portion of which has yet to be published.

rights against abridgements by the federal government.[50] New Hampshire's proposal that the Constitution be amended to provide, "Congress shall make no laws touching religion,"[51] well reflected this concern that the new government not involve itself with religion. What became the First Amendment was adopted largely to respond to the concern of the anti-Federalists about impingements on state authority.

At the time of the Bill of Rights, seven states retained what we now consider forms of establishments. Enough people criticized these arrangements as establishments so that members of Congress and legislators from these states might have hesitated to accept a provision that was purely *anti*establishment. We can best understand the clause as one that people with opposing views about establishment could have endorsed. A clause that forbade establishment of a national religion *and* interference with state establishments meets this criterion.

This understanding receives a degree of further support from the way the final language of the clause related to earlier proposals. Madison's original proposal included "nor shall any national religion be established,"[52] and at least six successive proposals conveyed a prohibition of Congress establishing religion or establishing *a* religion.[53] Only when a joint committee from the two houses met did the final phraseology of "no law respecting an establishment of Religion" emerge.[54] If the substitution of this language about "respecting," not found in any state constitution, was more than a stylistic change, it was probably designed to render the clause more neutral between establishment and antiestablishment.

Those arguments render plausible the notion that the Establishment Clause did actually provide some protection for state establishments (although the view that the clause was exclusively *anti*establishment is also a reasonable one).[55] But even if the important claim about original protection of state establishments is granted, we must be cautious about its force. That state establishments were safeguarded from federal interference is asserted by *both* a purely jurisdictional reading of the Establishment Clause (which would leave Congress free within federal domains to act as could a state) *and* a reading that Congress may not establish a religion for the country as

---

[50] A consistent theme of Federalist defenders was that speech and religion were subjects of state authority, not within the delegated powers of the federal government. See Lash, note 45 supra, at 1085–86.

[51] Amar, note 41 supra, at 247.

[52] Witte, note 2 supra, at 81.

[53] Id. at 81–88.

[54] Id.

[55] See, e.g., Laycock, note 49 supra.

a whole, do so within federal domains, or interfere with state establishments. Thus, much of the historical evidence scholars have adduced in favor of a jurisdictional reading is perfectly consistent with a reading of the text that is much more natural. The evidence, thus, does not support a view that Congress's power within federal domains was as unfettered in regard to religion as was the power of states inside their borders.

With this sense of the natural reading of the text, we can look at what Congress actually did regarding religion within federal domains. If Congress apparently felt as free to legislate as would a state, that would bolster the view that Congress did not see the Establishment Clause as affecting its power within exclusively federal domains. If Congress legislated to a degree about religion but not in a manner that most members would have regarded as tending to establish religion, its measures would have fitted best the understanding I have claimed is more persuasive. In this review of congressional action, we can find *some basis* to discern what kinds of actions members regarded as establishing religion.

Although actions by Congress both before and after adoption of the Bill of Rights can shed some light on how members understood the religion clauses,[56] most of them had not thought much about the precise scope of the Bill of Rights, and legislators often vote for laws without considering constitutionality seriously.

The major relevant actions by Congress were the appointment of congressional and military chaplains, the opening of sessions of Congress by prayer, religious exemptions from import duties and from property taxes in the District of Columbia, and various recognitions of religion in the regulation of the territories.

Congressional chaplains were established in 1789.[57] Congress made military chaplains "an official part of the American armed forces in 1791" and fifteen years later passed an act that "earnestly recommended to all officers and soldiers diligently to attend divine service."[58] When the federal government took over the District of Columbia, it continued the tax exemptions for churches that existed within Virginia; and Congress refunded duties on religious articles to importers when a House committee recommended.[59]

---

[56] Of course, what Congress did before adoption did not present the potential of an immediate direct conflict with the First Amendment. So long as it did not infringe the original Constitution, the first Congress was free to enact laws that might prove at odds with the language of the not-yet-approved First Amendment.

[57] Lash, note 45 supra, at 1133.

[58] Id. at 1132.

[59] Id. at 1127–29.

Congress opened its sessions with prayers, and the First Congress recommended "a day of public thanksgiving and prayer."[60] Presidents from George Washington forward issued Thanksgiving proclamations.[61]

These limited actions by Congress hardly provide genuine support for the claim that the Establishment Clause was understood to be purely jurisdictional. Since most members of Congress would not have regarded any of the measures as an establishment, they certainly do not tell us that Congress saw itself as having as great a freedom within federal domains as states had within their own borders. These actions *do* suggest that members of Congress did not suppose that every favoring of religion whatsoever violated the Establishment Clause, and we can infer that courts of the time would have taken a similar view.

In governing the territories, Congress set aside land for religious purposes, and it financed missions, even naming particular religious groups to receive funds.[62] Territorial regulations included coerced observance of restrictions on Sabbath activities and prohibitions against (Christian) blasphemy.[63] A frequently cited provision of the Northwest Ordinance was worded: "Religion, morality, and knowledge being necessary to good government and the happiness of mankind, schools and the means of education shall forever be encouraged."[64]

These actions might at first glance seem to support the jurisdictional view that Congress could treat religion as it wished within the territories, but the more likely explanation is that legislators did not perceive what they did as prohibiting free exercise or establishing religion. Even nonestablishment states then had laws restricting Sabbath activities and forbidding blasphemy. The grants to particular religious groups were mainly to educate and "Christianize" Native Americans and were given to the only organizations equipped to carry out the task.

Congress was operating under the Articles of Confederation when it originally approved the frequently quoted language about education and religion;

[60] Id. at 1124.

[61] Id. at 1123–24. Thomas Jefferson and Andrew Jackson did not do so.

[62] Id. at 1119–22.

[63] Id. at 1118.

[64] Id. With an eye toward recent Establishment Clauses challenges to the phrase "under God" in the Pledge of Allegiance, the 107th Congress emphasized the Religion, Morality and Knowledge Clause of the Northwest Ordinance in the course of reaffirming the Pledge and "In God We Trust" as the national motto. See Act of November 13, 2002, Pub. L. No. 107–293, § 1(5), 116 Stat. 2057 (finding that "[o]n July 21, 1789, on the same day that it approved the Establishment Clause concerning religion, the First Congress of the United States also passed the Northwest Ordinance, providing for a territorial government for lands northwest of the Ohio River, which declared: 'Religion, morality, and knowledge . . .'").

the First Congress under the Constitution "reenacted" the Ordinance (or at least revised it in certain respects)[65] before it settled on the final wording of the Establishment Clause. Although members of Congress may not have focused on the relationship between provisions of the Constitution and territorial governance, one may draw at least a mild inference that Congress would not have proposed a constitutional prohibition it believed was at odds with language it had recently adopted for the Northwest territories.

In 1789 most education was carried out under religious auspices. The comparatively few public schools did teach religion to some extent, and during the nineteenth century, when public schools took over the main burden of American education, they taught from a nondenominationalist Protestant perspective and engaged in devotional Bible reading. In 1789, the vast majority of legislators, whether from states with tax support for churches or from disestablishment states, would have assumed that education should include religion. The Northwest Ordinance reflects that view.

This conclusion tells us nothing at all about whether the Establishment Clause was purely jurisdictional. When public education developed in states that no longer had establishments, no one assumed that a dose of religion in their schools amounted to an establishment. If its members had assumed that the Establishment Clause barred Congress from establishing religion in federal domains, few, if any, would have perceived any difficulty with the clause in the Northwest Ordinance. The setting aside of sites in land grants to encourage religion may well be subject to similar analysis.[66]

In short, given the uncertainty and disagreement about what support amounted to an establishment and given the widespread assumption that many connections between government and religion did not do so, nothing the First Congress did indicates that its members regarded the Establishment Clause as purely jurisdictional, as leaving Congress relatively wide scope to legislate a religious establishment in the territories and other federal domains.

---

[65] Thomas Nathan Peters, "Religion, Establishment, and the Northwest Ordinance: A Closer Look at an Accommodationist Argument," 2000–2001 *Kentucky Law Journal* 743, 747, 771–72, n. 189, suggests that "reenactment" is not a correct characterization of what Congress did. The First Congress enacted two technical amendments. One substituted "the President of the United States" for all references to "the United States in Congress assembled." Act of August 7, 1789, chap. 8, § 1 Stat. 50, 52–53. The other provided that the secretary of the territory should perform the duties of the governor in the event of a vacancy. Id. § 2, 1 Stat. at 53. The text of the Northwest Ordinance was reprinted in a footnote to the amendments. 1 Stat. at 51–52 n. (a). Peters defends a very restrictive view of what the clause about religion and education means.

[66] If the government controls a large tract of land, reserving some parcels for religious institutions might seem appropriate to accommodate the exercise of religion. Modern zoning laws in many states require that towns make places for houses of worship.

If one were a strict originalist, believing that original understanding of constitutional provisions should control modern interpretation, *and* one were guided exclusively by the understanding at the time the Bill of Rights was adopted, *and* one tried to discern a median or consensus view (as contrasted with the strong disestablishment convictions of Jefferson and Madison), one would interpret both religion clauses more narrowly in many respects than has the modern Supreme Court. For example, most states had laws regarding religion, such as oaths of office with religious content and clergy disqualifications from office, that are now uncontroversially thought to violate the Free Exercise Clause. And very few people would then have thought that prayers and Bible reading in state-run schools established religion.

This exact originalist approach to interpreting the religion clauses lacks any semblance of a defense. If what should count in interpretation is original understanding, we cannot ignore understanding at the time of the Fourteenth Amendment when we consider the rights that the amendment guarantees against the states. In light of suggestions by Kurt Lash and Akhil Amar (among others) that the prevailing views of both free exercise and nonestablishment were more expansive in the mid-nineteenth century than in the late eighteenth century,[67] any serious originalist must grapple with how free exercise and nonestablishment were regarded at the later time.

The Establishment Clause and Incorporation through the Fourteenth Amendment

We have seen that the most plausible reading of the Establishment Clause includes an antiestablishment principle for the federal government in federal domains. We have also seen that supporters of nonestablishment have always perceived a strong connection between nonestablishment and free exercise. According to modern constitutional doctrine, the Fourteenth Amendment made most prohibitions in the Bill of Rights that originally applied only against the federal government applicable against the states. Nonetheless, various reasons have been advanced why the Establishment Clause is unfit for incorporation in this way against the states.

Joseph Snee once suggested that the Establishment Clause created a political duty, not an individual right.[68] Although we might understand such an

---

[67] Kurt T. Lash, "The Second Adoption of the Establishment Clause: The Rise of the Nonestablishment Principle," 27 *Arizona State Law Journal* 1085 (1995); Amar, note 41 supra, at 246–57.

[68] Joseph M. Snee, S.J., "Religious Disestablishment and the Fourteenth Amendment," 1954 *Washington University Law Quarterly* 371.

assertion in three or four different ways,[69] our concern here is whether casting it as a political duty might render the Establishment Clause unsuitable for incorporation against the states. The Due Process Clause of the Fourteenth Amendment forbids state deprivations of "liberty"; the Privileges and Immunities Clause forbids abridgments of the "privileges or immunities of citizens." Whether one focuses on the Due Process Clause as the engine of incorporation (the Supreme Court's approach) or the Privileges and Immunities Clause (the more promising vehicle), a political duty account of the Establishment Clause presents an impediment. A political duty of Congress is not a "liberty" of persons or a "privilege or immunity" of citizens, so the argument goes.

However, our review has shown that opponents of establishment regarded free exercise of religion and nonestablishment as very closely tied. Many of the strongest arguments against what dissenters perceived as establishments were cast in terms of liberty of conscience[70] and equal civil rights.[71] Central features of the established church in England undoubtedly impinged on the

---

[69] The phraseology could be employed as an alternative way of proposing that the clause was purely jurisdictional, that it concerned relations between the federal and state governments, not whether individuals in states or federal domains would be subject to an established religion. We may put this possible fourth understanding aside, having concluded that the clause was both jurisdictional and substantive.

Second, the distinction between political duty and individual right might be understood at the level of political philosophy. Thus, a right to free exercise might be seen as a natural right, a prohibition on establishment as a matter of institutional arrangements.

Third, one *conceivable* legal consequence of the distinction would be that individuals would not have standing to challenge violations of the Establishment Clause. However, individuals who are injured may sue even if the basic constitutional duty is owed to a different political branch rather than to individuals. Thus, we might say that the federal government owes a political duty to states not to interfere with purely intrastate commerce, but an individual adversely affected by a law that exceeds the authority of Congress can challenge the law on the ground that it impinges on the sovereignty of states. No straightforward connection exists between "political duty" and a lack of standing for individual claimants. Exactly who has standing to sue for violations of the Establishment Clause is a complex question. In general, federal taxpayers do not have standing to sue to claim constitutional violations, but in 1968, in *Flast v. Cohen*, 392 U.S. 83, the Supreme Court allowed taxpayers to raise Establishment Clause challenges to expenditures of federal money. In 2007, the Court declared that taxpayers could not contest administrative (as opposed to legislative) decisions. *Hein v. Freedom From Religion Foundation, Inc.*, 127 S.Ct. 2553. Even when federal taxpayers lacked standing in establishment cases, states often conferred standing for local and state taxpayers to challenge government spending, and the Supreme Court consistently reviewed such cases. I do not deal with the intricacies of standing in this volume, but they obviously matter for the effective judicial enforcement of constitutional limits on what federal, state, and local governments may do.

[70] Feldman, note 47 supra.

[71] Philip A. Hamburger, "Equality and Diversity: The Eighteenth-Century Debate About 'Equal Protection and Civil Rights,' " 1992 *Supreme Court Review* 295.

liberty of dissenters, and a common antiestablishment claim in the early republic was that a government violates liberty of conscience when it taxes
individuals to support religions to which they do not subscribe. One may
easily translate claims about equal rights into ones about free exercise—
when people suffer discrimination in rights because of their religion, that
impairs their free exercise—but, even if equality is treated as distinguishable
from free exercise, a claim of equal rights concerns individual rights. Such a
claim for equality could cover any preferences given to one denomination,
or to many, to the exclusion of others. In brief, whatever the perceived substantive coverage of the Establishment Clause, people did not understand it
in a political sense as divorced from individual rights. And it would require
much too refined a distinction to suppose that, according to language or
intention, all individual rights claims about religion were packed into the
Free Exercise Clause, leaving for the Establishment Clause *only* those aspects
of establishment that did not concern individual rights. So long as one sees
disestablishment as connected to liberty of conscience, and equality of rights,
the Fourteenth Amendment, including the Equal Protection Clause, could
well make much of its content applicable against the states.

It remains to address three other objections to incorporation of the Establishment Clause: (1) the whole doctrine of incorporation is misconceived;
(2) since the Establishment Clause was designed substantially to protect state
establishments, it should not have been read later to bar state establishments;
and (3) some *particular* violations of the Establishment Clause should not
be seen as involving individual rights.

I shall say little about the general debate over incorporation. It is still
sharply contested whether the adopters of the Fourteenth Amendment intended to restrict the states by a panoply of rights previously held only
against the federal government. Assuming that the adopters intended to create some new rights against the states (beyond whatever equality rights the
Equal Protection Clause guarantees and the evident procedural rights of the
Due Process Clause), it is arguable whether they intended to guarantee the
same rights one finds in various clauses of the Bill of Rights or rather a more
fundamental core of rights, such as rights "implicit in a concept of ordered
liberty."

I believe many of the adopters of the Fourteenth Amendment did mean to
protect basic federal rights against the states. Whether they meant to protect
rights to exactly the same degree as against the federal government is hardly
clear, but federal courts needing to elaborate rights against both federal and
state governments reasonably treat the rights as having the same scope. To

put the point concretely, it makes sense for courts to regard the same kinds of actions as unconstitutional impingements on freedom of speech or freedom of religion, whether the infringing government is federal or state. That, in any event, is the approach the Court has taken, and it is now a well accepted aspect of constitutional law.[72]

One argument against incorporation of the Establishment Clause in particular is that if the clause was originally understood in 1789 to reserve to states the power to establish or disestablish religion as they chose, it violates that aspect of the clause to regard it now as imposing *anti*establishment restrictions on the states. The claim would be plausible if the jurisdictional component of the clause had remained a constant. The answer to the claim lies in history. In 1833, Massachusetts repealed its system of support for religion. Although many states continued practices we might now regard as establishments, including Bible reading in public schools and religious tests for office, no state then had a structure of relations between government and religion that people of the time regarded as establishing religion. Thus, any jurisdictional aspect of the Establishment Clause, any aspect that protected state decisions to establish, had disappeared in significance by the mid-nineteenth century. People *then* regarded the clause as stating a basic principle of government appropriate for states as well as the federal government, and a number of states created before the Civil War had constitutions including establishment clauses modeled on the federal provision. These clauses were indisputably antiestablishment in their content.[73] Well before 1866, the substantive, antiestablishment aspect of the clause far exceeded any jurisdictional aspect in public perception. Thus, we can comfortably conceive the adopters of the Fourteenth Amendment as making the antiestablishment aspect applicable against the states.

Another argument against incorporation plays on the individual rights theme but in a more complicated way than the theory that the Establishment Clause was exclusively about political duty. According to this argument, the Fourteenth Amendment protects free exercise and equality rights against the states. The coverage of the Establishment Clause overlaps with the Free Exer-

---

[72] However, Justice Thomas has recently questioned whether the Establishment Clause should be applied to restrict the states at all or to the same extent as it restricts the federal government. See *Elk Grove Unified School Dist. v. Newdow*, 542 U.S. 1, 45–46 (2004) (Thomas, J., concurring in the judgment) ("I would acknowledge that the Establishment Clause is a federalism provision, which, for this reason, resists incorporation. Moreover, as I will explain, the Pledge policy is not implicated by any sensible incorporation of the Establishment Clause, which would probably cover little more than the Free Exercise Clause"); see also *Zelman v. Simmons-Harris*, 536 U.S. 639, 678–79 (2002) (Thomas, J., concurring).

[73] Amar, note 41 supra, at 249.

cise[74] and Equal Protection clauses.[75] The proper approach is to treat the Fourteenth Amendment as reaching *only* those violations of nonestablishment that *also* violate one of these other clauses. Thus incorporating the Establishment Clause, which does not *sound* like an individual right, is unnecessary, because the other two clauses will do whatever work is called for. In practical terms, aspects of the Establishment Clause that do not concern free exercise or equality would not apply against the states.

This approach is coherent, but it is probably *too* refined for wise decision. Any support for some religions over others implicates concerns about equality (and even support for religion in general could deny equality to nonreligious or antireligious claimants);[76] and many establishment problems involve concerns about the exercise of religion by outsiders or dissenters. For judges to try to skim off those laws or practices they would want to characterize as actual violations of the Establishment Clause (were the federal government to engage in them) but not as violations of free exercise or equal protection by states might not be worth the effort.[77] Incorporating the Establishment Clause, whose substantive content broadly implicates both free religious exercise and equality, is much more straightforward.

A major movement to amend the Constitution in respect to religion that occurred in the 1870s is not an obstacle to incorporation of the Establishment Clause. The amendment, proposed by Representative James G. Blaine in 1876 in response to pressure for public assistance to Roman Catholic parochial schools, explicitly applied to the states. Containing language like that in the religion clauses, his original proposal also provided that "no money raised by taxation in any state for the support of public schools, or derived from any public fund therefor nor any public lands devoted thereto, shall ever be under the control of any religious sect or denomination; nor shall any money so raised . . . be divided between religious sects or denominations."[78] The Senate failed to give the requisite two-thirds support to a somewhat revised version of the proposed amendment. In subsequent years, many states adopted constitutional provisions with language resembling that

[74] In the volume on free exercise, we saw many areas, including judicial abstention from determining matters of church doctrine, in which the Supreme Court relies on both religion clauses.

[75] If one thinks of religious classifications as "suspect," one will regard the Equal Protection Clause as overlapping significantly with both religion clauses.

[76] See, e.g., *Welsh v. United States* 398 U.S. 333, 356–57 (1970) (concurring opinion of Harlan, J.).

[77] Much would depend on how extensively courts construed the Free Exercise and Equal Protection clauses and whether they interpreted the Establishment Clause as placing serious limits on aid received by religious groups according to neutral, nonreligious criteria (a practice they would not be likely to view as violating free exercise or equal protection).

[78] Witte, note 2 supra, at 121 n. 1.

of the Blaine Amendment; many of their bans on using public money for religious education were even broader than that in the federal proposal.[79]

The Blaine Amendment and its subsequent state counterparts do not show that the Establishment Clause's incorporation is misguided.[80] Debate about the amendment centered on the issue of public aid to sectarian schools. Granted that people at the time may not have supposed that the Fourteenth Amendment had incorporated most of the Bill of Rights, one partial explanation is that the 1872 Slaughter-House Cases had shut off an expansive reading of the Privileges and Immunities Clause.[81] The near passage of the Blaine Amendment does not reveal an opinion that the Establishment Clause was particularly disqualified for incorporation. Insofar as the amendment poses a problem for incorporation, it suggests that contemporary opinion was contrary to the whole notion of incorporation, not that people had a particular view about the unsuitability of the Establishment Clause being applied to the states.

CONCLUSION

The most plausible reading of the original Establishment Clause—based on its text, the history leading up to its enactment, and legislation enacted by Congress—is that Congress could not establish a national religion, could not enhance or interfere with state establishments, and could not establish religion within exclusively federal domains. A purely "jurisdictional" reading that Congress could have established religion within federal domains is mistaken. Actions by the First Congress under the Constitution do, however, suggest that its members did not have an expansive view of what measures were "respecting an establishment of religion."

Because any jurisdictional aspect of the Establishment Clause that protected state establishments had vastly diminished in significance by the time of the Fourteenth Amendment, that clause, as well as the Free Exercise Clause, has sensibly been incorporated against the states—assuming that incorporation of other clauses of the Bill of Rights is appropriate. The mod-

---

[79] New York's constitution, for example, proscribes the use of "any public money" to aid "schools or institutions of higher learning wholly or in part under the control . . . of any religious denomination, or in which any tenet or doctrine is taught." Walter Gellhorn and R. Kent Greenawalt, *The Sectarian College and the Public Purse* 173 (Dobbs Ferry, N.Y.: Oceana Publications, 1970).

[80] Steven K. Green, "The Blaine Amendment Reconsidered," 36 *American Journal of Legal History* 38 (1992).

[81] 83 U.S. (16 Wall.) 36 (1872).

ern Supreme Court's treatment of the scope of the religion clauses cannot be justified on originalist grounds, whether one concentrates on the original understanding of forbidden practices at the time of the adoption of the Bill of Rights or the original understanding of forbidden practices when the Fourteenth Amendment was adopted, but the latitude with which the Supreme Court has departed from these original understandings is no greater than it has exhibited with other parts of the First Amendment and with other guarantees in the Bill of Rights. Whatever bases one may have to criticize the Supreme Court's religion clause jurisprudence, it is not *distinctly* unfaithful to original understandings.

CHAPTER 3

The Development of Doctrine and Its Significance

This chapter provides a summary account of the Supreme Court's doctrinal development of the Establishment Clause. With chapter 1's treatment of Establishment Clause values and their relation to equality, it sets the stage for the analytical discussion of particular issues in the chapters that follow. Along the way, I identify some major themes and tensions in approaches to the Establishment Clause, comment on a strong objection to the Supreme Court's use of the metaphor of church and state, and sketch the differences between fundamental principles, tests of constitutionality, standards of judgment, and relevant factors.

THE ESTABLISHMENT CLAUSE UP TO *EVERSON V. BOARD OF EDUCATION*

Not until 1947, in *Everson v. Board of Education*, did the Supreme Court first apply the strictures of the Establishment Clause to states and localities.[1] The Court had previously rendered three rulings permissive of aid to religious organizations. Two of these addressed and rejected challenges to such aid as an impermissible establishment; one sustained aid without reference to the Establishment Clause.

In 1899 the Court upheld an agreement by the District of Columbia to build a hospital that was to be administered by a Roman Catholic order.[2] It relied partly on the absence of a reference to religion in the hospital's certificate of incorporation and said the hospital must be managed in accord with its defined secular purposes. Nine years later, the Court approved the use of trust funds held by the federal government on behalf of Indians to pay the Bureau of Catholic Indian Missions for providing education.[3] Finally, in

---

[1] 330 U.S. 1 (1947). It had indicated it would do so seven years earlier in the free exercise decision of *Cantwell v. Connecticut*. 310 U.S. 296 (1940).

[2] *Bradfield v. Roberts*, 173 U.S. 296.

[3] *Quick Bear v. Leupp*, 210 U.S. 50 (1908).

1930, without considering any Establishment Clause argument, it sustained the use of state funds to supply textbooks in parochial and other private schools against the claim that such aid served no appropriate public purpose.[4]

This brings us to *Everson*'s challenge to the payment of bus transportation for children attending local Catholic schools. The Court applied the Establishment Clause to the states without addressing any of the arguments why that might be misguided. The Court upheld the state's paying for children to take buses to school, but in a manner that foretold that substantial aid to religious schools would not pass muster. The Court's majority assumed, in accord with the state statute, that aid was also available for any students attending other nonprofit private schools, as well as public schools. Passages of Justice Black's opinion for the Court point in different directions, and they have proved protean, exploited by later justices with their particular views. Although some language intimates that aid is all right if it goes to children or parents rather than parochial schools themselves, and some language may imply that parochial schools must not be treated better or worse than other nonprofit private schools, the central theme is that bus transportation for schoolchildren is a public service, like fire and police protection. On this interpretation, *Everson* stands for the proposition that only assistance that is peripheral to the educational process of religious schools is permissible. This interpretation is strengthened to a degree by the fact that four out of nine justices thought that even the payment for transportation had gone too far. All nine justices took Madison and Jefferson as their guides to the meaning of the Establishment Clause, not questioning whether these two founders were fairly representative of the diverse members of Congress and state legislatures; and Justice Black's opinion gave prominence to Jefferson's phrase about a "wall of separation" between church and state.

Let us pause at this point to identify some broad possibilities for interpretation of the Establishment Clause. The most quoted passage from *Everson*, and perhaps from any case interpreting the religion clauses, is the following:

The "establishment of religion" clause of the First Amendment means at least this: Neither a state nor the Federal Government can set up a church. Neither can pass laws which aid one religion, aid all religions, or prefer one religion over another. Neither can force nor influence a person to go to or remain away from church against his will or force him to profess a belief or disbelief in any religion. No person can be punished for entertaining or professing religious beliefs or disbeliefs, for church attendance or non-attendance. No

[4] *Cochran v. Louisiana State Board of Education*, 281 U.S. 370.

tax in any amount, large or small, can be levied to support any religious activities or institutions, whatever they may be called, or whatever form they may adopt to teach or practice religion. Neither a state nor the Federal Government can, openly or secretly, participate in the affairs of any religious organizations or groups and *vice versa*. In the words of Jefferson, the clause against establishment of religion by law was intended to erect "a wall of separation between church and State."[5]

A subsequent passage says that a state "cannot exclude individual Catholics, Lutherans, Mohammedans, Baptists, Jews, Methodists, Non-believers, Presbyterians, or the members of any other faith, *because of their faith, or lack of it,* from receiving the benefits of public welfare legislation."[6]

Justice Black's language clearly states that a state cannot aim to aid religious groups in their religious activities and it cannot expend tax funds for those activities. But what if religious groups provide a service, such as a hospital or school, that other private organizations also provide? Is it all right to fund these activities? Language that suggests that people cannot be denied benefits because of their faith or lack of faith seems to point toward a principle of equal treatment, but the assertion that taxes may not support any religious institutions seems more restrictive, as does the metaphor of "a wall of separation between church and state." If one concentrates on what most justices in *Everson* had in mind, the answer is the more restrictive principle. The four dissenters thought payment for bus transportation crossed the constitutional line, and Justice Black intimated that the law approached "the verge" of state power. If payment for bus transportation is barely allowable, payment for the educational programs of religious schools is not allowable.

We have long passed the point, however, at which discerning the drift of the *Everson* opinion is what is crucial for interpreting the Establishment Clause. Rather, justices must decide in light of subsequent cases and their own views about nonestablishment what is the comparative importance of equal treatment versus no aid. Undeniably, a tension exists between the two approaches in respect to assistance granted according to nonreligious criteria.

The Metaphor of Separation of Church and State

From the time of *Everson* forward, opinions have referred to the wall of separation, although with increasing acknowledgment that complete separation is impossible. Recently, Philip Hamburger has attacked the whole no-

---

[5] 330 U.S. at 15–16.
[6] Id. at 17.

tion of separation of church and state as unfaithful to original ideas of disestablishment.[7] His claim warrants thoughtful examination, because a
rejection of the metaphor of separation could signal a radical change in the
law of the Establishment Clause.

Hamburger's underlying thesis is that a robust concept of separation—
requiring disconnection between the activities of government and religion—
is historically distinct from the more constitutionally legitimate ideal of disestablishment—which requires only elimination of favoritism toward people
or groups based on their religious identity. The ideology of anti-Catholicism
in particular, and of anticlericalism more generally, has driven historical understanding of separation and has grossly distorted historical reality, Hamburger asserts. But by emphasizing certain facts, by treating the historical
record in a way that understates close connections between disestablishment
and separation, and by giving separation of church and state a solidity and
decisive logic that it lacks in actuality, Hamburger's account overstates the
importance of a distinction between disestablishment and separation.[8]

To evaluate the significance of a distinction between disestablishment and
separation, we need to understand that fuzzy, general political concepts like
disestablishment develop over time, and that dominant concepts may alter
without a large shift in what government practices are accepted as legitimate.
More precisely, in considering the importance of a shift from "disestablishment" to "separation," we cannot merely compare a modern idea of separation with a concept of disestablishment drawn from over two hundred years
ago. We need to assess roughly what might be the differences between reasonable modern conceptions of disestablishment and separation, taking account of how disestablishment, like other major constitutional concepts,
would have developed over time.[9] In my opinion, such development is
healthy, even necessary, if a constitutional order is to flourish through the
years, but even if a critic regards this development as regrettable, he must
acknowledge that it has characterized the Supreme Court's treatment of virtually every domain of constitutional law. In comparing "separation" with
modern "disestablishment," we would, in addition to taking into account
the likely growth of "disestablishment" over time, need to prune from the
separationist position certain broader political ideals that do not concern

---

[7] Philip Hamburger, *Separation of Church and State* (Cambridge: Harvard University Press, 2002).

[8] My comments here are excerpted from a much longer critique. "History as Ideology: Philip Hamburger's Separation of Church and State," 93 *California Law Review* 367 (2005).

[9] Virtually all the protections in the Bill of Rights have undergone extensions that are far from
trivial. The modern understandings of freedom of speech, freedom of the press, and the privilege
against self-incrimination forbid many laws and practices the Framers would have accepted. And, of
course, the Supreme Court has read the Equal Protection Clause of the Fourteenth Amendment to
forbid certain racially discriminatory practices and to protect groups, such as women, that the enacting legislators did not have in mind.

legal coercion[10] and ideals for law that virtually no modern believer in separation would support.[11] Only if we grasp a concept of separation that is
stripped of excesses and a concept of disestablishment that fairly reflects how
that concept would have developed will we be able to evaluate the extent to
which a shift in the prevailing metaphor from disestablishment to separation
would represent a real difference in legal substance. Of course, people would
not agree on the exact parameters of a concept of disestablishment that is
given its fair modern scope, any more than they agree on what the Free
Speech Clause should protect; but we can be sure that the modern scope of
disestablishment would not replicate precisely an eighteenth-century sense
of what counted as forbidden establishments.

As we approach various topics in the book, we may ask ourselves whether
"separation" has a force that differs significantly from that of "disestablishment." I believe that the force of the two concepts does differ for the very
important subject of "neutral" aid given without respect to religion, but not
for most other topics.

DECISIONS AFTER *EVERSON* AND GENERAL APPROACHES

A few years after *Everson*, the Supreme Court approved a program to excuse
children from public schools to go to religious instruction off the school
premises.[12] Justice Douglas's opinion struck a very different note than had
Justice Black's in *Everson*. He said, "We are a religious people whose institutions presuppose a Supreme Being" and talked of the desirability of accommodating the public service to people's spiritual needs.[13] This theme of accommodation is one on which later justices have drawn frequently.

In 1961, the Court upheld Sunday closing laws, despite their undoubted
origin in religious convictions, as serving a valid secular objective of a uniform day of rest;[14] and, as we saw in the free exercise volume, the Court
rejected the claim of a Sabbatarian for an exemption.[15] Chief Justice Warren
wrote in a plurality opinion in the latter case that a law indirectly burdening
religion could be valid if its "purpose and effect" are to advance the state's
legitimate goals.[16]

---

[10] I have in mind here such "separationist" ideas as that clerics should not be active in politics.

[11] One example is the possibility that churches not be allowed the legal protection of incorporation.

[12] *Zorach v. Clauson*, 343 U.S. 306 (1952).

[13] Id. at 313–14.

[14] *McGowan v. Maryland*, 366 U.S. 420.

[15] *Braunfeld v. Brown*, 366 U.S. 599.

[16] Id. at 607.

The Court's next important cases involved Bible reading and school prayer to open the public school day. The Court held both to be unconstitutional.[17] In the second of the cases, *Abington Township v. Schempp*, Justice Clark wrote that the state must be "neutral" toward religion. Drawing from the Sunday closing law cases, he said, "The test may be stated as follows: what are the purpose and primary effect of the enactment? If either is the advancement or inhibition of religion, then the enactment exceeds the scope of legislative power as circumscribed by the Constitution."[18]

When it next considered school aid, the Court sustained the loan of public textbooks to parochial school students. Justice White's opinion for the Court noted that the benefit went to children, not schools; he also invoked the *Schempp* test and emphasized the secular benefits of parochial education.[19]

Rejecting a challenge to property tax exemptions given to churches, the Court emphasized that taxing would entangle the state much more with religious institutions than granting an exemption.[20] In 1971, in *Lemon v. Kurtzman*,[21] another school aid case, the Court drew the elements of purpose, effect, and entanglement together into a comprehensive test or guide for Establishment Clause cases. Under the *Lemon* test, a challenged law is valid only if it (1) has a secular purpose, (2) does not have a primary effect that advances or inhibits religion, and (3) does not foster an excessive entanglement. For the next two decades, the Court used this formulation as its standard for judging establishment challenges.

As the test was elaborated, a secular purpose could suffice even if there was an equally strong religious purpose. A primary religious effect, however, could lead to invalidation even if a secular effect was as great or greater. The main concern about entanglement has consistently been administrative or institutional entanglement. Some opinions suggested that divisive political potential is a separate kind of entanglement. Later cases indicated that this potential should not be treated as an independent element that could lead to invalidation, but various opinions of individual justices have emphasized the danger of political divisions that track religious differences. The Court has continually repeated that an effect of inhibition of religion could violate the Establishment Clause, even though one might think such a problem would

---

[17] *Engel v. Vitale*, 370 U.S. 421 (1962) (school prayer); *School District of Abington Township v. Schempp*, 374 U.S. 203 (1963) (Bible reading).

[18] *Schempp*, note 17 supra, at 222.

[19] *Board of Education v. Allen*, 392 U.S. 236 (1968).

[20] *Walz v. Tax Commission*, 397 U.S. 664 (1970).

[21] 403 U.S. 602 (1971).

naturally be treated under the Free Exercise Clause.[22] More importantly, the Court has also consistently ruled that some accommodations to religion are permissible, though saying such accommodations are secular in purpose and effect is a bit awkward.

By the mid-1990s, a total of seven justices, proposing various substitute approaches in a range of concurring and dissenting opinions, had said they did not think the *Lemon* test should be used as a comprehensive approach to establishment cases.[23] However, the Court has yet to explicitly disavow the test in a majority opinion. The consequence is that lower courts must continue to apply that test; and various decisions rendered under *Lemon* and the individual elements of the test, especially the effects element, continue to influence the Supreme Court's judgment. In one case, Justice O'Connor wrote for the Court that entanglement should be treated not as a separate criterion but as one aspect of effects.[24]

A major alternative to the standard *Lemon* test is an inquiry about endorsement, whether a law or practice endorses (or condemns) a particular religion or religion in general. Justice O'Connor first proposed this approach as a "clarification" of the purpose and effect elements of *Lemon*;[25] but the approach has subsequently been regarded more often as a competitor to *Lemon*. Endorsement has become the controlling standard for religious symbols on public property,[26] and has been referred to more broadly.[27]

"Neutrality" has often been suggested as a kind of polestar for religious clause interpretation. Sometimes the term has seemed little more than a conclusion that an appropriate balance of values has been struck. More recently, neutrality in the sense of equal treatment of religious and nonreligious groups has emerged as "the key" in cases involving financial support from the government. That version of a "neutrality" approach allows substantially more aid to religious schools than have prior applications of the *Lemon* test. This was shown by the most important religion case of the new century, in which the Court approved a voucher plan by which state money flowed

---

[22] That is, if a law discourages religion in general, it would seem to impede free exercise rather than establish religion.

[23] See Kent Greenawalt, "Quo Vadis: The Status and Prospects of 'Tests' under the Religion Clauses," 1995 *Supreme Court Review* 323, 359–60. The main alternate approaches are set out briefly in what follows and in more detail in chapter 10. In chapters devoted to specific subjects, particular opinions in which justices rejected the *Lemon* test are summarized.

[24] *Agostini v. Felton*, 521 U.S. 203, 218, 232–33 (1997).

[25] *Lynch v. Donnelly*, 465 U.S. 668, 688–89 (1984) (concurring opinion).

[26] See *County of Allegheny v. American Civil Liberties Union*, 492 U.S. 573 (1989); *Capitol Square Review and Advisory Bd. v. Pinette*, 515 U.S. 753, 773–75 (1995) (concurring opinion of O'Connor, J.), 798–800 (dissenting opinion of Stevens, J.), 817–18 (dissenting opinion of Ginsburg, J.).

[27] For Justice O'Connor, it became a much more dominant standard for resolving cases under the Establishment Clause.

through parents to religious schools with no strings attached.[28] The Court subsequently resisted the more sweeping neutrality claim that a state that helped finance private college education had to include education for the ministry.[29] The state was allowed to rely on its own constitutional provision that restricted aid for religious education.

Other tests or approaches that have had some influence are coercion and history. Under a coercion test, the main distinction between permissible and impermissible state action is coercive effect. The Court relied on such an effect in 1992 to hold prayers at public high school graduations unconstitutional.[30] Since the Free Exercise Clause protects against direct coercion, the Establishment Clause makes a significant addition in this respect only if it reaches out to more diffuse, weaker forms of coercion.

All the justices have treated history as relevant in one respect or another. The most common approach in establishment cases has been to identify the underlying values the Establishment Clause was designed to protect (typically presented in a way that reflects the views of the particular justices on what values the clause should protect) and to give these a modern application. Under this approach, the precise practices of the founding and post—Civil War periods have not been determinative. Some justices have urged a more rigorous adherence to historical practices. For them, if a practice was accepted historically, that is a very powerful argument that it, and other practices that are closely similar, are constitutional.

Before we engage particular perspectives on establishment of religion in the chapters that follow, it may help to say a few words in general about doctrinal approaches that the Supreme Court has offered for establishment cases, categorizing somewhat different kinds of norms that matter in constitutional cases and noting some bases on which such norms are criticized.

Establishment Clause Tests and Other Criteria for Decision

Much of the controversy about the law of the Establishment Clause swirls around the appropriate tests or standards courts should use in evaluating particular disputes. Among the proponents of various positions lie substantial differences over the values underlying the clause, over the right kind of criteria for constitutional interpretation, over a desirable division of function

---

[28] *Zelman v. Simmons-Harris*, 536 U.S. 639 (2002).

[29] *Locke v. Davey*, 540 U.S. 712 (2004).

[30] *Lee v. Weisman*, 505 U.S. 579 (1992).

between legislatures and courts, and over ways to curb judicial discretion, insofar as that is desirable.

There is a large gap between the language of most constitutional provisions and concrete controversies. At the most general level are what we may call fundamental principles, such as separation of church and state or nonestablishment, but these will not usually carry a court very far toward a decision. As in other areas of constitutional law, the Supreme Court over the years has used narrower standards or tests to which it looks when it considers individual cases. People, Supreme Court justices as well as scholars, who talk about "constitutional tests" are not always clear what they mean; this is largely the consequence of the absence of any precise definition of the term.

On the most expansive version of the term "tests," any standard that helps decide a constitutional issue qualifies; on a more restrictive version, a test is a standard whose satisfaction determines constitutionality or unconstitutionality. I employ the more restrictive sense here in order to clarify an important distinction. According to the threefold test of *Lemon v. Kurtzman*, if a law has a secular purpose, does not have a primary effect that advances or inhibits religious, and does not excessively entangle the government with religion, the law does not violate the Establishment Clause.[31] What made this standard of judgment a test in the narrower sense was that, at least over a period of time, the Supreme Court's resolution of constitutionality depended on its judgment about how a law or practice fared under the standard. That approach, it must be acknowledged, did not remove considerable flexibility about *how* the test applied, a subject I will take up below.

In *Marsh v. Chambers*,[32] the Supreme Court evidently assumed that the practice of having chaplains who were hired from public funds opening legis-

---

[31] Putting the test differently, if the law lacks a secular purpose, if it has a primary effect that advances or inhibits religion, or if it creates an excessive entanglement of government with religion, it violates the Establishment Clause. As the *Lemon* test shows, a component of a test of constitutionality can, standing alone, be a test of unconstitutionality. That is how any of the three standards in the *Lemon* test functioned. If a law lacked a secular purpose, it was unconstitutional whatever else might be said about it. And so on. But having a secular purpose did not make a law constitutional. In that direction, purpose was only one component of a larger test. The *Lemon* test purports to apply to Establishment Clause cases in general, but any single constitutional provision may be interpreted to have different tests applying to different kinds of legal problems. That, indeed, has been the fate of free speech law, and is becoming the fate of Establishment Clause law.

A judge *could* use a hierarchy of criteria, each of which would function as a test in the restrictive sense. Suppose a Supreme Court justice assumes that decisions should always reflect the principles of the enactors, that the *Lemon* test does so, and that the proper inquiry under that test, when the government allows private religious speech on public property, is whether the government has endorsed religion. The justice could consistently declare that he is, in those cases, using endorsement, *Lemon*, and enactors' principles as tests, each controlling and yielding identical results.

[32] 463 U.S. 783 (1983).

lative sessions would not pass the *Lemon* test. Yet it upheld the practice as warranted by its acceptance from the time of the founding to the present. After *Marsh*, we could no longer say that *Lemon* was always a decisive test of unconstitutionality; but if *Marsh* seemed a highly unusual case, the status of *Lemon* had not changed very much. If the Supreme Court began to decide that many practices that *Lemon* would condemn were nonetheless valid, *Lemon* would no longer be a *test* of unconstitutionality in the restrictive sense.

A court may use other "standards" whose satisfaction or not bears significantly on a judgment of constitutionality but does not determine the result. As with "tests," "standards" has no precise sense, but I employ it here to refer to formulations that lack the feature of determining results that characterize tests.[33] That would be the situation if the Court typically applied the *Lemon* criteria but also looked at other standards and with some frequency did not decide as the *Lemon* criteria indicated. We may think of "factors" as characteristics of a situation that count for or against constitutionality but do not amount to broadly formulated standards. Thus, in some school aid cases, opinions have noted that a high proportion of private schools are Roman Catholic parochial schools; but no justice has ever formulated an explicit standard of how that bears on constitutionality.

The case of *Rosenberger v. Rector and Visitors of the University of Virginia*[34] provides an apt illustration of how a given consideration might work. In that decision, the Court held that money from a student fund at a state university could not be denied for a magazine that proselytized students to become Christians. For Justice Souter, in dissent, any use of public money for such a purpose was unconstitutional.[35] Thus, for him, one test of unconstitutionality is whether public money is used to support proselytization. Justice O'Connor, concurring, took a different view. In general, such use of money was barred, but here the principle of no aid to religion ran up against a principle of neutrality, that religious groups should be treated like nonreligious ones. In the circumstances of the case, the neutrality principle prevailed.[36] For O'Connor, the principle that public money should not be used for religious evangelization was a standard that did not necessarily determine

---

[33] A particular criterion of judgment, e.g., whether a law endorses religion, could function as a test in one direction and only as a standard in the other. That is, it could be that endorsement always renders a law invalid; but that an absence of endorsement only points toward a finding of constitutionality. Thus, if one asks whether any particular criterion is a test in the restrictive sense, one must be careful to ask both about validity and invalidity.

[34] 515 U.S. 819 (1995).

[35] Id. at 868.

[36] Id. at 847–48.

the outcome.[37] Among the relevant *factors* that mattered to her (and to the majority) were that the student fund was not drawn from general taxes, and money went to the printer of the magazine, not directly to the student organization. No one has formulated a test or a general standard in terms of these factors.[38]

The significance of individual factors calls for a closer look at what I have assumed could be a genuine test, the *Lemon* formulation. Its terms are vague and uncertain in application; what counts as a primary religious effect and what is excessive entanglement? On "excessive" entanglement the Court may be left to do little more than weigh an array of relevant factors. As this illustration shows, courts may assess factors within a preformed test or may simply, but much less usually, identify relevant factors and weigh their relative importance in relation to the formulation that is provided by the constitutional provision itself. Tests can be precisely or loosely formulated.

Problems with Tests, Global Skepticism, and the Significance of Tests

Why might a justice refuse to accept a test that has prevailed in previous cases or been proposed? We can identify various defects that a justice might perceive in a test (these might coalesce in particular instances).

Most obviously, the justice might think that accurate application of the test yields results that are mistaken under the constitutional provision. That is what most of the Court concluded in *Marsh v. Chambers* about the *Lemon* test for invalidity. Legislative chaplains were constitutional although they would be condemned by *Lemon*. A variation on the point about inaccuracy is a belief that a test asks the wrong question, given the historical understanding or basic values of a constitutional provision. Even if it yields correct

---

[37] The difference between tests that determine results and "mere" standards that do not is not just a question of whether one has explicitly conceptualized a higher-order criterion of decision that would settle the issue of constitutionality. One gathers from Justice O'Connor's opinion that she does not think one can formulate when the "neutrality" should triumph over the "no aid" principle. She has no higher-order test to determine the outcome, only the two standards, whose importance must be evaluated in context.

[38] Is there any fundamental difference between standards (that are not tests) and factors? Could one reformulate any relevant factor as a standard that suggests unconstitutionality or constitutionality—e.g., "When money goes to a printer rather than a religious publication itself, the grant is presumptively constitutional, but this is only one standard of judgment among many"? I doubt that there is a sharp conceptual distinction between "standards" and "factors," but the distinction is important in practice. Mere "factors" are likely to be of relatively less weight in isolation, and they are likely to refer to much narrower elements than most standards.

results on occasion, a test is obviously not appropriate if it is asking the wrong set of questions. A more general theme about incorrect results is that various subject matters call for different tests. Were this critique sound, no single test for the entire Establishment Clause could yield sound results for all subject matters.

A justice might think that a test otherwise well reflects values of the religion clauses, but calls on judges (or juries) to answer questions that are simply not appropriate for them. We saw in examining free exercise cases the Court's sense that judges should not be in the business of weighing religious burdens against state interests.[39] A good bit of thought about Establishment Clause interpretation also revolves around what questions judges or juries can sensibly answer.

Closely related to the last point are concerns that a test is unduly vague. One can distinguish two objections here. The first is that judges are left with too much discretion about how to apply a test. Justices such as O'Connor who believe in case-by-case adjudication under flexible standards are not disturbed by such vagueness; justices such as Scalia who think judges should decide according to clear criteria developed in advance regard such vagueness as a fatal defect. A second objection focuses more on general clarity and notice to the public (though this is tightly connected to the issue of undue discretion). A test may look clear and decisive, but if it is filled with holes that are bound to be filled in unpredictable ways, it is not much of a real guide to anyone. One may object to apparent clarity that is delusive.

Three forms of global skepticism exist about tests for the Establishment Clause. One is that doctrinal tests in general never affect legal results; they are merely a cover for what judges otherwise want to do. This skepticism is unfounded in any extreme form. Since tests reflect what judges think should be done, it is hardly surprising that the results they yield are often those that the judges would reach without the tests. But it is also true that judges do with some frequency reach results under controlling tests that they would not otherwise reach.

The serious version of skepticism is that opinions routinely overstate the importance of tests. That happens in two ways. Tests are sometimes wheeled out to support results reached on grounds not reflected by the tests. Or the crucial step is filling in some vague component of the test, and that decision could easily go in favor of either party. Both these things often happen in Supreme Court and other judicial opinions. But to say that opinions often

[39] *Employment Division v. Smith*, 492 U.S. 872 (1990).

overstate the determining power of tests is hardly to conclude that tests inevitably are mere surplusage.

A third skepticism, one particularly directed at the religion clauses, is that the clauses reflect such complex, often conflicting, values, that no tests can do them justice. How does one respond to such skepticism? Our lives are complex and we must resolve issues in which values compete. We manage to do this, but how adequate is our conceptualization of what we do? Justices can resolve cases under the religion clauses, and they can do so according to some coherent pattern, but whether that pattern can be verbalized into a coherent set of tests and standards is debatable. Part of the problem is doubt whether various trade-offs among values and principles can be rationally explained; and part of the problem is that no two justices agree on exactly what those trade-offs should be. These are serious obstacles, but one needs a closer look at issues under the religion clauses before admitting defeat. We concluded in volume 1 that free exercise tests as stated are commonly misleading, but that a rationally explicable, coherent approach to free exercise issues is possible. Part of the effort in this book is to evaluate the various tests and standards for resolving Establishment Clause cases. These have been sharply criticized as astonishingly inadequate if not fundamentally incoherent. I find much to criticize about the Supreme Court's performance in the pages that follow, but I also contend that what the Court has done in respect to establishment is, overall, more cohesive and reasonable than many scholars of the religion clauses believe.

CHAPTER 4

Government Aid to Religion and Promulgating Religious Doctrine

This chapter explains two related core aspects of the Establishment Clause: the government should not provide assistance to religious organizations to carry on their religious activities, and the government should not claim the truth of particular religious doctrines. We shall examine the basic grounding of these aspects, and look at their implications and controversial applications, as well as possible qualifications.

No Aid to Religious Organizations for Religious Activities or Based on Religious Criteria

As we saw in chapter 2, the classic established religion in Western history involved a state church, an official religion of the government. Short of designating, say, the Roman Catholic, Episcopalian, or Presbyterian Church *the* official religion, a state could conceivably decide to assist one and only one religion on the basis that it represents the soundest theological position or serves the largest number of citizens. We might imagine a southern state giving a direct grant to the Southern Baptist Church to pay its ministers and build its churches. No one doubts that such a grant violates the Establishment Clause.[1] To revert to the passage from the *Everson* case about what the Establishment Clause means, Justice Black, in language apparently accepted by all nine justices, commences: "Neither a state nor the federal government can set up a church. Neither can pass laws which aid one religion, aid all religions, or prefer one religion over another."[2] If the grant to one religious group would not "set up a church," it certainly would "aid one

---

[1] I assume here and in what follows (unless I indicate to the contrary) that the Establishment Clause does apply against the states through the Fourteenth Amendment. For someone who rejects the notion that the Fourteenth Amendment should be understood as making the Establishment Clause reach states and localities, the federal constitutional questions a court *should* be asking about such a law are whether it violates the Free Exercise Clause (assuming that clause does apply to the states) or the Equal Protection Clause. A state establishment clause would almost certainly bar this support in any event.

[2] 330 U.S. 1, 15 (1947). Five justices joined the exact language. Four dissenters thought restrictions on state aid were even more stringent than did the majority.

religion" and "prefer one religion over another." As chapter 3 of the volume on free exercise notes, classifications that favor some religious groups over others can be viewed as establishing the favored groups and impairing the free exercise of those that suffer a comparative disadvantage. Perhaps the establishment element seems to predominate if the favored groups are few; the free exercise element if the favored groups are many and the excluded groups are few; but the basic principle remains the same. Discrimination that prefers some religious groups over others violates the religion clauses.

As we saw in chapter 2, the religion clauses originally applied only against the federal government. Various states then provided assistance to multiple religious groups—only Christian groups, sometimes only Protestant groups. Given the country's increasing religious diversity and modern understanding of the proper scope of equality concerning religion, all the justices from *Everson* forward, as well as virtually all legal scholars, have assumed that outright favoritism for Christian groups in the provision of public benefits, to the exclusion of Jews, Muslims, Hindus, and so on, is unconstitutional.

In casting the relevant principle as "the government should not provide assistance to religious organizations to carry on their religious activities," I am putting aside major questions about government support for religious groups because they provide valuable secular services, such as assistance to the poor and education. Later chapters will discuss aid given according to "neutral" criteria that happens to go to religious groups providing secular services. Here it is sufficient to note that the Constitution does not allow government officials to decide which groups to finance on the basis of religious criteria. If the state aids groups because they provide a general "secular" benefit, such as running hospitals, officials cannot choose one group over another (a Roman Catholic hospital over a Presbyterian one) because they believe that group's religious views are true (or better).

We need to recognize three clarifications or qualifications to the principle that the state cannot aid religious activities of particular groups. The first is that in certain instances, the state may directly compensate for a cost it imposes. If designation of its house of worship as an historical landmark makes it more expensive for a group to keep its church in good condition, perhaps the state may provide assistance to make up for the loss it has imposed.

The second clarification or qualification concerns accommodations in general. Whether accommodations are formulated in terms of specific religious groups, they may be mainly designed with one group in mind. An exemption from the law that prohibits the use of peyote for worship services is responsive to the practice of the Native American Church.[3] In a sense, the exemp-

---

[3] See chapter 5 of volume 1.

tion undoubtedly aids the group in its religious activities, but permissible accommodations to burdens the state has imposed do not count as aid banned by the Establishment Clause. We investigated the blurry line between permissible accommodation and impermissible aid in the volume on free exercise, and chapter 17 of this volume explores that issue in more depth.

A third qualification concerns restricted environments. The government may be able to provide assistance to religious groups to serve the religious needs of military personnel and prisoners within its control, choosing whom to aid largely on the basis of the religious composition of the communities in which they will serve. Chapter 12 is devoted to these precise situations.

The *Everson* opinion says that the Establishment Clause bars aid to "all religions." This principle has proved much more controversial than the bar on aid to particular religions. It definitely goes beyond what many of the founders and the adopters of the Fourteenth Amendment believed. States in both periods routinely had laws restricting Sunday activities (in order to protect Sunday worship) and forbidding blasphemy (according to Christian notions). These laws, of course, would now be viewed as favoring the Christian religion in relation to (some) non-Christian religions,[4] but they clearly evidence a willingness of legislators in earlier eras to promote and protect religion to a degree. Some justices and scholars have urged that the government should be able to promote religion in general.

A comparison with favored religious groups may be made vis-à-vis atheist (or agnostic) groups or vis-à-vis groups that are not directly concerned with religion. In chapter 16 of the free exercise volume, we considered the state's stance in respect to atheism and agnosticism. I urged there that these do not count *as religions* but that the state cannot favor groups according to the answers they give to religious questions. Were the state to be able to aid religious groups *in general*, it should be required to give similar aid to groups whose very purpose is to promote negative answers (atheism) or skeptical answers (agnosticism) to religious questions.[5]

The serious issue is the relation between religious groups and nonreligious groups. May the state aid religions and not aid other nonprofit activities, such as universities and museums? May it aid universities and museums and not religious groups? The answer *Everson* provides is that the state may aid other groups and withhold aid from religious ones; it may not aid religious

---

[4] For Sunday closing laws, everything depends on whether the laws are seen as now promoting Sunday worship or a (secular) uniform day of rest.

[5] See Andrew Koppelman, "Secular Purpose," 88 *Virginia Law Review* 87, 130–39 (2002). One might reasonably argue (in contrast to my position) that groups whose purpose is only to express positions, not engage in activities comparable to corporate worship, need not be treated like those for which collective worship (or some secular analogue) is vital.

ones exclusively. The basic idea is that aid to religious groups, even in general, does constitute a form of establishing religion, and thus is barred by the Establishment Clause. The Supreme Court continues to rely on this premise, but it is subject to challenge in a stronger and a weaker form.

The weaker challenge is embodied in this illustration. Suppose all voluntary associations are given grants on the premise that a vibrant civil society promotes social health and good government,[6] and the grants are unrestricted, allowing each group to use its money as it chooses. Treating religious groups like other voluntary groups would not "establish religion." Indeed, the challenge goes, to treat religious groups worse than the others would be discrimination against religion. Chapters 18 and 19 address this issue of grants according to neutral (nonreligious) criteria that may be used for religious purposes.

The stronger challenge is that government should be able to favor religion over nonreligion; it should be able to limit aid to religious groups if it wants. This challenge may rest on the claimed historical ground that the founders never assumed that government would not aid religion, on the widespread conviction in this country that religion is specially valuable, and on the content of existing law. The historical argument suffers from a serious flaw, at least insofar as it rests on the actual view of many founders that the Christian religion could be favored. Virtually no one now contends that we should rely on that particular historical view as the basis for a modern constitutional law that would allow favoring Christianity over all other religions. It is implausible that a view that Christianity may be favored should, nevertheless, carry great weight for modern judgments about whether aid to all religions is all right.[7]

As for the modern conviction that "religion is specially valuable," some observations are in order. No one believes all religion is valuable. However universalist a person's sentiments may be, she will think some religions are seriously misguided and harmful. Someone might believe, however, that *al-*

---

[6] See Robert D. Putnam, *Bowling Alone: The Collapse and Revival of American Community* (New York: Simon and Schuster 2000).

[7] Justice Rehnquist's dissenting opinion in *Wallace v. Jaffree*, 472 U.S. 38, 104–6 (1985), reflects this gap in logic. More recently Justice Stevens has criticized Justice Scalia's position that the government may support monotheism on this basis. *Van Orden v. Perry*, 545 U.S. 677, 695–96 (2005) (Stevens, J., dissenting). Justice Scalia responds in a dissenting opinion in *McCreary County v. American Civil Liberties Union of Ky.*, 545 U.S. 844, 897–98 (2005). Claiming both that much historical work about the Establishment Clause is "bad history," slanted to support one substantive view or another, and that history cannot resolve present issues, Steven K. Green, " 'Bad History': The Lure of History in Establishment Clause Adjudication," 81 *Notre Dame Law Review* 1717 (2006), has recommended that courts sharply curtail their relaince on history to settle modern controversies.

most all religions are valuable and that the government should not decide which are and which are not; and that, therefore, aiding all religious groups is a good thing. Of course, many people in the United States who regard religion as very important in their own lives *do not* think most religions are valuable; they believe that their own religion is life-giving, that other religions (however categorized) are harmful or at least unhelpful. So it is doubtful what proportion of the population really regards religion in general as specially valuable.

Even if most religions are valuable, or are so regarded by many citizens, it does not follow that aid to most religions is desirable. Perhaps religion best flourishes if it is not assisted by government. Western European countries and Canada have provided much more aid to religion than American governments; religion in those countries is embraced by many fewer citizens. This fact hardly *proves* anything about aid in the American context, but it at least gives pause about whether public support will really help religion in the long run.

A different challenge to the "no aid" principle starts from existing law. The law is full of tax benefits that help religious groups, as well as various other provisions that favor religious groups and their leaders. What are we to conclude about these forms of assistance? One possibility is that all of them should be eliminated, or at least all of them except those in which religious groups can qualify under broad nonreligious criteria (such as "charitable organizations"). A second possibility is that these tax benefits show that the "no aid" principle is based on hypocrisy. Aid is everywhere, and we should acknowledge that it is proper. The third possibility is that tax exemptions, and other similar benefits, really do differ from positive aid— that we can accept those benefits and still believe direct aid is improper.[8] We shall explore these possibilities in chapter 15 on tax relief.

No Government Promulgation of Religious Doctrine

In a political community that adheres to a principle of no established religion, the government does not announce that any particular religious doctrines are true. Although the *Everson* opinion does not say directly that agencies of government may not promulgate religious doctrines, such as "Jesus

---

[8] As with measures that aim to benefit specific religious groups, the bar on aid to religious groups in general raises the question of drawing the line between impermissible aid and permissible accommodation, a subject chapter 17 tackles.

Christ is the true son of God the Father, and every person's salvation depends
on acknowledging him as the Lord of their lives; all others are condemned
to hell," its bar on aid to religions implies that prohibition. Justice Fortas,
writing for the Court in an opinion holding that a state may not ban the
teaching of evolution, was more explicit. "Government . . . must be neutral
in matters of religious theory, doctrine, and practice. It may not . . . foster
. . . one religion or religious theory against another."[9]

The Connection to Aid to Groups, and Forms of Government Support

Whatever *Everson* may strongly imply and whatever Justice Fortas may actually state, why should we assume that the government's sponsorship of religious ideas is to be treated like its aid to religious groups? State constitutions
at the founding themselves asserted religious principles, such as the obligation to worship God according to one's conscience; and in the nineteenth
century many Protestants who strongly objected to any financial assistance
to Roman Catholic schools had no compunction about the nondenominational Protestant flavor of the public schools. Perhaps the Establishment
Clause should be regarded as about institutional relations, *not* about religious ideas.[10]

The problems with such an approach are not hard to see. Suppose the
government sponsors particular religious ideas *and* imposes disabilities on
all those who do not subscribe to the ideas. Suppose, further, that these ideas
correlate closely with one or a few particular religious groups. Let us say
that no one will be allowed to hold government office or attend a state university unless she signs a pledge of belief in the doctrine of adult baptism,
that is, that adults but not babies and small children are fit persons for baptism. That this would have the effect of establishing Baptist groups, and
related groups with the same view about adult baptism, seems evident. The
government could promote a group by conditioning benefits on belief in its
doctrines (as well as by aiding the group as a corporate entity).

---

[9] *Epperson v. Arkansas*, 393 U.S. 97, 103–4 (1968). In *School District of Grand Rapids v. Ball*,
473 U.S. 373, 385 (1985), Justice Brennan declared for the Court that the Establishment Clause
"absolutely prohibits government-financed or government-sponsored indoctrination into the beliefs
of a particular religious faith."

[10] A highly qualified form of this position is advocated by Noah Feldman in "A Church-State
Solution," *New York Times Magazine*, July 3, 2005, 28. Professor Feldman would not accept disabilities for those who do not accept the religious ideas the government supports. A fuller exposition of
Feldman's views is in *Divided by God: America's Church-State Problem—and What We Should Do
about It* (New York: Farrar, Straus and Giroux, 2005). I respond to Feldman's approach in chapter
21, infra.

This conclusion does not change if a required belief cross-cuts organized religious groups or is much more encompassing. My hypothetical statement about Jesus and personal salvation is one to which evangelical Christians of various denominations subscribe. Within many denominations, many members would agree with the statement, though others would not. The statement tracks denominational membership less closely than the pledge about adult baptism, but the core notion that the state cannot promote particular religious doctrines includes doctrines that cross denominational lines.

The Supreme Court's modern encounter with a doctrinal criterion set by government involved a Maryland oath for officials that required belief in God. This, of course, encompassed the belief of a high proportion of American citizens, but the Supreme Court had no difficulty deciding in *Torcaso v. Watkins*[11] that it was unconstitutional. The Court relied mainly on the Establishment Clause, but also referred to the Free Exercise Clause. Justice Black's opinion treated the Maryland oath as discriminating among religions, because some religions do not accept the notion of a single Supreme Being. Few people would like to see the outcome of this case reversed.

Matters become more arguable if the government's endorsement of religious doctrine carries no exclusionary consequences.[12] The government adopts a particular religious position, but does not reward those who agree or penalize those who disagree.

Here we must consider the strength of the government's statement, the narrowness of the ideas it sponsors, and the contexts in which those ideas are received. At one end of the spectrum are religious ideas that a wide range of our citizenry endorses, that are communicated in a context that demands nothing of the recipients, and that may seem to many citizens to be only a kind of pro forma or weak endorsement by the government. Although some Americans may feel genuinely offended that they must handle currency with the theological message "In God We Trust," most citizens take the motto on currency as not very significant. The status of "under God" in the Pledge of Allegiance, taken up in chapter 6, is more debatable. But suppose a state legislature, whose members feel hampered by *Roe v. Wade*'s creation of a constitutional right of abortion,[13] adopts a statute that reads: "The Bible,

---

[11] 367 U.S. 488 (1961).

[12] An intermediate circumstance is one in which the government allows private individuals to discriminate along certain doctrinal lines but not others. An example would be a law forbidding discrimination by private firms against "anyone who accepts Jesus Christ as Lord." This law would allow discrimination against Jews, Muslims, atheists, etc., but not against (most) Christians. I assume that laws can no more draw such lines than engage the government itself directly in discriminating.

[13] 410 U.S. 113 (1973).

including both Old and New Testaments, is the word of God. A reading of the following passages [five passages are quoted] tells us that abortion is deeply sinful. Any woman who has an abortion commits a grave offense against God and places her soul in immortal danger." The legislators who pass this law are serious and the law clearly and strongly expresses specific religious ideas that many citizens reject. One might well see such legislative expressions as designed to marshal public opinion to condemn (on religious grounds) everyone who seeks an abortion or performs one. I conclude from this example that legislatures could definitely be engaged in establishing religious ideas even if the laws themselves impose no adverse consequences on dissenters. If legislatures are capable of violating the Establishment Clause by propounding religious doctrines, so also are public schools. The very important, particular issues regarding schools are addressed in subsequent chapters.[14]

Although the basic ban on government promulgation of religious doctrines is relatively simple, some complex problems, in addition to those of mild endorsements, arise at the edges. These are well revealed by four questions, the first three of which we shall examine in this chapter. (1) May the government take *no actions* that indicate positions about religious doctrines? (2) What expressions count as those of the government? (3) What constitutes the teaching of doctrines in the forbidden sense? (4) How far may the government inform people, especially students, about religious practices and doctrines that it may not teach as true or false?

Implications of Government Policies

Our first question is easiest to answer—many laws and policies, as well as ethical principles taught in public schools, inevitably imply that religious doctrines that are diametrically opposed to the laws, policies, and ethical principles are mistaken. A government that maintains strong military forces and engages in armed conflict implies that pacifist religions are in error; one that forbids racial discrimination implies that religions based on racial inequality are misguided.[15]

---

[14] See also a more extended treatment in Kent Greenawalt, *Does God Belong in Public Schools?* (Princeton: Princeton University Press, 2005).

[15] One might try to avoid the conclusion that government policies, such as racial equality, imply the incorrectness of some religious doctrines by arguing that the government acts *only* on the basis of secular reason and is *not* making a judgment overall about what is right or wrong. However, officials do not often promote ethical principles they believe violate God's law, and citizens understand this.

Although the state unavoidably carries out actions that imply that certain religious doctrines about social justice and order are unsound, never, or rarely, need its policies imply *the correctness* of any particular religious understanding. Because nonreligious reasons based in liberal democracy (and multiple religious understandings) can underlie racial equality, for example, the state's adoption of that principle need not imply that any particular religious grounding is correct.[16]

The conclusion that public policies inevitably imply the falsity of some religious doctrines carries the corollary that, without aiming to, the government may disadvantage the religions whose doctrines are implicitly rejected. Suppose the religion teaches that polygamy is a duty or that members of different "races" should be segregated in all aspects of social life. Citizens may be hesitant to embrace a religion that teaches that the basic civic norms of their society are misconceived.[17] The unavoidable "fallout" for religions with rejected doctrines illustrates the wider truth that no government can be wholly neutral in its effects on different religions. In many subtle ways, what government does can indirectly aid or discourage the acceptance of particular religious ideas and the interests of various religious groups. Asking a government not to *aim* to promote or discourage any religion is a realistic political ambition; so also is asking the government to respond to unintended indirect effects by making accommodations. Asking the government to see that the effects of its actions are wholly neutral on various religious groups is to indulge in fantasy.

Which Actions Are Relevantly Those of the Government?

To answer our second question about which actions that announce or teach religious doctrines count as those of the government, we need to distinguish expressions of the government from the independent expressions of people who happen to work for it. Drawing this line is complicated because the purpose of the inquiry may vary. One may be asking: (1) what speech should entail the legal consequence of being by the government? or (2) should an

---

[16] See Andrew Koppelman, "No Expressly Religious Orthodoxy," 78 *Chicago-Kent Law Review* 729 (2003). My conclusion does not address the historical question whether a society would have accepted any particular principle but for a widely held religious understanding. Nor does the conclusion address whether reasons that on their face are not religious are persuasive independent of religious premises. Thus, someone might believe that all arguments for human equality fail, unless grounded in God's relations to human beings. See, e.g., Michael J. Perry, *The Idea of Human Rights: Four Inquiries* (New York: Oxford University Press, 1998).

[17] Of course, if the government is highly unpopular, its adoption of a policy could have the contrary effect, actually strengthening religions that lie in intransigent opposition to it.

official regard her speech as being sufficiently connected to the government
to make her announcement of a religious doctrine a violation of the Establishment Clause, even if a court would not impose any legal consequence?[18]
or (3) should an official regard her support of religious doctrine as inappropriate according to cultural norms or standards of political philosophy, even
though not strictly unconstitutional? A further complexity concerns "either-
or" classification as contrasted with judgments of "degree." Although from
the standpoint of political responsibility one might conceive matters of degree—with some speech being *more* for the government than other speech—
when officials apply legal rules, they typically need to regard particular expressions as being "for the government" or "not for the government."

Among the expressions that clearly count as government speech are statutes,
executive orders, and court orders and opinions. On the other hand, when
officials are definitely not acting for the government, they are legally free to
express religious sentiments, whether implicitly by attending worship services
or explicitly by revealing their religious opinions in speeches or interviews.[19]

Some officials, leading elected officials especially, often speak in a way that
attaches to their position but may not be quite "for the government." Two
striking examples are senators' speeches on the floor of the Senate and opinions by individual judges that are not for their court. Whatever the legal
consequences may be of a succession of floor speeches that indicate a religious aim in adopting legislation, individual senators are legally free to express their opinions about pending bills, including conclusions drawn from
religious premises.

Individual judicial opinions are more troublesome. Judges occasionally
comment about their own personal backgrounds and outlooks in concurring
and dissenting opinions that are not "for the court." Nevertheless, formal
opinions, which remain important parts of the judicial record, are too close
to being "for the government" to warrant a judge asserting the truth of any
doctrinal religious proposition as if it should carry direct weight in a case.
Thus, a judge should not say, "I refuse to uphold any imposition of capital
punishment because it violates God's will." But if a judge says, "As a believing Roman Catholic, I think capital punishment is morally unjustified,
but our law provides otherwise," that is all right, because judges not infre-

---

[18] A court might not impose legal consequences because according to administrable standards of
constitutional law, such speech does not count as an announcement for the government. It might also
not impose legal consequences because the announcement has no relevant effect on anyone. I have in
mind here mainly the former reason.

[19] Good judgment in light of one's public position, however, should impose restraints—a Supreme
Court justice who told a reporter for publication that damnation awaits all who do not accept Jesus
Christ as their personal redeemer would act irresponsibly.

quently express their personal views about laws they think are undesirable but nevertheless uphold as constitutional, because our judge is merely indicating the source of his personal view and is not aiming to persuade judges or citizens who have a different view, and because his comment does not carry legal consequences.

Because of their particular roles, schoolteachers raise special concerns. Is a classroom teacher always speaking "for the state," or may each teacher express her own views, including views about religious truth, expecting students to realize that she speaks for herself? Within public universities, professors should be able to say whether they think an argument in favor of the existence of God is sound and strongly points toward the reality of a Supreme Being; but that approach is not workable for third-grade teachers. If their primary teacher tells third graders what she thinks is true about religion, her pupils will not easily separate what she believes from what the school is teaching. The issue becomes more arguable as students become older and have multiple teachers during the same year, but I shall suggest in a subsequent chapter that public school teachers should not assert in classrooms that particular religious propositions are true.

This conclusion raises a troubling question that is not always honestly faced: does such a restraint unfairly discriminate against religion in comparison with other subjects of human concern? On the one side, those favoring a strong separation of religion and government say that religion is a subject for outside school; opponents say the schools have their own religion of secularism. We need to understand fairly what transpires and why people react so differently.

Any discrimination, if it exists, is among ideas or subjects, not directly among students, but people care about what they believe. If school gives their beliefs short shrift, children may feel they are unfairly dealt with. And parents may worry that schools are unfairly inducing their children to develop false outlooks, contrary to the beliefs and values they are imparting to their offspring.

Although the rule that schools may not teach claims of religious truth or falsity includes a bar on teaching "secularism," *if* secularism is understood as a philosophy that asserts that God does not exist or is unimportant, a school that teaches almost everything but religious truths implicitly may convey the pervasive message that life and social relations can be understood without reference to God. That is a message to which many deeply religious people object.[20] But, as we have seen, the most obvious alternative, teachers

---

[20] Is it possible to deflect the concern about religion in the following way? "In liberal democracies, schools should not endorse one or another conception of the good life. Religion is not unique; the

teaching the truth of religious propositions, is even worse.[21] We shall in a subsequent chapter examine how far this problem can be rectified or ameliorated by a strategy of teaching *about* religion.

What Is an Unacceptable Teaching of Religious Ideas?

We now reach our third question: what actions the government takes overstep the line of announcing or teaching doctrines of religion?[22] Two aspects of that subject that we will address subsequently are teaching about religion and what we may call mild supports, expressions that are undoubtedly by the government but may be so innocuous they create no serious problem. Once we put these aside, we are left with government approval of particular religious views, of more widely shared religious premises, or of religion.

If Congress may not legislate that the doctrine of transubstantiation accurately portrays what takes place when a Roman Catholic priest performs the Mass,[23] or that "symbolic representation" is the true understanding of communion,[24] may it declare the truth of Christianity, the existence of a beneficent God, or the value of religion? I have strongly suggested that what-

---

schools take no position on the good life." This conceivable rejoinder has at least two fundamental flaws. First, public schools in the United States are generally not neutral about the good life. They teach students that serious work is desirable, that taking drugs and using alcohol heavily are undesirable, that maintaining a healthy body and developing broad cultural interests are desirable, etc.; and they should continue to so. Second, everyone agrees that schools should teach about justice, principles of mutual respect and fairness that are at the core of principles of liberal democracy. They should teach students to respect each other, to treat each other as equals, to be tolerant of opposing views (at least in public life), to be honest, and so on. However one distinguishes justice from the good life (and however difficult that may be), most religions have a lot to say about justice, for example, teaching respect for others, teaching that human beings are equal in God's eyes. If schools present claims of justice in a manner that excludes religion, deeply religious people may object that the most fundamental reasons why people should treat each other justly are omitted.

[21] That is not to say it will be worse for those religious people who want their doctrines taught in school and succeed in having their way.

[22] For analytical purposes, I have distinguished the questions of whether something counts as a relevant government action from whether the content of a message is an unacceptable promotion or teaching of religious doctrine. One needs to be cautious about this, however. Let us assume that statutes, formal presidential messages, and Supreme Court opinions are all expressions of the U.S. government. It is conceivable that language that would violate a principle of nonestablishment if placed in a statute would be permissible if placed in a presidential message or Supreme Court opinion, each of which is less formal than a statute.

[23] Limits on legislatures also apply to executive officials and judges. In their formal announcements, they cannot declare that the doctrines of a particular religious organization or perspective are true, or false.

[24] Lest it be objected that with its limited powers Congress would have no business adopting any such law, quite apart from the Establishment Clause, the answer is that states and localities, whose powers are not similarly limited, are also barred from such legislation.

ever may have been true in the nineteenth century,[25] at this stage of history a formal declaration that Christianity is the true religion would be improper. All sections of our country have many non-Christians. A modern judge may describe the country as Christian, in the sense that Christianity remains the dominant religion, and she may note that Christian ideas have significantly influenced legal developments, but she should not assert that we are a Christian country in the sense that implies that Christianity is the one true religion or is *the* religion of the United States.

Statements about a beneficent God are subject to a similar analysis. Some religions believe in no God and others in many gods. Although assertions about a beneficent God were prevalent at our country's founding, are contained in the Declaration of Independence, and remain in many state constitutions,[26] nevertheless government should not now make formal, serious claims about a beneficent God.[27]

We reach more difficult terrain if what officials assert is the value of religion in people's lives. One cannot coherently assert that "religion is true," because different religions assert propositions that are not consistent with each other. But one might coherently assert that religion is valuable, meaning that people's lives are enriched, or that they have a truer understanding of life's significance, if they practice some religion.[28] Would this be an appropriate message for a statute, a formal presidential order, a judicial opinion, or school teaching? I think not, but that view depends on the controversial conclusion that the government should not promote religion over nonreligion or irreligion, a point we considered in connection with aid to religious groups.

INDIRECT GOVERNMENT SUPPORT OF RELIGIOUS TEACHING

Two significant Supreme Court cases, both in the mid—twentieth century, concerned state involvement in religious teaching rather than direct teaching by government officials. These cases can be seen as being about aid to religious groups or about the promotion of religious ideas; they include both

[25] One could find in the nineteenth century judicial opinions saying that the United States is a Christian country and that Christianity is a part of the common law. *Vidal v. Girard's Executors*, 43 U.S. 127 (1844); *Holy Trinity Church v. United States*, 143 U.S. 457 (1892).

[26] See *ACLU v. Capitol Square Review and Advisory Bd.*, 243 F.3d 289, 296 n. 6 (6th Cir. 2001).

[27] This conclusion carries the implication that state constitutions with such language now violate the federal Establishment Clause *unless* one conceives the language as having mainly historical significance, not as representing a present and substantial doctrinal statement.

[28] Even here, one could not speak without qualification; if most religions are enriching, some may be destructive. But one might assert that the vast majority of religions are enriching.

elements. In the first case, *McCollum v. Board of Education*,[29] the Court reviewed a "released time" program under which teachers drawn from private religious groups instructed children whose parents wished, for half an hour each week during the regular school day, within the public schools. The students had either to attend religious instruction or to pursue secular studies at some place within the school building. The instructors in religion were employed by an interfaith Champaign Council on Religious Education, but were subject to the approval and supervision of the school superintendent.

The case was decided one year after *Everson*, and Justice Black again wrote for the Court. Because tax-supported property was used for religious instruction, school authorities cooperated closely with the interfaith council, and pupils "compelled by law to go to school for secular education were released in part from their legal duty upon the condition that they attend the religious classes,"[30] the program fell under the bar of the Establishment Clause.

Four years later, in *Zorach v. Clauson*,[31] the Court sustained New York's "released time" system. Under that state's law, students could be released from public school for religious instruction away from the school premises.[32] The case is notable for its shift from the controversial result in *McCollum*, and for its highly "accommodationist" general language, penned by Justice Douglas, who paradoxically later became the Court's most vehement separationist. Justice Douglas analogized the permission to attend religious instruction to individual requests by parents to have children excused for religious occasions.[33] Douglas did not deny a point stressed by all three dissents, that the program did not simply excuse all students from school, it required that students not attending religious instruction stay in school. Nor did he deny that a student who failed to go to religious instruction would be regarded as a truant.[34] For the dissenters, the fact that a student who was excused for religious instruction and did not attend would be a truant made the program essentially indistinguishable from that condemned in *McCollum*;[35] but Jus-

---

[29] 333 U.S. 203 (1948).

[30] Id. at 209–10. In a concurring opinion, Justice Frankfurter cautioned that decision should be about particular released time systems with judicial scrutiny "of the exact relation between religious instruction and the public educational system in the specific situation." Id. at 225.

[31] 343 U.S. 306 (1952).

[32] Students whose parents did not request their release were kept in school.

[33] *Zorach*, note 31 at 311, 313.

[34] Justice Douglas declared that no finding of coercion has been made, but he recognized that the compulsory school attendance law involved a degree of coercion. Indeed, his analogy to the parental request that a child be excused for an individual religious occasion supposes that "the teacher, in order to make sure the student is not a truant, goes further and requires a report from the priest, the rabbi, or the minister."

[35] Id. at 315–17 (Black, J., dissenting), 324 (Jackson, J., dissenting).

tice Douglas treated this as a form of state cooperation with parental wishes.[36] His use of children being excused for individual religious occasions, such as Yom Kippur, is illuminating. Typically parents may request that their individual children be excused from school for all sorts of reasons, *including* but not limited to religious ones, and rarely when individuals are excused is the school instruction for other students affected. By contrast, the released time program was specifically *for religious instruction*, with the nearly inevitable result of the program that enough students left school so that those who remained had some kind of study hall or review session. Nonetheless, Justice Douglas characterized this as appropriate cooperation.

In a passage often cited by those protesting against any rigid separationist view of the Establishment Clause, Douglas wrote:

> We are a religious people whose institutions presuppose a Supreme Being. We guarantee the freedom to worship as one chooses. We make room for as wide a variety of beliefs and creeds as the spiritual needs of man deem necessary. We sponsor an attitude on the part of government that shows no partiality to any one group and that lets each flourish according to the zeal of its adherents and the appeal of its dogma. When the state encourages religious instruction or cooperates with religious authorities by adjusting the schedule of public events to sectarian needs, it follows the best of our traditions. For it then respects the religious nature of our people and accommodates the public service to their spiritual needs.[37]

In dissent, Justice Black urged that any use of the state's coercive power "to help or hinder some religious sects or to prefer all religious sects over nonbelievers or vice versa is just what I think the First Amendment forbids."[38]

Zorach relies on an understanding of permissible accommodation that is not easily defended. The school week constitutes roughly 32 hours. Even when one takes into account after-school activities such as sports and clubs, and ample time for homework, enough time remains for children to receive religious instruction. *Unless* one thinks of public education as replacing education in ordinary subjects that is substantially religious, regular education does not "squeeze out" religious instruction. Assuming that children are up

---

[36] Id. at 311–13.

[37] Id. at 313–14.

[38] Id. at 318. Justices Frankfurter and Jackson, dissenting, also emphasized the impermissible use of the state's coercive power, with Jackson concluding, "Today's judgment will be more interesting to students of psychology and of the judicial process than to students of constitutional law." Id. at 325.

to receiving more than 32 hours of instruction per week (much less than the hours spent in school in many other countries), the plan accepted in *Zorach* did not really respond to some state-imposed disadvantage, or even to a disadvantage imposed by private parties. The true "benefit" of the plan was that it made religious instruction more palatable to students and increased the chances of attendance. Participating students did not need to sacrifice "free time," they missed only a boring study hall. We shall leave for a later chapter a fuller exploration of how courts should draw the line between permissible accommodation and impermissible aid or sponsorship, but whether *Zorach* is correctly decided under a desirable approach is very doubtful.[39]

DISESTABLISHMENT AND SEPARATION

I have proceeded through this chapter without once employing the metaphor of separation of church and state. When one considers government aid to religious organizations for their religious activities, or aid to those organizations on the basis of religious criteria (even if the aid goes for hospitals, adoption agencies, etc.), and when one considers a bar on state promotion of religious doctrines, one need not refer to any concept of separation that distinguishes itself from disestablishment. For government to aid religious activities or to sponsor religious doctrines is to "establish" the favored religious organizations and doctrines. Although I have noted respects in which modern constitutional principles on these subjects exceed what the founders regarded as establishments of religion, modern principles are based on the kind of developing notion of disestablishment that we could have expected, even if separation of church and state had never become the dominant phrase for what the Establishment Clause demands. At least as to these subjects, the shift in terminology seems not to have made a practical difference.[40]

---

[39] My judgment on this issue may well be affected by the fact that my father was Zorach's counsel. I was sixteen at the time, and recall his surprise and acute disappointment over how the Court had resolved the case.

[40] Someone might counter that, at least for the *Zorach* case, separation was a stronger objection to the New York plan. However, the New York plan understandably favored religion over nonreligious activities, and it practically favored religions big enough to mount regular after-school instruction over other religions, so it is far from clear that "disestablishment" arguments were weaker than separation arguments. And, in any event, since the Court approved the New York plan, *Zorach* indisputably is not an example in which the Court ruled a law invalid under the Establishment Clause because it had the ill-wisdom to rely on a principle of separation.

CHAPTER 5

Religious Words and Symbols in Public Places

One way a government may endorse or support particular religious ideas is by displaying signs with religious words or by using religious symbols. Were all a state's official buildings to have inscribed "Jesus, our Redeemer," or to display crosses in prominent places, that would recognize Christianity. The interesting, and constitutionally troublesome, issues arise in more ambiguous situations, in which it is unclear either whether words or symbols are religious or whether the state supports the religious message that they indisputably convey. The Supreme Court has decided six important cases involving religious messages in public places. We will examine those in due course, but I first consider the appropriate use of words and symbols detached from the nuances of Supreme Court opinions.

APPROPRIATE USE OF WORDS AND SYMBOLS

A government that should refrain from sponsoring any particular religious message should obviously avoid using words or symbols that imply its view that a particular religion is true. It follows that despite the large number of Christians in the United States, its governments should not employ Christian texts or symbolism to indicate that Christianity is the true, or best, religion. Were it all right for the government to promote Christianity in general, one would face the problem that versions of scriptural texts and the forms of some symbols, most notably crosses, differ among different Christian branches.[1] But the major concern is the presence of many non-Christians.[2]

A once religious symbol may become nonreligious over time, an evolution people may or may not understand. Many European countries have crosses on their flags or royal coats of arms. In their origin, these symbols signified that the country was Christian. But now citizens think of these crosses

---

[1] One might tell from whether the crosses did or did not have on them the crucified Christ whether the Christianity was Roman Catholic or Protestant. The Eastern Orthodox churches use crosses that differ in form from those of Catholics and Protestants.

[2] It is a more difficult question whether a display of Christian messages would be all right if everyone were Christian. On the view that people are free not to continue to be Christian, that the govern-

mainly as features of the countries' historical flags, not as endorsing Christianity.[3] The present meaning of other symbols is murkier, and their past
more complicated. The evergreen tree, a symbol in pre-Christian celebrations, was used by Christians to represent faith in everlasting life; a cut and
decorated evergreen is now commonly associated with Christmas and presents, but very few Christians or non-Christians have any sense of what it
may signify in religious terms.[4]

A rather different kind of situation involves the government's display of
symbols or texts that retain an undoubted religious significance but one that
the government does not support. State museums display early religious texts
(such as Books of Hours and the Gutenberg Bible) and paintings with religious symbols and figures. These texts and paintings convey religious messages, but that is not why the museum shows them. Viewers comfortably
draw a distinction between the verbal or symbolic message, and the aesthetic
and historical reasons that explain the choice to display these items in a
public museum.

It is when the main content of a message, or the degree of government
endorsement of its religious aspects, is uncertain, or viewers' reactions are
predictably mixed, that the more difficult problems arise. Officials should
not use symbols to promote a religion, even if they believe most citizens
will fail to grasp what they are doing. And, whatever their actual purposes,
officials also should avoid using symbols in a way that most citizens will
take as an endorsement. What if officials do not intend an endorsement, and
they are confident most citizens will not perceive one, but they realize that
a minority of citizens will believe the state is supporting a religion? When
citizens mistakenly think the government is promoting their own religion,
that is unfortunate. When citizens mistakenly think the government promotes a religion other than their own, and they sense that they are outsiders,
that is still more unfortunate. Although officials cannot base their actions
on how the most sensitive citizens will react, they should hesitate to use
symbols in a manner that many citizens will take as supporting a religion,
especially if most of the citizens who perceive an endorsement do not accept
the religion they feel is being endorsed.

---

ment is not competent about religion, and that sponsoring religion is not its business, the government
should not convey Christian messages even if everyone is Christian.

[3] However, some people may still regard the flags as one representation of the continuing Christian
heritage of these countries, most of which still retain a diluted form of an established church.

[4] Nevertheless, these trees are unmistakably associated with Christmas as a holiday, and everyone
understands that Christmas is a celebration of the birth of Christ.

Whether the government itself displays a text or symbol on public property, or allows a message it owns to be displayed on private property, its involvement suffices to generate concern about support or endorsement.

The primary controversies over actual texts have involved displays of the Ten Commandments in public schools and inside or outside state buildings. No one doubts that the Ten Commandments (in its various versions)[5] are substantially religious. Jews and Christians regard the Ten Commandments as among the most important biblical texts.[6] The first five commandments concern relations of human beings to God. To argue that display of the Ten Commandments does not involve endorsement of the Jewish and Christian faiths, one must rest on a claim that it reflects an important historical source of American law and morality or that it is one among a number of examples of lawgiving, most of which are secular.

The most common disputes about nontextual symbols have concerned Christmas decorations and crèches: portrayals of Jesus, Mary, Joseph, shepherds, wise men, and animals around a manger. We can examine the general issues about texts and symbols in light of that example, imagining that a city council considering whether to place a crèche in its city square during the Christmas season is aware that it should not support or endorse Christianity. What reasons, nonetheless, might be offered council members for displaying the crèche?

One conceivable possibility is that the crèche in context is not really religious, but rather a familiar cultural symbol of the Christmas season. However, the crèche has not, for most people, transmuted into a nonreligious symbol. It calls up the miraculous events surrounding the birth of Jesus, told in three of the four Gospels.[7] If the city wants symbols that are arguably nonreligious, it can use Santa Claus,[8] reindeer, and Christmas trees; these would not seem to endorse Christianity.[9]

Assuming the crèche conveys a religious message, perhaps council members could believe that its display will not sponsor that religious content. However, in contrast to the religious paintings and sculptures one finds in a

---

[5] Formulations of the Commandments differ in Protestant, Catholic, and Jewish Bibles.

[6] For one Muslim view of the Ten Commandments, see I. A. Arshed, "Islam Supports Bible's Ten Commandments," http://www.islam101.com/religions/TenCommandments/tcQuran.htm (visited July 24, 2006).

[7] The Gospel of Mark has no birth story.

[8] Santa Claus is another name for Saint Nicholas, and thus has a religious lineage; but most people do not think of Santa Claus as religious.

[9] However, one might think that any Christmas symbols count as religious because Christmas is a Christian celebration.

museum, the typical outdoor crèche has no, or little, artistic merit, and it does not appear with other, nonreligious, works of art. Thus, artistic merit is not a basis for the council to conclude that the city will not be endorsing the crèche's religious message.

Can the members regard a display as merely reflecting the city's recognition of understandings and sentiments deeply rooted in the country's history? Such a claim about historical tradition comes down to this: Government appropriately recognizes dominant themes in American history; most Americans have been Christians who have treasured the story of the birth of Jesus. Our city recognizes that history, but without endorsing the crèche's religious message. This approach draws an overly subtle distinction and opens a gaping hole in the principle that the government should not promote religion.

The overly subtle distinction is between belief and historical recognition. Most citizens and officials are Christian. If, during the year, the crèche will be the only display that seems primarily religious, it is doubtful whether members of a council can distinguish in their own minds between what they take to be a healthy representation of the relationship between Christianity and our country, and what they regard as of historical importance. Even were they to successfully perform this exercise in mental gymnastics, how will most members of the public react? Will they discern that the city is merely acknowledging the historical importance of Christian beliefs, not implicitly endorsing the belief-system associated with the story of Jesus' birth? Not likely.

If cities could display crèches to reflect historical traditions, why could they not present detailed accounts of dominant Christian doctrines on the same basis? For the principle that bars government promotion of religion to have significance, it cannot be evaded by turning every presentation of the dominant religion into a paean of faithfulness to the country's traditions. To make the historical claim on behalf of displaying the crèche at all credible, one would have to add the further ingredient that the promotion of religion is not very significant.

One might think that the state has some latitude to celebrate Thanksgiving or to sponsor such relatively bland ideas as does "under God" in the Pledge of Allegiance, topics we shall take up in the next chapter. But the crèche, a powerful and distinctly Christian symbol, resists such an analysis. The government has no latitude to endorse a single religion, not even the religion of most of our citizens.

The city council could try to meet this difficulty by presenting symbols associated with various religious traditions at various times of the year, but this strategy creates its own problems. Choices to include or not would become troublesome. And if the city presented a symbol of Judaism—the menorah—during the Christmas season, it would seem to give Chanukah an importance it lacks within the Jewish tradition. Other religions whose symbols might be displayed in December could be similarly distorted.

Understanding that they should not endorse Christianity, responsible council members must ask themselves not only whether some nonreligious justification might possibly support putting a crèche in the public square, but also whether many citizens, particularly non-Christians, will perceive support of Christianity. If they will, that itself is a strong reason not to display the crèche.

Thus far, I have focused on the crèche alone, with some reference to concerns about other religions. But with the crèche, as with many other free exercise and establishment problems, the relation between it and nonreligious texts and symbols is also of interest. No one could object if on July 4, the council displayed a representation of the Declaration of Independence, implying that the Revolutionary War was justified and that the Declaration states principles of governance that deserve our continued support.[10] As chapter 4 has suggested, although the government properly teaches ideas in moral and political theory as valid, it should not sponsor claims of religious truth.

What if, rather than sponsoring any messages on its own, the council makes a forum available for all kinds of displays? May it allow religious messages along with others? Must it allow religious messages with others? If a city makes a space available for people to display whatever messages they want, if the space is open to everyone on an equal basis, *and* if the public understands that the state is not endorsing any of the messages, the council has no good reason to exclude religious messages. However, if the infrequency and timing of actual displays would leave uninformed citizens with the impression that the government was itself conveying certain messages, actual perceptions could undermine the government's policy of neutrality.

Were a state to react by allowing all but religious messages, that would create its own difficulties. Government should not discourage private communication of religious messages in comparison with nonreligious ones, by making public property available for *all* but religious messages. Think of Speaker's Corner in London's Hyde Park, where people gather to deliver and hear ideas of every kind. It would be odd for the government to announce that the one thing people cannot say anything about is religious truth

---

[10] One does not often see in public squares portrayals of events in American history of which we are now ashamed, such as the slave trade and the pillage of Native Americans.

and falsity. If only private messages are involved, if the only state contribution is the provision of space, a much more natural approach is the nondiscriminatory policy of allowing every kind of message. If officials are worried that citizens will perceive that some private religious messages are carrying state endorsement, the best remedy, if feasible, is to permit all messages but to make very clear that the state is not endorsing any of them.

Constitutional Principles and Major Cases

Controversies over religious texts and symbols in public places have produced six major Supreme Court decisions involving the Ten Commandments (three cases), Christmas season displays (two cases), and a cross. None of these cases was decided before 1980. Part of the explanation is that the Supreme Court did not review some disputes resolved by lower courts, but the deeper reason is that various long-standing practices reflecting a Christian point of view have grown to seem more problematic than they had to earlier generations.

In the first of the six, *Stone v. Graham*,[11] a Kentucky statute required that public schools post the Ten Commandments in every classroom. Although each copy had at the bottom a comment about the secular adoption of the Ten Commandments as the fundamental legal basis of Western Civilization and the common law, the Supreme Court had no difficulty concluding that the Ten Commandments was a sacred text and that the principal purpose of the law was "plainly religious."[12] The Court was obviously right that no one could suggest such a pervasive displaying of the Ten Commandments because of its influence on secular law in the Western world. As I have mentioned, the first five commandments concern relations to God that are not a direct concern of modern law, and most of the prohibitions of the second five commandments involve precepts against killing, stealing, lying, and so on, that any legal system will have. No doubt the Ten Commandments has influenced moral attitudes and affected some legal norms (especially about Sabbath observance and sexual practices), but its influence on the common law overall has not been very great.

The Court's next case, *Lynch v. Donnelly* in 1989,[13] involved a crèche. That case, in which the "endorsement test" first emerged as a distinctive

---

[11] 449 U.S. 39 (1980) (per curiam).
[12] Id. at 41.
[13] 465 U.S. 668.

approach,[14] provides a window into how justices can use, and manipulate, doctrinal tests to reach results they regard as suitable.

The Christmas display, owned by the City of Pawtucket, Rhode Island, and erected in a shopping center owned by a nonprofit organization, included a crèche, as well as a Santa Claus house, reindeer pulling Santa's sleigh, a Christmas tree, carolers, cutout figures of a clown and some animals, and a banner reading "Season's greetings."[15] The challenge was to the crèche. The district court found that by including the crèche the city had "tried to endorse and promulgate religious beliefs," with the "effect of affiliating the City with . . . Christian beliefs."[16]

The Supreme Court disagreed. Chief Justice Burger's opinion suggests various theories, sowing confusion about which, individually or together, were sufficient to carry the day. The opinion signals a certain discomfort with the strong rhetoric of earlier cases, commenting that the metaphor of a "wall of separation" is "not a wholly accurate description of the practical aspects" of church-state relations.[17] In respect to the *Lemon* test, Burger noted, in a manner that would mislead any but the well-informed reader, "our unwillingness to be confined to any single test or criterion in this sensitive area."[18] After this caution, he proceeded to treat the case under *Lemon*'s three standards of purpose, effect, and entanglement.

The opinion refers to the adoption of a statute providing paid chaplains in the House and Senate by the Congress that proposed the First Amendment. Subsequent actions show "an unbroken history of official acknowledgment by all three branches of government of the role of religion in American life."[19] These include recognition and subsidization of religious holidays, the national motto of "In God We Trust," and the language "One nation under God" in the Pledge of Allegiance, religious paintings—predominantly Christian--in the National Gallery, and a frieze of Moses and the Ten Commandments in the Supreme Court.

[14] Id. at 688–94.

[15] Id. at 671.

[16] Id. at 672. The court also said that the resulting political divisiveness amounted to an excessive entanglement. The court of appeals affirmed.

[17] Id. at 673.

[18] He cited two cases in which the test was actually used despite mild disclaimers. He then suggested that in two other cases the Court did not apply the test, but he failed to remark that one of these involved discrimination between religions, and that the Court used the stricter approach according to which the law could not stand unless the state satisfied the compelling interest test. *Larson v. Valente*, 456 U.S. 228 (1982). As Justice Brennan's dissent pointed out, 465 U.S. at 696, only in a case involving legislative chaplains, *Marsh v. Chambers*, 463 U.S. 783 (1983), had the Court sustained a practice that did not appear to be valid under the *Lemon* standard.

[19] *Lynch*, note 13 supra, at 674.

The city, according to the Burger opinion, had a secular purpose to celebrate the Christmas holiday, and this purpose included the crèche.[20] The Court could not find a "primary effect" to advance religion because the crèche was not "more beneficial to and more an endorsement of religion" than other laws and practices the Court had sustained, such as textbook loans, grants for college buildings, tax exemptions, and Sunday closing laws.[21] Rather, any benefit to religion was "indirect," "remote," or "incidental" and thus permitted under the effects prong of the *Lemon* test.[22] In answer to Justice Brennan's dissent, Chief Justice Burger acknowledged the important religious meaning of the crèche, but he maintained that in the display the crèche was a reminder of the origins of Christmas.[23]

We can discern from the opinion three possible bases for the Court's decision, none of which is convincing in this context. The first ground is that the display as a whole is secular, and that the crèche's inclusion does not really endorse or support religion. The analogy to religious paintings in government museums is crucial here. The problems with the analogy are that the city has no aesthetic reason to display an ordinary crèche and that secular reasons to display other Christmas symbols do not justify including a powerful religious symbol.

The second approach is that whatever support or endorsement of religion is given is *of a kind* that was historically accepted. For this line, the analogy to legislative chaplains and early days of Thanksgiving and prayer is most relevant. Were this approach to dominate judgment, courts would assess the permissibility of modern practices against the views of the First Congress (and presumably the Congress that proposed the Fourteenth Amendment) about what was acceptable. As I have suggested in chapter 2, a faithful employment of this approach would sustain many practices the Supreme Court has declared invalid. It would also be impossible to square with the *Lemon* test, because the founders would have accepted various measures that had a religious purpose and a main effect of supporting religion. As earlier chapters explain, the development of constitutional concepts is a healthy aspect of interpretation of a written constitution; judges should not focus narrowly

[20] Id. at 681.

[21] Id. at 681.

[22] About entanglement, the chief justice found little evidence of divisiveness, and noted that "this Court has not held that political divisiveness alone can serve to invalidate otherwise permissible conduct." Id. at 683–84.

[23] Id. at 680, 683. "If the presence of the crèche in this display violates the Establishment Clause, a host of other forms of taking official note of Christmas, and of our religious heritage, are equally offensive." Id. at 686.

on practices that were deemed acceptable when constitutional safeguards were originally adopted.

The third approach involves measuring the *magnitude* of support and endorsement against widely accepted practices and earlier case decisions. The crèche, according to this approach, is no more supportive of religion than are days of Thanksgiving, textbook loans, tax exemptions, and Sunday closing laws. Were one to refine this approach further than the Court does, one would need to distinguish between endorsement from other forms of support, because this approach makes no sense for many forms of support. A crèche provides no support other than endorsement. Textbook loans may provide significant financial support to parochial schools but little endorsement. The opinion implies that the amount of support to religion that is constitutionally permissible is independent of secular benefits a practice confers. That is strikingly mistaken, at least about support other than endorsement.[24] The greater the secular purpose and benefit of a law or practice, the greater one would expect the permissible amount of support to religion to be. For tax exemptions and Sunday closing laws, which are thought to achieve very significant secular purposes, one might regard the actual benefit to religious groups as substantial without thinking it "primary." But were the same benefits to religion to accompany a trivial secular objective, one might well judge support of religion to be a primary effect.[25] The whole Christmas display made, at best, a slight contribution to secular welfare, and any *extra* secular benefit of including the crèche was slighter still. One could not conclude that the amount of support to religion was all right because it did not exceed that provided by a tax exemption.

Lynch shows us just how flexible the *Lemon* test can be about both purpose and effect. In finding a secular purpose, the Court rejected Justice Brennan's argument that the city could have achieved all its secular purposes without including the crèche.[26] And it set the "purpose" bar very low; a law is invalid only if "motivated wholly by religious considerations."[27] It is not

---

[24] One *might* think that endorsement is an either-or question and that the degree of secular benefit does not matter for the degree of permissible endorsement. But the opinion does not recognize, much less resolve, that issue. Justice O'Connor's opinion in the "under God" case, discussed in the next chapter, suggests that secular benefit may affect whether one would find an endorsement at all; I express strong skepticism about that view as applied to "under God" in the Pledge of Allegiance.

[25] To employ an extremely crude mathematical representation, one would not regard a religious effect of twenty units as "primary" if the secular benefit was one thousand units, but it would be primary in comparison with a secular benefit of three units.

[26] Id. at 681, in response to id. at 699 (Brennan, J., dissenting). Brennan argued that *if* you can accomplish all your secular purposes without a crèche, the aim in including the crèche must be a sectarian one.

[27] Id. at 680.

hard to see that when one looks at effects of supporting religion, one person's (forbidden) primary effect can be another's (allowed) incidental effect.[28] But a fair appraisal of the facts of *Lynch* should have led to the conclusion that the effect of including the crèche in the display was dominantly to provide some (mild) support to Christianity. The issue about purpose is slightly more complex because officials might have been motivated only by a desire to please consumers and help merchants. Nonetheless, a conscious effort to achieve these ends by providing a religious message counts as a religious purpose even if individuals in the government were personally indifferent to furthering Christianity.

Although the Court's reliance on various approaches makes it hard to say just what *Lynch* stands for,[29] Justice O'Connor, who also joined the Court's opinion, did develop a clear theory about what should count.[30] Her concurring opinion offered what she called "a clarification of our Establishment Clause doctrine."[31] The clause "prohibits government from making adherence to a religion relevant in any way to a person's standing in the political community."[32] The typical "infringement is government endorsement or disapproval of religion . . . [which] sends a message to nonadherents that they are outsiders, not full members of the political community, and an accompanying message to adherents that they are insiders, favored members of the political community."[33]

According to Justice O'Connor, "a statement's meaning for its audience depends both on the speaker's intention and on the 'objective' meaning of the statement in the community."[34] The forbidden purpose under *Lemon* is the intent to convey endorsement or disapproval. The forbidden effect is a perception by citizens that the government is endorsing or condemning a religion. She determined that the crèche display involved neither form of

---

[28] As we have seen, the Court, by comparing the magnitude of support to religion of the crèche display with the magnitude of support for programs that yield much greater secular benefits, gives to its conclusion that religious support is only incidental a big boost that lacks theoretical justification.

[29] One does not know whether the chief justice simply chose to throw out various strands of defense, or wrote as he did to compromise among a variety of positions held by justices joining the opinion.

[30] Her vote was necessary to make up a majority.

[31] *Lynch*, note 13 supra, at 687.

[32] Id.

[33] Id. at 688. The focus on "institutional entanglement and on endorsement or disapproval of religion clarifies the *Lemon* test as an analytical device." Id. at 689. For Justice O'Connor, potential for political divisiveness is too speculative in individual cases and "should not be an independent test of constitutionality." Id.

[34] One must look at both "the subjective and objective components of the message . . . to determine whether the action carries a forbidden meaning." Id.

endorsement. The purpose of the city officials was to celebrate "the public holiday through its traditional symbols."[35] As for effect, although the setting did not neutralize the religious significance of the crèche, it did, as with a religious painting in a museum, negate any message that the state endorses the religious content.[36] The crucial constitutional inquiries were, she said, not matters of simple historical fact but legal questions requiring "judicial interpretation of social facts." This chapter's final section marks some of the crucial questions about O'Connor's endorsement test and its viability; my own critical analysis of endorsement is reserved for chapter 10, which addresses various Establishment Clause tests and standards.

Justice Brennan, joined by Justices Marshall, Blackmun, and Stevens, wrote a lengthy dissent in *Lynch*.[37] Drawing from *Stone v. Graham*, Brennan inferred a religious purpose for the crèche, given that all valid secular objectives could be accomplished by a display without a crèche.[38] The primary effect "of including a nativity scene" is "to place the government's imprimatur of approval" on Christian beliefs.[39] About the Court's suggestion that

[35] Id. at 691. The district court's finding of a purpose to endorse was clearly erroneous, she concluded.

[36] Id. at 692. The same is true, she asserted, about government celebration of Thanksgiving, legislative prayers, "In God We Trust" on coins, and the opening of court with "God save the United States and this honorable court." Id. at 693. "These government acknowledgments of religion serve, in the only ways reasonably possible in our culture, the legitimate secular purposes of solemnizing public occasions, expressing confidence in the future, and encouraging the recognition of what is worthy of appreciation in society." Id. This language of Justice O'Connor foreshadows her approach to "under God" in the Pledge of Allegiance, discussed in the next chapter.

[37] He remarked that "the Court's less than vigorous application of the *Lemon* test may suggest that its commitment to it is only superficial." Id. at 696.

[38] Letters to city officials about "keep[ing] Christ in Christmas," made it impossible to conclude with confidence "that a wholly secular goal predominates." Id. at 701. Justice Brennan remarked in a footnote that inclusion of the crèche would fall under a criterion he suggested in *Schempp*, namely that government should not use religious means to serve governmental ends when secular means would suffice.

[39] Id. at 701. Despite its secular setting, the prominently displayed crèche "retains a specifically Christian religious meaning." Id. at 708. It is a "mystical re-creation of an event that lies at the heart of the Christian faith." The crèche, in this context, does not play the same role as a painting in a museum. Id. at 712. Nor is it like studying *Paradise Lost* in a literature course or gothic cathedrals in an architecture course.

Brennan suggested that when the power of government is placed behind a religious belief, minorities are put under an "indirect coercive pressure" to conform. Id. at 702. Since a crèche in a Christmas display will hardly exercise much pressure on people to conform, a crèche in this kind of Christmas display, or even in a display where it dominates, will not exert much pressure on non-Christians to conform to Christian practices (though it may cause a sense of exclusion). Thus, one doubts that pressure to conform is a crucial aspect of objections to this form of government sponsorship.

Near the end of his opinion, Justice Brennan quoted Justice Frankfurter from *McGowan v. Maryland* to the effect that the Establishment Clause "withdr[aws] from the sphere of legitimate legislative concern and competence a specific, but comprehensive, area of human conduct: man's belief or disbe-

government acknowledgments of religion are acceptable, Brennan wrote that if a government chooses to incorporate an arguably religious element into a public ceremony, its acknowledgment must not promote one faith or sponsor religion generally.[40] For Brennan, historical acceptance could not alone justify a challenged action; the central inquiry should be whether practices "threaten those consequences which the framers deeply feared."[41]

The next public display case, from Pittsburgh, involved two challenges, one to a crèche owned by the Holy Name Society that had been put on the Grand Staircase of the County Courthouse, the other to a Chanukah menorah placed next to a Christmas tree and a sign saluting liberty outside the city-county building.[42] Four justices thought both displays were acceptable; three justices thought both were unacceptable; Justices Blackmun and O'Connor, whose votes determined the outcomes, thought the second display was acceptable, but the first was not. These two justices united with their three colleagues who thought both displays unacceptable in adopting "endorsement" as the controlling inquiry for public displays.[43]

In the interim since *Lynch*, Justice O'Connor had explicated her endorsement approach in somewhat greater detail in a case reviewing a "moment of silence" in public schools.[44] The relevant issue under the effects test, she said, was whether an objective observer, "acquainted with the Free Exercise Clause and the values it promotes and with the text, legislative history, and implementation of the statute, would perceive a law as a state endorsement" of religion.[45]

---

lief in the verity of some transcendental idea and man's expression in action of that belief or disbelief." Id. at 726.

[40] Id. at 714. Brennan wrote that permissible acknowledgments may have shifted from being religious to being secular, as with Thanksgiving celebrations, or may recognize religious beliefs and practices "as an aspect of our national history and culture," as with "In God We Trust" on coins. Id. at 715–16. Brennan is straining when he talks of Thanksgiving as "unquestionably secular and patriotic," an occasion at which we are free "to address that gratitude either to a divine beneficence or to such mundane sources as good luck or the country's abundant natural wealth." Id. at 716.

[41] Id. at 719. In asking whether a particular practice is justified on historical grounds, Brennan argued that the Court had previously limited its inquiry to that particular practice; the Framers had no view about public displays of nativity scenes since the widespread celebration of Christmas did not emerge until the nineteenth century. Many of the sects who were foes of established religion also opposed the celebration of Christmas.

[42] *County of Allegheny v. American Civil Liberties Union*, 492 U.S. 573 (1989).

[43] In a part of his opinion that is for himself and Justice Stevens, Justice Blackmun called the rationale of the majority opinion in *Lynch* "none too clear" and embraced Justice O'Connor's approach, which "rejects any notion that this Court will tolerate some government endorsement of religion" and articulates a method for determining whether the government has endorsed religion. Id. at 594–95.

[44] *Wallace v. Jaffree*, 472 U.S. 38, 67–84 (O'Connor, J., concurring) (1985).

[45] Id. at 83, 76.

In a part of his opinion that was for the Court, Justice Blackmun concluded that in contrast to *Lynch*, nothing detracted from the religious message of the crèche inside the courthouse.[46] In a part of the opinion that represented his views only, Justice Blackmun said that the menorah has both religious and secular dimensions; with the menorah standing next to the Christmas tree and a sign saluting liberty, the city communicated its "secular celebration."[47] Justice O'Connor considered the menorah to be a religious symbol, but she thought that the city's "combined display does not convey a message of endorsement of Judaism or of religion in general."[48] Justice Brennan, with Marshall and Stevens, thought that display of the menorah "works a distortion of the Jewish religious calendar," in which Chanukah is a minor holiday,[49] and that the display did show favoritism toward Judaism.[50]

Justice Brennan did not struggle with the question whether anyone in a dominantly Christian community would understand the placing of the menorah as showing government favoritism of Judaism over Christianity--an unlikely supposition--but one might reasonably think that the menorah would seem to favor Judaism (as inside the general culture) in relation to other non-Christian religions (as outside). The issue of "favoring" minority religions is addressed at greater length in chapter 14.

Justice Kennedy, with Chief Justice Rehnquist, Justice White, and Justice Scalia, argued that the Establishment Clause allows governments some latitude to recognize the role of religion in our society.[51] Judges should be guided by practices that have long gone unchallenged or that the Court has accepted, determining the meaning of the Establishment Clause "by reference to historical practices and understandings,"[52] and permitting practices with no greater potential for establishment than ones the Court has considered legitimate. A limiting principle (which subsequently provided the Court's basis for holding graduation prayers unconstitutional) is that government may not coerce people to support religion or participate in any religious exercise.[53] By these standards, both the menorah and crèche were

---

[46] *County of Allegheny v. American Civil Liberties Union*, note 42 supra, at 598.

[47] Id. at 616.

[48] Id. at 634.

[49] Id. at 645.

[50] Id. at 637.

[51] Id. at 657.

[52] Id. at 670. Kennedy regarded *Marsh v. Chambers*, the case upholding legislative chaplains, as standing for this proposition, rather than the idea that specific practices common in 1791 are an exception to otherwise applicable principles.

[53] Id. at 659. Another limiting principle for Kennedy is that government may not give direct benefits to religion that establish a state "religious faith, or tends to do so." Id. (quoting *Lynch*, note 13 supra, at 678).

all right.[54] According to this view, government need not limit itself to acknowledging the secular aspect of a holiday with both religious and secular components.[55]

A crèche standing alone inside a courthouse conveys a religious message. A critical point of division among the justices continues to be whether there are some genuinely religious messages that it is all right for American governments to convey. I evaluate this general issue in the chapter that follows.

In 1995, the Court addressed another public display case, one involving Ohio's Capitol Square.[56] The regulating board, which the Court assumed allowed a wide range of unattended displays, had refused to allow the Ku Klux Klan to erect a cross, on the ground that the cross was a religious symbol.[57]

Justice Scalia, for a plurality, wrote that government, in opening up a forum for private speech, may not discriminate against religious speech.[58] If the government refrains from content discrimination, what it does is permitted whether or not some observers might mistakenly perceive an endorsement.[59]

Justice O'Connor, joined by Justices Souter and Breyer, defended use of the endorsement test for this kind of case. Although she agreed with the plurality about many of the relevant factors, she noted that a sign disclaiming government sponsorship could be important when religious symbols are placed close to government buildings.[60] She worried that were a private religious group to dominate a public forum, "a formal policy of equal access" could be "transformed into a demonstration of approval."[61]

---

[54] Id. at 664. Were the government permanently to erect a large Latin cross on the roof of city hall, that would represent an impermissible attempt to proselytize, id. at 661, but the seasonal recognition of religions is acceptable.

Justice Kennedy complained that the majority had rejected the Court's opinion in *Lynch* in favor of Justice O'Connor's concurrence. He said that "stare decisis directs us to adhere not only to the holdings of our prior cases, but also to their explications of the governing rules of law." Id. at 668.

[55] Justice Blackmun, for the Court, responded that Justice Kennedy's approach would gut the Establishment Clause. The country's history contains numerous examples of official acts endorsing Christianity; but "history cannot legitimate practices that demonstrate the government's allegiance to a particular sect or creed." Id. at 603. Justice O'Connor wrote that history is relevant to evaluation of whether a practice conveys a message of endorsement, but history cannot justify endorsements. Id. at 630.

[56] *Capitol Square Review and Advisory Bd. v. Pinette*, 515 U.S. 753.

[57] The district court had issued an injunction requiring the board to issue a permit to the Klan, and the court of appeals had affirmed. As the Supreme Court considered the case, the cross had actually been erected. The Court did not consider possible political reasons for refusing a permit to the Klan.

[58] *Pinette*, note 56 supra, at 760–63.

[59] Id. at 762–63. There is, thus, no appropriate place for what Justice Scalia labels a "transferred endorsement" test.

[60] Id. at 776. Justice Souter concurred that the board erred in denying the Klan's application "because of the possibility of affixing a sign to the cross adequately disclaiming any government sponsorship or endorsement of it." Id. at 784.

[61] Id. at 777.

Justice O'Connor compared her objective observer to a reasonable person in tort law, "a personification of a community ideal of reasonable behavior."[62] In a sweeping non sequitur, she rejected the idea that the endorsement test should focus on individual observers, because under such an approach a religious display would be "necessarily precluded so long as some passersby would perceive a governmental endorsement."[63] Contrary to what O'Connor assumes, a court might focus on actual observers and require for a finding of endorsement that most or many of them perceive an endorsement. An approach that makes crucial actual or probable subjective reactions need not give the most sensitive passerby an effective veto.

Justice Stevens would have created a "strong presumption against the installation of unattended religious symbols on public property."[64] His test of a "reasonable observer" would take special account of those who do not share the religious belief a symbol expresses.[65]

At least if nonreligious displays also occur *and* signs clearly indicate that the presence of a private display of a religious symbol does not represent government endorsement, such displays should be permitted; but Justice Stevens is on solid ground in his concerns about misperception and about the reactions of those who do not adhere to the religion the symbol represents.

In 2005, the Court resolved two Ten Commandments cases. These revealed a sharply divided Court, which may well take a new direction with Justice O'Connor's retirement. In one case, two Kentucky counties had posted the King James version of the Ten Commandments on their courthouse walls.[66] When suits were brought challenging these displays, the counties surrounded the Ten Commandments with other texts that had religious references. After a preliminary injunction was issued against the second displays, the counties surrounded the Commandments with copies of documents including the Magna Carta, the Declaration of Independence, the Bill of Rights, and lyrics of "The Star-Spangled Banner." In this third display, a comment to the Ten Commandments explained that they "provide the moral background of the Declaration of Independence and the foundation of our legal tradition."[67]

---

[62] Id. at 779–80. The observer "must be deemed aware of the history and context of the community and forum in which the religious display appears." Id. at 780.

[63] Id. at 779.

[64] Id. at 797.

[65] His way of putting the test was this: "If a reasonable observer could perceive a government endorsement of religion from a private display, then the state may not allow its property to be used as a forum for that display." Id. at 799.

[66] *McCreary County, Ky., v. American Civil Liberties Union of Kentucky*, 545 U.S, 844 (2005).

[67] Id. at 2731.

The second case involved a six-foot high monument inscribed with the Ten Commandments on the grounds of the Texas State Capitol, which also contained sixteen other monuments--on such assorted subjects as volunteer firemen, Confederate soldiers, and heroes of the Alamo--and twenty-one historical markers.[68] The Ten Commandments monument had been presented by the Fraternal Order of Eagles four decades earlier when Cecil B. DeMille was filming the movie *The Ten Commandments*; apparently he had cooperated with the Eagles in developing the kind of granite monolith that Texas and many places throughout the country then received.[69]

Eight justices thought the two cases should come out the same way, but they split four to four on what that way should be. Justice Breyer thought the two cases should come out differently, and so they did. Not surprisingly, the opinion for the Court holding invalid the Kentucky displays did not correspond with the plurality opinion sustaining the Texas monument.

Justice Souter wrote for the Court in the Kentucky case. The displays in the courthouses reflected an "ostensible and predominant purpose of advancing religion," a taking sides that violated the "central Establishment Clause value of official religious neutrality."[70] The initial solo displays of the Ten Commandments, a central text in Jewish and Christian understandings that proclaims obligations to a monotheistic God, were as evidently meant to promote religion as the schoolroom displays the Court had held invalid in *Stone v. Graham*. The purpose of the displays at the final (third) stage needed to be seen in relation to the history of the preceding stages; the district court and court of appeals rightly did not suppose that the counties had somehow purged their actions of their overriding religious significance. Although Justice Souter's opinion did not refer directly to the endorsement test, he not only talked about an "ostensible and predominant purpose," he also referred to an "objective observer" and suggested that if legislators cleverly and successfully disguised their religious intent, that "does nothing to make outsiders of nonadherents."[71] Justice O'Connor, who also joined the Court's opinion, explicitly connected the purpose of the displays to "an unmistakable message of endorsement to the reasonable observer."[72]

Writing for the four dissenters, Justice Scalia urged that the county display had an adequate secular purpose.[73] He repeated past objections to the purpose test, and argued that the Court had made finding a secular purpose

[68] *Van Orden v. Perry*, 545 U.S. 677 (2005).

[69] Id. at 713–14 (Stevens, J., dissenting).

[70] *McCreary County*, note 66 supra, at 860.

[71] Id. at 863.

[72] Id. at 883 (O'Connor, J., concurring).

[73] Id. at 902–12.

more difficult than it previously had been, subjects chapter 10 takes up in more detail. In a part of his opinion joined by Chief Justice Rehnquist and Justice Thomas, Scalia rejected the Court's basic assumption that the government should be neutral about religion. Historical practice demonstrates that public acknowledgments of the Creator are not barred by the Establishment Clause.[74] My degree of disagreement with Justice Scalia's approach is explained in chapter 6.

Four of five of the justices in the majority in the Kentucky case dissented in the Texas case. The phrase "I AM the LORD thy God" appears in larger letters than the rest of the text on the Texas monument.[75] The quotation is framed by Stars of David and by the Greek letters representing the monogram of Christ. According to Justice Souter in his dissent, nothing detracts from the monument's religious message. Because the seventeen monuments on the grounds share no common theme, an observer would take each monument on its own terms. The impression is very different from that given by the frieze in the Supreme Court in which Moses is placed among history's great lawgivers, most of whom were not religious leaders.[76]

Chief Justice Rehnquist's plurality opinion acknowledged that the monument has some religious significance, but it also has historical meaning, recognizing the role the Commandments have played in America's heritage.[77] The placing of the monument was much more passive than the classroom use of the texts in *Stone v. Graham*, and it did not involve the special concerns about messages directed at schoolchildren.[78] According to Rehnquist, the monument fits comfortably with other recognitions of our religious heritage, and does not violate the Establishment Clause.[79]

Although he joined the Rehnquist opinion, Justice Scalia also wrote that he would have preferred to rule "that there is nothing unconstitutional in a State's favoring religion generally, honoring God through public prayer and acknowledgment or, in a nonproseltyzing manner, venerating the Ten Commandments."[80]

---

[74] Id. at 885–900.

[75] *Van Orden v. Perry*, note 68 supra, at 739 (Souter, J., dissenting).

[76] Id. at 740. In a footnote, Justice Souter distinguishes other displays in federal buildings from the Texas monument. Justice Stevens wrote a dissent that, among other things, defended his presumption against displays of religious symbols on public property. Id. at 707–10.

[77] Id. at 688–71.

[78] Id. at 689–92.

[79] Id. at 686–92. The analysis "is driven both by the nature of the monument and by our Nation's history." The *Lemon* test is "not useful in dealing with [this] sort of passive Monument." Id. at 686.

[80] Id. at 692 (Scalia, J., concurring). Justice Thomas wrote a longer concurring opinion urging a radical shift in Establishment Clause jurisprudence that would return to original intent. Id. at 692–98.

We come to Justice Breyer's opinion, which explains how he, alone among the justices, found himself able to vote with the majority in both cases. Before we engage the opinion itself, it is worth setting it in the context of the Court's composition. In most Establishment Clause cases after the appointment of Justice Breyer, if either Justice Kennedy or Justice O'Connor voted for the "separationist" side, the side claiming that a law or practice violated the Establishment Clause, that side won. When Justices O'Connor and Kennedy voted to sustain a law or practice, they were joined by Rehnquist, Scalia, and Thomas, and the constitutional challenge failed. *Van Orden* is the first case in that period, indeed in Justice O'Connor's entire tenure, in which she regarded something as a violation of the Establishment Clause and was on the losing side. For that case Justice Breyer was the swing vote, and one would therefore look to his opinion to predict the future direction of the Court. But Chief Justice Rehnquist's death and Justice O'Connor's retirement change that perspective. The Bush administration has done much to inject religion into our public life. Chief Justice Roberts and Justice Alito may well take a view closer to Scalia's or Rehnquist's, and to Justice Kennedy's in the *Allegheny County* case, than to Breyer's. If this happens, five votes will be available to sustain public displays of religious themes, and Justice Breyer's agreement will not be necessary.

Now to the Breyer opinion. Justice Breyer acknowledged that the text of the Ten Commandments has a religious message, emphasizing the Deity,[81] but in context the display also conveys a moral and historical message. The physical setting of the Texas monument and the surrounding monuments do not suggest the sacred, and the monument's forty-year presence without controversy indicates that people have not regarded it as a detrimental favoring of a system of religious beliefs by the government.[82] Although the display might pass muster under the purpose and effect aspects of the *Lemon* test, Breyer preferred to rely more directly on the basic purposes of the religion clauses. He referred back to a concurring opinion of Justice Goldberg's in *Schempp*, the 1963 school prayer case, which cautioned against " 'untutored devotion to the concept of neutrality' " which could partake " 'of a brooding and pervasive devotion to the secular and a passive, or even active, hostility to the religious.' "[83] Concerned about the prospect of divisiveness along religious lines, Breyer feared that invalidation based on the religious text of the monument would exhibit a hostility toward religion that might generate disputes about other depictions of the Ten Commandments in and

[81] Id. at 700–701.
[82] Id. at 701–2.
[83] Id. at 699.

around public buildings, and create the very divisiveness the Establishment Clause seeks to avoid.[84] Breyer does not quite say this, but one senses he has weighed the benefits of court-ordered removal of routine displays of the Ten Commandments against the public conflict that would be likely to generate, and opted for the less disturbing alternative. (This topic is explained further in the next chapter.) In any event, given the Breyer opinion and the seating of two new justices, the prospect for future challenges to displays of the Ten Commandments outside of the public school setting may not be promising.

The Endorsement Test

Chapter 10 discusses various Establishment Clause tests, including endorsement, but because the endorsement test has been so important for displays of texts and symbols, it may help to mention some of the puzzles about it here. Justice O'Connor's endorsement test figured prominently in the last two decades. One reason is that O'Connor has been the crucial swing vote in many cases under the Establishment Clause and she has reviewed most of them in terms of endorsement. Litigators and lower-court judges have been fully aware of this; and other justices writing opinions may have drawn from endorsement language partly to satisfy Justice O'Connor. With her retirement, the fate of the endorsement test is uncertain. The test, at least in its basic outline, has considerable appeal, but its proper boundaries and status are elusive, and these bear importantly on how, in my judgment, courts should respond to texts and symbols that people may perceive differently. We can identify nine important inquiries about endorsement.

Relation to the *Lemon* Test and to Concepts of Promotion and Support

Justice O'Connor initially presented endorsement as a clarification of the purpose and effect strands of the *Lemon* test, but the endorsement test has usually been considered as an alternative to *Lemon*. How should the relationship between the two approaches be understood?

Purpose versus Effect

Justice O'Connor has considered inquiries about endorsement to concern both purpose and effect. But her version of endorsement involves what an objective observer with full information perceives about a law or practice.

[84] Id. at 704.

Would such an observer ever conclude that officials had a significant religious purpose without also finding that a significant effect was to create a perception of endorsement, or vice versa?

The Nature of Endorsement

Assuming that government officials act transparently, making their objectives clear, what behavior exactly amounts to an endorsement? In particular, can there be endorsement if the government has no aim to communicate any message?

Range of Application

In various concurring opinions, including one in the moment-of-silence case, Justice O'Connor indicated that endorsement is a crucial inquiry in the broad range of establishment cases. Other justices (who accept the approach at all) have not denied that endorsement could be relevant elsewhere; but a majority has treated the inquiry as central only in the public display cases. What range of application does, and should, the endorsement test enjoy?

The Relevance of Political Status

In *Lynch*, the original crèche case, Justice O'Connor wrote, in language she has subsequently repeated, that the government must avoid sending a message that nonadherents are not "full members of the political community," and that adherents are "favored members of the political community."[85] Did O'Connor mean *only* that the relevant community is one defined by political boundaries or that one's sense of his *political status* is crucially affected? A Jew or Muslim may not doubt that he is a full citizen but still feel he is a religious and social outsider. Is the endorsement test critically about people's political status, or is it about more general feelings of exclusion and alienation, with "political" circumscribing the relevant community that counts?

Subjective or Objective, Affiliated or Not

As elaborated by Justice O'Connor after her initial account in *Lynch*, the endorsement test is highly objective, its application not depending on the actual perceptions of real people. One element of this objectivity is that the observer is detached, not a member of any particular religious group. The perspective

[85] Note 13 supra, at 688.

is that of a hypothetical observer who lacks a feature that all real people have, some particular perspective (even if completely negative) about religion. Is such a standard for whether endorsement has occurred flawed because it is removed from the perceptions of citizens who may feel excluded or favored and because it is unrealistic in abstracting from aspects of human belief and identity that are universally present?

Comparative Relevance of Majority and Minority Outlooks

Texts and symbols may be appraised somewhat differently by members of the majority and those of minorities. Most Christians may pass a crèche in a public space without giving it a second thought; it may have more significance for most Jews. To take a more personal example, when I was a public school student, we sang Christmas carols around a centrally located tree in the main hall for fifteen minutes or so every morning for a week or two; and we (the students under the music teacher) put on a Christmas pageant. I took all this for granted, but I now wonder how Jewish students in the school regarded it.

The direct reactions of members of different groups are barred by the detached character of Justice O'Connor's observer, but suppose her nonaffiliated observer reaches the following conclusion. "I think this is the sort of practice most reasonable outsiders would perceive as an endorsement, but most reasonable insiders would not." Should the observer give special weight to the likely feelings of reasonable members of minorities?

Degrees of Knowledge and Understanding

As she developed her understanding, Justice O'Connor said the relevant observer will know the history of laws and practices and will understand the constitutional values at stake. Her observer is thus far better informed than the ordinary reasonable person. Along with other features, this aspect of the hypothetical observer renders a potentially disturbing discrepancy between what he may perceive and what most actual people will perceive. Most people may reasonably perceive an endorsement, though the objective observer knows better. In such a case, accurate use of the endorsement test, as formulated, will not forestall reasonable feelings of exclusion and fortified inclusion. Is the test *too* objective, or is that objectivity necessary to permit the Supreme Court to develop a national standard, rather than leaving final assessments about endorsement to local juries and courts, who are better able to reflect perceptions about displays in different communities?

The Desirability of the Endorsement Test

The endorsement test has a considerable appeal in focusing on what may seem most important in display cases, among others. But serious uncertainties and difficulties surround its application, not to mention the problem that different judges—seeking honestly to replicate the objective observer—may reach very different conclusions about the line between endorsement and no endorsement.

The whole approach has been challenged as focusing too much on symbolism rather than concrete advantages and disadvantages and as resting on some illusory ideal of neutrality.[86] Should endorsement in some form be a dominant or significant aspect of Establishment Clause jurisprudence? We shall examine this, and the other questions, more closely in chapter 10.

---

[86] See especially Steven D. Smith, "Symbols, Perceptions, and Doctrinal Illusions: Establishment Neutrality and the No Endorsement Test," 86 *Michigan Law Review* 266 (1987).

CHAPTER 6

Mild Endorsements and Promotions

As we have touched on in the previous chapter, federal and state governments in the United States engage in a number of practices that seem, at first glance, to endorse religion and religious activity. Our currency says "In God We Trust"; the Pledge of Allegiance includes the words "under God"; presidents declare days of Thanksgiving; legislatures pay chaplains and open sessions with prayers; and the Supreme Court commences its own sessions with the words "God Bless the United States and this Honorable Court." What are we to make of these practices? They certainly appear to embody religious assumptions, even if their effect on people's lives is unprofound. And, picking up on points made in chapter 4, most of the practices reflect only some, not all, religions. References to God, most importantly, connote a single God, not multiple gods or a nontheistic religious premise.

Tensions and Possible Approaches to Reconciliation

In the total compass of our society's life, these practices do not loom as very important, but they nonetheless pose acute questions about how to understand the Establishment Clause. Two opposing positions are rather straightforward. Both assume that many, if not all, of these practices are genuinely at odds with the principle that government should not sponsor or promote religious ideas.[1] Those who approve the principle conclude that a wise and courageous Supreme Court would draw the inevitable conclusion that the practices are unconstitutional. Those who cannot imagine that our law would, or should, actually bar such practices believe that they show that the Supreme Court's approach to government sponsorship of religious ideas

---

[1] As we shall see, not all these practices need be subject to exactly the same analysis. One might, for example, say that legislators should be able to begin with a prayer if most of them wish, and that concerns about pressure and inequity are much less important for adults (most legislators are not even in attendance for opening prayers) than for schoolchildren whose classes might start the day with prayer.

is fundamentally unsound—that government should be able to sponsor religious ideas around which many citizens coalesce.[2]

Is there some means of reconciliation of these practices with Establishment Clause principles that avoids each of these stark alternative conclusions? One way out is to discern that many of the references to religion have lost real religious significance, that they perform exclusively some civil ceremonial function. Although this may well be the approach the Supreme Court will eventually take about Thanksgiving and "under God" in the Pledge of Allegiance, and is a line that some believers in separation of church and state adopt when these practices are thrown up at them, I shall argue in this chapter that it is patently absurd. I shall concentrate on the opinions in a 2004 case dealing with the Pledge,[3] but my basic observations apply to Thanksgiving as well. That holiday may well have civil ceremonial significance, but its religious content has certainly not disappeared. A "giving of thanks" is ordinarily conceived as a giving of thanks to someone, not just a grateful reflection on good fortune. In light of their actual religious beliefs, we can be confident that most Americans continue to regard Thanksgiving, as it was in its historic roots, as a giving of thanks *to God*.

A second mode of reconciliation is a variation on the first. The practices, it acknowledges, do have *some* religious significance, do involve *some* sponsorship, but their civic nonreligious aspect overwhelms their religious significance.

Two other modes of reconciliation, which can be fruitfully combined, are more promising. The third mode is historical tradition. Certain practices have a long historical pedigree; and purists about constitutional principle should not insist on uprooting them. Perhaps these practices should never have been started; or perhaps they were entirely appropriate for the country at the time they began. In either event, they are now moderately out of joint with the principles that should guide the behavior of the state. But long historical customary practice underlies an argument for continuance. Governments and societies are not entirely rational in their applications of valid first principles. The development of public institutions is messier than that. Continuity and stability matter in social life, and history has its claims.

The fourth mode of reconciliation emphasizes the minor significance of these various practices. Yes, they have religious content, but it does not figure importantly in anyone's life. Perhaps a kind of de minimis approach should

---

[2] The opinions of Justices Scalia and Thomas in the Ten Commandments cases, *McCreary County v. American Civil Liberties Union of Kentucky*, 545 U.S, 844, 885–912 (2005) (Scalia, J., dissenting); *Van Orden v. Perry*, 545 U.S. 677, 692–98 (Thomas, J., concurring), express this view.

[3] *Elk Grove Unified School Dist. v. Newdow*, 542 U.S. 1 (2004).

treat practices as tolerable if they involve no serious impairment of appropriate church-state relations.[4]

Why should even minor deviations from a fundamental principle of no sponsorship be tolerated? One possible answer is that the deviations are *so slight*, they are beyond constitutional cognizance. Another answer employs the historical rationale; minor (but not major) deviations should be accepted if they are deeply rooted in historical practice.

A more complex form of reconciliation—one purists on either side find objectionable—equivocates about whether the government should refrain entirely from sponsoring religion:

> We are a country with a rich religious heritage; many settlers came to our shores for religious reasons and regarded the society they founded as a City upon a Hill, as a religious example. That heritage has by no means disappeared. Given the modern diversity of religious views and the presence of many serious citizens who do not have religious convictions, the government should refrain from promoting religion. Still, some weak references to a religious understanding, ones not likely to exclude and offend religious dissenters, are appropriate.

On this view, the weak promotion of nonexclusionary religion still has a place, although nonpromotion should guide government action that has a substantial influence on people.

I have put this last form of reconciliation as if it represents a desirable constitutional approach given the country's history and present population. A close cousin of that approach adopts a hard-boiled realistic account of how the Supreme Court should act. Here is a possible version of it.

> According to constitutional principle, mild endorsements should be declared unconstitutional, and that indeed is what the Supreme Court should do were the politicians and citizens willing to stand still for that approach. But if we did not know beforehand, we have learned from the widespread outrage over the Ninth Circuit's decision that "under God" in the Pledge is unconstitutional that Supreme Court invalidation of these practices would create a firestorm of criticism that would be very costly for the Court[5] (and not warranted by the importance of the issue)[6] and would likely be practically futile, because

---

[4] One finds hints of this approach in Justice Breyer's concurring opinion in Van Orden v. Perry, note 2 supra, at 697–705.

[5] See Richard H. Fallon, Jr., *Implementing the Constitution* 54–55 (Cambridge: Harvard University Press, 2001).

[6] One might compare *Brown v. Board of Education* and *Roe v. Wade* as highly controversial, but having profound practical effects.

a "corrective" constitutional amendment would follow. The end result would be worse for the "no sponsorship" principle than if the Court winked at these minor deviations. Justices rarely, if ever, admit they take such political realities into account, and scholars disagree about whether they should, but the Court does well to understand itself as a political institution that needs to be responsive to opinions of other officials and of citizens.

We shall explore and assess these various alternatives in more depth when we examine the issue of "under God" in the Pledge.

THE PRELUDE TO *NEWDOW*

One might reasonably regard the cases about religious symbols on public property we have just reviewed as being about one form of mild endorsement; but if we put these aside, the Supreme Court has actually decided on the constitutionality of only one mild endorsement—paid legislative chaplains, very likely the least mild of the bunch.[7] In *Marsh v. Chambers*,[8] a majority of the Court upheld the hiring of chaplains paid by state governments to open legislative sessions with prayers. It sustained the practice on historical grounds. Chief Justice Burger's opinion noted that from the beginning of the Republic, Congress had hired chaplains to say opening prayers, and state legislators had done the same. Over the strong protests of dissenters, the Court declined to apply the threefold test of *Lemon v. Kurtzman*.[9] *Marsh* was decided during the period when the Court consistently applied the *Lemon* test to Establishment Clause problems; this was the one case in which it upheld a practice without doing so.[10] One must infer that the justices recognized that paid chaplains in legislatures would fail the purpose and effects strands of the test—that is, their main purpose and a primary effect were to aid or sponsor religion.[11] (Perhaps paid chaplains would also be at odds with the rule that government should not be excessively entangled with religion.)

---

[7] That is, paying legislative chaplains to say prayers at the beginning of legislative sessions is a stronger endorsement of religion than having a crèche display at Christmas.

[8] 463 U.S. 783 (1983).

[9] 403 U.S. 602 (1971).

[10] As I noted in the previous chapter, the Court employed the strong version of a compelling interest test in *Larson v. Valente*, 456 U.S. 228 (1982), a case of discrimination among religions. That test was harder for the state to satisfy than the *Lemon* test.

[11] The argument that chaplains are necessary to protect free exercise, an argument that supports chaplains for military personnel and prisoners, is not relevant for legislators, who have ample opportunity to engage in religious exercises outside of legislative sessions.

Chief Justice Burger was not quite clear whether historical entrenchment as strong as existed for legislative chaplains would be sufficient to sustain *any practice*—definitely *not* the Court's approach to many religion clause issues—or whether the constitutionality of a practice depends on a joining of historical acceptance with a less than grave breach of the values served by contemporary constitutional standards. One gathers the latter.

Various opinions for the Court and of individual justices since *Everson* have remarked on other mild supports. Justice Douglas alone hinted that most of these practices may be unconstitutional.[12] Other justices, as in the Court's opinions in *Marsh v. Chambers* and in *Lynch v. Donnelly* (the first crèche case),[13] have presumed their constitutionality and drawn comparisons between them and the challenged practices that the Court was then reviewing. The strategies of analysis are of two kinds. Justices who would accept a practice, say of a crèche display or graduation prayer, cite longstanding practices like Thanksgiving and "In God We Trust" on coins as showing that some government support for religion is acceptable, and that allowing the challenged practice follows closely in this tradition.[14] In this analysis, the presumed validity of mild supports underpins an argument in favor of more substantial supports. In contrast, justices who vote to invalidate a display of a crèche or a graduation prayer undertake to explain why the mild supports are different.[15] The typical claim of difference, offered as early as 1963 by Justice Brennan in the Bible reading case, is that those mild supports have lost religious meaning, that they now signify a kind of national civil unity.[16]

"UNDER GOD" IN THE PLEDGE OF ALLEGIANCE

The Pledge of Allegiance, as enacted by Congress in 1942 in connection with a codification of customs relating to the American flag, then read: "I pledge allegiance to the Flag of the United States of America, and to the Republic for which it stands, one Nation indivisible, with liberty and justice for all." In 1954 Congress amended the pledge to include "under God" after "Nation." The sponsor of the change stated that the aim "was to contrast this

---

[12] *Engel v. Vitale*, 370 U.S. 421, 437–44 (Douglas, J., concurring).

[13] 465 U.S. 668 (1984).

[14] See, e.g., id. at 674–77, and *Lee v. Weisman*, 505 U.S. 577, 633–36 (1992) (dissenting opinion of Scalia, J.).

[15] See *Lynch*, 465 U.S. at 715–17 (Brennan, J., dissenting), and *Lee v. Weisman*, 505 U.S. 596–97.

[16] *Abington Township v. Schempp*, 374 U.S. 203, 303–4 (concurring opinion).

country's belief in God with the Soviet Union's embrace of atheism."[17] In accordance with California law, which provides that public elementary schools are to conduct patriotic exercises that can be satisfied by performing the Pledge of Allegiance, the Elk Grove Unified School District requires each elementary school class to recite the Pledge every day. Children who object, or whose parents object, to their participation may be excused.

In response to the challenge of a girl's noncustodial biological father, an atheist, the Ninth Circuit Court of Appeals held "under God" to be unconstitutional. Its purpose and effect (under the *Lemon* test) were to support religion; it endorsed a religious view (thereby violating the "endorsement test"), and its use in the public school was sufficiently coercive to render it unconstitutional according to a test that focuses on coercion.

The Supreme Court reviewed the case but failed to resolve the basic issue. It determined that as a noncustodial father, who disagreed with the mother's wish to have her child participate in the Pledge, Newdow lacked standing.[18] The ruling about standing involved a complex mix of federal and state law, and we need not pursue it here, except to say that some members of the Court may have preferred not to make a decision on the merits of an issue that had generated such heated emotions. Three justices disagreed. Each of these did resolve the merits, and each voted to sustain "under God."

Justice Thomas took the occasion to reject the Supreme Court decision that held graduation prayers for public schools to be impermissibly coercive;[19] he intimated doubts about the Court's invalidation in 1962 and 1963 of classroom prayer and Bible reading;[20] and he suggested that only establishments violating liberty interests should be regarded as forbidden to the states. Having reviewed the nature of traditional establishments of religion and the possibility of a government imbuing a religion with its authority, Thomas wrote, "It is difficult to see how government practices that have nothing to do with creating or maintaining the sort of coercive state establishment described above implicate the possible liberty interest of being free from coercive state establishments."[21] Like the Ninth Circuit Court of Appeals, Thomas regarded the school's use of the Pledge as at odds with Su-

---

[17] *Elk Grove Unified School Dist. v. Newdow*, 542 U.S. 1, 25 (2004) (quote is from Rehnquist, C. J., concurring).

[18] Newdow and the mother had never married.

[19] *Newdow*, note 17 supra, at 45–49.

[20] Id. at 53. He quoted with approval Justice Stewart's dissent in the prayer case, *Engel v. Vitale*, 370 U.S. at 445. Quoting a dissent would not necessarily signal disagreement with a result, but the point for which Stewart is quoted goes to the heart of the case, and Justice Thomas has shown little respect for precedents he believes were wrongly decided.

[21] *Newdow*, note 17 supra, at 53.

preme Court precedents; his response was to disapprove the precedents and their underlying theory.[22]

Chief Justice Rehnquist and Justice O'Connor strove to perform the more difficult feat of reconciliation. Each fails badly if one takes what they say at face value, but with some modifications one can build a coherent, if not persuasive, defense of "under God." Both justices argued that "under God" now has civic, not religious meaning. O'Connor joined Rehnquist's opinion, but she also presented a theory that was worked out more fully than was his. Since O'Connor had been with the majority in the graduation prayer case and Rehnquist had dissented, it may well be that Rehnquist's efforts at reconciliation were less sincere than hers.[23] We shall look briefly at his opinion before turning to hers.

For Rehnquist, "Reciting the Pledge, or listening to others recite it, is a patriotic exercise, not a religious one; participants promise fidelity to our flag and our Nation, not to any particular God, faith or church."[24] After cataloging various references to God in the country's political history—Thanksgiving proclamations, presidential addresses, "In God We Trust" on currency, and the words with which each Supreme Court session opens—Rehnquist wrote that "these events strongly suggest that our national culture allows public recognition of our Nation's religious history and character."[25] "Under God," he said, is a "descriptive phrase"[26] (a bizarre characterization that also finds its way into Justice O'Connor's opinion). Some may disagree with "under God," but they, no more than those who might disagree with "liberty and justice for all," should have a veto power over the ability of willing participants to pledge allegiance in public schools.[27]

Here are some problems with Rehnquist's approach. Granted that the Pledge is mainly a patriotic exercise, it *may also* include endorsement of a religious view and involve participants in affirmation of that view. Were "under God" to involve *only* a recognition of the country's religious character, that could fairly be called other than a religious exercise and "descriptive," but the historical examples Rehnquist relies on—proclamations of

---

[22] We will have occasion to review most of those decisions in subsequent chapters. We have considered the Pittsburgh crèche case, *County of Allegheny v. American Civil Liberties Union*, 492 U.S. 573 (1989), in the previous chapter. Justice Thomas called that result "silly." *Newdow*, note 17 supra, at 45 n. 1.

[23] I do not mean this as a criticism. Within our system of following precedents, judges often find themselves "distinguishing" cases whose principles they reject.

[24] *Newdow*, note 17 supra, at 31.

[25] Id. at 30.

[26] Id. at 33.

[27] Id. at 32.

Thanksgiving and so on—are not themselves references to historical under-standings, they recognize God and call on God's help. The language of the Pledge is not historical. It sounds as if the Nation *is* "under God," not that historically many citizens have believed that the nation is under God. So understood, it is not a "descriptive phrase" in any relevant sense. (One may think, and indeed I do think, that claims about God's existence and qualities are descriptive claims, as contrasted with normative claims, imperatives, ex-clamations, etc., but the rule against government endorsing religion is a rule that covers this class of claims, whether they are descriptive or not.) Finally the comparison with people who object to "liberty and justice for all" is beside the point. The government can sponsor political positions; it cannot sponsor religious ones. That some people might object to political sentiments reflected in the Pledge has nothing to do with the status of religious senti-ments to which a minority of the population objects.

Justice O'Connor made a much more strenuous effort than the chief jus-tice to explain that "under God" is not really an assertion of a religious proposition. Before getting to the heart of her position, it helps to clear away two unconvincing observations that are less than central. In an effort to avoid the force of the school prayer cases, O'Connor emphasized that the Pledge is not a prayer.[28] No, it is not a prayer, but neither is the Apostle's Creed said in churches. A pledge is an affirmation of conviction and loyalty. Suppose the Pledge read: "one Nation, under the lordship of God the Father and our savior Jesus Christ, upon whom our salvation rests." This would not be a prayer, but no one would doubt that it would be religious.

Justice O'Connor's version of the "merely descriptive" nature of "under God" is that even "if taken literally . . . it purports only to identify the United States as a Nation subject to divine authority."[29] But, taken literally, the phrase in the Pledge is about religious reality, that God exists and that our Nation is subject to God's providence and authority. *These* are religious propositions of the sort ruled out by the bar on government endorsement of religion.

Justice O'Connor's central argument was that saying "under God" in the Pledge is an act of ceremonial deism, not religious affirmation. As she indi-cated, the constitutional test to be applied to this kind of case is the same she used for religious symbols: whether or not the government endorses a religious view. The reason why endorsements of religion are unconstitutional is that they send "a message to nonadherents that they are outsiders . . . and

---

[28] Id. at 39–40. She also said that the stating the Pledge is not an act of worship.

[29] Id. at 40.

an accompanying message to adherents that they are insiders" in the political community.[30] As we saw in the previous chapter, whether an endorsement is present is determined by a reasonable, well-informed observer. After a sentence in which she wrote that an observer would judge that many "facially religious references" do not signify an endorsement of either "any specific religion, or even of religion over nonreligion,"[31] O'Connor went on to say, "There are no *de minimis* violations of the Constitution—no constitutional harms so slight that the courts are obliged to ignore them."[32]

According to O'Connor, various references that are cast in the language of religion serve essentially secular purposes, commemorating the role of religion in our history and solemnizing occasions instead of invoking divine provenance.[33] "Under God" in the Pledge is a form of "ceremonial deism" rather than endorsement of religion.

To reach this conclusion, Justice O'Connor relied on a number of factors. "Under God" has been part of the Pledge for fifty years, a significant portion of the nation's history; it has been rarely challenged; if some legislators in 1954 had religious objectives in mind, they also had secular purposes, and, in any event, in the ensuing fifty years, the words have lost any "religious freight";[34] although no "brief solemnizing reference to religion . . . would adequately encompass every religious belief expressed by any citizen of this nation," the phrase "under God" is inclusive and not designed to favor any belief system;[35] finally, it has minimal religious content. These factors together mark "under God" as other than a sponsorship of religious ideas.

Insofar as Justice O'Connor claims that "under God" involves no endorsement of a particular religious view or of religion, it is singularly unpersuasive. People may take "In God We Trust" on coins as other than serious religious assertion, but a pledge involves affirmation. Perhaps many children and adults now say the Pledge of Allegiance by rote and take it as signifying no more than some vague statement of national loyalty and of approval of the country as it is, or as it aspires to be. (Whatever one's political outlook, one cannot sensibly believe that the United States *now enjoys* "liberty and justice for all.") But some people do pay attention to the words of the Pledge, and some may be influenced by the words even if they are not paying attention. As one who grew up when the Pledge did not include "under God,"

[30] Id. at 34.
[31] Id. at 36.
[32] Id. at 36–37.
[33] Id. at 35–36.
[34] Id. at 41.
[35] Id. at 42.

my sense is that it did well enough at solemnizing one's relation to the nation before those words were added. It is evident that the words "under God" taken literally have religious significance, however vague. These words trouble some of the small percentage of young people who do not believe in a single God. My already strong intuition that this must be so was confirmed by an atheist student in a seminar describing how uncomfortable, how much an outsider he felt, when the Pledge was recited at his school.

The *Newdow* case raised both the constitutional validity of the Pledge in general and its being said in class every day at a public elementary school. Whatever one might think about the notion that adults do not perceive that the religious language is to be taken seriously, that it serves a secular solemnizing function, can we really suppose that second- and third-graders participating in a pledge will so understand "under God"? A pledge is not a song. We all, including small children, sing songs whose lyrics may not reflect our sentiments and attitudes; we do not pause to ask whether we affirm whatever it is that the lyrics assert. But in a pledge, we are undertaking to affirm the content of the pledge. That is what a pledge is. Undoubtedly, there are sophisticated views that what we affirm in a creedal statement or secular pledge need not be its content as delimited by its ordinary language—such perspectives allow many Christians to say the Apostle's Creed as a traditional statement of faith without believing that Jesus was "born of the Virgin Mary" in the literal sense that Mary had not ever had sexual intercourse prior to his birth. But not everyone feels comfortable approaching creeds in this way— I, for example, usually omit language in creeds that does reflect my sense of what is true. And, much more important, we definitely cannot assume that most second graders will bring such a nuanced view to "under God." For them, that language will be an affirmation of *a* religious belief. For this point, it does not really matter whether the language is substantially inclusive; it is not, as O'Connor acknowledges, reflective of all religious beliefs, and it is definitely at odds with the beliefs of atheists and agnostics. If people really regard "under God" as having the bland content O'Connor assumes, one wonders how genuinely solemn those words and the rest of pledge are taken to be.

Justice O'Connor's position that "under God" involves no endorsement of religion is unconvincing. Perhaps we can write off "In God We Trust" on coins and "God Bless the United States and this Honorable Court" as historical formulations that really do not any longer convey a significant religious message, but we cannot fairly conclude that about "under God" in the Pledge, *especially* when it is said day after day by youngsters. We might better view "under God" as a form of "civil religion," understood as broad support for a political order that relies on watered-down, widely shared, but genuine religious premises.[36]

A more plausible variation on O'Connor's position would be that degrees of endorsement must be measured against the independent secular functions of religious language. If endorsement is relatively slight and secular solemnization is substantial, perhaps that is constitutionally acceptable. (This position could have allowed O'Connor to maintain her stance that there are no de minimis violations of the Constitution, but she would have needed to acknowledge that some de minimis endorsements do not constitute constitutional violations.)

This suggestion raises sharply the delicate question whether some weak sponsorship of religion by federal and state governments is all right. Against any such sponsorship is the reality that such government involvement can easily trivialize the profound beliefs of people who are seriously religious. And for many people, watered-down religion is inauthentic religion. Nevertheless, given the history of the country and its present religious composition, I believe it is too harsh to say that every religious endorsement must now be purged. In order to draw the line between the acceptable and unacceptable, the factors Justice O'Connor relies on are relevant: the inclusiveness of the view that is endorsed, historical pedigree, the brevity of references to religion. These factors bear on how specific and how intense is a sponsorship and endorsement. One might address these concerns with a focus on the religious message standing alone or by comparing that message with the secular solemnization the words perform.

The Pledge, as such, may be acceptable under such an approach; but it remains difficult to justify the indoctrination of public school children.[37] True, any child objecting to the Pledge can either be excused or remain silent, but this is an insufficient corrective. Many children will hesitate to appear unpatriotic or unreligious or both, and part of the problem of the Pledge is that it has some weak tendency to indoctrinate the uncommitted.

This conclusion raises the question whether, nonetheless, the Court should approve the Pledge for schoolchildren because a firestorm of criticism would follow a contrary decision and a constitutional amendment to reverse the outcome would be fairly likely. To be clear, I believe the high probability is that the Supreme Court *will* accept the Pledge when the issue next arises.[38] I

---

[36] See, e.g., Robert Bellah, *Beyond Belief* 175 (New York: Harper and Row, 1970).

[37] See Steven H. Shiffrin, "The Pluralistic Foundations of the Religion Clauses," 90 *Cornell Law Review* 9, 73 (2004).

[38] Justice Scalia did not sit on *Newdow* because he had sharply criticized the Ninth Circuit decision. Justice Breyer's approach to the Ten Commandments monument may signal a willingness to accept

also do not doubt that Supreme Court justices are influenced to some degree by public opinion—they cannot help themselves. The question I am raising is whether a justice should ever consciously say to herself, "Apart from likely political reaction, I would decide this case in favor of the plaintiff, but given consequences that would follow from outrage over the decision, I regard it as desirable to decide for the defendant." I respect purists who say this basis for decision is never proper and I understand those who believe, to the contrary, such consequences should standardly be part of a justice's assessment. My own position is that justices should try to decide apart from such considerations except in very rare instances in which the predictable consequences would be severe and the benefit of a decision producing those consequences would be modest.

Since I assume, along with most other commentators, that courts should not acknowledge in their opinions that they are swayed by such political considerations, I accept that this is an unusual instance in which judges should not reveal an important basis for their decision.[39] Whether or not "under God" remains part of the Pledge of Allegiance that children say is not, standing by itself, of great practical importance. I do not have my hand on the political pulse of the country, but I believe that the widespread outrage and antagonism toward the Court, as well as a corrective amendment, which would be likely to be generated by a decision striking down "under God" in the Pledge for schoolchildren, do put this issue into the narrow category of circumstances when judicial responsiveness to strong political opinion is warranted. In any event, according to the analysis in this chapter, the decision that Rehnquist, O'Connor, and Thomas would have reached cannot be adequately defended in other terms.

"under God" in the Pledge. One would not expect the appointees of President George W. Bush to declare that part of the Pledge invalid. Whether a majority of the Court would rely on something like O'Connor's theory or more straightforwardly approve this endorsement of a religious view is uncertain.

[39] Laura Underkuffler, in "Through a Glass Darkly: *Van Orden, McCreary,* and the Dangers of Transparency in Establishment Clause Jurisprudence," 5 *First Amendment Law Review* 59 (2006), has suggested that there is value in the Court's propounding a principle of neutrality toward religion while accepting some practices at odds with that principle, that in this area, as in some others, one should not wish for full transparency.

CHAPTER 7

Public Schools: Devotions

In this chapter and the next two, we shall look at religion and public schools. What schools may and may not do with respect to religion are important practical questions, and the Supreme Court's most controversial decisions about the Establishment Clause have involved prayer and Bible reading in the schools. This chapter concentrates on those practices as well as that of taking a "moment of silence." The immediately following chapter discusses teaching about religion, permitted, even encouraged, by the Court's rhetoric. Chapter 9 takes up the problem of whether teaching about science and moral choices should make reference to religious perspectives or be influenced by those perspectives. I have chosen science and moral choice because knowledge in science is based on a widely accepted nonreligious methodology and no such methodology exists for moral choice. These three chapters cover a set of problems I have discussed in more detail elsewhere, but they are too important to omit from this volume.[1]

INITIAL SUPREME COURT DECISIONS ON PRAYER AND BIBLE READING

From their beginning, American public schools engaged children in the devotional practices of prayer and Bible reading. This chapter asks whether devotional practices sponsored by educational authorities violate the Establishment Clause or instead have a proper place in public schools.[2]

The Supreme Court in 1962 and 1963 held, with one dissenter in each case, that the Establishment Clause forbids school-sponsored devotional prayer and Bible reading in the classroom. Much more recently, it extended these rulings to sponsored prayer at public school graduations and football games.

Although these rulings have not themselves changed American life nearly as much as the Court's decisions about racial segregation and abortion, they have proved enduringly unpopular with many citizens. Widely disobeyed,

---

[1] Kent Greenawalt, *Does God Belong in Public Schools?* (Princeton: Princeton University Press, 2005).

[2] Devotion could be to gods or to some unifying force, but in this country, dominated by monotheist religions, devotion in public schools has been to God.

they also sparked a sharp increase in political involvement by evangelical conservative Christian groups dismayed over the country's drift toward secularism and amorality.

From the time of the rise of public schools in the nineteenth century until 1962, prayer and Bible reading had been common practices. During most of the nineteenth century the religious tone in public schools was Protestant—if a Bible was read, it was the King James translation—and one of the motivations for Roman Catholic parents to send children to parochial schools was the Protestant character of the public schools. Although before the mid-twentieth century, some state courts had held Bible reading to violate their state constitutions, in most cases the practice was upheld. During the late nineteenth and first part of the twentieth century, the Protestant tone had often given way to a more ecumenical one, and some schools abandoned devotional Bible reading and prayer; but they continued at many schools, and in other schools, including the one I attended, Christmas pageants and carol singing provided a Christian touch.

In 1962, the Supreme Court passed judgment on the following nondenominational prayer said by a teacher or chosen student at the beginning of the day in each class of the school district:

> Almighty God, we acknowledge our dependence upon Thee, and we beg Thy blessings upon us, our parents, our teachers and our Country.[3]

The State Board of Regents, responsible for public school education, had composed the prayer and recommended its use by local districts.[4]

Justice Black, writing for the Supreme Court, treated the practice as an obvious violation of the Establishment Clause. Calling the prayer "a religious activity . . . a solemn avowal of divine faith and supplication for the blessings of the Almighty,"[5] he repeated his rhetorical approach from the 1947 case of *Everson v. Board of Education*, and declared that the Establishment Clause "must at least mean" that "it is no part of the business of government to compose official prayers for any group of the American people to recite as a part of a religious program carried on by the government."[6] Although Black noted that when the government puts its power, prestige, and financial support behind religious beliefs, "the indirect coercive pressure

---

[3] *Engel v. Vitale*, 370 U.S. 421, 422 (1962).

[4] New York's highest court, the Court of Appeals, had upheld daily use of the prayer, on the understanding that no pupil would be compelled to join in over her objections.

[5] *Engel*, note 3 supra, at 424.

[6] Id. at 425. Justice Black wrote that those who fled to this country objected to prayers composed by government. But objectors typically opposed prayers whose content they did not accept, rather than any prayers composed by government.

upon religious minorities to conform . . . is plain,"[7] his stated constitutional principle directly emphasizes the government's participation rather than coercion; and it does not distinguish children from adults who might be the participants in a government-sponsored prayer.

Relying heavily on the history leading up to the Virginia Bill for Religious Liberty, Justice Black urged that by the time of the Constitution people knew that "the Government's placing its official stamp of approval upon one particular kind of prayer or one particular form of religious services" was one of the greatest dangers to freedom of worship.[8] That the prayer was "nondenominational" and that no direct government compulsion was involved were irrelevant.

Justice Stewart, dissenting, emphasized the wish of schoolchildren to say the prayer, and urged that they should not be prohibited from doing so. He objected to language about a "wall of separation" of church and state, as unfaithful to the way in which our religious traditions are "reflected in countless practices of the institutions and officials of our government."[9] Stewart's dissent in *Engel v. Vitale* is of a piece with his lone dissent in the Bible reading case, in which he emphasized the "substantial free exercise claim . . . of [parents] who affirmatively desire to have their children's school day open with the reading of passages from the Bible."[10] He worried there that forbidding such exercises would place religion "at an artificial and state-created disadvantage."[11]

In *Abington School District v. Schempp*,[12] the Supreme Court treated Bible reading as it had prayer. Justice Clark's opinion rejected a claim that Bible

---

[7] Id. at 431.

[8] Id. at 429. Quoting Madison's "Memorial and Remonstrance," Black said that history shows that the result of government joining religion is disrespect both for government and for the religion it supports. Near the end of the opinion, Black, in a footnote, addressed references to the Deity in historical documents, anthems that might be recited and sung in school, and "many manifestations in our public life of belief in God." These "patriotic or ceremonial occurrences bear no true resemblance to the [school prayer's] unquestioned religious exercise." Id. at 435, n. 21.

[9] Id. at 446. In a final footnote, he was "at a loss to understand" how the Court could distinguish the school prayers and other expressions of religious faith by government officials. Id. at 450.

[10] *Abington Township v. Schempp*, 374 U.S. 203, 312 (1963).

[11] Id. at 313. He argued that the danger of official support to instruction of the tenets of various sects was absent because the Bible reading was unaccompanied by comment. Id. at 314.

[12] *Schempp*, note 10 supra, at 203. A Pennsylvania statute and a Baltimore ordinance required a reading from the Bible at the beginning of each school day. In the Pennsylvania case, the complaining Unitarian father's testimony throws an interesting light on perceptions about pressure to conform. Edward Schempp said he considered asking that his two children be excused from the exercises, but he was afraid they would be regarded as "odd balls" by their classmates and teachers. Id. at 208–9. See also id. at 289–90 (Brennan, J., concurring). If the father was sincere and his willingness to expose his children to unfavorable criticism had not increased, it is remarkable that he thought that having his children excused would produce more negative feelings than his suing to have the entire practice

reading was designed for nonreligious moral inspiration; the practice was indisputably religious.[13] The state cannot prescribe religious exercises as "curricular activities of students who are required by law to attend school."[14] Since individual students chose the Bible readings in the Pennsylvania high school whose practice was challenged, the decision in *Schempp* makes clear that school sponsorship of devotional readings is unconstitutional, whether or not the government writes or selects the text.

Before I review various significant aspects of the *Schempp* opinion, it is worth pausing over the stark opposition between the *Engel* and *Schempp* majorities and Justice Stewart. For most constitutional lawyers, the Stewart dissents may not loom very large, but a radio interview that I once did turned out to be occupied entirely with the question: "What could possibly be wrong with the inclusive and innocuous prayer in *Engel v. Vitale?*" Justice Stewart's sentiments are shared by many of our citizens.

The most straightforward argument for allowing school-sponsored prayer or Bible reading is that they involve minor contact between the state and religion, and that state sponsorship of religion *in this way* and *to this degree* is acceptable. We have already reviewed arguments about modest supports of religion in the last chapter. It is hard to characterize classroom prayer and Bible reading as modest. Certainly they are religious, not solemnizing rhetoric that has lost religious significance. The basic principle that engaging in religious exercises is not an appropriate function for government in our society stands against classroom prayer and Bible reading. And the endorsement of a religious view in these practices is more than slight. If the constitutional standard turns on the degree of sponsorship, one could think prayer and Bible reading in public schools are all right only if one accepts substantial sponsorship.

Two arguments for devotional practices in school that rely more heavily on free exercise concerns focus on students as "captives" and on important occasions. The contention that because the government coerces students to attend school, it should institute devotional practices is weak. Students have ample opportunity during time away from school to engage in religious devotion.[15]

---

stopped. In the Baltimore case, the complainant was Madalyn Murray, an atheist who became a famous litigant in establishment cases and whose son was then in school.

[13] Id. at 224.

[14] Id. at 223.

[15] I am not addressing here the situation of students who believe they must pray at particular times of the day when they are in school. Schools should aim to accommodate the religious needs of those students insofar as they can without disrupting school.

The concern about "important occasions" is more troubling. Many parents and their children may believe that a group prayer, involving all participants who share a desire to join in, should precede major activities in life.[16] These parents wonder why they (and their children) have to sacrifice their wishes to have the school day begin with a prayer because a handful of parents (or children and their parents) object. So long as students may be excused, they think, others should be able to begin school with a formal class prayer or Bible reading. This argument underlies much of the appeal of Justice Stewart's dissent. Even if broader principles of liberal democracy and of constitutional law that protect minorities should bar class prayer and Bible reading, the ensuing frustration of those who would like to participate in a group prayer is a genuine cause for regret.

Before we reach a conclusion about the argument for devotional prayer or Bible reading, we need to look more specifically at how they might be carried out and at alternatives. Among other things, these inquiries illuminate the uncertain line between discrimination *among* religions and discrimination in favor of religion over nonreligion.

We can see quickly that no organized school prayer will satisfy everyone.[17] Suppose the teacher says a prayer written by the state or by himself. Any prayer referring to Christ does not represent non-Christian opinions. Any prayer to God, even the highly inclusive New York prayer in *Engel*, does not represent the views of those who do not believe in a single God. Perhaps unrepresented students will listen respectfully or substitute their own form of prayer; but they may feel excluded and offended. Even if they do not, the prayer cannot have the same significance for them as for students whom the prayer "fits." When states or teachers develop prayers that are as inclusive as possible, that may trouble some theologically conservative Christian parents, who do not want their children hearing a daily prayer that omits any reference to Christ. Because *no* prayer can be equally satisfactory to the members of every religion, the issue about prayer goes beyond the relation of religion versus nonreligion; it also concerns effective discrimination among diverse religious views.

In this regard, Bible reading is similar. Children who do not recognize the authority of the Jewish and Christian Bibles cannot participate fully in this form of devotion. Even if a Hindu child listens with respectful interest, the

---

[16] The common saying of grace before meals is one illustration of such a practice.

[17] It is possible, of course, that within any class, school, or district, a prayer will satisfy everyone or at least will not offend anyone.

reading will not be devotional for her in the same way it may be for a Christian;[18] and the Hindu may feel excluded, an outsider.

The problems do not stop there. If the teacher reads from the New Testament, Jews will not take that text as authoritative. And Christians themselves recognize different versions of the Bible; a number of translations are widely used, and the "Roman Catholic" Bible includes some books omitted from "Protestant" Bibles. In short, a teacher who reads consistently from one version of the Bible is bound to favor not only the religious views of groups who recognize the Bible as authoritative, but also the views of groups that use that particular version of the Bible.

Excusing children from the prayer or Bible reading eases the difficulty without solving it. A child who leaves the room each day for a standard school activity will feel more excluded than one who sits through religious devotions that are not compatible with her own beliefs. Even were excusal costless, it would not solve the dilemma of the parent who feels a sense of hurt that another religion is favored—say a Roman Catholic parent disturbed that the school uses the King James translation of the Bible.

When we attempt an overall appraisal of the claim to engage in devotional prayer and Bible reading in class, we need to consider possible alternatives. One conceivable alternative would be for a school to have oral prayer or Bible reading, or some suitably broadened set of possibilities, with individual students deciding what is to be said or read on any particular day. If each student picks a reading or says a prayer in turn, everyone has a chance to express his or her convictions, *and* the state stays out of the business of endorsing any religious text.

If students must say prayers or choose religious readings, this approach favors religious devotion over nonreligious approaches to life. That is troublesome, if the state should not be sponsoring religion *in general*. This problem might be met if teachers encouraged students to say or read whatever was meaningful to them, thus allowing an atheist child to express her antireligious views directly.

Even structured in this latitudinarian way, the program's effect would be to push majority perspectives and exert pressure against minority ones. In a fifth-grade class composed of twenty-two Christians, one Jew, one Muslim, and one atheist, with each child in turn saying an oral prayer or expressing his or her views, non-Christians will "have their chance," but only on three days out of every five weeks. On the twenty-two other days, Christian chil-

---

[18] I say "may be," because even a Christian student may hardly pay attention to a pro forma reading of the Bible to begin school.

dren may choose a Christian prayer that misfits the convictions of the outsiders. Unless the Christian children are tolerant, the outsiders may face hostility for being different or trigger evangelical efforts to bring them around. The child choice option could well put minority children under more pressure than when a teacher prays or does the reading.

Two more promising alternatives to oral prayer and Bible reading are a moment of silence, discussed in a subsequent section, and allowing students who wish to pray together for a few minutes before the beginning of school, but not in the organized classroom setting. This alternative is fine for older students; at least if the school also makes space available for other purposes, it should make space available for this purpose. To organize such an activity for children in elementary school without the leadership of a teacher is more difficult, but parents may be able to do what is needed without involving the school (except in providing space) or putting pressure on nonparticipating children.

Given the inevitable difficulties with any devotional program run by the school, and the reality that both a moment of silence and voluntary gatherings raise significantly less severe problems of sponsorship and coercion, I strongly believe the Supreme Court was right to decide that public schools should not include devotional practices as part of their school day.

The opinion in *Schempp* is notable in the history of establishment litigation in a number of respects. Responding sharply to the possibility of preferential aid to all religions, it "rejected unequivocally the contention that the Establishment Clause forbids only governmental preference of one religion over another."[19] Justice Clark emphasized "neutrality"—a word that has taken on different meanings in subsequent cases—as the key to the Establishment Clause; a state may not place official support behind "one or . . . all orthodoxies."[20]

Another important aspect of *Schempp* is its formulation of two-thirds of what soon became the standard Establishment Clause test. In order "to withstand the strictures of the Establishment Clause there must be a secular legislative purpose and a primary effect that neither advances nor inhibits religion."[21]

Responding to the claim that if religious exercises are omitted, a "religion of secularism" will be established in public schools, Clark remarked that the

[19] *Schempp*, note 10 supra, at 216.

[20] Id. at 222. The opinion also remarked that in previous cases, "the Court has consistently held that the clause withdrew all legislative power respecting religious belief and the expression thereof." Id.

[21] Id. Although noting the implicit coercive effect on children of having devotional practices as part of the curriculum, Justice Clark wrote that "a violation of the Free Exercise Clause is predicated on

state may not exhibit hostility to religion, and that schools may teach about comparative religion or the history of religion.[22] Complaints about a "religion of secularism" continue to fill the rhetoric of opposition to the Supreme Court's prayer and Bible reading decisions, and "teaching about religion" is one of the most important topics about religion and public schools.

Justice Brennan's concurring opinion, which occupies seventy-eight pages in the United States Reports and undertakes a comprehensive survey of related establishment problems, offers a purposive approach to the way in which history should matter for decisions of modern cases. In answer to the argument that Madison and Jefferson would have accepted devotional exercises in public schools, Brennan responded that a "too literal quest for the advice of the Founding Fathers upon the issues of the cases seems to me futile and misdirected."[23] At the time of the Bill of Rights, education was almost entirely private. Now, public schools—the primary means to educate children—"serve a uniquely *public* function: the training of American citizens in an atmosphere free of parochial, divisive, or separatist influences of any sort—an atmosphere in which children may assimilate a heritage common to all American groups and religions."[24] The proper inquiry is whether Bible reading tends "to promote that type of interdependence between religion and state which the First Amendment was designed to prevent."[25] In other words, one draws from history to discern the broad purposes of a constitutional provision and then assesses a challenged practice against these purposes.[26]

---

coercion while the Establishment Clause violation need not be so attended." Id. at 223. The exact place of coercion in respect to the Establishment Clause remains a substantial issue.

[22] The Bible may be studied "for its literary and historic qualities. Nothing we have said here indicates that such study of the Bible or of religion, when presented objectively as a part of a secular program of education, may not be effected consistently with the First Amendment." Id. at 225.

[23] Id. at 237.

[24] Id. at 242.

[25] Id. at 236. According to Brennan, the Court's decisions establish that all organs of government must maintain "a strict neutrality on theological questions." Id. at 243. That courts should not decide such questions was established in the post–Civil War case of *Watson v. Jones*, 80 U.S. (13 Wall.) 679 (1872), and was also reflected in *United States v. Ballard*, 322 U.S. 78 (1944).

In partial answer to the contention that the Framers of the Fourteenth Amendment did not intend to circumscribe activities that fall short of formal establishments, Justice Brennan quoted a letter from Justice Bradley that said the Constitution was adopted "with the fixed determination . . . to avoid all appearance even of a State religion, or a State endorsement of any particular creed or religious sect." *Schempp*, note 10 supra, at 258. Bradley went on to say that "our fathers . . . thought they had settled one thing at least, that it is not the province of government to teach theology . . . [W]e cannot legislate religion into the people." Id.

[26] Against the arguments that the Fourteenth Amendment should not be read to incorporate the Establishment Clause, ones we examined in chapter 2, Justice Brennan responded that all state estab-

Brennan remarked that the Maryland oath case and the Sunday closing law case suggest "that government may not employ religious means to serve secular interests, however legitimate they may be, at least without the clearest demonstration that nonreligious means will not suffice."[27] For this reason, religious exercises cannot be justified as helping to foster harmony and tolerance and inspire better discipline.[28]

PRAYERS AT GRADUATIONS AND FOOTBALL GAMES

The Court did not address school prayer in another full opinion until 1992, thirty years after *Engel v. Vitale*. In *Lee v. Weisman*,[29] the Court considered prayers at junior and senior high school graduation ceremonies.

Graduation from high school, and from other school levels, is a one-time only event for each student. Many students and their parents want a transcendental dimension to graduation ceremonies. Of course, parents or churches can organize religious baccalaureate ceremonies shortly before or after graduation, and a moment of silence is always a possibility. But many parents and students may feel that neither is quite the same as giving some recognition to God in the graduation ceremony itself. The basic conflict between majority wishes and minority protection is harder to resolve for graduation prayers than ordinary class prayers, just because the majority's wish to participate in shared acknowledgment of God's providence at one of life's most important occasion raises a stronger free exercise concern.

In the specific factual setting that the Court reviewed, a rabbi had delivered an invocation and benediction at a middle school graduation. He had been chosen by school officials, who had given him a pamphlet entitled "Guidelines for Civic Occasions," prepared by the National Conference of Christians and Jews and recommending that prayers be composed with "inclusiveness and sensitivity."[30]

The Court held, five to four, that the prayers were unconstitutional. Its opinion, written by Justice Kennedy, who had criticized the *Lemon* test in

---

lishments had been abolished three decades before the Fourteenth Amendment and that, with the Free Exercise Clause, the Establishment Clause is a co-guarantor of religious liberty. *Schempp*, note 10 supra, at 255–56. These comments by Justice Brennan provide the fullest explanation to be found in any Supreme Court opinion of why the Establishment Clause can be incorporated under a clause protecting liberty.

[27] Id. at 265.
[28] Id. at 280.
[29] 506 U.S. 577.
[30] Id. at 581.

an earlier Pittsburgh crèche and menorah case that we reviewed in the last chapter, emphasized the subtle coercion involved in graduation prayers.[31] In a formal sense attendance is voluntary, but graduation is one of the most important occasions in a young person's life, and attendance is effectively mandatory.[32]

Although concerned that the principal controlled the content of the prayers,[33] Justice Kennedy's main worry was that the graduation ceremony places public and peer pressure on students. Standing or maintaining polite silence could indicate merely respect for the views of others, but students may fear it will be taken to "signify adherence to a view."[34] The nonbeliever or dissenter may, thus, feel that religious practices in a school context are "an attempt to employ the machinery of the State to enforce a religious orthodoxy."[35] In his dissent, Justice Scalia ridiculed the idea that anyone would take standing or sitting in silence as signifying acceptance of a view. But even if dissenting students do not assume others will believe that they adhere to the views expressed in a prayer, they may feel offense in having to stand or sit through uncongenial religious practices at a school occasion.

Justice Souter, also joined by Justices Stevens and O'Connor, wrote to explain why the Establishment Clause forbids practices that do not favor one religion over another and why the graduation prayer could not be justified as an accommodation to religious exercise. Quoting language from earlier decisions,[36] and reviewing the text and history of the clause, Souter argued

[31] Four of the five justices in the majority continued to subscribe to the standard establishment test from *Lemon v. Kurtzman*; they said that the prayers had the effect of promoting religion. Presumably, the Court's opinion fell to Justice Kennedy because he was the fifth vote necessary to make up a majority. The concurring opinions of Justices Blackmun, id. at 604, and Souter, id. at 623, made clear that they did not believe coercion is required for a violation of the Establishment Clause.

[32] Id. at 586.

[33] Id. at 588. About the efforts of school officials to find a common ground, Kennedy said, "The suggestion that the government may establish an official or civic religion as a means of avoiding the establishment of a religion with more specific creeds strikes us as a contradiction that cannot be accepted." Id. at 590.

[34] Id. at 593.

[35] Id. at 592. According to Justice Kennedy, "the real conflict of conscience faced by the young student," id. at 596, distinguishes the graduation prayers from the legislative prayers upheld in *Marsh v. Chambers*, 463 U.S. 783 (1983). Id. at 596.

[36] He relied on a passage from *Wallace v. Jaffree*, 472 U.S. 38 (1985), saying that the First Amendment rests on the conviction "that religious beliefs worthy of respect are the product of free and voluntary choice by the faithful." (472 U.S. at 53–54), id. at 610, and discussed *Texas Monthly, Inc. v. Bullock*, 489 U.S. 1 (1989), which invalidated a tax that benefited religious periodicals in general. (Note that with tax measures, unlike prayers or Bible reading, it is possible to benefit religion in a nondiscriminatory way; although some religions may benefit more than others, no religion is really put at a disadvantage unless one conceives of a kind of strict competition between religions.)

that the phrase "an establishment of religion" most plausibly bars a nonpreferential establishment as well as the establishment of a particular religion.
He also noted that, in many contexts, including graduation prayers, a nonpreferential approach would require distinguishing forbidden sectarian religious practices from acceptable ecumenical ones, an endeavor for which
courts are ill suited.[37]

According to Souter, many accommodations to free exercise are appropriate and do not "signify an official endorsement of religious observance
over disbelief."[38] Accommodation "must lift a discernible burden on the free
exercise of religion."[39] Since students may express religious feelings before
and after the ceremony and may organize a privately sponsored baccalaureate, graduation prayers do not lift any burden.[40]

Justice Scalia, joined by three other justices, began his dissent by asserting
that the meaning of the Establishment Clause should be determined by references to historical practices and understandings. Under this approach, graduation prayers are perfectly appropriate, since "[t]he history and tradition
of our Nation are replete with public ceremonies featuring prayers of
Thanksgiving and petition."[41] For him, "The coercion that was a hallmark
of historical establishments of religion was coercion of religious orthodoxy
and of financial support by force of law and threat of penalty,"[42] not the
Court's "boundless, and boundlessly manipulable, test of psychological coercion."[43] In contrast to Brennan's historical approach, which focuses on

[37] In terms of the graduation prayers actually said by the rabbi, a nonpreferentialist would need
"to explain why the government's preference for theistic over nontheistic religion is constitutional."
Id. at 617. It would not solve this problem for the state to promote a "diversity" of religious views,
because courts would have "to make wholly inappropriate judgments about the number of religions
the State should sponsor and the relative frequency with which it should sponsor each." Id. at 617.

[38] Id. at 627–28. As volume 1 explains and subsequent chapters explore further, if religious believers are favored over similarly situated nonbelievers, it is not so easy to conclude that there is no
endorsement of religion.

[39] Id. at 629.

[40] Souter agrees with Douglas Laycock that people want government-sponsored prayers precisely
because they want a symbolic affirmation that government endorses their religion. Id. at 630. I do
not think this fairly captures the reason why many people want prayers at a graduation. Rather, they
want, as members of a group participating in an event of deep significance in the lives of graduates
and their parents, to acknowledge God and seek God's blessing.

[41] Id. at 633.

[42] Id. at 640. In addition our constitutional tradition "ruled out of order government sponsored
endorsement of religion (even without coercion) . . . where the endorsement is sectarian, in the sense
of specifying details upon which men and women who believe in a benevolent, omnipotent Creator
and Ruler of the world are known to differ (for example, the divinity of Christ)." Id. at 641.

[43] Id. at 632.

purposes of provisions cast at an abstract level, Scalia wants to generalize from specific practices that were then accepted to judge the appropriateness of different modern practices similar to the historical ones.

Justice Scalia stressed that most religious believers feel a need to acknowledge God's blessings as a people, a need recognized by the country's tradition of prayer at civic ceremonies. Such prayers are unifying, encouraging a toleration and affection among those of different faiths. Society should not be deprived of this unifying mechanism in order to spare "the nonbeliever what seems to me [a] minimal inconvenience."[44]

Justice Scalia's confidence that prayers are unifying is, at best, warranted only in some circumstances. Christians of a theologically liberal bent and many Jews may feel a sense of unity standing for the kind of prayer the rabbi delivered; but Hindus and atheists may feel excluded, and some Christians are likely to resent the absence of any reference to Jesus Christ. For some groups, having no prayer is going to be more unifying than a bland ecumenical prayer to God.

The Supreme Court's most recent engagement with organized school prayer occurred in connection with football games.[45] Under school policy, students had voted in favor of having invocations at football games and had selected a student to deliver them.[46] According to Justice Stevens's opinion for the Court, an objective observer would perceive a state endorsement of prayer. The government's removal from composing the prayer did not "insulate the school from the coercive element of the final message."[47]

In answer to the claim that attendance at football games was truly voluntary, Stevens responded that some students—members of the team, band, and cheerleading squads—had to attend and that many other students had a strong desire to do so.[48] But even if attendance were wholly voluntary, the prayer had "the improper effect of coercing those present to participate in an act of religious worship."[49] The school's policy, Stevens concluded, had an unconstitutional purpose, warranting invalidation on its face.

For me, the most difficult of all the prayer cases is the one involving graduation prayer. Whatever may be a widespread view in Texas about football games, high school sports events are routine aspects of school life, not mo-

---

[44] Id. at 646.

[45] *Santa Fe Independent School Dist. v. Doe,* 530 U.S. 290 (2000).

[46] Although the exact description of what the students voted to have delivered changed, after the initial policy was challenged, in order to make it less evident that what was intended was a prayer, the Court concluded that the school was inviting and encouraging religious messages.

[47] Id. at 216.

[48] Id.

[49] Id. at 217.

mentous occasions in the lives of students and their families. The argument that participants and spectators need a school-sponsored prayer to solemnize these events is much weaker than for graduations. Despite my regret at what may be lost when prayers are not said at graduations, I believe that the principle of nonsponsorship of religion is important enough to justify the Court's determination that even these prayers are unconstitutional.

The Court's decisions do not resolve some issues that lower courts have faced, including what to do about oral prayers and religious expressions that come from the initiative of speakers, not school officials. As I explain elsewhere,[50] I believe prayers at graduation ceremonies are inappropriate whether or not schools sponsor them. Religious expressions are different, because no member of the audience is necessarily expected to agree with what a speaker says; but speakers should not be chosen in order to deliver a religious message.

MOMENTS OF SILENCE

A substantial majority of states authorize classroom moments of silence.[51] Everyone understands that these are a kind of substitute for oral prayer, but if a teacher says, "We will begin with a moment of silence," any individual student can choose to use her moment for something other than prayer, neither the teacher nor any other student will know how a student is spending her moment, and no negative consequences will follow if someone chooses to reflect on last night's party. Do moments of silence violate the Establishment Clause?

In its one full consideration of such a law, *Wallace v. Jaffree*,[52] the Supreme Court in 1985 struck down Alabama's moment-of-silence law, but the opinions of the justices made clear that most such laws were acceptable. This odd combination of results was a consequence of special aspects of Alabama's law and the language in the concurring opinions. Given a law that already authorized silence for "meditation," the Alabama legislature

---

[50] *Does God Belong in Public Schools*, at 47–50. In the course of that discussion I criticize a 2003 Guidance on Constitutionally Protected Prayer in Public Elementary and Secondary Schools issued by the Department of Education, as mischaracterizing the content and implications of the Supreme Court decisions. In the same book, I also discuss the performance of religious choral music and the simulating of religious ceremonies to educate students. Id. at 50–57.

[51] According to Derek H. Davis, "Editorial: Moments of Silence in America's Public Schools: Constitutional and Ethical Considerations," 45 *Journal of Church and State* 429, 432 (2003), thirty-two states now permit or require moments of silence.

[52] Note 36 supra.

amended the law to include "voluntary prayer."[53] The sponsor had said that the law's purpose was to encourage prayer,[54] and the state had presented no evidence of a secular purpose.[55] This was sufficient for six justices to conclude that the law lacked any secular purpose and, therefore, failed the first prong of the *Lemon* test.

The crucial opinions in respect to other moments of silence proved to be those of Justice O'Connor and Justice Powell concurring. Employing the endorsement approach with which we have now become familiar,[56] O'Connor concluded that Alabama's new law did endorse voluntary prayer, but she made clear she would regard most moment-of-silence laws as constitutional. She indicated that a law would be all right if it did not "favor the child who prays" or give a child the message that she "should" pray.[57]

This exact way of putting matters is doubly obscuring. Even if students are urged to pray, the child who prays will not be favored in any ordinary sense over the child who daydreams, because the teacher will not know what each does. Telling a person he *should* do something is usually to suggest that he has a duty to do that—"You should tell the truth."[58] If the teacher says, "The legislature has set aside this moment to allow silent prayer, but you are, of course, free to use it as you wish," he *has encouraged prayer* but without telling his students they should pray. By formulating the issue as she did, Justice O'Connor made it easier than was warranted to conclude that most moment-of-silence laws do not endorse prayer. A more realistic appraisal is that most of the laws are passed in order to allow silent prayer, and that a high percentage of students and parents recognize this. Given this appraisal, the crucial question is whether such a mild form of encouragement or endorsement is acceptable—a question to which I shall return shortly.

In a concurring opinion mainly defending use of the *Lemon* test, Justice Powell agreed with O'Connor that most moment-of-silence statutes may be constitutional and discerned a similar view in the Court's opinion.[59] Since *Wallace v. Jaffree*, judges and scholars have assumed that the Supreme Court

---

[53] The Court dismissed as irrelevant that the new statute covered more grades than its predecessor.

[54] *Wallace*, note 36 supra, at 56–57, 43. In a dissent, Chief Justice Burger, with whom Justice White mostly agreed, rejected the majority's finding of an impermissible purpose. The sponsor's remarks were made *after* the legislature had passed the statute; there was no evidence that others shared his motive. Id. at 88.

[55] Id. at 57.

[56] *Wallace v. Jaffree* was an important case in her development of the test; she there sets out the main requisites of her objective observer who is the standard for the test's application.

[57] Id. at 17 (O'Connor, J., concurring).

[58] "Should" is also used in a conditional way. "If you want good grades, you should study hard."

[59] *Wallace*, note 36 supra, at 66. He overstated a bit what could fairly be found in the Court's opinion.

accepts standard moment-of-silence laws, and the Court has declined to review subsequent challenges to those laws.[60]

Whether the Supreme Court *should* accept such laws and whether legislatures *should* adopt them remain issues not so easily resolved. Of course, many legislators may disagree with the results in *Engel* and *Schempp* and wish to evade those to the extent they can;[61] but let us begin with legislators and justices who—like myself—believe these cases are correctly decided.

We know that a moment of silence is one in which participants may, but need not, pray. Whether participants assume that prayer is expected will depend on context. If, before a meal at which members of different faiths are present, the person at the head of the table says, "Before we begin, let's bow our heads for a moment of silence," those present are aware the speaker is mainly expecting personal prayers. But, if someone walks on the stage before an opera and says, "Please let us observe a moment of silence in honor of the memory of S who died this morning," a quiet reflection on S's life may be as apt as prayer.[62] A moment of silence to begin the school day may lack the obvious "nonprayer" alternative of reflecting on the life of someone who has died, but contemplation on what lies ahead in the school day seems much more of an option than in respect to dinner. Much, of course, depends on the history and religious life of a particular community, and on how a teacher tells students to engage in moments of silence. For example, if he says, "Let us bow our heads," that may point toward prayer. If the principles of the school prayer decisions are correct, teachers, and other officials, should indicate clearly that prayer is not a favored option.[63]

---

[60] In *Brown v. Gilmore*, 2000 U.S. Dist. Lexis 21623 (E.D. Va. Oct. 26, 2000), cert. denied, 534 U.S. 996 (2001), the Court did not review a failed challenge to a law that included "prayer" as one possible use of silence.

[61] If a legislator conscientiously believes the Supreme Court has been misguided, he will rightly perceive no obstacle to attempting whatever its decisions leave as possibly available options. To this extent, at least, legislators need not take what the Court says as the last word. I do not here delve into the more controversial question of how far legislators and other political officials should regard themselves as bound to comply with clear rulings of law by the Supreme Court made in cases to which these officials are not parties. In the decades since *Brown v. Board of Education*, the Court itself has consistently spoken as if it authoritatively declares the law of the Constitution, as well as resolving specific cases, but matters are more complicated than that. For a more extensive analysis of how judicial decisions should affect legislators and executive officials, see Kent Greenawalt, "Constitutional Decisions and the Supreme Law," 58 *University of Colorado Law Review* 145 (1987).

[62] I have put this contrast in "objective" terms, but its basis, since I have seen no poll on the topic, is subjective experience. I feel that a moment of silence before a meal is "meant for" silent prayer; I feel that a moment of silence in memory, a fairly common phenomenon at professional sports events, is much less pointed toward prayer.

[63] It may be that a moment of silence would not be instituted except for an aim that students who wish may have an opportunity to pray, but it does not follow that students should be encouraged to pray rather than silently reflect.

A legislator should ask herself whether instituting a moment of silence will *significantly* endorse prayer and will have a detrimental effect on those of minority faiths and nonbelievers. As my illustration about silence in someone's memory reflects, we can imagine moments of silence that do not involve endorsement of a religious practice.[64] Across a wide range, the honest answer about endorsement is one of degree. A participant may understand that a nonprayer option is all right, but that prayer is the most "natural" response. The "push" toward prayer may seem very light or quite substantial. If the legislator thinks that enacting a moment of silence will lead students who engage in such moments to suppose that the legislature or the schools, or both, strongly endorse silent prayer as the preferred activity, that should be a sufficient reason to vote against it; but she may accept a much slighter push toward prayer as an unavoidable adjunct of an otherwise desirable practice.

Moments of silence affect dissenters differently than do oral prayers. No one objects to moments of silence per se.[65] Although traditions differ about the comparative importance of oral and silent prayer, none is offended by silent prayer. The moment of silence does not require anyone to do anything against conscience; it does not create pressure on "outsiders" to ask to be excused or to submerge objections and participate in an offensive practice.

Even insofar as it does encourage prayer, the moment of silence carries out an approach of nonpreference better than can any oral prayer.[66] No one need listen to a prayer whose content she finds objectionable. Majority perspectives are not "favored" by frequency of repetition, as when individual students choose class readings.

In summary, except insofar as a moment of silence is understood to support or endorse prayer, parents and children cannot reasonably be offended by it. Insofar as silence is understood to support or endorse prayer, it may give some offense to nonbelievers, but the conflict between conscience and group practice is much less severe than with oral prayer. Weighing these considerations, a legislator might or might not support a moment of silence.

[64] However, in this culture, many people may assume that any moment of silence is meant mainly for prayer.

[65] We could imagine a religion that taught that all prayer should be oral and in groups. Knowing that many people will pray in a moment of silence, a member of such a faith might find moments of silence offensive in the same way that nonbelievers and believers who reject inclusive prayers might have been offended by the New York school prayer. But as far as I am aware, there is no such religion.

[66] One might think that moments of silence give slight support to religions for whom silence is highly significant, such as the Society of Friends, but people are unlikely to perceive such a preference because they understand *why* silence is chosen over oral prayer.

When we turn to constitutional judgment, three possible bases for upholding a moment of silence are that it entails (1) no endorsement, (2) only a slight endorsement, or (3) accommodation to religious exercise. I have already suggested that Justice O'Connor's approach that no endorsement is given is mistaken.

In answer to the federal government's argument that a moment of silence can be regarded as an accommodation to the desire of some children to pray, Justice O'Connor responded that accommodation must lift state-imposed burdens on religious activity; no state-imposed burden was there present.[67] As a later chapter will explain, I think this formulation is overly rigid. Some accommodations may appropriately relieve burdens imposed by the private sector. But O'Connor rightly discerned no relevant burden that would justify a moment of silence as a free exercise accommodation.

Moments of silence raise a difficult constitutional question, and some critics have argued that they should uniformly be held invalid.[68] Given the mildness of the endorsement of religion if prayer is not pushed on students by legislators or teachers, given the degree to which the practice goes some distance to meet the strong wish of a percentage of parents and children to begin the school day with a prayer, and given the slight imposition on anyone who dissents, I agree with the Court's assumption that moment-of-silence laws are constitutionally acceptable.

This conclusion does not by itself resolve what courts may do about teachers who encourage prayer more strongly. Parents may sue to challenge such individual departures from appropriate practice, but that is time-consuming and expensive. Moments of silence should be held invalid upon proof that teachers pervasively encourage prayer, but acquiring that evidence would be very difficult. Realistically, if such legislation adopting a moment of silence is upheld on its face,[69] one cost will be some unsanctionable encouragement

---

[67] About permissible accommodation, O'Connor commented: "It is disingenuous to look for a purely secular purpose" when a statute's objective is to facilitate free exercise," *Wallace,* note 36 supra, at 83, and she suggested that "[t]he solution to the conflict between the Religion Clause lies not in 'neutrality' but rather in identifying workable limits to the government's license to promote the free exercise or religion." Id.

[68] See Debbie Kaminer, "Barring Organized Prayers through the Back Door: How Moment-of-Silence Legislation for Public Schools Violates the Establishment Clause," 13 *Stanford Law and Policy Review* 267 (2002); David Z. Seide, "Note, Daily Moments of Silence in Public Schools: A Constitutional Analysis," 58 *New York University Law Review* 364 (1983); "Note, The Unconstitutionality of State Statutes Authorizing Moments of Silence in the Public Schools," 96 *Harvard Law Review* 1874 (1983).

[69] The difference between on-the-face and applied challenges is between holding that a statute is invalid as a whole as written and holding that it is invalid as applied in particular circumstances.

of prayer by some teachers. It falls upon teachers and school administrators to see that such encouragements are infrequent.

Justice Rehnquist's dissent in *Wallace* mounted a full-scale assault on Establishment Clause jurisprudence up to that time, propounding views that still belong to a minority but a minority that has become more than one. Rehnquist began by rejecting *Everson*'s version of history and the metaphor of "a wall of separation between church and state."[70] According to Rehnquist, Madison may well have been strongly separationist in his own convictions, but in working on the First Amendment he performed as "a prudent statesman seeking the enactment of measures sought by . . . fellow citizens," not attempting to place his own views into the federal Constitution. The Establishment Clause, Rehnquist writes, should be read only to prevent the government from establishing a national religion or preferring one sect to another.

Not only, for Rehnquist, has the Court's approach been too restrictive, it has failed to yield principled results,[71] causing the Court "to fracture into unworkable plurality opinions."[72] Rehnquist dismissed the purpose prong of the *Lemon* test; either it will have little practical effect—if it requires only a statement of a secular purpose—or it will reach too broadly to invalidate appropriate assistance to sectarian institutions.[73]

Elaborating his notion of a better approach, Rehnquist wrote, "The true meaning of the Establishment Clause can only be seen in its history. . . . As drafters of our Bill of Rights, the Framers inscribed the principles that control today. Any deviation from their intentions frustrates the permanence of that Charter and will only lead to the type of unprincipled decision making that has plagued our Establishment Clause cases since *Everson*."[74] This quote is striking in (1) its originalism, (2) its intentionalism, (3) its focus on the *drafters of the Bill of Rights*, and (4) its hint that unprincipled decision making inevitably follows deviations from original meaning.

Without explanation, Rehnquist omits five possibly relevant groups from his originalist account: the ratifiers of the Bill of Rights, the drafters and ratifiers of the Fourteenth Amendment, and the ordinary citizens of both eras. The suggestion that deviation from original understanding typically leads to unprincipled decision is simply implausible. (To take one example, modern equal protection law as it relates to women, which has no support

---

[70] Id. at 91–99.
[71] Id. at 107.
[72] Id. at 110.
[73] Id. at 108.
[74] Id. at 113.

in original understanding about forbidden practices, is neither more nor less principled than aspects of equal protection that can claim more grounding in original understanding.) In other chapters, we have seen and shall see the fundamental challenges to modern Establishment Clause law as they are formulated by Justices Scalia and Thomas.

CHAPTER 8

Public Schools:
Teaching about Religion

When the Supreme Court ruled in 1963 that devotional Bible reading in public schools was unconstitutional, it declared that the Constitution permits studying "comparative religion or the history of religion" and the Bible "for its literary and historic qualities."[1] Five years later, reviewing an Arkansas statute that forbade teaching of the theory that mankind descended from a lower order of animals, the Court stated that "the First Amendment does not permit the State to require that teaching and learning must be tailored to the principles or prohibitions of any religious sect or dogma."[2] Two decades later, the Court held invalid a Louisiana law that required that teachers who teach evolution also teach "creation science." Discerning a legislative purpose "to advance the religious viewpoint that a supernatural being created humankind," the Court held the law invalid.[3] These cases establish a clear conceptual line: public schools may teach *about religion* in various ways, but they cannot teach that particular religious views are true, and they cannot tailor their curriculum to conform with religious positions, even when conformance involves failure to teach material rather than directly teaching religious doctrines.

Many people in the United States are deeply disturbed by this interpretation of the Establishment Clause. They believe that we are a religious country, and that basic religious ideas, such as belief in a Divine Creator who is concerned with human welfare, and perhaps more specific Christian understandings, should be taught in public schools. I have suggested in chapter 3 some reasons why governments in the United States should not endorse or sponsor religious ideas. The Supreme Court's approach to religion in public schools carries out that understanding. As with the more general principle of nonsponsorship, the principle that public schools cannot promote some religious doctrines over others can be justified according to a broad idea of nonestablishment—such promotion would "establish" the favored doc-

---

[1] *Abington Township v. Schempp*, 374 U.S. 203, 225 (1963).
[2] *Epperson v. Arkansas*, 393 U.S. 97, 106 (1968).
[3] *Edwards v. Aquillard*, 482 U.S. 578 (1987).

trines. One need not resort to the metaphor of separation of church and state to conclude that the schools should not be teaching religious ideas as true.

In this chapter and the next, we shall explore public school instruction and religion. I first address teaching that is either directly about religious ideas or about the influence of religious movements on broader social developments. The next chapter considers teaching that is not on its face religious but that would not take the form it does were it not for religious views. I focus primarily on the controversial topic of evolutionary biology and competing explanations of the origins of life that are dominantly influenced by religious understandings. In that chapter, I also tackle teaching about morality in general and about specific behavior, such as the use of artificial contraceptives, that might or might not be heavily influenced by particular religious understandings. The teaching of morality is interesting for its own sake; it also presents an illuminating contrast in some respects with the teaching of natural science.

TEACHING ABOUT RELIGION: HISTORY AND SOCIAL STUDIES

Religious beliefs, organizations, and movements have played a tremendously important role in human history, and they continue to do so. Few doubt that the coverage given to religion in public schools is less than a fair reflection of its actual influence. Among the various explanations for this phenomenon, misapprehensions about the restrictions of Supreme Court decisions and fear of controversy and litigation are probably much less significant than a sense among major educators in the twentieth century that religion was "in decline," and doubts among text writers and teachers about their ability to present religious subjects in a fair and sufficiently objective way.[4]

Powerful educational reasons support saying more about religion in public school history courses. If students have little grasp of the influence of religion in history, they will be missing a key piece in understanding human societies and the development of our own culture. To take just three examples from U.S. history, the movements for abolition of slavery, prohibition, and civil rights were deeply penetrated by religious perspectives and religious organizations. And the strong influence of religious convictions continues over issues such as abortion, stem cell research, capital punishment, and the coun-

---

[4] I include the adverb "sufficiently" because no one can present these subjects in a completely objective way; I am assuming that presentations can be more or less objective.

try's policy toward the Middle East. Even citizens who have no personal involvement or interest in religion need to perceive the ways in which many of their fellow citizens are guided by religious premises in forming ethical and political opinions.

Another reason to teach about religion is so that youngsters can make an informed judgment about whether religion matters, or should matter, in their own lives. Neglect of religion may convey the message that religion is unimportant. I think we need to be careful here; we cannot be confident that more teaching about religion will produce adults who are more religious. Perhaps religious training at home will persist more often if young people don't learn much about opposing views; perhaps religion seems more challenging and exciting to some teenagers because it is covered little in their schools. Considerable education that adopts particular religious perspectives has not forestalled a strong movement toward secularization in most Western European countries. That experience should definitely make us skeptical that the state's *promoting* religious ideas in school will make citizens more religious; but it even casts doubt on the causal effects of teaching about religion. However, if, as I believe, we cannot be sure what the overall effect on the religious lives of citizens will be if schools do much more teaching about religion, that does not detract from the desirability of presenting religion as something students *may* choose to take seriously in their own lives. (And, of course, the desirability of students understanding how religion has functioned in our culture, and continues to influence many of their fellow citizens and peoples around the world, does not depend on whether teaching about religion makes students more or less religious.)

History courses should reflect the influence of religion on the development of civilizations. An account of European history should spend time on the spread of Christianity as well as the classical cultures of Greece and Rome. The Protestant Reformation should not be neglected in comparison with the Renaissance; it is hard to say which had a more profound effect on modern Europe. Students learning American history should understand the religious visions that brought the Pilgrims and Puritans to Massachusetts; they should also understand that many Protestants believed that Roman Catholicism was, literally, the religion of the Antichrist, and saw struggles between Catholics and Protestants as a profound conflict between evil and good. In confronting the horror of slavery, students should be taught not only the religious premises of abolitionists, but also that many Christian leaders found grounds to defend slavery.

What is true about Europe and the United States is true about other parts of the globe. Buddhism, Hinduism, Islam, and Judaism have been crucial components of the development of cultures. For many societies, perhaps one cannot clearly distinguish between religion and other aspects of culture. But this is no reason to disregard the features of these cultures that seem to us to fit into the category of the religious, and it *is* a reason to explain carefully to students that a differentiation of religious practice from other cultural aspects is by no means a given for social life among human beings, that it is more characteristic of "advanced" civilizations than smaller, more cohesive groups, and that something like the older practice exists within smaller units in our society, such as the Amish and Hasidic Jews.

The recommendation that religion should be accorded its fair place in history courses, and the premise that teaching about the place of religion in history should not inculcate any particular religious view, are fairly straightforward; but they raise three questions that are not so simple: (1) Do the dangers of incompetence and bias make this approach too risky in terms of values of nonestablishment? (2) What should texts and teachers do about perspectives on history? (3) Should teachers identify their own religious outlooks, encourage free discussion of competing views, and argue for their own views?

The first question connects to the other two in the following way: if texts and teachers try to do too much, their level of competence and fairness may be lower than if their aspirations are more modest. And, indeed, I shall suggest that even able text writers and teachers should be circumspect when they deal with religion. But, for now, let us suppose that we can identify a treatment of religion that would be appropriate in the hands of a text writer or teacher who has a reasonable grasp of various religious perspectives. Is the risk of incompetence or bias so great among actual writers and teachers that they should do less? The risk concerning writers of history texts is qualitatively different from the risk for teachers. Many texts are coauthored; a writer who recognizes that she cannot handle some religious topic as well as another writer can get help. More important, outsiders are capable of appraising texts. Schools or state boards can choose texts that are competent, and if they fail to reject texts that are partisan in favor of one religious view, courts can review books to see if they cross over the line that divides the permissible from the constitutionally impermissible.

The risk that individual teachers may not be able to handle religious subjects well is more worrisome, because it is less subject to review. A teacher who regards himself as unable to discuss religious matters adequately cannot call a friend to take over his class for these days; he must do the best he can, aided by the text. And some teachers may have very strong feelings about topics that arise. Let us suppose that the subject for the day is the life of

Mohammed and the rise of Islam. In general, it may seem easier to be reasonably objective about events long past than modern circumstances, such as the role of the religious right in the contemporary Republican Party (though perhaps the degree of objectivity is more accurately seen as the fruit of "the victors" writing history). But one question that is hard to avoid in the wake of September 11 is the status of violence in Islam. Those within and without Islam who speak to this topic quote different parts of the Koran; they refer to military conquests of Muslims or to their considerable tolerance of competing faiths; they compare the record of Islamic peoples with the record of Christian peoples, inheritors of a faith that most Christians do not regard as intrinsically militant. It is hard enough for experts to address this question without regard to events of the first part of the twenty-first century, and one gathers that not all the experts even try—rather using theories about "the nature of Islam" instrumentally to encourage developments within that religion or political responses to terrorist organizations and to Middle Eastern countries that they would like to see. An ordinary history teacher who has not made a close study of the origins of Islam may be strongly inclined to adopt a view about Islamic militancy that fits his present political views.

Three observations about the risks of incompetence and bias are extremely important. The first is that religion *is* special in an important sense, although the risks I have stressed are present for many areas of history instruction apart from religion. Does anyone suppose that most history texts and teachers give a fair account of citizens of the thirteen colonies who were conscientiously "loyal" to Great Britain during the Revolutionary War,[5] or delve deeply in the tension between the language of the Declaration of Independence and the practice of slavery? (These bits of bias *might* be defended on the ground that courses in American history should inculcate national loyalty.) To move forward to the time of my own high school education, one did not read or hear very much about what might be said in favor of communism or socialism as systems of government. What is special about religion is not the risk of bias, or incompetence, but its constitutional status. Teaching that praises American revolutionaries and neglects the loyalist perspective is not unconstitutional; teaching that praises Protestants and disregards Catholic perspectives is unconstitutional.

The second observation is that the long-term solution to problems of unacceptable bias and incompetence is better training of history teachers, including more attention to religious beliefs and movements in the colleges and graduate schools where prospective teachers study. But that cannot happen

---

[5] See Kenneth Roberts, *Oliver Wiswell* (New York: Doubleday, 1990), for a fictional portrayal.

overnight, and we have no assurance it will be a complete solution. If relatively few writers of academic history and university teachers are themselves interested in religion, they are likely to underemphasize it in what they do. No one will compel them to write and teach about it, if they are disinclined to do so. And some topics about religion may be so controversial, perhaps we should not expect enough treatments of them that are sufficiently unbiased.

This leads to the third observation. For many schools and teachers, a decision to do less about religion than would otherwise be appropriate can be defended as a reasonable choice to minimize the effects of incompetence and bias. In the short term, schools must take texts and teachers as they find them. No history course should, or could, disregard religion altogether; but some may, and probably should, devote less attention to religion than one would recommend for excellent texts and teachers.

I turn now to my narrower second question: what should texts and teachers do about perspectives in history? Each major religion in the world has its own perceptions about the unfolding of historical events. Very crudely, we might divide views about history into religious perspectives, antireligious perspectives, and agnostic perspectives. By an antireligious perspective, I mean one that asserts that all religious perspectives regarding history are misguided; such an approach will almost always be accompanied by a view that all religions are misguided, at least if evaluated according to some standard other than usefulness for human beings at various stages of history.[6] A Marxist approach to history is antireligious in both respects: religious ideas are illusions and material forces drive historical change. By an agnostic approach, I mean one that does not affirm or deny the correctness of religious views of history.

Texts and teachers should use an agnostic approach. Thus, given our constitutional values, a public high school text or teacher should not assert that history shows God's providential plan for human beings, or that historical events demonstrate that human life over the centuries is untouched by God's providence. Inevitably, in tracing nonreligious explanations for events, a teacher may implicitly make certain religious explanations seem less compelling. When the "black plague" struck Europe, killing a third of the population, many regarded it as a scourge of God against sinful activities or against the Jews.[7] If one can produce a scientific explanation for the spread of that

---

[6] I mean here to mark the idea that religious ideas may be useful for some human societies although they have no independent truth. Thus, someone may think it helps people to believe in God, although no God really exists.

[7] See Mark Lewis, "Plague to World: Drop Dead," *New York Times*, April 3, 2005, S7 at S22 (reviewing John Kelly, *The Great Morality: An Intimate History of the Black Death* (2005)).

fatal disease, that may make the idea that God was meting out punishment seem less likely (though it does not, of course, foreclose the possibility that God acted through infected insects, etc.). Here is an illustration of a phenomenon I mentioned in chapter 3. What is asserted on the basis of science or some other discipline may conflict directly with a religious claim (such as, the earth is the center of the universe) or make it seem less likely (such as, the black plague was God's punishment).

To say that history teachers in public schools should themselves adopt an agnostic approach to history, presenting events and explanations without an overriding religious or antireligious perspective, does not resolve how far they should try to present these perspectives from an objective point of view. As an aspect of an explanation of Puritan religious or Marxism views, should teachers elucidate a Puritan or Marxist view of history? Yes, to some extent. Perspectives *about history* are a significant component of many religious and antireligious positions, and educators should not neglect them, but they should also recognize pitfalls. Many religious Jews regard themselves as God's chosen people; many Christians in our country's history have regarded our nation as chosen by God. But what is it to be chosen? Is that mainly a matter of being favored, or having special obligations, or something else? That has been highly controversial, as is the question whether the idea of a nation's being favored is consistent with the dominant universalism of Christianity. (*For this purpose*, the idea that anyone who commits his or her life to Christ is saved and others are not is consistent with universalism, because no people or nationality is preferred.)[8] Given not only the complexity of many views, but also the diverse understandings within single religious traditions, even a sensitive text writer or teacher may find it impossible to expound the Jewish, or the Christian, or the Buddhist, or the Hindu view of history.[9] Greater success may be possible if she concentrates on the account of particular influential individuals, such as Augustine,[10] Jonathan Edwards,[11] or Reinhold Niebuhr,[12] but she must then be careful to explain that

---

[8] I am passing over two nuances. If one thinks belief depends on environment, one *might* think God favors those with a Christian upbringing and favors the people of countries in which most citizens are Christians. And, of course, this exclusivist version of Christian is directly at odds with the idea that God will treat members of all faiths (and nonbelievers) similarly.

[9] See Donald Mitchell, *Buddhism: Introducing the Buddhist Experience* (New York: Oxford University Press, 2002); Arvind Sharma, *Hinduism and Its Sense of History* (New York: Oxford University Press, 2003).

[10] See Peter Robert Lament Brown, *Augustine of Hippo: A Biography* (Berkeley and Los Angeles: University of California Press, 2000) (1967); St. Augustine, *The City of God*, Marcus Dods, ed. and trans. (New York: Hafner, 1948).

[11] See George M. Marsden, *Jonathan Edwards: A Life* 193–200 (New Haven: Yale University Press, 2003).

[12] Reinhold Niebuhr, *The Irony of American History* (New York: Scribner, 1952).

any one view is only a strand in a complex tradition. Overall, a teacher should probably be modest about the depth of her explanation of religious views of history that are likely to seem very peculiar to her, given her own training from a secular (agnostic) approach that does not seek religious explanations for events explicable in other terms.

The third question—whether teachers should identify their own religious outlooks, encourage free discussion of competing views, and argue for their own views[13]—also concerns modesty and depth. Since students will be interested and likely to speculate in any event, teachers should certainly be free to *identify* their own religious outlook. "Well, I happen to be a Lutheran, so I find Luther's position on faith to be appealing." "I'm not a church member now, but I was raised as a Roman Catholic and still consider myself a Christian." And so on. Such self-identification is more likely, I think, to give the students a basis to appraise what the teacher says than to push them toward his position.

It goes without saying that a teacher cannot argue for his religious views as the official position of the school—that would be a clearly forbidden establishment—but suppose one Lutheran teacher says, "I am going to tell you what I think and why, presenting my position as forcefully as I can; but you should understand that this is not the school's official position and you are free to form your own opinions." She then launches into a sharp attack on the Catholic Church at the time of Luther, and develops arguments from the Gospels and the letters of St. Paul why faith, not works, is the key to Christian salvation. Such teaching is appropriate in colleges and universities, even public colleges and universities, but I believe it is out of place in high school. Most high school students are not in a position to respond critically to the teacher's forceful presentation, and concerned parents will not be reassured that such presentations are only a feature of teaching about religion, not official endorsement of religious positions. (Viewed in isolation, such teaching might be appropriate for a small class of superbly educated and sophisticated high school seniors, but constitutional principles need to be administrable by educators and judges. The legal inquiry that an exception along these lines would require would be too refined and too uncertain in outcome to be practical).

My view is similar about critical discussions in class about these subjects, with the teacher withholding her own view. Here the main problem is that students with minority views may feel ganged up on and pressured by their peers; but there is also a risk that some students may think the teacher is favoring particular views by the way she directs the discussion. For rare classes, such discussions may work, but often they are inadvisable.

---

[13] Warren A. Nord, *Religion and American Public Education* 249–51 (Chapel Hill: University of North Carolina Press, 1995).

Thus, although history courses should cover religion, texts and teachers should exercise certain restraints that may not be necessary, or desirable, with nonreligious matters. If these limits are significantly overstepped, teaching about religion *in history* may turn into an unconstitutional endorsement or sponsorship of particular religious views.

Among the subjects to which religions throughout history have spoken are the organization of political and economic life. One thinks, for example, of injunctions in the Bible to care for the poor, of traditional Roman Catholic ideas about just price and just war, about Calvinist conceptions of a close linkage of political and religious purposes carried out by separate personnel of church and state, of various Christian socialist movements. Treatment of religious perspectives on political and economic life should not end with time past; courses dealing with government and economics as modern disciplines should provide students with some sense of how these subjects are seen from various religious standpoints.

The simplest illustration regards economics. Texts and teachers may tend to present neoclassical, market-based, economic theory as if it is the obvious foundation for a sound economic life. That theory focuses on consumer preference. Although the theory does not deny that a consumer's preference could be to assist those who suffer—for example, paying a higher price for goods so a surplus can assist earthquake victims—the ordinary assumption is that consumers are mainly self-interested and seek maximum satisfaction from material goods. In practice, the economic models of neoclassical theory do not leave much room for religious understandings. Even if teachers choose mainly to focus on neoclassical theory, they should make students aware that many religious leaders have criticized market-oriented economies as helping to produce a culture of selfishness and materialism. One striking example of such a critique was a 1986 pastoral letter of American bishops entitled "Economic Justice for All," which sharply criticized the great discrepancy between rich and poor—a gap that has widened in the ensuing two decades—and the undervaluing of meaningful work.[14] In sum, teachers should make students aware of religiously based critiques of modern economic life and of competitors to neoclassical theory, including some competitors that derive from religious understandings.

The conclusion I have reached about teaching modern economics applies to political subjects such as democracy, human rights, and war. Nearly every-

---

[14] National Conference of Catholic Bishops, "Economic Justice for All," in Hugh J. Nolan, ed., 5 *Pastoral Letters of the United States Catholic Bishops* 371 (Washington, D.C.: National Conference of Catholic Bishops, 1988).

one is aware that some Islamic fundamentalists are sharply critical of modern culture—terrorism does a superb job of capturing public attention—but how many high school students understand critiques and defenses of political arrangements made by more moderate religious groups within the Christian, Jewish, and Islamic traditions? As I was writing this section, I read a column by Kenneth L. Woodward about the choice to be made of a new pope.[15] He wrote that the lines of continuity left by John Paul II are "likely to be extended: a body of social teachings based on the dignity of the human person; a powerful critique of war; a preoccupation with the world's poor; a vibrant 'Gospel of Life' that stands against the growing global acceptance of abortion, euthanasia, and the destruction of human embryos for scientific purposes." Many citizens are aware of the official Roman Catholic stance on issues about which they feel strongly, such as abortion and capital punishment, but how many non-Catholics have a sense of any overarching perspective that unites the various Catholic positions? If they do have such a sense, it is unlikely to come from courses in public schools. Yet the development of Catholic views on these subjects, as well as on democracy and religious toleration, is a significant aspect of the last half century. Protestant views are less easy to encapsulate, given their diversity and the absence in most denominations of anyone entitled to speak authoritatively for that denomination; but these have also been influential, with a powerful shift from the dominance (in expression at least) of liberal views during the civil rights movement and opposition to the Vietnam War to the key role of religious conservatives in the Republican Party and its policy in the early part of the twenty-first century. As difficult as it may be to teach these matters in an appropriately objective way, texts and teachers should make the effort.

One possible objection to such teaching might be that political decisions should be made on the basis of reasons that are "accessible" to everyone, such as basic premises of liberal democracy and ordinary techniques of determining facts, and that religious reasons—not accessible to those who do not believe in the religion from which the reasons derive—lie outside this category. Therefore, political issues, including the shape of the economy, should be analyzed in nonreligious terms. If that conclusion is correct, does it follow that this is how public schools should approach these subjects?

The idea of "public reasons" is a complex topic, on which I have written at length elsewhere[16] and examine more summarily in chapters 23 and 24.

---

[15] Kenneth L. Woodward, "Progressive, Conservative or Rock Star?" *New York Times*, April 11, 2005, A19, col. 1.

[16] *Religious Convictions and Political Choice* (New York: Oxford University Press, 1988); *Private Consciences and Public Reasons* (New York: Oxford University Press, 1995).

My own view is that a stringent recommendation to citizens, religious groups, and legislators to rely only on public reasons is definitely not a requirement that can be lifted out of the Establishment Clause and that such a recommendation is also unsound as a claim about the political theory of liberal democracy. But, whether I am right or wrong about the latter point, this is a controversial subject about which students should be exposed to a diversity of views. Part of understanding whether reliance on religious reasons is appropriate or not is having a sense of what religious reasons are advanced for various positions. Further, even if one thought religious reasons should be excluded from public dialogue, one need not look far to realize that many religious groups and individuals, including many public officials, take a different view. One cannot grasp the political life of our society as it is without a sense of positions that are based on religious premises that influence our law and public policy. Thus, even if one grants that "public reasons" *should* dominate political life, students have a need to learn about the actual place of religious reasons that do not fit this paradigm.

Literature

I need say relatively little about religious writings and literature. The Bible and other religious texts, as well as novels, poetry, and essays with religious themes, properly enjoy a place in literature courses.

In all literate cultures, core religious texts have played an important part, and a succession of years of study of literature that omits these texts altogether gives a misleading picture of literature. Just how teachers should present such texts is a more difficult problem. They should explain their religious significance, the basic religious understandings that underlie the texts. But it is doubtful whether teachers should go further and try to explain in depth the fundamental religious understandings of the nature of sacred writings, such as what Jews and Christians mean when they say the Bible is the Word of God, a phrase that carries vastly different significance for those within both broad traditions. Most present teachers of English literature may not be equipped to explain the subtle variations among such positions.

With respect to authoritative religious texts, choices of what to teach risk conveying approval of some religious views over others. I shall discuss a similar problem about comparative religion in more detail; compilers of books and teachers should use three criteria for inclusion: (1) literary quality, (2) significance in terms of the world's religions, and (3) connection to the culture of the students. Classes should balance biblical texts with texts from other religious traditions, but teachers in typical American school districts need not spend as much time on Hindu texts as on the Bible. This conclusion that the Bible should not receive exclusive focus has been challenged.[17] If one looks at English and American literature, it is rife with allusions to biblical stories; modern students understand the Bible much less well than earlier generations; they cannot well understand the deposit of literature in English unless they have a basic grounding in the Bible. This argument is strong enough to justify an optional course for high school students that covers both the Bible itself *and* its uses in literature written in English; but a course that covers just the Bible is not warranted for high school students, and it is definitely inappropriate for younger students.

As literature teachers should not steer clear of sacred writings, so also they should not avoid novels, poems, and essays with religious, and antireligious, themes.

COMPARATIVE RELIGION

One form of teaching about religion is in a course on comparative religion. So long as no religious position is endorsed, such a course is perfectly appropriate. As I have noted earlier in this chapter, religious perspectives remain a major way of understanding human life, and religious groups play vital parts in most societies.

Not many public school teachers may now be competent to teach such courses, and those who are must make difficult judgments in selecting which religions to teach, and how to cover the religions they do teach. Although one *might* aim to expose students to the greatest possible range of religions or to treat equally religions with the most significance worldwide, teachers may decide to pay particular attention to the religions mainly represented in this country.

A school could not justify a greater concentration on Christianity than other religions on the basis that it is the truest religion, but it might defensibly treat importance in the society as one criterion of choice. Perhaps if a course devotes attention to religions based on both worldwide and local importance, children of minority religions, such as Hinduism, might feel at some disadvantage; but if teachers give even moderate attention to the Hindu reli-

---

[17] A comment along these lines was made by my colleague Robert Ferguson at a discussion of my *Does God Belong in Public Schools?*

gion, they may dispel the nearly complete ignorance of most American students regarding its beliefs and practices.

Decisions about what to teach about various religions are also difficult. Teachers should expose students to writings from within a religious tradition, so they can develop a sense of the religion from the inside. Teachers should describe practices and basic doctrines, but how far should they probe fundamental premises and understandings? For reasons that I suggested in the section on history, it would be risky for a teacher to explore in depth the biblical and theological arguments in favor of justification by faith. Although a teacher might attempt to lay out opposing positions without tipping her hands as to which she believes are correct, high school students might mistakenly think that propositions were being claimed as true when teachers were withholding judgment on that score. Further, the teacher's choice of doctrines and practices for intensive examination might seem to convey a judgment about their intrinsic merit and importance.

Rather than presenting positions herself, a teacher might invite "outsiders," clergy and active laypersons, to put forward various perspectives. If students heard from a range of outsiders, none would appear to carry the state's endorsement. In principle, this strategy for educating students about a broad spectrum of religious understandings is a sound one, but it must be done in a way that avoids proselytizing and favoritism toward particular views. Choosing exactly which outside speakers to participate will often be difficult, and in some communities parents will object to advocates teaching their children religious views that compete with their own. Individual communities will have to decide whether the possible benefits of such a program make it worth trying.

Few high school teachers are now competent to teach a course in comparative religion. Even well-trained teachers will have to be thoughtful about what religions they teach and about the depth of their coverage of diverse religious approaches. Making courses in comparative religion optional mitigates some of these risks.

CONSTITUTIONAL REVIEW

Although I have referred relatively little to constitutional law in preceding sections, constitutionally permissible teaching largely coheres with what I have claimed is appropriate or desirable teaching. Teaching religion as *true* is unconstitutional; teaching *about* religion in various forms is constitutional.

Schools are *allowed* to teach less about religion than might be desirable from an educational point of view.

Judges reviewing school efforts to teach about religion face hard questions about supervision and control. Inevitably, some teachers, self-consciously or not, will intimate that certain religious views are true or false; inevitably some students will mistakenly understand teachers to have asserted the truth of religious positions, although a balanced evaluation would suggest otherwise. How should a court respond to this reality?

When teachers dominantly convey religious messages or students dominantly, and reasonably, receive their teaching in that way, the teaching has crossed the constitutional boundary. Although in theory a court could determine that, in an individual instance, what purports to be teaching about religion has become, in purpose or effect, teaching of the truth of certain religious positions,[18] in practice, few parents will bother to sue individual teachers. If such suits constituted the only safeguard against impermissible establishments, most teaching labeled *about* religion would enjoy a free ride.

Realistic prospects of challenge are greater if objecting parents can show that in respect to some program, the apparent objective is to promote a particular religious view, or that many teachers are crossing the constitutional threshold, or are using as authoritative a text that does so. In that event, a court could declare the whole endeavor unconstitutional. It might also reach that conclusion if a program lacks sufficient supervision to forestall teaching of religious truth.[19] Finally, courts might consider whether available teachers are adequately trained. Giving some deference to the judgments of educational authorities, a court that finds that teachers are woefully equipped to teach about religion might decide that the near certain result will be an impermissible teaching of religious truth. That, also, could be the basis to hold a program invalid.

---

[18] Justice Scalia and others who are skeptical of subjective purpose as a test of violations of the Establishment Clause have not addressed whether such a test could be relevant if the actions of a single individual are in question. As chapter 10 explains, given the legal approaches to determining unacceptable discriminations of various sorts, I do not think it is defensible to foreclose consideration of an individual's purpose if the claim is that he or she has violated the Establishment Clause.

[19] When the courts deal with parochial schools, monitoring to avoid promotion of religion may slide into impermissible entanglement between government and religion, but that would not be a problem here. Public authorities would be monitoring what occurs in public classrooms. The judgments that supervising authorities would make about programs would correspond with those that text writers and teachers should have been making. It is not entanglement for higher educational officials to make sure that teachers have not overstepped the line in their evaluations of religious ideas and in their styles of presentation.

CHAPTER 9

Public Schools: Teaching Whose Content Rests on Religious Views

In this chapter we turn from teaching about religion—as an acceptable alternative to teaching of religious truth—to teaching that is not explicitly religious but whose content is determined by religious views. Religious views could determine what is not taught as well as what is taught. To take a (now) fatuous example, if a teacher did not mention religion but asserted that the earth was the center of the planetary system, his religious view would be determining the teaching if his only, or primary, reason for his belief about the place of the earth was his reading of the Bible. If, because of his religious belief, he did not mention anything about what body lies at the center of the planetary system his failure to mention that all ordinary evidence demonstrates that planets revolve around the sun would be determined by his religious understanding. I will consider examples drawn from the teaching of biology and from the teaching of moral choices. These subjects differ mainly in that natural scientists have shared techniques for determining scientific truth, whereas people disagree over how to discern moral truth.

EVOLUTION, CREATIONISM, AND INTELLIGENT DESIGN

The major controversy about religion and teaching in the public schools has occurred over evolution. Is it appropriate for schools *not* to teach evolution because of religious objections? Should courses in biology offer "scientific creationism" or "intelligent design" as an alternative to evolution? The Supreme Court has answered some of these questions. Here, I defend those answers as sound and go on to explore in some depth the issue about the constitutionality of teaching intelligent design, both because that issue is relatively novel and because I believe it is more complex than either proponents or opponents have recognized.

Let us start with the Supreme Court's major decisions about evolution and creationism, which I have noted in earlier chapters. In 1968, the Court reviewed an Arkansas law that forbade teaching of the theory that mankind descended from a lower order of animals.[1] The Arkansas Supreme Court had sustained the law, finding it unnecessary to resolve whether the statute "prohibits any explanation of the theory of evolution or merely prohibits teaching that the theory is true."[2] The U.S. Supreme Court decided that the law was unconstitutional in either event.

Justice Fortas wrote for the Court that the law proscribed a segment of the body of knowledge "for the sole reason that it is deemed to conflict with . . . a particular interpretation of the Book of Genesis by a particular religious group."[3] Although courts should not often intervene in curricular decisions,[4] states cannot require that teaching conform to the principles of a religious doctrine.[5]

When, two decades later, the Supreme Court reviewed a more complicated Louisiana law that required that *if* teachers were to teach evolution, they must also teach creation science, the Court reached a similar conclusion.[6] Proponents of creation science claimed that substantial scientific evidence supported that perspective,[7] but the Court determined that the law's purpose was to advance religion.[8]

Mentioning the "historic and contemporaneous link between the teachings of certain religious denominations and the teaching of evolution,"[9] Justice Brennan wrote for the Court, "The preeminent purpose of the Louisiana legislature was clearly to advance the religious viewpoint that a supernatural being created humankind."[10] During the legislative process, "creation science" was treated as including belief in a supernatural creator.[11] Since an

---

[1] *Epperson v. Arkansas*, 393 U.S. 97. There was no record of prosecutions under the statute, but a science teacher challenged the law.

[2] Id. at 101 n.7.

[3] Id. at 103.

[4] Id. at 104.

[5] Id. at 106. No one had suggested that the law was justified by "considerations of state policy other than the religious views of some of its citizens."

[6] *Edwards v. Aguillard*, 482 U.S. 578 (1987).

[7] Id. at 581.

[8] The law defined the theories of evolution and creation science as "the scientific evidences for [creation or evolution] and inferences from those scientific evidences." Officials claimed that the act's purpose was academic freedom, but Justice Brennan wrote that it furthered neither the goal of providing a more comprehensive science curriculum nor the goal of freeing individual teachers to instruct as they thought best. Id. at 586–87.

[9] Id. at 590.

[10] Id. at 591.

[11] Various efforts after the law was adopted to define "creation science" without reference to a supernatural creator were not relevant to what the legislature's purpose had been. Id. at 595–96.

improper purpose rendered the statute invalid, the district court properly decided the case prior to a trial on the basis of summary judgment.[12]

Justice Powell, concurring, emphasized that in ordinary usage "the theory of creation" is that God created the world and its life-forms out of nothing.[13] What were apparently the major organizations supporting creation science, the Institute for Creation Research and the Creation Research Society, both conceived their mission as encouraging belief in a Divine Creator.[14]

Justice Scalia's lengthy dissent undertook a sweeping attack on any "purpose" test that depends on the subjective motivations of legislators,[15] a subject that the next chapter will consider. Scalia went on to argue that even were the purpose of the legislature a proper test of constitutionality, the legislative history revealed sufficient claims about the scientific evidence for creation science, so that legislators may have had a valid secular purpose.[16]

To evaluate the Court's decisions in its two evolution cases, and to draw out the implications of those decisions, we need to say a little more about the theories of evolution and creationism.

Charles Darwin was not the first scientist to suggest the idea of evolution, but his 1859 *The Origin of Species* amassed all the evidences for evolution from various scientific fields.[17] Darwin suggested that the primary engine of development for this evolution with modification was a process of natural selection, according to which whether a characteristic that individual animals possessed from birth was passed to succeeding generations of offspring depended largely on whether the characteristic had over time contributed to the species' survival and reproduction.[18] Darwin's own approach has been filled out in very important ways, notably by genetic theory, and some of Darwin's

---

[12] Justice Brennan also urged that the statute discriminated in favor of creation science as against evolution because it provided curriculum guides and resource services (supplied by a panel of creation scientists) for the former, but not the latter. The easy answer to this contention is that the legislature understood that science teachers in the main believed in evolution, and since plenty of teaching materials were available, no curriculum guides or resource services were needed for evolution. See Justice Scalia's dissent at id. 630–31.

[13] Id. at 598–599. In its earlier drafts, the bill talked of creation ex nihilo by God. Only in subsequent stages was explicitly religious language eliminated, and there was no indication that the underlying purpose was then altered.

[14] Members of the latter had to subscribe to the historical and scientific truth of all assertions in the Bible. Id. at 602.

[15] Id. at 636–39.

[16] Id. at 619–36. A law's purpose, Scalia urged, is not necessarily to advance religion simply because it coincides with the tenets of a religion. The legislators' idea of academic freedom was that students not be "indoctrinated" in evolution.

[17] Jeffrie Murphy, *Evolution, Morality, and the Meaning of Life* 47 (Totowa, N.J.: Rowman and Littlefield, 1982).

[18] Darwin's account covers plants as well as animals. For the sake of simplicity, I limit myself to animals.

particular views have been supplanted; but ideas prevailing now fit within a general frame of Darwinian evolutionary theory, a neo-Darwinian synthesis.[19]

According to modern scientific understanding, the earth has existed for more than four billion years. It took a long time—a billion years or so—for any life to develop. The first life-forms were single-cell organisms. Only a long time later—two billion years or so—did multicell organisms arise. All complex animals (and plants) developed out of the original single-cell organisms. The main engine for change, but not the only one,[20] has been a process of natural selection: random mutations in genes produce organisms with different characteristics; if characteristics contribute to the survival and reproduction of an organism, they are more likely to be passed on to the next generation. Thus, gene alterations with survival value are carried forward; those without survival value expire. Neo-Darwinians disagree over some details, but all suppose that natural selection based on random mutations has played a crucial role.

It is not hard to see why Darwin's theory was, and neo-Darwinian theory is, disturbing to many traditional Christians. One central difficulty is that it seems to remove human beings from their exalted status in God's plan of creation. According to Genesis, God created man (and woman) in his own likeness and with dominion over the animals. If God created human beings to rule the earth, it is easy to conclude that they have rational and moral capacities qualitatively different from those of other animals. According to evolutionary theory, once simple organisms are in place, the development up to and including human beings can be explained without reference to God's creative hand. If human beings are one link in a long continuous chain, it is harder to suppose that a vast gulf separates their qualities from those of similar animals.

The deterministic quality of Darwinian evolution and its dependence on random changes have also disquieted some of those who believe that life on earth is part of God's plan and that human beings can achieve their own true good by responding rationally to that plan. Ever since Darwin wrote, many religious believers have regarded his theory as threatening the grounds of religious belief and of morality.[21]

---

[19] Philip Kitcher, *Abusing Science: The Case Against Creationism* 17 (Cambridge: MIT Press, 1982).

[20] Neo-Darwinian theory attributes some development to recombination of genetic characteristics (if one hundred blue-eyed and one hundred brown-eyed human beings intermarry, more than 50 percent of their children will have brown eyes because the brown-eye gene is dominant) and to "genetic drift" that is not explained by the survival value of genes.

[21] However, the precise grounds of complaint have varied, and the intensity of objections has waxed and waned.

Whether drawn directly from the book of Genesis or bolstered by claimed scientific findings, the creationist account most familiar to Americans differs radically in nearly every respect from neo-Darwinism. The earth is young—perhaps six thousand to ten thousand years old. All kinds of plants and animals that have ever existed were created within a span of days; they did not develop from single-cell organisms. The only development over time is within kinds, not from one kind to another.[22] Notably, human beings did not grow out of any nonhuman species of animal.

Because the scientific evidence for the major aspects of the neo-Darwinian story is so overwhelming and the scientific evidence for the competing creationist account so weak or nonexistent, little can be said from a scientific standpoint for factual claims that correspond with the passages in Genesis.[23] For example, many scientific disciplines, including geology, astronomy, and physics, unite in positing an ancient earth; and fossil dating powerfully confirms that small simple creatures preceded large complex ones by many eons. If, as I assume, the scientific evidence is extraordinarily weak that the earth and its population appeared as a literal reading of Genesis indicates, creationism should not be presented in a science course as a plausible scientific alternative to evolution. Even though scientific theories themselves evolve and once dominant theories are modified or abandoned, the possibility that scientific evidence will eventually support belief in facts that fit Genesis, read literally, is exceedingly slight.[24] A common argument for teaching creationism is that students should be able to examine competing theories and choose among them; the answer is that texts and instructors should not treat as plausible science what is not so. The only plausible reason to teach this form of creationism in biology is religious conviction, and the Supreme Court is right that doing so amounts to an impermissible teaching of religion. This conclusion does not rest on what particular state legislators may or may not have thought about the scientific credentials of creationism.

---

[22] Whether, according to this view, natural selection can explain development from one species to another depends on exactly how "species" is defined. Although "kind" is not a precise designation, cats definitely are not of the same kind as dogs and human beings are not of the same kind as apes or monkeys.

[23] The sentence in the text includes a version of life's development that omits explicit claims about God, referring in more neutral language to "spontaneous appearance," and does not use the standard Genesis story with its reference to God's creation.

I am not a scientist. I report dominant evaluations, filtered through some standard of what seems reasonable to me. Thus, a claim that a great flood made unreliable all modern dating of rocks does not seem to me a reasonable support of a view that the earth is only ten thousand years old, particularly given the confirmation of an ancient earth by disciplines such as astronomy that do not depend on dating earthly substances.

[24] I put aside here a possible shift in scientific thinking caused by divine intervention.

What might public schools teach about creationism? Science teachers may note that some people regard biblical texts, or some other religious authority, as a more reliable way of discerning what really is true than scientific conclusions.[25] And without claiming that any of them are literally true, schools could teach various theories about the origins of life, including the Genesis story along with accounts drawn from other religions. What the schools cannot do is teach creationism in its familiar form *as natural science*. (More broadly, they cannot teach as sound history or political science factual claims that receive no support from techniques within those disciplines.)

This conclusion does not quite answer the question about forbidding the teaching of evolution. Because the main outlines of that theory are so strongly supported by scientific evidence, and that theory is a central aspect of biological study, such a prohibition is bound to rest on religious convictions, and will be so perceived by those who are affected by the prohibition.[26] It is a modest extension of a principle that schools cannot teach material just because it fits religious beliefs to a conclusion that the state cannot forbid the teaching of material because it does not fit religious beliefs. In its first evolution case, the Supreme Court held invalid a state prohibition of teaching evolution.[27] If a state cannot forbid such teaching, it should follow that a particular school district or high school that offers a biology course cannot decide that evolution will not be taught.[28] This judgment rests on the assumption that any biology course in high school would teach evolution, central as it is to the subject, were it not for religious objections. The Supreme Court

---

[25] The teacher may point out that many scientific conclusions seem to receive confirmation of their truth by their ability to predict consequences of various sorts.

[26] For this purpose, I am treating a decision not to offend parents whose views rest on religious convictions as similar to a decision that rests directly on such convictions.

In conversation, Robert Audi pointed out to me that decision makers might rely on religious convictions in a way that would not be apparent to others. I am inclined to think that when such convictions are, in fact, *the* reason not to teach material, this amounts to an impermissible purpose to promote a religious view, even if the reason is not transparent to others. But that is a harder problem than what I am assuming about not teaching evolution.

[27] *Epperson*, note 1 supra.

[28] The 1999 decision of the Kansas Board of Education to remove evolution from its seventeen-page required science curriculum probably should also be viewed as having been unconstitutional, inexplicable as it was except as a response to religious objections. See Steven Benen, "Evolution Evasion," 52 *Church and State* 4 (1999). But see Derek Davis, Editorial, "Kansas Schools Challenge Darwinism: The History and Future of the Creationism-Evolution Controversy in America," 41 *Journal of Church and State* 661 (1999), concluding that this attempt to limit instruction in evolution would not be likely to be invalidated by a court. For an account of battles over the content of science teaching in Kansas and contests over membership on the State Board of Education, see Ralph Blumenthal, "In Kansas, Evolution's Backers Are Mounting a Counterattack," *New York Times*, August 1, 2006, A1, col. 1; Monica Davey and Ralph Blumenthal, "Fight over Evolution Shifts in Kansas School Board Vote," *New York Times*, August 3, 2006, A15, col. 1.

did not say, and I have not claimed, that any influence of religious convictions on the subject matter of science courses is necessarily unconstitutional; perhaps a degree of such influence is acceptable when the subject is one that might reasonably be taught or not taught if one focused exclusively on the subject's relevance from the standpoint of science and practical effect.

Some texts and schools districts have followed yet another strategy: labeling evolution as "only a theory." This strategy should also be regarded as unconstitutional.[29] The labeling implies a status for evolution that is misleading. One can speak of a theory that the earth moves around the sun, but we assume to a high degree of certainty that the earth really does move around the sun. As this illustration shows, a "theory" may be consonant with great certainty about relevant facts. Aspects of the theory of evolution, such as an ancient earth, the priority in time of single-cell organisms, and the evolution of multicell organisms from the single cells, are accurate to a very high degree of certainty (judged by scientific criteria).[30] Even the more controversial role of natural selection is as well established as the facts assumed by many scientific theories. To label evolution alone as "only a theory" is to suggest that its scientific credentials are weaker than most of what is taught in science courses. That is what is misleading. And because the choice to engage in such labeling is based on particular religious beliefs, that choice slides over into an impermissible favoring and endorsing of those beliefs.

I turn now to a theory that requires a more complicated analysis than any version of "scientific creationism" that fits the Genesis account. The idea of "intelligent design" is, or can be, much more modest in its challenge to neo-Darwinism theory. No doubt, many supporters of intelligent design believe in their heart of hearts that the Genesis account is true; but they are willing to settle now for what they think they might shoehorn into public schools—namely, some vague version of intelligent design. But when its crucial premises are spelled out, intelligent design need not dispute most features of neo-Darwinism. Its central claims are that natural selection, even when supplemented with other devices of the dominant theory, cannot explain all development of life, *and* that one can understand what is missing only as the

---

[29] See *Kitzmiller v. Dover Area School Dist.*, 400 F.Supp. 2d 707, 708–9, 762–64 (M.D.Pa. 2006); *Selman v. Cobb County School Dist.*, 390 F.Supp. 2d 1286, 1311 (N.D.Ga. 2005).

[30] I do not believe there is some sharp break between scientific methods and ordinary ways of discerning truth about the natural world (that is, ways that do not depend on assumptions about possible transcendent realities). See *Does God Belong in Public Schools?* 111 (Princeton: Princeton University Press, 2005). But, whether that view is correct, and whether, if correct, it reaches all or only some scientific methods, there are widely accepted methods of discovery in natural science.

consequence of intelligent design. "Intelligent design" is required to explain some features of complex life as we know it.[31]

The strongest candidates for intelligent design are highly complex organs, such as the eye and the wing, and highly complex single cells. Although more recent writing has concentrated on complex single cells,[32] I shall use the eye for illustrative purposes, since the way it works is roughly familiar to readers. The basic argument takes this form. The eye has a great many individual parts that must function together for animals to see. One cannot imagine that genetic mutation would have produced the beginning of these various parts all at the same time, and one cannot imagine that the earliest stages of most of the parts, standing alone, would have made any contribution to survival. Therefore, undirected natural selection would never have allowed the parts to persist, and to develop into an eye that sees. Not only does such complexity give the lie to natural selection as its primary cause, it points to the active involvement of an intelligent designer. Thus, intelligent design in the development of life can be detected empirically.[33]

Notice that this is *not* a theory about what stands behind every aspect of life on earth. Many religious people believe that God has created, and continues to sustain, everything in the universe, including its physical laws. In this understanding, God's design is perfectly consistent with explanations according to natural principles of science; these principles reflect the manner in which God's design is fulfilled. In this understanding, the complete truth of neo-Darwinism need not threaten belief in God's design.[34] The "intelligent design" that matters for our purposes is a partial alternative to neo-Darwinian theory, not an ultimate explanation that stands behind all physical reality.

---

[31] Among the writings supporting "intelligent design" are Michael J. Behe, *Darwin's Black Box: The Biochemical Challenge to Evolution* (New York: Touchstone Books 1998) and William A. Dembski, *The Design Inference* (Cambridge: Cambridge University Press, 1998). Robert T. Pennock, ed., *Intelligent Design Creationism and Its Critics* (Cambridge: MIT Press, 2001), contains a wide-ranging collection of essays supporting and criticizing intelligent design theory.

[32] See Behe, note 31 supra.

[33] The theory of intelligent design has been said to involve two basic assumptions: intelligent causes exist, and they can be detected empirically (by discerning specified complexity). Access Research Network, "FAQ" about intelligent design (2001; visited December 3, 2002, at http://www.arn.ord/id_faq.htm).

[34] However, a number of scientists and philosophers of science have contended that a benign, powerful Deity would not "choose" natural selection, with its randomness, wastefulness, and pain. See Philip Kitcher, *Living with Darwin: Evolution, Design, and the Future of Earth* 117–66 (New York: Oxford University Press, 2007). For me, the "problem" of believing in a benign Creator and natural selection is one facet of the problem of natural evil, i.e., the problem of why a benign God would allow terrible things to happen that are not caused by the exercise of human freedom.

The theory of intelligent design standing alone does not tell us much about the designer.[35] If we knew that the eye was designed by an intelligent being, we could infer that the designer made it for seeing; but we might not know whether the designer was highly intelligent or only moderately so, fully effective in carrying out plans or often ineffective, benign or malevolent; or, indeed, whether the designs we identify came from many intelligences or one. If we relied exclusively on evidence of life on earth, we might wonder whether the designer gave creatures eyes so that they could flourish, or in order to empower them to destroy each other in increasingly sophisticated and fascinating ways. Most people who believe in intelligent design no doubt have in mind a benign and extremely powerful creator; but the theory, in and of itself, does not get us there. The gap must be filled in accordance with religious premises or traditions, or by what we may glean from the philosophy of religion.[36]

We can split intelligent design theory into negative and positive inferences. The most modest negative claim is that neo-Darwinian theory, as it now exists, does not have an adequate explanation for the rich complexity of many organs and individual cells. The next negative claim is that neo-Darwinian theory will not in the future be able to explain such complexity. Finally, it is claimed that no ordinary scientific theory will be able to do so (for reasons I shall explain, intelligent design does not count as an ordinary scientific theory). The positive inference is that intelligent design is the causal explanation for many important aspects of life's development over time.

The counters to intelligent design theory are that neo-Darwinism is adequate to the task and that, even if it should somehow prove lacking, other scientific principles, not intelligent design, will fill any gaps. Notably, some theorists have urged that principles of order not yet discovered (but eventually discoverable) will help explain life's development,[37] just as the discovery of the function of DNA helped to explain how one-cell embryos grow into babies.

Because nonscientists must participate in decisions about school curricula and in legal judgments about what is constitutionally permissible, they cannot leave all claims and counterclaims to the experts.

Here is my decidedly nonexpert appraisal. Neo-Darwinians do not assert that they have any clear picture, much less proof, of particular stages of

[35] Behe, note 31 supra, at 97, suggests that it is possible to infer design "without knowing anything about the designer."

[36] I have in mind here possible philosophical arguments in favor of a deity with certain characteristics.

[37] See, e.g., Stuart Kauffman, *At Home in the Universe* (New York: Oxford University Press, 1995); Gordon Rattray Taylor, *The Great Evolution Mystery* (New York: Harper and Row, 1983). One

development of complex organs and cells. Among other problems, the eye and other soft-tissue organs do not make fossils; we have *no* fossil record of how the eye developed in various species. But if natural selection is by far the soundest explanation of changes that we can observe and of which we do have fossil records, it is probably the soundest explanation of changes about which we have less information. And it is an intrinsically plausible explanation.[38] Early stages of features of the eye may have given a helpful sensitivity to light, useful though far less so than a functioning eye. Or, these early stages may have aided animals in some other respect. Given the hundreds of millions of years over which eyes took to form, the slow process of natural selection could well have produced them. If for some reason natural selection does not provide the dominant explanation for how particular aspects of complex life developed, most scientists assume that another ordinary scientific explanation will do so.

We have, at the outset, to recognize that scientists will never be able to establish beyond any cavil of doubt the inaccuracy of intelligent design. At its most modest, that theory asserts only that intelligent design played some role in the development of life. However complete a scientific explanation of evolution may be, it can never *demonstrate* that nothing happened beyond what natural selection, and other natural factors, can account for (just as a doctor cannot demonstrate that the cure of any particular illness happened because of natural processes and owed nothing to divine intervention).

If people entertain enough doubt about whether natural selection can explain *as much* as neo-Darwinians now suppose to make us wonder whether something else is (and was) going on, should they conclude that the something else necessarily (or probably) has been intelligent design? The assertion that it has been draws from William Paley's famous argument that if one finds a watch in a heath, one knows it was designed by an intelligent creator.[39] The claim is that one can draw a similar inference about complexity in nature. This move from inferences about human creativity to causes of complexity in nature is too hasty. That is, inferences about human design within a world whose objects we understand reasonably well are an *insecure* basis to determine what aspects of nature require an assumption about design that reaches beyond ordinary scientific principles. When they first realized that tiny one-cell embryos consistently grew into babies of their parents' species, human beings might have concluded that no natural explanation

---

possible explanation that differs from both neo-Darwinism and intelligent design theory (as I take it) is that aliens placed complex life-forms on earth.

[38] See, e.g., Richard Dawkins, *The Blind Watchmaker* 77–86 (New York: Norton, 1987).

[39] William Paley, *Natural Theology* 9–10 (New York: American Tract Society, n.d.).

would suffice, that an active creator must be at work; but now we have a convincing natural explanation of how embryos develop.

To make a long story short, in counterposition to intelligent design theorists, if natural selection falls short, the explanation for complexity in life may well be an understandable principle of natural order, rather than intelligent design. The rest of this section is based on this set of assumptions about the challenge of intelligent design to neo-Darwinian theory.

Is intelligent design a scientific theory, and does it belong in science courses? The argument that intelligent design theorists mount against natural selection as the explanation for complex organs and cells is that their development by a slow process of random mutations with survival value is impossible, or so extremely improbable as to be practically impossible. This argument relies upon claimed inferences from facts, without explicit reliance on religious claims. It is not merely that we intuit that complexity *must* be the product of intelligent design. A necessary component of the argument for intelligent design is that natural selection simply does not work in the way scientists suppose to produce eyes or complex cells. The decisive evidence, beyond discovery of how many parts make up complex cells and exactly how these parts cooperate, is the account the neo-Darwinians themselves have provided about how natural selection works. It is as if a theorist carefully explained how people are able to jump off the ground and then asserted that people once were able to jump twenty feet high (on earth). A critic could use the explanation of "how" to show that the claimed twenty-foot jumps could never have taken place.

Does intelligent design itself provide *an explanation* for how things have happened? That depends on how much one demands of an explanation.[40] Imagine you are walking along the beach and see a construction of twigs and pebbles that funnels water into a small dish. Aware that no beavers are around, you are sure that only a human being would have produced this funnel, but you have no idea what this particular builder was like or why she would have wanted to build what she did. You have no idea when, if ever, she will build another similar funnel or what precise conditions would cause her to do so. Suppose your six-year-old child asks where the funnel came from. You say, "Water and wind would not make this, and I'm sure no animal around here could. A person definitely built it, but I don't have a clue why she wanted to get water into a dish in this way."

Intelligent design theory, standing alone and without any input from religious premises, provides an explanation that is even thinner. It can't tell us

---

[40] On the ambiguity of the term "explanation," see Robert T. Pennock, *Tower of Babel*, 185–89 (Cambridge: MIT Press, 1999).

much about the qualities of the designer, except that the designer is very powerful. It can't tell us why the designer chose to create particular kinds of cells (or eyes);[41] it provides virtually no basis to predict when and how the designer will act in the future.

Can a theory with these drawbacks be "scientific"? Let us suppose for the moment that the theory is highly plausible, that available evidence strongly supports the inference of an intelligent designer. Without wandering too far into the morass of just how one decides if a theory is scientific or not,[42] we come up against the hard fact that intelligent design does not provide a natural explanation. Insofar as it is an explanation at all, it is an explanation that reaches beyond the natural, earthly order of things. In this respect, it resembles the explanation of the funnel, which reaches beyond the natural order of sea, wind, and sand to posit human intervention.

Does the analogy to the funnel suggest that intelligent design could one day become a natural explanation? We might one day discover who made the funnel and, if we knew enough about what made that person tick, we might, relying on psychology and related human sciences, understand just why she acted as she did and what would cause her to produce a similar device in the future. Could the same be true for the designer intelligent design theory posits? Indulging fantasy, we might imagine that a single intelligent designer would one day reveal herself by unmistakable signs and also reveal all the springs of her actions and capabilities, allowing us to predict and explain her actions according to a set of psychological principles. But no one thinks ordinary human beings on earth will ever have this kind of knowledge about an intelligent designer.[43]

Intelligent design theory, at its most modest, relies on natural data, and on the scientific theories that try to explain these data, to reach beyond scientific

---

[41] In urging that one can infer design "without knowing anything about the designer," Michael Behe, note 31 supra, at 97, overstates slightly. At least if a design is functional, one can attribute to the designer an aim to realize that function.

[42] See *McClean v. Arkansas Board of Education*, 529 F.Supp. 1255, 1267 (E.D. Ark. 1982), and the criticism of that approach in Larry Laudan, "Commenting on Ruse: Science at the Bar—Causes for Concern," in M. LaFollette, ed., *Creationism, Science, and the Law: The Arkansas Case*, at 161–66 (1983). In arguing that intelligent design qualifies as a scientific theory, David K. DeWolf, Stephen C. Meyer, and Mark Edward DeForest, "Teaching the Origins Controversy: Science, or Religion, or Speech," 39 *Utah Law Review* 29, 66–72 (2000), cite challenges like Laudan's to any "definitional" or "demarcation" theories of science, and claim that naturalistic and nonnaturalistic theories of origins are metaphysically equivalent. For an account of the characteristics of scientific theories, see Philip Kitcher, *Abusing Science: The Case Against Creationism* 35–42 (Cambridge: MIT Press, 1982).

[43] Many religious people do believe we know very important truths about God, but those are not mainly gleaned from the natural sources on which science relies; and it would generally be regarded as blasphemy to claim that we understand God so well we could predict all God's creative actions according to psychological explanations.

explanation. It asserts that within a domain where natural science claims to provide (at least potentially) full causal explanations, natural science cannot do so. It is best understood as a theory about the limits of science.

It helps, I think, to contrast *intrinsic* limits of science—basic limits that are set by the domains of scientific endeavors—with *contingent* limits—limits on what science is able to explain, within the domains that scientific inquiry covers. Why anything exists at all and whether we should be moral are intrinsic limits; science, by its nature, cannot answer these questions.[44] If science cannot explain certain events that transpire in the natural world, such as a claimed miraculous cure from illness, the limit is contingent.[45] In this sense, the theory of intelligent design is a claim about a contingent limit of science.

What is the place for discussion within science courses of contingent limits of science? We may initially rule out any full discussion of claims about limits drawn directly from religious sources. But the asserted bases for intelligent design, as we have seen, are different from any direct reliance on religious sources. The theory takes the empirical data available to scientists and concludes that scientific efforts are doomed to impotency in providing a full explanation.

Research biologists are, in the main, committed to an approach called methodological naturalism. They seek to provide full natural explanations for phenomena in nature. For them to pause long over intelligent design would be to concede that no natural explanation may be forthcoming. We should not be surprised that few scientific researchers are among the proponents of intelligent design. When the Ohio Board of Education considered intelligent design in 2002, critics warned that the theory had not been subject to "repeated experimentation and discovery," that its speculation about an ultimate agent was "the antithesis of true science," that proponents were trying to force unanswerable questions about the instigation of life into a curriculum that should be directed to the "rigorous proofs of science."[46]

A science teacher's role is not exactly that of a researcher. One might well think that part of the teacher's job is to suggest contingent limits of science, if empirical data and scientific theories indicate such limits. If one is theoriz-

---

[44] My conceptual point does not depend on the accuracy of these two examples.

[45] For there to be a genuine limit, it must be that a scientific explanation would not succeed, even if we had much more knowledge than we now possess.

[46] Francis X. Clines, "Ohio Board Hears Debate on an Alternative to Darwinism," *New York Times*, March 13, 2002, A16, col. 1. The proposal that the board finally approved in December 2002 is that students in biology classes be taught critiques of evolutionary theory. See transcript, *NPR Talk of the Nation/Science*, Friday, November 8, 2002, 9 (comment of board member Deborah Owens-Fink). In February 2006, the Board of Education reversed the earlier position. Jodi Rudoren, "Ohio Board Undoes Stand on Evolution," *New York Times*, February 15, 2006, A14.

ing about *the limits of science*, one can hardly expect "rigorous proofs" based on "repeated experimentation and discovery" of the sort often possible with fully natural explanations. In the Columbus debate, an advocate of teaching intelligent design argued that the methods of science "are part of the debate that teachers should air." Some philosophers coming from religious perspectives have, indeed, urged that scientists should abandon methodological naturalism,[47] but I see the issue as narrower. Within a general practice according to methodological naturalism, should science teachers acquaint students with possible contingent limits of science, when empirical data and the failures of fully natural explanations to explain the data point to such limits?

My answer to this question is a guarded yes. It is yes because teaching about the limits of a discipline is an appropriate aspect of the discipline. Someone instructing students about predictions of human behavior based on economic analysis or political polling rightly tells them just how these techniques fall short, insofar as we understand why they are imperfect predictors of what people do. My answer to the question is guarded because I have not yet addressed the issue of plausibility in this context. Science teachers should not be explaining contingent limits of science because a few eccentric theorists argue that the empirical data and inadequacy of natural explanations reveal such limits. An overwhelming majority of research scientists reject intelligent design out of hand.[48] Science teachers should not be introducing theories about contingent limits unless those are grounded solidly within the sources with which scientists occupy themselves. It is at just this point that one's estimate of plausibility becomes crucial.

As I have noted, intelligent design theorists advance three skeptical conclusions and one positive claim. The skeptical conclusions are (1) natural selection, as presently conceived by neo-Darwinian theory, cannot fully explain the development of complex life (even when it is supplemented by subsidiary elements of that theory); (2) no reformulated or developed neo-Darwinian account will do the job; (3) no combination of natural explanations will ever account persuasively for the development of complex life. The positive claim

[47] See Alan Plantinga, "When Faith and Reason Clash: Evolution and the Bible," in Pennock, note 31 supra, at 139–41; Philip Johnson, *Reason in the Balance* 107 (Downers Grove, Ill.: Intervarsity Press, 1995); Nicholas Wolterstorff, *Reason within the Bounds of Religion* 77 (Grand Rapids, Mich.: Eerdmans, 1976).

[48] The American Association for the Advancement of Science, the nation's largest scientific organization, recently adopted a resolution that said: "The intelligent design movement has failed to offer credible scientific evidence to support its claims. The intelligent design movement has not proposed a scientific means of testing its claims. And, therefore, it is resolved that the lack of scientific warrant for so-called intelligent design theory makes it improper to include it as part of science education." See NPR transcript, note 46 supra, at 3.

is that the actions of an intelligent designer are a required component of any full explanation.

To this nonexpert, skeptical claim 1 may well be sound. Evolutionary theory has developed significantly since Darwin wrote *The Origin of Species*, and I see no reason to believe we have arrived at a terminus. That we have not is suggested both by very substantial ignorance about many details of the development of complex life and by quarrels among evolutionists themselves about those details.[49]

Skeptical conclusion 3 is closely tied to the positive claim about the place of intelligent design. Design theorists assert that we can infer design from complexity, but I have explained why I do not think we can move so quickly from inferring human design in complex objects we find on this earth to inferring a transcendent design in complex natural life-forms. May there not be natural principles of order in the universe that are susceptible to natural explanations but which we have not yet discovered? Modern scientific inquiry is only a few centuries old; modern theories about life's development derive largely from Darwin's work a century and a half ago. Given the amazing history of science so far, it is highly likely that major discoveries lie in the future, possibly including novel natural explanations for the development of complex life.

Without knowing what new factual evidence may be adduced and what course the development of neo-Darwinian theory may take, *and* without undertaking the tedious task of trying to figure out when a theoretical account would change so radically that it would no longer be neo-Darwinian, we are in a poor position to estimate whether a full explanation of the life's development might be neo-Darwinian or would include elements that neo-Darwinism would not accommodate. But the crucial issue is not about the ultimate status of neo-Darwinian theory but about the adequacy of natural explanation. The answer to the skeptical claim that it cannot be adequate is that *some* natural explanation may suffice, even if the now dominant theory should prove to fall short.

How does all this translate into teaching of biology in public schools? One reasonable choice would be to teach neo-Darwinian evolutionary theory, with the caveats that all scientific theories are subject to revision over time and that scientists are more confident about the development of complex life from simple life-forms than they are about the exact role of natural selection

---

[49] Behe, note 31 supra, at 69, makes the following use of a dispute over "gradualism" in evolutionary theory: "Each side points out the enormous problems with the other's model, and each is correct."

in relation to other causes of development postulated by the dominant theory. According to this reasonable choice, teachers would say nothing about intelligent design.

Another reasonable choice would be to inform students that a relatively few scientists matching empirical data against the theory of natural selection believe it cannot explain nearly as much about the evolution of complex life as neo-Darwinian theory assigns to it. If this skepticism proves accurate, undiscovered principles of natural order may help explain this development, although it is possibly a product of intelligent design not itself explicable according to natural principles.

It would *not* be a reasonable choice to present neo-Darwinism in more or less its present form and intelligent design as the two most plausible alternatives.

Contrary to what one might think at first glance, the very concept of intelligent design is not necessarily religious. The mere fact that empirical evidence and scientific theory might point to something transcendent does not make the theorizing itself religious.[50] An investigation of a cured illness is not unscientific because it eventuates in a conclusion that the cure is probably beyond ordinary explanation. Neither the inference to intelligent design nor mention of intelligent design is itself enough alone to make teaching religious.

However, if scientific evidence is highly inconclusive about what natural explanations might be forthcoming for the development of complex life, it *is* religious teaching to present neo-Darwinian theory and intelligent design as *the* two alternatives. Without a basis of religious convictions, I do not believe one can reasonably conclude that intelligent design is *the* necessary supplement for whatever natural selection (with the subsidiary elements of neo-Darwinian theory) might not satisfactorily explain.[51]

Another basis for the religiosity of intelligent design theory was relied on by the district court passing on the mention of intelligent design in biology classes in Dover, Pennsylvania.[52] It found the history of that theory was so closely linked to a religious creationist view that the theory was indelibly

[50] The court in *Kitzmiller*, note 29 supra, at 735, apparently reached a different conclusion, though the court's main emphasis was on the reasons why mention of intelligent design was introduced by the school board.

[51] In reaching this conclusion, I am rejecting arguments to the contrary that Behe, note 31 supra, and other intelligent design theorists explicitly advance. For an extended argument that teaching intelligent design is not teaching religion, see DeWolf, Meyer, and DeForest, note 42 supra, at 79–100. For a contrary view, see Jay D. Wexler, "Note, Of Pandas, People, and the First Amendment: The Constitutionality of Teaching Intelligent Design in the Public Schools," 49 *Stanford Law Review* 439, 460–68 (1997).

[52] See *Kitzmiller*, note 29 supra, at 735–46.

religious. An otherwise acceptable theory should not be indefinitely tainted by religious roots, but the court reasonably took the history of this theory's development as a strong indication of its character.

The mere fact that people would be uninterested in alternatives to evolution were they not disturbed about evolution for religious reasons is not alone enough to condemn the alternatives as religious. Suppose that whatever teachers might say about possible alternatives is itself intrinsically unobjectionable; but that no one would worry about qualifying the teaching of natural selection *except that* it is at odds with many people's religious convictions. Perhaps many scientific theories are as vulnerable as natural selection, but if they do not touch religious beliefs, no one worries about presenting qualifications and alternatives. Thus, we might conclude that what is said as a hedge about neo-Darwinian theory is said because of people's religious beliefs. This causal relation between the content of teaching and religious conviction is not enough to make the teaching religious in a sense that makes it unconstitutional. Of course, in practice, judges will be hard put to establish an exclusive religious cause for teaching that is otherwise appropriate, but let us assume they are sure that doubts about natural selection would not be aired but for religious understandings. If the doubts are reasonably supported by empirical data and genuine explanatory difficulties of natural selection, and the teaching about the doubts is sound and is not itself religious, the teaching should not be treated as religious simply because no one would have pressed for it, had evolutionary theory not been disturbing to some citizens on religious grounds. Of course, if an alternative theory is pushed *because of* its religious content—what the district court decided had occurred in Dover[53]—then an unconstitutional purpose to endorse religion condemns its being taught.

To summarize, intelligent design theory, taken as asserting that neither neo-Darwinism nor any other ordinary natural explanation can fully account for the development of complex life on earth, is a theory about the limits of science that claims to be grounded on indisputable empirical data and the incapacity of scientific principles to explain those data. The vast majority of scientific experts reject intelligent design theory, but assertions about the dominant role of natural selection are less than airtight. As a nonexpert looking at scientific claims, I believe one cannot reasonably doubt that natural selection has had a very large role in the development of life, but one can reasonably doubt it has had *as* dominant a role as neo-Darwinism assigns to it. Textbook authors and teachers may decide to discuss

[53] Id. at 90–132.

doubts about the role of natural selection and a range of possible alterna-tives. Given the likelihood that other natural principles could well fill in any details now missing, one cannot reasonably suppose intelligent design is *the* alternative to the prevailing evolutionary theory. To teach it as such in public school science courses is an impermissible teaching of religion, whether or not one can show that those who authorize such teaching have religious objectives in mind.

MORALITY AND MORAL CHOICE

Teaching about morality and moral choice presents an interesting contrast with teaching about natural science. We have no settled nonreligious way to resolve moral questions. Although most people may agree in their actual moral judgments across a wide range of behavior, they disagree about how to reach these judgments, and they disagree sharply about the morality of some courses of action, such as the acceptability of abortion or of removing a feeding tube from a person who has been in a persistent vegetative state for a long period of time.[54] Many Americans rely heavily on religious sources, particularly the Bible and church authority, to decide moral questions; oth-ers, including many people who are religious, make moral judgments in a way that is substantially independent of religious sources.[55] Schools may teach about moral choice; and various subjects, such as sex education, raise issues about particular decisions students might make. I shall focus mainly on the second topic, which involves the issue of nonreligious content being dictated by religious belief, but I turn first to teaching about morality.

Because there is no settled methodology for resolving moral questions, teachers addressing moral choice in general should either incorporate major religious perspectives as possible approaches to moral decision-making or should carefully explain that the course limits itself to nonreligious ap-proaches although many people reply on religious sources to resolve moral questions. In no event should teachers present a particular nonreligious per-spective (one that implicitly excludes religious approaches) as the *proper* way to make moral choices. The once popular "values clarification" ap-proach exhibited this defect, or came very close to doing so. Based on the notion that students should freely choose their values after careful consider-

[54] See, e.g., *Schiavo ex rel. Schindler v. Schiavo*, 357 F.Supp. 2d 1378, 1387–88 (M.D.Fla. 2005).

[55] I say "substantially independent" because religious people are likely to be affected to a degree by what they perceive as implications for morality of their religious views, and even nonreligious people are affected by the general culture, including religious traditions, in which they live.

ation, the approach implicitly rejected the idea that moral values may be a matter of obligation connected to a transcendent source.

For those teachers who undertake to explain some major religious approaches to moral choice, the question arises about an appropriate depth of coverage. Probably, teachers would do well not to probe too deeply into the nuances or the logical roots of various positions. They might, for example, note that many Protestants rely heavily on the Bible, and have students read some of the passages that are thought to bear on important moral questions. But a teacher should not aim to develop in depth various strategies for interpreting biblical passages or the full theology that lies behind according such high authority to the Bible. She should explain that Roman Catholics rely heavily on natural law (premises about morality that do not depend on particular religious convictions) and on church authority, that Catholics are (in the church's view) free to dissent from some positions taken by the hierarchy, but not others. She should not try to explain fully the precise relations between natural law and church authority, or the religious conceptions that accord these two sources their places.

Schools teach that some moral choices are right and others are wrong. They teach that people should be honest and considerate, and that students should develop their talents, not undermine themselves by a heavy use of drugs or alcohol. So long as the school's position conforms with the great majority of religious (and nonreligious) views in the community, there is no problem, although teachers might indicate just how widespread are the positions they are offering.

The difficult questions arise if the community is badly split over the propriety of some moral choice, such as whether older high school students should engage in sexual intercourse. In most such instances, the schools may do well to refrain from teaching any particular answer as the correct one. Typically, they should tell students that various religious traditions have different views about the choice, if that is the fact. Without explaining just how the religions have arrived at their positions, a teacher might say the Roman Catholic Church and some Protestant and Jewish groups oppose premarital intercourse but that many Protestants and Jews (and some individual Catholics) think it is morally acceptable. If the class is in sex education, not approaches to moral choice, the teacher should probably not delve into the arguments for competing positions.

This kind of avoidance may not be appropriate if the moral issue concerns social justice. Public schools should teach the equal status of women and men, even if some religious groups in the community believe that women should occupy a subordinate role. Teachings about social justice are typically about premises on which liberal democracy rests. The strongly prevailing view in American society, supported by many laws, is that women deserve equal treatment as citizens. Although a teacher's statement that some religions oppose what she presents as a demand of social justice may risk a dilution of the force of the teaching or a putting down of the religions as benighted, nonetheless, she probably should mention that the school's view about social justice is not universally held, is opposed by some religions represented in the community.

A rather different problem arises if, with or without addressing issues about moral choice, the school tailors its teaching not to offend the religious convictions of some members of the community. The most striking example is a decision *not* to teach about contraceptive use in many sex education courses for high school students. This is a complex topic, and I will settle for a brief summary here.[56]

If the materials or the teacher indicate that abstinence before marriage, or until adulthood, is a sacred obligation to God, then the school is teaching a particular religious point of view as sound, in violation of the Establishment Clause. But suppose the teacher offers nonreligious reasons for abstinence, such as the danger of sexually transmitted diseases and the desirability of postponing what can be a very powerful emotional experience. There *are* substantial nonreligious reasons to think (or at least for parents and other adults to think) that abstinence is preferable to other alternatives. These alone, however, cannot explain why nothing is said about contraceptive methods. That silence *might* be defended on the ground that young people who engage in sex outside of marriage or use contraceptives commit grossly immoral acts that should not be facilitated whatever the consequences. Most teenagers do engage in sexual intercourse before they are eighteen. Even most adults who would strongly prefer abstinence by high school students do not condemn engaging in sex as grossly immoral, and they may accept the use of contraceptives. At present, only those with a strong religious view are likely to condemn premarital intercourse with contraceptives as grossly immoral.

An alternative argument for silence about contraceptives is the consequential one that if abstinence alone is emphasized, many fewer teenagers will have sex. Teaching about contraceptives is, in this view, an encouragement of dangerous sexual behavior. The reality is apparently otherwise. About the same number of teenagers will engage in sexual intercourse whether or not

---

[56] I have a somewhat longer discussion in *Does God Belong in Public Schools?*, note 31 supra, at 147–48.

they are educated about contraceptives; for these teenagers, the greater danger lies in ignorance of contraceptive use.

If neither the immorality argument nor the consequential argument can stand as a good reason for public schools to neglect teaching about contraceptive use in high school sex education courses, the only basis for that neglect is that such teaching is offensive to the religious views of members of the community. These views *should* be represented in discussions of alternatives but they *should not* block the teaching of content that would obviously belong in a course, were it not for religious opposition. Because this problem is more complicated than that of what belongs in biology courses, it is less clear how courts should respond, but I conclude that a failure to teach about contraceptive use in sex education courses for high school students, like a failure to teach evolution in biology courses, amounts to an establishment of religion.

CHAPTER 10

Establishment Clause Tests and Standards

Having examined a number of specific problems in applying the Establishment Clause, we are ready to pause and review the standards that Supreme Court justices have used to resolve those problems. This review can provide a dimension of depth regarding the constitutional issues we have considered so far, and it introduces the controversial subjects that lie ahead, the two most important of which are the limits of accommodation and the permissibility of aid that goes to religious groups but is granted according to nonreligious criteria (such as the provision of hospital or educational services).

The various approaches that members of the recent Supreme Court have used to resolve Establishment Clause issues include (1) the threefold test of *Lemon v. Kurtzman*,[1] about which I will say more shortly, (2) endorsement, (3) consistency with historical practice or understanding, (4) coercion, and (5) decision of specific issues in light of the values of nonestablishment but without any guiding standard. Justices have used some of these approaches as comprehensive tests, in the sense that the application of that test by itself determines how a challenged law or practice fares. That has been the typical use of the *Lemon* test: a law that satisfies all three branches is constitutional; a law that fails any branch is unconstitutional. And at least as to public displays of religious symbols, that is how endorsement has figured. Whether a display is constitutional depends on whether religion is endorsed. Other tests may be partial, or one way. A determination that a practice coerces religious exercise signals unconstitutionality, as it did in the Supreme Court's decision that sponsored prayers in graduation ceremonies of public schools were invalid;[2] but the absence of coercion will not assure that a practice is constitutional. Or, as I explained in chapter 3, the Court may employ standards or rely on factors that count for or against constitutionality without those standards or factors necessarily determining the outcome. Thus, a justice might think that consistency with historical practice counts in favor of a challenged activity, but that some activities that satisfy the standard are

---

[1] 403 U.S. 602 (1971).
[2] *Lee v. Weisman*, 507 U.S. 577 (1992).

nevertheless unconstitutional (and that some novel connections of government and religious activities are constitutional).

Chapter 5, on religious symbols in public places, has a preliminary discussion of endorsement. After focusing on the basic, much criticized *Lemon* test, this chapter considers the endorsement test and offers briefer comments on coercion and on references to historical understanding.

THE *LEMON* TEST: PRELIMINARY REFLECTIONS

Under *Lemon v. Kurtzman,* a law or government practice is invalid if it (1) lacks a secular purpose, (2) has a primary effect of advancing or inhibiting religion, (3) or involves excessive entanglement between government and religion. In some early formulations, "entanglement" included political divisiveness, as well as administrative entanglement. More recently, most justices have dropped this as a separate inquiry for particular cases.[3] And, as of 1997, the Court has treated administrative entanglement not as a separate strand of a threefold test but as one relevant factor in determining effects.[4]

We have explored some nuances of the *Lemon* formulation in previous chapters, but together the secular purpose requirement and the rule against an effect of advancing religion have barred serious government promotions of religion. In most establishment cases, the effect inquiry has proved crucial, although an improper purpose to advance religion has been decisive in a recent Ten Commandments case[5] and in some public school cases at which we have looked.

The Court has said that the purpose standard is satisfied by *a* secular purpose, even if that is accompanied by an equally strong religious purpose. Asymmetrically, a substantial religious effect can be primary, even if there are equally substantial nonreligious effects. Imagine that a law is backed by two purposes, S (the secular purpose to facilitate hospital care) and R (the religious purpose to further the religious ideas of the religious groups running hospitals) of exactly equal strength, and that it causes major effects of

---

[3] I put the point this way because members of the Court have not denied that preventing political divisiveness was one reason for bars on the establishment of religion. Justice Breyer emphasized the dangers of divisiveness along religious lines in his dissenting opinion in *Zelman v. Simmons-Harris,* 536 U.S. 639, 717–29 (2002). And for Breyer, a concern that a ruling that would require removal of depictions of the Ten Commandments from public buildings would generate divisiveness on religious lines constituted one reason to uphold the monument on the grounds of the Texas State Capitol. *Van Orden v. Perry,* 545 U.S. 677, 703 (concurring opinion).

[4] *Agostini v. Felton,* 521 U.S. 203, 232–33 (1997).

[5] *McCreary County v. American Civil Liberties Union of Ky.,* 545 U.S. 844 (2005).

these kinds that are also of exactly equal strength. (This notion of exact equality is an analytical construct. No one could estimate that the two kinds of purposes and effects were exactly equal.) According to the *Lemon* test, as it has been applied, the law has *a* secular purpose, adequate to pass the purpose strand; but it has *a* primary religious effect, enough to condemn it under the effects test.[6] This disparate treatment is part of what has helped to make effects analysis central. If this treatment of purposes and effects of comparable strength can be justified at all, it represents a degree of deference to legislative aims and a hesitancy of judges to determine what purposes are really dominant.

One might initially suppose that the purpose and effect strands of the *Lemon* test are at odds with any accommodations to free exercise, whether a legislature grants these or a court imposes them under the federal or a state free exercise clause. The concern is that any accommodation to free exercise, such as a legislative exemption that allows members of the Native American Church to use peyote in worhip services,[7] involves a purpose to advance religion and a parallel effect, just what the *Lemon* test forbids. One way to deny this apparent contradiction is to understand permissible accommodations as not advancing religion but merely as making up for a disadvantage religion would otherwise suffer. In this view, equalizing the playing field is one kind of secular purpose and effect.[8] Another approach is to understand *Lemon* as containing an implicit qualification to the rule against advancing religion, such that any permissible accommodation, though it advances religion, is nevertheless allowed.[9] The second approach is clearer and more satis-

---

[6] Acknowledging the language of some earlier cases suggesting that a law would fail the purpose test only if entirely motivated by religious considerations, Justice Souter's opinion for the Court in *McCreary County*, id. at 860–61, 863–65, indicates that the inquiry is whether the "predominant" or "preeminent" purpose is religious. As I suggested in chapter 5 and develop further in this chapter, the endorsement test developed by Justice O'Connor makes judicial inquiry into purpose and effect nearly indistinguishable. That is not because an "endorsement" approach *as such* has this implication. One might imagine a legislative purpose to endorse that is carried out in such a subtle or inept way that people do not perceive an endorsement, and one certainly may imagine circumstances in which people perceive an endorsement though none was intended by legislators. But Justice O'Connor used as her standard an extremely well-informed reasonable observer. She did not suggest how such an observer could find a purpose to endorse but no such effect, or vice versa.

[7] In *Employment Division v. Smith*, 494 U.S. 872 (1990), the Supreme Court, although rejecting the claim that the Constitution itself generates such a privilege, made clear that legislatures could choose to create one.

[8] See Justice White's opinion for the Court, *Corporation of the Presiding Bishop of the Church of Jesus Christ of Latter-Day Saints v. Amos*, 483 U.S. 327, 335–36 (1987).

[9] See Justice O'Connor's concurring opinion in id. at 348–49. For Justice O'Connor the crucial question is whether government action endorses religion. Steven D. Smith has criticized this technique to draw the line between permissible accommodation and impermissible advancement on the ground

factory,[10] but whatever conceptual devices one uses to reconcile *Lemon* with free exercise accommodation, the salient point is that Supreme Court justices, with the possible exception of Justice Stevens (in some of his opinions), have never supposed that free exercise accommodations are all forbidden establishments of religion.

The serious problem is not that the *Lemon* test and accommodation are radically irreconcilable, but rather the limited assistance the test affords to judges in deciding challenges to accommodations. If permissible accommodations do not *relevantly* advance religion, then a determination that a law is meant to benefit religion and will have a substantial effect of this kind will not resolve the constitutional issue. One must proceed to ask if the accommodation is permissible, a multifaceted inquiry that will engage us in a later chapter.[11]

Although for decades, the Court employed the *Lemon* formulation in almost every establishment case, it did not do so in *Marsh v. Chambers*,[12] a challenge to a state's hiring of a legislative chaplain and to the legislature's beginning every session with a prayer. As we have seen in chapter 6, such a practice was impossible to square with *Lemon*'s language. Chief Justice Burger's opinion for the Court, sustaining these practices because of their long historical pedigree, indicated that *Lemon* was a guide but not the final standard of what counted as an establishment. *Marsh v. Chambers* left open just how the Court would decide *when* to rely on the guidance of *Lemon* and when not to. For many observers and some justices, *Marsh* provided evidence that the *Lemon* test was ill conceived. By 1995, seven justices had expressed doubt that *Lemon* should be employed as a comprehensive test for all establishment cases. Although an opinion of the Court (for a majority of justices) has yet to so rule, *Lemon*'s day as a complete test has already passed;[13] but that does not mean its various elements are irrelevant. Not only

---

that "accommodation" and "endorsement" will often coincide. Smith, "Symbols, Perceptions, and Doctrinal Illusions: Establishment Neutrality and the 'No Endorsement' Test," 86 *Michigan Law Review* 267, 282 (1987). See also Michael W. McConnell, "Religious Freedom at a Crossroads," 59 *University of Chicago Law Review* 115, 151 (1992).

[10] One reason is that the same kind of purpose and effect may underlie permissible and impermissible accommodations, which may be distinguished only by the magnitude of the burden imposed on outsiders.

[11] See note 6 supra, for the possibility that a determination about endorsement will provide a basis for resolution. I shall explore that possibility in chapter 17.

[12] 463 U.S. 783 (1983).

[13] For example, Chief Justice Rehnquist, writing for four justices upholding a monument containing the Ten Commandments on the grounds of the Texas state capitol, said, "Many of our recent cases simply have not applied the *Lemon* test. . . . Whatever may be [its] fate in the larger scheme of Establishment Clause jurisprudence, we think it is not useful in dealing with [this] sort of passive

do opinions consider those elements, cases decided under *Lemon* are treated as authoritative. For those reasons, and also because other suggested approaches to establishment cases are best understood either as versions of or alternatives to *Lemon* as a whole, or to its various components, we need to examine those components closely.

THE *LEMON* TEST: PURPOSE

In this section, I consider *Lemon*'s most controversial, though perhaps least practically important, element, purpose. As a 2005 opinion puts it, "[L]ooking to whether government action has 'a secular legislative purpose' has been a common, albeit seldom dispositive, element of our cases."[14] Although this chapter's focus will be on the use of purpose to invalidate laws or practices as establishments, as in the moment-of-silence case,[15] the statute providing for the teaching of "scientific creationism" in science courses,[16] and the placing of copies of the Ten Commandments in county courthouses,[17] we should keep in mind that similar issues about purpose can arise if people claim that a law violates their free exercise of religion by discriminating against them or by targeting their particular religious practices,[18] subjects taken up in the first volume.

Under the *Lemon* test, a law must have a secular purpose. According to the Supreme Court, this does not mean that its *exclusive* or *main* purpose must be secular. It is enough that it have a substantial secular purpose, even if it also has a religious purpose. In the various cases in which the Supreme Court has declared that a law or practice fails the purpose test, it has deemed the overriding purpose to be religious. In discerning purpose, the Supreme Court has relied on the language of laws, on what a new law adds to preex-

---

monument." *Van Orden v. Perry,* note 3 supra, at 681. Concurring, id. at 703–4, Justice Breyer relied "less upon a literal application of any particular test than upon consideration of the basic purposes of the First Amendment's Religion Clauses themselves." In *Board of Education of Kiryas Joel Village School District v. Grumet,* 512 U.S. 687 (1994), Justice O'Connor, concurring, devoted four pages of her opinion to suggesting that a single unified test for Establishment Clause cases was a bad idea, that the Supreme Court would do much better to break down cases into discrete categories, with their discrete tests. "If each test covers a narrow and more homogeneous area, the test may be more precise and therefore easier to apply." Id. at 721. She discerned a powerful drift away from the standard threefold test of *Lemon,* and declared it to be good.

[14] *McCreary County,* note 5 supra, at 859.

[15] *Wallace v. Jaffree,* 472 U.S. 38 (1985).

[16] *Edwards v. Aguillard,* 482 U.S. 578 (1987).

[17] See note 13, supra.

[18] See, e.g., *Church of the Lukumi Babalu Aye, Inc. v. City of Hialeah,* 508 U.S. 520 (1993).

isting law, and on indications from the legislative history about the objectives of legislators.

On the subject of what counts as a permissible purpose, I have already mentioned that a purpose to accommodate religion may be acceptable, whether or not one calls it "secular." Another point worth noting is that a remote secular purpose will not validate a direct purpose to promote religion. A legislature may not (at least in most settings)[19] promote the practice of religion on the ground that religious involvement will further the secular value of good citizenship. With these understandings, we can formulate the purpose element of *Lemon* as follows: To be valid, a law must have either a secular purpose (that is not only the remote objective of a more direct purpose to promote religion) or a purpose to accommodate religion in a permissible way (chapter 17 explores the boundaries of permissible accommodations).

When we compare *Lemon*'s purpose test with Justice O'Connor's inquiry about when government is endorsing religion, we can see that the two overlap to a very large degree, but impermissible purpose is a somewhat broader category. If a law or practice endorses a particular religion or religion in general, that improperly promotes religion under *Lemon*. Suppose a law announces that the pope is the father of the genuine Christian Church and that transubstantiation is the correct doctrine about the significance of communion; the law has *no* practical consequences, it does not make any rights or duties turn on whether someone accepts the pope or believes in transubstantiation. Nevertheless, the law both undoubtedly endorses the Roman Catholic religion and has the forbidden purpose under *Lemon* of promoting that religion.

But a legislature could have an invalid purpose to advance religion without having a purpose to endorse that religion. A small county legislature is choosing where a highway will be built. Many members of the legislature belong to a Baptist church located in the general area over which the highway will travel. Proposed Route A will go right through the site of the Baptist church. Route B, which will be thirty miles distant from the church and the residences of most of its members, will draw housing and commerce away from the community. Route C, which will traverse five miles from the church and the center of the community in which most of the Baptists live, will leave their residential life undisturbed, will draw potential church members into the area, and will make getting to church easier for those members who live

---

[19] I add this qualification because it is arguable that the government may encourage religious practice in settings in which it largely controls the lives of individuals, such as public orphanages, prisons, and the military.

many miles away. The legislators agree among themselves that if they regarded the interests of the Baptists as no weightier than those of the many other religious groups in the area, as well as nonreligious ones, their ordering of choices would be A, B, C. Nevertheless, out of religious conviction and also political ambition,[20] they want to further the religious efforts of this particular Baptist church and its members, and they choose Route C. Their purpose in choosing C over the other two routes is to advance a particular religion, but they have no desire to have this aim recognized publicly. They would have a forbidden purpose to aid but not a purpose to endorse.[21]

Without exploring various subtleties about judicial determinations of improper purpose, one is hard put to understand why the Court's reliance on improper purpose has aroused such intense oppositions and why the future status of a purpose test is in doubt. In what is perhaps the most thoughtful analysis of a purpose test, Andrew Koppelman remarks both that a "growing faction of the Court . . . may be ready to scrap the secular purpose requirement" and that "[t]he secular purpose requirement follows directly from a principle at the core of the Establishment Clause: that government may not declare religious truth."[22] Justice Souter, for a bare majority of five, wrote in the Kentucky Ten Commandments case that when the government's "ostensible and predominant purpose" is to advance religion, it violates the "central Establishment Clause value of official religious neutrality."[23]

One major question about the kind of purpose that renders legislation or an executive practice invalid is whether an improper purpose involves the

[20] I assume here that if a legislator is personally indifferent about the Baptist religion but sees a chance to win votes by acting to help Baptists *in promoting their religion* to the comparative disadvantage of other religions, his purpose is improper. (Anyone who has doubts about this assumption can take the illustration as exclusively involving legislators trying to promote their own religious faith.) As chapters 23 and 24, infra, indicate, I am *not* suggesting here that all legislative reliance on religious convictions is improper. On the importance and difficulty of identifying the class for comparison against which one measures privileges, see Andrew Koppelman, "Is It Fair to Give Religion Special Treatment?" 2006 *University of Illinois Law Review* 571.

[21] It is an interesting question how the endorsement test would handle this example, if it were offered as a total approach. It is hard to believe that anyone would say the purpose here *is permissible*. One might say that there is an endorsement, whether the legislators want it perceived or not, but that seems strained. One might say that if these facts were understood, the choice would have the effect of endorsing, despite the absence of a purpose to endorse. One *might* say that the legislative decision is actually acceptable, as far as judicial review is concerned. Justice Souter in the Kentucky Ten Commandments case, 545 U.S. at 860, says the government violates neutrality if it "acts with the ostensible and predominant purpose of advancing religion. . . ." His opinion does not address the example of a predominant purpose that is knowable but not ostensible. For further discussion, see the section "The Endorsement Test" in this chapter.

[22] Andrew Koppelman, "Secular Purpose," 88 *Virginia Law Review* 87, 88–90 (2002).

[23] *Van Orden v. Perry*, note 3 supra, at 862.

"subjective" attitudes of legislators (or other officials), a more objective measure of what they have done or communicated—including their statements
about what they have been doing and the history of their actions—or an aim
that is unmistakable from the face of the particular statute or behavior that
is challenged. Related to this inquiry are five others. (1) Is it only *ostensible*
purpose that renders a law invalid? (2) Is purpose genuinely distinguishable
from effect? (3) Is the purpose standard for individual administrative decisions the same as the purpose standard for legislative actions? (4) Is the
disagreement on the Court over purpose really about the use of legislative
history and the deference judges should give to legislators? (5) How do approaches to the purposes that count when judges ask if laws are constitutionally invalid relate to the way judges discern purposes in order to interpret
the content of legislation? Finally, the members of the Court undoubtedly
disagree over exactly what purposes are proper or improper. For example,
as chapter 5 indicates, a minority (that may possibly have become a majority
by the time this book is published) thinks it is all right for legislators to
support belief in a monotheistic God in various ways; the majority, so far,
has disagreed. Having examined such questions about which purposes are
improper in preceding chapters, here we concentrate on the nature of improper purposes, not their content. Later chapters return to questions about
which purposes are flawed; and chapters 23 and 24 present a sustained discussion of reliance on religious convictions to adopt legislation on subjects
such as capital punishment and welfare support.

"Purpose" might refer to the actual aims of those who perform an action,
their "subjective" purposes or aims, or it might refer to some more objective
standard of the significance of what the actors have performed.[24] Whether a
majority of Supreme Court justices believed as of the summer of 2007 that
subjective purposes of legislators are relevant is difficult to tell.

We have seen that the Court in the Kentucky Ten Commandments case
talks of an "ostensible and predominant purpose of advancing religion"; it
goes on to say that "an understanding of official objective emerges from
readily discoverable fact, without any judicial psychoanalysis of a drafter's
heart of hearts."[25] Koppelman is clear that the relevant purpose does not depend either on what particular legislators thought or felt or on how individuals

---

[24] A distinction is sometimes drawn between a legislator's sense of the purpose of a statute, say to
subsidize wheat farmers, and his motive, to win the votes of wheat farmers in the next election. My
discussion here concentrates mainly on purpose in the sense of direct objectives of legislation, but I
do consider whether certain background motivations, such as winning converts to one's church, are
inappropriate.

[25] *McCreary County*, note 5 supra, at 862.

have responded to what they have done, but what the government's speech act means,[26] on how "native speakers of English" would understand it.[27]

The basic disagreements over purpose in Establishment Clause jurisprudence do not turn on a distinction between objective and subjective, but if we are to grasp what *is* at stake, we need to explore that distinction and in particular the possibility that subjective purpose might be relevant. The distinction between subjective and objective purpose is, to begin, less sharp than might first appear. If one inquires about the understandings of native speakers of English, one is asking how most people in that class would (subjectively) take something.[28] And the way "native speakers of English" understand ordinary communications is typically in terms of what they believe writers or speakers are trying to communicate, that is, in terms of their estimate of what a speaker or writer is subjectively trying to communicate. Were one's sense of "objective" purpose to rest completely on the idea that the meaning of communications depends on how they would be taken by normal speakers of the language;[29] estimates of subjective aims and understandings would hardly be removed from the analysis.[30]

The language of the Kentucky case hardly gives us a clear theory about objective versus subjective purpose. We are told that secret aims will not count, that legislators will not be psychoanalyzed, that courts will rely on objective manifestations; but do the justices suppose that they are coming up with an "objective" purpose that is quite separable from what the actual legislators were trying to accomplish, or do they, instead, believe they can infer from objective manifestations what actual legislators were trying to accomplish to a rather high degree of reliability (as in ordinary conversation we infer what speakers have in mind from what they say)?

Having cast some doubt on the degree to which objective and subjective purpose are sharply distinguishable, I want to suggest that the only plausible arguments for courts *not* paying attention to subjective purpose concern the nature of legislators and courts, and their interrelations. Such arguments cannot be directed to all official action. I point out along the way that a

---

[26] Koppelman, note 22 supra, at 112. See also William P. Marshall, "The Concept of Offensiveness in Establishment and Free Exercise Jurisprudence," 66 *Indiana Law Journal* 351, 374 (1990–91).

[27] Koppelman, note 22 supra, at 115.

[28] This is not the same as how people in the class *feel* about what is communicated, but a reference to "native speakers" must rest on a cumulation of likely subjective perceptions of individuals about what is meant.

[29] To be clear, I do not take Koppelman to be relying exclusively on such a view.

[30] I explore the complexities in much greater depth in Kent Greenawalt, "Are Mental States Relevant for Statutory and Constitutional Interpretation?" 85 *Cornell Law Review* 1609, 1657–68 (2000).

theory that courts should *never* rely on considerations of legislative purpose is indefensible, and that arguments about purpose for invalidation (the issue that concerns us) are subtly different from arguments about how purpose should be understood when courts interpret the content of statutes.

Although not the first to make the argument, Justice Scalia has become the strongest opponent of reliance on the subjective purpose of legislators to hold laws invalid.[31] He is also the strongest opponent of reference to subjective purposes and of reliance on the history of legislation (as it moves from bill to law) to interpret legislation.[32] This is hardly a coincidence. In both contexts, Scalia contends that judges are unable to discern the subjective purposes of legislators and that what really matters is what legislators do, not what they may think and feel about what they do. I have disagreed with Scalia's position about statutory interpretation, urging that what legislators actually aim to do should matter, if it can be discerned, and that use of legislative history is one appropriate method to discern what they aim to do.[33] But here I draw out one obvious implication of Scalia's position and note two important differences between interpretation and invalidation.

Justice Scalia has never insisted that purposes that can be discerned from the language of a statute itself cannot be used for interpretation.[34] Similarly, in respect to invalidation, he does not rule out a conclusion about purpose evident from the statute. In the Santeria case he was willing to rely on the language of Hialeah's ordinances to conclude that they were targeted against the practices of that religion.[35] As far as I am aware, Justice Scalia has never denied that an explicit statement of purpose *within* legislation could itself render a law invalid under the Establishment Clause. To illustrate how this might work, suppose the preamble for a moment-of-silence law states: "Acting in response to the Supreme Court's ill considered judgments that the schools of this country cannot promote Protestant Christianity, and wishing to encourage Protestant Christian prayer insofar as the courts will allow, we hereby institute a moment of silence."

A very strong skeptic about judicial reliance on purpose might claim that a statement of purpose in a preamble has no constitutional relevance, so long as the operative provisions can be sustained by a secular purpose and

---

[31] See *Edwards*, note 16 supra, at 610 (Scalia, J. dissenting).

[32] See, e.g., Antonin Scalia, *A Matter of Interpretation: Federal Courts and the Law*, Amy Gutman, ed. (Princeton: Princeton University Press, 1997).

[33] See Kent Greenawalt, *Statutory Interpretation: Twenty Questions* 91–200 (New York: Foundation Press, 1999).

[34] However, for Scalia, such purposes could ordinarily not overcome the plain meaning of applicable language.

[35] *Hialeah*, note 18 supra, at 520 (Scalia, J. concurring).

secular effects. But that position is not maintainable. Under such an approach, Congress and state legislatures could do a great deal of promoting of *very specific* religious views in preambles. If my earlier claim in chapter 4—that statutes cannot announce the truth of Christianity—is sound, however, it follows that preambles may neither state nor more obliquely imply that truth.

A skeptic about purpose *might* accept the conclusion that such a preamble would be unconstitutional, but contend that its invalidity would not undermine the operative provisions establishing the moment of silence; these would remain intact without the preamble. The problem with this approach is that a preamble stating a purpose, especially if it is widely publicized, will affect how people understand a statute and the practices it institutes. The preamble *is* relevant to the constitutionality of a statute's operative provisions. If a court struck down the preamble, and it alone, and this was publicized in state newspapers, then school officials, teachers, and informed students would remember why the legislature formally said that it instituted a moment of silence. I conclude that a "loaded" preamble could render an entire law invalid,[36] whatever might be the fate of a similar, subsequently enacted, law that omitted the preamble.

Two important features distinguish objections to judges using purpose to discern the content of laws from objections to their relying on purpose to hold laws unconstitutional. One can reasonably argue that when officials create legal norms, these should be interpreted in accord with what their words in context convey to readers, not in terms of the subjective intent of the persons who issue the norms. Thus, one *could* defend this reader-centered practice for interpreting directives issued by a single executive official as well as for interpreting laws adopted by legislatures. As we shall shortly see, a similar approach definitely does not work across the board for invalidation, because subjective motives are indisputably relevant for many actions by individual officials.

Another special aspect of invalid action concerns the Constitution's application to officials other than judges. Ordinarily, no constitutional problem is presented if legislators have subjective aims that differ from the purposes

---

[36] A determined critic of reliance on purpose might argue that an undesirable "purpose" can never undermine an otherwise permissible statute, but that a preamble is part of what a statute *does* and thus is part of its effects. If the preamble is sufficiently interconnected with the operative provisions, and the preamble creates the effect of an unacceptable promotion of religion, the entire package may be invalid, but this invalidation depends on effect and is not *really* on the basis of purpose. The only problem with this logic is that it turns a formal statement of purpose into the producer of one relevant effect. Such a transformation is fine, but it hardly establishes the irrelevance of purpose.

one would discern from the language of a statute. But legislators should not self-consciously attempt to achieve unconstitutional objectives.[37] They *should* restrain themselves, in the sense of voting for legislation only if they believe it is warranted on proper constitutional grounds. If judges considering constitutionality disregard the actual purposes of legislators, they implicitly accept the possibility that legislators' disregard of constitutional obligations will pass beyond review. That conclusion can be defended, but it requires more powerful reasons than one would need to believe that the subjective intentions of legislators should not matter for judges who are determining the content of statutes.

Could someone reasonably claim that subjective purposes never have anything to do with whether an official decision is invalid? The answer to this question is easy—no—but understanding that answer is a first step toward clarifying more serious challenges to purpose analysis.

The idea that all that matters are official actions and the relevant factors that *might* cause them to be undertaken, not *why* officials actually make the decisions they do, is plausible when relevant factors definitely *call for* a particular decision or definitely *rule it out*. Suppose that a school board requires the teaching of the truth of papal authority and transubstantiation. No permissible considerations could support such a decision. We know that the decision impermissibly promotes religion, whatever the subjective purposes of the board members. Suppose that the board of a new school requires the teaching of American history. It so happens that all members of the board are virulently anti-Catholic, and their dominating reason for wanting American history taught is that it will show the comparative strength and truth of Protestantism. Their purpose is improper. But any serious educator, and virtually all parents, think that children in the United States should learn American history. If the board demands no more American history than the

---

[37] There is a special wrinkle about legislative restraint that I shall not explore in depth. Suppose a legislator believes firmly, contrary to the Supreme Court's view, that government promotion of religion is all right according to the best understanding of our Constitution. Is he justified in voting for a bill because it will serve this purpose, which he believes is constitutional but the Court has said is not? Perhaps. Legislators should seriously consider what the Court has determined about constitutional principles, and, in the interest of orderly governance, they should defer in most instances when the matter seems arguable to them; but if legislators develop a firm conviction that the Court has mistakenly interpreted the Constitution, they should feel able to act on their own understanding. This is especially true if their doing so will not create continuing direct conflict between the legislature and the judiciary. If a law is supportable by secular purposes and these are announced, no conflict between the two branches will be created if some legislators vote for the law for religious reasons they regard as constitutionally acceptable, despite the Court's view to the contrary. See Kent Greenawalt, "Constitutional Decisions and the Supreme Law," 58 *University of Colorado Law Review* 145, 156–68 (1987).

minimum anyone else would urge, their indisputably correct decision may not be undermined because its actual motivation was defective.[38]

So far, so good. But the strategy of looking only at official action and not at its purpose self-destructs for actions that are optional. Officials have a vast range of discretion about what they do; they may reach a great number of alternative decisions, all of which are acceptable to courts. They have a power to reach one of a number of decisions within the permissible range, but they should not settle on one of the options for an unacceptable reason. A district attorney is hiring a lawyer for his office. He might reasonably choose any of five candidates. The DA chooses the one white male (E), rejecting the other four candidates because they are women or members of a minority. Under any version of constitutional or statutory antidiscrimination law, covered in chapter 18 in the free exercise volume, the DA will have acted illegally. He has done something wrong, not merely done the right thing for the wrong reason.

How will anyone ever know why the DA acted as he did, and what can a court do about it? He may be stupid enough to say to his longtime deputy, "I can tell you, I ruled out A, B, C, and D right from the start. I don't want women, blacks, or Hispanics in my office, and I shall never hire one. If you wish to know why E got the job, that's the story." If the deputy testifies to this effect, the evidence of discrimination will be very strong. Alternatively, a pattern of hiring only white males may make discrimination look extremely likely. What a court can do in response to such discrimination is somewhat more troublesome. It can award damages to those injured; it can order that one or more of the victims be hired with the next openings in positions; and it could undo the original decision (though courts do not often do that about discriminatory hiring).[39]

We can see easily how this analysis familiar from employment discrimination applies to the actions concerning religion. A decision by an administra-

---

[38] This may be like an instance when A saves B's life, only because he hates C, B's rival. We do not think A's behavior was wrong, that its consequences should be undone, because his purpose was an immoral one.

[39] Perhaps it might be contended that even on this example, it is not really purpose that makes *the action* of hiring the white male wrong, if it is wrong. If of all the five possible decisions, one would really have been best, that decision might have been to hire E. A judge does not know who should have been hired; all she can say is that the chances of a wrong decision were high if the DA relied completely on unacceptable reasons. The judge appropriately treats the DA's decision as if it were wrong, because the chances of its being wrong were high. But it was not his purpose that made it wrong.

This explanation of what is occurring turns out to be misconceived, because the law would treat any of the five decisions as right if it had been made for acceptable reasons. The law treats the decision as wrong, once it identifies the impermissible motive as having generated the decision.

tor motivated by an aim to hurt one particular religion or to discriminate among religions would be wrongful. Were the superintendent of roads to choose to build a road that would necessitate demolishing a church, just because she detests that religion, her decision would be invalid, even though a road built on that path would be among a set of reasonable alternatives. To see that a decision made in order to benefit a religion could be invalid, even though the same decision might have been made for other reasons, we need only revert to a variation on my earlier illustration, assuming that the decision in favor of Route C is made by an individual administrator rather than an administrative board. Routes A, B, and C are presented to the administrator, who is a member of the Baptist community, and he knows his fellow Baptists want Route C. Acknowledging to himself that Routes A and B are otherwise preferable, he chooses Route C because it will help his church. And he tells this to his deputy, who then discloses the conversation. A court should not try to decide what route *really* is best *or* what route the administrator would have chosen had he not had the impermissible motive. It should declare his decision to be invalid, and if plans have not gone too far, it should have someone else make the decision or instruct the administrator to revisit the issue without giving weight to the special benefits for his own church.

Improper purpose can certainly render official decisions wrongful and invalid in the law. And we can quickly see that this conclusion could apply to a general rule that an administrator creates as well as a hiring decision. Were an executive to set a "No headgear in the office" rule, only because he wants to make sure no Orthodox Jewish men will work in the office, that would constitute impermissible religious discrimination (which could be proved were the evidence strong enough).

The serious issues about attributing improper purposes to legislators involve the nature of legislative bodies and the relations between legislatures and courts. We can identify three threads of the claim that courts should not invalidate legislation on the basis of purpose. (1) With statutes, the aims of individual legislators are irrelevant. (2) Courts should attribute the best purposes possible to the legislature. (3) Courts should not investigate legislative history to discern purpose, they should rely only on what a statute says and actually does. These strands are interrelated, and all may draw to some extent on the difficulty of discerning what a diverse group of legislators is actually aiming to achieve.

Part of the general argument over how statutes should be interpreted *and* how their constitutionality should be assessed is whether the aims of individual legislators matter. The claim that they do not rests either on a skeptical view that groups do not have intentions or on the idea that, whatever may be true for groups in general, what counts with *statutes* is *the language* that legislators adopt. The first claim is not convincing; nor is the second claim, at least absent an extensive political theory to support it.

We have already reviewed two reasons not to embrace complete skepticism about group intent as a basis for invalidation. First, the Constitution bears directly on the behavior of legislators themselves—they are required to act upon permissible objectives. If almost all of them act for the same impermissible objectives, it is a short step to saying that the legislature has done so. Second, an impermissible purpose stated directly in a law itself is easily conceptualized as a purpose of the legislative body. A more general and fundamental flaw with skepticism about group intent is that we comfortably speak of groups having an intent when most members of the group have the same objective in undertaking an action. Yet more to the point in relation to law, it can be important to evaluate the objectives of many participants of a group, even if we would hesitate to ascribe their objectives to the group as a whole.[40] Suppose we are concerned that an official decision may discriminate against some individual or group; *perhaps* it should be sufficient to overturn the decision if enough participants have had impermissible objectives to have determined the decision's content. We can easily see in our highway and hiring examples how a collection of members less than a majority might steer the decision toward their favored outcome by presenting ostensibly appropriate grounds as a cover for their improper ambitions.[41]

A stronger argument for courts not considering the aims of individual legislators is that in our system what counts is the adopted statute. This view need not denigrate the obligation *legislators themselves* have to rely only on proper purposes, nor need it reject an attribution of purpose that is evident from the face of the statute and surrounding circumstances. Yet, an argument that judges should rely exclusively on the "adopted statute" is not self-evidently correct. Views expressed by individual legislators may be relevant to *explain* what the legislature has done or to show that it has acted on improper grounds.[42] An approach to invalidity that includes reliance on what legislators say about what they do might be rejected on the ground that

[40] See generally Greenawalt, note 33 supra, at 98–100.

[41] Suppose a committee of four is doing the hiring. Initially, one of the four believes E, the white male, is really the best qualified. Two other committee members back A and B respectively. The fourth is sure A is best qualified, but wants to hire only white males. We can see how his backing of E's candidacy could lead to E's being hired, although his three peers are acting conscientiously.

[42] An argument for not going beyond the statute that is based on "notice to the public" is much more relevant for interpretation of what a law provides than for the question of whether the law is invalid. In respect to interpretation, advocates of judges' relying exclusively on the statutory text have claimed that the views of individual legislators do not fairly represent what legislators in the other branch or the chief executive may have thought. Whether this claim has equal force for the question of invalidity turns on whether an impermissible purpose in one house would be sufficient to make a

legislators' objectives will rarely be so clear as in my hypothetical highway board vote. According to a long-standing tradition, courts attribute public-regarding purposes to legislatures; and in Commerce Clause and substantive due process cases it has stretched to find acceptable purposes, even when these were hard to come by.[43] A critic of purpose analysis might say this. "Whatever may be true about a legislator's responsibility, whatever may be true about the purposes of groups and members of groups generally, whatever may be true about attributions of purpose for statutory interpretation, courts considering constitutional invalidation should assume the best possible purposes consistent with the statutory language."

Although courts have generally ascribed benign purposes to legislators, they have not done so routinely in cases involving "suspect classifications" or important individual rights. The practical import of a stringent compelling interest test—with legislation sustained only if it serves a compelling government interest that cannot be achieved by less restrictive means—is to render invalid much legislation that was likely based on an impermissible purpose to favor dominant groups over minorities or to suppress individual rights, such as free speech. Because religious classification is one form of suspect classification, such an approach may take care of cases of religious discrimination and, to a lesser extent, cases of adverse targeting of particular religious groups,[44] but what are courts to do with claims that the legislature is aiming to promote religion in a way at odds with the Establishment Clause? Courts should be able to rely on what leading legislators say during the political process to discern the objectives of legislators.

In a number of purpose cases under the Establishment Clause, the Court has looked at statements of individual legislators, particularly sponsors of bills.[45] Justice Scalia, and others, have protested. They complain both about reliance on what individual legislators may be aiming to do and about the use of legislative history. Someone who thinks individual aims are irrelevant is likely to think reliance on legislative history that contains them is also

---

law invalid. If invalidity turns on both houses having an impermissible purpose, one could make the analogous argument that one should not generalize from the events in one house to the perspectives of the other. I do not find this argument to be compelling for issues of either interpretation or invalidity.

[43] Early on, the Supreme Court declined to investigate whether a state land grant by Georgia's legislature had been procured by bribery, *Fletcher v. Peck*, 10 U.S. (6 Cranch) 87 (1810), although it may have been crucial for the Court's decision that the land had already passed to innocent purchasers.

[44] A problem with targeting cases is that one needs to identify the targeting before the compelling interest test comes into play. That test will not determine how to handle a case in which targeting is not evident from the face of the law.

[45] The cases are discussed in *McCreary County*, note 5 supra, at 862–63. In that case and others, the Court also relied on the history of measures adopted by legislators as evidence of the purpose of the latest round of legislative action.

inappropriate.[46] But even someone *otherwise* open to judges considering individual purposes might balk at combing the legislative history, on the ground that it reveals little about the aspirations of most legislators. I shall not here undertake a full defense of use of legislative history, but if the inquiry about invalidity is largely about whether legislation would have been enacted but for the wrongful purposes of legislators, legislative history is a promising source of information.[47]

Against the argument that using legislative history to determine whether statues are constitutionally valid invites the legislators to enact (or reenact) laws while veiling their true aims, there is a triple answer.[48] First, legislators often are not careful, and, further, certain legislators now discern political advantage in coming out foursquare in favor of promoting religion. The remote possibility that down the road a court may rely on what they said to find an improper purpose may not affect their candor. Second, were legislators to believe that they could not divulge a purpose to promote religion, they might become more restrained about promoting religion. Third, the values of nonestablishment are undermined to a degree if aims at odds with these values are spread upon the public record and widely reported. Thus, legislative veiling of purposes itself could be of some benefit.[49]

I conclude that the Supreme Court has, in Establishment Clause cases up until now, been right to inquire about the actual purposes legislators entertain and to use legislative history as one device to discern those purposes.

THE *LEMON* TEST: EFFECTS

The second strand of the test of *Lemon v. Kurtzman* is that a law or practice violates the Establishment Clause if it has a primary effect of advancing or inhibiting religion. This, as we shall see in subsequent chapters, has proved

[46] In Greenawalt, note 33 supra, at 192–98, I discuss Ronald Dworkin's suggestion that legislative history counts because it has conventional weight.

[47] One's view of ways of discerning purposes could affect one's view of *what* purposes could invalidate. A purpose to endorse is likely to appear on the face of the statute. A purpose to advance religion without endorsing is not likely to appear on the face of the statute. One who takes a very restrictive view of how courts can determine purpose might decide that the only invalidating purpose should be endorsement or condemnation.

[48] Koppelman, note 22 supra, at 113–16, answers what he calls the "rubber stamp" and "evanescence" objections to reliance on purpose, pointing out that some laws have no plausible secular purpose.

[49] One might take the Kentucky Ten Commandments case as indicating that only "ostensible" purposes could render a law invalid. My analysis strongly suggests that some laws could be unconstitutional (the highway example) although outsiders would be unaware of a purpose to promote religion. Of course, a court is usually unlikely to discern a law's invalid purpose unless the purpose is ostensible.

practically the most significant part of the entire test, and in one sense the least controversial. It is the least controversial in that everyone agrees that some effects of laws are forbidden by the Establishment Clause. But critics may nonetheless take the view that the formulation of the effects rule, as such, is so vague, misleading, and unhelpful that it should be abandoned. We need to consider these related points: (1) the relation of purpose to effects; (2) effects judged by principle and effects judged by particular consequences; (3) primary effects and remote or incidental effects; (4) effects under *Lemon* and under endorsement; (5) the inclusion of inhibiting religion as an Establishment Clause violation (when it might seem more natural for that to raise concerns under the Free Exercise Clause); and (6) the possibility that the effects test, whatever its abstract theoretical soundness, is unhelpful for courts deciding controversies.

Most important cases resolved under the *Lemon* test have been decided under the effects strand. On occasion, the Court has said that a law is invalid under both purpose and effect or both effect and entanglement. And when the Court has relied on impermissible administrative entanglement alone, the scheme that was deemed to be excessively entangling was designed to avoid what the Court had previously said were forbidden effects. Typically, when the Court has found an improper purpose, it would have proceeded to say that there were improper effects, had it undertaken that inquiry. A simple example was the state law requiring the posting of the Ten Commandments in all school classrooms. The Court discerned a forbidden purpose to promote religion;[50] had it looked at effects, it would certainly have found a primary effect of promoting religion, and more particularly those religions that recognize the authority of the Bible.

This linkage of purpose to effect is hardly fortuitous, and is one reason why elimination of a separate inquiry about purpose could have limited practical import. If a law's purpose is to promote particular religious ideas by putting them forward as approved by government, one effect will be that people understand that the government is indicating its approval. If the legislature intends to aid a particular religion by making a large grant to it, its aim may be to provide material support rather than indicate approval. But the effect of the support will still be to aid the religion, and people aware of the law may take the law as implicitly expressing endorsement of that religion.

Independent purpose analysis may seem more indispensable if officials aim to aid religion, but not in a manner that people will perceive.[51] The highway

---

[50] *Stone v. Graham*, 449 U.S. 39 (1980).

[51] Few actual legal cases fit within this category, because secret purposes are usually not discovered.

board decides on Route C in order to aid a particular religion, but presents other plausible reasons for its choice. People may perceive neither material aid nor approval. Although we can rightly say that the aiding of religion is an impermissible effect here, that hardly shows that purpose analysis is unnecessary. Had Route C been chosen for reasons having nothing to do with religion, its effects on different religions would be viewed as remote or incidental. The reason why religion is being directly aided is because that is the objective of those who have chosen the road. In this circumstance, we must know their purpose to decide if aid is direct or incidental.[52]

Unacceptable effects need not depend on impermissible purposes. A state legislature may have an objective to promote secular education, but, according to a number of Supreme Court decisions we will consider in chapter 19, it may allocate money in a way that has a primary effect of advancing religion. Thus, we may say that an improper purpose is highly likely to produce improper effects, but that improper effects may also flow from acceptable purposes.

Supreme Court justices are divided on the fundamental question whether they should evaluate consequences in particular instances or judge legislative schemes on a more abstract basis. If aid is going to all private nonprofit schools, does it matter what percentage are religious, what percentage of those belong to one denomination, what percentage of religious schools provide an education that is pervasively sectarian? Such facts have sometimes figured in the Court's treatment of public aid to schools, and in the Court's acceptance of greater aid for colleges and universities than it has allowed for schools. Under this approach, the notion of a "primary religious effect" is an open-ended and flexible one; it is applied according to an evaluation of various relevant factors. An opposing approach is more formal, distinguishing between kinds of effects that are or are not qualitatively invalid. In a case we will examine in the next chapter, for example, Justice Souter contends that any public aid that supports religious endeavors such as worship and proselytizing is unconstitutional.[53] One need not look at the magnitude of

---

[52] A conceivable way to avoid this conclusion is to say that whenever purpose becomes known, as it must if a court is to rely on it, *then* people will become aware of an effect of aiding religion. Therefore, purpose alone is irrelevant. This proposal is subject to two objections. One is that the original decision is unconstitutional, whether or not people ever become aware of its nature; it does not become unconstitutional the moment evidence in court reveals its basis. The second objection is that even granting the point that publicity turns purpose into effect, the forbidden effect is still totally dependent on people understanding the underlying purpose. Thus, in these cases of secret purpose and effects that are not obviously direct, purpose remains a necessary separate component of the analysis.

[53] *Rosenberger v. Rector and Visitors of the University of Virginia*, 515 U.S. 819, 868 (1995) (dissenting opinion).

aid or the context in which it is granted. In a more recent aid-to-school case, Justice Thomas takes a strikingly formal approach, though one that differs strongly from that of Justice Souter. According to Thomas, so long as the government's criteria for aid are neutral, not depending on religious affiliation, and the aid itself is not of a religious sort, it does not matter who is receiving the aid or what they do with the aid after they get it.[54] Under a principled approach that forbids certain kinds of aid but not others, any question of "primary effect" becomes a question about the qualitative nature of assistance, not a matter of the degree of aid turning what would otherwise be permissible into the impermissible.

The division on the Court over how far effects should be evaluated by formal standards, which distinguish among *kinds* of effects, and how far by investigations into actual consequences in particular circumstances, relates to a more general dispute in constitutional law between formal approaches and approaches that demand contextual judgments about particular circumstances. Once we recognize this disagreement, we can see that justices who favor a dominantly formal approach are likely to prefer to move away from the "primary effects" language of *Lemon*. "Effects" has a consequentialist ring to it. If the Court should be looking only at whether legislation formally provides a forbidden form of assistance, or uses impermissible criteria for assistance, or explicitly sponsors religious positions, a court could refer directly to those defects; it would not need to speak of primary effects. Even if one grants that under *Lemon*'s threefold test, most crucial matters are *better* categorized as concerning effects than as purpose or entanglement, one might think that the *best* categorization would be in other language altogether. Thus, we can understand the sharp division on the present Court over what kinds of effects are forbidden as raising implicitly the question whether "primary effects" is itself a desirable phrase to distinguish the allowed from the forbidden.

How does the standard *Lemon* test about effects differ from an endorsement approach to effects? As I noted in respect to purpose, direct state sponsorship or endorsement of religious ideas would have the effect of advancing religion under *Lemon*. But the state might also advance religion in ways that would not generally be perceived as an endorsement and that it did not wish people to perceive in that way. The Supreme Court has consistently said, for example, that substantial direct aid to parochial education is forbidden even

---

[54] *Mitchell v. Helms*, 530 U.S. 793, 809–10, 821–25 (2000) (plurality opinion of Thomas, J.). If, for example, the government helped private colleges construct science laboratories, it would not offend the Establishment Clause if one year after construction a religious college converted the laboratory into a chapel.

if the state has no aim to promote religion. Under an endorsement approach, the question of endorsement or not is *the* crucial criterion for whether a law or practice is constitutional. Although it is difficult to say just how much of a difference this makes,[55] the comparative emphasis on various factors is likely to shift depending on whether endorsement or the standard "effects" test is at the center of the inquiry.

The *Lemon* test has always been cast as making a primary effect of inhibiting religion a forbidden one. If as I have contended in the volume on free exercise, atheism and agnosticism should not count as religious under the religion clauses, this is a dubious exercise in classification, but one of little or no practical importance. If a law inhibits a particular religion unacceptably, we may fairly say that it helps to "establish" its competitors. But what of a law that is aimed against religion in general? Suppose that instead of receiving a tax deduction, those who made contributions to religious organizations had to pay, over and above the income tax, a stipend to the government equaling their religious contribution. Such a tax would violate the Free Exercise Clause (and no such tax will be adopted in any foreseeable future), but it is hard to say that the tax discouraging religious exercise is an establishment *of religion*.[56] Although no practical consequences whatsoever are likely to flow from this aspect of *Lemon*, it is a confusion that would better be eliminated.[57]

Although almost any position about the Establishment Clause will include some inquiry about the effects of laws and practices, one might reasonably believe that *Lemon*'s casting of the constitutional test is unhelpful. We have already reviewed one such objection: that the test loosely implies that inquiries into particular consequences are called for, whereas the correct standards of adjudication are relatively formal criteria such as neutrality or sponsorship. A different objection is that *Lemon*'s "effects" test is so vague it provides little assistance to courts. According to this critique, application of

[55] How "endorsement" deals with material aid, in comparison to the standard effects test, is one crucial question. Under the standard test, apparent government sponsorship or promotion may certainly be one element in an overall appraisal of effects; but that inquiry takes priority under endorsement. A defender of endorsement *might* say that whenever substantial aid goes to religion, that *represents* an endorsement, whether or not so intended or perceived, or that it would be perceived by a reasonable person as an endorsement. Under such an approach, everything relevant under a standard *Lemon* approach might be squeezed under the rubric of endorsement, but the weight of various factors could still be affected.

[56] One might respond that it is a law "respecting the establishment of religion," the actual language of the First Amendment, that it favors some views over others, and that the subject of the disfavored views is religion.

[57] This confusion has been carried over by Justice O'Connor into her endorsement standard, which suggests that a message that religion in general is disfavored would be an establishment of religion.

the test is not much more than adherence to prevailing precedents and an assessment of circumstances in light of religious clause values. Speaking of "primary effects of advancing religion" may not do great harm, but we should not fool ourselves into thinking that it gets us very far. The distinction between primary effects and incidental ones is more a conclusion reached at the end of a process of evaluation than a basis for analysis.

I believe that the distinction between primary and incidental effects is indeed highly flexible, but I also believe for many matters, a fairly contextual approach is the best one for the Court to take. I, thus, conclude that the "primary effects" language, or something similar like "significant effects" or "substantial effects," is appropriate; but any terms of this sort do leave a great deal open. In the course of subsequent chapters, we will review crucial questions about how effects are evaluated, including the issue whether significant effects of promoting religion should be a basis for invalidity even if a law yields substantial secular benefits.

THE *LEMON* TEST: ENTANGLEMENT

According to *Lemon*, a law or practice is invalid if it requires (or involves) an excessive entanglement of the government with religion. The Court has spoken of institutional entanglement, which includes both what we may call intertwining and misplaced authority, and political divisiveness. This chapter briefly discusses the two kinds of institutional entanglement and then considers whether political divisiveness should be an element of any approach to establishment issues.

In a 1997 school aid case, Justice O'Connor wrote for the Court that entanglement should not be a separate inquiry but one aspect of an effects test.[58] It is hard to know how much difference this may make. Entanglement is (generally) one kind of effect, so saying that it belongs under "effects" may seem uncontroversial, but treating entanglement as something other than an independent element of a threefold test appears to downgrade its significance. Summing up entangling effects with other effects, instead of treating them as an independent criterion of invalidity, will reduce the likelihood that they will determine invalidity. If other effects are not troublesome, worrisome entanglements may be more easily tolerated than would happen were they examined alone.[59]

---

[58] *Agostini*, note 4 supra, at 232–33.

[59] The opposite result *could* sometimes occur. Suppose other effects of a law are almost, but not quite, sufficient for a court to invalidate it, and that an entanglement is troublesome but not grave

Most of the Court's decisions about excessive entanglement, as we shall see when we consider school aid and government funding of religious organizations providing social services, have turned on an intertwining of government with religious endeavors. It is not a good thing for government administrators to engage in close and continuing surveillance of religious activities. For the most part, it is the Court's conclusions about how aid may cause impermissible effects of advancing religion that have created the need for such entangling relations. A state that institutes schemes of supervision to avoid aiding religion may fall afoul of the bar on excessive entanglement.

This approach to entanglement raises two fundamental questions. The first is why we should worry if the religious groups are willing to accept detailed supervision in order to get funds. The answer to this is that the value of independence of religion from government is not something that it should be up to church officials simply to waive. Among other reasons, leaders of religious groups now needing financial assistance may underestimate the corrosive effects on religious independence over time, especially if they fail to take into account that degrees of supervision may increase as the government's financial stake in activities grows.

The second question is how to distinguish permissible from impermissible supervision. State governments already supervise religious schools in various ways, requiring that they meet educational standards. How much does the supervision necessary to prevent religious uses of public money differ from ordinary, acceptable supervision? In some cases, the Court assumed a significant degree of distrust whether teachers left unsupervised would promote religion. Recent cases have reflected a higher degree of trust that officials will not overstep constitutional boundaries,[60] and thus have required less supervision. The Court has never made clear, and perhaps the subject does not admit of it, just when supervision crosses over the line to excessive entanglement. Virtually everyone agrees that some intertwining could be unacceptably harmful, but judgments differ about when the point of unacceptability is reached.

In other circumstances, the basic problem is not intertwining but a religious body exercising political authority or a political body exercising religious authority. In a case involving the former problem, a church was able to make the final decision about whether someone could receive a liquor license close to its premises.[61] Here there was no real intermixing of govern-

---

enough for a court to invalidate on that basis alone. Added together, all the effects might lead to invalidation.

[60] See *Agostini*, note 4 supra.

[61] *Larkin v. Grendel's Den, Inc.*, 459 U.S. 116 (1982).

ment officials and religious institutions. The church made its decision, and
that settled things. But churches should not exercise the power of government. In a later chapter, we shall examine much more difficult instances,
including laws relating to *kosher* and *get* practice.

Just as religious institutions cannot act for the government, the government cannot make certain fundamental religious decisions, such as who a
church should hire as a minister. Further, the government cannot make applications of the law turn on the resolution of debatable points of religious
doctrines and practices; it must avoid what may be called "doctrinal entanglement."[62] Concerns of this sort are primarily regarded as free exercise issues, and they are treated in the volume on free exercise, but chapter 14 in
this volume treats in some detail the relation of civil law to two aspects of
Jewish law.

In some cases, the Court has spoken of a separate element of entanglement, likely politically divisive struggles along religious lines. One might
quarrel over whether this concern is really about "entanglement"; but in any
event, the Court has dropped divisiveness as a separate independent element.
Some justices have warned that people opposed to a form of aid should not
be rewarded by *making* the issue politically divisive.

What role should political divisiveness play in church-state law? Worries
about political struggles along religious lines had something to do with why
people valued nonestablishment, but that does not tell us whether divisiveness should figure independently in actual cases.

Divisiveness should not be a separate element that, in and of itself, could
condemn a law or practice that was otherwise unobjectionable, but a potential for political division should be *a* relevant factor in otherwise close cases.
A court should ask the question about divisiveness in terms of a broad category of laws or programs, not in terms of the history of one particular law
or program. Thus, it might ask whether substantial financial aid to religious
schools is likely to be divisive, even if aid is given according to neutral criteria.[63] In this respect, the inquiry could be one aspect of a more general inquiry
about effects.

---

[62] Scott C. Idleman, "Religious Premises, Legislative Judgments, and the Establishment Clause,"
12 *Cornell Journal of Law and Public Policy* 1, 37–47 (2002). One problem here is intertwining,
that the government could make such decisions only by involving itself deeply in church affairs. But
intertwining is not the only problem. The government cannot choose ministers no matter how simply
it might be able to do that.

[63] See Justice Breyer's dissenting opinion in *Zelman*, note 3 supra, at 723–61. For a carefully developed argument that political divisiveness should not figure as an element in Establishment Clause
analysis, see Richard W. Garnett, "Religion, Division, and the First Amendment," 94 *Georgetown
Law Journal* 1667 (2006).

Neutrality

A number of Supreme Court opinions have referred to "neutrality" as relevant to Establishment Clause evaluation. As Justice Souter noted in a dissenting opinion, the Court has used this term in at least three different ways.[64] Initially, the Court meant a kind of equipoise between encouragement and discouragement of religion, the steering of "a neutral course between the two Religion Clauses."[65] In this vague form, neutrality could be fulfilled by applying whatever test of nonestablishment was appropriate, and indeed Justice Clark used language about neutrality in his opinion declaring that class Bible reading was unconstitutional, an opinion that also referred to a test of a legislature's secular purpose and a primary effect that neither advances nor inhibits religion.[66] In this sense "neutrality" is more a guiding principle and a conclusion reached at the end of the day than a concrete standard to judge constitutionality.

In other cases, "neutral" was used to refer to secular benefits, benefits other than religious ones. When public money was given to religious groups, it had to go for secular, or neutral, objectives rather than religious ones. In this sense, aid's being neutral was a precondition of its being permissible.[67]

A third sense of "neutrality" is now dominant. In this sense, a law's relevant classification is neutral if it does not, by its explicit terms or in its obvious coverage, distinguish between religious individuals or groups and nonreligious ones. We have seen this usage in free exercise law, which now affords no constitutional right of religious exercise when the law that forbids behavior is, like Oregon's ban on the use of peyote, a neutral law of general application.[68] When it comes to government aid, a law is neutral in this sense if it treats religious enterprises like nonreligious ones. For some justices, neutrality of this sort may amount to a guarantee of constitutionality; for others neutrality is one among other relevant factors. As we shall see in the chapter on school aid, this difference comes close to encapsulating the sharp division among the justices over aid that goes in large proportion to parochial schools but is distributed without reference to religious criteria.[69]

---

[64] *Mitchell*, note 54 supra, at 878 (Souter, J., dissenting).

[65] *Walz v. Tax Commission*, 397 U.S. 664, 668 (1970).

[66] *Abington Township v. Schempp*, 374 U.S. 203, 222 (1963).

[67] That did not necessarily assure that the aid was constitutional, since other factors might render it impermissible.

[68] *Employment Division v. Smith*, note 7 supra.

[69] See especially *Zelman*, note 3 supra.

The Endorsement Test

As we have seen in previous chapters, one Establishment Clause test examines whether the government has endorsed or disapproved of a particular religion or religion in general. This approach, developed mainly by Justice O'Connor, sees endorsement (or disapproval) as fatal because it sends a message to nonadherents that they are outsiders, not full members of the political community, and a message to adherents that they are favored members of the community. Chapter 5 has already suggested many of the perplexities about endorsement as a standard. Here we shall examine the present status of the test and the way in which these various difficulties might be resolved. This affords us a basis to evaluate how far endorsement should figure as a constitutional inquiry. It also gives us some ground to estimate how much that test is likely to influence the Supreme Court in deciding cases now that Justice O'Connor has retired.

Our initial inquiry concerns the relationship between endorsement and the *Lemon* test. The relevance of this inquiry does not depend on the survival of *Lemon* as a comprehensive test because, as I have suggested, the Court has continued to pay attention to the kind of purposes and effects that have led it to decide laws are invalid under *Lemon*, even when it does not refer to that test in its entirety.

In her initial explication of the endorsement test, Justice O'Connor's concurring opinion in *Lynch* indicated that it was a clarification of the purpose and effects prongs of the *Lemon* test.[70] For the most part, however, endorsement has been viewed as an approach that is an alternative to the *Lemon* test. In thinking about the relation between the two approaches, we need to distinguish among kinds of cases. Suppose a challenged government practice centrally involves communication—a city places a crèche in the town hall. Whether the city is advancing the Christian religion—the inquiry under *Lemon*—is virtually indistinguishable from whether the city is endorsing Christianity. For these cases, one can reasonably suppose the endorsement test is a desirable clarification of what matters under *Lemon*, or is a substitute with little practical difference. But what of the case in which the highway board chooses a route to benefit a particular church, but strongly wishes to keep that secret. The board has supported a particular religion without endorsing it; and even if the secret comes out, it is highly artificial to identify

---

[70] *Lynch v. Donnelly*, 465 U.S. 668, 688–89 (1984). Justice O'Connor here treated entanglement as a separate standard. Later, as we have seen, she wrote the Court's opinion in *Agostini* that treated entanglement as one element of effects.

the crucial flaw in the board's action as a kind of endorsement. To generalize, for cases in which communication is not highly significant,[71] the *Lemon* test is broader in scope than an inquiry about endorsement and disapproval, and, depending on how far endorsement might be stretched, could well yield different results.[72]

It is hardly a coincidence that endorsement has won acceptance of a majority of justices as *the* constitutional test only in cases of public displays. For other cases, it is often mentioned as a relevant consideration but definitely not treated as the exclusive one.[73] Other courts, aware of Justice O'Connor's position as a likely "swing" vote, have often undertaken a separate examination of endorsement. It remains to be seen how much attention opinions of the Supreme Court and of lower courts will give to endorsement in domains where it is not the prevailing inquiry, now that Justice O'Connor has left the Court.

As we proceed to examine various nuances of the endorsement test, it is useful to keep in mind that the degree to which it is flawed depends partly on how extensively it is to be used. For now, we can conclude that endorsement is a plausible approach only in respect to some of the purposes and effects that have been relevant under *Lemon*.

Although her *Lynch* opinion suggested that the perceptions that counted were those of ordinary people, fairly soon thereafter Justice O'Connor made clear that she thought that judges should imagine an objective observer, not attached to any religious group.[74] This objective observer is familiar not only with a law's[75] text, legislative history, and implementation, but also with free exercise values (and presumably other relevant constitutional values). Since one could well imagine an endorsement test that focuses on perceptions differently conceived, the advantages and disadvantages of this formulation are highly important.

We need first to put aside two red herrings. Justice O'Connor has suggested after *Lynch* that a subjective test of people's actual reactions would leave the government vulnerable to the most sensitive of its citizens—would preclude a display "so long as some passers-by would perceive a governmen-

---

[71] For all ordinary laws, of course, communication is important in that legislators communicate what behavior the laws permit or forbid, encourage or discourage.

[72] In *Lynch* Justice O'Connor appeared to treat endorsement as the relevant inquiry for all issues of purpose and effect. Id. at 691–92.

[73] As Smith, note 9 supra, at 275, says, "The Court seems disposed to accept the *expansive* implications of the test, and thus to employ 'endorsement' as an additional ground for finding an impermissible purpose or effect."

[74] *Jaffree*, note 15 supra, at 76 (concurring opinion).

[75] Id. at 83.

tal endorsement."[76] The fallacy is plain; a court could ask if most, or many, citizens would perceive an endorsement, thus disregarding the reactions of the most easily offended. The second red herring is to imagine that the relevant test would have to be wholly objective or wholly dependent on people's actual reactions. A court might employ a subjective test, constrained by some notion of reasonableness. Thus a court might decide not to count reactions based on demagogic appeals or a failure to grasp basic constitutional principles. Even if most people might perceive a failure to have teachers lead prayers in public schools as a disapproval of religion, a court could decide not to count that reaction if it first determined that having such prayers would be unconstitutional.

Some of the disadvantages of a wholly objective test strike one in the face. To a degree at least, such a test detaches itself from the underlying reason to inquire about endorsement. Reasonable adherents and nonadherents of a religion might perceive an endorsement, and experience feelings of favoritism and exclusion, although the superbly informed objective observer would realize no endorsement was present. Because the objective observer has no religious affiliation or beliefs (or lack thereof), he does not possess a crucial component of the identity that real people will bring to bear in their perceptions of these matters. Further, the "objective observer" seems so unmoored to people's actual experiences that analysis in these terms may come down to little other than whether a particular judge perceives endorsement. Such an approach invites variations according to the distinctive outlooks of different judges (and scholars)[77] and may produce a high degree of unpredictability.

The objective approach carries the advantage of not requiring judges to figure out how most people perceive the significance of government action, but perhaps its main virtue is that it allows the Supreme Court to resolve cases without depending on what local judges and juries believe about perceptions in particular localities. Since actual perceptions may well vary in different places, a dominantly subjective standard might yield the result that precisely the same practice that was an endorsement in Tennessee might not be an endorsement in Maine. Unless the Supreme Court employed a subjective standard that estimated the reactions of people nationwide, the subjective approach would require a degree of deference by that Court to the determinations of those more familiar with local sentiments.

---

[76] *Capitol Square Review and Advisory Bd. v. Pinette*, 515 U.S. 753, 779 (1995) (concurring opinion).

[77] See Smith, note 9 supra, at 301. However, lower-court judges may follow the applications of the Supreme Court for situations closely similar to those reached by the Supreme Court, and a string of cases may yield predictable reactions of individual judges. And we should not suppose that a subjec-

Were judges to inquire about the actual reactions of real people, they would have to decide how much to count the perceptions of nonadherents and adherents. With various Christian symbols and references to God, those in the majority may take them for granted and not perceive an endorsement. But nonadherents, more sharply aware that they are left out in a sense, may think the government is endorsing the majority perspective. If it is the feeling that one is an outsider that is particularly detrimental, perhaps the sentiments of nonadherents should be given extra consideration, as Justice Stevens has suggested.[78]

The "objective observer" approach may seem to avoid this problem. *If* it does so, it fails to give special regard to minority sentiments without an explanation of why that makes sense. But I am inclined to think the objective approach does not really avoid the problem. A judge trying to imagine the reactions of an "objective observer" can hardly pay no attention to the perceptions of well-informed actual people. Suppose the judge concludes that an objective observer would grasp that most reasonable, well-informed nonadherents would see things differently from most reasonable, well-informed adherents. The observer, to oversimplify, would have to decide whether his perception of endorsement, or not, would follow the perceptions of most reasonable people (most of whom are adherents) or of most nonadherents. Rather than being resolved or avoided, the question of how to treat divergent perceptions of adherents and nonadherents is pushed by the objective approach into the murky recesses of uncertain evaluation.

The *Lemon* test draws a clear distinction between purpose and effects. In numerous cases the Supreme Court has found a secular purpose but nonetheless held that a primary effect of advancing religion renders a law invalid. (It is more doubtful whether one could have a perceived absence of a legitimate purpose without also having impermissible effects, and no case represents that combination.) What is the relation between purposes and effects under the endorsement test? In *Lynch*, Justice O'Connor still treats these as separate,[79] but once she clearly adopts the standard of a hypothetical, very well informed objective observer, it is harder to see how a judge could find a permissible purpose but not permissible effects. The observer assesses purpose in light of his complete knowledge of the text and what has transpired in the legislative process, and he assesses effects in light of how a law would be perceived by someone with this full knowledge, not by the perceptions of

---

tive test would be much more certain in application, given the difficulty in assessing the reactions of most people to the often subtle question about endorsement.

[78] *Pinette*, note 76 supra, at 785–86 (dissenting opinion).

[79] Note 70 supra, at 690 (concurring opinion).

ordinary, less informed people. With such evaluation, the observer could hardly take a different view of whether endorsement was a purpose and endorsement was an effect.

However, one feature of judicial evaluation, and possibly another, could lead to invalidation under effects but not purpose. In the moment-of-silence case, Justice O'Connor wrote that "the inquiry into the purpose of the legislature . . . should be deferential and limited."[80] If the objective observer considering effects took account of matters like a sponsor's postenactment testimony that would not play a role in determining purpose,[81] then the results of the two inquiries could differ.

Another *possible* difference replicates a point made about purpose and effect under *Lemon*. For the most part the Court has treated an important and fairly direct advancement of religion as an impermissible "primary" effect even if it does not dominate nonreligious effects. By contrast, a secular purpose has sufficed even if accompanied by a religious purpose. Thus, as I imagined for the twofold purpose and effect of aiding hospital care and promoting the religions that are running hospitals, if there are two equally strong religious and secular purposes and two equally strong secular and religious effects, a law would be valid in terms of purpose and invalid in terms of effects. This asymmetry *could* carry over to endorsement. Although Justice O'Connor tended to write of endorsement as either-or, present or not present, and to suggest that if a law did endorse religion, it was invalid, one might reasonably think of degrees of endorsement being measured against secular purposes and effects. In that event, an objective observer finding some endorsement *and* substantial secular purposes and effects might declare a law to have impermissible effects although not an impermissible purpose.

What exactly did Justice O'Connor, and the other justices insofar as they followed her, have in mind as constituting a relevant endorsement of religion? We can deal with four points fairly quickly. Justice O'Connor talked of a person's standing in the political community. Government messages might make someone feel like a social outsider even though she does not believe she has less than equal status as a citizen.[82] England has an established (Anglican) Church of England. English law endorses Anglicanism in various ways. Non-Christians and Christians who are not Anglicans *may* feel somewhat on the outside in respect to traditional English culture, but most do not regard themselves as less than full citizens. Whatever Justice O'Connor

---

[80] *Jaffree*, note 15 supra, at 74 (concurring opinion).
[81] Id. at 75.
[82] Smith, note 9 supra, at 305–9.

herself may have thought, one should take the crucial question about endorsement as whether within the boundaries of our political community, a law conveys a message that nonadherents are outsiders. It should be enough that they are made to feel like social outsiders; they would not have to feel they are being treated as less than equal citizens.

The forbidden endorsement must be in respect to religion. That standard, of course, raises the underlying question what counts as religion for these purposes. In most cases what is relevant religion will not be in dispute; what is contested is whether the government is endorsing it. But whether what the government may be endorsing counts as religious may sometimes be in doubt. In chapter 8 of volume 1 we looked at a challenge to a course on Transcendental Meditation in the New Jersey public schools.[83] Assuming that one regarded offering the course as a kind of state endorsement of that practice, judges applying the endorsement test would need to decide whether Transcendental Meditation was religious. As the chapter in the free exercise volume suggests, I believe such questions need to be approached by drawing analogies to what is indisputably religious.

A third point concerns the attitude of legislators. One possible position is that the state is endorsing religion only if the officials themselves have that objective, and that the state is *not* endorsing religion if officials are merely making concessions to the sentiments of their constituents. Since nonadherents are not going to feel much better if they realize that their fellow citizens have pushed laws favoring the dominant religion through a pack of indifferent legislators, it should not matter whether an endorsement is based on the independent convictions of legislators themselves or derives from their wish to please the majority of voters.

One cannot resolve the issue of endorsement by asking whether a law accommodates the religious needs of citizens. A law could *both* accommodate religious exercise and represent an endorsement of the religion that is accommodated.[84] What is true about accommodations is that legislatures may be inclined to grant them without endorsing the positions that receive the accommodations. Allowing pacifists to qualify as conscientious objectors is not to endorse pacifism. No doubt, such an accommodation does reflect a degree of sympathy for the view that is accommodated—legislators will hesitate to vote for accommodations specifically designed for religious positions they regard as despicable. But a minimal degree of sympathy should

---

[83] *Malnak v. Yogi*, 592 F.2d 197 (3d Cir. 1979).

[84] See Smith, note 9 supra, at 279–282. I agree with Professor Smith that "accommodation" and "endorsement" are "[f]ar from being mutually exclusive," id. at 282, but I do not agree that they "are much more likely to coincide."

not be taken as an endorsement. Thus, inquiry whether a law represents a reasonable accommodation to pressing religious needs is one appropriate aspect of an evaluation of whether the law endorses religion; but it cannot be the final word.[85]

This brings us to the hard questions about endorsement. What kind of government position amounts to an endorsement and how does one determine whether it is adopting that position? "Endorsement" in the usual sense means openly expressing approval or support.[86] Many laws and government practices are not designed to express anything.[87] Could such a law amount to an endorsement of religion?

Suppose a prominent scientist has lived all his life in the South. He is offered a position at a northern university that is regarded as the country's best in his field; the offer includes salary, research help, and other perquisites superior to those at his present institution. He refuses the offer. When asked why, he says, "I am happy where I am." He has frequent relations with northern scientists and has wished not to ruffle any feathers. He has intentionally not communicated anything negative about the North as a place to live in comparison with the South. Nonetheless, an observer might say, "By declining this extremely attractive offer, one at which almost any scientist would jump, he has implicitly expressed his approval of southern life and his comparative distaste for life in the North." *If* the endorsement test were to be used as the test in respect to purposes and most effects (those other than entanglements), the force of laws that are not designed to communicate messages about religion would have to be dealt with in something like this fashion.[88] Thus, a large official grant to a religious organization, like a large campaign contribution, could represent an endorsement. The difficulty of discerning implicit messages in acts that are not designed to communicate is one reason why it makes sense not to make "endorsement" *the* Establishment Clause standard, but to limit its possible dominance to displays, school prayers, and other practices that are mainly communicative.

[85] It could be the final word about unconstitutional endorsement only if one initially decided that an otherwise reasonable accommodation would be constitutionally permissible whether or not it also endorsed religion.

[86] See Merriam Webster's Collegiate Dictionary, 10th ed. 1993.

[87] See Smith, note 9 supra, at 286–91. Of course, all laws are meant to communicate to others the extent of their coverage; but, in the relevant sense, "Please pass the salt" and "Do not park from 11:00 a.m. to 2:00 p.m." are not designed to express anything.

[88] See Joel S. Jacobs, "Establishment Clause as Adoptive Action: A Suggested Definition of, and an Argument for, Justice O'Connor's Endorsement Test," 22 *Hastings Constitutional Law Quarterly* 29, 42, 51–52 (1994), who would have a court ask if the government action expresses approval or disapproval of religion. For acts that are not primarily communicative, the court would see if there is a persuasive explanation that does not depend on an impermissible religious preference.

The kind of expressed approval that should be impermissible for laws and for officials when they speak directly for the government includes not only some exclusive preference for a particular religion but also indications that particular religions or religious views are true or good, or that religion is peculiarly valuable or preferable to various nonreligious endeavors. As we shall see in chapters that follow, I believe that in certain restricted settings, particularly military and prison life, the government may take actions that are rightly seen as endorsing religion but are nonetheless permissible.

The way I have formulated the forbidden expressions of approval, and the way Justice O'Connor has understood the approach, render impermissible a serious government endorsement of monotheism or monotheist religions. (Recall that Justice O'Connor treated "under God" in the Pledge of Allegiance as no longer, if it ever did, having true religious significance.)[89] It is not a coincidence that justices who believe that American governments can express belief in God also reject the endorsement test.[90] One *could* support an endorsement test that was qualified to allow government support of religious propositions that are relatively general and have been widely shared throughout the country's history; but such an approach would hardly be faithful to the whole rationale of the approach. If a (or the) crucial concern of the Establishment Clause is not to make people feel like outsiders, second-class citizens, and one thinks of Buddhists, Hindus, agnostics, and atheists, all of whom do not believe in a single God, it is hardly reassuring that the great majority of Americans have believed and do believe in such a God. Indeed, one's feeling of exclusion or alienation may be more intense if the government adopts a position held by a large proportion of the citizens than if most citizens are outside of the favored religious position. The rationale that lies behind the endorsement approach provides a strong basis to reject the notion that the government can endorse or approve monotheism in a powerful way.

Whether one employs a highly objective approach, as Justice O'Connor has, or asks about how reasonably well-informed actual persons would respond, the perception that should matter is whether someone perceives that the government is expressing approval of a religious position or of religion. That perception would be based on the ordinary significance of communicative acts and of what is implicitly communicated by acts that are not primarily communicative.[91] The inquiry should not be a direct one about feelings

[89] See chapter 6, supra.

[90] In the *McCreary* case, Justice Thomas and Chief Justice Rehnquist joined Justice Scalia's defense of the state's approval of monotheism.

[91] See Jacobs, note 88 supra, at 48–52.

of offense[92] or exclusion. People may react very differently to perceptions that as far as religion is concerned they are outsiders. An atheist may be seriously troubled by government recognitions of God, or he may suppose with equanimity that less enlightened individuals will always use religion as a crutch and draw the state's support. What matters constitutionally is that one recognize that the state is approving religion, not how one person or most nonadherents *feel* about that. A focus on cognitive perceptions rather than feelings leaves open whether the perceptions of nonadherents are especially important. I think they should be.

The endorsement test has been criticized as a jurisprudence of symbolism, disregarding tangible aids and impediments to religion in favor of the symbolic significance of laws and government practices.[93] For laws whose dominant feature is to assist or retard religion in concrete ways, this criticism is largely on point. The main constitutional focus should be on what a law does, not what it implicitly symbolizes in terms of approval or disapproval.[94] But when the challenged law or practice involves a display or a school prayer, its main significance lies in its communicative or symbolic effect. If one believes, as I do, that the government should not be expressing serious approval of religious positions, an inquiry about endorsement is one appropriate way to sift the permissible from the impermissible. And I strongly believe that a state's communicative acts can violate the Establishment Clause, even if they carry no negative practical consequences for nonadherents.

As Steven Smith has urged, the endorsement test is one reflection of the general drift toward neutrality (in the sense of equal treatment) in adjudication under both the Establishment and Free Exercise clauses.[95] The test depends on a fundamental notion that citizens should regard themselves as equals and be so regarded by their governments. In both this volume and the one on free exercise, I have resisted the idea that the religion clauses are only, or fundamentally, about equality; but I have also argued that equal treatment is a critical component of how the clauses should be understood. I agree with Smith that what constitutes "neutral" treatment is often elusive and dependent on the baselines that one chooses, but we have some sense of what it means to treat all religious perspectives and organizations

---

[92] See William P. Marshall, "The Concept of Offensiveness in Establishment and Free Exercise Jurisprudence," 66 *Indiana Law Journal* 351 (1991), pointing out that feelings of offense are usually not treated as relevant for purposes of free speech analysis.

[93] Smith, note 9 supra, at 316–20.

[94] If an objective observer is sensitive to constitutional values, his conclusions about endorsement will be largely affected by whether a law fits with those values as they bear on assistance independent of expressions of approval.

[95] Smith, note 9 supra, at 313–31.

equally or neutrally. That ideal is plainly *not* realized by a formally established church or a serious legislative declaration that a single God rules the universe. As I explain in chapter 20, I think neutrality has more effective content than does Smith. Thus, I do not think the understood connection to ideas of neutrality is a basis to reject the endorsement test. However, we have identified a number of aspects of Justice O'Connor's formulation of that approach that could be clarified or improved upon, and we have also found a number of reasons to think that test is most apt as the dominant approach for only a limited domain of subjects, namely government acts that are mainly communicative in the sense I have used here. For other subjects, it may be appropriate to ask as part of an overall assessment whether what the government has done implicitly expresses approval or disapproval of particular religions or of religion, but that inquiry should usually be subsidiary to analysis of more direct aims and practical consequences.

Coercion

Coercion may seem an odd test for the Establishment Clause, since one thinks of coercion respecting religion as violating rights of free exercise; but the Supreme Court's invalidation of graduation prayers was grounded in Justice Kennedy's theory that students were subject to unacceptable pressure to appear to endorse the prayers.[96] The idea is that coercive pressures more modest than would constitute a violation of free exercise may nevertheless amount to an establishment. An inquiry about coercion could never amount to a complete establishment clause test, because some noncoercive measures undoubtedly constitute establishments, but coercive elements count against a law or practice challenged as an establishment, and in some cases these elements may prove decisive.

History

Chapter 2 sketches claims about the relevance of history for constitutional adjudication. Justices and scholars are divided about how much historical practices and attitudes should count, and about how they should count. No

---

[96] *Lee v. Weisman*, note 2 supra. All of the other four justices joining his opinion would have found the prayers unconstitutional apart from any coercion. Thus, the Court's opinion being cast in those terms was largely the product of Justice Kennedy's being the necessary fifth vote to constitute a majority.

justice denies the relevance of history; but some believe it should be largely dispositive, others that it is one factor among many to be taken into account.

Various opinions by the justices treat history in three different ways. One reliance on history is to conclude that if the very practice that is challenged was accepted without controversy at the founding, that counts powerfully against a conclusion that the practice is unconstitutional. This was the Court's conclusion about legislatures paying chaplains and opening their sessions with prayers. A broader reliance builds analogies from historically accepted practices. If the law or practice that is challenged resembles what was historically accepted or is no more contrary to the values of nonestablishment than were those practices, then it is probably constitutionally acceptable. This, in part, was Justice Scalia's argument in favor of graduation prayers, and it was Justice Kennedy's argument in favor of allowing the display of a crèche in a courthouse. We can say with confidence that were those the main uses of history, the Supreme Court would have permitted practices that it has declared invalid.

A third use of history encourages more flexible constitutional development. One looks to the basic evils nonestablishment was meant to correct and asks whether the challenged practice presents some of those evils. For example, Justice Brennan claimed that the Framers meant to foreclose "involvement of religions with secular institutions which (a) serve the essentially religious activities of religious institutions; (b) employ the organs of government for essentially religious purposes; or (c) use essentially religious means to serve government ends, where secular means would suffice."[97] Under such an approach, a modern court could easily identify public school teaching from a nondenominational Protestant point of view as an employment of government organs for religious purposes, an unacceptable endorsement of one religious view, even though the vast majority of members of the founding generations might have taken such teaching as uncontroversial.[98]

This third use of history is familiar in the opinions of justices with an expansive view of the Establishment Clause. They are quite willing to hold invalid practices that people once considered constitutionally acceptable. If these justices *also* believe the founders would have condemned the very practice that is challenged, they do not hesitate to rely on that as well.

As chapter 2 explains, vital and controversial questions about the development of constitutional law are encapsulated in disputes about the relevance

---

[97] *Schempp*, note 66 supra, at 230 (concurring opinion); *Walz*, note 65 supra, at 680 (concurring opinion).

[98] In fact, there were few public schools at that time, but such teaching pervaded the public schools that developed in the first half of the nineteenth century.

of historical practices and ideas. In that chapter, I briefly defended an approach to constitutional rights that goes well beyond inquiry about what laws and practices the founding generation would have accepted. When courts must interpret a constitution that endures over time, that is very hard to amend, and that is a powerful civic symbol within our political order, they need to be able to develop the fundamental values the constitutional text represents in light of changing social conditions and evolving moral and political premises.[99]

---

[99] I explore this issue and defend my position in Kent Greenawalt, "Constitutional and Statutory Interpretation," in Jules Coleman and Scott Shapiro, eds., *The Oxford Handbook of Jurisprudence and the Philosophy of Law* 268 (Oxford: Oxford University Press, 2002).

CHAPTER 11

Equal Facilities and Freedom of Speech

This chapter explores the subject of equal treatment of religious and nonreligious endeavors from the perspective of freedom of speech guaranteed by the Free Speech Clause. With the exception of the Ku Klux Klan request to place a cross on Ohio's Capitol Square,[1] discussed in chapter 5, we have thus far paid little attention to this piece of the puzzle of constitutional doctrine. The First Amendment's speech clause has been interpreted to forbid many classifications based on the content of communications; when the government makes available a public forum for private communication, it cannot, in general, bar worship and religious expression if it allows other expressions.

The circumstance on which this chapter focuses is when the government allows private groups to hold meetings or communicate messages on public facilities. The broad questions we shall consider are whether officials can limit availability to religious groups only, or to nonreligious groups only, or must they treat nonreligious and religious groups equally. Of the six Supreme Court cases on this subject, five involve public educational institutions, and four of these concern students ranging from universities to elementary schools.

One can quickly surmise that free exercise arguments press toward granting religious groups treatment that is equal to that given nonreligious ones, or perhaps, as I shall discuss, special (more favorable) treatment. Arguments against establishment of religion *might* suggest less favorable treatment for religion. The free speech principle that the government should not bestow advantages or disadvantages because of the views that people express points toward equal treatment.

LEGISLATIVE CONSIDERATIONS

In thinking about the availability of public facilities for private groups, we may start with the premise that they should be available on an equal or neutral basis, barring some reason to the contrary.

---

[1] *Capital Square Review & Advisory Bd. v. Pinette*, 515 U.S. 753 (1995).

Are there reasons why public facilities, say meeting rooms in town halls or public universities or schools, should be *specially* available to religious groups? Since a state should definitely not favor some religious views over others, we know that if any religious groups are to be favored, all should be. States should refrain from judgments about the fundamental truth of religion and they should not try to implement secular values, such as community and good citizenship, by favoring religious groups; but a state might decide that religion enjoys distinctive constitutional protection and is especially important in the lives of its citizens.

What would follow from these judgments? Here, we need to distinguish ordinary conditions of access from conditions of scarcity or extensive supervision. Most religious groups have their own places of worship, and those that do not can often hold their own worship services within the structures of other religious groups. Religious groups have no special need to use public facilities. And most public facilities can accommodate the needs of all groups who wish to use them, given regulation about times of use. There is no reason to make public facilities available only for religious groups or to give some special preference to religious meetings.[2]

Conditions of scarcity could vary this conclusion. Let us imagine a new settlement in a remote area of Alaska or a town that has suffered extensive flood damage. The government owns the only building in which people can hold meetings. In that setting, according a high priority to people's desire to worship, giving a preference to worship services over meetings of the Rotary Club or 4-H would be reasonable.

Circumstances of close supervision may also be special. A prison might have ample space to permit various kinds of meetings, but prisoners do not enjoy all the ordinary opportunities for social life, and prison authorities make judgments about what forms of socializing are desirable. Prisons do, and should, allow inmates to worship, without allowing the general range of group meetings that might take place in free society. In any event, with the exception of scarcity and close supervision, officials should not favor religious groups in the use of public facilities.

What reasons might support giving access to nonreligious groups but not religious ones? If officials allow religious groups to use public facilities, they might appear to sponsor those religions, but they can largely meet this problem by making clear that the facilities are available to everyone, that religious groups have no special status or privileges. A problem may remain if, given

---

[2] Were the government to prefer religious groups, it would provide a direct support for religion that could not be justified as a needed accommodation to free exercise.

access, religious groups would so dominate the use of facilities that their main use will end up being religious. Whether this is a concern will depend on local conditions. However, if officials reasonably fear that such domination will lead to a public perception that the state is promoting religion, the best response may be not to open up the facilities for public groups, rather than to open them up to all but religious groups.

A conceivable reason to deny use of facilities to religious groups has to do with the fundamental idea that citizens should not be taxed to benefit religion. Madison, and others at the time of the founding, regarded it as a violation of religious conscience for people to be forced to support religions to which they did not subscribe. Given that individual citizens pay compulsory taxes that are used for all sorts of purposes they abhor, including fighting wars to which they may be conscientiously opposed, a conscience argument against support for religion seems less an independent reason for government to avoid that support than a consequence of a determination that it is inappropriate on other grounds. Even if the conscience argument has some force for monetary or other tangible support, especially if the support is specifically designated for religious groups,[3] we should probably think of the ability to use ordinary public facilities as in the general category of benefits available to everyone (such as police and fire protection), not as involving distinctive tax support.

We, thus, may conclude that in ordinary circumstances, when states make facilities generally available, they should make them available for use by religious groups. That approach best reflects a stance in which the state neither assists nor disadvantages religion.

Constitutional Principles

Ideas of equal treatment have figured in Supreme Court opinions under the Establishment Clause since the time of *Everson v. Board of Education*, when Justice Black wrote that a state cannot exclude people "because of their faith,

---

[3] On this point, we shall shortly review an exchange between Justices Thomas and Souter over whether Madison opposed any use of tax funds to support religious organizations or only funds that were part of a program to aid religion. Reformulating this question, we might ask whether people would have a legitimate claim of conscience not to have their taxes spent on religious groups, regardless of whether a program was to benefit religious groups or extended more generally. If we ask how people would *feel*, the answer is that some might be specially offended if religious groups are favored; others might not care very much just what kind of program benefits the religious groups with which they disagree.

or lack of it, from receiving the benefits of public welfare legislation."[4] But not until 1981 did the Court consider a state's explicit denial of equal facilities to religious groups. A branch of the University of Missouri permitted registered student groups to use its facilities, but prohibited use "for purposes of religious worship or religious teaching."[5] Members of Cornerstone, an evangelical Christian organization, whose typical meetings included prayers, hymns, Bible commentary, and discussion of religious views and experiences, challenged the prohibition.

Eight-to-one, the Supreme Court held the prohibition in *Widmar v. Vincent* invalid. By accommodating student meetings, the University had created a forum that was generally open. Rejecting Justice White's argument, in dissent, that worship should not count as speech for free speech purposes,[6] the Court treated religious worship as one form of speech and regarded the prohibition of religious worship as discrimination based on the content of speech. Such discrimination violated the constitutional protection of freedom of speech unless it was necessary to serve a compelling state interest and was narrowly drawn to achieve that end.[7] Any regulation that was required under the Establishment Clause *would* serve a compelling interest. But an "equal access" policy would not offend the federal Establishment Clause. It would have a secular purpose and would avoid entanglement;[8] and any benefits to religion would be incidental, not primary, given that the forum would be open to a broad class of speakers and the university would not be endorsing any particular point of view.[9]

The Court left open the possibility that advancement of religion might be the primary effect if religious groups dominated the open forum. It is not so easy to imagine such domination if all that is involved is use of space in classrooms. Even if 75 percent of the meetings are religious, why should this matter if everyone is free to have the meetings they wish? Such domination is readily conceivable if the audience is not self-selecting. If public school students are told to make oral classroom presentations on subjects of their

[4] 330 U.S. 1 (1947).

[5] *Widmar v. Vincent,* 454 U.S. 263.

[6] Id. at 285 (dissent of White, J.).

[7] Id. at 270.

[8] Id. at 277. In fact, the entanglement between state and religion would be greater if officials had to determine which activities were excluded.

[9] Id. at 274. The Court also rejected Missouri's argument that its policy implemented a state constitution whose establishment provision might be more restrictive than that of the federal Constitution. Without determining whether a state interest deriving from its own constitution could ever outweigh federal free speech interests, the Court decided that it could not do so here, given the protection of separation of church and state already provided by the federal Constitution. Id. at 275–276.

choice, and seventy-five speak on why they have turned their lives over to Jesus, the effect on the class might well be to promote that religious view. (Although such a consequence of student choice might not actually be unconstitutional, it would be of sufficient concern for a wise teacher to constrain the range of student topics.) Something similar could happen if the available space is a park area that is used continually by one or more religious groups, whose worship activities are witnessed by nonparticipants.

In 1989 Congress enacted an Equal Access Act that extended the principle of *Widmar* to public secondary schools receiving federal financial assistance. In the Court's next decision about equal facilities, *Board of Education v. Mergens*,[10] school officials had denied students permission to form a Christian club that would use classrooms after school. The Court decided that the federal statute had been violated[11] and that the statute was constitutional; thus, it did not need to decide whether the school's policy was directly violative of the Constitution.[12]

Writing for herself and three colleagues on the constitutional issue, Justice O'Connor applied the *Lemon* test, saying "the logic of *Widmar* applies with equal force to the Equal Access Act."[13] "Congress's avowed purpose—to prevent discrimination against religious and other types of speech—is undeniably secular."[14] Even if some legislators were motivated by a concealed aim to promote religious practice, that would not undermine the law's secular purpose. In seeming to imply that even if all legislators had such religious objectives, the secular purpose would stand, O'Connor suggested a difference between purpose (public, knowable aims) and motive (unrevealed aims). I have suggested in the previous chapter (with my highway choice example) that unrevealed religious objectives could make a law unconstitutional, however unlikely it may be that a court would have enough informa-

---

[10] 496 U.S. 226 (1990).

[11] The statutory issue concerned the circumstances in which a school created a "limited open forum," requiring equal access to groups without discrimination based on "religious, political, philosophical, or other content" of speech. Id. at 235. A limited open forum was created when a school opened its facilities to "noncurriculum related student groups"; the Court took this phrase to include a chess club and stamp-collecting club that did not relate directly to school courses. Id. at 239–240. The high school had a number of such clubs. Justice Stevens, dissenting, proposed a much more purposive approach to the ambiguous phrase in the statute, one "revealed by its overall structure and by the legislative history." Id. at 271. For him, "noncurriculum related" included only clubs part of whose purpose is "the advocacy of partisan theological, political, or ethical views." Id. at 276. According to this understanding, the high school had not opened a public forum, and had not violated the statute.

[12] Id. at 247.

[13] Id. at 248.

[14] Id. at 249.

tion to decide a case on that basis. Because Justice O'Connor did not pause to develop her distinction between purpose and motive, it is hard to know how she would have regarded my claims about secret aims to advance a religion.

On the question of primary effect, Justice O'Connor urged that the school would not be endorsing the religious message of private student groups and that secondary school students are mature enough to understand this.[15] Faculty members would not control or participate in the meetings of religious groups; and the broad spectrum of student clubs would counteract any possible message of endorsement.[16]

The Court's next encounter with equal access problems, *Lamb's Chapel v. Center Moriches Union Free School District*,[17] involved a New York law that authorized school boards to make facilities available to private groups for various purposes, not including religious purposes. A local school board, applying a rule (Rule 7) prohibiting use of its facilities for religious purposes, had denied the use of school facilities to an evangelical group that wanted to show a six-part film series addressing family life from an evangelical Christian perspective.

The Court unanimously held that the exclusion was unconstitutional. The application of Rule 7 constituted "viewpoint discrimination" (by now regarded as a particularly suspect form of content discrimination) because school property could "be used for the presentation of all views about family issues and child rearing except those dealing with the subject matter from a religious standpoint."[18] Under the *Lemon* test, an equal access approach would be acceptable; thus, the school had no compelling interest in excluding religious speech.

Justices Kennedy, Scalia, and Thomas all agreed with the result but objected to use of the *Lemon* test, which according to Justice Scalia is "[l]ike

---

[15] Id. at 250.

[16] Id. at 252–53. Justice Kennedy, with Justice Scalia, concurring in the judgment about constitutionality, objected to O'Connor's emphasis on "endorsement." Id. at 261. For him, the crucial question was "whether the government imposes pressure upon a student to participate in a religious activity." Justice Marshall, with Justice Brennan, concurred in the judgment. He argued that the school's message about existing clubs was one of endorsement, an encouragement to become well rounded. If the religious club was the only advocacy-oriented group, the school had to positively disassociate itself from the religious activity. Id. at 266–70.

[17] 508 U.S. 384 (1993).

[18] Id. at 393. Were the film shown after hours and under a general policy of access to many groups, there would be "no realistic danger that the community would think that the District was endorsing religion or any particular creed."

some ghoul in a late-night horror movie that repeatedly sits up in its grave and shuffles abroad after being repeatedly killed and burned."[19]

In 1995, the Supreme Court decided two equal facilities cases. I shall return shortly to the more important of the two, which involved state financing of religious proselytizing.[20] The other, *Capitol Square Review & Advisory Bd. v. Pinette*,[21] we reviewed in chapter 5 on public displays. In a plurality opinion, Justice Scalia indicated that if Ohio makes the space in front of its capitol available on a nondiscriminatory basis, it has acted constitutionally. Agreeing with the result that the state board could not forbid display of a cross, Justice O'Connor, concurring, was unwilling to conclude that a nondiscriminatory policy was automatically constitutional. She thought that "a private religious group may so dominate a public forum that a formal policy of equal access is transformed into a demonstration of approval."[22] Thus far, a majority of the Court has retained the possibility that a policy of nondiscrimination could nonetheless result in a promotion or endorsement. Justice O'Connor suggested that relevant factors include the geography and nature of the public space and the character of the religious speech.[23] Steven Gey has argued that a crucial question is whether religious dissenters are forced to "opt out" of a public forum; the answer will depend partly on the scale, form, and repetitiveness of the religious speech.[24] Discussing a decision that a municipal festival could not include a Roman Catholic mass, because a village had seemed to sponsor the mass and encourage attendance at it,[25] Gey contends that its likely effect on participants at the festival was sufficient reason to bar the mass even had the village not actively sponsored it. When exactly general availability to all forms of speech can slide into promotion or sponsorship of religion is a difficult question, but Justice O'Connor was definitely right to suppose that a policy of nondiscrimination does not *necessarily* satisfy the demands of the Establishment Clause.

In *Rosenberger v. Rector and Visitors of the University of Virginia*,[26] the Court decided by one vote that a state university that funded the printing of a broad

---

[19] Id. at 398. Scalia pointed out that six sitting justices had on various occasions objected to use of the test. Justice Kennedy also objected to the majority's reference to "endorsing religion," which "cannot suffice as a rule of decision." Id. at 397.

[20] *Rosenberger v. Rector and Visitors of the University of Virginia*, 515 U.S. 819.

[21] Note 1 supra.

[22] Id. at 779 (O'Connor, J., concurring in part and concurring in the judgment).

[23] Id. at 778.

[24] Steven G. Gey, "When Is Religious Speech Not 'Free Speech'?" 2000 *University of Illinois Law Review* 379, 437, 444–45.

[25] *Doe v. Village of Crestwood*, 917 F.2d 1476 (7th Cir. 1990).

[26] Note 20 supra.

range of independent student publications had to fund a Christian evangelical journal urging commitment to a Christian life. The case is significant both for what it says about viewpoint discrimination and because it extends the facilities cases to the expenditure of public money for religious activities.

Under university guidelines, funds were unavailable for a religious activity, one that "primarily promotes or manifests a particular belie[f] in or about a deity or an ultimate reality." The organizers of the magazine *Wide Awake* complained that the university's refusal of funding violated the principle that the state should not discriminate among speech on the basis of content. The university interposed the Establishment Clause as a justification for its content-based guidelines.

Rosenberger is a difficult case because the "facility" involved was the actual expenditure of public money, sought to finance an undeniably religious message. Although the general university program of paying for student publications had a secular purpose, the particular disbursements for *Wide Awake* would support religious advocacy, something that had never been allowed in school aid cases. Justice Kennedy wrote for the Court, with Justice O'Connor, a necessary fifth vote for the majority, adding a concurring opinion.

The justices disagreed initially over the classification the university guidelines created. By now, free speech jurisprudence distinguished between viewpoint discrimination and other discrimination according to content. A rule allowing financial support of publications praising the government but not of ones criticizing it would constitute viewpoint discrimination. A rule forbidding support of all endorsements of political candidates would classify according to content but not by viewpoint.[27] Because the government's treatment of speech in public forums should not depend on whether it likes the opinions expressed, viewpoint discrimination is very hard to justify.

Justice Kennedy said that the guidelines favored nonreligious messages over religious ones and thus involved viewpoint discrimination. He emphasized the point made in *Lamb's Chapel* that to favor nonreligious discussions of social problems, such as racism, over religious ones is to prefer nonreligious perspectives to religious ones.[28] Justice Souter, dissenting, emphasized that the guidelines did not distinguish among religious, atheist, and agnostic writings; it treated equally all writings that manifested a belief "in or about a deity or ultimate reality."[29] Because the guidelines did not choose among competing viewpoints on that subject, they did not discriminate by viewpoint.

[27] See *Lehman v. Shaker Heights*, 418 U.S. 298 (1974) (plurality opinion).

[28] *Rosenberger*, note 20 supra, at 831.

[29] Id. at 894–99. Luba L. Shur, in "Content-Based Distinctions in a University Funding System and the Irrelevance of the Establishment Clause: Putting *Wide Awake* to Rest," 81 *Virginia Law Review*

The truth lies somewhere between the positions of Justices Kennedy and Souter.[30] Insofar as the guidelines covered materials that mainly addressed the possible existence and nature of God or ultimate reality, they did not classify according to viewpoint. Insofar as the guidelines covered comment on social problems from various perspectives, they did discriminate against religious perspectives. *Rosenberger* shows, among other things, just how hard it can sometimes be to distinguish viewpoint discrimination from other content discrimination. The consequence of *Rosenberger* is a considerable lack of precision and an unfortunate expansion of the concept of viewpoint discrimination.

Given its conclusion about viewpoint discrimination, the Court could sustain the guidelines' application to bar funding for *Wide Awake* only if that was necessary to achieve some compelling interest. The university's most promising claim about compelling interest was the necessity of complying with the Establishment Clause.

The four dissenters and Justice Thomas, in a concurring opinion, adopted straightforward positions about what constitutes an establishment. We can best understand the more nuanced approaches of Justice Kennedy for the Court and Justice O'Connor concurring, against the simpler alternatives. For Justice Souter, the case involved a use of public funds to subsidize prose-lytization. He wrote, "Using public funds for the direct subsidization of preaching the word is categorically forbidden under the Establishment Clause, and if the Clause was meant to accomplish nothing else, it was meant to bar this use of public money."[31] Justice Souter claimed that, although neutrality in the sense of evenhandedness between religious and nonreligious groups had been a relevant factor in some previous establishment cases, it had never been sufficient by itself to justify a program of public support to religion. In this case, were the state to finance publication of *Wide Awake*, it would be spending public money for religious purposes. Public aid to religious preaching is impermissible, whether money comes from student fees or taxes, goes to an outside printer or the religious group itself, and is or is not part of a program in which other journals also receive money.

Justice Thomas's concurrence casts doubt on the premises of much of Establishment Clause jurisprudence. His opinion interpreted Madison's "Memorial and Remonstrance" in a way that Justice Souter rejected. According

---

1665, 1680–82, 1705–6 (1995) is highly critical of the Court's treatment of viewpoint discrimination. She also argues that the *Rosenberger* decision infringes the university's range of educational judgment.

[30] I discuss this issue in more detail in "Viewpoints from Olympus," 96 *Columbia Law Review* 697 (1996).

[31] *Rosenberger*, note 20 supra, at 868.

to Thomas, Madison did not assume that religious entities "may never participate on equal terms in neutral government programs," nor did he "embrace the argument . . . that monetary subsidies are constitutionally different from other neutral benefits programs."[32] For Thomas, the Establishment Clause allows the distribution of funds to religious groups, as well as their use of public facilities, on a basis that is neutral between them and nonreligious groups. Although in *Rosenberger* Thomas wrote only for himself, his approach to government spending was embraced in a 2000 school aid case by three others justices.[33]

In *Rosenberger*, Justice Kennedy and Justice O'Connor steered between the approaches of Souter and Thomas. Both opinions mentioned various factors that differentiated funding of a student religious publication from tax support of the religious activities of churches. Funding money was derived from a student fee, not general taxes; the government program would be neutral toward religion if all kinds of publications were funded, implying no endorsement; and direct payments went to the printer, not to *Wide Awake* itself.[34]

Justice Kennedy's strongest argument for the permissibility of aid for the publication of *Wide Awake* drew by analogy from the equal facilities cases we have just reviewed. Physical facilities require payment for upkeep, computer facilities are not different in principle from meeting rooms, and paying printers is not different in principle from allowing groups to use computer facilities.[35]

According to Justice O'Connor, the case lay at the "intersection of the principle of government neutrality and the prohibition on state funding of religious activity."[36] The Court, therefore, had to undertake "the hard task of judging—sifting through the details and determining whether the challenged program offends the Establishment Clause."[37]

Although I am sympathetic with Justice O'Connor's effort to examine all relevant factors, I do not agree with the Court's conclusion. Whether it comes from student funds or taxes, financial assistance by a state university for a publication of a journal whose major aim is religious proselytizing

---

[32] Id. at 854. For Justice Souter's views to the contrary, see id. at 868–71.

[33] *Mitchell v. Helms*, 530 U.S. 793 (2000) (plurality opinion of Thomas, J.).

[34] Both opinions also remarked that students with a conscientious objection to use of their fees for political or religious messages (unlike ordinary taxpayers) might have a constitutional right not to pay. Id. at 840 (opinion of the Court); id at 851 (concurring opinion of O'Connor, J.). This possibility now seems foreclosed by *Board of Regents v. Southworth*, 529 U.S. 217 (2000).

[35] *Rosenberger*, note 20 supra, at 842–44.

[36] Id. at 847.

[37] Id.

oversteps the uncertain boundary of what should be regarded as permitted under the Establishment Clause.[38] One thing that is notable about the opinions in *Rosenberger* is that none of them employs the *Lemon* test in its familiar form and that the opinions of Kennedy and O'Connor do not really rely on *any test* in the strict sense. Justice Kennedy's majority opinion stressed that funding of *Wide Awake* would allow religious advocacy to be treated equally with other subjects of student concern. He emphasized that no settled principle barring government funding of religion precluded the payments. He discussed various cases decided under the "effects" strand of *Lemon*, but nowhere mentioned the precise *Lemon* formulation about impermissible effects.[39] Justice O'Connor treated as significant what she saw as safeguards against any perception that the university would be endorsing the magazine's religious perspective, but she did not here present "endorsement" as an overarching test. Instead, she repeated an observation from an earlier case that "experience proves that the Establishment Clause . . . cannot be reduced to a single test."[40]

Justice Souter's opinion, at one point, indicated that a crucial issue was whether "the law is truly neutral with respect to religion (that is, whether the law either 'advance[s] [or] inhibit[s] religion' . . .)";[41] but he did not offer the *Lemon* test as the correct way to approach the establishment question, sticking instead to the narrow preclusion of public funding. In sum, not a single justice in *Rosenberger* relied on *Lemon* as a comprehensive test for determining whether funding violates the Establishment Clause. In this respect, it resembles a number of recent cases, which do not explicitly reject the *Lemon* approach, which rely on cases decided under that approach, but do not use the approach as *the* vehicle to resolve issues.

Both Kennedy and O'Connor referred to "neutrality" and "no funding" principles as important, but they did not propose a "test," because they provided no criterion for settling a conflict between the two principles. Justice O'Connor, at least, was self-conscious about this. She not only rejected

[38] For a more extended analysis of the case, see Kent Greenawalt, "Quo Vadis: The Status and Prospects of 'Tests' under the Religion Clauses," 1995 *Supreme Court Review* 323, 326–27, 375–79.

[39] Indicating that the Court's approach, which required no review of material, would entail less official entanglement with religion than if the Guidelines were used, Justice Kennedy cited *Walz v. Tax Commissioner*, 397 U.S. 664 (1970), a pre-*Lemon* decision sustaining tax exemptions for churches, at 515 U.S. at 845. The cite is not offered directly but in a quote from *Widmar v. Vincent*, 454 U.S. 263 (1981).

[40] 515 U.S. at 852 (quoting *Board of Education of Kiryas Joel Village School District v. Grumet*, 512 U.S. 687, 720 (1994) (concurring opinion)).

[41] 515 U.S. at 879 (quoting *Allegheny County v. American Civil Liberties Union*, 492. U.S. 573, 592 (1989)).

a "Grand Unified Theory," as she put it, she did not provide any explicit formula for resolving cases within this discrete domain. For something to be a definitive test, in a strict sense, one would need to say that if its conditions are met, the outcome will be in one direction, and if the conditions (or one of them) are not met, the outcome will be in the opposite direction. If a justice says that, when a practice conflicts with the no-funding principle but is compatible with the neutrality principle, we do not know yet whether it is constitutional, then neither "no funding" nor "neutrality" is operating as a test in the sense that *Lemon* previously operated in the vast majority of cases. Justice O'Connor was very clear that, for her, neither of these two principles operated as a test in this way.[42]

Rosenberger extends the equal facilities cases toward funding and other forms of aid. Justice Thomas's opinion suggests an "evenhandedness" approach to all kinds of government assistance. If aid is given equally to all groups, religious and nonreligious, *and* the basis for aid is a valid secular purpose, the aid would be permissible under his approach.

Such an approach might or might not be qualified if the great majority of recipients were religious organizations, a question that relates partly to whether the Court takes a "formal" or "realistic" approach to aid. In *Rosenberger*, the justices treated as important the fact that the great majority of recipients of funding for publication were not religious groups. The balance is quite different in school aid cases, to which chapter 19 is devoted. The *full logic* of the evenhandedness approach would allow direct funding of churches, with churches spending their assistance on core religious activities, *so long as* assistance is not based on religious practice but goes, for example, to all participatory membership organizations in the private sector.

A later equal facilities case involved an elementary school that had refused to allow a Good News Club, a Christian club for children from ages six to twelve, to meet right after school.[43] The club's activities included worship and evangelical outreach. The federal statute was not applicable because it applied only to secondary schools, but the Court held nonetheless that the school could not exclude the club while making the rooms available to other groups that "promote the moral and character development of children." The Good News Club promoted such development from a religious perspec-

---

[42] For Justice Souter "no funding" is a test of unconstitutionality; if something counts as funding religion, it is not permitted. For Justice Thomas neutrality as evenhandedness seems to be a test of constitutionality; neutral aid is constitutional. (Note that a test of unconstitutionality need not be a test of constitutionality. Justice Souter might decide that funding of religion is not involved but that other factors render a practice unconstitutional.)

[43] *Good News Club v. Milford Cent. School*, 533 U.S. 98 (2001).

tive; to exclude it amounted to viewpoint discrimination. According to a principle of neutrality, it could not be treated differently from groups like the Boy Scouts. Justice Thomas's opinion for the Court rejected the claim of three dissenters that religious worship and religious proselytizing were distinctive, not like ordinary speech, and were likely to introduce divisiveness.[44]

Against the argument that elementary school children might be particularly subject to pressure and to misperceptions about whether the school endorsed an activity, Justice Thomas responded that parents, not the children themselves, would decide on their participation, and that parents would not be likely to be confused about school endorsement.[45] Thomas did not address the possibility that parents unconfused about school sponsorship might yield to the pressure of young children who might insist on joining an activity in which many classmates participated and which they believed the school was endorsing. And, even if parents decided free of pressure, it is undesirable for the actual participants in the activity—that is, the children—to believe the school is sponsoring a particular religion's point of view.

Good News Club extends the requirement that public facilities be equally available for religious worship and speech from college and secondary schools to elementary schools. That the case involved an outside group seeking to evangelize and that its meetings were to be directly at the end of the school day are disturbing features of the case. Although as James Underwood has emphasized, the decision assures only equal treatment of religious groups, not that religious groups will be allowed to meet at whatever time and place in the school they request,[46] I believe the Court should have reached the contrary result. School authorities may have genuine concerns that immature students may not understand the absence of school sponsorship and that they may feel pressured to join religious meetings held on school premises. If a school district or legislature decides that these risks are worth taking, that may be all right, but a school's choice to avoid these risks, in respect to lower grades not addressed by Congress or the state legislature, should have been respected.

---

[44] See id. at 130–32 (dissent of Stevens, J.); id. at 136–39 (dissent of Souter, J.).

[45] Id. at 115.

[46] James L. Underwood, "Applying the *Good News Club* Decision in a Manner That Maintains the Separation of Church and State in Our Schools," 47 *Villanova Law Review* 281, 291–93 (2002).

CHAPTER 12

Chaplains in the Military and in Prison

Federal and state governments provide chaplains and special opportunities to worship within the armed services and within prisons.[1] These practices may seem hard to square with a principle that the government should not promote religion, and they raise significant constitutional questions. If they appear at odds with principles we have thus far accepted, should we conclude that the government should cease employing chaplains, should we abandon the principles that seem to condemn them, or may we discern a reconciling strategy that allows us to embrace both the principles and the practice?

ESTABLISHMENT PROBLEMS WITH MILITARY CHAPLAINS

The history of chaplains for the military is as old as the country. During the Revolutionary War chaplains of state militia became part of the national army, and in 1791 Congress authorized the appointment of an army chaplain.[2] Although they must initially be endorsed by their respective denominations, military chaplains are government employees. They receive military training (except for training in arms), and they are subject to military regulations and orders.[3] The government's employing persons to perform the duties of clerics seems to constitute a direct promotion and endorsement of religion, and it may inhibit the free exercise of its chaplains.

---

[1] For a sense of the conditions under which prisoners may engage in religious practice, see U.S. Department of Justice, Federal Bureau of Prisons, Program Statement: Religious Beliefs and Practices (2004). http://www.bop.gov//policy/progstat/5360_009.pdf (accessed September 27, 2007).

[2] See *Katcoff v. Marsh*, 755 F.2d 223, 225 (2d Cir. 1985). For a series of essays on military chaplains, see Doris L. Bergen, ed., *The Sword of the Lord: Military Chaplains from the First to the Twenty-First Century* (Notre Dame, Ind.: University of Notre Dame Press, 2004).

[3] Katcoff, note 2 supra, at 226. Only since early in the twentieth century have chaplains had ordinary military ranks. Rycroft, "Is the Military Chaplaincy Constitutional?" 37 *Church and State* 20 (1984). As of 1986, the annual cost of the military chaplaincy was estimated at $85 million. Julie B. Kaplan, "Note, Military Mirrors on the Wall: Nonestablishment and the Military Chaplaincy," 95 *Yale Law Journal* 1210 (1986). For a very thorough and perceptive evaluation of the extent to which various aspects of the military chaplaincy may be justified as permissible religious accommodations,

In thinking about constitutional problems with military chaplains, we can helpfully distinguish between the minimum necessary to provide military personnel with religious guidance and access to worship, and additional features of the chaplaincy as it now operates. These additional features may generate issues of establishment by involving (1) more active promotion of religion than is justified; (2) provision of chaplains in settings where they are unnecessary; (3) a tighter connection between the military and chaplaincy than is warranted; (4) relatedly, unnecessary constraints on the religious exercise of chaplains; (5) favoritism of some religions over others.

Providing Clergy for Military Personnel: The Basic Issue

The crucial premise in a defense of army chaplains is that the military withdraws soldiers and sailors from ordinary life. They are not free to go wherever they want whenever they want, to arrange their schedules to attend church or consult ministers. Military life is exceptionally stressful for many service personnel. Going into battle, knowing that one may be killed, is among the most frightening experiences anyone can have; but even ordinary, routine military life, with its demands of training and its isolated social environment, takes its toll. Soldiers may suffer "tensions created by separation from their homes, loneliness when on duty in strange surroundings involving people whose language or customs they do not share, fear of facing combat or new assignments, financial hardships, personality conflicts, and drug, alcohol, or family problems."[4] For many of these people, having spiritual comfort and guidance can be vitally important.

To evaluate the army chaplaincy, we need initially to determine a baseline. Is the appropriate baseline what military life would be like without chaplains, in which event the provision of chaplains undoubtedly stands as a promotion of religion? Or is civilian life the appropriate baseline, in which event we can view chaplains as compensation for a deprivation? Here, the answer is plain for both draftees and volunteers—the right baseline is civilian life. If a government conscripts young men (and perhaps in the future women) out of civilian life for reasons unrelated to any fault of theirs,[5] it

---

see Ira C. Lupu and Robert W. Tuttle, "Instruments of Accommodation: The Military Chaplaincy and the Constitution," 110 in *West Virginia Law Review* 89 (2007).

[4] *Katcoff*, note 2 supra, at 228.

[5] I mention the absence of fault, because someone might think the analysis for prisoners, who have committed wrongs against society, is different. However, even if one thought the intrinsic right of prisoners to exercise their religion was somehow less than that of civilians, one should recognize that depriving those who must spend time in jail of spiritual support is pointless and that, insofar as the aim is to prepare prisoners to reenter ordinary life, religious practice can be an important and positive element of that life.

should make up for the deprivation of spiritual support. The answer is nearly as obvious for a volunteer army. Although young people then make the choice whether to join the military, they should not be forced to choose between civilian life and a spiritually barren life in the military.

The provision of military chaplains easily surmounts the first hurdle of possible objections; the practice is warranted to preserve opportunities for religious exercise that exist in civilian life. But a defense of the practice as it exists faces other hurdles: the government's *degree* of support; unnecessary intertwining of religion and government; inequality among religions; and the special treatment accorded religion.

The Status of Military Chaplains

Chaplains in the United States military are members of the armed services; they wear uniforms and have rank; they are subject to the Code of Military Justice; they have military duties in addition to their ordinary responsibilities as clerics. These realities raise two questions: (1) Should the government be paying chaplains? (2) Should the clerical and military roles be as tightly connected as they now are?

Government support would be reduced if religious groups supplied chaplains at their own expense; and government influence on religion would be reduced if chaplains were not subject to military control. The financial issue is the more straightforward. Obviously, privately financed chaplains would involve the government in supporting religion less than do paid chaplains; but would private financing yield chaplains where and when they are needed? Chaplains are most needed when troops are shipped out from the United States, and units often deploy after twenty-four or forty-eight hours notice. Would privately financed chaplains be willing to accompany units wherever they go, even to combat and dangerous "peacekeeping" areas, and would the military, in light of concerns about supervision and security, be willing to take chaplains along without assurances that they would be trustworthy? Would private groups pay enough money to supply an adequate number of chaplains? No one can be sure of the answers to these questions. The government would have to engage in some screening of any personnel it might take into combat zones.[6] But the government's control is greatest if it is paying someone's salary. One point the problem about financial depen-

---

[6] However, it does accommodate Red Cross personnel who are employees of that organization, and increasingly has allowed defense contractors into dangerous areas. One possibility would be to treat chaplains as a similar auxiliary force. See William T. Cavanaugh, Jr., "Note, The United States Military Chaplaincy Program: Another Seam in the Fabric of Our Society," 59 *Notre Dame Law Review* 181, 221 (1993).

dence indirectly supports is this: the government should not be paying chaplains to function in circumstances where ample civilian religious resources are available, unless these chaplains are attached to a group of personnel that may be shipped to a location in which ordinary religious resources will not be available.[7]

Another benefit of government payment is that it prevents a kind of discrimination in effect against religious groups, and their military personnel, that are too poor to pay the costs of chaplains. Although some groups may comfortably be able to support chaplains, others may not be.

Chaplains paid by religious denominations will inevitably be less subject to control than chaplains paid by the government, but the question of control is distinguishable from that of financial support. The military hires some clergy to perform specific services on a contract basis.[8] These are paid by the government but are not military personnel. There can be no doubt that from the standpoint of religious freedom and nonestablishment, having chaplains who are not part of the military chain of command is preferable. The "institutional duality" of military chaplains is bound to create "role tension."[9] In particular, a cleric who is directly subject to military discipline, whose promotion depends on the approval of other military officers, is not likely to speak critically about a war in which the country is engaged.[10] (We should not be surprised that expressions of concern about the military chaplaincy arose at the time of the unpopular Vietnam War.) On the other hand, chaplains who are members of the military may be best able to perform functions, such as attending to the wounded in combat, that are valuable in providing crucial spiritual support, as well as for military objectives. It is arguable that the combination of military and religious roles is better designed than any alternative to provide spiritual assistance to service personnel.

Promoting Religion

The uncontroversial purpose of military chaplains is to provide spiritual help for those who desire it. Chaplains are also instructed that part of their job is to encourage the religious interests of the troops.[11] At first glance, this task

---

[7] Field training exercises in the United States are often in remote, inhospitable locations.

[8] See Kaplan, note 3 supra, at 1217.

[9] See Cavanaugh, note 6 supra, at 190–96.

[10] See Harvey Cox, "Introduction, The Man of God and the Man of War," in Harvey Cox, ed., *Military Chaplains* x (New York: American Report Press, 1972).

[11] Kaplan, note 3 supra, at 1212 n. 16. According to *Katcoff*, note 2 supra, at 228, chaplains are not permitted to proselytize. Under such a rule, encouragements to religious involvement must fall short of proselytization.

seems directly opposed to the notion that the government should not promote religion in general. We can imagine three possible responses.

First, it *might* be said that chaplains do not reach out to nonbelievers or
apathetic personnel to encourage them to become involved in religion, that
insofar as the language in chaplains' manuals about encouraging religious
interests may seem to suggest otherwise, the manuals are not now to be taken
seriously. Whether this response is at all accurate depends largely on what
chaplains actually do. If the response *is* accurate (and constitutes the primary
basis for deflecting this challenge to military chaplaincies), formal government documents should be altered to eliminate this purpose of chaplains.

A second response is that ministers, priests, rabbis, and imams generally
encourage people to become involved in religion, whether or not they are in
the military, although the degree of encouragement varies significantly
among groups. Chaplains who encourage in this way are merely doing what
clerics ordinarily do. Were *this* to be the justification for chaplains encouraging religious participation, that activity should be left to the discretion of
individual chaplains, not required by official policy.

A third possible response poses much deeper issues about government and
religion. It is that in specific contexts where individuals live in total (or near
total) government environments, government promotion of religion is acceptable, both for the welfare of individuals and in the interest of broader
government objectives. Very roughly the argument would be that religion
is good for individuals and for society, that the government refrains from
involvement in that sphere largely because the subject is best left to the voluntary actions of religious communities and private choices among families,
but that absent a relevant private sector, the government can play a role that
would normally be barred to it.

The argument is appealing when the government raises children in a public
orphanage, without parents to make choices about suitable religious activities for their children. Those running the orphanage might encourage children to involve themselves in religious worship, because that is what most
parents in the United States would want for their children, and because many
individuals do find their lives enriched by religious involvement.

In respect to the totality of official control, jail is not so different from the
orphanage. If most people in jail are poorly integrated into society, hostile
and alienated, their lives may be better if they become involved in religion.
Further, their chances of committing crimes when they are released may be
reduced. (We shall later consider how far this argument may reasonably be
taken.) Although military personnel are adults who have not gotten into
serious trouble, they are mostly immature and they find themselves in novel,

highly stressful situations. Religious involvement may help them cope with the strains of military life, and it may make them better soldiers. In sum, perhaps in the military as well as orphanages, the government should be able to implement a judgment about the value of religion that is rightly foreclosed to it for ordinary civilian life. Federal law, if long-standing language is still to be taken seriously, seems to confirm this position with its comment in respect to the duties of naval chaplains that "it is earnestly recommended to all officers, seamen, and others in the naval service diligently to attend at every performance of the worship of Almighty God."[12]

As far as the military is concerned, this possibility is subject to two powerful objections. The first is that those in the military are neither children nor convicts; they may be isolated physically, but they maintain contacts with family and friends, they continue to be subject to private influences. The government should not be deciding whether religion is good for their lives. The second objection is that insofar as the government's aim is to promote its own patriotic and military purposes, the religions that it favors are bound to be ones that are patriotic and favorable to the government's choices of military involvement. What the government will promote will not be exactly religion in general, but religious views compatible with its military missions. That the government would use religion for its own military ends is a cause for concern; that doing so involves a kind of discrimination among religious approaches is independently troublesome.

Effective Discrimination among Religions, and Related Concerns about Free Exercise and Free Speech

One of the most powerful principles of the religion clauses is that the government may not favor some religions at the expense of others. Military chaplaincies impinge on that principle in various ways, only some of which involve intentional discrimination.

We have already examined the most obvious problem. If chaplains are military officers, in the chain of command, they are not likely to express hostility to military missions. The whole system favors religious views that are congenial with the country's military commitments. Now, to some extent this may be an inevitable consequence of the government's providing clerics for military personnel, however it does so. Even if private religious groups made clerics available, the military would not tolerate spiritual guidance that

---

[12] 10 U.S.C. § 6031(b).

was vehemently opposed to military participation. A degree of restriction is a necessary accommodation to the needs of military discipline, but the favoritism toward patriotic religion is almost certainly greater if chaplains are themselves military officers.

The government's requirement that chaplains be available for members of all religions, as well as its encouragement of ecumenical religion and its discouragement of proselytizing (which is more exclusive in its import than an encouragement of religious activities),[13] pose a different problem of effective discrimination. Insofar as these policies trench on what chaplains may say without fear of penalty, they touch potential rights of free exercise and free speech.[14] Each of these policies may favor clerics who are open to and tolerant of other religions, in comparison with those who believe the road to salvation is narrow, and they are traveling on it. Federal law assures that a naval chaplain "may conduct public worship according to the manner and forms of the church of which he is a member"[15]—that is, he need not conduct some form of nondenominational service with which he is uncomfortable. But that does not settle exactly what he can say.

We face here another genuine conflict of possible military need and maximum religious freedom. Given a limited number of chaplains, having chaplains of one faith available to help personnel of different faiths is undoubtedly desirable; and the last thing the military wants is intense conflict over religious belief and identity. When chaplains perform in official situations involving members of widely diverse faiths, they can be expected to do so in a way that does not exclude participants whose religious identity does not match their own. However, matters are different when they are holding worship services according to their traditions. Although a tolerant, ecumenical atmosphere may fit military objectives better than exclusivist messages,[16] chaplains should have wide latitude to preach what they believe in their worship services. A chaplain should not receive a low rating for saying "men

[13] In 2005, the deputy chief of air force chaplains drew a distinction between acceptable "evangelizing" of the unchurched and unacceptable trying to convert people in an aggressive way. Laurie Goodstein, "Evangelicals Are a Growing Force in the Military Chaplain Corps," New York Times, July 12, 2005.

[14] See CDR William A. Wildhack III, CHC, USNR, "Navy Chaplains at the Crossroads: Navigating the Intersection of Free Speech, Free Exercise, Establishment, and Equal Protection," 51 Naval Law Review 217 (2005).

[15] 10 U.S.C. § 6031(a).

[16] However, in recent years evangelical groups have been more supportive of military objectives than mainstream denominations, and the increased interest of evangelical clerics in military service may be one explanation for a growth in the number of evangelical chaplains reported in Goodstein, note 13 supra.

who call themselves Christians should live as Christians."[17] That conclusion is bolstered by a decision ruling that chaplains could urge their congregants to support overriding a veto of the Partial Birth Abortion Act, despite the government's claim that that would violate Department of Defense regulations and the Anti-Lobbying Act.[18] The judge determined that application of these restrictions was barred by the Religious Freedom Restoration Act.

Sources of favoritism that are not easily defensible are standards of hiring. One concern is credentials. Present requirements call for chaplains to have undergraduate degrees and three years of postgraduate education, typically leading to a master of divinity degree or an equivalent.[19] This directly disadvantages individuals who want to be chaplains and who are recognized clerics within their own denominations, but who lack that much education; and it disadvantages the religious groups whose clerics have a much lower average level of education.[20] Why should not designation by a religious group itself be sufficient as a qualification to be a chaplain? The military may respond that educational qualifications are required because of the multiple functions that chaplains serve, and that chaplains, like lawyers and doctors, are professionals whose perspectives will be broadened by graduate education, but few other military positions require three years of graduate education. That requisite seems hard to justify as an absolute requirement, given its uneven effect.

Another troubling hiring issue concerns the mix of religions represented. At a point in the past, some military branches tried to key hiring to religious

---

[17] See this and similar claims in *Adair v. England*, 183 F.Supp. 2d 31 (D.D.C. 2002). In February of 2006, the air force softened its guidelines to make clear that chaplains would not have to offer nonsectarian prayers. Alan Cooperman, "Air Force Eases Rules on Religion: New Guidelines Reflect Evangelicals' Criticism, General Says," *Washington Post*, February 10, 2006, A05. In *Veitch v. England*, 2005 U.S. Dist. Lexis 6257, aff'd, 471 F.3d 214 (D.C. Cir. 2006), a former chaplain claimed he had suffered discrimination because his supervisor had criticized the content of his sermons, which emphasized the authority of scripture. The supervisor denied that his criticisms were directed to the doctrines Veitch preached. The courts did not resolve the substance of Veitch's claim.

[18] *Rigden v. Perry*, 962 F.Supp. 150 (D.D.C. 1997). The case is discussed in Steven H. Aden, "The Navy's Perfect Storm: Has a Military Chaplaincy Forfeited Its Constitutional Legitimacy by Establishing Denominational Preferences?" 31 *Western State University Law Review* 185, 198–203 (2004). However, as recently as September 2006, a naval chaplain received a letter of reprimand for appearing in uniform at a news conference protesting a navy policy that requires that chaplains who offer prayers for occasions that are not religious services make their prayers nondenominational. *New York Times*, September 14, 2006.

[19] Kaplan, note 3 supra, at 1214; Cavanaugh, note 6 supra, at 191–92.

[20] A 1973 report of the United Church of Christ, *Ministries to Military Personnel*, at 30, indicated that these standards excluded some of that denomination's clergy, over half of the clergy of American Baptists, and nearly all of the clergy of some denominations.

affiliations in the population at large.[21] Now, the services have no explicit standard of distribution, although a suit against the navy claimed that it had an informal policy of hiring one-third Roman Catholics, one-third "liturgical" Protestants (despite a much smaller percentage of such Protestants in the navy), and one-third nonliturgical Protestants (more informal, typically evangelical, groups) and clerics of special religions such as Jewish and Muslim.[22]

Especially given the desirability of having some chaplains who can serve members of smaller religious groups, one should not expect any tight correlation of percentages of chaplains and percentages of members of denominations, but if any standard is to be used for appropriate proportions, it should be the proportion in the service that is involved;[23] and indeed the government should make some effort to see that major groups in the various services are adequately represented. If, as has been asserted, the number of nonliturgical Protestants in the navy is far greater than the number of liturgical Protestants, an explicit policy to hire one-third liturgical Protestants could not be justified. (It would be a different matter if the higher proportion of liturgical chaplains could be explained on the basis of stronger educational credentials or a willingness to carry forward the navy's policy of assisting members of other faiths, though each of these reasons carries its own worry about favoritism.) In recent years, the percentage of nonliturgical Protestant chaplains has risen significantly, no doubt in substantial part because of greater sympathy of those groups than mainline churches with the country's recent military endeavors.[24] Any explicit favoritism in promotion for liturgical Protestant chaplains could no more be justified than preferences in hiring. Disappointed members of the chaplaincy have charged such discrimination, but no court has yet made a finding to that effect.[25]

---

[21] See *Katcoff*, note 2 supra, at 226.

[22] *Adair v. England*, note 17 supra. The district court in *Larsen v. U.S. Navy*, 486 F.Supp. 2d 11 (D.D.C. 2007), ruled that if the navy had ever followed such a policy, it was not doing so now, rather taking into account a variety of factors related to the needs that chaplains meet.

[23] A 1999 newspaper article said that each service tries to appoint chaplains according to the "number of followers of various faiths," though with far from full success, partly because of the difficulty of hiring Roman Catholic priests. *Patriot Ledger*, December 8, 1999, 5. The rest of the article makes it clear it is the followers in the service that matter.

[24] See Goodstein, note 13 supra; Kristin Henderson, "In the Hands of God," *Washington Post*, April 30, 2006, at W08 (magazine), asserts that more than a third of military chaplains are Christian fundamentalists and evangelicals but less than 20 percent of service members come from these denominations.

[25] For recent cases involving claims about such favoritism, see *Larsen v. United States Navy*, 346 F.Supp. 2d 122 (D.D.C. 2004); *Adair v. England*, note 17 supra; *Wilkins v. United States*, 2005 U.S. Dist. Lexis 41268 (S.D. Cal. 2005). These cases are discussed by Aden, note 18 supra, who assisted counsel for some of the plaintiffs.

Whatever the method of selecting chaplains, most military personnel who belong to minority religions with minute representation in the population will have to do without their own chaplains. Insofar as many modern Protestant denominations resemble each other in belief and practice, this may not be too troublesome. Because it was our local "community" church, I was confirmed in the Dutch Reformed religion; but, had I been in the military, I would have been as comfortable with chaplains of other mainstream Protestant denominations as with a Dutch Reformed chaplain. One cannot, however, be so sanguine about Hindus or Muslims. No Christian or Jewish chaplain will meet their religious needs very well (especially if the country or group against which the country wages war is identified as Hindu or Muslim). And membership in the same denomination is no guarantee of compatibility. A "born again," theologically conservative Baptist soldier may be uncomfortable with a liberal Baptist chaplain. As the country's religious diversity increases,[26] so may the number of soldiers without appropriate chaplains.

With a volunteer army, members of fringe religions may be less likely to join the American military; but if one of their reasons is their awareness that they will not receive the religious support they want, that accentuates, rather than ameliorates, the concern about unequal representation. Soldiers lacking a chaplain with whom they feel comfortable may experience that as a kind of discrimination, even if the selection process is the best that it can be.

When one reviews the various features of the chaplaincy as it now exists, one recognizes that both overrepresentation of clerics who do not object to the country's military policy and a kind of advantage for military personnel who associate with religious groups large enough to have many chaplains are inevitable, but other sources of favoritism could be avoided, making the system more neutral, in the sense of responding to the preferences of service members themselves.

Can Religion Be Special?

It remains to consider one final issue, the distinction between religious groups and practices and other groups and practices. When people join the military, they forgo many aspects of a richer civilian life. The military supplies some facilities and opportunities, including athletic ones, that are supe-

---

[26] In 2005, out of a total of 280,000 air force enlistees, 3,500 said they were Hindus, Buddhists, Muslims, pagans, druids, or shamans, 1,600 said they were atheists, and about 50,000 said they had no religious preference. Goodstein, note 13 supra.

rior to those usually available in civilian life; but it does not attempt to maintain anything like the diverse organizational life many citizens enjoy. It may allow soldiers to continue to participate in private organizations when that is convenient, but it neither provides military representatives of civic organizations nor allows those organizations to supply representatives to military units. There is no secular "chaplain" for NOW or the NAACP, or for the Democratic or Republican Party, or for the Sierra Club. A particular soldier might feel, "This nonreligious activity means as much to me as religious participation does to many others; I would like a representative available to help and guide me." To take just one illustration, a young woman who is outnumbered by and subject to degrees of harassment by male peers might welcome a representative of a woman's organization.

Nonreligious organizations play an absolutely central role in some individuals' lives, and in times of stress the companionship, advice, and support from an officer of such an organization might be of tremendous assistance. But, *in general*, the attachments of people to formal nonreligious groups are less vital to their identity, less a source of personal consolation and support, than are attachments to religious organizations. Even if one concludes that government should not generally support religious practice, it reasonably treats religious chaplains and activities within the military differently from representatives and activities of other groups. This conclusion fits with my claim in volume 1 on free exercise that some distinctions between religious practices and other practices are justified; and, as we have seen, the fundamental justification for having religious chaplains derives from the desirability of free exercise for service men and women.

CONSTITUTIONALITY OF MILITARY CHAPLAINS

The Supreme Court itself has never passed directly on military chaplains. In concurring opinions, various justices have embraced the free exercise justification for that practice, not mentioning the further constitutional obstacles that lie in the way even if one believes that military personnel deserve to have clergy supplied in some fashion.[27] I believe that, even apart from possible discrimination and interferences with the free religious expression of chap-

---

[27] *Abington School Dist. v. Schempp*, 474 U.S. 203, 296–98 (1963) (Brennan, J., concurring) (includes prison chaplains), 306 (Goldberg, J., concurring), 308–9 (Stewart, J., dissenting); *McCollum v. Board of Education*, 333 U.S. 203, 254 (Reed, J., dissenting). Apparently only Justice Douglas has suggested that paid chaplains are unconstitutional. *Engel v. Vitale*, 370 U.S. 421, 437 (1962) (concurring opinion).

lains, there is a substantial constitutional argument that the present "military chaplains" system is invalid in light of alternatives, notably an extension of the use of contract chaplains, that would diminish government control and support, and reduce effective favoritism for some religions over others.[28] However, one cannot imagine that firmly entrenched practice being treated as unconstitutional by the Supreme Court in any foreseeable future.

That judgment is confirmed by the Second Circuit's response to such a claim in 1985 in *Katcoff v. Marsh*.[29] The court believed that a failure to supply chaplains would deprive soldiers of their free exercise of religion and would constitute an inhibition of religion forbidden under the Supreme Court's interpretation of the Establishment Clause.[30] Noting that the country's survival depends on its military forces, and that religious support could be vital for military personnel, the court treated the provision of chaplains under the war power as presumptively valid.[31] Considering the risks of a system in which chaplains were supplied by religious groups, the judges rejected the challenge to the present approach, reserving only the possibility that a fuller record might reveal that chaplains should not be supplied for retired personnel and for "armchair" personnel who commute to work.[32] Given the uncertainties of how a radically different alternative would work, and the fact that chaplains presently are an integral part of the military, with extensive training and serious responsibilities in combat zones and elsewhere, the court was right to reject the major constitutional challenge.[33] However, its dismissal of the alternative of religions supplying chaplains as "border[ing] on the frivolous" was gratuitous and mistaken.[34] Voluntary supply of chaplains by religious groups is a reasonable alternative that one might well recommend were one setting up a system at the outset.[35]

---

[28] See Kaplan, note 3 supra, at 124–32, who concludes that the present system fails constitutional requisites of neutrality and nonentanglement.

[29] *Katcoff*, note 2 supra.

[30] Id. at 234.

[31] Id.

[32] Id. at 238. Plaintiffs dropped the case after the court of appeals decision, so the district court had no occasion to resolve the narrower question.

[33] Id. at 232–33.

[34] A case in which a court did not defer to military necessity involved rejection of the requirement that cadets and midshipmen attend chapel at the military academics. *Anderson v. Laird*, 466 F.2d 283 (2d Cir. 1972).

[35] Some of the court's doctrinal analysis is puzzling. It remarked that the military chaplaincy is all right under *Everson*; but fails to satisfy all three strands of the *Lemon* test. Nonetheless, because the Supreme Court has declared its unwillingness to be bound by a single test, the military chaplaincy, which has the same historical imprimatur as chaplains in Congress and is supported by both war powers and free exercise considerations, is valid. What is puzzling is that the court does not acknowl-

Prison Chaplains

In most American jurisdictions, the government also provides chaplains in prisons, to conduct worship services, marriages, and funerals, and to engage in counseling and staff support. According to a survey published in 1998, out of forty-eight jurisdictions that responded, thirty-three paid for chaplains out of public funds and another ten used both public and private funds.[36] The others admitted clerics to perform worship services in prison.[37] Whatever their approach for allowing religious services and using chaplains, prison systems generally do not afford similar treatment to most nonreligious activities and leaders of nonreligious groups.

As a matter of principle, ministers for prisoners should be supplied by religious groups, not employed by the government. Apart from officials whose job is to coordinate religious activities within prisons, the argument for clergy to be hired by the government is weaker for prisons than for the military. Ordinary ministers can work part time in prisons, and they will not need to move with units that might be shipped thousands of miles to foreign lands.[38] Federal and state governments do have a legitimate interest in what chaplains say to prisoners. They may reasonably exclude clerics who encourage prisoners to break the law—even if the encouragement takes a form that would be constitutionally protected outside the prison walls[39]—and they may certainly exclude clerics who promote terrorist activities—a concern that has been raised about some Muslim imams.[40] One would expect that these interests

---

edge that, whatever its phrasing, the purpose and effect prongs of the *Lemon* test have consistently been taken to allow accommodations to free exercise and that what amounts to *excessive* entanglement undoubtedly depends on circumstances. Because of the religious needs of military personnel, basic features of a military chaplaincy are much easier to defend under *Lemon* than are legislative chaplains, although that defense may not extend to aspects of the present system that needlessly favor certain religions and religious views over others.

[36] See "Religion Behind Bars," in A. de Groot, ed., *Corrections Compendium*, April 1998, at 8, 14–16. I am assuming that "inmate welfare trust funds" are public; if not, three more jurisdictions would have public and private funding.

[37] However, the District of Columbia provided no services while being absorbed by the Federal Bureau of Corrections.

[38] However, it has been suggested that "volunteers—for security reasons—can't mix casually among the prisoners apart from scheduled monitored activities." Becky Beane, "Chaplains: Prison Padres," *Jubilee*, Winter 2001, at 6.

[39] The basic standard for speech urging illegal behavior is set by *Brandenburg v. Ohio*, 395 U.S. 444 (1969). I explore the content and implications of the case at length in Kent Greenawalt, *Speech, Crime, and the Uses of Language* (New York: Oxford University Press, 1989).

[40] According to Marci Hamilton, *God vs. the Gavel* 145–49 (New York: Cambridge University Press, 2005), this problem is very serious and is heightened because of the groups that propose imams for prison service. In *A Review of the Federal Bureau of Prisons' Selection of Muslim Religious Ser-*

can be safeguarded without making clergy government employees so long as officials carefully check the backgrounds of participating clergy and closely review what goes on between clerics and prisoners.[41] Since some states now rely on private financing, volunteer ministers, or contractual arrangements,[42] other states can investigate how well systems work that do not involve chaplains employed by the government; the risks of switching from government chaplains are not nearly as severe as with military chaplains.

Although I would expect many courts to accept government employment of prison chaplains, the constitutional basis for that practice is much thinner than for the analogous military practice. "Private" and "contractual" alternatives are realized in some states; there are fewer duties that hired chaplains can perform that outsiders could not; issues of training and subjection to orders are less acute; and what is at stake in trying an alternative to government employment is less momentous. Finally, as far as I know, the practice does not have the long historical pedigree of the military chaplaincy. Although states may allow religious meetings within prisons while denying meetings of other civilian associations, and they may also pay clerics on a contractual basis for the services they perform in prisons, it is doubtful whether they should be permitted to provide religious support by hiring clerics as government employees.

---

vices Providers (2004), the Office of the Inspector General of the Department of Justice stated that the dangers of extremist messages and the development of what is called "Prison Islam" were greatest when inmates led services, not when services were led by clerical chaplains, contractors, or volunteers.

[41] The OIG recommended that the Bureau of Prisons screen the doctrinal beliefs of Muslim service providers, supra note 40, at 50, and engage in more extensive supervision of services, id. at 53–54. For analysis of whether such measures violate the Free Exercise Clause or constitute impermissible religious or race-based discrimination, see Stephen Seymour, "The Silence of Prayers: An Examination of the Federal Bureau of Prisons' Moratorium on the Hiring of Muslim Chaplains," 37 *Columbia Human Rights Law Review* 523 (2006); John W. Popeo, "Note, Combating Radical Islam in Prisons within the Legal Dictates of the Free Exercise Clause," 32 *New England Journal on Criminal and Civil Confinement* 135 (2006).

[42] See, e.g., *Washington Post*, December 2, 1987, Metro, D1, indicating that except for the District of Columbia, local governments in the Washington area did not pay then for jail chaplain services, and that Virginia did not pay its state prison chaplains, who were paid by an organization of churches in Virginia. Chaplains in 1993 reported that prison administrators are cutting back on chaplains for financial reasons. "Gutting the Soul of America's Prisons," *Christianity Today*, March 8, 1999, 49. A tendentious editorial entitled "Norman Siegal and the Imam," *New York Sun*, March 13, 2006, 8, opined that the ACLU should (given its views on school vouchers) regard public employment of clergy as unconstitutional, and it commented that Chicago uses volunteers to meet prisons' religious needs. A story the following day, Russell Berman, "Chaplains Cost City Taxpayers $1 M a Year," *New York Sun*, March 14, 2006, estimated the cost of New York City's chaplain program.

CHAPTER 13

Religious Groups Exercising
Government Power

A common feature of traditional established churches was that religious leaders occupied government positions or directly exercised authority over matters that modern states place within the domain of civil government, or both. Supreme Court justices and scholars agree that assigning government power to religious leaders or groups violates the Establishment Clause. According to the threefold *Lemon* test of unconstitutionality, this is one form of entanglement, a form that needs to be distinguished from administrative entanglement and political divisiveness. In two Supreme Court cases this kind of entanglement has played an important part. We shall look at those cases and their implications, also inquiring about one accepted form of clerical involvement in civil government, the performance of marriages, and about a much more controversial engagement by religious organizations, the running of selected prison programs.

The following chapter focuses on two interactions between civil law and religious standards: state enforcement of kosher standards and encouragement of Orthodox and Conservative Jewish husbands to grant their wives a religious divorce, called a get.

CHURCHES DECIDING ON LIQUOR LICENSES,
AND CLERGY AUTHORITY TO MARRY

The Supreme Court case most clearly representing the principle that religious groups cannot exercise government authority involved a challenge to a trivial law.[1] In Massachusetts, towns were not allowed to issue liquor licenses to premises within five hundred feet of a church or school if its governing body objected in writing. A church close to the Grendel's Den restaurant had opposed its receiving a liquor license. The highest court in Massachu-

---

[1] *Larkin v. Grendel's Den*, 459 U.S. 116 (1982).

setts treated the church's power as a "veto"; the church did not need to offer reasons for its stance, and the license could not be issued over its objections.

The Supreme Court regarded the state law as delegating a zoning power ordinarily vested in government agencies to private, nongovernmental entities. According to the Court, the "wall" of separation designed to insulate government and religion from each other "is substantially breached by vesting discretionary governmental powers in religious bodies."[2] The assignment of such a veto power was unnecessary. Public officials could, instead, make decisions about liquor licenses after hearing the views of affected private institutions, or the law could create a blanket rule against the issuance of liquor licenses for premises near to "churches, schools, hospitals, and like institutions."[3] The law provided no guarantee against religious congregations using their power for explicitly religious ends, vetoing licenses for strangers and approving licenses for church members. Thus, churches might use their delegated power for religious rather than secular purposes. Further, "[T]he mere appearance of a joint exercise of legislative authority by Church and State provides a significant symbolic benefit to religion."[4] According to the Court, the law had a primary effect of advancing religion, and its enmeshing of churches in political processes constituted an impermissible entanglement.[5]

The Court's opinion is not entirely clear on what would have been the result if a legislature chose to grant a "veto" power, but extended it to a category of institutions as broad as that encompassed by the laws relieving charitable, educational, and religious organizations from paying property taxes. One could not find any symbolic favoritism of religion, and the veto power each organization would enjoy might seem less like an exercise of government authority. Still, churches would be making final determinations whether enterprises would or would not receive liquor licenses; still, churches could exercise that power to favor their members or those with compatible religious views. This should be enough to create unacceptable effects and entanglement.

When the Court framed its alternatives to the Massachusetts regime, based partly on the laws of other states, it assumed a wider range of protected institutions than schools and churches. What would it have said if the legisla-

[2] Id. at 122–23.

[3] Id. at 124.

[4] Id. at 125–26.

[5] Id. at 126–27. Chief Justice Burger referred to the danger of political divisiveness on religious lines, but the state law did not seem to pose a major threat in this respect, since all houses of worship had the same privilege.

ture created a flat ban on liquor licenses within five hundred feet, or made available a hearing process, but chose to limit these safeguards to *only* schools and churches? Especially considering that a high proportion of private schools are religious, probably such an approach impermissibly favors religion—even absent a veto power (although conceivably the state could justify granting churches and schools extra protection in respect to liquor sales that hospitals and other charities can do without). Thus, a veto power for churches over who receives liquor licenses should be unconstitutional however broadly the power extends, *and* a unique protection for religious groups regarding liquor sales within their vicinities should be unconstitutional even if the protection is not a veto power.

The Court unsurprisingly gave no hint that religious marriages are unconstitutional, but do they not involve members of the clergy performing government functions? In European countries governed by the civil law, one's marriage must be by a public official if it is to have civil authority.[6] In many American states, only public officials and clerics can perform valid marriages.[7] Clerics have an authority that is denied to other private citizens. As familiar as this pattern is, on reflection we must recognize that it does entail an exercise of government power by the clergy and *some* symbolic union of religious authority and government.

The exercise of government authority in marrying couples differs in significant respects from what *Grendel's Den* involved. For many centuries, priests and ministers have had the authority to perform marriages; we do not have a *new* assignment of civil power to religious groups. Perhaps more important, the power is not discretionary in the same sense as is the denial of a liquor license. A cleric may decline to perform a marriage, and many clergy do so for religious reasons (not making their services available to those whose religious perspectives differ radically from their own); but couples can find someone else to marry them, and, if they qualify for a marriage license, they have a right to be married by civil authorities. Thus, no single member or a combination of the clergy can prevent eligible couples from getting married. Further, marriages are not disputed. If we disregard emotional upset and private relations regarding property, the marriage of two people does not hurt

---

[6] "French law [requiring a civil marriage] served as a model for many states in the world, where marriage as a legal institution was freed from all religious elements and put under the exclusive jurisdiction of the state's laws and institutions." Dagmar Coster-Waltjen and Michael Coster, eds., *International Encyclopedia of Comparative Law*, vol. 4, *Persons and Family*, Mary Ann Glendon, ed., chap. 3, sec. 118, p. 75 (Tübingen: Mohr; The Hague: Mouton, 1997).

[7] Uniform Marriage and Divorce Act § 206(a). I put aside here any special powers for captains of ships and any special accommodation to religious groups, such as the Society of Friends, that do not have clergy.

third persons in the way that a restaurant is harmed if a church prevents it from receiving a liquor license. For all these reasons, and perhaps others, the ability of clergy to marry has not seemed threatening in the manner that the Court regarded the church's veto power over a liquor license.

Recently this widely accepted clerical exercise of civil authority has come under scrutiny in connection with the controversy over gay marriage. Some have proposed that the civil law should impose no requirements regarding the gender of two people to be married; religious groups would be left to celebrate and recognize marriages on whatever basis they chose.[8] Advocates of this approach hope it would diminish religiously based objections to acceptance of gay marriage by state laws. Were such a proposal adopted, it would make sense to require that all marriages carrying civil authority be performed by public officials (or by any private citizens who apply for that privilege). Were members of the clergy to lose any special authority in respect to civil marriages, their religious status would no longer carry this particular form of government power.

A School District Drawn on Religious Lines

The second important Supreme Court case was more complicated and more controversial, and it suggests much deeper issues about religious liberty. The New York village of Kiryas Joel was an enclave of 320 acres composed entirely of Satmar Hasidim who practiced a strict traditional form of Judaism.[9] The Satmars had been able to create their village out of a larger town according to a neutral procedure provided by state law. The community educated its children in private religious schools, but it faced a problem with its handicapped children. The private schools could not afford to offer distinctive, expensive, programs for these children, who were eligible for extensive state assistance. According to then prevailing Supreme Court doctrine,[10] the state services could not be provided within religious schools; they could be offered only in public schools or in detached units. The Satmar parents initially sent children needing special education to surrounding public schools, but they subsequently withdrew all of the children because they

---

[8] See, e.g., Alan M. Dershowitz, "Commentary: To Fix Gay Dilemma, Government Should Quit the Marriage Business," *Los Angeles Times*, December 3, 2003, at B15; William Raspberry, "Marriage Rites and Wrongs," *Washington Post*, December 13, 2004, at A21.

[9] *Board of Education of Kiryas Joel Village School District v. Grumet*, 512 U.S. 687 (1994).

[10] *Aguilar v. Felton*, 473 U.S. 502 (1985), subsequently overruled in *Agostini v. Felton*, 521 U.S. 203 (1997).

experienced fear and trauma at being with children who were so different. In order to meet the needs of the handicapped Satmar children, the state legislature created a special school district consisting only of the village. The village then created a school providing special education that was attended by its own handicapped children and handicapped Hasidic children from nearby areas.

The challenge that the Supreme Court considered was to the legislature's creation of the special school district. Six justices agreed that the action of the New York legislature was unconstitutional, but they did not agree entirely on why that was so. The opinions left it unclear just what kinds of legislative measures were impermissible, and implicitly raised the troubling question whether a village that in practice supported a cohesive Satmar community could be all right if a similarly drawn school district was not all right.

The two basic rationales for the decision were that the legislature had drawn the school district to grant power to a religious group (or along religious lines) and that it had favored the Satmars. We shall look at the second theory first.

In a part of Justice Souter's opinion that was for the Court (picking up Justice O'Connor's vote as well as the votes of three justices who joined his entire opinion), he wrote that the Court could not know whether the legislature would pass a similar special act for another religious group having the same need as the Satmars.[11] This potential for arbitrary favoritism precluded assurance that government authority would be exercised in a neutral way,[12] since courts would not normally be in a position to review legislative failures to act.[13]

Considering that the failure of neutrality here concerned *possible* inaction in respect to a similar future request, Souter seemed to condemn any accommodation granted for a specific religious group, because it is always possible that the legislature will fail to treat another group similarly.[14] It is

---

[11] *Kiryas Joel*, note 9 supra, at 702–3.

[12] In her concurring opinion, Justice O'Connor also remarked on the possibility that the legislature might not treat another group similarly.

[13] Id. at 703. Addressing the possibility that the law creating the special school district might be justified as an accommodation, Souter wrote that "neutrality as among religions must be honored" for an accommodation to be acceptable. Id. at 707.

[14] See Abner S. Greene, "*Kiryas Joel* and Two Mistakes about Equality," 96 *Columbia Law Review* 1, 61 (1996). The language also casts some doubt on any accommodation framed in terms of a particular practice, such as using peyote in worship services—because the legislature might not treat as favorably a nonidentical but similar practice engaged in by other religious groups. The consequences of a broad reading of this neutrality language for specific legislative accommodations would be striking. Whenever a legislature grants an exemption for a specific practice, it *might* in the future deal less generously with a claim for exemption from another group that is equally pressing and no more

highly doubtful that most justices joining the majority intended anything so dramatic.[15]

Justice Kennedy, concurring, and Justice Scalia, dissenting, sharply attacked this theory of nonneutrality based on potential legislative failures in the future. As Kennedy put it, the Satmars were singled out because of their specific need; *if* the legislature failed to provided relief for another religious community with the same burden, that community could then challenge New York's discriminatory treatment of the two religious groups.[16] The majority provided no convincing explanation why courts could not exercise adequate judgment in the future to address and correct failures to grant similar relief when they occurred.[17]

In the portion of his opinion that won the votes of only three other justices, Justice Souter compared the creation of the school district to the law in *Larkin v. Grendel's Den, Inc.* The state had delegated its civic authority to operate a school district to a religious group, "giving the sect exclusive control of the political subdivision."[18] In form, the delegation was to the political unit of the village, but in reality the legislature had intentionally delegated discretionary power to a community based on its religious identity. Clear evidence for this was the extraordinary nature of this newly created district, one much smaller than other districts in the state. The result was a forbidden "fusion of governmental and religious functions."[19]

For Justice Kennedy, the vice in New York's statute was in "drawing political lines on the basis of religion."[20] Justice Stevens, concurring, was particu-

---

threatening to state interests. All specific accommodations *might* be viewed as insufficiently neutral. See Michael McConnell's critical comments in "The Church-State Game: A Symposium on *Kiryas Joel*," *First Things*, November 1994, 42.

[15] Perhaps the concern about possible legislative failures to act in the future relates only to specific grants *of political power*, but Justice Souter did not explain why that factor might be especially important in such a case rather than for all grants of privileges for religious exercise. Another sentence of the Souter opinion was much narrower in scope, including the comment that "we have never hinted that an otherwise unconstitutional delegation of political power to a religious group could be saved as a religious accommodation."

[16] *Kiryas Joel*, note 9 supra, at 726–27. See id. at 745–47 (Scalia, J., dissenting).

[17] See Greene, note 14 supra, at 60 (drawing a comparison with Title VII enforcement against discrimination).

[18] *Kiryas Joel*, note 9 supra, at 698. It is something of a puzzle why Justice Kennedy was not willing to join this part of the opinion. His view that a state may not draw "political boundaries on the basis of religion," id. at 722 (concurring opinion of Kennedy, J.), is not far off from Souter's explanation. See Douglas Laycock's comments in "The Church-State Game," note 14 supra, at 38. For Laycock, the simple issue in the case was whether the state was "letting a religious organization run its own government."

[19] *Kiryas Joel*, note 9 supra, at 702.

[20] Id. at 722. He perceived this as a much narrower ground than the Court's reliance on a failure of neutrality.

larly troubled by the state's legislating to assist the Satmars in segregating their children from their neighbors.[21]

One crucial question about *Kiryas Joel* is what, if anything, distinguishes the village from the school district drawn along the same lines. All the opinions assumed that the creation of the village presented no constitutional problem, although its boundaries were drawn to include only land owned and inhabited by Satmars. For Justice Souter there was a crucial difference between a delegation based on religion—the creation of the school district— and "a delegation on principles neutral to religion, to individuals whose religious identities are incidental to their receipt of civic authority."[22] And in answering Justice Scalia, Souter wrote that the Court was not disabling "a religiously homogeneous group from exercising political power conferred on it without regard to religion."[23] As far as the state legislature is concerned, this distinction makes sense. *It* is not acting with respect to religion if a group of citizens who are living near each other and happen to use the procedures to create a village do so because they want to live in an exclusive religious community. A court should not accept criteria for school districts that are formally neutral but evidently designed by the legislature to accommodate a particular religious group,[24] but we have no reason to suppose that New York's village law reflected such a design. So far as we know, it was developed without an aim to benefit any particular group of citizens.

Whether the state legislature *should* be able to design school district lines on the basis of the religious affiliations of those within the district turns out to be a difficult question. One might avoid this question for *Kiryas Joel* by pointing out that nothing in the law creating the district mentioned religion and, although the new district was unusually small in size, the legislature could have been responding to purely cultural factors, not attending at all to religion. The majority of justices were right not to take such a formalist approach. The legislature was trying to meet the needs of the Satmars, and relevant cultural factors, such as use of Yiddish, were bound up with and largely determined by religious perspectives.

---

[21] Id. at 711. Nathan Lewin, counsel for the Satmars, was especially disturbed by this opinion, which was joined by Justices Blackmun and Ginsburg, as being insensitive and hostile to religious perspectives. "The Church-State Game," note 14 supra, at 39–40. Christopher L. Eisgruber, "Political Units and the Powers of Government," 41 *U.C.L.A. Law Review* 1297, 1325 (1994), suggested that the basic interest accommodated by the new school district was the inappropriate one of separating students who were unlike one another.

[22] *Kiryas Joel*, note 9 supra, at 699.

[23] Id. at 708.

[24] After the Court's decision in *Kiryas Joel* the New York legislature adopted such a law, which was found to be unconstitutional in *Grumet v. Cuomo*, 90 N.Y.2d 57 (1997).

But perhaps trying to meet the needs of a religious group in these circumstances was appropriate. One might think that the Satmars should be able to exercise their exclusivist view of what *their* society should be like and to receive some help from the state.[25] That is the crux of the broader issue about *Kiryas Joel*. In thinking about this problem, we need to distinguish minority religious groups that undertake some form of interconnected, perfectionist social life[26] from dominant religions and from minority groups that do not aim to create exclusive communities. We need also to focus on why the group wants a school district of its own and on what basis the officials in charge will, or are likely to, run the district.

Imagine this case. Members of a religious group, the Starites, constitute the only occupants of a village; they have convictions and practices like a mainstream Protestant denomination except for a belief that daytime is for rest and recreation and nighttime is for work and attendance at school. The group has no exclusivist aspirations. Parents will not send their children to school in the daytime, but they would be happy to have their children mix with those of other religions, so long as school is at night. All public schools in the state provide daytime instruction, and the larger school district in which this small village is situated is unwilling to make any exceptions. The state legislature responds by carving out a school district whose borders track exactly the area in which the Starites live. The schools in the new district operate exactly as others in the state, except at night. As in *Kiryas Joel*, the legislature has created a highly unusual small school district to meet the needs of a religious group, but it has not supported an ideology or practice that is separationist in its aspirations, and it has no reason to suppose that, except in meeting time, the district's public schools will be unusual. One might think that were there any small community in which the vast majority of parents wanted their children to go to school at night—say for medical reasons or the work schedules of the parents—creating an independent district would be appropriate, and that the connection to religious belief here would be fortuitous. In a sense it would be true, to take the language of Justice Kennedy's concurring opinion, that the legislature was "drawing political lines on the basis of religion,"[27] but one would hesitate to say, as

---

[25] See Greene, note 14 supra, at 8–56.

[26] See id. at 9–10 ("insular normative communities"); Mark D. Rosen, "The Outer Limits of Community Self-Governance in Residential Associations, Municipalities, and Indian Country: A Liberal Theory," 84 *Virginia Law Review* 1053, 1064 (1998) ("political perfectionism" based on ideas of government socialization and interconnected welfare).

[27] *Kiryas Joel*, note 9 supra, at 722.

did Justice Souter's plurality opinion, that the legislature had given "the sect exclusive control of the political subdivision."[28]

In *Kiryas Joel*, the opinions did not directly suggest that the school district itself was operated in a way that manifested a religious purpose. The teachers and therapists were from outside the district and boys and girls were not put in separate classes, as would accord with Satmar tradition.[29] But one wonders whether the justices were influenced by the fact that in all aspects of life, members of the community accepted the authority of their rebbe. Imagining that those elected to run the schools would be genuinely independent was difficult. This reality provides a tie to other aspects of village governance, and sharply raises the concern how those aspects should be viewed. However they may have been created, should villages like Kiryas Joel themselves be viewed as unconstitutional because religious leaders are exercising political authority or because public acts are bound to have a religious purpose, or for both reasons?

The initial creation of the village of Kiryas Joel arose during a zoning dispute in the Town of Monroe.[30] As Nomi Stolzenberg has explained, Hasidic Jews commonly object to the single-family zoning of well-to-do suburbs.[31] When a group like the Satmars acquires enough property, it is in a position to create a village and adopt its own rules about zoning. The Satmar Hasidim are a "tight-knit, pervasively regulated traditional holistic community"[32] who perceive the sacred as pervading all of life, who recognize no sharp distinctions of religious and secular.[33] The Grand Rebbe of the community "exercises charismatic authority over every aspect of his followers' lives."[34] Control of private property is a primary device by which the Satmars can maintain their exclusive community,[35] but they have also used the powers of local government for that end.[36] Given the nature of the community, one

---

[28] Id. at 698. That is partly because one would not think of the Starites as a cohesive unit whose practices press toward consensus. Whether a court should get in the business of assessing cohesiveness and pressure to conform is, however, arguable.

[29] See the dissenting opinion of Justice Scalia, id. at 733.

[30] Id. at 691.

[31] Nomi Maya Stolzenberg, "The Puzzling Persistence of Community," in David N. Myers and William V. Rowe, eds., *From Ghetto to Emancipation: Historical and Contemporary Reconsiderations of the Jewish Community* 75, 77 (New York: University of Scranton Press, 1997).

[32] Id. at 78.

[33] Id. at 92.

[34] Id. at 79.

[35] Id. at 88.

[36] *Kiryas Joel*, note 9 supra, at 79, 89–90. In the famous case of *Shelley v. Kraemer*, 334 U.S. 1 (1948), the Supreme Court held that racially exclusionary covenants in property could not be enforced

can hardly imagine that zoning rules would be adopted that did not have a purpose and effect of benefiting the community religion. As Professor Stolzenberg writes about another Hasidic community, "Naturally, a population of voters that follows the authority of a Rebbe is going to elect town officials who (usually) act in accord with the Rebbe's expressed wishes. Local zoning ordinances are designed to permit the land uses favored by the Rebbe and the Skverer community at large . . . [and] to exclude the land uses favored . . . by others."[37]

How should a court view a multifamily residence provision in the zoning law, in reality designed to preserve the community as a haven for the Satmars, in accord with the wishes of the rebbe and virtually all members of the community? Such an ordinance appears to serve a religious purpose, it will have a substantial effect of promoting a particular religion and of endorsing that religion, and it may show that political power lies in the hands of a religious leader. Can it be defended against the argument that it violates all three strands of the *Lemon* test, as well as the endorsement test?

Such cases rarely come before courts. Not too many outsiders will be anxious to buy property in the midst of a community like the Satmars', and not too many citizens will concern themselves with the independent operations of small religious communities. Once state funds are expended, however, state officials may raise objections, and organizations committed to separation of church and state may support taxpayer claims. In any event, the absence of challenge does not settle whether such zoning laws are constitutional.

If a court considered the zoning ordinance that supports continuation of an exclusive religious community, it could adopt a formalistic analysis that sharply restricts judicial investigation of legislative behavior. The zoning ordinance is not on its face about religion; it could have been adopted for secular reasons, and indeed one might say that the choice of members of the community to live in multifamily dwellings is as much cultural as religious (though the members themselves would not draw that distinction). As far as the rebbe's authority is concerned, that is not conferred *by* the civil government because of his religious position. Either village officials choose to be guided by him or he has been elected to a public position by democratic

---

consistent with the Equal Protection Clause. The status of enforcement of covenants that require sales to members of one religion or forbid sales to members of certain religions is not settled. The covenant that excludes members of particular religions should be treated like the racial covenant. The covenant that limits sales to members of a particular religion may be supported by a free exercise argument. Both kinds of covenants seem to violate the terms of the federal fair housing law.

[37] Nomi Maya Stolzenberg, "The Return of the Repressed: Illiberal Groups in a Liberal State," 12 *Journal of Contemporary Legal Issues* 891, 934–35 (2002).

processes. In neither event does he *as a religious leader* have the kind of authority conferred on him that churches had in *Grendel's Den*.

This kind of formalist approach seems appropriate for the rule that government authority cannot be assigned to religious leaders and groups. One cannot say that all legislation is invalid if individual legislators are moved by the judgments of religious leaders. (The place of religiously grounded judgments in political life is taken up in a chapters 23 and 24.) And it is hard for the law to draw a line based on the percentage of legislators influenced by a particular religious leader and on the degree of the independence of judgment about what the leader proposes. Many Roman Catholic legislators in the United States may be influenced by what the pope says about moral and political issues, but most of them believe that as to such matters they are not constrained to do what the pope recommends.

According to such a formalist approach, states would not be permitted explicitly to confer political authority on religious organizations, as New Jersey did for the Ocean Grove Camp Meeting Association of the Methodist Episcopal Church,[38] but if local government officials happened to be uniformly loyal to a particular religious authority, that would not violate the principle established in *Grendel's Den*. A harder, intermediate case for the formalist was presented by the City of Rajneeshpuram in Oregon. According to facts assumed at that point in the litigation, the city was completely composed of followers of the Bhagwan Shree Rajneesh.[39] The purpose of the corporate commune was to build "a religious community where life is, in every respect, guided by [his] religious teachings." The organized religious community had control of all the city's land, and residence was limited to followers of the religion.[40] Apparently the commune could effectively fire any city officials who were disloyal by ousting them from residency.[41] Resisting the granting of state funds to the city, Oregon claimed that under these circumstances, and when the raison d'être of a city was the practice and advancement of religion,[42] it would be unconstitutional to give the city municipal power and status. The federal district court agreed, rightly refusing to dismiss the state's claim prior to a hearing at which the actual facts could be developed. When such formal legal arrangements are present, a

---

[38] *State of New Jersey v. Celmer*, 404 A.2d 1 (N.J. Sup. Ct. 1979).

[39] *State of Oregon v. City of Rajneeshpuram*, 598 F.Supp. 1208 (D. Ore. 1984). The city had made a motion to dismiss the state's complaint. At that preliminary stage, the court assumes a plaintiff's factual claims to be true.

[40] Id. at 1213.

[41] Janice L. Sperow, "Rajneeshpuram: Religion Incorporated," 36 *Hastings Law Journal* 917, 937–38 (1985).

[42] *Rajneeshpuram*, note 39 supra, at 1213.

court may assume, subject to a contrary showing, that a city government is indistinguishable from religious authority.

That conclusion alone does not answer the question whether such a legal arrangement is constitutionally impermissible if it arises from actions of the religious group itself carried out according to general legal provisions having nothing to do with religion (rather than resulting from the kind of a special grant of authority involved in *Kiryas Joel* or from a general law that confers a privilege on religious groups as a class, as in *Grendel's Den*). Resolution of the question of constitutionality *should* depend substantially on how one views measures taken by the municipal government within such a locality.

A local zoning ordinance that is neutral on its face but designed to preserve an exclusive religious community is one example of such an issue. Considering that the Court has taken legislative history into account in establishment cases, an approach I have defended, one could not, consistent with that practice, offer a purely formalist account to answer all the relevant questions about purpose, effect, and endorsement. If the indisputable import of the municipal government is to promote a religion, it should not be crucial that its ordinances themselves do not refer directly to religion. If everyone understands that the zoning law is mainly designed to serve religious objectives, should it matter whether local officials say so? One could hardly feel comfortable about such a formalist approach if diverse citizens of a community designed their property law intentionally to keep out members of one religion[43] or race or ethnic group.[44]

A more substantive (less formal) defense of a zoning ordinance that is designed to keep a community exclusive is that it does reflect how members of the community wish to live, *apart* from any exclusionary objective. A village needs some law about zoning. What law should it have if not one that fits its own community preferences? According to this approach, the ordinance would not be all right if the village adopted a zoning scheme that is obviously preferred only because of its ability to exclude.[45] Under this approach, a court would not need to indulge the fiction that the village's citizens sharply distinguish between secular and religious matters. Their preference to live in multifamily dwellings could well be religiously based, as is the preference of many citizens to have Sunday as a day off, or to treat

---

[43] See *United States v. Village of Airmont*, 67 F.3d 412 (2d Cir. 1995), discussed in Stolzenberg, note 31 supra.

[44] The Court's thinking about religious exclusion may well be influenced by legal responses to racial segregation. See Greene, note 14 supra, at 63–70.

[45] Thus, the choice to build a highway on a certain route *because* it would help a particular church (discussed in earlier chapters) would be unconstitutional.

Christmas as a holiday. The local government would be allowed to respond to *that preference*, although it could not implement a religious wish to promote a favored religion to the exclusion of others.

A different, more sweeping defense of local legislation designed to preserve a cohesive religious community is that such communities should have a chance to exist in a larger liberal society. A person can choose to allow only co-religionists on his own private property. Perhaps the same should be true for a small religious group that lives together on conjoined pieces of property. From one perspective, this accommodation approach could be seen as a free exercise argument about what the broader law should permit. From another perspective, the purpose and effect of promoting religion would be regarded as all right *if* the religion that is promoted is shared by every (or nearly every) member of the community; and endorsement would not be a problem *if* there would be no nonmembers (in the community) who could feel like excluded outsiders. This proposal brings us to the core issue about political liberalism and illiberal perfectionist communities and about how constitutional law should respond to such communities.

As Mark Rosen has pointed out,[46] insular, perfectionist communities, religious and secular, have existed for much of the country's history, and he suggests that the willingness of the broader society to accept such communities has diminished over time.[47] Some believe that because such closed communities do not themselves accept political liberalism as a guide to their corporate lives, their exclusiveness should not be encouraged within a liberal democracy.[48] Arguing to the contrary, Abner Greene draws on the writings of Robert Cover in developing the affirmative value of insular communities living by their own law,[49] and Rosen makes a strong argument that allowing such communities to flourish is actually most consistent with political liberalism.[50] Their members are able to exercise their strongest religious and social convictions without disturbing the broader society of which they are part. If one imagines only adult members who self-consciously choose to live in such small communities, I think this argument is persuasive. (I consider much larger communities below.) Judgment becomes more difficult when one considers that children born within a community may not enjoy the range of choices available to those living outside it. Despite this concern,

---

[46] Rosen, note 26 supra, at 1063–89.

[47] Id. at 1088.

[48] Eisgruber, note 21 supra, at 1302.

[49] Greene, note 14 supra, at 8–16.

[50] Rosen, note 26 supra, at 1089–1124 (contending that the political liberalism of John Rawls is best understood as consistent with such communities, despite Rawls's own belief to the contrary).

exhibited to a degree by the education of Amish youngsters,[51] such communities should be allowed to flourish, so long as they can do so on the basis of voluntary choices about social contacts, property relations, schooling, and the like.[52]

Whether they should be able to engage the power of government directly on their behalf is much more doubtful. Suppose we start with the tentative proposition that small minority exclusivist religious groups should be able within localities in which they are the sole residents to further their religious aims by some local ordinances and government policies.[53] Such a proposition immediately calls for various qualitative distinctions and measures of degree. Two basic distinctions are between majority groups and minority groups and between groups that have a genuine encompassing vision of social life and those that do not. Among other lines that any such constitutional principle would need to mark out would be ones concerning size of territory, percentage of adherents to the insular religion, and precise measures of assistance to a religion that would be permitted.

Without exploring these matters in detail, we can quickly recognize some dilemmas. Were a religion that represented a majority over a large area—say the state of Utah—to establish small local communities excluding outsiders, the result could be serious oppression of nonadherents—something not caused by a village of Satmars. And it is highly doubtful whether members of a religion should be able to use government to promote their religion by excluding outsiders, if they have no plan for a close integrated social life, only a wish not to live near nonadherents.

The questions about size of territory and percentage of adherents relate to each other. If the village government of Kiryas Joel can act to promote an exclusive community, should the result be different if one nonadherent lives within its borders? Perhaps not, but one balks at the idea that once a group attains a voting strength sufficient to elect the entire local government (51 percent or even less, given the failure of many citizens to vote), the government can do whatever it could do for a community made up only of Satmars. An exclusivist small village is one thing, a large metropolis or state another. For example, a group like the Church of Jesus Christ of Latter-day Saints should not be able directly to promote Mormonism in the state of Utah or one of its major cities.[54]

---

[51] Volume 1, at pp. 86–106, discusses *Wisconsin v. Yoder*, 406 U.S. 205 (1972).

[52] For a brief comment on how far the government can enforce property restrictions that require sale to members of particular religions, see note 36 supra.

[53] This is a position that both Greene, note 14 supra, and Rosen, note 26 supra, appear to support.

[54] Possibly, if any privilege to promote religion were limited to highly cohesive, perfectionist groups, the problem of size would take care of itself.

Were a constitutional principle explicitly to allow small exclusivist groups to use local government on their behalf, there would need to be limits to what measures the government could adopt. The government might engage in religious expressions[55] and undertake zoning regulations to protect the character of the community, but presumably it could not require attendance at worship services, make it unlawful for anyone who has fallen away from the faith to live within village boundaries, or assign taxpayers' money directly to the favored church. In short, whatever the locality might be able to do, it could not set up a local established church of the kind that existed in centuries past. Courts would need to decide whether any particular measures to aid the exclusivist faith fell on the permissible or impermissible side of the line.

Deciding just what to make of these potential difficulties is not simple. One might respond that cases challenging religious promotion by local governments of exclusive religious communities are rare, that courts will be able to handle sensibly the infrequent contests that do arise. But I believe the extraordinary complexity of developing a position that is fully defensible counts against a constitutional law that recognizes any privileges for small religious groups to use government on their behalf. Courts should be relatively generous in attributing secular rationales to laws like a zoning ordinance that reflects living patterns the residents prefer, but they should not carve out special privileges to promote particular religions, applicable only to the governments of small communities occupied entirely (or almost entirely) by members of highly cohesive, exclusivist sects. An additional reason for this conclusion is doubt that the communities really need such help, since many small communities survive reasonably well over time without holding the reins of local government.[56]

Our long detour about how municipal governments within localities like Kiryas Joel should be regarded brings us back to the precise issue in that case. If, contrary to what I have suggested, courts should accept local governments like Kiryas Joel actually promoting the exclusivist religious life of their communities in various ways, then it would *also* be appropriate for state legislatures to draw political lines to further that process. (So long as the religion is one of a small minority, a state legislature should not be viewed as endorsing it.)[57] On that view, the case was wrongly decided. However, if

---

[55] Richard C. Schragger, "The Role of the Local in the Doctrine and Discourse of Religious Liberty," 117 *Harvard Law Review* 1811, 1874–91 (2004), argues that local government should have flexibility about expression, but does not support "nonneutral" financial or political assistance. Id. at 1890.

[56] Of course, it would be less expensive for any religious group if the state would help pay for religious education as an aspect of public education within the locality.

[57] The next chapter deals with a possible qualification to this point. A state legislature might endorse one minority religion over another without endorsing the first over Christianity.

as I believe, local community governments should not be able to promote religion, then a state legislature should have to constitute local governments according to criteria that do not include religion. On that view, the New York legislature's creation of a special school district only for the Satmars was rightly rejected by the Court, independent of whether the schools themselves were operated to promote a particular religious perspective.

RELIGIOUS ORGANIZATIONS AND PENAL REHABILITATION

We turn now to examine one aspect of a problem that lower courts have faced but that has not been addressed by the Supreme Court: involvement of religious groups in the process of rehabilitation for those convicted of crimes in a manner that is arguably an exercise of government power by these groups. In its strongest form, religious groups actually take over the supervision of a portion of prisoners at an institution. In a weaker form, the religious group provides one component of a required program of rehabilitation. Both forms raise questions about advancement of religion and endorsement characteristic of state support of religious providers of other social services. These questions are addressed in chapter 18. Here I comment briefly on the possibility of unacceptable delegation of a government function to religious organizations.

One specific issue that lower courts have faced about a component of a rehabilitation program is whether states may condition a grant of probation (rather than time in prison) or of early release from prison on participation in a "twelve step" program, such as that of Alcoholics Anonymous or Narcotics Anonymous, that may be significantly religious.[58] It is arguable whether these programs are religious enough to raise a constitutional difficulty, but let us suppose that they are. Under what conditions, if any, might a person convicted of a crime be told that participation is the alternative to time in prison?

The voluntary participation of someone who is convicted of a crime in a religious rehabilitation program raises no problem, even if officials in the criminal justice system give some consideration to that involvement, along with other factors, in determining how an individual is treated. AA is not performing a discretionary government function if it does not determine whether an individual will go to prison, beyond perhaps reporting atten-

---

[58] See, e.g., *Boyd v. Coughlin*, 917 F.Supp. 828 (N.D.N.Y. 1996); *O'Connor v. State*, 855 F.Supp. 303 (C.D. Cal., 1999); *Stafford v. Harrison*, 766 F.Supp. 1014 (D.Kan. 1991).

dance at meetings and progress in the program and leaving it to state officials to determine the consequences of attendance or nonattendance. So long as AA (1) provides a program that is available to persons whether or not they are entangled in the criminal justice system; (2) concentrates its efforts on recovery from addiction, not more direct government objectives; and (3) does not itself determine the status of individuals vis-à-vis the government, *except* in reporting attendance at meetings and progress in the program, the government's conditioning freedom from prison time on participation in AA does not run afoul of the principles of *Grendel's Den* and *Kiryas Joel*.

The constitutional issue looks different if the state actually turns over to a private religious group the operation of its prison program, authorizing the private group to control the activities of prisoners and make determinations about how particular prisoners will be treated. According to Justice O'Connor's opinion for the Court in *Agostini*, entanglement is to be regarded as one aspect of effects,[59] and it may be that the reason not to allow religious groups to act for the government comes down to concerns that religious views will be promoted or endorsed. Nonetheless, the particular problem of religious organizations performing government functions is distinctive enough to warrant a special focus on that.

Were a state to turn over its entire prison system to an unambiguously religious organization, such as the Methodist Church, that would be clearly unconstitutional. Operating a prison system is a core government function, one that dwarfs in magnitude decisions about liquor licenses near churches, the determinations religious groups could not make in *Grendel's Den*. As unwise as it probably is, states are within their constitutional authority in farming out the operation of penal institutions to some private organizations, but farming out to a church is special. Unconstitutionality would be obvious if the penal regime had a strongly Methodist component. Suppose, to move to the other end of the spectrum of possible practices, the Methodists had no religious components in their regimes for prisoners, or allowed worship of different kinds on an equal basis. Still, the danger would be too great that prisoners embracing Methodism would be more favorably treated, and the state's decision to contract out to the Methodists would seem to be an advancement and endorsement of their religion.[60] Matters would become more arguable if the Methodist organization purported to hire prison em-

---

[59] *Agostini v. Felton*, note 10 supra, at 232–33.

[60] This concern would be alleviated *somewhat* if the government contracted out to a variety of religious organizations and assigned prisoners according to their religions. But the danger of promotion of particular religions by organizations performing a government function would still exist; and, of course, no assembly of organizations could fit the religious convictions of all prisoners.

ployees regardless of religion and assured officials that there would be no connection between their prison program and anything distinctively Methodist or Christian. Even here, it would probably be unacceptable for the state to contract out its entire prison program to one religious organization, in part but only in part because of dangers that despite its announced policies, the program might advance Methodism in various ways.

The programs that actually exist in some states differ from this hypothetical in three respects. The operators are not attached to a specific religious denomination, they do not operate an entire system but supervise the programs of only some prisoners, and participation is voluntary. In Florida, Texas, Iowa, and elsewhere, the contracting groups have been evangelical Christian, with programs that strongly reflect this point of view, aiming to transform prisoners through their building a relation with Christ.[61] Although this religious perspective transcends formal denominational lines, it represents one particular stance within the broader Christian tradition. A committed evangelical group could no more be given authority to run an entire prison system than could the Methodist Church.

The relevance of a group's supervising a limited number of prisoners concerns the voluntariness of participation, and this bears on whether one should conclude that the religious group is performing a government function. If no tangible advantages flow from being a participant in the program run by the religious group, one might regard the choice as fully voluntary. But if conditions within units operated by the religious group are significantly less harsh, as a federal court determined about the Iowa's Inner-Change program,[62] prisoners have a significant inducement to choose the religious program. More important for our purposes here, if conditions within the unit operated by the religious group are better than those outside, a decision to drop someone from participation is to consign him to less favorable prison conditions. The federal court in Iowa noted that "both the Dept. of Corrections and InnerChange have the right to expel inmates from Inner-Change."[63] From the standpoint of InnerChange, one basis for such a decision could be a prisoner's failure to achieve spiritual growth or participate

---

[61] The Iowa program, like that in Texas operated by the InnerChange Freedom Initiative, is described in detail in *Americans United for Separation of Church and State v. Prison Fellowship Ministries*, 432. F.Supp. 2d 862 (S.D. Iowa 2006). Douglas Roy, "Doin' Time in God's House: Why Faith-Based Rehabilitation Programs Violate the Establishment Clause," 78 *Southern California Law Review* 795, 798–806 (2005), discusses the Lawtey facility in Florida. For an account of the Christian interest in prison reform, see Chris Suellentrop, "The Right Has a Jailhouse Conversion," *New York Times*, December 24, 2006, at S6 (magazine).

[62] See note 61 supra.

[63] *Americans United for Separation of Church and State*, note 61 supra, at 903.

in religion-centered activities with the right attitude.[64] Of course, it makes sense to allow those operating a rehabilitative program to dismiss those who are not participating in a cooperative way; but in this context, a prisoner may be effectively returned to much less tolerable living conditions because of a judgment that his religious opinions and spirit are deficient.

Considering the question of entanglement, the federal court reviewing the Iowa program concluded, "For all practical purposes, the state has literally established an Evangelical Christian congregation within the walls of one of its penal institutions, giving the leaders of that congregation, i.e., Inner-Change employees, authority to control the spiritual, emotional, and physical lives of hundreds of Iowa inmates."[65] In short, the state has surrendered a standard governmental function to a private religious group that it has chosen, a troubling relationship under the principles of *Grendel's Den* and *Kiryas Joel*.

The worry would be softened, though not eliminated, if the state's basis for its choice had nothing to do with the religious character of the group. That certainly was not the court's view of the situation in Iowa, where from the beginning it was understood that InnerChange "was the only real competitor in the search for a values-based provider."[66] But, more generally, we can hardly be confident that any group proposing a similar program would be regarded similarly. Would any American state confer the same responsibility on a conservative Islamic organization? That is highly doubtful.

At least when conditions within the unit run by a religious organization are substantially preferable to the conditions other prisoners endure,[67] assignment to a religious group of responsibility for the entire schedule of some prisoners' lives, and for their continuance (or not) within the religion-centered program, violates the basic principle we have examined in this chapter that religious groups should not perform government functions.

---

[64] Id. at 908.: "One prisoner was told that though his conduct was excellent, his demanding and manipulative ways meant that he simply was 'not displaying the growth needed to remain in the program. Your focus is not on God and His Son to Change you.' "

[65] Id. at 933.

[66] Id. at 883.

[67] Were the conditions not more favorable, one might consider dismissal from the religious program for rehabilitation as not involving a government function.

CHAPTER 14

Religious Law and Civil Law:
Using Secular Law to Assure Observance of
Practices with Religious Significance

This chapter addresses two complex problems regarding ordinary secular law and Jewish law. The analysis touches questions of accommodation and concerns about establishment. In pursuing various nuances, we can see just how debatable are some connections between civil law and religious practice. Civil law in the United States ordinarily does not help to enforce religious standards for behavior, yet the law of some American states does so with respect to certain observances of Orthodox and Conservative Judaism, with effects extending over the entire jurisdiction, not just one geographical locality. Some states enforce kosher requirements, to which Orthodox and some Conservative Jews adhere. The laws, which penalize fraud in the labeling of products as kosher, serve the secular interest in preventing deception of consumers. but they require officials to decide when religious regulations have been violated.

Orthodox and Conservative Jewish divorces generate another involvement. According to Jewish law, a woman who is divorced under the civil law may not remarry unless her husband grants her a get. A husband who refuses to do this may effectively block his wife's remarriage. New York has adopted statutes that aim to induce a divorcing husband to grant a get to his wife, and judicial decisions in some other states exert a similar influence. These laws and rulings contribute to civil equality of men and women, and they give practical substance to the wife's civil right to remarry, but the cost is the state's interference with what is, in a sense, a religious matter.

I concentrate here mainly on issues of constitutionality, but I comment in passing on matters of legislative and judicial wisdom. The analysis reveals the significance of a number of questions. One involves the favoring of Orthodox Judaism over other forms of the Jewish faith. Should application of religion clause tests be influenced by the minority status of all the religions that are mainly affected? A connected question concerns denominational preference: what is a court to do if the law actually speaks in terms of one "denomination," but members of other relevant denominations may believe that the law's doing so is appropriate? A third question, raised by the *Kiryas Joel* case in the previous chapter, concerns the possibility that other groups might, in the future, need and want the help that one group now receives. Is that relevant to the validity of the present benefit? A narrower question concerns judicial appraisal of the tenets of religious views. When should judges accept the sincere understandings of affected individuals as controlling; when should they seek to discern dominant understandings within a religious group; when should they decline to make such inquiries at all? Both kosher laws and civil law involvement with the get raise significant issues of equality and fairness. In respect to kosher laws, these mainly involve various groups; for the get, equality between the two divorcing partners is the main focus.

The two specific subjects of study in this chapter yield a number of broader conclusions, including ones about when civil authorities may make determinations that rest on religious law, about when a possible favoring of one minority group over another may be unconstitutional, about the effectiveness of private enforcement of religious standards not supported by focused state coercion, and about when a court's inquiry should be about an individual's convictions and when about dominant views within a religious group.

KOSHER LAWS

Many states and some cities have laws that are designed to see that those who advertise their products as kosher have, in fact, observed kosher requirements.[1] Literally, "kosher" means something like "fit" or, for food, "suitable for consumption." Deriving from biblical passages and rabbinical interpretations, kosher requirements concern classes of foods, ritual slaughter, and the handling and preparation of foods. Some animals, such as pigs and shellfish, may not be eaten in any circumstance. An animal that is regarded as clean, or *tahor*, must be killed by a ritual slaughterer according to an approved procedure. Its blood must be immediately drained and the meat soaked and salted to draw out remaining blood. Kosher foods must not be stored or prepared with nonkosher foods; meat and dairy products must be stored apart, prepared with different utensils, and eaten separately.[2]

---

[1] See *Barghout v. Bureau of Kosher Meat and Food Control*, 66 F.2d 1337, 1340 n. 5 (4th Cir. 1995).

[2] See generally Gerald F. Masoudi, "Comment, Kosher Food Regulation and the Religion Clauses of the First Amendment," 60 *University of Chicago Law Review* 667–71 (1993).

This summary of overarching principles hardly does justice to the complexity of kosher requirements, about which, a court said in 1918, "thousands of volumes have been written."[3] For example, the knife with which an animal is slaughtered must be free of nicks or imperfections, and requirements for cleaning animals, and even vegetables, can be highly detailed. As food technology advances, novel determinations must be made, such as whether cheese can be kosher if made from an enzyme that is engineered from a pig's gene.[4]

The three main branches of American Judaism, Orthodox, Conservative, and Reform, have different attitudes toward kashrut, that is, Jewish dietary laws. Orthodox and a minority of Conservatives are observant, although the Orthodox practice is stricter in some respects. Some Reform Jews observe aspects of kashrut, but they do not consider the rules binding.[5] Judaism within the United States is not hierarchical. Although broad agreement exists about most aspects of kosher practice, no one enjoys central authority to settle disagreements that arise. On disputed matters, observant Jews follow the judgments of rabbis whom they trust.

Kosher requirements were religious in their origin and retain religious significance. Even if the beginnings of kashrut also reflected a concern for physical health, no one who now focused only on physical well-being would arrive at exactly those standards.

Nonetheless, many consumers besides religious Jews buy kosher products. Some of these, such as Muslims, who do not eat pork, have religious dietary

---

[3] *People v. Atlas*, 170 N.Y.Supp. 834 (App. Div. 1918).

[4] This and related issues relating to biotechnology are discussed in Kathleen Day, "Modern Science Meets Ancient Ritual; Advances in Biotechnology Raise Issues About What Is Kosher," *Washington Post*, March 26, 1994, A1.

[5] See 6 *Encyclopedia Judaica* 27 (1971). The basic understanding of Reconstructionist Jews is that kosher laws, like other rituals, are cultural practices rather than binding requirements. Mordecai Kaplan refers to them as "folkways," which may be valuable in preserving Jewish culture. See Mordecai Kaplan, *Judaism as a Civilization: Towards a Reconstruction of American Jewish Life* 433 (Philadelphia: Jewish Publication Society and Reconstructionist Press, 1984). With regard to kashrut practices, Kaplan writes that even though the requirements cannot be understood as divine ordinances, "[T]he fact remains that because of the dietary inhibitions the Jewish civilization has acquired a high degree of distinction and dignity. . . . [W]hy then should not the Jews avail themselves of those of their folkways which might energize the deeply ingrained habit of transforming the act of eating, as it were, into a sacrament." Id. at 440. In practice, Reconstructionist Jews often follow kosher guidelines to some extent for the spiritual values they believe doing so entails. In a 1996 survey commissioned by the Jewish Reconstructionist Federation, 34 percent of Reconstructionist respondents said that they keep kosher as compared to 24 percent of Conservative Jews who affirmed that position in a recent Conservative movement survey. But even those who keep kosher are not as concerned about technicalities as Orthodox Jews would be. See "Reconstructionist Survey Finds Inclusiveness Attracts," *Metrowest Jewish News*, December 12, 1996, at 8.

restrictions similar to those of Orthodox Jews. Others have no religious motivation, but they believe that kosher products are especially carefully prepared, or taste good, or they buy products without realizing that they are kosher.[6] One estimate is that only about one-fourth of those who buy kosher products are Jewish.[7] Since some individuals will buy only kosher products and are willing to pay more for them, sellers have an incentive to claim fraudulently that nonkosher products are kosher.

Much enforcement of kosher requirements is private. For example the Union of Orthodox Jewish Congregations of America inspects and approves manufacturing facilities; manufacturers then put the symbol Ⓤ on their products. Local rabbis inspect stores and restaurants and guide followers about which of them observe kosher requirements. Such private "enforcement" by itself raises no problem of legislative wisdom or constitutionality. These problems arise only when the state enters the picture. The state may limit itself to backing up private enforcement with damages for trademark infringement or penalties for fraudulent claims of approval. Or the state can undertake direct enforcement, with inspections and determinations whether practices conform to kosher requirements.

An outline of these possibilities quickly reveals three points. *Purely* private enforcement, with no state involvement at all, may be less effective than would be desirable. Suppose a manufacturer puts pork in its frankfurters but nonetheless uses the Ⓤ symbol. The Union of Orthodox Jewish Congregations could rely on publicity, directed at stores and consumers, to expose the fraud,[8] and it could sue for misappropriation of a trademark, but it might face difficulties if manufacturers use unfamiliar brand names, or sell the frankfurters through butchers who do not use brand names. Further, the manufacturer could avoid the risk of liability under trademark law by claiming its frankfurters are kosher but not using the symbol of any standard organization that reviews kosher practice. A second point is that a mix of alternatives is possible. Some matters might be left to private enforcement aided by state penalties when symbols of approving bodies are fraudulently

---

[6] Vegetarians, for example, may believe that a restaurant that holds itself out as kosher, and as serving dairy products but not meat products, is unlikely to have any meat particles in its food.

[7] See "Around the Island/Crime and Courts/Suit Says a N.Y. Law Is Simply Too Kosher," *Newsday*, Nassau and Suffolk Edition, May 21, 1996, A27; "The Brave New World of Kosher; Foods Exert a Growing Appeal That Isn't Just for Jews," *New York Times*, November 15, 1996, B1, col. 2 (estimates 29 percent). Such estimates become less illuminating as more and more ordinary products, such as Coca-Cola, are prepared to qualify as kosher, id.

[8] Purely private enforcement may be sufficient for highly observant Jews who pay close attention to the guidance of their rabbis, but it works less well for strangers visiting unfamiliar settings and for those who wish to observe kosher laws without investing much personal effort.

used; other matters might be subject to direct state enforcement. The third point is that the methods of direct state enforcement can vary significantly. Enforcement officials could be secular administrators or rabbis; the state could decide what counts as kosher or accept the determinations of rabbis or Jewish organizations; the law could, or could not, create a defense for those who sincerely believe their products are kosher.

Constitutional conclusions may depend on the precise scheme the state has chosen. One crucial question under a sensible constitutional analysis is whether a scheme with fewer troublesome features can yield adequate enforcement.

We shall move from less intrusive state involvements with kosher requirements to greater ones, asking at each stage what values are compromised. If kosher laws purposefully favor or endorse some religion over other religions, they create a suspect classification, are subject to strict scrutiny, and are effectively unconstitutional. Otherwise, we must look for guidance to *Lemon*'s elements of purpose, effect, and entanglement, to Justice O'Connor's endorsement approach, and to the principle (explored in chapter 16 of volume 1) that civil courts may not resolve arguable matters of religious doctrine and practice.

State Support of Private Enforcement

The most modest state involvement is backing up private enforcement of kosher rules. The state could remedy trademark infringement suffered by the organizations whose symbols are improperly used; it could go further and employ the law of criminal and civil fraud. So long as the state deals similarly with other fraudulent claims of endorsement, it neither singles out religion for special treatment, nor favors one religion over another.

Does the state's backing up private enforcement impermissibly enforce religious law? Although some people want to eat kosher food for nonreligious reasons, the importance of kosher standards remains largely religious. They are about ritual observance. In Judaism, culture and religion are intermingled; but any idea that kosher requirements have moved, like Santa Claus (St. Nicholas), from being primarily religious to being predominantly secular would be specious.

Nevertheless, the state has a legitimate secular interest in preventing fraud, even if the reason why people want a kind of product is mainly religious. Suppose that someone sold crosses with the claim, "Personally Blessed by the Pope." The state properly prevents such fraud. As chapter 7 of volume 1 explains, officials cannot assess the truth of essentially religious claims, and they should sometimes avoid determining the sincerity of people who offer claims about their religious views, but a simple determination that the pope did not bless particular crosses raises no such problems. Neither does a determination that a seller claimed falsely its meat was approved by a private kosher enforcement organization. These straightforward factual judgments are undoubtedly proper.

Direct State Enforcement

Serious issues about the state's role arise only when the state's involvement increases. Many states and cities with laws regulating kosher advertising have directly enforced kosher rules, investigating and determining whether kosher standards have been violated. Although major cases have declared such schemes unconstitutional, they still exist in a number of jurisdictions.[9] In considering direct enforcement, we need to distinguish the bare minimum of any scheme from complexities that intensify constitutional doubts. The two main complexities are (1) use of rabbis as state officials responsible for enforcement and (2) resolution of disagreements about what is kosher. When judges and advocates have indicated that enforcement of kosher laws is unconstitutional, they have not always been clear whether the basic scheme of enforcement is invalid or complexities make it so.

The Basic Scheme

A statute makes it illegal for someone to advertise as kosher food that he realizes is not kosher. As the New York law, which served as a model for other states, provided up to 2002: "A person who, with intent to defraud, sells . . . food . . . [that he] falsely represents . . . to be kosher . . . is guilty of a . . . misdemeanor."[10] Kosher was defined in New York and most other jurisdictions as being in accord with "orthodox Hebrew religious require-

---

[9] Both New Jersey and New York abandoned such direct enforcement after courts held their laws invalid. Among states that continue to provide for enforcement that requires official decision whether products are kosher are California, Connecticut, Illinois, Ohio, Pennsylvania, and Texas.

[10] New York Agricultural and Markets Law § 201-a (McKinney 2006). The basic New York kosher law was declared unconstitutional in *Commack Self-Service Kosher Meats, Inc. v. Weirs*, 294 F.3d 415 (2d Cir. 2002). The present law provides that producers, distributors, and sellers of food who wish to say it is certified as kosher must provide information on the organization or person giving the certification. New York Agriculture and Markets Law § 201-a. See also New Jersey's law, NJ Admin. Code § 13:45A-21.1–21.8 (2006), which requires that establishments claiming to sell kosher food fully disclose the bases on which their claims are made.

ments," although some laws did not make explicit reference to Orthodox Judaism.[11] Is such a law constitutional?

The circumstances most favorable to that conclusion would be if enforcement were by ordinary officials and applications of the concept of kosher were easy and undisputed. Everyone agrees that pork is unacceptable according to traditional Jewish standards. A seller who falsely claims that meat containing pork is kosher violates the law. The state *does* determine that someone has violated religious law but, in aiding people to avoid deception, it refrains from any judgment about what is religiously correct and from any debatable judgment about how religious precepts should be understood and applied. It does not say people should follow kosher requirements. Since the determination that Jewish tradition treats pork as unacceptable is indisputable, the government does not intermingle in doctrine or practice as it would by taking sides on arguable issues for which it lacks competence.[12]

Does the state favor or endorse one religion to the disadvantage of other religions or nonreligion? We can examine this question in terms of actual present discrimination or potential discrimination. Whether the state engages in present favoritism depends on whether competing versions of kosher are unprotected and on whether other similar desires to be free of fraudulent representations are unsatisfied. Suppose that each major branch of the Jewish faith had its own kosher standards; and the state chose to enforce only Orthodox Jewish requirements. That law would favor Orthodox Judaism over other branches of Judaism and would reasonably be viewed as an endorsement of Orthodox Judaism in comparison with them (although not in comparison with Christianity or other religions). Such a law would be unconstitutional. The conclusion differs if other Jews accept the Orthodox tradition as providing the measure for whether foods are kosher;[13] in that event, kosher laws would not impermissibly favor the Orthodox over other Jews.

---

[11] See Masoudi, note 2 supra, at 672–73. If enforcement officials in states where the statutes and regulations do not refer directly to Orthodox standards end up referring to those standards, the constitutional analysis differs little from that for states whose laws explicitly refer to Orthodox standards.

[12] Some language in the opinion holding New York's kosher law invalid seemed to suggest that the state could not adopt a position on a point of religious doctrine, regardless of the clarity of the answer, *Commack*, note 10 supra, at 427, but the court also relied heavily on the fact that kosher standards are disputed.

[13] On this view, other Jews may be less rigorous in their *observance* of kosher requirements than Orthodox Jews, but lack (for the most part) independent standards of what counts as kosher. See Judge Lay's opinion in *Barghout*, note 1 supra, at 1341–41 n. 9, quoting from an amicus brief of the New Jersey Association of Reform Rabbis et al. (representing the entire spectrum of Jewish practice) in *Ran-Dav's County Kosher, Inc. v. State of New Jersey*, 129 N.J. 141, 608 A.2d 1353 (1992). This suggestion is decisively rejected by the *Commack* court, note 10 supra, at 426, which found evidence that disagreements over kosher standards have existed for a long time. Among other sources, it cites

Do kosher laws effectively establish an existing religious view to the exclusion of one that might emerge as religious understandings shift? Suppose, to imagine an artificially stark illustration, a leader arose who claimed that Jews should evolve a new understanding that considers any food to be kosher if produced in the right spiritual environment. His farming and meat-producing community wishes to use the label kosher for frankfurters in which pork is used. When the law forbids this labeling, does it establish the old religious view over the novel understanding? The answer is no.

For the vast majority of Jewish consumers, that is, according to the dominant understanding of those who care most whether products are kosher, "kosher" is a shorthand for "acceptable according to traditional Jewish standards." If the community's frankfurters were labeled kosher, without further information, that would deceive most consumers. The law appropriately requires labeling that accords with heavily dominant views, if these can be identified. Unless, and until, the leader manages to persuade many Jews to adopt his view of what is kosher, his labeling is fraudulent.

Whether kosher laws aid or endorse Judaism over other groups because they provide a special protection is more debatable. Here the answer depends on whether any non-Jewish groups have similar needs that are disregarded. If so, one might reasonably speak of discrimination and a forbidden aid to one religion in relation to another.[14] The day may come when a legislature's failure to protect followers of Islam who wish to adhere to their dietary restrictions might amount to unacceptable discrimination.[15] Thus far, how-

---

Samuel H. Dresner, Seymour Siegel, and David M. Pollock, *The Jewish Dietary Laws* 55–56 (New York: Rabbinical Assembly of America, United Synagogue Commission on Jewish Education, 1982).

[14] Further, if the state failed to assist a secular group wanting similar protection against fraud, say strict vegetarians, one might worry about its protecting religious needs in comparison with analogous nonreligious ones. A counter to this worry might be that people are especially concerned not to eat food they believe is unacceptable for religious reasons, and that, therefore, the state may concentrate efforts against fraud as to that. The court in *Commack*, note 10 supra, at 431, suggested that any singling out of religious rules for protection against fraud might be invalid because general enforcement against fraud would safeguard secular interests.

[15] Muslims have dietary requirements to eat foods that are halal (lawful or permitted). The main restrictions concern meats, although alcohol and other intoxicants are prohibited. The intricacy of restrictions governing meat resembles that found in kosher practices, with detailed analysis of the acceptability of gelatin and of meat from animals slaughtered by Jews and Christians ("people of the Book"). Kosher standards do not track exactly the standards of halal, and Muslims could benefit from clearer labeling of what conforms to their standards. Although the precise number is disputed, there are now approximately as many Muslims as Jews within the United States. If, within a state, as many or more Muslims follow halal as Jews follow kosher, and Muslims need the kind of protection kosher laws provide for observant Jews, the potential for a claim of discrimination exists. However, one cannot fault state legislatures for failing to provide equal treatment at this point in time. The population of Muslims has increased greatly in recent years; and so far the main efforts in regard to

ever, neither Muslims nor any other sizeable group (religious or secular) has sought and failed to receive the kind of protection afforded by the kosher laws. So long as this is true, basic kosher laws do not presently favor or endorse Judaism.

What is the relevance of potential discrimination? In *Kiryas Joel Village v. Grumet*, which we considered in the last chapter, five justices suggested that a potential for subsequent discrimination was one reason to invalidate the legislative creation of a special school district for a village made up entirely of members of the Satmar Hasidic sect of Judaism.[16] According to the Court and Justice O' Connor, a legislature that affords such a special benefit to one religious group might fail to afford the same benefit to other similar groups. Because a failure to grant a benefit is not reviewable, the courts are not in a position to prevent legislative favoritism along religious lines, and the existing benefit therefore is not neutral in the sense required under the Establishment Clause. Were this theory to prevail in future cases and be given a generous extension, it would threaten kosher laws. The possible future failure to treat other groups equally would mean that an existing kosher law would lack adequate neutrality.

We have strong reasons to doubt this theory will be used to undermine kosher laws. As Justice Kennedy's concurrence and Justice Scalia's dissent in *Kiryas Joel* pointed out, many specific legislative concessions have been granted, and the Supreme Court has approved such concessions in principle.[17] Courts have not assumed that the possibility of some future discrimination makes such exceptions invalid; rather they have supposed that courts can measure claims of actual unfair treatment according to equal protection and establishment criteria when these claims arise.[18] The mere possibility of some future legislative discrimination does not itself make kosher laws presently unconstitutional.

Troubling Complexities

Disagreements over what food is kosher and the state's reliance on religious leaders for enforcement complicate constitutional analysis of kosher laws and make their defense much more difficult. Both factors influenced the New

---

halal have been to get some manufacturers to observe its standards and provide appropriate labeling, not to get state governments to set up regimes of enforcement.

[16] 512 U.S. 687, 702–5 (opinion of the Court), 716–17 (concurring opinion of O'Connor, J.).

[17] Id. at 725–27 (concurring opinion of Kennedy, J.), 745–48 (dissenting opinion of Scalia, J.).

[18] They can then extend the legislatively granted benefit to the similar group or hold the original benefit invalid.

Jersey Supreme Court,[19] the Fourth Circuit Court of Appeals,[20] and the Second Circuit Court of Appeals[21] to hold kosher enforcement laws invalid. Using the *Lemon* test, the New Jersey court determined that the state's regulations unduly entangled the government with religion and also had a principal or primary effect of advancing religion.[22] The court emphasized disagreement about the interpretation of laws of kashrut within Orthodox Judaism and between it and other branches of Judaism. Even if such disagreements may occur infrequently, when they do, the state will be "seeking to impose and enforce its own interpretation of Orthodox Jewish doctrine."[23]

For the court, the religious qualifications of enforcement officials confirmed that "the regulations themselves have a principally religious meaning."[24] The chief of the Bureau of Enforcement was an Orthodox rabbi, and an Advisory Committee, which consisted of nine Orthodox rabbis and one Conservative rabbi, "was constituted as it was precisely because rabbis have the expertise, education, training, and religious authority to interpret, apply, and enforce the regulations."[25]

In a 1995 decision, three Fourth Circuit judges unanimously held Baltimore's ordinance enforcing kosher laws to be unconstitutional.[26] Two judges adopted different theories of unconstitutionality and the third judge embraced both. Judge Lay emphasized that the ordinance, by requiring that the Bureau of Kosher Meat and Food Control consist of three Orthodox Rabbis and three laymen chosen from a list supplied by two Orthodox associations, impermissibly employed religious officials to exercise secular power, unac-

[19] *Ran-Dav's*, note 13 supra.

[20] *Barghout*, note 1 supra.

[21] *Commack*, note 10 supra.

[22] It said, "Our primary ground for [holding the regulations invalid] is that [they] impose substantive religious standards for the kosher-products industry and authorize civil enforcement of these religious standards with the assistance of clergy, directly and substantially entangling government in religious matters." *Ran-Dav's*, note 13 supra, at 145–46, 608 A.2d at 1355. The regulations could not be justified, as the dissent proposed, as an accommodation to religion, because they responded to no burden on religious exercise.

[23] Id. at 162–63, 608 A.2d at 1364. The dissenters urged that all branches of Judaism recognize Orthodox Judaism as setting the standards for what is kosher. "[T]o the extent the New Jersey regulations refer to commercially-recognized and sufficiently definite standards, they are facially valid" and do not unacceptably entangle the state in "monitoring religious practices." Id. at 185, 608 A.2d at 1375. The regulations focused mainly on display, identification, and verification requirements, and neither the record nor secondary sources "establish that those disputes (over *kosher* food preparation) are so pervasive and substantial as to engender a dispute over religious doctrine in the routine enforcement actions contemplated by the regulations." Id. at 182, 608 A.2d at 1373–74.

[24] Id. at 158, 608 A.2d at 1361.

[25] Id. at 157, 608 A.2d at 1361. The dissent regarded the composition of the State Kosher Advisory Committee as irrelevant, because the committee was not required by the regulations.

[26] *Barghout*, note 1 supra.

ceptably entangling religion and government.[27] He also concluded that the ordinance, separate from general provisions on fraud, had created an impermissible symbolic union of church and state.[28]

Judge Luttig, in a concurring opinion, wrote that the ordinance, by defining kosher according to "orthodox Hebrew religious" standards, "has unquestionably expressed an impermissible intrafaith denominational preference for Orthodox Judaism."[29]

Reviewing the New York law, the Second Circuit later held that it was invalid because it involved the state in resolving religious questions, favored Orthodox views of kosher standards over Conservative ones, and included persons chosen as Orthodox rabbis in its enforcement activities (as members of an advisory board).[30]

These cases are complex. When people challenge an entire scheme of regulation, judges should assess both the presence of clerical enforcement officials and the importance of disputes over kosher rules, including the relevance of a possible sincerity defense.

RABBINICAL INVOLVEMENT

When the crucial state officials are rabbis, and particularly when the law requires that they be so, the state is dangerously entangled with religion. This is partly because administrative judgments are likely to be made directly on the basis of the rabbis' own religious understandings, and also because the appearance that judgments are made on this basis matters. It is partly because the state employs religious leaders, as such, to make governmental determinations.

Because a large aspect of practical compliance with kosher requirements involves submitting to rabbinical supervision, clerics are inextricably involved. Just as secular officials can identify whether someone who asserts the priest-penitent privilege has been ordained, secular officials may determine whether rabbinical supervision has occurred. However, when rabbis as rab-

---

[27] For him, what the ordinance required was closely similar to the Massachusetts law, struck down in *Larkin v. Grendel's Den, Inc.*, 459 U.S. 116 (1982), which permitted churches to veto the issuance of liquor licenses within five hundred feet of their buildings. According to Judge Lay, the ordinance could not have been cured by giving secular officials the power to determine kosher violations, because such officials may not decide matters of religious significance. *Barghout*, note 1 supra, at 1344.

[28] Id. at 1345.

[29] Judge Lay disagreed, reasoning that "all of the various sects of the Jewish faith agree that kosher standards are determined by reference to Orthodox Jewish law." Id. at 1341 n. 9. "The mere fact that various sects have different interpretations does not create an intra-faith dispute as to the basic meaning of what is and what is not kosher."

[30] *Commack*, note 10 supra, at 427–30.

bis are the state officials who directly determine exactly what kosher rules apply or whether they have been observed (or who assess whether adequate rabbinical supervision has taken place), the situation is different. Such enforcement signals that laypersons may be incapable of making the civil legal judgment. If laypersons are incapable of deciding whether kosher requirements have been observed or whether adequate rabbinical supervision has occurred, the determinations themselves look fundamentally religious, and therefore outside the proper domain of state authority.

DISAGREEMENTS ABOUT KOSHER STANDARDS

The crucial questions about disagreements are more complicated. What matters are their frequency and significance, their correlation with distinct groups, and the state's response to them. Many violations of kosher laws are clearly agreed upon, but some issues, such as the status of sturgeon and pheasants, are disputed. Any statute (or regulation) that refers explicitly to Orthodox understanding aligns the state with Orthodox positions against competing non-Orthodox views. I shall initially assume that a state carries out such language in its literal sense, treating as nonkosher products that most Orthodox Jews generally believe are not kosher but which most Conservatives accept as kosher, such as sturgeon.

If the state takes a position on such questions, does it not make an essentially religious judgment? One way to avoid this conclusion would be to say that the state is relying on consumer understanding of what counts as kosher. But if Conservatives have a different understanding of whether certain things really are kosher than do the Orthodox,[31] the state's adoption of Orthodox standards is one-sided and, depending on the number of Conservatives who observe kosher standards, might be impossible to justify in existing consumer assumptions.[32]

[31] If Conservatives were merely less observant in some respects than Orthodox but accepted Orthodox standards for what counts as kosher, using Orthodox standards of what is kosher would fit broad consumer understanding.

[32] There is a more complicated argument for such a grounding. Suppose Conservative Jews broadly conceive some independent standards of kosher but recognize, as consumers, that the civil laws are keyed to Orthodox positions. Thus, the state might claim that its standards do fit consumer understanding, and its choice of Orthodox approaches does not represent an intrinsically religious judgment. The flaw with this argument is its circularity. Consumer understanding (I am assuming) is here based on what the state has chosen to enforce in the past, not some independent understanding of what constitutes kosher observance. The state's initial choice to enforce Orthodox views of kosher laws is not rendered nonreligious simply because non-Orthodox consumers learn what the state is doing and have come to take it for granted.

We can imagine a response that when a particular kosher law was adopted, the Orthodox view was dominant, and the basis for consumer understanding of state labeling was set before Conservatives

The state's enforcement of Orthodox views does not present the most stark kind of conflict. Conservatives do not find food that meets Orthodox standards unacceptable to eat. The problem is that Conservatives may want to use a broader range of products than the Orthodox find acceptable; but the state gives them no help in drawing their line between kosher and nonkosher when it differs from that of the Orthodox. The state, in effect, gives Orthodox Jews assistance it declines to offer Conservatives, who are prohibited "from using the *kosher* label in accordance with their religious beliefs."[33]

The intensity of comparative disadvantage for Conservatives who disagree with Orthodox standards depends on three factors, two of which at least civil courts may determine. The first factor involves the relevant standards of Conservatives. The disadvantage arises when Conservatives, accepting some products Orthodox regard as nonkosher, but rejecting other related products, do not receive the help the state gives the Orthodox. The second factor is the practicality of giving similar aid to Conservatives. Are Conservative standards sufficiently stable for a regime of enforcement? A third factor is more amorphous. How do Conservatives regard themselves in respect to kashrut? If they see themselves as having their own relatively stable standards of what products are kosher, state enforcement only of Orthodox standards is unfair. If, instead, they see themselves either as outright innovators *or* as followers of Orthodox practice, with minor deviations, they may not perceive kosher enforcement of Orthodox standards as advancing Orthodoxy. Because judges could assess this third factor only by appraising the variant understandings among Conservative Jews who observe kosher standards, an inquiry that hovers uncomfortably close to making forbidden judgments about which religious doctrines and practices are true to a tradition, this factor should play little, if any, role in constitutional evaluation.

One technique for understanding whether a religion is impermissibly advanced is to ask if it is endorsed by the state. No one can reasonably take kosher laws as endorsing Judaism over Christianity. The serious question is whether the state endorses Orthodox Judaism over Conservative Judaism.

---

were such a large group. If the factual conditions for this response could be met, the response should nevertheless fail. The state should not be able to enforce the practices of one group indefinitely because the group was dominant when enforcement began. However, since the law could enforce accurate labeling that indicates kosher compliance by Conservative as well as Orthodox standards, it is arguable that the state is justified in continuing existing enforcement practices until Conservatives press for parallel enforcement of their own standards.

[33] *Commack*, note 10 supra, at 430. Reform Jews might complain that kosher laws accord recognition and prestige to Orthodox Judaism in comparison with their branch, but since they accept no dietary requirements, any disadvantage they suffer is too slight and oblique to matter constitutionally.

Justice O'Connor, the main proponent of endorsement analysis, has opted, as we have seen, for a test that relies on a reasonable observer with no specific religious affiliation. Most non-Jews are substantially ignorant about kosher enforcement, but study might lead a reasonable observer to consider the effect on Conservative Jews and to wonder[34] how most of them regard those laws. If Conservatives reasonably feel that kosher laws represent a public statement that the authentic Judaism is Orthodox Judaism, then, especially if the Orthodox share this opinion, the "observer" should reach the same conclusion. When the issue is the possible endorsement of one minority group over another, the reasonable reactions of members of those groups should be of overarching significance, although a court may find it hard to achieve resolution if reactions are substantially divided.

For constitutional review of kosher regulations, the incidence of disputes may matter. If I have been right that a basic scheme of enforcement is constitutional, marginal worries in rare cases should not alter that judgment. On the other hand, if many instances of arguable violations of kosher requirements concern substantive disputes between Orthodox and Conservatives, a major component of enforcement efforts would involve taking sides between groups, each of which has a substantial number of adherents to the competing views about kosher practice. This defect would render the scheme as a whole unconstitutional.[35]

My conclusions about laws that enforce Orthodox standards to the exclusion of Conservative ones involve the assumption that it is possible to enforce both Orthodox and Conservative standards when these differ. One method of doing this is for the state to employ the option left open by the three courts

[34] As I have.

[35] Just how should judges estimate the relevant percentages of disputes about the content of kosher requirements? The crucial disagreements are over what food *is* kosher, when enforcement of Orthodox standards leaves Conservatives without help in enforcing their own variant standards. Judges might estimate the percentage of these disagreements, relative to the overall use of kosher symbols. They might, instead, assess instances of such disputed standards as a percentage of cases in which many people believe that manufacturers or sellers have claimed to conform to kosher requirements, but have failed to do so. Finally, judges might see how often disputes over standards arise in enforcement.

All these approaches may be relevant, but the first seems the most important. The "actual enforcement" approach is simplest; but enforcement officials may steer away from disputed standards. A scheme that puts the state in the business of resolving debated matters is not rendered innocuous by officials who sidestep controversial applications. Further, enforcement of a law embodying Orthodox standards might not reveal most disputes that exist because other Jews accept different standards. For both these reasons, a court should not stop at actual enforcement or beliefs about fraudulent claims, but also inquire how far disputes over standards figure in patterns of kosher observance.

that have invalidated schemes of kosher regulation—state prosecution for false claims of private approval. Private enforcement agencies can hold themselves out as applying particular standards of judgment; consumers can know whether approval is according to Orthodox or Conservative standards. Another method would be for the state to require labeling that indicates whether food is kosher under stricter Orthodox standards or more lenient Conservative ones. Finally, state enforcement officials might decide to accept claims that food is kosher when those claims have substantial Conservative support, even if the state statute is cast in terms of Orthodox requirements.[36]

When we think about constitutionality, we need to distinguish between a general challenge to the law and a challenge to the law as it applies to a seller who has self-consciously conformed to Conservative standards of kosher while violating Orthodox standards. The case-specific challenge should definitely succeed. It is unconstitutional for the state to convict those who follow widespread Conservative understandings of kosher observance. As Marc Stern has written, "[T]he State could not invoke the kosher food laws against someone who, in good faith reliance on the decision of the Conservative rabbinate, sold swordfish or gelatin as kosher."[37]

Whether a general challenge should succeed, as it did in the New Jersey Supreme Court, the Fourth Circuit, and the Second Circuit is a closer question. But I believe that any scheme that unambiguously involves enforcement of Orthodox requirements to the exclusion of Conservative ones should fail, since a legislature can accomplish its legitimate objectives without that differentiation.

Patterns of actual enforcement could focus less on Orthodox requirements than one might gather from the statutory language. Despite the statutory language, the chief enforcement official in New York, the state with by far the most extensive history of enforcement,[38] once suggested that distinctive Orthodox standards do not play a crucial role in the statute's application. Ac-

---

[36] It might be argued that a state's failure to treat Orthodox and Conservative standards similarly does not constitute present discrimination. The position of observant Conservatives who do not receive enforcement of their distinctive standards might be seen as like that of followers of Islam. The law does not monitor claims about Muslim dietary standards, and it could do so, but Muslims have not pressed for such help. If Conservatives have not made a serious effort to get similar assistance, perhaps no one should not be heard to complain that the present law unfairly assists Orthodoxy. The difficulty with this position is that the law explicitly, and I assume unnecessarily, enforces only Orthodox requirements of kashrut; the preference for Orthodox Judaism over Conservativism is much more direct than any preference of Judaism over Islam.

[37] Marc D. Stern, "Kosher Food and the Law," 39 *Judaism* 390, 397–98 (1990). The plaintiff in *Commack*, note 10 supra, cited four times for violations in how it processed meat, had been relying on the judgment of a Conservative rabbi.

[38] "Around the Island," note 7 supra. See also Masoudi, note 2 supra, at 671–72.

cording to a newspaper story, he "acknowledges that state law cites 'Orthodox' standards but said that has never been a consideration in enforcement."[39]

When one evaluates possible nonenforcement against those who conform with Conservative standards, it helps to distinguish a "sincerity defense" from what we may call equal treatment. The theory of a "sincerity defense" would be that a seller has failed to adhere to statutory standards, but is not guilty of fraud because he believed he was complying, believed that food of the character he sold was kosher.[40] A defendant would be immunized from liability if he sincerely thought his food was kosher and believed that his position would receive fair support among rabbis. Such a defense would not eliminate worries about uneven enforcement.

One difficulty is that officials may initially resolve whether basic requirements have been met. If they decide S is selling kosher food, he will not need to show his sincerity. If they decide S's food is not kosher, S is forced to persuade someone that he is sincere. Further, the group whose position on kosher is opposed to S receives endorsement of its view of kosher. A second, related, difficulty is that S's efforts to convince someone he is not lying may entail an expensive process, with an uncertain end. A third difficulty concerns subsequent occasions. Perhaps S must accept the state's determination once it has been rendered. These three difficulties show why a sincerity defense does not remove the constitutional problems if state determinations of what counts as kosher follow Orthodox requirements.

An "equal treatment" approach is more promising. Under this approach, all claims of kosher that have significant rabbinical support would be treated as valid. It is worth pausing to emphasize that this is the approach enforcement agencies *must take* to conflicting claims among Orthodox rabbis given a statute like the one that New York used to have.[41]

---

[39] "Around the Island," note 7 supra. However, the court in *Commack* took a decidedly different view. Note 10 supra, at 421, 427–28.

[40] In *Ran-Dav's*, the New Jersey case, the majority assumed that a sincere belief that food was kosher was not a defense, note 13 supra, at 153, 608 A.2d at 1359–60, if the state determined that food was not kosher. It relied on an apparent shift in the position of the attorney general about the possibility of such a defense. The dissenters wrote as if good-faith reliance on the representations of suppliers would be a defense. Id. at 169–70, 608 A.2d at 1367. The Fourth Circuit in *Barghout* apparently accepted the constructions of the Maryland Court of Appeals that persons were not guilty under the Baltimore ordinance "who sincerely believe their food products are kosher." Note 1 supra, at 1344. Marc Stern describes a number of cases in which courts have considered it important that statutes did not apply to those with a belief that their products were kosher . Stern note 37 supra, at 391–96.

[41] Disagreement among Orthodox Jews about kosher requirements is a fact of life. Some groups are stricter than others, and no centralized authority exists to resolve disagreements. When Orthodox

The "equal treatment" approach would extend state neutrality to disagreements that fall mainly along Orthodox-Conservative lines. Such equal
treatment would eliminate any problem of preference, except for two possible wrinkles. The first wrinkle concerns the statutory language itself. Whatever officials actually do, the reference to Orthodox requirements may seem
to endorse and advance Orthodox Judaism. If enforcement is evenhanded,
the impact of the bare statutory language may be minimal, but it does not
disappear.[42]

The second wrinkle is still more troublesome. For merchants, what matters
is not only outcomes at the end of the day, but also the process of enforcement.
Someone who is being investigated not only bears expense and inconvenience,
he may lose the confidence of customers. If many investigations are aimed
against those who follow Conservative standards but fail to conform to Orthodox ones, the law in practice can effectively discriminate against Conservatives, even if courts and high enforcement officials ultimately treat differing
Orthodox and Conservative standards as equally authoritative.

Conclusion about Kosher Laws

The best approach to kosher rules involves state enforcement against fraud
involving claimed approvals of private organizations and individual rabbis
for all levels at which that is feasible. What I have called the basic scheme
of direct state enforcement should also be viewed as constitutionally permissible, if the necessary conditions for that scheme exist. However, if a significant number of arguable violations of kosher rules involve disagreements
about standards between Orthodox and Conservative Jews, and the law embodies Orthodox standards, leaving Conservatives without similar protection, direct state enforcement should be regarded as unconstitutional. Probably such unequal treatment should be regarded as a denominational
preference; in any event, it unjustifiably promotes Orthodox Judaism at the
expanse of Conservatism. Unconstitutionality is more straightforward when
clergy have heavy direct involvement in state kosher enforcement, impermissibly entangling civil government with religious authority.

Jews differ about kosher requirements, states cannot declare one position to be valid to the exclusion
of another.

[42] A court conceivably might take the step of striking a phrase like "Orthodox requirements" from
a statute or regulations.

Civil Involvement in Granting of the Get

Traditional Jewish law regarding divorce can be seriously unfair to wives, and is decidedly out of step with modern notions of equality. Should civil judges intervene to combat unfairness and to promote equality between divorcing spouses? Is that intrusion on the religious life of its citizens unconstitutional?

Under Jewish law (*halachah*), a marriage may be dissolved by the husband's signing and delivering to his wife a bill of divorce, or get.[43] A typical get written in Aramaic says: "I release and set aside, you, my wife, in order that you may have authority over yourself to marry any man you desire. . . . You are permitted to every man. . . . This shall be for you a bill of dismissal, a letter of release, a *get* of freedom. . . ."[44] Because the procedures for granting a get are complicated, the aid of a rabbinical court, or *beth din*, is usually needed. Typically, the get is invalid if the husband signs under duress.

The choice whether to divorce is not exclusively a husband's.[45] In some circumstances, wives have a right to be divorced. And the wife's assent is now necessary for a divorce. The involvement of the *beth din* has allowed substantial pressure to be put on husbands.[46] Thus, the traditional Jewish law of divorce gives wives some protection, but a wife is still much more vulnerable than a husband, mainly because a failure to divorce carries uneven consequences.

---

[43] See Irving A. Breitowitz, *Between Civil Law and Religious Law*, 5–39 (Westport, Conn.: Greenwood Press, 1993); Elliot Dorf and Arthur Rosett, *A Living Tree* 512–65 (Albany State University of New York Press, 1988). The book by Professor Breitowitz is a comprehensive and careful study of the get problem; it treats in detail not only civil cases but also the complex issues of Jewish religious law. Breitowitz has also written an article, "The Plight of the *Agunah*: A Study in *Halacha*, Contract, and The First Amendment," 57 *Maryland Law Review* 312 (1992), which covers most of the same subjects in shorter compass. I here cite the relevant passages in the book.

[44] See Blu Greenberg, "Jewish Divorce Law: If We Must Part, Let's Part as Equals," *Lilith*, Summer 1977, at 26, 27.

[45] Breitowitz, note 43 supra, at 10–11, explains that the major shift toward equality was under Rabbi Gershon in the tenth century. See also Blu Greenberg, *On Women and Judaism: A View from Tradition* 125–45 (Philadelphia: Jewish Publication Society of America, 1981); Eliezer Berkovits, *Not in Heaven: The Nature and Function of Halakha* 32–45 (New York: KTAV Publishing House, 1983). See generally David Werner Amram, *The Jewish Law of Divorce in the Bible and Talmud* (New York: Herman, 1968); Ze'ev Falk, *Divorce Action by the Wife in the Middle Ages* (Jerusalem: Hebrew University, 1973).

[46] For some instances, at least, even physical compulsion has been regarded as an appropriate technique to force husbands to agree to comply with an order of a *beth din*. Moses Maimonides explained that physical compulsion is applied to force the husband to do what he truly desires—to comply with Jewish law. See Breitowitz, note 43 supra, at 34–35.

Since Jewish law does not recognize civil divorce, one spouse's refusal to participate in a religious divorce prevents the other from marrying within the Orthodox and Conservative faiths. But a husband's refusal affects his wife much more severely than her refusal affects him. When a husband leaves his wife and cohabits with an unmarried woman, he violates Jewish law against polygamy; but children of the new union do not have a reduced status. Once he divorces under Jewish law, he may marry that partner. A wife who is divorced under civil law but has not received a get is considered an *agunah*, or chained (anchored) woman. If she cohabits with a man, they are guilty of the very serious offense of adultery; she may not marry that man when she later receives a get. Children born of that union are deemed *mamzerim*, a stigma indicating that they were born within an incestuous or adulterous relationship. These children may not marry other Jews, except for converts and other *mamzerim*. Thus, the wife who has not received a get must either refrain from sexual involvement or commit a grave violation of Jewish law that carries a stigma for herself and any new children.

These realities create a serious problem when a husband chooses not to grant a get to his wife or uses his power to withhold a get as a bargaining chip in negotiations over property and child custody. Estimates vary wildly, but one is that fifteen thousand Orthodox and Conservative Jewish women are *agunot* in New York state;[47] the social problem is substantial where the Orthodox and Conservative Jewish communities are large. The husband's power to restrict the wife's freedom is especially troubling when the wife is a victim of physical abuse; and some observers regard inequities that are embodied in get practice as symptomatic of the "exclusion of women from power and authority in traditional Judaism."[48]

In various ways, civil judges and legislators have tried to induce husbands to give *gittin* to their Orthodox and Conservative wives. Except for two possible difficulties, these inducements are appropriate and beneficial. One potential difficulty, about which I will say little, is that civil force might render a get invalid as a product of duress, thus defeating the purpose of intervention. The difficulty we shall examine is that civil law may trespass on religious liberty and involve the state unacceptably in religious matters. We will consider in turn contractual enforcement, statutory protection, and judicial doctrines of equity and tort.

[47] See id., at 2. Part of the disagreement is over who exactly qualifies as an *agunah*. Perhaps the crucial number is women who seriously want a get and do not receive one in due course.

[48] Judith Plaskow, "Jewish Feminism: The Year of the Agunah," *Tikkun*, September–October 1993, at 52.

The Nature of a Get

Is granting a get a secular or religious matter? No doubt, a system of law parallel to the law of the state could conceivably be cultural and not religious. For some individuals, the get may be cultural in this way. However, the great majority of Jews who regard divorce requirements as important understand them as related to their religious practice and belief.[49] As one writer proposes, the get procedure is religious, according to a test that asks whether it has "any rational justification other than the significance that some religion puts on it."[50]

This conclusion about the significance of the get does not settle how husbands regard the act of granting or withholding one. Do husbands see their behavior as religious, in the sense of being governed by spiritual or ecclesiastical considerations, or in some other sense? When Jewish law requires a husband to grant a get, many husbands will feel obligated to comply, especially if a *beth din* tells them that is their duty. A husband's sense of obligation connects to his religious identity and practice. But, for our purposes, a sense of religious obligation to grant a get is not very important. The state will intervene only to encourage, not discourage, the granting of a get; thus, the critical question about the feelings of husbands concerns those who refuse to give their wives religious divorces.

If a husband heading for civil divorce felt a religious obligation not to submit the possibility of divorce to a *beth din* or not to give a get after a *beth din* had instructed him to do so, then the state's interference would intrude on his religious conscience. One cannot rule out this possibility. A man who

---

[49] For Orthodox and Conservatives, the Jewish law of divorce, like kashrut, has cultural aspects, but these are intertwined with religion. Further, the tribunal that typically assists the divorce is made up of rabbis or includes a rabbi; this gives it at least a quasi-religious status.

[50] Lawrence C. Marshall, "The Religion Clauses and Compelled Religious Divorces: A Study in Marital and Constitutional Separations," 80 *Northwestern University Law Review* 204, 219 (1985). Someone might resist the conclusion that delivery of the get concerns religious practice in the following way. "Jewish law was developed to regulate the whole life of Jewish communities. Although all of the law was believed to derive from divine revelation, one could perceive a rough division of religious from secular subjects. Marriage and divorce were essentially secular, rabbis having authority to marry and divorce, just as clerics have authority in common-law countries to perform marriages with civil validity. Within Jewish law, marriage and divorce are not essentially religious; and divorce remains a secular concern."

This neat argument is confused. What might be an appropriate conceptual division within a society governed by Jewish law is not a defensible perspective in societies, like American society, whose separate secular law governs the marriages and divorces of all people. There, Jewish law has, by itself, no civil consequences. A wife who does not receive a get is harmed only because she and others have a religious and cultural sense that the get is important. For them, the get's significance is largely religious.

was once an Orthodox Jew and who has become an evangelical Christian might regard any participation that recognizes the authority of Orthodox Jewish practices as violative of his religious conscience. Still, the delivery of the get requires no affirmation of faith or religious ceremony. Neither cases nor other published materials, nor discussion with persons familiar with Jewish divorce practice, suggest that many husbands have this kind of religious objection to the involvement of a *beth din* or to granting a get.[51]

Perhaps inquiring about a sense of religious obligation puts the question too narrowly. A husband lacking such a sense might nevertheless believe that his refusal is part of the practice of his religion (or nonreligion) tied to his identity. That identity might be as a Reform Jew, a Christian, or an atheist. Such a husband could have a serious religious problem with submitting to a *beth din* even though he does not feel that refusal to give a get is a religious obligation.[52]

In summary, the acts of granting and receiving a get are not distinctively religious acts, like prayer and communal worship. Most husbands who withhold *gittin* do so for nonreligious reasons. However, the act of granting a get has significance within a distinctively religious system of law (as that system exists in the United States) *and* the act removes what is primarily a perceived religious impediment to remarriage and bearing children. This fundamental religious significance is alone enough to make state intrusion a matter of concern under the religion clauses, and the concern increases if the husband has a significant religious objection.

In examining various legal bases for civil involvement in get practice, we will move from contractual bases, the easiest grounds to defend, to statutory provisions, and then to common-law bases other than contract.

Contractual Enforcement

Wives sometimes rely on premarital agreements by husbands to provide *gittin* should their marriage end in civil divorce, or on agreements reached during separation or civil divorce proceedings. I shall concentrate on agreements

---

[51] One atypical husband claimed that giving a get would compromise his present religious beliefs, but his offer to deliver the get if his wife invested twenty-five thousand dollars in an irrevocable trust gave the court a solid basis not to believe him. *Burns v. Burns*, 223 N.J. Super. 219, 538 A.2d 438 (1987).

[52] Paul Finkelman has suggested that this attitude will most commonly arise when a husband has shifted away from Orthodoxy or Conservatism during his years of marriage or when a wife has shifted toward such traditional practice. See Finkelman, "A Bad Marriage: Jewish Divorce and the First Amendment," 2 *Cardozo Women's Law Journal* 131, 146–52 (1995). Finkelman says of the husband in *In re Goldman*, 554 N.E. 2d 1016 (Ill. App. Ct. 1990), "He had not been married in an Orthodox ceremony and he truly despised Orthodox rituals and beliefs." Id. at 148.

made at the time of the marriage; if these are appropriately enforceable, then obviously so also are agreements made when a couple has decided to separate or divorce. "Agreements" made at the time of marriage differ in specificity and apparent force, and in the degree to which the parties are aware of them.

Highly Specific Agreements

At one end of the spectrum lie agreements like that drafted in the 1970s by a commission of the Rabbinical Council of America (the major Orthodox rabbinical group) and later withdrawn. Under a prenuptial agreement that was a separate civil agreement, a husband and wife agreed to give and receive a get within thirty days of civil divorce, and they agreed that an Orthodox *beth din* would arbitrate any disputes about whether they had fully performed.[53] Is there any objection to civil enforcement of such an agreement?

In recognizing the authority of a *beth din*, a court ordinarily need not resolve any disputed questions of Jewish law. Given that Orthodox wives will not otherwise feel free to marry, and will not be regarded as divorced by the Orthodox men they would want to marry, the husband's performance of his agreement bears on the practical value of his wife's civil right to remarry after a civil divorce. That constitutes a sufficient secular interest for the state to enforce the agreement, and establishes that enforcement does not promote religion inappropriately. So long as enforcement is straightforward, a court need not go beyond "neutral principles of law," of the sort the Supreme Court has said courts may use to resolve disputes about church governance.

Yet a question about ordering specific performance remains. The state should not compel intrinsically religious acts, even if people have agreed to perform them. Imagine that H plans to sue G for hitting him; but their minister persuades H to forgo the suit if G will confess his wrong to the entire congregation. G and H sign an agreement to that effect. A court would not order G to confess publicly in a worship service, though it would deny him the benefits of the agreement if he does not confess.

Ordering specific performance to submit to a *beth din* is not beyond the pale in this respect. Appearing before a *beth din* and even granting a get are

---

[53] See Debbie Eis Sreter, "Nothing to Lose but Their Chains: A Survey of the *Aguna* Problem in American Law," 28 *Journal of Family Law* 703, 722–24 (1989–90). The sanction for nonperformance was daily liquidated damages, a consequence intended to fall short of duress that would make performance invalid. Since most Orthodox couples have not signed such explicit civil agreements, the potential enforcement of such agreements does not eliminate the *agunah* problem for Orthodox wives.

not intrinsically religious for most recalcitrant husbands. Civil courts may compel those acts, as they order people to donate money to churches if they have made legal agreements to do so, without violating constitutional principle.[54] When spouses have agreed to be bound by the decision of a *beth din*, civil courts should also be ready to enforce what the *beth din* directs, if that is necessary.

Shifts in a husband's religious beliefs could raise a greater concern with specific performance. Suppose he (sincerely) says, "My religious views have altered since my marriage agreement; participating in a Jewish divorce would *now* offend my religious conscience." Whether a court should still order him to appear before a *beth din* or grant a get is debatable. Nevertheless, since the husband need not affirm beliefs or participate in typical religious acts to deliver a get, a court appropriately would enforce a clear civil contract, making the husband do what his earlier convictions led him to agree to do.

Vague, General Understandings

At the other end of the spectrum of specificity of agreements is the general *ketubah* that is a part of all Orthodox and Conservative wedding ceremonies that lack a more complicated undertaking. This is usually written and read in Aramaic.

Spouses who utter a general *ketubah* at their marriage should not ordinarily be understood to have agreed to provide a religious divorce or submit to a *beth din*. This is especially true when a couple cannot reasonably be supposed to be aware of that potential significance. Considering a general *ketubah* under which the husband agreed to fulfill obligations to cherish and support his wife under the "laws of Moses and Israel," the Court of Appeals for Arizona ruled that "such a vague provision has no specific terms describing a mutual understanding that husband would secure a Jewish divorce."[55]

Even if a court concluded that the husband and wife agreed to civil law consequences, what exactly the husband must do remains a question of the predominantly religious Jewish law. Although the usual requisites of delivering a get are straightforward, a civil court may sometimes have trouble

---

Some of the problems under Jewish law with the enforcement of agreements are explained in Breitowitz, note 43 supra, at 77–86, 93–96.

[54] See, e.g., *Waxstein v. Waxstein*, 394 N.Y.S. 2d 253 (App. Div. 2d Dept. 1977) (wife had already performed part of her agreement).

[55] *Victor v. Victor*, 866 P.2d 899, 902 (Ariz. App. Div. 1 1993). It continued, "If this court were to rule on whether the ketubah, given its indefinite language, includes an unwritten mandate that a husband under these circumstances is required to grant his wife a get, we would be overstepping our authority and assuming the role of a religious court."

deciding if a husband has fulfilled all his obligations under Jewish law. This potential difficulty for civil courts strengthens the conclusion that general language in a *ketubah*, like that in the Arizona case, should not be construed as a civilly enforceable agreement by the husband to deliver a get.

Intermediate Specificity

The genuinely debatable cases arise when the *ketubah* is much more concrete, but lacks both the detail and the explicit reliance on civil law found in the agreement drafted by the commission of the Rabbinical Council of America. Many Conservative marriages are performed with *ketubahs* that fit this description.[56] The New York Court of Appeals considered one of them in *Avitzur v. Avitzur*.[57] At their marriage, the Avitzurs signed a Hebrew/Aramaic *ketubah*, declaring their "desire to . . . live in accordance with the Jewish law of marriage throughout [their] lifetime" and further agreeing "to recognize the *beth din* of the Rabbinical Assembly and the Jewish Theological Seminary of America" (a Conservative seminary) or its representatives "as having authority to counsel us in the light of Jewish tradition . . . and to summon either party at the request of the other, in order to enable the party so requesting to live in accordance with the standards of the Jewish marriage throughout his or her lifetime. We authorize the *beth din* to impose such terms of compensation as it may see fit for failure to respond to its summons or carry out its design."[58]

A majority of the Court of Appeals treated the agreement like other agreements to submit disputes to a nonjudicial forum: the case could be decided by neutral principles, "without reference to any religious principle." The three dissenters took a sharply different view, regarding the attempt to obtain what they regarded as a religious divorce as "a matter well beyond the authority of any civil court."[59] They argued that a definition of the wife's rights under the *ketubah* required "an examination into the principles and practice of the Jewish religion." Although the document reads as if the sum-

---

[56] See Greenberg, note 44 supra, at 135–36, discussing the Lieberman *ketubah*.

[57] 58 N.Y. 2d 108, 446 N.E.2d 136, 459 N.Y.S. 2d 572 (1983). The case and its implications are discussed illuminatingly in Breitowitz, supra note 43, at 361–70, and Finkelman, note 52 supra, at 156–58. Lawrence M. Warmflash, "The New York Approach to Enforcing Religious Marriage Contracts: From Avitzur to the *Get* Statute," 50 *Brooklyn Law Review* 229, 231 (1984), supports the approach of that case but not more extensive state involvements to encourage recalcitrant husbands.

[58] 58 N.Y.2d at 112, 446 N.E. 2d at 137, 459 N.Y.S. 2d at 574.

[59] 58 N.Y.2d at 121, 446 N.E.2d at 142. 459 N.Y.S. 2d at 578.

mons to appear must come from the *beth din*, the wife argued for a construction that the husband must appear upon her summons.[60]

The most disturbing point in the dissent is that civil courts may have to interpret Jewish law even to determine whether Mr. Avitzur must appear before a *beth din*. The appropriate view is that civil judges can enforce a clear obligation to appear, even if they must make some reference to religious law.[61] However, when a husband's duty to appear is debatable, civil courts face a genuine dilemma. A civil court might declare that, since it should not resolve controversial issues of religious procedure, it should not enforce obligations that demand resolution of such matters. Alternatively, the court might apply a general, neutral principle of law that favors initial submission to an "arbitrator" when the arbitrator's jurisdiction is disputed, leaving it to the arbitrator initially to resolve the jurisdictional issue in light of the body of law that applies. Probably the latter course makes more sense here. A civil court could order a husband to submit to *beth din* in some conditional way, leaving it to the *beth din* to determine whether he must submit to full proceedings regarding his divorce.

Statutory Protection

Thus far, only New York has passed legislation focused on the get. Given the large number of Orthodox and Conservative Jews that live within the state, the statutes have a practical importance that far exceeds New York's status as one among fifty states. The statutory provisions also pose sharply some issues about civil law and religious law that are closely similar to those generated by judicial reliance on equity and tort doctrines, a reliance that may occur in any state.

New York has adopted two measures to induce husbands to grant *gittin* to their wives.[62] A 1983 statute provides that if a cleric solemnized the marriage, a person seeking divorce must allege that he or she has taken or will take "all steps solely within his or her power to remove any barrier to the

---

[60] The husband, in turn, claimed that he had no obligation to appear because his earlier request for a convocation of such a body was refused. The dissenters concluded, partly from the witnesses the wife planned to offer at trial, that a court would need to delve into Jewish law to some degree to decide whether the husband would actually have to appear before the *beth din*.

[61] Such a determination resembles civil courts determining which religious tribunals have authority (within religious legal systems) to make decisions, something they must do to give effect to decisions of authoritative religious tribunals. (See volume 1, chapter 16.)

[62] The laws can require behavior of a wife as well as a husband; but since wives refusing to receive *gittin* have generated little difficulty, the main force of both laws is to motivate husbands and to offset their imbalance of power.

defendant's remarriage" following the divorce.[63] If the cleric who married the couple certifies that the plaintiff has not taken all steps to remove barriers, the court may not enter a final divorce. In 1992, New York, to cover gaps left by the original statute, amended its equitable distribution law to provide that courts "shall, where appropriate" take into account barriers to remarriage when they decide on the distribution of marital property and the amount and duration of maintenance.[64]

New York's Precondition for Acquiring a Civil Divorce

The 1983 law does not directly force anyone to do anything. By making the granting of a get a condition of receiving a civil divorce, it ingeniously avoids the worry that a get obtained under duress may be invalid under Jewish law. But the device of imposing a condition for the receipt of a benefit does not obviate constitutional problems. The state cannot ordinarily condition a benefit as important as a divorce on someone's behaving in a manner that the state could not compel.[65]

The constitutional problems would be minimal if the law were essentially secular, with some applications happening to involve religious institutions. But this law is limited to religious marriages, and specific authority is given to the clerics who performed the ceremonies. Barriers to remarriage are defined as those that exist "under the principles held by the clergyman . . . who has solemnized the marriage."[66] The only barriers the statute now covers derive from Jewish law;[67] the aim of the statute was to cover the Jewish get.[68] When a statute covers religious divorce proceedings of only one religion, when it deals with marriages entered by religious ceremonies, when it assigns

---

[63] N.Y. Dom. Rel. Law § 253 (McKinney 2006). Before a court will grant a final divorce, the plaintiff must swear that he has removed all barriers. In consent divorces both parties must file statements to that effect.

[64] N.Y. Dom. Rel. Law § 236 B(5)(h), (6)(d) (McKinney 2006).

[65] The Supreme Court spoke of divorce as a "right" in *Boddie v. Connecticut*, 401 U.S. 371 (1970).

[66] N.Y. Dom. Rel. Law § 253(6) (McKinney 2006).

[67] Probably the basic language of the statute does not apply to Roman Catholics. Roman Catholics may suffer an impediment to remarriage that in some ways resembles the problem with the get, except that the impediment works equally for men and women and does not depend alone on the voluntary choice of either spouse. A request for an annulment may come from either party, and an annulment may be granted even if the other party refuses to participate. Any uncertainties about possible coverage of Roman Catholics are removed by § 253(6), N.Y. Dom. Rel. Law (McKinney 2006), which provides: "All steps within his or her power shall not be construed to include application to a marriage tribunal or other similar organization . . . of a religious denomination which has authority to annul or dissolve a marriage under the rules of such denomination."

[68] As the governor's signing message shows. See Edward S. Nadel, "New York's *Get* Laws: A Constitutional Analysis," 27 *Columbia Journal of Law and Social Problems* 55, 71 (1993).

direct authority to the marrying cleric, and when its undoubted impetus was concern about the power to refrain from religious divorce within the one religion the law covers, the law must be regarded as dealing with just that subject.

As with kosher laws, we can helpfully consider first a minimal "basic statutory scheme," and then investigate features that raise further complexities. The basic scheme here is that an Orthodox or Conservative Jewish husband receives a civil divorce only if he conveys a get to his wife.[69] Assuming that a civil court may make any necessary determinations without religious judgment, would the purpose and effects of such a law be secular or religious, and, if religious, permissibly or inappropriately so? Relatedly, does the law endorse any religion?

The vast majority of adults marry, and most of those who are divorced want to remarry and do. Children of divorce may fare better if the spouses remarry. Certainly children denominated *mamzerim* suffer restrictions among Orthodox and Conservative Jews in relation to their own future marriages. This combination of strong individual wishes to remarry and the possible welfare of children forms a sufficient secular basis for the state to want people who are civilly divorced to feel free to remarry and be so regarded by others. However, if the *barrier* to remarriage comes from people's sense of religious obligation and their wish to be accepted within a religious community, does that make a statute's purpose or effects inappropriate?

About purpose, the state can respond: "We would want to eliminate such barriers wherever they appear, especially when inequality systematically favors husbands. Our aim does not concern religion." This argument easily establishes a secular purpose.

The possibility of improper religious effects is more serious. Indisputably, the law affects whether wives and potential marriage partners feel an obligation not to marry that relates to their religious identity and practice. Undoubtedly the law has some effect on religious practice. But this effect alone does not really advance or inhibit religion.

Against the concern that the law harms these forms of Judaism by interfering with their internal legal regimes, it is at least a partial answer that most Orthodox and Conservative rabbis and members want the state to encourage recalcitrant husbands to grant religious divorces; and the law was adopted in response to urgings from the Orthodox community. The law's attention

---

[69] The law's coverage of those infrequent situations when a Jewish wife adamantly refuses to receive a get does not alter the analysis in the text.

to practices of Orthodox and Conservative Jews does not itself prefer or endorse those religions, since only they raise this divorce problem.

A more troubling question is "condemnation," which has a constitutional status similar to "endorsement." Justice O'Connor, the primary proponent of endorsement analysis, has said the government may not send "a message to nonadherents that they are outsiders, not full members of the political community."[70] Condemnation of the views of a minority sends the forbidden message even more directly than the more benign endorsement of the majority's position. Condemnation definitely can "inhibit" the religion that is its target. One issue for a get law is whether it impermissibly condemns traditional Jewish practice by sending the message that the husband's power to withhold a get, and the consequences that flow from that power, are unjust.

A get law is not an impermissible condemnation for three reasons. First, implicitly labeling one practice as unfortunate, because of undesirable secular effects, is within the range of what the government may do.[71] Second, if most Orthodox and Conservative Jews welcome the state's intervention, it is hard to conclude that the law significantly condemns their faith in some symbolic way. Third, one may view the state's involvement as compensating for power it has removed from religious tribunals. Traditionally, religious courts could put pressure on husbands they no longer have available. The situation that the state intervenes to stop—unfettered discretion of divorcing husbands to deny *gittin*—is one generated partly by the shift to divorce by civil authorities. Thus, what the law mostly condemns,[72] if it condemns anything, is the regrettable consequence of religious law in combination with a diminution of authority for religious courts.

Two considerations complicate the questions whether the get law "advances" or "inhibits" religion. First, the statute may involve a very subtle promotion of Orthodox and Conservative Judaism over Reform Judaism. Most Reform Jews reject the whole notion of separate Jewish divorces. The statute implicitly treats that procedure as important by inducing husbands to grant *gittin*. Absent state interference, the injustice of traditional get practice might generate greater discontent among Orthodox and Conservative Jews,

---

[70] *Lynch v. Donnelly*, 465 U.S. 668, 688 (1984) (concurring opinion).

[71] As I have noted in chapter 4 of volume 1, ordinary criminal laws reach some practices of some religions; effective condemnation of particular practices is an inevitable, and therefore acceptable, aspect of government regulation. The get law is pointed more directly at one (or two) religions, but that is because only they raise the problem the law covers.

[72] I say "mostly" because even if the religious tribunals had all the power they once had, there would still be some injustices to wives according to modern secular values.

especially women.[73] The government, by making a practice of Orthodox and Conservative Judaism more palatable, may indirectly support them against Reform Judaism.

Second, the law is bound to influence Orthodox and Conservative Judaism to some degree. By pushing husbands to perform their responsibilities within a system of religious law, the state may aid the religion, but the law may have a deeper effect on Orthodox and Conservative Judaism. For modern sensibilities, the plight of the *agunah* is a cause for concern, or even outrage. Were the state not to involve itself at all, the pressure for reform within the more traditional branches of Judaism might increase. If state influence successfully combats the injustice of their present practice, Orthodox and Conservative Judaism may have less pressure to change.

When one compares these subtle influences on religion to the secular interest in having civilly divorced women feel free to remarry, the religious effects of the law, rather than being "primary" or "direct and immediate,"[74] are minor enough to be regarded as what the Supreme Court has called "incidental," and are therefore acceptable.[75]

In respect to effects (and purpose), a defender of the law has another string to his bow; he may claim that if the effects are primarily religious, they represent an acceptable accommodation to the religious exercise of the wife. To be acceptable on this basis, the law must accommodate the wife's religious exercise *and* impose appropriately on the husband. Any doubts about the interference with the ordinary husband are misplaced.[76] Strong pressure on the husband is similar to coercing employers to make reasonable accommodations to the religious requirements of employees, discussed in volume 1. Since the typical husband's refusal to grant a get is not a matter of religious obligation or serious religious concern for him, the state's "encouragement" of that is within the range of what a permissible accommodation may require.

Whether the law appropriately accommodates the wife's religious exercise is more complicated. Does the law aid the wife's religious exercise, and, if

---

[73] I do not mean that many people would on this basis alone reject these more traditional forms of Judaism. But discontent with the inequities of traditional divorce practice might have an influence on people shifting to embrace Reform Judaism as a preferable alternative.

[74] See Nadel, note 68 supra, at 88.

[75] Similarly, if attention to the get represents a slight "favoring" of traditional branches of Judaism, it is far from amounting to an endorsement.

[76] One commentator has argued that the law indirectly coerces the husband, and that the Supreme Court's accommodation cases do not support coercion, or coercion of religious practices. See Nadel, note 68 supra, at 88. See also Ilene H. Barshay, "The Implications of the Constitution's Religion Clauses on New York Family Law," 40 *Howard Law Journal* 205, 234–35 (1996).The distinction between coercion and coercion of religious practices is crucial. No accommodation case supports

so, does it properly respond to some impediment to that exercise? The law helps remove a barrier that her religious sense (and that of potential husbands) imposes on her, but does this removal really increase her ability to exercise her religion? She can adhere to her religion whether she refrains from remarriage from a sense of religious obligation or undertakes marriage because she is free to do so. However, a wife without a get may be tempted to remarry, and the law that pressures her husband to grant a get transforms an attractive illegal act (under Jewish law) into one that is permitted. That shift alone might be said to assist religious exercise by eliminating a conflict of desire and obligation.

One writer has urged a more powerful argument that religious exercise is aided: "In Judaism, marriage is central to religious life. Significant religious obligations that are fulfilled within the domestic sphere devolve upon the observant Jewish woman. Because freedom to enter into a Jewish marriage is important to a Jewish woman's religious observance, it falls within the protection of the free exercise clause."[77] A court, of course, cannot decide what is really central to Jewish religious life; but it can accept a plausible claim that for many traditional Jewish women, a family is significantly part of that life.

The accommodations that are easiest to justify are those in which the state makes up for an impediment it has caused. The source of the get problem may be regarded as arising from the combination of Jewish law and the civil law of divorce.[78] The rules of Jewish law themselves may give rise to injustice (according to modern secular standards) when husbands refuse to divorce wives, but the state exacerbates the difficulties by allowing a civil divorce separate from a religious divorce and by disallowing some forms of pressure religious communities have employed against recalcitrant husbands. The get law might be seen as responding to the contribution of the civil law to the resulting injustice. More importantly, as I shall argue in chapter 17, not all accommodations need respond to state-imposed impediments. The legitimacy of accommodation, thus, does not depend on casting the state as the main source of the difficulties facing Jewish wives who are civilly, but not religiously, divorced.

---

coercion of genuinely religious acts. But some coercion of private individuals and enterprises has been regarded as acceptable.

[77] Tanina Rostain, "Permissible Accommodations of Religion: Reconsidering the New York Get Statute," 96 *Yale Law Journal* 1147, 1165–66 (1987).

[78] Breitowitz, note 43 supra, at 277. It is countered that the basic problem already exists within Jewish law, as is evidenced by the extent of identical difficulties in Israel, which lacks civil divorce. Finkelman, note 52 supra, at 134.

In summary, a basic get law is an appropriate accommodation to the wife's religious exercise, and its pressure is acceptable for most husbands who wish not to grant a get or not to appear before a *beth din*. Nevertheless, the constitutional argument that the law serves secular objectives and that all relevant religious effects are incidental is simpler and perhaps more decisive than the argument that the law properly accommodates religious exercise.

The uncommon situation in which the husband has a genuine religious sentiment that he should not give a get to his wife presents a special issue for the statute's application. Then the statute does directly interfere with religious liberty.[79] For husbands with substantial claims of religious conscience, courts should employ some version of the compelling interest test to assess the law's application. One may argue that the state has a very strong interest in protecting the right of wives to remarry, and in meeting serious dangers of fraud. But elimination of a barrier to remarriage that arises only out of a sense of religious tradition and obligation should not be regarded as powerful enough to require acts that offend the husband's religious identity.[80]

When we move beyond the "basic scheme" to New York's actual statute, we find religious elements that create extra constitutional vulnerabilities. Even apart from the law's failure to assist wives who sue husbands for divorce, the statute benefits only some wives who need a get. The law applies only to people who have had religious marriages, and the definition of barriers is cast in terms of principles of the marrying cleric.[81] What of a couple who has a Reform marriage and then becomes Orthodox or Conservative before the husband seeks a civil divorce? No barriers would exist according to the principles of the rabbi who performed the marriage.[82] The failure of

[79] For such a case, it might be argued that under *Employment Division v. Smith*, 494 U.S. 872 (1990), the husband has no special privilege based on his religious claim. But that case, which deals with a secular neutral statute prohibiting behavior, should not be regarded as applicable to statutes that require an act of predominantly religious significance. Moreover, New York courts may employ the compelling interest standard under their state constitution. See *Rourke v. New York State Department of Correctional Services*, 159 Misc. 2d 324, 603 N.Y.S. 2d 647 (Albany County Supreme Ct. 1993), aff'd, 201 A.D. 179, 615 N.Y.S. 2d 470 (3d Dept. 1994) (using strict scrutiny under state law after *Smith*).

[80] However, the manner in which courts have actually applied the compelling interest test in the free exercise area is to reject claims of religious conscience when the dangers of fraud are significant. Under that approach, a court might reasonably conclude that the compelling interest test is satisfied if the dangers of fraud appear very high.

[81] How the statute applies if the marrying rabbi has shifted his or her religious allegiance between the marriage and the divorce is not clear. But presumably his principles at the time of marriage control (at least if the couple has not also shifted their allegiance).

[82] It is doubtful how the law applies to couples married in a civil ceremony who then become Orthodox or Conservative and go through an appropriate marriage ceremony. The statute covers

the law, as written, to protect some women who require a get is troubling, but should not undermine the statute's constitutionality.

The provision granting the marrying rabbi authority to prevent a civil divorce by certifying that the husband has not taken all steps to remove barriers is more intractable. The drafters probably assumed that the husband's having or not having taken necessary steps was a simple matter of fact, with the marrying rabbi a neutral figure well placed to make the determination. But they may also have wanted to eliminate worries that state courts would have to discern Jewish law to see if a husband has taken necessary steps. The statute's "solution" is, nevertheless, inadequate. The less serious difficulty is that, since the marrying rabbi may have died or be unavailable, the court will then have to accept at face value the husband's affidavit that he has eliminated any barriers to remarriage; or it will have to make its own determination. Second, more fatally, the statute appears to give the rabbi absolute authority to block the civil divorce. This feature does not undermine the whole scheme, but itself is unconstitutional; it could be "corrected" by a court's giving the rabbi's certification presumptive weight but not final authority.[83]

The Equitable Distribution Law

The equitable distribution law of 1992 avoids the possibly arbitrary limitation to religious marriages and the assignment of civil authority to rabbis, but one of its features raises a problem not present in the 1983 statute. From the standpoint of Jewish law, enforcement of the 1992 law may involve unacceptable duress by imposing a financial loss,[84] and this creates a conceivable constitutional issue. If the alternative to an invalid get is no get at all, the civil law has done no harm. But perhaps a husband would have given a get without civil duress. How serious is this concern? Given intricacies about

---

marriages "solemnized" by a cleric. For the state, the crucial marriage is the initial civil marriage, not the subsequent religious marriage. Nevertheless, a generous interpretation would include a marriage "solemnized" by a cleric after a valid civil ceremony.

[83] One other complication alters the "basic scheme." Taken together, the law's provisions either (1) treat affidavits by husbands as conclusively accurate, capable of being trumped only by denials of marrying rabbis, or (2) call on courts to make decisions about the removal of barriers to remarriage. When such decisions are difficult, they would entangle the state with religion more than would straightforward factual determinations. Deference to the marrying rabbi's determination is one acceptable way to avoid difficult decisions. When the marrying rabbi is unavailable, a court should be able to reject a husband's affidavit if it is patently false.

[84] If civil law imposes unacceptable duress, then the get a husband grants will be invalid from a religious viewpoint. See Breitowitz, note 43 supra, at 212–19.

when serious pressure on husbands is appropriate, and disagreements and uncertainties among Orthodox and Conservative Jews about the limits of acceptable pressure, assessment by an outsider is not easy. A court cannot enter the thicket of debatable issues of Jewish law. It should not strike down the provision on this ground in the absence of clearly determinant opinion in the Orthodox and Conservative communities that the law creates unacceptable duress. No such opinion is now in evidence.

For standard civil constitutional analysis, the other issues concerning interference with religion are mainly similar in the new and old statutes. In certain applications, the equitable distribution provision is easier to defend. Insofar as the inability to remarry affects a wife's prospective financial status, courts appropriately take her failure to obtain a get as bearing on her financial future. That narrow economic rationale does not cover a court's responding punitively to a husband's unfairness or its employing the lever that it will impose an unfavorable settlement unless a husband grants a get.[85] When a court acts for these reasons, the constitutional problems of affecting religion are at least as great as they are for the earlier statute.

In summary, statutes designed to induce husbands to go through Jewish divorces do present serious issues of wisdom and constitutionality, but the basic features of those statutes should be accepted.[86] Some details raise further problems, and the assignment of final authority to marrying rabbis in the 1983 law should be regarded as constitutionally impermissible.

Equity

When courts act on their own motion, the constitutional issues are closely similar to those generated by legislation. In some cases, courts have invoked equitable principles, in effect, to preclude a husband's achieving an unfair advantage by refusing to grant a get.[87] Generalizing about these kinds of cases is hard, because so much depends on particular circumstances. The argument for equitable relief from an agreed settlement is strongest when husbands have explicitly used their power to withhold a get in order to bargain successfully for more favorable terms. Perhaps a secular state should have no policy about imbalances of power for purely religious divorces,

[85] Of course, it is possible that the threat of such a response might help achieve economic fairness indirectly by encouraging more reasonable settlements.

[86] For one case accepting the 1992 provision, see *Becher v. Becher*, 66 N.Y.S. 2d 50 (App. Div. 1997), decided below by a judge who said that he has seen the coercive withholding of a get on occasions "too numerous to count."

[87] See *Segal v. Segal*, 650 A.2d 996 (N.J. Super. Ct. 1994); *Schwartz v. Schwartz*, 583 N.Y.S.2d 716 (1992).

viewed in isolation; but the state rightly determines that the leverage pro-vided by an imbalance should not benefit the stronger party in the civil di-vorce settlement.

Whether equitable relief should be given if the husband has never agreed to obtain a get and has never bargained about it is more difficult. As I have said in respect to New York's 1992 statute, the state properly treats a wife more generously if she has bleaker financial prospects because her husband refuses to give her a get. The serious questions arise when the court goes further to pressure the husband to grant a get or to penalize him for failing to do so. If the husband himself seeks a civil divorce, the constitutional issues about judicial use of equity are the same as under the New York statutes. A defendant husband who resists a divorce has a somewhat stronger argument that the state should not indirectly coerce him to give a get by diminishing his share of the settlement. Nevertheless, the constitutionality of civil law prodding to grant a get should not depend on whether the husband is a plaintiff or defendant, or on whether he is found to be "at fault."

Tort

Another way in which civil courts might act on their own is to allow a wife recovery in tort law for a husband's refusal to grant a get. The most apt form of action is the tort called the intentional infliction of emotional distress, covered in chapter 17 of volume 1. This tort involves the intentional or reck-less causing of severe emotional suffering by outrageous conduct. Many wives who are divorced civilly but denied a religious divorce undoubtedly suffer greatly. Some husbands may actually wish to impose such suffering. Even those who do not are probably aware that suffering is substantially likely, and this awareness is sufficient to support a finding of recklessness. Is the behavior outrageous? When a husband acts purely from spite, a court comfortably concludes that his effort to prevent a remarriage for his wife and to cause her acute distress is outrageous. A husband with a genuine conviction that he should not participate in the get procedure is not acting outrageously. The most difficult case is one in which a husband withholds a get in order to get a better bargain in the civil divorce. Bitter negotiations are a common, if unfortunate, element of many modern divorces. Not infre-quently, people may use as a bargaining chip something, such as custody of children, that they may not really want, in order to be able to "concede" this in return for something else they do want. If such bargaining were often treated as raising claims of intentional infliction of emotional distress, di-vorcing couples might "up the ante" in conflicts already full of emotional hostility. Although courts *might* make a judgment that bargaining about the get is especially unfair, and therefore outrageous, I do not think bargaining about the get should be given this special status for purposes of tort law. I would limit tort recovery to circumstances in which the husband's motivations are clearly spiteful.[88]

Conclusion about Civil Pressure to Grant a Get

Although the constitutional issues are difficult, I have concluded that states may appropriately aim to encourage recalcitrant husbands to give wives the *gittin* that are necessary for remarriage within Orthodox and Conservative religious communities. The state's secular interest in freedom to remarry and its interest in accommodating religious exercise are strong enough to support such encouragement, although these interests probably do not override a husband's claim of religious exercise in the unusual instance when a husband has a genuine opposition of religious conscience to submitting to a *beth din* or providing a get. Whether a state should take the step of adopting a statute or remain within the limits of common law and equity will depend on the capacity of courts to address the problem within the constraints of judge-made law. One straightforward mode of judicial involvement is enforcement of prior agreements. When husbands have clearly agreed to civil law enforcement of a promise to submit to a *beth din*, courts should regard themselves as free to compel that, so long as they need not resolve any debated issues of Jewish law.

GENERAL CONCLUSIONS

In this final section, I draw together some threads in the analysis to see what broader lessons close study of our two problems about civil law and Jewish law have revealed.

Specific Doctrinal Conclusions

1. Civil determination of *debatable* issues of religious law is generally unacceptable; but straightforward determinations of religious requirements by civil courts may be appropriate if these determinations serve secular interests. Just as the priest-penitent privilege and civil deference to religious

[88] For a more expansive recommendation about the use of tort law, see Barbara J. Redman, "Divorce: What Can Be Done in Secular Courts to Aid the Jewish Woman?" 19 *Georgia Law Review* 389 (1985).

tribunals demand some recognition of religious law, so also do typical kosher laws and civil pressure in regard to *gittin*. But recognition of religious law does not by itself render these civil involvements unconstitutional.

2. Similarly, civil pressure to perform acts of religious obligation may, by itself, be all right, so long as secular reasons exist for performance of the acts. Thus, the fact that, once a *beth din* orders him to grant a get, a husband may feel some religious obligation to do so, does not make civil pressure on him to grant the get unconstitutional.

3. The strict compelling interest test, applicable when there is a direct attack on a religion or conscious discrimination among religions, should not apply when the government promotes a secular interest in a manner that may cause some religion comparative disadvantage.[89] These situations should be dealt with under other Establishment Clause principles.

4. In determining whether a religion is impermissibly assisted, a court should ask whether other groups have similar needs that are unmet. Thus, kosher and get laws do not aid Orthodox Jews impermissibly against Reform Jews, who do not observe kosher standards or engage in religious divorces.

5. Ordinarily, despite some language in Supreme Court opinions, a possibility of a future failure to extend the same benefit to another similar group should not render a benefit unconstitutional. One can never be sure what legislatures will do or what claims of religious groups may develop. Thus, if the legislature provides protection against fraud involving kosher products, it is always conceivable that a similar group will arise and not be similarly treated. If that possibility were alone sufficient to render the initial benefit unconstitutional, legislatures could not act to give benefits[90]— even essentially secular benefits—that are focused on any particular religious community. However, such benefits are not always invalid.[91]

6. In an Establishment Clause analysis of whether effects are acceptable, the feasibility of alternative schemes that generate fewer negative effects should be relevant. "Least restrictive means" is a familiar component of free exercise analysis used in the Religious Freedom Restoration Act. Alternative means should also make a difference when courts review Estab-

[89] However, if a state does support Orthodox views of kosher in preference to Conservative ones, that does probably amount to conscious discrimination.

[90] More strictly, it could not give benefits that were not already required by the Constitution or by a generally worded statute like the Religious Freedom Restoration Act.

[91] If contrary to what I have just said, such focused laws are unconstitutional, legislatures could respond by adopting generally worded laws, such as the New York get provisions, that would cover other similarly situated groups as they arise. With ingenuity, a legislative drafter could find general language to cover food requirements of various religions, leaving it to administrators to concentrate on kosher requirements.

lishment Clause challenges. This point is strikingly illustrated with respect to kosher enforcement. Civil determinations of what are kosher require- ments present definite constitutional difficulties; whether these difficulties should be accepted depends partly on whether civil enforcement of fraud involving authorization by private groups will provide consumers ade- quate protection. If a court is confident state support of private enforce- ment will work effectively, that is a reason to hold that more extensive state involvement is unconstitutional.

7. A plain effect within religious law could conceivably bear on constitution- ality under civil law. Notably, if state pressure on husbands to grant *gittin* plainly rendered their acts ineffective under Jewish law, that would consti- tute a ground for concluding that the law, in paradoxical opposition to its aim, "inhibits" religion unacceptably. (Apparently measures taken by leg- islatives and courts thus far have not undermined their purposes in this way.)

8. For most free exercise purposes, the religious views that count are those of the person or persons advancing the free exercise claim, regardless of whether those views are widely shared by others. Thus, a husband could raise a serious free exercise objection to being pressured to grant a get if doing so would violate his religious conscience. However, if only a very small percentage of persons in a regulated class have sincere religious ob- jections, and members of the class have a substantial incentive to claim such objections falsely, and if determining sincerity is very difficult, courts might reasonably decide not to accede to such objections. They might conclude, instead, that the government has a compelling interest in not making any exceptions.

9. For establishment purposes, it is the views of people more generally that matter; and this is true whether one asks about advancing or inhibiting religion, or about endorsement. If a court asks whether kosher laws aid or endorse Orthodox Judaism in comparison with Conservative Judaism, the views of most Conservative Jews, not isolated individuals, matter. If the great majority of Conservatives who observe kosher actually wel- comed enforcement of Orthodox standards, that would be a reason to conclude that such enforcement does not unacceptably disadvantage Con- servative practice. Similarly, if most Orthodox and Conservative Jews want the state to pressure husbands to grant *gittin*, that is evidence that the law does not "inhibit" those religions. No doubt, courts are not well suited to figure out exactly how many members of a religion take particu- lar positions; but they should be able to discern heavily dominant opinion on these subjects, when it exists.

10. For endorsement analysis, the relevant comparison may concern the relative position of two minority religions (or two branches of one minority religion). It is a stretch to think of kosher or get laws as having much, if anything, to do with the place of Christians in relation to Jews. If any endorsement (or condemnation) exists, it is of one branch of Judaism vis-à-vis another. Such an endorsement is undoubtedly possible—a legislature that is mostly Christian might effectively endorse some branch of another religious tradition as authoritative. The major opinions employing endorsement analysis have thus far proceeded as if the views of a hypothetical reasonable person of no distinct religious understanding determine whether a law, in purpose or effect, does endorse a religion. If that approach is carried over to the problems I have discussed here, the relevant reasonable person would need to evaluate how members of the minority religions would be likely to react to what the legislature has done. It is hard to see how this can be done without inquiry into how members of those religions *do* react. A non-Jewish judge who tries to replicate the reasonable observer will be hard put to assess how a reasonable Conservative Jew who observes kosher requirements will regard enforcement of Orthodox standards without some knowledge of what Conservative Jews think about that.[92]

11. Endorsement analysis sometimes seems very close to more general analysis of advancements of religion, but this is not invariably so. If one asks whether typical kosher laws aid Orthodoxy over Conservatism, one will look to their effect on Conservative practice and perhaps at how Conservative Jews regard the laws; these factors will also bear on whether the state has endorsed Orthodoxy. On the other hand, the argument that the get law impermissibly aids Orthodoxy by moderating the harsh effects of one of its practices has little relation to endorsement. For areas of establishment law other than public symbols (for which endorsement is already the dominant approach), it remains an open question how significant a role endorsement analysis will play. As this question is addressed, courts need to think carefully about when endorsement terminology is closely similar to other inquiries about aid and when the questions are genuinely different.

12. Reliance on decisions of rabbis about matters of Jewish law is a reasonable response to the difficulty of ordinary civil officials making decisions

---

[92] I am contending implicitly that reflective Christians will have a *better* sense of how Christians and others will react to a cross in a courthouse than of how members of branches of non-Christian religions regard subjects unfamiliar to Christians. (I, in fact, doubt that most Christians have an adequate sense of how Christian symbols affect members of other religions.)

about Jewish law, and to the unconstitutionality of such officials resolving debatable questions of religious law. But it is not permissible for kosher laws to make rabbis, as rabbis, the public officials who render final determinations for the state. Nor may the state assign private rabbis unreviewable authority over whether people can acquire civil divorces. The way out of this dilemma is for civil officials, not themselves chosen *as clerics*, to defer to the decisions of religious authorities (including here individual rabbis) on subjects of religious law, but not to confer ultimate civil authority upon those authorities. Among the various ways in which this can be done, a court can treat a *beth din* as it might some other civil arbitrator, accepting its judgments about the Jewish law of divorce.

Overall Summary

These individual conclusions illustrate, as the main study topics of this chapter have done, the complexity of considerations that bear on how civil law should permissibly involve itself in matters of religious significance. The aspiration for simple approaches is either deluded or badly misguided. It is deluded if a proponent believes simple approaches will yield results sensitive to the nuances of our religious and social life; it is misguided if it recognizes the Procrustean quality of simple approaches, but thinks their clarity and determinacy are worth the price of unhappy outcomes.

CHAPTER 15

Tax Exemptions and Deductions

Religious organizations benefit from various tax exemptions and deductions, granted federal, state, and local levels. Perhaps most important, churches and other places of worship are exempt from local property taxes, a privilege guaranteed in state constitutions and statutes. Religious organizations need not pay income tax on income connected to their religious functions, and they are also relieved from federal unemployment and social security taxes. Relief is also accorded in the form of deductions from taxable income for those who contribute to churches and other religious organizations. These deductions benefit the organizations indirectly. People in high tax brackets who live in states with substantial income taxes will save more than forty cents (from their federal and state taxes together) for each dollar they donate to a church;[1] thus someone who feels she can be out of pocket six thousand dollars will be able to donate ten thousand dollars. Yet a different kind of tax relief is exemption from sales taxes for the sale of religious publications. And a special rule that a cleric need not count a church's provision of a parsonage as income reduces the tax burden on the minister and indirectly allows her church to pay her a lower salary.

The exact details of many of these forms of relief vary from state to state; and judicial decisions depend significantly on the precise wording in state constitutions and statutes, wording not always chosen with a careful eye to the desired scope of a privilege.[2] The treatment of religious organizations raises fundamental questions of tax policy and constitutional law. Among the issues of policy are whether exemptions should be regarded as subsidies and whether religious organizations can fairly be distinguished from many other nonprofit organizations. A subsidiary question, reserved for the last part of the chapter, concerns limits on the political activities in which churches and other charities are allowed to engage.

---

[1] That is, the total of federal and state income tax will be more than 40 percent at the margin, so that each dollar subtracted from income will reduce the tax bill by more than forty cents.

[2] Arvo Van Alstyne, in "Tax Exemption of Church Property," 20 *Ohio State Law Journal* 461 (1959), long ago described the details of a good deal of the constitutional and statutory language, and judicial responses to that language. A common example of careless language is that exempted property be "used exclusively for religious worship." Id. at 464. A court would not be likely to take

The constitutional questions involve both religion clauses. A religious claimant may assert that the Free Exercise Clause requires an exemption, or at least that it requires an exemption if certain other organizations are receiving one. Those who object to exemptions for religious organizations may claim that such a subsidy for religion always violates the Establishment Clause, or does so unless similar exemptions are given to a much broader class of nonprofit organizations and activities. Supreme Court cases dealing with these claims raise crucial questions about how tax exemptions compare with grants and about acceptable classifications of beneficiaries.

POLICY CONSIDERATIONS

When one thinks about tax policy for religious organizations, getting a handle on the appropriate standards of evaluation is not easy. Two major issues concern the right perspective to take about exemptions and deductions and the design of categorizations for organizations that might benefit from them.

In examining the first topic, we can concentrate on exemptions from property taxes. In terms of economic effect, there is little or no difference between a tax exemption and a grant of money. Suppose church property is worth $1,000,000 and is appraised at that value. The normal property tax is 2 percent of appraised value. The church saves $20,000 a year if it is not taxed; enjoying the same financial benefit as if it received yearly an unrestricted grant of $20,000. If churches should not receive unrestricted grants from the government, why should legislatures give them property tax exemptions?

But there is another way of looking at the problem. The government's declining to take in taxes is not formally the same as its giving away public money in grants. Its refusal to tax reflects the independence of church from state; its giving of grants would reflect the dependence of churches upon the state. If we think, naively perhaps, of money that the church *would pay* as its own until the government takes it, not paying a tax is quite different from receiving a grant.

In an influential defense of exemptions and deductions, Boris Bittker made the related point that exemptions could easily be reformulated as limitations on the original tax base.[3] Instead of exempting nonprofit institutions from the income tax, Congress might draft a law taxing profit-making organiza-

---

such language as precluding preparation of food for a church supper or using a room to care for infants while their parents worship. Id. at 467–68.

[3] Boris Bittker, "Churches, Taxes and the Constitution," 78 *Yale Law Journal* 1285, 1288–89 (1969).

tions and natural persons. Inevitably, taxes are imposed only on some organizations or activities to the exclusion of others. One should not view every untaxed organization or activity as being subsidized by the government.

A partial response to this general line is to regard tax policy as based both on revenue considerations and independent social objectives. According to what is commonly called a tax expenditure analysis,[4] we should regard the pursuit of independent objectives through tax laws as a kind of government expenditure. Those objectives should not be implemented in the kind of haphazard, politically motivated manner that characterizes much of the tax law; they should be scrutinized with the sort of care given to outright grants. This approach conceives of some ideal tax based on revenue considerations; Bittker's answer is that we have no objective measure of what the ideal tax would look like.[5]

Bittker's argument is sufficient to caution us that an exemption from taxes cannot be equated simply with a subsidy from a grant. Nevertheless, however difficult characterizing exemptions in general may be, we can quickly see that designating certain groups to receive exemptions while denying them to others that share the relevant characteristics would be unjust. Suppose that property tax exemptions were given only to Presbyterian churches and denied to all other religious groups. We do not need a complete view of an ideal tax to know that this is not acceptable.

A critical question is whether it could be appropriate to exempt religious groups, and not to exempt charitable, educational, and other nonprofit groups. This is one form of the general issue of whether religion should receive special or equal treatment. Were an exemption limited exclusively to religious organizations or activities, the justification could not be simply that religious groups are not out to make a profit, or that they confer benefits on the community, because that much is true about many nonreligious, nonprofit groups as well. Legislators can more easily justify an exemption extended widely to an umbrella of organizations within which religious organizations happen to fall than an exemption given only to religious groups.[6]

---

[4] See, e.g., Donna D. Adler, "The Internal Revenue Code, the Constitution, and the Courts: The Use of Tax Expenditure Analysis in Judicial Decision Making," 28 *Wake Forest Law Review* 855–68 (1993); Erika King, "Tax Exemptions and the Establishment Clause," 49 *Syracuse Law Review* 971, 994–1001 (1999).

[5] Bittker, note 3 supra, at 1296, writes that " 'ideal' taxes are hard to come by, even if our models are academic projects rather than statutes shaped by the interaction between relentless lobbyists and harried legislators."

[6] Of course, the category in which the religious groups fall must be natural. An exemption limited to farmers who earn less than thirty thousand dollars, to people who use solar heat in their homes, and to religious groups would not be natural in this sense. The reasons to exempt farmers and users

Does it follow that membership in a larger category is a sine qua non for whether an exemption may appropriately be granted to religious groups?[7] That exemptions are exclusively for religious organizations does not *necessarily* condemn them. Everyone agrees that direct grants to churches for general church purposes are unacceptable if the grants go only to religious groups, but one might think that exemptions limited to religious groups are a reasonable accommodation to the free exercise of religion. That argument will be especially appealing if there are few nonreligious analogues to the religious activity that is favored—the tax benefit for parsonages located next to the churches may afford an example.[8] But legislators might suppose more broadly that religion is special, and may be favored even when one can easily imagine otherwise similar nonreligious groups or activities that *might* be exempted.

Related to free exercise reasons to protect religion are particular worries about government involvement with religious groups. One reason not to impose property taxes on churches is the difficulty of appraising their property. Appraisal is hardly an exact science; and in many communities appraised value is self-consciously set at well below market value. Whatever the methodology, appraisal reflects a delicate individual assessment. Were church properties appraised for taxes, that would open the door for negotiation between influential church officials and government administrators, and allow room for favoritism or prejudicial disadvantage. The correct methodology would itself be troublesome. Should appraisal be according to value "as a church" or according to market value? Suppose that a church attracting mainly parishioners of modest means happens to be in a section of a city that is undergoing rapid development, with a steep rise in property values. If its land is assessed by market value, property taxes could overwhelm the church, with its limited income. The consequence would be to drive many churches out from valuable commercial areas of the city, depriving surrounding residents of continuity in their places of worship. (Of course, were very few residents left in the vicinity, closing the church might seem desirable.)

---

of solar heat would have virtually no contact with the reasons to exempt religious groups. The exemption for religious groups would then have to stand on its own.

[7] If one thinks that even outright grants to religious groups for general church purposes are appropriate *if* those groups happen to fall within some larger category of beneficiaries, tax exemptions on that basis will seem unexceptionable. If one thinks that grants to churches to be used for general church purposes are unacceptable (the prevailing view and my own view), then the existence of a larger category will matter for exemptions, only if exemptions differ in principle from grants.

[8] Ellen P. Aprill, "Parsonage and Tax Policy: Rethinking the Exclusion," *Tax Notes*, August 26, 2002, 1243, has urged extending the parsonage exclusion to employees of any public charity.

Appraisal according to value "as a church" raises other difficulties. How does one set the monetary value of church property "as a church"? According to what some other religious group might pay for the property? If the property is that of a Roman Catholic church in a heavily Catholic neighborhood, no other church might be interested in it. Perhaps, an appraiser would need to ask what the Roman Catholic church would pay to get the property, if it did not already have it, or what another typical denomination would pay if the surrounding population were members of that denomination. These methodological problems may not be insurmountable, but they combine with worries about individualized assessments to give one pause about any system that requires such evaluations.

Of course, similar appraisal problems exist to a degree with any charitable institutions. Located in a city and area in which property values are rapidly increasing, would the property of Columbia University be valued as the site of a university or according to what commercial developers might pay for its land? One can well imagine a major university or museum suggesting that it will leave a city if its property is appraised at too high a value, and one would expect officials to take such threats seriously. But a basic difference between most charitable institutions and churches is that no fundamental constitutional principle stands in the way of the government favoring one charity at the expense of another, similar to the principle against favoritism of one religious group vis-à-vis others. Although the imprecise science and policy of appraisal presents similar and disturbing opportunities for favoritism, the concerns about government entanglement with religious groups do not apply with the same force to ordinary charities and educational institutions.

Legislators may reasonably adopt different attitudes toward the significance of exemptions as contrasted with grants and toward the significance of a larger category, as opposed to "for religion only." Many legislators will hesitate to break with historical practice. States in this country have uniformly adopted property tax exemptions for churches. Similar exemptions can be traced back to the ancient world, and historically grounded perceptions that churches (or the church) should be separate from the state may continue to exert some influence.[9] To eliminate all property tax exemptions would be a radical shift in the status quo, with disastrous effects on many churches. Even if one thinks the status quo has a dose of illogic in distinguishing so sharply between grants and exemptions, eliminating all exemptions will not seem the course of legislative wisdom. Nevertheless, legislators should not regard complete exemption from property taxes as forever im-

[9] See King, note 4 supra, at 973–79 (1999).

mune from review.[10] In stages of English and American history, the acquisition and maintenance of property by churches has been regarded as a serious threat to the economy.[11] That could happen again,[12] and legislators might decide in the future that the property of churches, and other charitable institutions, needs to be taxed.

Although some particular tax benefit limited to religion might be defended as needed for accommodation or because religious groups happen to be the only members of a reasonable class of potential beneficiaries, property tax exemptions are easiest to justify if religions fall within a larger category of beneficiaries that includes other nonprofit organizations that are devoted in some expansive sense to public welfare, including museums, universities, charities, and independent groups that promote nonreligious ideas. This inclusive approach fits best the pattern of exemptions in American history and our modern concern about fairness between religious and other groups.

CONSTITUTIONAL PRINCIPLES

Thus far having discussed tax relief as a matter for legislative choice (although one informed by the values of free exercise and nonestablishment), we turn now to constitutional principles that may restrict legislative choice. Arguably, some forms of tax relief are required by federal and state free exercise clauses, and many state constitutions have specific provisions guaranteeing exemptions from property taxes. The Establishment Clause and its state variants foreclose certain forms of tax relief.

Whether relief is permitted, required, or barred can depend how categories of beneficiaries are defined. A form of categorization that is never, or almost never, acceptable is extending a benefit to some religions to the exclusion of others in a manner that signals comparative approval and disapproval.[13]

[10] Of course, if a state constitution requires an exemption, then legislators meeting in ordinary sessions must accept it. In general, state constitutions are much easier to amend than the federal document.

[11] In *Walz v. Tax Commission*, 397 U.S. 664, 715–716 n. 17 (1970), Justice Douglas, dissenting, quoted President Grant's 1875 State of the Union Message expressing concern over the increasing value of church property and recommending its taxation. When Henry VIII ruled in England, one-third to one-half of the country's wealth may have been held by the church. See Michael S. Ariens and Robert A. Destro, *Religious Liberty in a Pluralistic Society* 686 (Durham, N.C.: Carolina Academic Press, 1996).

[12] A genuine need to assist the economy may be hard to separate from a wish to curb the power of churches. Grant's proposal to tax church property may well have been influenced by anti-Catholicism.

[13] Categorization by size of income or numbers of members would probably be all right, applied to religious groups as well as other nonprofit organizations.

Notably, the Supreme Court upheld a challenge against a Minnesota scheme of tax relief that imposed more onerous reporting requirements on groups that raised much of their money from nonmembers, a class into which the Unification Church happened to fall.[14] A ban on discrimination among religions is the least controversial aspect of the religion clauses together.

With respect to tax law, the problem is less that the statutes and regulations directly discriminate among religions than that they generate opportunities for administrative discrimination. The approach of the Internal Revenue Service to what counts as a church is an enumeration of fourteen factors whose presence helps signal a church. Among the factors are "a recognized creed and form of worship," "ordained ministers," and "established places of worship."[15] An organization can qualify as a church if it satisfies some but not all of the factors. Without doubt, the IRS needs an approach to distinguish from genuine religions bogus religions that have been created to avoid taxes,[16] and the Service has adopted one form of the analogical approach to "defining" religion that I have supported in chapter 8 of the volume on free exercise. Still, such flexibility does create the risk that an unpopular movement will be classified as nonreligious.

Another risk of discriminatory treatment is created by determinations regarding charitable contributions. In *Hernandez v. Commissioner of Internal Revenue*, the Supreme Court upheld the decision of the IRS that a "fixed donation" for religious education services ("auditing" and "training") was a quid pro quo that could not be deducted as a contribution to the Church of Scientology.[17] In light of the practice of the IRS allowing as deductions other fixed payments, such as pew rents and tithes, two dissenters believed that the record established discrimination against the Church of Scientology.[18] I believe there is an important distinction between fixed payments that are for the benefit of the church as a whole and payments for services for one's particular spiritual and psychological health (as in the Scientology "donation"), but at the edges that line may become thin indeed, as may be seen if we ask whether pew rents are mainly a form of support for the church or a way to assure oneself a good seat. Risks of administrative discrimination are unavoidable whenever officials have to apply general standards to com-

---

[14] *Larson v. Valente*, 456 U.S. 228 (1982). The case is discussed in more detail in chapter 3 of the volume on free exercise. As I indicate there, exactly why that law was treated as discriminatory was not clear from the opinion.

[15] *Church of Eternal Life and Liberty, Inc. v. Commissioner*, 86 T.C. 916, (Tax Court 1986) (libertarian organization without most of the characteristics of ordinary churches).

[16] See, e.g., id.

[17] *Hernandez v. Commissioner of Internal Revenue*, 490 U.S. 680 (1989).

[18] Id. at 712 (O'Connor and Scalia, JJ.).

plex and variant situations, but legislators and administrators who draft standards and judges who review individual applications should attempt to prevent discrimination insofar as they reasonably can.[19]

The category arguments that mainly occupy us in this chapter involve comparisons, not among religious groups, but between religious groups and nonreligious ones.

A Free Exercise Right to Tax Relief

The first three cases in which the Supreme Court dealt with tax relief involved free exercise objections to taxes that municipalities imposed on religious activities. In the 1942 case of *Jones v. Opelika*,[20] Jehovah's Witnesses who went from house to house and distributed their literature for money, claimed they should not have to pay a licensing tax the city imposed on booksellers. The Supreme Court, by a five-to-four margin, rejected their free exercise argument: the government could charge reasonable fees for the privilege of using commercial methods of sale in canvassing.

A year later, in *Murdock v. Pennsylvania*, a change in Court membership yielded a different result.[21] Here, the flat license tax was for the privilege of canvassing or soliciting orders for articles. Noting that the "hand distribution of religious tracts is an age-old form of missionary evangelism," and analogizing the sale of literature to passing the collection plate in church, the Court said, "[T]he mere fact that the religious literature is 'sold' by itinerant preachers rather than 'donated' does not transform evangelism into a commercial enterprise."[22] A person engaging in religious activities may have his income taxed but he cannot be taxed for delivering a sermon. Remarking that Thomas Paine's pamphlets were not distributed free of charge, the Court referred to "freedom of speech, freedom of the press, [and] freedom of religion [as] available to all, not merely those who can pay their way."[23] The Court placed some emphasis on the fact that a license fee of a set amount operates in advance; it is "a prior restraint that tends to suppress the exercise of those constitutional liberties of press and religion."[24]

---

[19] Part of the problem for judges is how much deference they should give to administrative judgments.

[20] 316 U.S. 584.

[21] 319 U.S. 105 (1943). Justice Rutledge, who joined the new majority, had replaced Justice Byrnes, who had rejected the constitutional claim in *Jones*.

[22] Id. at 111.

[23] Id.

[24] Id. at 114.

A year later in *Follett v. Town of McCormick*,[25] the Court applied the rule of *Murdock*, and compared a Jehovah's Witness who lived in the community and earned his living exclusively by selling religious literature to preachers of a more orthodox faith, who are not engaging in commercial undertakings simply because they earn their livelihood by their calling.

One may look at *Murdock* and *Follett* as protecting the particular activity of religious preaching or evangelism or as implicitly standing for a broader principle. The analogies of the itinerant evangelist to the preacher, and of sales of literature by evangelists to plate donations at church, provide a focus on religion, rather than some broader class of activities.[26] If the crucial comparison is with plate donations, which the Court assumes cannot be subject to a license tax, perhaps it should matter whether an evangelist sets up shop and sells items at a fixed price without much personal interchange or reaches out to individuals, speaks her message to them, and sells her literature at a price that varies according to what the "customer" can, or is willing to, pay.[27]

The language in *Murdock* about freedom of speech and of the press suggests a broader First Amendment basis. Perhaps someone spreading a nonreligious message door to door and sustaining herself by selling pamphlets could not be subject to a license tax any more than could Murdock. On this view, the tax relief that the Court grants would cover all itinerant preachers of ideological messages who sustain themselves by selling pamphlets and other literature.[28]

Whatever are the characteristics of the evangelist selling literature that makes him enough like the ordinary preacher living from plate donations, we can imagine nonreligious counterparts. A person might live by giving

---

[25] *Follett v. Town of McCormick*, 321 U.S. 573 (1944).

[26] I explain in chapter 8 of volume 1 why I count the Ethical Culture Society as religious, so I assume even the narrow focus would cover such organizations.

[27] The Court does not engage these various nuances, each of which weakens or strengthens the analogy to orthodox ministers and plate donations.

[28] A relatively recent case that supports a treatment of religious solicitation like that of door-to-door advocacy for other causes is *Watchtower Bible & Tract Society of New York, Inc. v. Village of Stratton*, 536 U.S. 150 (2002), which held that an ordinance requiring a license for those promoting any cause on private residential property was invalid as it applied to religious proselytizing and anonymous political speech. Although a decision to protect itinerant sellers of pamphlets conveying their messages from being taxed would need to explain why an ordinary bookseller does not enjoy a similar benefit, those who live by small numbers of sales of messages of their faith, religious or secular, may be differently situated from those whose business is selling a wide range of publications. This particular division would pose a hard case if a bookseller sold only one kind of book and claimed that was his ideology. An example could be owners of stores that sell only the literature of a single religion.

lectures and accepting donations afterward. If that activity could not be subject to license tax, then one who goes house to house and sells pamphlets with a nonreligious message about environmental protection might also be protected from a license tax. Even if one takes the guiding analogy as being to the ordinary preacher, one might conclude that the crucial ground of protection should be the Free Speech and Free Press clauses rather than the Free Exercise Clause.

By treating a flat license tax as a prior restraint, discouraging the exercise of religious expression, the Court adopts a rationale that could easily reach other forms of expression.[29] A core basis, some would say the basis, for the First Amendment protection of freedom of speech and of the press was to forbid prior restraints, the kind of licensing censorship of publications that had existed in England. Once the Court characterizes a restriction on expression as a prior restraint, it is highly likely to hold it invalid.

In subsequent decisions, the scope of *Murdock* and *Follett* as protections against taxes has been cabined. In 1990, the Court, distinguishing earlier decisions on the ground that a license tax differs sharply from taxes imposed on sales when they occur, unanimously rejected a claim that California could not apply its sales and use tax to religious magazines, books, tapes, and records.[30] Although the Court had no need to settle whether the kind of tax imposed in *Murdock* and *Follett* would also be invalid as applied to someone going door to door and selling nonreligious political tracts, it referred to a nonreligious press case that upheld a tax because it was unlike the license taxes of those two cases.[31] In summary, we can conclude that there is still a fairly narrow free exercise right not to be subjected to a particular form of tax on selling religious literature, and that there may well be a parallel right in respect to nonreligious, noncommercial literature. I believe both that the narrow right is one that should continue to be recognized *and* that it should be understood to reach nonreligious ideological literature.

A Free Exercise Right to Discriminate?

A different kind of free exercise claim arose when the Internal Revenue Service interpreted a generally worded statute providing a tax exemption for educational organizations to the effect that a school or university that dis-

---

[29] See id.

[30] *Jimmy Swaggart Ministries v. Board of Equalization of California*, 493 U.S. 378, 386–88 (1990).

[31] Id. at 387–88, referring to *Minneapolis Star & Tribune Co. v. Minnesota Commissioner of Revenue*, 460 U.S. 575 (1983).

criminated on racial grounds did not qualify.[32] Reading the exemption provision in light of the companion section on deductions,[33] the Supreme Court concluded that in order to qualify, an educational institution had to meet the requisites of a common-law charity, and not act contrary to public policy.[34] Given a strong public policy against racial discrimination in education, racially discriminatory schools and universities were not entitled to an exemption.[35] Thus, Bob Jones University, which did not allow interracial dating, and a school that discriminated in admissions were liable for federal unemployment and Social Security taxes. Bob Jones University claimed with considerable plausibility that this interpretation was not what the statutory language suggested or what those adopting it had in mind; but that argument failed, the Court reasoning that the IRS was acting within its proper authority,[36] and that Congress had acquiesced in its interpretation.

A second argument of the university and religious school was that the statute, interpreted in this way, denied their free exercise of religion. They did not claim that the government had to grant them a favorable tax status, but that it could not deny that status on the basis of a religiously grounded policy to treat members of races differently. The Court assumed that the religious educational institutions had made a substantial free exercise argument, one that could be trumped only by a showing that denying them tax exempt status served a compelling government interest. The Court quickly decided that the interest in eliminating racial discrimination in education was sufficiently compelling.[37] This decision about a university and school does not tell us what the Court might decide were Congress or the Internal Revenue Service to take away tax benefits from actual churches, synagogues, or mosques because they discriminate on grounds of gender or race in choos-

---

[32] The Internal Revenue Service initially adopted this approach after a three judge district court had forbidden it from giving tax exempt status to racially discriminatory private schools in Mississippi. *Green v. Kennedy*, 309 F.Supp. 1127 (D.D.C.), app. dismissed sub non *Cannon v. Green*, 398 U.S. 956 (1970).

[33] The exemption section is 26 U.S.C. § 501 (c)(3); the deduction section is 26 U.S.C. § 170.

[34] *Bob Jones University v. United States*, 461 U.S. 574 (1983). Justice Powell, concurring, id. at 609–10, objected to the Court's suggestion that an organization must comport with "the common community conscience," as failing to give due recognition to value of tax exempt organizations promoting diverse and conflicting views. See also Charles O. Galvin and Neal Devins, "Tax Policy Analysis of *Bob Jones University v. United States*," 36 *Vanderbilt Law Review* 1353, 1366–67 (1983).

[35] In large part, the concern was that private schools discriminating on racial grounds were created to evade racial desegregation of public schools.

[36] For the view that such policy judgments should be made by Congress, see Galvin and Devins, note 34 supra, at 1371–74.

[37] See note 30 supra. In a famous article, "Nomos and Narrative," 97 *Harvard Law Review* 14 (1983), Robert Cover lamented the Court's casual approach to the free exercise issue, though not its ultimate conclusion.

ing leaders or members.[38] As I have suggested in chapter 20 of the volume on free exercise, such discrimination by a church itself should, for the most part, be regarded as protected under the Free Exercise Clause. Eliminating a tax exemption because of such discrimination would constitute an unconstitutional failure to protect.

Property Tax Exemptions and Establishment

In the years after *Everson v. Board of Education*,[39] when the Supreme Court was taking a narrow view of permissible financial aid to religious schools, an owner of private property in New York challenged the constitutionality of the exemption from property taxes of properties used exclusively for religious purposes. Every state then did, and now does, exempt churches from property taxes and in most, including New York, the exemption is protected in the state constitution. In the 1970 case of *Walz v. Tax Comm'n of New York City*,[40] the Supreme Court sustained the exemption. Some aspects of the Court's decision are straightforward; one crucial aspect is more elusive.

Chief Justice Burger's opinion rejected the relevance of the economic argument that an exemption is equivalent to a subsidy. He relied heavily on the uniform historical acceptance of such exemptions and on an argument about entanglement. The standard practice of granting property tax exemptions showed that at the time of the adoption of the Bill of Rights (and of the Fourteenth Amendment), no one considered such exemptions to be an impermissible support of religion. Although the Court did not treat historical acceptance as settling the issue of constitutionally,[41] it did take the history as helping to show that the tax exemption was a form of "benevolent neutrality toward . . . religious exercise," not the first step on a path toward forbidden establishment.[42]

It was in *Walz* that the Court first emphasized entanglement as a component of Establishment Clause analysis. The chief justice reasoned that were the government to appraise property and collect a tax, that would entangle

---

[38] Douglas Laycock, in "Tax Exemptions for Racially Discriminatory Religious Schools," 60 *Texas Law Review* 259 (1982), urged that such a course would be unconstitutional as an undue infringement on religious conscience and church autonomy and as a form of discrimination against religious believers in these forms of different treatment. Laycock further believed that pervasively religious schools should have received similar protection if they did not impose substantially on outsiders.

[39] 330 U.S. 1 (1947).

[40] Note 11 supra.

[41] Id. at 681. In this respect the case differs from *Marsh v. Chambers*, 463 U.S. 783 (1983), involving legislative chaplains.

[42] *Walz*, note 11 supra, at 681.

it much more with religion than did allowing an exemption. Thus, possible entanglement was here a ground to sustain a benefit for religion, in contrast to most later cases in which concerns about entanglement served to invalidate schemes of aid.[43]

What is less clear about the case is the importance of the extension of the exemption to a wide range of charitable activities. On this point, Justice Brennan and Justice Harlan, in separate concurrences, took a somewhat different slant from the Court. Justice Brennan thought that the exemption was permissible because religious organizations, like the other exempted nonprofit organizations, "contribute to the well-being of the community in a variety of unreligious ways"[44] and because they "uniquely contribute to the pluralism of American society by their religious activities."[45] Justice Harlan, after highlighting the importance of preventing government involvements in religious life that may lead to strife and may strain the political system,[46] urged that neutrality requires the avoidance of "religious gerrymanders."[47] Because New York offered the exemption to historical and literary societies and to associations "for the moral or mental improvement of men," churches fall naturally within this broader class and properly receive the exemption even apart from any conventional charitable activities they perform.[48]

Although the majority gave some emphasis to the breadth of the exemption, Burger's opinion does not explicitly make that critical. Rather, stressing our early history, in which churches were the dominant beneficiaries of property tax exemptions, it found that the exemption was a valid safeguard against hostility toward religion. And because entanglement of the state with nonreligious charities would not present a significant constitutional problem, the Court's reliance on nonentanglement could itself be taken as a basis to permit an exemption to religious groups, independent of any larger package of exemptions.

Whether religious organizations *must* fall within a broader class if an exemption for them is to be valid has been a subject of continuing controversy, and competing sides have debated the true significance of *Walz*. It is helpful to distinguish two different arguments about the broader class into which religious organizations might fall, arguments that connect to two different

---

[43] Most of these cases are discussed in chapter 19, infra.
[44] *Walz*, note 11 supra, at 687.
[45] Id. at 689.
[46] Id. at 694.
[47] Id. at 696.
[48] Id. at 696–97.

purposes for exemptions. One argument is that religious organizations should receive an exemption as one among groups that perform socially beneficial activities that the government would otherwise have to undertake. Many churches have various outreach programs that benefit the community. This could entitle them to be treated like other charities. A problem with this rationale is that many religious groups do not undertake significant programs of this sort, but one must agree with Chief Justice Burger that the state should not judge the precise degree of outreach of any single church.[49] Thus, one might justify giving any exemption to all religious organizations because many of them do substantial charitable work.

The second argument concerns the efforts of religious organizations to promote moral and mental improvement. That is a purpose of all religious organizations, even those that benefit only members and even those whose only significant activity is worship. Most religious groups might formulate their mission in terms of spiritual sustenance rather than mental improvement, but participation in spiritual life can be one form of mental improvement. For this rationale, stressed by Justice Harlan, outreach activities are not crucial. What is crucial is that the category of organizations receiving exemptions include others whose main purpose is to enlighten and teach, whether or not they provide charitable assistance to the broader public.

If an exemption for religious organizations is to be justified on this basis, it cannot be because the government could undertake what they do. The government can undertake various activities for moral and mental improvement, but it cannot do what most religious organizations do. Nor can it declare that particular religious beliefs and practices are true.[50] But if it exempts other nonprofit organizations devoted broadly to personal improvement, it can treat religious approaches equally. Indeed, not to do so might discriminate against religion in a way that would be unconstitutional.

Whatever one regards as its exact parameters, *Walz* clearly established the acceptability of property tax exemptions as they are now commonly formulated. The decision erased as well any doubts about income tax relief for churches and income tax deductions for contributions to religious groups, also part of a much broader package of available charitable deductions.

The next important taxation case involved a state statute that exempted from sales and use taxes "periodicals . . . published or distributed by a religious faith . . . consist[ing] wholly of writings promulgating the teachings of

---

[49] Id. at 674.

[50] However, as chapters 7–9 explain in relation to schools, the government can present ideas as true that are in conflict with various religious claims.

the faith and books . . . consist[ing] wholly of writings sacred to a religious faith." The Court struck down the law in *Texas Monthly, Inc. v. Bullock*,[51] but without a majority opinion. Justice White thought there was a simple violation of the Free Press Clause, because the law discriminated by the content of publications.[52] Five justices voted to invalidate the law based on the Establishment Clause. Justice Brennan, with Justices Marshall and Stevens, wrote the plurality opinion. Justice Blackman, joined by Justice O'Connor, adopted a narrower principle of decision.[53] We can best understand the Blackmun opinion against that of Justice Brennan, and it is the latter who draws most of the fire of Justice Scalia's dissent.

According to Justice Brennan, the purpose and effects test of *Lemon* establishes that government "may not place its prestige, coercive authority, or resources behind a single religious faith or behind religious belief in general."[54] Referring to *Walz* and other cases, Brennan stressed that the benefits flowed to a large number of nonreligious organizations as well as religious ones. Had only religious organizations benefited, the state would have been sponsoring religion, and "we would not have hesitated to strike [the laws] down for lacking a secular purpose and effect."[55]

In one of the more serious efforts to draw a line between permissible accommodation and impermissible establishment, Justice Brennan wrote that a subsidy to religious groups "that is not required by the Free Exercise Clause and that either burdens nonbeneficiaries markedly or cannot reasonably be seen as removing a significant state-imposed deterrent to the free exercise of religion" unjustifiably assists religious organizations and conveys a message of endorsement.[56] This formulation's suggestion that *either* a marked burden on nonbeneficiaries *or* a failure to remove a state-imposed deterrent to free exercise can be enough to make favorable treatment of religion invalid, de-

[51] 489 U.S. 1 (1989).

[52] Id. at 25–26 (concurring opinion). We have seen that a similar point of view carried the day in the later case of *Rosenberger v. Rector and Visitors of the University of Virginia*, 515 U.S. 819 (1995), dealing with the state's refusal to fund the publication of a student religious periodical.

[53] *Texas Monthly*, note 51 supra, at 26–29. Since their votes were critical to invalidation, one might reasonably say that their opinion best represents what the case stands for.

[54] Id. at 9. In this connection, Brennan cited Justice O'Connor's comments about endorsing religion in *Wallace v. Jaffree* and in *Lynch v. Donnelly*.

[55] Id. at 11. Brennan acknowledged that in *Walz* the Court had not found it necessary to justify the exemption on the basis of social welfare services or good works of churches, but "we in no way intimated that the exemption would have been valid had it applied *only* to the property of religious groups." Id. at 12 n. 2.

[56] Id. at 15. Whether a burden on nonbeneficiaries or a failure to remove a significant state-imposed deterrent is enough alone to make a law invalid is a subject to which we shall return in chapters 16 and 17.

notes a fairly narrow scope for permissive accommodation—one that, as I explain in chapter 17, is too narrow. Texas's tax exemption failed on both counts, Brennan said. It did not remove a state-imposed deterrent on religious exercise and it burdened nonbeneficiaries who would end up paying higher taxes.[57] An exemption cannot be limited to discussion of religious issues, let alone to publications advocating religious belief.[58]

In response to the state's argument that had it failed to exempt religious publications, it might have violated free exercise rights, Brennan found no evidence that application of the sales tax would offend religious beliefs or inhibit religious activity.[59] He acknowledged that his approach was at odds with some "sweeping statements" in *Murdock*. Insofar as the language of that case suggested that the sales of religious publications cannot be taxed, Justice Brennan disavowed "those dicta."[60] But the results in *Murdock* and *Follett* could be justified on the free exercise ground that a state may not impose a flax license tax that applies to commercial salesmen on religious missionaries who "occasionally sell religious tracts for small sums."[61]

Justice Brennan added an entanglement argument. Officials administering the exemption, and determining what is a religious publication within the meaning of the statute, might engage in inconsistent treatment or become embroiled in controversies over religious doctrine.[62]

For Justice Blackmun, the case presented a conflict of free exercise and no establishment values.[63] Believing that the Texas statute engaged in unacceptable preferential support for religious messages,[64] he suggested that an exemption statute might be all right if it included "philosophical literature distributed by nonreligious organizations devoted to such matters of conscience as life and death, good and evil, being and nonbeing, right and wrong."[65]

Joined by Chief Justice Rehnquist and Justice Kennedy, Justice Scalia, dissenting, pointed out that many states have exemptions for religious publica-

---

[57] Id. at 19 n. 8.

[58] Id. at 16.

[59] Id. at 18. In any event, *United States v. Lee*, 455 U.S. 252 (1982), suggests that the government can collect taxes even when to do so does violate religious tenets. Id. at 19–20.

[60] Id. at 21, 24.

[61] Id. at 23.

[62] Id. at 29.

[63] Id. at 26–27. He thought that Justice Brennan's opinion sacrificed free exercise in relation to no establishment and that Justice Scalia's dissent sacrificed no establishment in relation to free exercise.

[64] Id. at 28.

[65] Id. at 27–28. Justice Blackmun seemed to assume that Brennan would not accept such an exemption, but that is unclear to me from Brennan's opinion.

tions,[66] and that the Court's ruling could well undercut other tax benefits that are limited to religious groups. Justice Scalia contended that *Walz* strongly supported the Texas exemption, based as that case was on the historical record and a judgment that an exemption may guard against hostility to religion. Tax exemptions for religions are justified as a permissible accommodation to religious practice, not because religious groups fit within some broader class of beneficiaries.[67]

Justice Scalia granted that distinguishing accommodation from promotion may not always be easy, but withholding of a sales tax for "religious materials is not even a close case."[68] Whether or not *Murdock* established that the exemption was constitutionally required, it at least showed that it was constitutionally permissible.[69]

Both because of the division of the justices and because the case involved a distinction based on the content of publications, *Texas Monthly* does not settle the status of various exemptions granted on the basis of religion alone. Most notable may be the parsonage exemption that allows clerics not to count as income the provision of a house or housing allowance by their churches.[70] It should not be sufficient that religion is singled out simply because the government can choose to favor religion in granting exemptions. Something else is needed. The something else could be the absence of nonre-

[66] Id. at 30.

[67] Id. at 38. Justice Scalia argued that Justice Brennan wrongly attributed to the Court his own theory for resolving *Walz*. He claimed, further, that Justice Brennan's opinion confused cases in which breadth of categorization matters because aid is given to activities that achieve a particular secular goal, such as education, with cases in which accommodation to religion is the underlying rationale (for which breadth is not required). Id. at 39–40.

[68] Id. at 40. Justice Scalia implicitly rejected Justice Blackmun's approach without analysis. Justice Blackmun had suggested that accommodation may underlie a benefit, but that Establishment Clause values may then help determine the scope of coverage, the position I have taken with respect to conscientious objection and some other matters. If the Blackmun opinion indicated just how far a majority of the Court was willing to take nonestablishment at that point in time, Scalia's disregard may seem surprising. I can only guess at the following explanation. Justice Brennan, the senior member in the majority, assigned himself the opinion. He circulated an opinion, hoping it would attract five votes. Justice Scalia wrote and circulated his dissent. Justice Blackmun then circulated his concurrence. Recognizing both that his substantive claims answered Justice Blackmun as well as Justice Brennan, and considering Brennan's opinion a clearer and more inviting target, Justice Scalia decided not to clutter his opinion with references to Justice Blackmun.

[69] Id. at 41. Just one year later, Justice Scalia's opinion in *Employment Division v. Smith*, 494 U.S. 872 (1990), sharply circumscribed what the Free Exercise Clause *requires*; one supposes he had already probably decided that the Texas tax exemption was not actually constitutionally required.

[70] For competing views, see Dean T. Barham, "The Parsonage Exclusion under the Endorsement Test: Last Gasp or Second Wind," 13 *Virginia Tax Review* 397 (1993) (valid), and Matthew W. Foster, "The Parsonage Allowance Exclusion: Past, Present, and Future," 44 *Vanderbilt Law Review* 149 (1991) (invalid).

ligious activities that are significantly parallel, a similar forum of treatment of nonreligious activities under some other provision, the relief of some government-imposed burden on religion, or a substantial justification in terms of avoiding entanglement between government and religion.

In favor of the parsonage allowance, it may be said that other charities do not have the tradition of their leaders living next to the main locus of their activities, and that clerics who reside within the boundaries of their church properties consistently make their living spaces available for church activities.[71] Further, were the government to tax the provision of such a house as income, determining how much a minister might subtract because she uses the house for her work might prove very complicated. Of course, this rationale does not apply with full force to ministers who buy or rent property away from their churches, but that extension might be justified as needed to achieve fairness among ministers and among churches. Nonetheless, including as it does residences that are far removed from the churches themselves, a housing allowance limited to clerics is difficult to defend.

Another distinction in federal law is between churches (including synagogues, mosques, etc.) and other religious and charitable organizations. Churches are free of reporting requirements that everyone else must satisfy.[72] One might worry that church reporting and government auditing would tangle religion and the state unduly or suppose that some small, informal churches (unlike other religious organizations and charities) would find it difficult to make the needed financial reports; but one needs to stretch to come up with a plausible justification for favoring churches in this way.

CONDITIONS OF ELIGIBILITY

Charities may maintain their tax exempt status only if they do not engage in "substantial" lobbying efforts "to influence legislation"[73] and do not support or oppose political candidates.[74] The latter restriction is absolute, although it is not simple to say exactly which activities are covered,[75] and

---

[71] I do not mean to suggest that *only* clerics use their houses in this way. Many universities provide houses for their presidents that are on or adjacent to their campuses, and they do so with the expectation that the presidents will use the houses for university functions.

[72] See John M. Swomley, "The Impact of Tax Exemption and Deductibility on Churches and Public Policy," 22 *Cumberland Law Review* 595, 599 (1991–92), for a critical discussion.

[73] 26 U.S.C. § 501(h).

[74] 26 U.S.C. § 501(c)(3).

[75] See Steffen N. Johnson, "Of Politics and Pulpits: A First Amendment Analysis of IRS Restrictions on the Political Activities of Religious Organizations," 42 *Boston College Law Review* 875, 880,

religious groups have found ways to indicate their support of particular candidates indirectly. The Supreme Court has upheld the restriction on lobbying in respect to a nonreligious group,[76] and we have no reason to think it would take a different view of either requirement as it applies to religious groups.[77] So long as contributions to lobbying efforts and to campaigns are not tax deductible, the government has an interest in seeing that money for these purposes is not funneled through religious and charitable organizations,[78] but that hardly seems to justify the absolute rule against candidate support.

Whatever may be true about other charities, the application of these restrictions to religious organizations may interfere with a group's sense of its mission.[79] If a church regards racial discrimination or abortion as evil, it may feel constrained to support candidates who oppose these practices. From a wider standpoint, if churches are independent organizations that can benefit the polity as a whole by opposing arbitrary government power, these restrictions limit their efforts in this respect. With some exaggeration, it has been urged that the law attempts to move religion into the private sphere.[80] A further concern is that the vagueness of "substantial" in respect to lobbying, the uncertainty about exactly which efforts count as support of candidates, and the impossibility of full enforcement create unfortunate opportunities for discrimination by those administering the law. Some restrictions on political activities are warranted for religious groups, as well as other charities, that benefit from tax exemptions and deductions, but the formulation about candidate support is now too uncertain in its coverage and too restrictive in its scope.

895–99 (2001); David D. Kirkpatrick, "Pastors' Get-Out-the-Vote Training Could Test Tax Rules," *New York Times*, March 21, 2006.

[76] *Regan v. Taxation With Representation*, 461 U.S. 540 (1983).

[77] Religious groups would have a possible claim under the Religious Freedom Restoration Act, but, given judicial deference to Congress about tax policy, such a claim would be unlikely to succeed.

[78] See Johnson, note 75 supra, at 893–94.

[79] Edward McFlynn Gaffney, Jr., "On Not Rendering to Caesar: The Unconstitutionality of Tax Regulation of Activities of Religious Organizations Relating to Politics," 40 *DePaul Law Review* 1 (1990).

[80] Richard W. Garnett, "A Quiet Faith? Taxes, Politics, and the Privatization of Religion," 42 *Boston College Law Review* 771, 774 (2001). It is because churches are still completely free to express positions on issues of social justice that I see this understanding as exaggerated.

CHAPTER 16

Religion and the Exemption Strategy

Among the most troubling questions about the Free Exercise and Establishment Clauses are when exemptions from ordinary regulations are warranted and how any exemptions, and other benefits going to religious groups, should be formulated. Religious individuals or groups may want badly to engage in activities that legislators have reasons generally to forbid. For example, legislators believe they should forbid the use of hallucinogenic drugs, including peyote, traditionally used by the Native American Church; church members regard peyote as a crucial element of their religious ceremonies. Conversely, some religious individuals believe they should not perform acts that a legislature designs as general duties, such as jury service or compulsory military service.

Looked at from the broadest perspective, the central question about exemptions is whether they are warranted at all. On this issue, we can see religious exemptions as a subclass of exemptions that might legitimately be granted; and it is instructive to compare claims for them with arguments that the state should provide exemptions for threatened minority cultures.

If any exemption is warranted, how should its boundaries be drawn? In this respect too, the comparison with cultural claims is illuminating, as is the possibility that all those whose need for exemption rests on conscience or deep concern should be granted one.

The free exercise volume, and, to a lesser extent, this volume, say a good deal about these subjects in relation to religion, but here I supply a wider theoretical frame and draw the threads together in a general overview. I consider with much more care than I have previously the arguments against exemptions.

In this chapter, we will look at these questions: (1) Are exemptions from general laws ever warranted? (2) If so, is the granting of exemptions always a matter of legislative grace or discretion, or is it sometimes a matter of justice or duty? (3) What are legitimate reasons for granting exemptions? (4) How frequently is the exemption strategy warranted, and how frequently is it required as a matter of justice? (5) If exemptions are to be granted, are the claims of religious persons to receive them among the strongest that the state faces? (6) Is the state ever justified in granting exemptions only to religious persons? (7) Is the state ever justified in granting exemptions only to persons within religious groups, or within named religious groups? (8) If the state is sometimes justified in granting an exemption only to religious persons, is it always justified in limiting the exemption to them, or should it sometimes extend the exemption further? (9) How far, if at all, should the granting of an exemption be a matter of constitutional right, enforceable by courts, within a polity that has a guarantee of the free exercise of religion? (10) How far should a free exercise right, or a rule of nonestablishment of religion, or both, restrict the boundaries of categorization if a legislature grants an exemption? (11) In particular, may a legislature, consistent with the Constitution, limit an exemption to religious individuals, to members of religious groups, or to members of named religious groups?

These eleven questions raise three others: (12) Insofar as a line between religious and nonreligious claims is acceptable, how should religion be understood? (13) How far should the understanding of what counts as religion be developed by courts as a matter of constitutional principle? (14) When the state grants an exception (or other benefit) or requires private persons or companies to grant an exemption, does the issue of constitutionality turn on whether the state has itself caused the conditions that generate the need for the exemption or benefit?

My answers to these questions, as I explain below, are these: (1) Exemptions are sometimes warranted. (2) They are sometimes matters of duty or justice. (3) Grounds for exemption may be to relieve burdens upon deep concerns, to protect against unfair treatment, but not to assure survival of religious groups or understandings. (4) The exemption strategy is warranted more than rarely. (5) More than rarely, it is required by justice. (6) The state is sometimes warranted in granting exemptions only to religious persons. (7) Less frequently, it is justified in limiting the exemption to members of religious groups; it should never limit an exemption to members of named groups, but it can include members of named groups as beneficiaries. (8) The state should sometimes extend an exemption to nonreligious persons. (9) Some claims for exemption should be matters of constitutional right, enforced by courts. (10) Both free exercise and nonestablishment provisions limit the boundaries of acceptable classification. (11) Sometimes they preclude an exemption limited to religious persons and members of religious groups. Always they preclude an exemption limited to members of named groups.

My answers to questions (12) and (13) are developed in chapter 8 on the concept of religion in volume 1. I there conclude that religion should be understood in an analogical way and that the courts should play a role in developing the boundaries of religion as an aspect of constitutional interpretation. The issues raised by question (14) are reserved for the following chapter, which considers a range of ways in which courts might distinguish between permissible accommodations and impermissible establishments. That chapter treats exemptions as one very important form of accommodation, but also discusses other kinds of accommodations, such as the state's providing resources to religious groups to carry out their endeavors or undertaking practices—moments of silence are an example—in which everyone may engage, but which are adopted to allow religious exercises. The division between exemptions and other accommodations is not a sharp one. A released time program that allows children in public schools to use part of the school day for religious instruction is an exemption from a requirement to remain in the public school; it is also a grant of the resource of time for religious instruction.

We need to distinguish outright exemptions from other ways in which religious or cultural understandings could affect criminal or civil liability. Suppose the law of child neglect requires parents to seek medical assistance for children who are seriously ill, but, in respect to criminal penalties for serious parental failures, it contains an exception for parents who believe that faith healing is preferable to ordinary medicine. That is an exemption. But liability can be influenced in more subtle ways. Religious or cultural beliefs may bear on crucial mental states. Manslaughter may require a reckless disregard for life, in a sense that requires that someone be subjectively aware of a risk.[1] A parent who is absolutely certain that faith healing will work is not reckless in failing to consult an ordinary doctor for an ill child (although he may well be guilty of the lesser crime of negligent homicide).[2]

THE EXEMPTION STRATEGY: A MATTER OF JUSTICE?

Let us suppose that the government has some good reason to forbid an activity, such as riding a motorcycle without a helmet. Members of a particular

---

[1] In some states, an unreasonable failure to recognize risk is the basis for some level of manslaughter, but in these states, actual awareness of risk typically underlies a graver degree of manslaughter.

[2] Someone who kills intentionally may have his liability reduced from murder to manslaughter if he acts from an emotional disturbance for which there is a reasonable explanation or excuse. A man who kills his wife because she has committed adultery might conceivably succeed with this defense of mitigation if his culture and religion tell him that he should act in this way.

group strongly want not to be subject to such a regulation, because wearing a helmet and also wearing a head covering called for by their religion and culture is physically impossible. Sikh men, for example, may believe that they should wear turbans as aspects of religious observance.[3] What should the legislature do?

It has three options. One is to adopt the regulation without any exceptions. Another is to decide against requiring anyone to wear helmets. The third option is the exemption strategy. People, in general, are required to wear helmets, but an exception is made for a limited class of persons. If the legislation pursues the exemption strategy, it must define the category of those who will receive the exemption.

An exemption might be cast in terms of an activity, a belief, or a status, or some combination of these. Thus, an exemption from combatant military service granted to all those who are conscientiously opposed to such service is phrased in terms of belief. An exemption from a prohibition on the use of peyote given for use in worship services by members of religious congregations that standardly use peyote in worship, such as the Native American Church, would be formulated in terms of activity (use in services) and status (membership in a group of this kind).

Any intuition we may have that the state should sometimes make concessions to strong religious claims needs to be tested against arguments that exemptions are misguided, or at most are a subject of legislative grace. This exercise can help us to identify appropriate grounds for exemptions.

It helps initially to draw two distinctions. The first is emphasized by Jeremy Waldron.[4] The instances for which an exemption is sought may or may not present the danger that underlies the regulation. Waldron discusses a strange case in which an Afghani immigrant was prosecuted for having mouth-genital contact with his infant son.[5] Apparently it is a customary practice in Afghanistan for a father to kiss the penis of his baby son. The law was aimed at sexual abuse; the contact in the case was not sexual. Similarly, it may be said that one reason an exemption from a prohibition on drinking of alcoholic beverages is warranted for communion is that the extremely small amount of wine people consume then presents no danger of intoxication.[6]

---

[3] I am assuming here that it is not easy to construct helmets large enough to cover turbans.

[4] Jeremy Waldron, "One Law for All? The Logic of Cultural Accommodation," 59 *Washington and Lee Law Review* 3, 5–9 (2002).

[5] *State v. Kargar*, 679 A.2d 81 (Me. 1996).

[6] However, a small sip might conceivably lead a congregant to want more to drink, and a priest who consumes consecrated wine remaining after the ceremony might possibly drink enough to become intoxicated.

In other circumstances, the actions for which exemption is sought do involve the dangers a regulation is designed to curb. If Sikhs wear turbans instead of helmets when they ride motorcycles, they suffer the ordinary risks of riding helmetless. If a reason to prohibit peyote is to prevent hallucinatory effects, that reason covers religious ceremonies during which these effects are understood to have deep religious significance. A claim for an exemption is strengthened if the instances to be exempted do not involve the harm that underlies a regulation.

Drawing from a different dichotomy proposed by Christopher Eisgruber and Lawrence Sager, we can distinguish between claims that a belief or activity should be specially privileged and claims that it should be protected against unfair treatment.[7] The idea underlying privilege is that religion, or culture, or conscience deserves special consideration, because it is particularly valuable or important, or because many people care intensely about it.

One argument based on privilege is that the state should aim to preserve a way of life that is intimately connected to the practice for which an exemption is sought. Reserving other claims of privilege for later consideration, we may dispose of the preservation argument, as far as religion is concerned. A liberal state cannot have the *aim* to preserve a religion, in the sense that some multiculturalists believe the state should try to preserve minority cultures.[8] Whatever may be a desirable approach to minority cultures,[9] a liberal state should be neutral among religious perspectives, not aiming to get citizens to adopt one particular religion or another. Barring past or present oppression by the government or other members of a society, the government should not try to preserve a religion that might otherwise disappear; doing so would be aiming to get some citizens to continue to adhere to that religion.

---

[7] Christopher L. Eisgruber and Lawrence A. Sager, "The Vulnerability of Conscience: The Constitutional Basis for Protecting Religious Conduct," 61 *University of Chicago Law Review* 1245, 1248 (1994).

[8] See, e.g., Irwin Deutscher, *Accommodating Diversity: National Policies That Prevent Ethnic Conflict* (Lanham, Md.: Lexington Books, 2002); Dean Harris, ed., *Multiculturalism from the Margins: Non-dominant Voices on Difference and Diversity* (Westport, Conn.: Bergin and Garvey, 1995).

[9] There is a complexity here that I will remark but not try to resolve. If the government legitimately tries to maintain a minority culture, such as that of the Inuit, that culture will include religious elements, and these are not likely to be sharply distinguished from other aspects of culture. A policy to maintain the culture cannot easily aim to maintain the culture minus those religious elements. What is the government then to do? One might say it can include religious elements with all others, attempting to preserve them as aspects of culture, not because they are religious. But probably the government should concentrate on nonreligious elements, insofar as possible, allowing the religious elements to be preserved only because they are connected to other elements that are supported. In any event, this problem would not affect the legitimacy of a policy to preserve Christian Science or Mormonism, religions not connected to any minority culture.

It may be said, to the contrary, that James Madison relied in the Federalist on the diversity of religions in the United States,[10] that were this diversity to diminish, it would be harmful politically and spiritually. Further, in *Wisconsin v. Yoder*, the Supreme Court was apparently influenced by expert testimony that were Amish children required to attend school until they were sixteen, this could threaten the existence of the Amish community.[11]

The answer to the argument from Madison is that diversity of religions may indeed be beneficial spiritually and politically but that does not mean it should be a conscious objective of the state. Moreover, given the extraordinary religious diversity that now exists in the United States, and will exist in any foreseeable future, it is wholly fanciful to imagine that preservation of some small religious group that might otherwise die out is needed to maintain adequate religious diversity. As for *Yoder*, insofar as a group's survival is relevant, it matters because it shows the group's intense concern about the practice it wants to maintain, and bears on the harshness of the government's forbidding that practice, not because the state should have an objective to keep religions alive.

We can see the idea of protection as the safeguarding of those who seek an exemption to avoid treatment that is unfair in relation to how others are treated. Most straightforwardly, the claim may be that treatment is really unequal, despite formal or surface equality. When claims for exemptions are viewed in this way, proponents and opponents may dispute what kind of treatment is "really" equal, or, more precisely, which kind of equality is normatively most important.

Unfair treatment can take the form of self-conscious discrimination, but it can be more subtle, involving only conscious indifference (e.g., regulators are not aiming to harm a group, but they are aware the group will suffer badly and do not care) or inadvertent neglect (e.g., regulators are not aware of how a group will suffer). Among critical issues about protection are whether the intentions and awareness of legislators matter and whether judges can reasonably decide if a failure to exempt involves one of these forms of unfair treatment.[12]

---

[10] One possible basis to support a minority religion would be to compensate for past oppression of that religion, as occurred with regard to Native American religions in the United States. To take a simple, extreme, example, if a government tried to suppress a religion by burning its houses of worship, it could later rebuild those. A government might also respond to oppression by groups of citizens. Thus, fearing antagonistic actions by members of a Hindu majority, the government of India might aim to protect Muslim practices.

[11] 406 U.S. 205 (1972).

[12] One possible approach would be to "objectify" the inquiry, asking what a person who has voted as have the legislators would probably think rather than asking what the actual legislators probably thought.

We turn now to what we may call exemption-skepticism. The most important arguments against a use of the exemption strategy are based on rule of law, equality, and administrability. As Waldron has noted, one aspect of Dicey's concept of the rule of law is that laws apply to all persons, not providing one rule for officials, another for citizens, one rule for nobility, another for commoners.[13] Dicey's main target was those in power privileging themselves, but we can extend the rule-of-law concern to other special exceptions to ordinary standards of behavior. An exception granted exclusively on the basis of *activity* is not in tension with the rule of law, so long as any person may participate in the activity that enjoys the exception.[14] But exceptions granted on the basis of belief or status do threaten the realization of this ideal.

The concern about equality relates closely to that about rule of law. An exemption treats some people differently from others; it allows some to do what others may not do. This difference in treatment requires justification.[15]

The worry about administrability applies to beliefs and, less strongly, to status. Any exemption requires enforcement officials to identify who qualifies. That will be simple if the exemption extends to all those engaging in an easily observable activity, such as wearing a turban. Identification is more complicated if officials must ascertain membership or another kind of status, but *usually* saying whether someone belongs to a particular group or occupies a particular position will not be too hard. Ascertaining beliefs is much more troublesome. It may take a substantial administrative apparatus to determine if someone is a conscientious objector, and determinations may often be erroneous. Much the same is true if an exemption turns on how important a belief or practice is within an individual's or group's overall set of beliefs.

The force of these various concerns may lead us to wonder if an exemption strategy is ever justified. If some people have a very strong reason not to be subjected to a regulation, that is a good reason not to impose the regulation on anyone; if the government has a powerful reason to regulate, perhaps it should make no exceptions. Perhaps withdrawing exemptions already

---

[13] Waldron, note 4 supra, at 3.

[14] If the activity is one that only some people can comfortably undertake, such as the practice that once existed of allowing men who paid a high fee to be excused from compulsory military service, an exemption cast in terms of an action may be regarded as unfairly depending on a kind of status. For any exemption based on action, one can ask if it connects unfairly to status or belief. With respect to some activities, such as wearing turbans, that only a specific group of people wish to engage in, an exemption based on an activity may in reality be limited to people with a particular membership or status.

[15] Again, this problem does not arise if the exemption is cast in terms of an activity that does not connect significantly to membership or status.

granted would be impolitic, but, in principle, the government should be very hesitant to grant them. This view is powerfully defended in *Culture and Equality*[16] by Brian Barry, who employs a "pincers" approach: "Usually . . . either the case for the law (or some version of it) is strong enough to rule out exemptions, or the case that can be made for exemptions is strong enough to suggest that there should be no law anyway."[17]

Among the subjects Barry discusses are requirements of humane slaughter, the wearing of motorcycle helmets, the attachment of a red and orange triangle to the back of slow vehicles, and school clothing that excludes head scarves. His rich discussion of these examples and others is not easily summarized, but I can provide enough of their flavor to indicate his overall position.

Humane slaughter laws require that animals be stunned before they are killed. According to Jewish kosher and Muslim halal standards, slaughter should be by their traditional methods, which Barry calls "a euphemism for bleeding animals to death while conscious."[18] Barry notes that in some countries that do not make exceptions, rabbis have accepted the stunning of animals and that Jews and Muslims unwilling to make this adjustment are free to become vegetarians.[19] Barry clearly believes that the interest in preventing animal suffering is sufficient to sustain an exceptionless law.

He takes a similar view about the requirement that slow vehicles display a red and orange reflective triangle on their rear.[20] Skeptical of the strength of the claim of a subgroup of the Amish that the symbol was too "worldly," and crediting the testimony of experts that no alternative would provide as much protection as this internationally recognized symbol, he regards the state case decided in favor of the Amish as "absurd."

Barry's position about motorcycle helmets is more complex.[21] He is attracted by the idea that Sikhs, like everyone else, actually have an opportunity to ride with a helmet, and that if they do not wish to do so, they can forgo riding motorcycles. He also recognizes that there may be strong reasons of religion and custom, and of preference, to ride without helmets. Given these reasons, he thinks it is arguable whether the helmet requirement should be imposed on any one, despite the safety considerations, mainly paternalistic ones, in favor of the rule.

[16] Brian Barry, *Culture and Equality* (Cambridge: Harvard University Press, 2001).

[17] Id. at 39.

[18] Id. at 41.

[19] Id. at 35.

[20] Id. at 184–87.

[21] Id. at 33–34, 49. Barry writes that "it is questionable that the wearing of a turban is a religious obligation for Sikhs, as against a customary practice among some," id. at 33, but that doubt is not crucial for his analysis.

About head scarves, Barry recognizes a strong cultural and religious basis for their use; but if schools and employers are to allow Muslim women and girls to wear them, perhaps the best approach would be to allow their use by everyone.[22]

These examples give us a sense of Barry's pincers. He acknowledges that once exemptions have been granted, eliminating them may create practical problems, including bad effects on relations among religious groups and alienation among minorities who have received the exemptions.[23] But if we ask whether exemptions should be granted in the first place, Barry responds, "Once we accept . . . that the case for exemption must be based on the alleviation of hardship rather than the demands of justice, it seems to me much more problematic to make it out than is widely assumed."[24] To "make sense," the exemption approach "requires a combination of very precise conditions that are rarely satisfied all together. It must be important to have a rule generally prohibiting conduct of a certain kind. . . . [but] having a rule must not be so important as to preclude allowing exceptions to it."[25] Not too many cases fit these conditions.[26]

Evaluating the strength of the argument against exemptions depends on assessing equality and rule of law concerns, and on deciding whether the reasons to exempt some persons can be fairly distinguished from reasons that those who do not benefit from an exemption may have not to comply. In one simple form, the antiexemption claim is that people with strong preferences to commit otherwise illegal acts do not receive exemptions and that reasons of conscience, religion, and culture are not relevantly distinguishable from strong preferences. Therefore, the exemption strategy is misguided. The argument, at least in this simple form, is misconceived not only in its equation of conscience and religious observance with strong preferences—the typical objection—but also in its assumption about the status of strong preferences.

Let me take the second point first. Prohibitive laws do not exempt those with strong desires to engage in the forbidden behavior. Indeed, many serious criminal laws are aimed primarily at just those who have such desires, since

---

[22] Id. at 57–61.

[23] Id. at 50.

[24] Id. at 39.

[25] Id. at 62.

[26] Id. A formulation that sounds somewhat more receptive to religious exemptions is at id. at 175, but he repeats his observation that exemptions are not required by justice. In discussing this chapter, Akeel Bilgrami has suggested that the typical circumstance in which an exemption is warranted may be when the wisdom of a restriction is itself doubtful. Perhaps many justified exemptions may be so explained, but not all. For example, compulsory military service was undoubtedly warranted for World War II, but so also was an exemption for conscientious objectors.

most people are effectively constrained by their moral sense from committing murder, rape, and so on. But when we come to regulations involving motorcycle helmets, regulations mainly designed to protect the very people whose actions are restrained, is it so obvious that no exception should be made for those with intense preferences not to wear helmets?

To pose this question in principle, we need first to put aside problems of administrability. Measuring intensity of preference is well nigh impossible;[27] and people with some desire to engage in a prohibited activity have an incentive to overstate that desire if those with strong preferences are to be excused. The only way in which a strong preference exception could be administered would be by having people purchase a license to ride without a helmet or make some other sacrifice that most people would not be willing to make. Short of such a scheme, a prohibition cannot, practically, make exceptions for those with strong preferences. But that does not tell us whether such exceptions would be otherwise desirable; and that alone is not a powerful reason to deny more limited exemptions that are administrable.[28]

We need first to assume that the strong preferences in question are not immoral, self-destructive, or developed in a manner that perpetuates social inequality. A strong preference would be immoral if it is unduly neglectful of the interests of others. A preference would be self-destructive (and perhaps immoral) if its indulgence would harm its holder. Preferences of alcoholics to drink and of addicts to use hard drugs are self-destructive in this way, and a legislature might well decide not to yield to preferences whose fulfillment is damaging. The idea about preferences that perpetuate inequalities is harder to pin down, but seems partly to underlie assumptions that those with expensive tastes should not be rewarded by getting a greater share of goods. Barry uses the example of people with a strong desire to eat plovers' eggs and drink vintage claret.[29] Poor people are not likely to develop these tastes, and someone's developing of the tastes may seem self-indulgent. If the issue is distribution of economic resources, it seems unfair that *others should have less* because the people with expensive tastes have powerful desires for food that costs more.

We should not leap from a conclusion about expensive tastes and the distribution of limited resources to a conclusion about all strong preferences

---

[27] More precisely, it is virtually impossible to measure the intensity of A's desire to do x against B's desire to do x. Measuring A's desire to do x against A's desire to do y or z is not so hard.

[28] However, if strong preferences should be exempted, but for problems of administration, there could be some concern about whether those with such preferences are fairly treated if others are exempted.

[29] Note 16 supra, at 34–35.

and all prohibitions. Most people have intensely positive feelings about some activities in which they engage. The activity that most commonly creates intense physical pleasure and satisfaction is sexual relations. Let us imagine that for some few individuals—ecstatic riders—riding a motorcycle without a helmet is like a sexual experience, and riding with a helmet is terribly unsatisfying. Riding without a helmet definitely increases physical risk, but is the increase in safety of a restriction worth the cost? If we focused only on the pleasure of sexual relations, putting aside its connections to love, companionship, and procreation,[30] and we supposed that sexual relations carried risks comparable to those of riding without helmets,[31] we would still be very surprised if a legislature would forbid all sexual acts. Legislators would not deem the reduction in physical risk to be worth the cost to the quality of life. It follows that in regard to the ecstatic riders, viewed as a separate class, the balance of benefit and harm of regulation is unfavorable. Would it not make sense to exempt them *if* they could be easily identified?[32] Note that excusing the ecstatic riders would not impose on other riders who are required to wear helmets, in the manner that a shift of tangible resources does.[33] This hypothetical raises some serious questions about a premise that, in principle, those with strong preferences do not warrant exemptions; but I shall not pursue these further.

Assuming that strong preferences do not warrant exemptions, how should we compare strong preferences with conscientious opposition or with a need that connects to participation in a group or to activities that carry a deep meaning beyond extreme physical satisfaction? Here Barry's stance resists distinctions and comparisons that are often made. His basic position is that people have an opportunity to do things, whether or not their disinclination to do them is based on strong preference or conviction. Remember that in discussing humane slaughter and motorcycle helmets, Barry points out that people with religious objections need not eat meat or ride motorcycles. The state does not demand that they violate their religious sentiments; their problem arises only because they have a powerful wish to eat meat or to ride a motorcycle.[34]

---

[30] In the near future, artificial means may suffice for procreation.

[31] Of course, some sexual relations do carry grave risks.

[32] If one reason to require helmets is to reduce medical expenses for society, we might require the riders to pay a special fee or carry insurance.

[33] Those with weak preferences are denied a privilege afforded the ecstatic riders, but they are in the same boat, whether or not an exemption is given. I put aside here the reality that when accidents kill riders or render them unconscious, the roads are more dangerous for others.

[34] About kosher slaughter, Barry writes that "an appeal to religious liberty provides only spurious support for this and other similar exemptions, because the law does not restrict religious liberty, only the ability to eat meat." Note 16 supra, at 44.

Even when the government creates a direct conflict by forbidding an act a person thinks is required by conscience or religious practice, or by requiring an act the person thinks is forbidden, Barry does not see much of a distinction between these conflicts and conflicts with strong preferences. If it is said that beliefs cannot easily be changed, the same can be said about many preferences.[35] Responding to the comparison between persons with claims of conscience and those with physical disabilities, Barry says that to "suggest that they are similarly situated is in fact offensive to both parties."[36] A person with a physical inability to perform an act lacks an opportunity that is qualitatively different from a conviction against doing the act; and a person who "freely embraces a religious belief" does not perceive it "as analogous to the unwelcome burden of a physical desirability."[37]

In considering the comparison of strong preferences to convictions, and to desires to engage in religious or cultural practices with deep meaning, I shall start with direct conflicts, and then turn to restrictions that do not generate direct conflicts.

For direct conflicts, as when the government requires jury service that an individual resists, the difference between preference and conscience hits us in the face. If I have a conscientious belief that I should not perform an act, I believe it would be deeply wrong for me to do so; I believe I should not do so even if the cost is a very considerable sacrifice of my own welfare. A person with a conscientious objection to combatant military service believes it would be better to die than to kill in war.[38] A genuine objector to jury service need not believe service would be worse than death but she must believe she should undergo real hardship rather than serve. The person who has only a strong preference feels she should forgo satisfying the preference if the advantages are substantial. Moral conviction is not a barrier. The government should usually not try to compel people to do what they are opposed in conscience to doing. A conflict between legal requirement and conscience creates a much more severe opposition[39] than a conflict between legal requirement and strong preference, even a very strong preference.

Matters are more complicated when one addresses aspects of religious or cultural practice that are not exactly required by conscience, but connect in

---

[35] Id. at 35–36.

[36] Id. at 37.

[37] Id.

[38] This is not to say the sincere objector necessarily will have the courage to die, but he believes he should. Some objectors believe they can serve in noncombatant roles, and if their applications for conscientious objector status are granted, they are assigned to such roles.

[39] Either the requirement fails to compel, as with objectors to military service who go to jail, or the requirement succeeds and the objector feels he has been forced by the state to violate his deepest moral sense.

a deep way with religious or cultural identity, as when someone feels strongly drawn to an act as an expression of her deepest beliefs and social ties. A church member might have this attitude about using peyote in a worship service, believing that participation with peyote in the service is deeply meaningful but not thinking it would be worth spending a month in jail for, something we might suppose that an objector to jury service might think she should be willing to undergo.[40] In any event, the crucial comparison, here, is not with claims of conscience but with strong preferences; actions one wants to perform because of their powerful tie to deep beliefs and social ties have a status different from most acts that one wants to perform because of "detached" preferences (i.e., preferences *not* connected to conscience, deep beliefs, or strong social ties). Although one cannot be dogmatic about this, the performance of acts of religious and cultural practice usually connects to people's sense of themselves and their place in the community to a much greater degree than does the satisfaction of preferences like the experience of riding without a helmet.[41]

To sum up about direct conflicts, we cannot easily move from an assumption that strong preferences do not deserve exemption to a conclusion that claims of conscience and claims that connect to deep beliefs and profound social ties do not either.

Analysis of situations when the law does not impose direct conflicts involves an extra element. To take the motorcycle example, why not say with Barry that all the law forbids is riding a motorcycle without a helmet and that no Sikh believes that as a matter of culture or religion he must ride a motorcycle? Thus, all that the law frustrates is a strong preference. The degree of appeal of this argument depends in part on how essential the activity is to the frustrated individual. If motorcycles and bicycles were the primary modes of transportation for poor people, a helmet requirement would severely circumscribe enjoyment of a wide range of opportunities for poor Sikhs, even if all their difficulties could be capsulated as involving preferences rather than convictions or acts with deep meaning. But even if the frustrations are minor, there is a problem with the law effectively preventing people from enjoying some opportunities, because they are barred from performing

---

[40] As I remarked in note 38 supra, the main question is not what one would actually be willing to sacrifice, but what one thinks she should be willing to sacrifice.

[41] The reason why we cannot be dogmatic is that for some people certain detached preferences may lie at the core of their identity. Waldron, note 4 supra, at 15–17, makes the important point that typically claims based on religion or culture invoke a regime of social regulation outside that of the state. However, some religious claims are based on individual convictions that may not flow from a regime of social norms of existing religions groups.

other acts that would correspond with their consciences or with deep cultural practice. If virtually everyone in the culture has an opportunity to ride a motorcycle, it seems unfair (barring dangers or costs to third persons) to deny that chance to someone because he cannot bring himself to comply with an ordinary condition for use. We saw similar examples in chapter 21 of volume 1, in which I argued that it is not enough to say to a doctor or a nurse who feels she cannot participate in an abortion, "Well, you don't need to be in this profession if you don't want to perform the ordinary procedures."

If *either* (1) exemptions might make sense for strong preferences *or* (2) claims of conscience and of needs that are connected to powerful beliefs or strong social ties can be relevantly distinguished from strong preferences, an exemption strategy can make sense, in principle. Although because of difficulties of administration, it might conceivably always be a bad idea to grant exemptions, a legislature can make a principled decision to have a general requirement from which some people are exempt.

Could an exemption be a matter of justice, that is, could those who want to receive an exemption have a valid claim of justice on their behalf? Barry writes that the case for group-differentiated rights is that "departures from equal liberty . . . can be supported pragmatically"[42] and that "the case for exemptions must be based on alleviation of hardship rather than the demands of justice."[43]

In addressing the question whether exemptions may be required by justice, we need initially to clarify six points. One major issue about exemptions is whether they should be determined by legislatures, administrators, or courts. Americans used to the notion that an exemption required by constitutional right falls within the domain of justice can easily slip into the fallacy that if legislatures are the proper bodies to determine exemptions, these must be subjects of discretion, or grace, or pragmatic judgment. However, in some countries, no constitutional rights enforceable by courts exist.[44] Even in countries like the United States with its extensive constitutional rights, many issues of social justice are left to legislative decision. In the United States, legislatures decide whether or not to impose capital punishment for murder, an issue that certainly concerns justice. Legislative determinations about tax rates mix issues of prudence and justice. Scholars who argue for no or limited judicial review of legislation commonly contend that legislatures, not courts,

---

[42] Note 16 supra, at 12.

[43] Id. at 39. See also id. at 175. A less absolute statement is at id. at 33.

[44] Great Britain has long been the most notable example, but membership in the European Community now carries obligations not to violate basic rights that are enforceable by European tribunals.

should be the final arbiter of disagreements over what justice requires.[45] Because a claim that legislatures should typically decide about exemptions does not resolve whether they may be required by justice, we should not conflate Barry's preference for legislative choice with his assertions that exemptions are matters of (mere) prudence.[46]

Second, saying exactly when a claim at hardship becomes more than a prudential claim and turns into a claim of justice is not simple. The basic claim about just treatment concerns fairness, what burdens one can fairly be asked to bear and what benefits one is entitled to as a member of the political community. Although a claim of justice can be overcome by competing considerations, the claim involves something more than an assertion about the balance of advantages.

Third, the fact that people may reasonably disagree about whether an exemption should be given does not establish that if one is given, the reason is a prudent exercise of discretion rather than acknowledgment of a valid claim of justice. A claim of justice may be both debatable and, on balance, convincing. Fourth, arguments about exemptions often mingle discussions about justice and more prudential considerations, especially the ease or difficulty of administering whatever exemption might be granted. If the arguments for an exemption that are based on justice are strong and the prudential and justice-based arguments against the exemption are not too powerful, justice might require an exemption.[47]

A fifth clarification is that when we ask about claims *of justice*, we must be careful what alternative we have in mind. The standard argument of justice supposes that legislators have adopted, or will adopt, a regulation, and the question is whether they should grant an exemption. If one compares an exemption with the option of no regulation, things will look different. Unless a regulation protects innocent victims,[48] no one has a complaint *of justice* if

[45] E.g., Jeremy Waldron, *Law and Disagreement* (New York: Oxford University Press, 1999).

[46] The two issues are, however, connected in the following way. If Barry is right that claims for exemption are not based on justice, that is a substantial reason to assign decision to legislatures.

[47] This manner of putting it does concede that strong prudential arguments against an exemption might lead to a conclusion that justice does not require what justice might require in the absence of the prudential considerations. I prefer this way of speaking to the following alternative: "Justice requires an exemption, but it would be imprudent; therefore, on balance, the government should not grant an exemption required by justice."

[48] If a regulation would protect innocent victims, they may have a claim of justice to have it imposed. In that event, for the claim of justice of those who seek an exemption to be sound, it must be powerful enough to offset or outweigh the claim of justice of victims to have the regulation apply across the board. Thus, imagine that a draft is to be introduced because a volunteer army unjustly casts the burden of dying for one's country on the poor. If the mostly affluent and educated conscientious objectors are to receive an exemption on grounds of justice, their claim must be strong enough

the state decides not to regulate. Thus, it could be a matter of prudence whether to have no regulation or regulation with an exemption, a matter of justice whether to have regulation of all persons or to create an exemption for some.[49]

Finally, we need to understand that a valid claim of justice could be based on a sound argument either about privilege or about equal or fair treatment. Not every claim of justice is based on a comparison of how different people are treated. The conscientious objector urges that society acts unjustly if it demands that people who object in conscience to killing prepare themselves to kill others. Put in this simple form, the claim is one of justice based on the violation of an objector's moral right not to be forced to kill. That is a claim of privilege.

A claim of justice based on protection is perhaps even easier to identify, but we must work harder to pin it down satisfactorily. Against the view that he is treated equally with all those who are subjected to a regulation, the person who claims he should receive an exemption urges that his treatment is unequal (or at least unfair). He contends that he is not situated similarly to others who are subject to the regulation. The issue of how strong preferences compare with claims of conscience now emerges as part of the question whether exemptions are required by justice.

The member of the Native American Church who wants to use peyote in his religious ceremonies can offer two useful comparisons. He, first, points out that when legislatures have adopted prohibitions of alcohol use they have made exceptions for the sacramental use of wine. Given that alcohol is at least as damaging to people as is peyote,[50] the church member argues that his treatment is unfair in comparison with the position of those who use (and have used) wine in religious ceremonies within jurisdictions that forbid use of alcohol.[51] He asserts with confidence that the government would not ban all use of peyote were it a common feature of worship in mainstream

---

to outweigh the concern that the exemption will have some tendency to burden the poor.

In all cases in which the claim for exemption is to allow some people (especially parents) to treat others in a manner that would normally be regarded as unjust, as imposing serious corporal punishment, concern for potential victims is a central factor.

[49] Even if we focused on no regulation or regulation with an exemption, we might think the arguments for regulation with exemption are mainly prudential ones, the arguments against exemption mainly ones of justice.

[50] I am putting aside Waldron's point that use of peyote in worship involves some "harms" against which a regulation is aimed, something not true about minimal use of alcohol. This point could be developed as part of a counterargument. My aim here is to show the structure of the claim, not to resolve whether, on balance, it is convincing.

[51] He may, of course, add that a total ban on religious use of peyote reflects a kind of contempt for Indian religion.

churches. He should not be denied an exemption because he is part of a small, powerless minority.

The church member's second comparison is with those who want to use (or would use)[52] peyote for recreational purposes. If he does not think it is positively mandatory to use peyote in a religious ceremony, he may nevertheless regard it as the central element of his deepest religious (and cultural) experience. The prohibition will then operate on him much more harshly than it does on a recreational user, even one who believes use of peyote yields profound experiences and insights. Thus, the church member claims he is not similarly situated to others who are subject to the law. Though the law operates with formal equality, it operates unfairly by imposing a deprivation that a legislature would never impose on a substantial part of the population.

On examination, the force of this argument cannot depend exclusively on a particularly intense desire to ingest peyote or on the fact that there would be no ban if most people badly wanted to use peyote. Barry points out that all criminal laws operate with unequal effect. That some people would like to commit particular crimes much more than would other people does not make the laws unequal or unfair in their operation. And what any society regulates depends largely on the values held by most members of that society. An activity that is forbidden in society A, say riding without a helmet on a motorcycle, is allowed in society B, where many people highly value riding without a helmet. To some extent, majorities in various societies regulate on the basis of their values, and the minority with different values must go along. That legislation would be different if most people had the values of the minority does not necessarily show injustice.

What more is needed to sustain the protection argument for injustice? Perhaps claimants must show that they are being disregarded in terms of some form of identification, such as religion or culture, as to which the majority should not ride roughshod over a minority, or that their ground of action has some claim to being privileged (this approach combines aspects of privilege and protection), or that what the legislature has done in respect to them imposes harm so disproportionate to benefit that it amounts to comparative unfairness.

In any event, the central points here I have made so far are that an exemption may be required by justice even if decision is rightly assigned to the legislature, even if the wisdom of an exemption is arguable, even if considera-

---

[52] It is commonly said that peyote is not a drug of choice, a fact that might suggest that if the members of churches that use peyote have a strong claim, the result should be no regulation, rather than rule and exemption. Insofar as the "not a drug of choice" conclusion rests on the availability of

tions of prudence mix with those of justice, and whether the fundamental reason to exempt is to privilege certain activities or to assure fair treatment. Once we grasp these points, we can see that some exemptions are more than a good idea, they are required by justice.

Here is an example provided at a conference by William Galston in response to Barry's book. In some jurisdictions, the bodies of people who were not under the care of a physician when they died are subjected to an autopsy. An objective of the autopsy is to identify possible foul play. In circumstances in which death appears to be natural—an elderly man of limited means dies in his sleep at home—the chances that an autopsy will reveal foul play are very slight, but having the autopsy may remain a desirable safeguard, as well as serving unrelated medical purposes. Some religious groups, including Orthodox Jews, have very strong objections to autopsies. Were most people in society to regard autopsies as negatively as do members of these groups, a requirement that autopsies be performed whatever families wish would be less broad. For members of such groups, it may be necessary to perform autopsies if the circumstances of death suggest a real possibility of foul play, and the autopsy can reveal cause of death and yield other important evidence. But the claim of Orthodox Jews not to have the bodies of loved ones disturbed, and their claim in the present not to have their own bodies disturbed in the future, seem strong enough to outweigh the need for an autopsy when death occurs in circumstances that give no hint of any wrong.[53]

This claim against being subjected to an autopsy can be seen as one of justice. It is both a claim that the state wrongs people if it trespasses on this deep-seated conviction without a more substantial need and a claim that the state would not perform routine autopsies if many Christian groups shared the attitude of Orthodox Jews. If the claim to be free of a routine autopsy is strong enough to warrant an exemption, the exemption may be required by justice, whether or not that decision is left to the legislature and whether or not the arguments on each side are fairly even.

This is not to say that every warranted exemption is required by justice. Sometimes the crucial arguments will be ones of mere prudence; and often the arguments against an exemption will be strong enough so that a legislature may properly deny it without acting unjustly. A reasonable decision to grant the exemption will then not be required by justice.

---

other illegal drugs that are more pleasant to consume, it seems to me a dubious starting point for analysis. Probably one has to ask if people would choose to use peyote if related prohibitions were effective.

[53] My use of this example (which fits my understanding of Galston's original comment) is not meant to precisely describe the law of any state or country as to the exact circumstances when autop-

It is not my aim here to say just when justice, rather than utilitarian or prudential considerations, is dominant, or to say just what exemptions justice may require. It is simply to rebut any contention that justice *never* requires an exemption,[54] that whenever legislatures are considering exemptions, they need focus only upon prudential considerations.

To show that the exemption strategy is desirable in a considerable number of circumstances *and* that exemptions are sometimes required by justice, one would need to consider a wide range of possible examples. Rather than undertaking that task here, I remind the reader of the variety of examples that the volume on free exercise covers, which I believe strongly support both claims.[55]

RELIGION AND OTHER POSSIBLE BASES FOR EXEMPTIONS

Religious claims indisputably form one basis for various exemptions. Claims based on culture, personal nonreligious convictions, and strong preferences are other possible bases. The sorting of claims into qualifying and nonqualifying can be avoided by a system of self-selection. As I argue about conscientious objection in volume 1, a workable system of self-selection is actually preferable to having officials decide whether someone qualifies for an exemption. Self-selection *is feasible* only when those who want an exemption badly pay for it or make some other sacrifice that most people would not be willing to make to receive the same privilege.[56] Thus, to take an example we have

---

sies will be performed regardless of family wishes. The example exhibits the kind of argument for an exemption that may seem forceful.

[54] I should say that taking Barry's book as a whole, it is doubtful whether it does advance such a contention, although some individual sentences support it. At the conference discussing the book, Barry was clear that some exemptions might be required by justice.

[55] The claim that justice requires an exemption is easiest to make when the activity the claimants want to protect does not present the dangers that concern the government, but I am assuming, as with the autopsy example, that justice may require an exemption on some occasions in which the dangers do arise. (That is, the danger of not having an autopsy is the same if an Orthodox Jew dies in innocent-appearing circumstances as when anyone else does so.)

[56] Self-selection *might not* be fair if the alternative needs to be so onerous to exclude others than those with reasons of conscience that the cost to those with reasons of conscience is too great. If, for example, it was necessary to conscript 95 percent of the young population for military service and alternative civilian service had to be set at six years (compared with two years of military service) in order for self-selection to yield adequate military personnel, that could be unfair.

One might say that self-selection is feasible if ordinary people would not be interested in engaging in the prohibited behavior. But if the only people who want to perform the acts are those who seek the exemption, granting them an exemption will produce the same practical effect as not having a regulation; thus, the state can decide between exceptionless regulation and no regulation.

considered, a state might allow motorcycle riders to go without helmets if they pay a thousand dollars a year for the privilege.[57] Insofar as such a market approach favors the rich—for a millionaire who rides for recreation a thousand dollars may be only a minor annoyance, for a farmworker who rides to work a thousand dollars may be prohibitively expensive—a state might make the fee proportional to income or wealth, or impose nonmonetary service, such as the alterative service that conscientious objectors had to perform.

Short of instituting a scheme of self-selection, a state should not extend an exemption to all those with strong preferences. We may take strong preferences here as the *same kinds* of wishes and desires that many people have but ones that greatly exceed their ordinary strength.

As I have explained, the reason why people with strong preferences should not receive an exemption is not that in principle one could never be warranted. Rather, such an exemption would generate three related problems connected to its administration. First, even if claimants are honest and articulate, and possess morally acceptable preferences developed independent of the regulation in question, officials (whether law enforcement officers on the spot or administrators issuing licenses) would find it difficult to decide when the standards for the exemption had been satisfied. Second, claimants would have powerful tactical incentives to overstate their preferences in order to gain a cost-free exemption. If all that was at issue was someone's strength of preference, administrators would not easily spot liars. Third, claimants would form and articulate their preferences in response to the boundaries of an exemption. A regulation could actually influence the precise strength of a preference—a rider who was aware that riders with preferences of a certain strength did not need to wear helmets might develop such a preference, as many young men whose primary objection was to U.S. involvement in Vietnam managed to persuade themselves that they were objectors to all wars.[58] Further, whatever the exact strength of a preference, a claimant needing to articulate his feelings verbally may come to believe that his preferences possess the strength demanded by the law's imprecise formula for exemption.

---

[57] Something like this approach has been used in connection with air pollution; companies are allowed to deviate from standards of air quality if they pay for the privilege.

[58] I recently talked to a Lutheran who said he was still troubled by his successful claim to be a conscientious objector. He initially put the point as if the issue was, whether, as a faithful Lutheran, he could be a pacifist. I pointed out that, as he well knew, the law did not require membership in a pacifist denomination and that some Roman Catholics, not members of a pacifist religion, were pacifists. I also pointed out that his claim was certainly religious, and asked whether the crux of the problem did not come down to whether, in some sense, he was "really" a selective objector rather than a pacifist. He said the answer was yes, although there was no doubt that at the time he applied,

For all these reasons, governments cannot grant exemptions to all those whose strength of preference exceeds a certain margin. The grounds for an exemption must rest on something qualitatively different from the typical reasons that would lead most people to wish to perform acts forbidden by law. Three major candidates are religion, culture, and nonreligious conscience. (One might, as Christopher Eisgruber has suggested, reasonably view required accommodations for people with physical and mental disabilities as a form of exemption from having to meet ordinary standards of performance. So understood, these accommodations are one uncontroversial form of exemption not based on belief, attitudes, or attachments.)

Some initial cautions are in order about the distinctiveness of religion, culture, and conscience. The category of "nonreligious" conscience assumes, as chapter 8 in volume 1 argues, both that people may develop conscientious reasons or feelings against committing acts that have nothing to do with religion in any ordinary sense (an obvious point), and that a person's being conscientiously opposed to performing an act does not automatically *make* his opposition religious.

The relation of religion and culture is more complex. Often these will be interwoven, and that is especially true within societies that draw no sharp distinction between religion and other aspects of culture.[59] Frequently cited modern examples are the Jewish law of kashrut and the caste structure of Hinduism; these are religious and cultural. Such an interweaving, by itself, need not create a problem if a practice evidently qualifies, whether an exemption requires a religious ground or a cultural ground. Thus, humane slaughter laws might exempt approved methods of kosher slaughter as a religious *or* as a cultural practice.

A problem arises if the law does not treat cultural practices as qualifying and it is hard to say whether a culturally rooted practice is sufficiently based in religion to qualify as "religious"; or if the law does not treat religious practices as qualifying and it is hard to say whether a religiously based practice is sufficiently cultural to qualify under the term that the law requires. For example, British law forbids discrimination on grounds of ethnicity but not religion.[60] If someone asserted that prohibition of a religious practice amounted to "ethnic" discrimination, she would need to show that the practice was part of the culture of her ethnic group. A practice common to all Roman Catholics, such as celebration of the mass with wine, and the paci-

---

he did believe himself to be a general objector. The matter that troubled him was not whether he had lied, but whether he was a victim of some subtle self-deception.

[59] This is said to characterize what are sometimes called "traditional" societies.

[60] See Barry, note 16 supra, at 34.

fism of members of the Society of Friends, a mainstream religious group, are not "cultural" in the relevant sense (which generally refers to discrete minority cultures). Were an indigenous tribe to have fished certain waters for generations (waters to which they attach no special religious significance), they might have a cultural, nonreligious, claim to continue. (I use this illustration only to differentiate kinds of claims, not to express a view on the strength of such a claim.)

We have seen in chapter 8 of volume 1 that determining the boundaries of religion is far from simple; the categories of culture and conscientiousness present similar difficulties of line drawing. When exactly does someone's moral objection to doing something cross over the line of being a "conscientious objection," and what are the boundaries of cultural claims? Difficulties of drawing boundaries are one reason *not* to pursue an exemption strategy, but, taken in general, they are not a good reason to prefer some other categorizations to categorization in terms of religion.[61]

How should religious claims for exemptions be regarded in relation to other possible claims? Many of the most powerful reasons people have not to adhere to general regulations concern their religion. For most religious people in the United States, religious responsibilities involve a sense of duty to a transcendent power, but even for those who do not believe in God, or gods, religion can be a powerful source of identification and community.

It would definitely not make sense to exempt nonreligious conscientious objectors and fail to exempt religious conscientious objectors; such a comparative hostility to religious grounds would be unjustified. With certain qualifications, we can reach the same conclusion about exempting cultural practices, practices connected with "ethnic" groups, and not exempting religious practices.[62] Legislators might limit protection to cultural practices because they worry that members of minority cultures are being oppressed or face unfair disadvantages, whereas members of most religious groups fare reasonably well, or they might conclude that in their society the clashes between general legal requirements and other perceived obligations typically involve minority cultures. Such limited protection might be part of an effort to preserve minority cultures or to make up for past oppression;[63] but apart from these possible purposes, one cannot see why, in principle, cultural prac-

---

[61] However, for any particular subject matters, classification by one category or another may prove simpler.

[62] According to Barry, England's law against racial and ethnic discrimination has this effect. Note 16 supra, at 34.

[63] One thinks of special accommodations that might be made to Native Americans in the United States, the aborigines of Australia, or the aboriginal peoples of Canada.

tices should receive exemptions and (other) religious practices denied them. Of course, many protected cultural practices, such as wearing turbans and kirpans (knives) by Sikh men, would also be religious. But not all important religious practices are significantly attached to specific cultures (other than the dominant culture). Given the perceived strength of religious responsibilities, legislators should not typically protect cultural practices (religious and nonreligious) and fail to protect religious practices that are not aspects of minority cultures but may be valued by religious minorities within the dominant culture.

Harder questions are posed by the possibility of restricting an exemption to religious persons, to members of religious groups, or to members of named religious groups. Analysis is simplest if we take these possibilities in reverse order.

A fundamental principle of liberal democracy, though one not observed to its fullest extent in countries with established churches, is that the government should not favor one religious group over others. An exemption limited to members of named religions begins with an initial strike against it. If two religious groups are relevantly similar, they should be treated similarly.

The best that can be said for an exemption restricted to a named group is that no other group may be relevantly similar. Part of the rationale for excusing the Amish from paying Social Security taxes is that members of that community will not receive Social Security from the government, and that because the Amish have a long historical continuity and relatively few members leave the community,[64] the government is assured that not many elderly former Amish will need government assistance. If no other group quite meets these requisites, why not cast an exemption in terms of the Amish?

The problem is that over time some other group might qualify. Were legislatures constantly attentive to such developments, one might say, "Let them include another group when, and if, it comes along," but legislators are not attentive in this way, *and* success in legislation often depends on political pressure. A statute limited by name to the Amish invites future unfairness. A legislature should adopt a general formula that fits the Amish and could include other groups in the future.[65]

Is it all right to name the Amish at all? I think the answer here is yes, though the point is debatable. If the legislature knows it wants to exempt

[64] Barry says that 20 percent leave before baptism. Note 16 supra, at 242. He also points out that a powerful reason for the elderly not to leave is that they have no external means of support.

[65] Finding a general formula *may* prove somewhat difficult, especially if individual legislators disagree over just *why* the Amish deserve an exemption.

the Amish, it may say so. The risk is that over time the Amish may lose some of the characteristics that warrant an exemption. Further, one may worry that naming constitutes a subtle endorsement. However, when the group named is a small minority obviously not being endorsed as the "true faith," the convenience of naming an obvious beneficiary should outweigh the concerns about future inappropriate application and implicit approval.[66]

Turning to the question whether group membership should ever be a requirement of exemption, we can distinguish between exemptions that are intrinsically *for* groups, or require group participation, and those that are intrinsically *for* individuals. An exemption from a requirement that applies to organizations obviously would cover organizations; for example, religious organizations may discriminate on grounds of religion in their employment decisions. Other exemptions presuppose group concerns and activities. Thus, the government might decide to allow indigenous groups to kill a limited number of a protected species of whale.[67] The general prohibition on killing whales would apply to individuals (as well as companies); the exemption would turn on the need of some identifiable group.

Other exemptions could, in principle, go to individuals whose claims need not attach to membership in groups. Two examples are exemptions from military service and exemptions from bans on the use of peyote. My general position, developed in chapters of the free exercise volume, is that much depends on the nature of an exemption, how it is administered, and possibilities of fraud. Conscientious objection to military service is an individual matter, and an administrative screening process allows scrutiny of sincerity. Especially given the fact that those committing outright fraud can easily join a pacifist religious group and feign pacifist beliefs, it does not make sense to require group membership. However, an individualized privilege to use peyote or marijuana as a personal act of worship, applied after the fact, opens up the law to extreme administrative difficulties and abuse. If an exemption is to be given, requiring that use be within a group setting (and possibly requiring that the user be a member of the group) makes sense.

The most serious questions about categorization are the following: (1) Should nonreligious conscientious beliefs and deep-seated practices be treated as favorably as religious ones? (2) Should nonreligious cultural prac-

<hr />

[66] Nevertheless, the position that legislation should operate only by general formulas, even when the obvious aim is to reach a particular group, is a reasonable alternative.

[67] An isolated individual would be unlikely to have a cultural or religious practice of killing a whale, and the state's interest in protecting whales should not yield to such an individual, were there one.

tices be treated as favorably as religious practices? The answer to each question could be always, sometimes, or never.[68]

We can reject the "never" answer straightaway for both questions. In some circumstances, nonreligious conscientious claims will seem about as pressing as religious ones and roughly as easy to administer. That is the case in respect to conscientious objection. An administrative structure that determines whether claimants are honest can assess the convictions of nonreligious pacifists about as well as those of religious ones.[69] As far as cultural beliefs and practices are concerned, we can imagine nonreligious convictions or practices that are so deeply rooted that, if a particular kind of practice is to receive an exemption, a cultural ground should be included. Inclusion has the further advantage of not requiring an official to decide whether a belief or practice is religious as well as cultural.[70]

The hard issues are whether, if exemptions are to be given to religious claimants, they always, or only sometimes, should extend to conscientious nonreligious claimants or to claimants who rely on cultural practices. My answer is "sometimes," that for some exemptions religion may be special.

One might offer prudential, historical or cultural, and principled grounds for treating religion as special. By prudential grounds, I refer to convenience in categorization and administration. Even though a perfect categorization, perfectly applied, might not draw the line at religion, religious claimants could overlap nearly completely with those who should be exempted, and sorting out the merits of nonreligious claimants might be very difficult. Under these conditions, a law justifiably would limit an exemption to religious claimants. An exemption of Amish, and other similar religious groups, from requirements of schooling beyond a particular age provides an illustration. We can imagine a stable nonreligious community whose members feel as strongly as the Amish that schooling beyond the eighth grade is destructive of values they hold dear and jeopardizes the fundamental welfare of the children exposed to further school, and we can further imagine that few

[68] One might think that in some situations, a choice either way would be reasonable. One might believe even that the choice comes down to a close prudential judgment that precludes saying that either decision is right or wrong. I mean here not only that making the assessment is extremely difficult, but that even someone with full information who has done the assessment of values would not use the terminology of right and wrong.

[69] No doubt, a member of a pacifist church needs to explain less about his own point of view, but some religious claimants will not belong to pacifist churches. Further, one who sets out to commit systematic fraud will not find it very difficult to feign whatever religious beliefs, if any, are required to join a pacifist church. I add the "if any" because my impression is that many Quaker congregations are extremely inclusive in terms of belief.

[70] However, for nonreligious practices, this addition demands decision whether the practice is relevantly cultural.

children leave this community upon becoming adults. However, a careful look at historical sources fails to reveal that any such community has ever existed. Given the evanescence of virtually all nonreligious voluntary communal experiments, which history also reveals, we further conclude that the emergence of such a community is extremely unlikely. Under these circumstances, a legislative choice to limit an exemption to religious groups would make prudential sense.

By a historical or cultural justification, I mean that within a particular society religion is considered special.[71] Such a view might actually be embodied in a constitution. Thus, it may plausibly be claimed that that the religion clauses of our federal Constitution instantiate the view that religion is special. An argument that the special place of religion is enshrined by history or accepted in modern society need not rest on a principled defense of the special place of religion; it is enough for political leaders, and judges, to implement the fundamental cultural value, at least it is enough if giving religion that place is not positively unjust.[72]

Can one offer a principled defense for treating religion as special, a defense that does not rely only on history, existing culture, or prudence, and that could counter arguments that affording a religion a special place is unjust? Here we may begin with defenses that rely on the truth, or possible truth, of religious premises. Defending a special place for religion is easiest if one relies directly on religious premises, such as the premises commonly held in the United States that religion concerns the relation of human beings to a transcendent God and that this relation supersedes in importance all human relations, including one's responsibility to comply with law.

This defense of distinguishing religious claims for exemption from nonreligious ones faces three difficulties. First, a reasonable representative government is not likely to adopt measures that legislators believe require citizens to violate actual obligations to God. So the more precise justification for an exemption must be that the government, insofar as is feasible, should not require people to violate what *they* perceive as their obligations to God. To this extent, at least, the exemption will go to people who are seen by most members of a society as having a mistaken sense of their obligations to

---

[71] This conclusion might, or might not, lead to a judgment that it is always constitutionally permissible to limit an exemption to religious claimants.

[72] If the special place of religion is not solidly entrenched in constitutional law, the argument that it justifies limiting exemptions to religious practices is open to the counterargument that societies have long accepted all sorts of unjust inequalities, that legislators should counter these, and that, if no principled distinction favors religion, a legislature's granting exemptions only for religious beliefs and practices is unjust.

God.[73] Second, this particular justification seems not to cover people who have a radically mistaken view about religion. What about religious people who worship ancestors, or thousands of divinities, or, though participating in some religion, do not believe in any god? Why should they get an exemption? (Perhaps "religion" is the best way to categorize, and these people will benefit indirectly from a justification based on sound religious views, but that justification that does not directly apply to them.) Third, it is highly doubtful in a liberal democracy, especially one with a rule against an establishment of religion, that the government should legislate on the basis of what is a "correct" theological view.[74]

A more modest approach is to say that within the individual lives of many citizens, religion has a special place. Many people perceive *their religion* as involving relations with a transcendent God. Whether they are wise or foolish, the government should not demand that they do what they believe God forbids them from doing, or does not want them to do. This justification does not depend on a claim about the actual existence of God and about God's nature and will. This justification does not itself pick up religious claims that do not posit any such obligations, but one might conclude that religion is the reasonable or required criterion of classification and that a high percentage of religious claims (in our culture) will concern perceived transcendent obligations. For officials, this version of the "in principle" argument is preferable to one that depends on the claimed truth of any religious view,[75] but many citizens attracted to the stronger assertion will reasonably accept exemptions on that ground.

A rather different basis for distinguishing most religious claims from most nonreligious claims of conscience is that the former derive from regimes of social regulation that are separate from the state's legal norms.[76] There may

---

[73] I can imagine at least one qualification. People might believe that various individuals have special vocations and that some of these vocations would preclude actions in which others engage. Thus, it might be thought that monks have a religious obligation not to serve on juries, although such service is fine for laypersons.

[74] Instead of supposing that a religious view based on a transcendental God is true, the government might instead assume that such a view may be true, and act accordingly. Michael McConnell writes of a political theory that includes the possibility of a transcendent God. McConnell, "Accommodation of Religion," 1995 *Supreme Court Review* 1, 15. A government would sensibly rely on such a theory only if it thought the probability of truth to be high (something very close to adopting it as a "correct" view) or if it deferred to the sentiments of most, or many citizens (the theory I discuss in the next paragraph).

[75] My reasons for this position are the same as those I explore in chapter 22 regarding justifications for the religion clauses.

[76] See Waldron, note 4 supra, at 16–18, 23–24. However, one could be a religious conscientious objector after developing individual convictions about war without being a member of any group with a norm against military service.

be value in letting such systems flourish, not supplanting them at every turn with the state's rules.[77]

With respect to the question whether any particular proposed exemption should be limited to religious claimants, officials should consider "in principle," historical and cultural, and prudential arguments. Sometimes these will justify limiting the category of claims to religious ones.

Constitutional Right or Legislative Choice

In regard to whether issues about exemptions should be regarded as matters of constitutional right or left to legislative choice, what is the best approach within the United States may not be apt for other liberal democracies.[78] Some assign greater responsibilities to the courts than do others, and the textual meaning and underlying understanding of specific constitutional provisions vary. For any challenge to a particular classification, it could make a controlling difference whether a constitutional text protects a right to conscience or a right to the exercise of religion or both, whether it forbids an establishment of religion, and whether it guarantees minority cultural rights. In most of what follows I concentrate on the United States, with its guarantee of the free exercise of religion, but not freedom of conscience, and its prohibition of an establishment of religion. Readers should be aware that many constitutions and international documents have no guarantee against established religion, and that some protect freedom of conscience, understood more broadly than religious conscience.

Unconstitutionality in the United States is most apparent when a classification favors some religions over others. A rule against no establishment bars favoring particular religions, and a principle of free exercise implies, at least in a regime with no establishment, that peoples of different faiths will have equal rights of religious exercise.[79] If some religions cannot be favored over others, an exemption given to members of one religion must be given

---

[77] See id. at 17–18, referring to Robert M. Cover, "The Supreme Court 1982 Term Foreword, Nomos and Narrative," 97 *Harvard Law Review* 4 (1983).

[78] We shall look at those questions, insofar as possible, without a general predisposition for or against judicial resolution of problems as matters of constitutional law. A person who believes that judicial review is unhealthy, that virtually all political issues should be decided by bodies that are politically responsible, will oppose judicial review if it is proposed and will wish to limit its scope if it is already entrenched.

[79] There is an argument that in the United States the original religion clauses contemplated that Christian religions could be favored over non-Christian religions, but virtually no one has defended this position for modern constitutional law, and I shall not pause to address it.

to members of another similarly situated religion.[80] Suppose two different religions require use of wine in family religious ceremonies; were a state that prohibits the drinking of alcoholic beverages to make an exception for family devotional use of one of the two religions, but not the other, its classification would be unconstitutional (unless the state could present a powerful nonreligious reason why the exemption should go to members of one religion and not the other).[81] This, indeed, is what the Supreme Court held about a benefit in terms of tax reporting that it assumed a state legislature designed to reach some religious groups and not others.[82] Any exemption formulated in terms of named religions risks such a finding of unconstitutional classification, because a court may find some other religion to be similarly situated.[83]

The reality that an exemption will benefit members of some religions more than members of others does not itself create a constitutional problem—a higher percentage of Quakers than Presbyterians happen to be pacifists—but ordinarily a legislature should not be allowed to make membership in a particular kind of religion a condition of receiving an exemption. Such a

---

[80] The sentence in text equivocates about what constitutes being similarly situated. If members of each group have the same interest in an exemption, clearly one group cannot be favored because officials want to advance it or regard its theological position as sounder. If the government is to distinguish among religions, it must have neutral, secular reasons for doing so.

[81] The issue of favoritism will look different in a country that has an established religion or a constitution that fails to guarantee nonestablishment. If a country has a traditional established church, with the government contributing to the salaries of clergy and to the upkeep of buildings of the established church, a constitutional right of free exercise would not assure equality in religious exercise, since members of the established church enjoy advantages that others do not. An exemption that went only to members of the established church or its members might be viewed as an aspect of the permitted establishment.

By a somewhat paradoxical logic, an exemption given to all but members of the established church might also be all right. Here, the reasoning would be that members of the established church have various political and financial advantages; a government might be able to offset them by extending exemptions to others. If an exemption aided members of some nonestablished religions but not the members of others, the argument would be stronger that a principle of equal free exercise was violated, but the government could argue that the existence of a religious establishment sets the understanding of free exercise as not involving an equality principle. We need not pursue how these various arguments would play out if the country has some kind of multiple establishment (in which some religions receive benefits others do not) or is allowed constitutionally to create an established religion although it does not then have one.

[82] *Larson v. Valente*, 456 U.S. 228 (1982). Michael McConnell, in "Accommodation of Religion: An Update and Response to Critics," 60 *George Washington Law Review* 685, 708 (1992), has written, "The test seems to be that accommodations need not be equal if there are neutral secular reasons, not based on religious favoritism for distinguishing among religious beliefs." At least in many contexts the government would need more than some such reason and would have to satisfy the compelling interest test that applies to suspect classifications.

[83] Upon such a finding a court may hold the existing exemption invalid, extend it to similarly situated groups, or give the legislature a limited time in which to resolve that issue.

strategy—for example, exempting only pacifists who belong to pacifist religions—might be defended on grounds of administrative convenience, but, in general, courts should regard it as unconstitutional when the exemption concerns individual activity. Among other reasons, the law should not encourage people who seek the exemption to join one religious group rather than another. When the exemption involves participation in worship services, or otherwise directly concerns the practice of a collectivity, an exemption may turn on the nature of the group in which one participates.

The distinction between religious and nonreligious claimants is most troubling. I assume that religion differs enough from (other) cultural practices that an exemption cast in terms of religion need not be extended to all nonreligious cultural usages. The hard question is whether an exemption cast in terms of religion needs to be extended to all individuals whose sentiment about engaging in the prohibited act is otherwise similar to that of the religious claimant. Nonreligious conscientious opposition to participating in war is a striking example.

I have suggested that in some instances, it makes sense, on principled, historical and cultural, and prudential grounds, to limit an exemption to religious claims. Although one can reasonably argue that a principle of nonestablishment or a more general principle of equality never allows the government to distinguish religious from comparable nonreligious claims,[84] I think this approach is too formalistic and demanding for situations in which a parallel nonreligious claimant is highly unlikely to arise.

This leaves the central question whether the government should be able to exempt a religious person but not a nonreligious one, when a belief (such as pacifism) or action has roughly the same significance for them. There is a constitutional argument flowing from the Free Exercise Clause that the government may always make that choice: The Constitution permits free exercise accommodations, even when it does not demand them; thus, a legislature may choose to accommodate religious exercise without accommodating similar nonreligious beliefs or practices.[85]

A technical legal argument to the contrary may be mounted on the basis of *Employment Division v. Smith*,[86] which, as chapter 5 of volume 1 explains, holds, with limited qualifications, that the Free Exercise Clause guarantees no right to exemptions. On that understanding, perhaps one should not think

---

[84] In its strongest variety, the argument asserts that the government must classify in a more general way, even if it expects the only persons who will qualify to be religious.

[85] This argument is not implausible, and three justices accepted it in *Welsh v. United States*, 398 U.S. 333, 371–73 (1970) (White, J., dissenting).

[86] 494 U.S. 872 (1990).

of religious exemptions created by legislatures as somehow extending a principle already built into the Free Exercise Clause itself. Scholars, like myself, who continue to be dismayed by *Employment Division v. Smith* will not find it a comforting premise from which to reason about limits on legislative power; but even if one accepts the principle of *Smith*, one may also believe that the Free Exercise Clause signals something special about religion, including the appropriateness of exemptions directed to religion.[87] It is not obvious that either the Establishment Clause or the Equal Protection Clause bars such exemptions, but they may bar some motivations for exemptions.

A broader argument against religion-only exemptions acknowledges that the Constitution and other legal materials are inconclusive, but relies on a modern constitutional principle that when people are otherwise similarly situated, those with certain kinds of beliefs should not be favored over those with other kinds. On this view, the combined effect of the Free Speech, Establishment, Free Exercise, and Equal Protection clauses bars a preference limited to religious grounds, unless the government has a reason for the limitation that goes beyond preferring religion. This broader argument can fit with a recognition that the Free Exercise Clause does require some exemptions. In these circumstances, that clause directly protects religious claimants; people with nonreligious but otherwise similar convictions may be swept into the ring of protection by the force of other constitutional clauses.

According to my understanding, courts should recognize a principle of prima facie equality between religious and nonreligious beliefs and activities, such that the government cannot treat religious activities more favorably than otherwise similar nonreligious ones, *unless* it has some substantial reason to do so *other than* a theological premise or popular opinion that religious beliefs and actions are more deserving than nonreligious views. The issue whether a legislature can treat similar religious and nonreligious beliefs and activities differently is a significant one for courts to resolve. They should leave a degree of discretion to legislatures but sometimes declare that the exclusion of similarly situated nonreligious people is a constitutional violation.

The central question that remains for us in this chapter is whether any exemptions from valid laws are constitutionally required and should be enforced by courts in the face of legislative inaction.[88] Let us assume that the

---

[87] Someone who thinks *Smith* is fundamentally about the limits of judicial competence may believe that legislatures have a constitutional obligation to create some exemptions that is not judicially enforceable.

[88] In describing a law as valid, I am assuming that the law is not, despite its general wording, actually aimed against a particular religion and does not in its purpose discriminate among religions. Rather, the complaint against the law's enforcement is that it effectively infringes upon an important

constitutional language and history are indecisive, as they are in the United States. Here we have the fundamental issue the Court addressed in *Employment Division v. Smith*, when it switched *from* a judicial test that allowed significant interferences with the exercise of religion only if they were supported by compelling state interests *to* a rule that a religious challenge (unsupported by any *other* constitutional right) could never succeed against a valid law of general application.[89] Thus, given a law against use of peyote, members of the Native American Church had no right to use peyote in their worship services, although that use was the very center of their worship, the church's most basic activity. According to the Court's approach, it was irrelevant whether the state had any need to extend its law to worship services and whether use in worship was supremely important. Many, including myself, reacted that this result was a travesty of free exercise protection, but perhaps that judgment was hasty.

The Court's approach might be defended on pragmatic or principled grounds. By pragmatic grounds here, I refer mainly to the functioning of courts. Perhaps judges are ill equipped to decide when exemptions should be given. A constitutional decision in favor of an exemption requires an assessment of sincerity, some measure of how much a belief or practice matters to an individual or religion, and some assessment of whether the government's interests will be unduly sacrificed by granting the exemption. These are not inquiries, the argument goes, that courts should be making; they are specially troublesome because courts should not enter the thicket of making judgments about religion. An alternative constitutional course of courts sustaining virtually all religious claims is even less palatable. Thus, courts should not be in this business at all, and free exercise rights should not include rights to exemptions. That, indeed, is the gist of Justice Scalia's opinion for the Court in *Smith*.[90]

Insofar as the critique of judicial assessment of claims for free exercise exemptions is sound, it also reaches any broad legislative authorizations to

---

religious belief or practice, in the manner that a general law about humane slaughtering would infringe Jewish beliefs and practices concerning kosher slaughter.

I leave aside here whether a law that may not be intended to discriminate and does not actually classify in terms of particular religions can nonetheless be regarded as discriminating between religions if the grounds of classification turn out clearly to include some religions and exclude others—a possible understanding of the issue in *Larson v. Valente*, note 82 supra.

[89] A similar question arises if during the period of constitutional design, the framers of a new constitution might or might not provide for constitutionally mandated exemptions.

[90] If this pragmatic approach provided the main support for the rule of *Smith*, one might believe that the legislature enforcing free exercise rights in good faith must, or should, provide exemptions but that courts cannot correct any failures on the part of legislatures. This understanding would have powerful implications for how legislators should regard their constitutional responsibilities.

courts to "balance" such claims against competing government interests, and shows that statutes like the Religious Freedom Restoration Act are unwise, if not unconstitutional, in the burdens they impose on courts. (The critique does not condemn specific legislative exemptions that courts can enforce without making difficult judgments on their own.)

Winifred Fallers Sullivan has challenged general protection of religious exercise in a book strikingly titled *The Impossibility of Religious Freedom*.[91] Sullivan recounts a Florida dispute between, on the one hand, family members who had installed upright monuments to commemorate loved ones and, on the other, the city of Boca Raton, which had restricted that part of its cemetery to flat memorials. The case involved the interpretation and application of the Florida Religious Freedom Restoration Act.[92]

Sullivan rightly points out how hard it is to interpret the act's requirement that a person's religious exercise be substantially burdened, when people advance religious reasons that connect to their respective faiths but do not involve standard requirements of the faith. Most of the reasons individual plaintiffs gave for choosing the memorials they did fit into this category. Sullivan rightly criticizes the trial judge's conclusion, subsequently embraced by the state supreme court, that a substantial burden on religious exercise necessarily involves a prohibition or requirement of a person's religion. Considering both the statutory language and the U.S. Supreme Court's approach to religious claims, the interpretation of the courts in the case is both too institutional—not adequately focused on an individual's beliefs and practices—and too demanding—excluding choices that someone thinks are supported by her religion but not required.

But Sullivan's main point is that the whole enterprise of discerning a substantial burden is too difficult. Early on, she writes, "Forsaking religious freedom as a legally enforced right might engender greater equality among persons and greater clarity and self-determination for religious groups and communities."[93] And the last sentence of her text suggests that a right to religious freedom "may not be best realized through laws guaranteeing religious freedom but by laws guaranteeing equality."[94] Greater clarity yes, but

---

[91] Winifred Fallers Sullivan, *The Impossibility of Religious Freedom* (Princeton: Princeton University Press, 2005).

[92] Two of the complexities of the case were that the rules clearly barred upright monuments and that cemetery employees had told people they could be installed. As long as other cemeteries were available, it is hard to see how religious exercise could be substantially burdened for someone who, knowing the rules, chose to use an area limited to flat monuments. A reliance argument built on what cemetery officials agreed to would not seem dependent on a religious claim.

[93] Note 91 supra, at 8.

[94] Id. at 159.

also better realization of religious freedom? It is hard to see how in the very case she discusses. If someone just preferred an upright monument in an area limited to flat monuments, she would be out of luck. Perhaps Sullivan would favor specific exemptions given to people on grounds of morality or conscience. This, in fact, is the general approach of the vast majority of laws that allow medical personnel to refuse to engage in certain medical procedures, and I believe it is often the best approach. (One might argue that the Free Exercise Clause itself somehow requires exemptions for conscience, religious or not, but Sullivan makes no such claim.) In respect to upright markers, distinguishing nonreligious claims of conscience from choices based on "mere" sentiment or aesthetic judgment would be very hard. So, as far as grave markers are concerned, the option of equality means that religious claims will end up being grouped with all other sorts of preferences and will inevitably yield to regulation.

Concerns about judicial competence undoubtedly have some force, but Justice Scalia's approach allows the effective destruction of a religion on a slight state interest in general regulation. That hardly seems a robust protection of the free exercise of religion. Granting that, as chapter 13 of volume 1 reveals, work needs to be done to develop the best formula for constitutional review of neutral laws that impinge on religion, the *Smith* alternative of no review whatsoever emasculates free exercise. Difficulties in standards of judicial review, hardly unique to free exercise, are preferable to sacrificing a fundamental constitutional guarantee.

What can we say about the principle of free exercise? Does it reasonably include only a right against discrimination? Without trying to answer this question for every political society, the United States is a modern liberal democracy with citizens of diverse religious views and many small religious groups, with idiosyncratic practices, who are not well represented in the legislative process. (With substantial immigration to other Western democracies, this description increasingly fits them.)

Early in this chapter, we saw that exemptions are sometimes required by justice. That does not itself show that exemptions should be matters for the judiciary, but when we add that a crucial aspect of constitutional rights should be the protection of minorities against disregard in the legislative process, the argument for judicial assessment builds. Of course, minorities cannot be protected in every respect—far from it—but religious practice is of great importance, and has long been regarded as a fundamental right. And religion has been a fertile source of unjust discrimination. Among minority beliefs and practices that should be protected, religion has a powerful claim.

One reason for constitutional exemptions is to prevent outright intentional discrimination, achieved by apparently neutral legislation, that courts are not in a position to identify. In this respect, the direct right to exemption is an indirect means to avert purposeful discrimination. But legislative neglect, which comes in the form of attentive indifference or ignorant disregard, is of much broader concern. Legislators may be aware that their general law will probably have detrimental, even devastating, effects on some religious practices or beliefs, but because those religions seem alien, strange, and indefensible, the legislators do not regard these effects as anything to worry about. This self-conscious attitude about effects approaches intentional discrimination, but does not quite move over the line according to some understandings of discrimination.[95] When an adversely affected minority religion is so far off the "radar screen" that legislators do not consider it at all when they adopt a general rule, we can talk of ignorant disregard.

Both these problems are well addressed by courts considering claims as ones of constitutional right. Indeed, Eisgruber and Sager build a complete theory of constitutional exemptions on the basis of protection against discrimination broadly conceived.[96] According to their approach, courts considering claims for constitutional exemptions should pose counterfactual questions about how legislators would have treated similar religious interests had they been part of mainstream religions. One need not accept either their rejection of all "privilege" arguments for exemptions or their precise recommendations about judicial approaches to see that protecting against unfair indifference and neglect is a strong reason for constitutional exemptions.

Ira Lupu has urged that judicial exemptions are constitutionally preferable to legislative ones.[97] He is concerned partly that legislators will undervalue minority religions and be insufficiently respectful of establishment limits. Whether one accepts or rejects (as I do) his recommendation that legislative exemptions be considered unconstitutional, he provides strong reasons for welcoming some judicial exemptions grounded in the constitutional right of free exercise.

If we conclude that courts should enforce some constitutional exemptions for religious claims, it *does not follow* that nonreligious conscientious claims must suffer by comparison. That religious claimants must be treated better

---

[95] In standard criminal law terminology, one might speak about recklessness regarding these harmful effects.

[96] See Eisgruber and Sager, note 7 supra; Christopher L. Eisgruber and Lawrence G. Sager, *Religious Freedom and the Constitution* (Cambridge: Harvard University Press, 2007).

[97] Ira C. Lupu, "Reconstructing the Establishment Clause: The Case Against Discretionary Accommodation of Religion," 140 *University of Pennsylvania Law Review* 555 (1991).

than most people who are subject to a restrictive law does not entail that they may be treated better than others whose nonreligious objections to a law resemble their own.

In summary, it is troublesome for courts to decide that some citizens will be relieved from obligations imposed generally, and it is troublesome for courts to make the necessary assessments about religious needs and state interests; but the *Smith* alternative involves such a blatant inattention to the fundamental political rights of citizens that it should be abandoned. If this analysis is correct, it leaves open just how courts should exercise their protection of free exercise rights and, particularly, just how much latitude they should leave for reasonable legislative judgments. But a constitutional rule that permits the prohibition of practices deemed fundamental by religious individuals and groups on the slenderest of public needs is intolerable. The combination of positions that I defend is that free exercise demands certain exemptions but that nonestablishment, equal protection, and free speech sometimes require extension to similarly situated nonreligious claimants.

REGULATION OF PRIVATE ENTITIES AND EXEMPTIONS

Thus far, we have been focusing on exemptions from behavior that government generally requires, such as wearing helmets or serving in the military. Yet more complex issues about exemption can arise when the government requires that private enterprises make exemptions from their ordinary rules. To take a standard example, an employer requires all workers to work on Saturday; may the government insist that the employer excuse those whose religion forbids Saturday work from working on that day?

We need here to disentangle elements of jurisdiction, protection of free exercise, and avoidance of establishment. In the federal system of the United States, there might be a question whether the federal government has general authority to promote the free exercise of religion. In this form, the question does not arise for individual states, which can promote all aspects of public welfare. Even for the federal government, if it otherwise has jurisdiction, say through the Commerce Clause, it can pursue a policy of protecting the exercise of religion *unless* the religion clauses themselves forbid it.

Here is an argument that governments in the United States cannot create religious exemptions from exercises of private power. The First Amendment forbids Congress, and now the states, from prohibiting the free exercise of religion. The government can "prohibit" only by its own action; no private action violates the free exercise guarantee. Thus the free exercise guarantee gives no support to regulating private responses to religious needs. The Establishment Clause forbids government preferences for religion. When government requires private entities to accommodate religion, it prefers religion and violates the Establishment Clause.

This neat argument is too neat. We may take, first, private insensitivity to religious needs that itself somehow derives from government action that violates religious liberty in some way or did so in the past. A corrective for past government violations might include requirements placed on private entities.

The hard question involves exemptions that do not respond to government action. Some opinions by Supreme Court justices have suggested that demands on private entities cannot be squared with the Establishment Clause unless they are part of a package of forbidding discrimination on religious grounds[98]—a power that the government uncontroversially has.[99] It is in this manner that the modest accommodations required of private employers under Title VII have been said to be appropriate.

I think it is reasonable to suppose that the government has authority to lift obstacles to religious exercise even when these are purely private. In employment, for example, the Establishment Clause should generally not be understood to bar the government's requiring accommodations by private companies that would clearly be proper were the government as employer to make them.

However, requirements of exemptions are subject to limits. One limit is that the government cannot seriously infringe *the religious exercise* of the private entities that are regulated. Another limit is that if the government insists on too much, even in the way of economic costs, it has crossed over the threshold of forbidden establishment. This is the best understanding of what condemned Connecticut's absolute requirement that employers give employees a day off on their Sabbath, in *Estate of Thornton v. Caldor.*[100] On this view, as the next chapter explores, the distinction between accommodation that the government may require and forbidden establishment can be a *matter of degree* rather than some *qualitative* difference in how a law operates or in the motivations that engender it. In *Estate of Thornton,* Justice O'Connor says that a defect of that law is that in favoring Sabbath observance over

---

[98] See especially the concurring opinion of Justice O'Connor, in *Estate of Thornton v. Caldor, Inc.,* 472 U.S. 703, 712 (1985), discussed in the next chapter.

[99] It is not entirely clear why one might not object that forbidding private religious discrimination and allowing political or ideological discrimination somehow establishes religion.

[100] Note 98 supra.

other religious practices, it endorses a particular religious belief.[101] But this seems a mistake. Any specific exemption will single out some features of religions over others. That is not enough to make an exemption invalid. Recognition of an especially strong need to accommodate is not necessarily an endorsement of the belief that supports the practice that is accommodated.[102]

The following chapter considers in greater detail how courts may distinguish permissible accommodations from impermissible establishments of religion.

---

[101] Id. at 711.

[102] One might concede my general point and still agree with Justice O'Connor that when a legislature requires employers to accommodate to religious practices of workers, it cannot specify a single practice for favored treatment.

CHAPTER 17

Limits of Accommodation

Among the most vexed questions in the law of the religion clauses is when a legal measure that might otherwise be justified as an accommodation to free exercise is instead a forbidden establishment of religion. The chapters in the free exercise volume as well as those in this volume up to this point provide some idea just how complex this question can be. We now tackle it head on. Scholars have fairly observed that the Supreme Court has given us no theory, or no tenable theory, for drawing the line between permissible accommodation and impermissible establishment. We will look at what the Court has said and done, as well as the writings of some scholars, to see whether we can discern bases for distinguishing accommodation from establishment. Analysis of major scholarly proposals that deviate sharply from the Court's approach is reserved for chapter 21.

It helps initially to set out some premises on which the remainder of the chapter rests and to note discrete subquestions. The premises are these: (1) A great many accommodations to religion are exemptions from rules that are generally applicable, but accommodations may take the form of assistance that is not an exemption, as exemplified by the presence of chaplains in the military and in prisons. (2) Accommodations may be constitutionally required or within legislative (and administrative) discretion. This chapter concentrates on accommodations legislators choose to grant. (3) Whatever one thinks about the implications of its precise language, the threefold *Lemon* test has never been regarded by most justices as barring all accommodations to religion. Either they have considered the purpose and effect of relieving burdens on religious exercise as one kind of secular purpose and effect (the majority position in *Amos*)[1] or they have considered the purpose and effect as being a permissible religious purpose and effect (Justice O'Connor's position in *Amos*).[2] Concerns about whether an accommodation is unconstitutional may be lessened when it is formulated in general terms and

---

[1] *Corporation of the Presiding Bishop of the Church of Jesus Christ of Latter-Day Saints v. Amos*, 483 U.S. 327, 336–37 (1987).

[2] Id. at 348–49 (concurring opinion).

not limited to religious claims;[3] but the Court has never indicated that all accommodations made explicitly to religious exercise are invalid. Indeed, in 2005, the Court unanimously sustained federal legislation requiring accommodations to religious claims within prisons,[4] and in 2006 it upheld the application of the Religious Freedom Restoration Act to protect the importation of an hallucinogenic tea for worship by a small Christian Spiritist sect with origins in the Amazon rainforest.[5] Given that justices who reject the *Lemon* approach have joined these opinions, the cases clearly indicate that the permissibility of some accommodations in terms of religion does not depend on the continuing status of the *Lemon* test. (4) Accommodations may not involve favoritism of one religious group over another similarly situated religious group. (5) As chapters 13 and 14 reflect, accommodations may not consist of conferrals of direct political authority upon religious groups. (6) Efforts to aid or promote religion that do not relieve any identifiable burden—sponsored oral prayer in public schools is an example—do not count as accommodations. A state may not single out religious groups for financial grants and call it accommodation. (7) An "establishment" concern may be generated by flawed legislative aspirations, by burdens imposed on those who bear the costs of accommodation, or by a failure to privilege nonreligious claims analogous to the favored religious claims. If the only problem is the failure to treat analogous claims similarly, a judicial corrective may take the form of extending the privileges.[6] In other instances, the "accommodation" is treated as invalid.

Some of the crucial questions are these: (1) Must the burdens that accommodation relieves be ones that the government itself has imposed? (2) Are all concerns about establishment removed if the classification for an exemption or other benefit is in nonreligious terms? (3) What determines whether a classification may permissibly be in terms of religion? (4) May the state accommodate by imposing burdens on private individuals and companies? (5) Are the distinctions between permissible accommodations and impermissible promotions of religion ones of qualitative difference or of degree, or of both? To put this last question in terms of the *Lemon* test, will the main

---

[3] As chapter 21 of volume 1 recounts, typical privileges not to participate in medical procedures are cast in this broader way.

[4] *Cutter v. Wilkinson*, 544 U.S. 709 (2005).

[5] *Gonzales v. O Centro Espirita Beneficente União do Vegetal*, 546 U.S. 418 (2006).

[6] *Welsh v. United States*, 398 U.S. 333, 357–58 (1970) (Harlan, J., concurring) (nonreligious conscientious objectors should be treated like the religious objectors Congress exempted from military service).

purpose or primary effect of a permissible accommodation be fundamentally different from the main purpose or primary effect of an impermissible establishment, or may the purposes or effects be of a similar nature but of a different magnitude?

A helpful way to illustrate some of the premises and to illuminate the questions is to focus on a Supreme Court case striking down an attempted accommodation.

THE PUZZLE OF *ESTATE OF THORNTON*

In response to a court decision declaring that its Sunday-closing laws were unconstitutionally vague, the Connecticut legislature allowed a greater number of businesses to stay open on Sunday, and it provided that "[n]o person who states that a particular day of the week is observed as his Sabbath may be required by his employer to work on such day."[7] A Presbyterian who wanted Sunday off sued after Caldor, Inc.'s, refusal to keep him in his management position if he refused to work on Sunday. The Connecticut Supreme Court ruled that the law did not have a "clear secular purpose" and had a primary effect of advancing religion, because it conferred its benefit on a religious basis.[8]

On review, the Supreme Court affirmed the decision, with an opinion by Chief Justice Burger that relied on the law's impermissible effect. By affording workers an absolute right not to work on their Sabbath, the law took no account of the convenience of employers and of other workers. If a business, such as a school, operated only five days a week, it would have to grant an employee one of those days off if that was his Sabbath. And workers with nonreligious reasons to have a day off would have to give way to those with religious reasons. This "unyielding weighting in favor of Sabbath observers" went beyond an incidental or remote effect; the statute had "a primary effect that impermissibly advances a particular religious practice."[9]

Justice O'Connor's two-page concurrence seemed to go further than the Court in various respects.[10] By singling out "Sabbath observers for special and . . . absolute protection, without according similar accommodation to ethical beliefs and practices of other private employees," the law conveyed

---

[7] *Estate of Thornton v. Caldor, Inc.*, 472 U.S. 703, 706 (1985).
[8] Id. at 707–8.
[9] Id. at 710.
[10] Id. at 711–712.

"a message of endorsement of the Sabbath observance."[11] According to O'Connor, the accommodations contemplated by the Free Exercise Clause are those that lift burdens imposed by the government, not by *private* employers.[12] Title VII (the basic federal statute barring discrimination),[13] which requires private employers to make reasonable accommodations to workers' religious needs (unless these would produce undue hardship for the employers), is justified, she wrote, because it is an antidiscrimination law and calls for reasonable rather than absolute accommodation.

Justice O'Connor's opinion intimated two sweeping limits to permissible accommodation that are neither supported by the Court's jurisprudence nor wise. The Connecticut law focused on Sabbath observance. *Any* specific legislative accommodation will be directed to some particular religious practice to the omission of others, for example, use of peyote in worship, or riding motorcycles without helmets. If every choice to protect one form of religious exercise is the endorsement or advancement of that form over others, every specific accommodation violates the Establishment Clause.[14] All that would be left for legislators to decide would be whether or not to grant a general accommodation, such as the Religious Freedom Restoration Act, that does not distinguish among forms of religious exercise. Yet it is highly desirable to leave some decisions up to legislatures, not courts, as to whether state interests will allow specific religious accommodations.[15]

If the choice to protect religious exercise over other nonreligious ethical beliefs and reasons inevitably advances religion in an impermissible manner, then *both* specific and general accommodations are invalid when they are formulated in terms of religion. As we have seen, the Court has consistently assumed, with Justice O'Connor's vote, that some accommodations in terms of religious exercise are all right; and I have defended that approach in both these volumes.

Chief Justice Burger's opinion for the *Thornton* Court was much more circumspect. It rightly held the state law invalid but left open the possibility that a more modest protection of Sabbath observance—one imposing fewer costs on employers and coworkers—might be acceptable. It eschewed the purpose argument adopted by the Connecticut Supreme Court. One can see

[11] Id. at 711.

[12] Id. at 712 (citing her opinion in *Wallace v. Jaffree*).

[13] See chapters 18 and 19 of volume 1.

[14] One might defend such an approach as appropriate in the context of privileges of workers vis-à-vis employers, but Justice O'Connor gives no such limited defense.

[15] See William K. Kelley, "The Primacy of Political Actors in Accommodation of Religion," 22 *University of Hawaii Law Review* 403 (2000) (arguing that legislators are particularly to be trusted when they protect minority religions by accommodations).

why. In any superficial sense—we shall later consider more complex arguments—it is hard to see that the legislative purpose to protect Sabbath observance differs depending on whether it gives absolute protection or a qualified protection to be balanced against the economic needs of employers and the claims of fellow workers. In treating *Sherbert v. Verner* (which held that a Seventh-day Adventist could not be denied unemployment compensation because her religious convictions precluded work on Saturday) as continuing to be valid constitutional law, the recent Court has assumed that a legislature might enact an exemption from Saturday work in its unemployment laws to accommodate those who worship on Saturday and consider it a day of rest.[16] The legislative purpose to protect workers from suffering conflicts between religious obligations (or needs) and the demands of employment does not in any obvious way alter with the degree of protection.

Whether an effect is incidental or primary can reasonably be seen as related to the weight of the imposition on others. If religious exercise prevails over all countervailing considerations, the advancement of religion is much greater than if the law requires only modest efforts to accommodate. At least subject to further analysis, *Estate of Thornton* seems to be a case in which degree is crucial. Effects of the *same kind*—that is, benefits to religious exercise at some inconvenience to employers and fellow workers[17]—are primary or incidental depending on their magnitude. The case, thus, raises a flag of caution about all efforts to distinguish permissible accommodations from impermissible establishments on the basis of qualitative (or categorical) differences.

REQUISITES FOR PERMISSIBLE ACCOMMODATIONS

Drawing from the Supreme Court's jurisprudence, we can identify the following requirements for a permissible accommodation to religious practice. A valid exercise in accommodation relieves a relevant burden on religious practice; its remedy is not intrinsically unconstitutional, does not impose

[16] *Sherbert*, of course, was a decision about a constitutionally required exemption. But if an exemption is required, it is obviously also one a legislature would be permitted to make. (And if one thinks *Sherbert* survived the more limited free exercise rights of *Smith* only because the Court had previously decided a number of unemployment compensation cases, *Smith* clearly would *allow* legislatures to carve out the privilege *Sherbert* requires.)

[17] One might distinguish unemployment cases as ones in which the government (and taxpayers in general) bear the burden, but in some states employer contributions to unemployment funds depend to a degree on how many of their employees draw unemployment compensation. See Kelley, note 15 supra, at 414.

unacceptably on others, and is not much more expansive than is needed; and its classification of beneficiaries is appropriate. We shall examine each of these requisites in turn, asking how far decisions about whether they are satisfied can be based on relatively straightforward classifications, demand nuanced judgments about how to apply categories, or call for outright balancing of conflicting interests. This examination is followed by an introduction to three scholarly proposals that would significantly alter how courts address issues of accommodation. The first two suggest simpler criteria, the last a large degree of deference to legislative judgment.

Relief of a Relevant Burden

According to modern Supreme Court doctrine, an accommodation of free exercise must relieve a burden on religious practice, not promote or sponsor that practice. But saying that an accommodation must relieve a burden does not tell us what counts as a burden. Is any tax a burden, or is a tax a burden only if it really interferes with religious practice or falls with particular weight on religious practice? In *Texas Monthly, Inc. v. Bullock*, Justice Brennan in his plurality opinion wrote that an exemption for religious publications from a state sales tax was not justified when (absent the exemption) the tax would fall equally on all publications and apparently would not offend religious beliefs or inhibit religious activity.[18] For Justice Scalia in dissent, it seemed sufficient that the exemption relieved religious groups of a tax they would otherwise have to pay.[19]

Justice Brennan said that when a subsidy goes exclusively to religious organizations and is not compelled by the Free Exercise Clause, it is in invalid if it "either burdens nonbeneficiaries markedly or cannot reasonably be seen as removing a significant state-imposed deterrent to the free exercise of religion."[20] The dissenters were much less demanding.

One might see this disagreement as over how great a burden must be or as whether relief of a burden should even be a requirement of permissible accommodation. Perhaps it should be enough that the government enables religious practice without coercion or sponsorship. Recall *Zorach v. Clauson*, the case in which New York allowed public school students to leave school for religious instruction.[21] Justice Douglas's opinion for the Court in that case is broadly positive about government accommodation to the reli-

[18] 489 U.S. 1, 18 (1989).
[19] Id. at 38–39.
[20] Id. at 15.
[21] 343 U.S. 306 (1952).

gious needs of citizens. If one thinks the case was correctly decided,[22] one might justify the result on the ground that mandatory school attendance did interfere with possibilities for religious instruction (thus imposing a burden) or simply on the ground that government may aid citizens who want to engage in religious practice, whether or not it responds to a burden.

In my judgment, the Court has been right to insist that an accommodation must relieve some burden on the exercise of religion; that requirement is a needed corollary of a rule against promotion of religion. But this conclusion alone does not settle the question of baselines that many chapters of this book have engaged. What exactly is the state of affairs against which the inquiry about burden should be put? In *Zorach*, is it a burden that mandatory regular education occupies much of a student's day? In respect to military chaplains, does one take as given the basic conditions of military life—or does one start with conditions of ordinary civilian life—in which event military life restricts religious practice in a manner chaplains can relieve? These issues about baselines need to be addressed individually. Some are easy and some are hard, but none are resolved by a general formulation that requires relief of a burden.

One fundamental question about burden is whether the burden must be state-imposed. The crucial passage from Justice Brennan's opinion in *Texas Monthly* talks of a "state-imposed deterrent" to free exercise,[23] and Justice O'Connor's opinion in *Estate of Thornton* emphasizes that free exercise accommodations must lift burdens imposed by the government, not private employers.[24] If this limitation is conceived as applying to all government accommodations to the exercise of religion, I believe it is misconceived. To begin, as I explain in chapter 18 of the free exercise volume, it is a strain to construe the accommodation required by Title VII as only about discrimination, as Justice O'Connor did. The statutory language demands that employers make some accommodations to religious exercise that go beyond preventing discrimination. O'Connor was on solid ground if all that she meant was that the terms of the Free Exercise Clause, which bar laws "prohibiting" religious exercise, seem to authorize only the lifting of burdens imposed by government.[25] (Although a state may "prohibit" the exercise of religion in a broad sense by failing to correct a burden *it* has imposed, its

---

[22] Believing that New York's law significantly promoted religious practice through the use of the state's requirement that children attend school, I do not think the case was correctly decided.

[23] *Texas Monthly*, note 18 supra, at 15.

[24] *Estate of Thornton*, note 7 supra, at 13.

[25] Michael W. McConnell, "Accommodation of Religion: An Update and a Response to Critics," 60 *George Washington Law Review* 685, 712 (1992).

failure to lift a privately imposed burden does not seem to involve it in prohibiting free exercise.) Still, burdens are often the consequence of an inter-
mingling of government and private power. Private practices are affected
by various laws, and many private enterprises rely heavily on government
purchases and various forms of cooperation. And one should conceive the
authority of governments to promote public welfare as including some lifting
of burdens on religious exercise that goes beyond the specific terms of the
Free Exercise Clause. That, I have argued in the previous chapter, is a much
more sensible approach to accommodation than treating every effort to lift
privately imposed burdens as invalid under the Establishment Clause. No
Supreme Court case has actually rejected an accommodation *because* it responds to a privately imposed burden, and it is fair to say that question has
yet to be carefully considered.[26]

Unconstitutional Forms of Relief

An accommodation cannot remedy a burden by a measure that is intrinsically unconstitutional. Two illustrations will suffice here. In *Board of Education of Kiryas Joel Village School District v. Grumet*, discussed in chapter
13, the New York legislature created a school district drawn on religious
lines.[27] That was regarded as impermissibly assigning political authority to
a religious group on the basis of religion.[28] Another measure that would not
be acceptable would be one that required courts to use criteria of judgment
that the Court has ruled out as themselves unconstitutional.[29] A state legislature could not accommodate the religious practices of frustrated members
of religious congregations by a law that assigned church property to the
faction that "has remained faithful to traditional doctrines and practices."
As chapter 16 of volume 1 explains, state courts cannot create and use such
standards, and they would be barred to state legislatures as well.

Some forms of relief may not be intrinsically unconstitutional but will
have features that count negatively in an overall appraisal of their validity.
The government is to remain neutral as to religion. If it attempts to accom-

---

[26] When an attempted accommodation raises Establishment Clause problems, perhaps the countervailing free exercise interests should count more strongly if the lifted burden has been imposed by the
government, but relief from private burdens should not be ruled out.

[27] 512 U.S. 687 (1994).

[28] Id. at 699 (opinion of Souter, J.), 722 (concurring opinion of Kennedy, J.). The two opinions
offer slightly different rationales, but the difference is not significant for this point.

[29] The language of the Texas statute ruled unconstitutional in *Texas Monthly* seemed to demand
difficult judgments about exclusion and inclusion, note 18 supra, at 5, but that feature did not figure
in the decision.

modate a religious practice in a manner that encourages people to join religious groups and to adopt or feign religious belief, that leans toward a form of establishment.

Given the absolute privilege it provided, the Connecticut law held invalid in *Estate of Thornton* could well have encouraged people to join religious groups that worship on the day they would want off. They could assume that the state would not check their church attendance every week, and even if they attended services regularly, that could leave much of the day for recreation. Sometimes the need for accommodation is great enough, however, to warrant a degree of unintended encouragement to join a religious group. No matter how a draft exemption for conscientious objectors is formulated (i.e., whether or not it is limited to religious objectors and does or does not require group membership), it provides *some* encouragement to join pacifist religious groups, since those deciding if an applicant is really opposed to participation in any war are less likely to determine that members of pacifist religions are insincere.[30]

Relation of Relief to Religious Need

If a legislative accommodation grants a benefit that is far more extensive than the burden to which it responds, the "accommodation" will become an unconstitutional promotion of religion. This principle was invoked by the complaining fired workers in *Corporation of the Presiding Bishop v. Amos*.[31] They claimed that the sensible privilege granted to religious organizations to discriminate on religious grounds when they employ persons in positions of religious leadership could not be extended to mundane forms of work unconnected to religious practice. The justices rejected their argument, on the ground that it would be burdensome for religious groups to have to explain why they should be able to use religious criteria in hiring and firing for various positions, but in doing so, the Court accepted the basic idea that the breadth of privilege should correlate reasonably with the breadth of the burden the privilege relieves.[32]

The Connecticut law reviewed in *Estate of Thornton* presented a problem of this kind, though not one on which the Court focused. The law gave workers their Sabbath off from work whether or not they objected in princi-

---

[30] This problem is discussed at length in chapter 4 of volume 1.

[31] 483 U.S. 327.

[32] Such a correlation is also required if Congress acts to "enforce" the Free Exercise Clause and the claim is that it has exceeded its jurisdictional authority. In *City of Boerne v. Flores*, 521 U.S. 507 (1997), the Court held that Congress could not justify the breadth of the Religious Freedom Restoration Act as a measure to prevent actual violations of the Constitution.

ple to working on their Sabbath, and could or could not combine worship and work on the same day. A large number of Christians have no objection based on their religion to working Sunday afternoon and evening.[33] Although the law's generosity in granting entire days off might be justified as a matter of administrative convenience, giving Sabbath observers so much more of a privilege than most of them needed could more reasonably be seen as excessive, amounting to promotion of Sabbath observance. We may generalize that the greater a law's privilege in relation to religious need, the more likely it will be that the legislature has gone beyond relieving a burden.

Permissible Classification

A legislative accommodation must classify beneficiaries in an acceptable way. Most obviously, the legislature cannot treat similarly situated religious groups differently. In chapters of both volumes, we have considered what features might make groups sufficiently dissimilar to make differential treatment acceptable. A particular problem raised by the *Kiryas Joel* case is whether a legislature may respond with focused legislation to a particular problem faced by one religious group, given the absence of a any assurance that it would treat another group similarly in the future. Justice Souter wrote for the Court that this potential for discrimination constituted an unacceptable failure to exercise authority in a religiously neutral way.[34] With Justice Kennedy,[35] I believe to the contrary that legislatures should be able to respond to pressing needs for accommodation; if unfair differentiation later occurs, judges can respond to it.

The more pervasive question about accommodation classification is whether religious groups and practices may be treated differently from analogous nonreligious ones. Much of volume 1 and chapters 15 and 16 of this volume address that question in various contexts, and it is a primary focus of chapter 21. The most sensible position, I have claimed, is that for some subjects religion may be treated differently, for others not.

If a legislature's initial classification is impermissible for one reason or another, the legislature can choose to withdraw the benefit altogether or to extend the range of beneficiaries. Unless and until the legislature acts, a court declaring a classification invalid must make a similar choice, based, it is often said, on its best judgment of what the legislature would want.[36] Much may

---

[33] One *might* think this superfluous degree of privilege was partly designed to give Christians no less of a privilege than Jews, who, if observant, do not believe they should work on their Sabbath.

[34] Note 27 supra, at 702–4.

[35] Id. at 726–27 (concurring opinion).

[36] *Welsh v. United States*, 398 U.S. 333, 357–58 (Harlan, J., concurring).

depend on the size of the pool the legislature intended to benefit in relation to the size of the pool needed to make a classification constitutional. If the intended religious beneficiaries numbered one hundred thousand and the nonreligious pool needed to make the classification acceptable numbered three thousand, one would assume the legislature would want an extension. Were the numbers reversed, one would think the legislature would prefer to withdraw the benefit.

If a legislature chooses to grant a benefit in a way that is not limited to religious claimants, the chances are significantly reduced that a court will find a violation of the Establishment Clause, even if the main body of intended beneficiaries have religious reasons to want the benefit. One option is to make the benefit available to anyone who wishes to take advantage of it. A prison concerned about religious objections of inmates to eating meat (or specific kinds of meat) may provide a vegetarian option, allowing any prisoner to choose the vegetarian meal. Concerned about religious scruples against oaths, the drafters of the federal Constitution itself allowed federal officials to be bound to support the Constitution "by Oath or Affirmation."[37]

Rather than granting a benefit to all who wish it, a legislature may set criteria that do not refer to religion.[38] It may, for example, allow nurses not to participate in medical procedures if they have a moral objection or an objection in conscience to doing so. Or parents may be excused from having their children vaccinated if vaccinations are contrary to their moral convictions. These criteria include religious convictions, but do not privilege them.

Although uses of these broader criteria sharply reduce concerns about violations of the Establishment Clause, they do not necessarily eliminate them. That is most evident with respect to constitutional objections that rest on the burdens that must be borne by others. Suppose the Connecticut law in *Estate of Thornton* had mandated a day off for all workers who had a reason of conscience not to work on that day. If an employer could show to the satisfaction of a court that the overarching aim and effect of the law was to protect Sabbath observance, it could presumably succeed on the argument that did succeed in the case—namely, that the legislature cannot protect the religious exercise of some citizens by imposing unduly on the interests of other citizens.[39] It is to this subject that we now turn.

---

[37] U.S. Constitution, Art. 6.

[38] A variation on this option is to include religion explicitly as a basis, but also to include other bases that reach all analogous reasons for wanting to behave in a particular way.

[39] A similar analysis may be made of claims of hospitals and patients that a privilege for nurses not to participate may interfere too greatly with the provision of medical benefits. See the discussion in chapter 21 of volume 1.

Who Bears the Burden of a Privilege and
How Great Is the Burden's Weight?

An accommodation relieves a burden on the religious exercise of certain individuals; sometimes, but not always, others have to bear the cost of the privilege that the accommodation grants. That can make a crucial difference for whether the accommodation is constitutional. In any realistic sense, some accommodations carry no burden to be borne by others. If officials or witnesses at trial can "affirm" rather than swearing an oath, no one is poorer (unless those who affirm are more likely to lie as a consequence). If members of the Native American Church can ingest peyote in worship services, no one else suffers as a result.[40]

Other privileges from accommodations do impose disadvantages on others. The cost may be a financial one for the government and thus for individuals as taxpayers. In *Texas Monthly*, Justice Brennan wrote that the exemption from the sales tax for religious publications "burdens nonbeneficiaries by increasing their tax bills by whatever amount is needed to offset the benefit bestowed on subscribers to religious publications."[41] Although such a cost may be of some concern, an otherwise valid accommodation would not be ruled unconstitutional because taxpayers have to foot the bill.

The real problems arise if the cost is borne by private persons and enterprises in a way that reaches beyond a marginal increase in their tax liabilities. These costs can be financial or in opportunities forgone; they can be in terms of religious exercise itself. In *Estate of Thornton*, either employers had to carry the costs of workers taking their Sabbath off, or other workers had to work on days they would have preferred to be home (mainly Sunday and Saturday), or both.[42] For the Court, the demands that Connecticut's absolute Sabbath privilege placed on employers and other workers were too great.

As I have suggested in my original account of the case, it is hard to understand the question of whether the burdens to be borne by others are too great

---

[40] That is, assuming that those who have ingested peyote do not go out and harm others (I am aware of no evidence that this happens), and putting aside feelings of possible discrimination among those who have nonreligious reasons to ingest peyote.

[41] Note 18 supra, at 19 n. 8 (plurality opinion).

[42] In *Estate of Thornton*, the original burden on free exercise came from employers who wanted work on Sunday (and other days that were the Sabbaths of workers), *and* the cost of the countervailing privilege not to work on one's Sabbath also fell on employers. These two features, source of burden and cost of its relief, typically combine, but they are distinctive. If the government gives an absolute Sabbath privilege to its own workers, the burden may fall mainly on other individual government workers, not the government and taxpayers in general. If the government gives special compensation to those who lose jobs in the private sector because they refuse to work on their Sabbath, the burden

as anything other than a matter of degree. A slight cost borne by private individuals will not violate the Establishment Clause; a heavy cost will amount to an advancement of religion at the expense of other interests. Jonathan E. Nuechterlein has suggested, however, that the case may be analyzed in terms of an inquiry about purpose. The legislature's extreme inattention to the interests of employers and other workers demonstrated that its purpose was to promote religion rather than lift a burden.[43] Although it is true that a failure to consider the interests of others can often be a signal of one's purpose, I am skeptical about this particular conclusion. Why should we not rather say that the legislators regarded an inability to worship on the Sabbath as a very heavy burden that needed to be lifted however high the cost on others?[44] In any event, if one standard for whether the legislative purpose was to promote religion is assessing the *magnitude* of hardship others must bear, we are still left to consider the *degree* of that hardship, to determine purpose.[45]

A special kind of burden that others might bear is an imposition on their own religious freedom. Michael McConnell has written, "An accommodation must not interfere with the religious liberty of others by forcing them to participate in religious observance."[46] McConnell is right to note the difference between an indirect economic injury and some form of forced participation in religious exercise. The latter will almost never be constitutionally allowable, but we cannot rule out completely the possibility that a law may appropriately pressure individuals to a degree to participate in a proceeding that has some religious significance but also gravely affects the value of civic rights of someone else. As we saw in chapter 14 of this volume, the law may justifiably impose certain negative consequences on divorcing husbands of the Jewish faith who refuse to appear before a *beth din*, in proceedings leading to a religious divorce for their wives.

---

would be privately created, but the expense of accommodation would fall largely on the government and its taxpayers.

[43] Jonathan E. Nuechterlein, "The Free Exercise Boundaries of Permissible Accommodation under the Establishment Clause," 99 *Yale Law Journal* 1127, 1141–43 (1990).

[44] The fact that the law gave workers their Sabbath off from work whether or not they objected in principle to working on their Sabbath, and had religious reasons not to work on their Sabbath, was a stronger signal of a purpose to promote Sabbath worship than the burden placed on employers.

[45] If the conclusion about purpose is, instead, simply a label one affixes once one has decided that a burden is disproportionate, then purpose itself plays no real part in the analysis at all.

I mean here to distinguish between assuming that legislators (or a reasonable !legislator) actually had in mind one objective or another, with degree of burden providing some evidence of actual intent, and treating the "purpose" as depending directly on the degree of burden apart from any assumption about people's actual objectives.

[46] Michael W. McConnell, "Accommodation of Religion," 1995 *Supreme Court Review* 1, 37.

A particular problem about bearing the burden of accommodation arises when a law accommodates by giving a private enterprise the right to treat someone (a worker) differently than it could treat that person if ordinary prohibitions applied. In *Amos*,[47] the Mormon gymnasium was allowed to fire a worker on religious grounds. Justice White's opinion for the majority suggested that if all the law does is to give a religious organization a privilege to engage in discrimination, if it chooses, the discrimination is not the responsibility of the government. On that view, the burden on the workers' free exercise of religion, namely that a deviation from Mormon practice might lose them their jobs, was not attributable to the government. The better view, that taken by the concurring justices, was that the interference with workers' religious exercise, authorized by the law, did need to be taken into account, but that it was justified in terms of the free exercise interests supporting freedom for the religious organization.[48]

A Brief Word about Major Alternatives

In chapter 21, we shall review two notable proposals, "substantive neutrality"[49] and "equal regard,"[50] that draw on aspects of what the Supreme Court has decided but would reform the law of the religion clauses to a considerable extent. Either of these proposals, if adopted, would affect how one would draw the line between permissible accommodation and impermissible establishment. Instead of working through separate inquiries about burdens, purposes, and effects, a court would ask how the law fares against an ideal of neutrality or equal regard. Under an ideal of neutrality, the government would aim to the greatest extent possible neither to encourage nor to discourage religious affiliation and practice. Under an ideal of equal regard it would aim to respect religious claims equally with nonreligious claims. Because the Connecticut law in *Estate of Thornton* could easily have encouraged people to join churches and gave unequal regard to religious and nonreligious claims to be free of Sunday work, we can see how either of these approaches might have yielded the result of that case.

[47] Note 1 supra.

[48] See the discussion at pp. 383–84 of volume 1.

[49] Douglas Laycock, "Formal, Substantive, and Disaggregated Neutrality toward Religion," 39 *DePaul Law Review* 993 (1990). This approach is criticized in Nelson Tebbe, "Free Exercise and the Problem of Symmetry," 56 *Hastings Law Journal* 699 (2005).

[50] Christopher L. Eisgruber and Lawrence G. Sager, *Religious Freedom and the Constitution* (Cambridge: Harvard University Press, 2007).

Two points about "neutrality" and "equal regard" approaches are important here. First, the apparent simplicity of each approach might lead one to think that they would permit straightforward categorical analysis, rather than balancing and assessing matters of degree. Chapter 21 shows how far that is from the truth. Second, even if one believes that neither approach captures all that is relevant under the religion clauses—and I shall argue in chapter 21 that neither does—the considerations they pick out as crucial are relevant in an overall appraisal of what constitute relevant burdens and acceptable effects.

Deference to Legislative Judgment

As with most individual rights questions, the Supreme Court has approached the bulk of religion clause cases without affording great deference to legislative judgment. William Kelley has urged that this approach is misconceived as far as accommodations are concerned because they typically assist minority groups, and legislatures can be trusted when they reach out to protect minorities.[51] Insofar as it is sound, this argument would apply when legislatures choose to protect minorities, not when they refuse to do so. Two problems with the argument concern its level of generality. Major pieces of accommodation legislation, such as the federal and state RFRAs, and the Religious Land Use and Institutionalized Persons Act, have been strongly supported by leading religious groups. Legislators may be disinclined to oppose that powerful set of lobbyists.[52] And legislators who may be trusted not to exaggerate the needs of minority religions over the welfare of the general populace may not care very much about the small number of nonreligious people with claims analogous to religious ones, such as nonreligious objectors to vaccinations. As to the choice whether to include nonreligious claimants in an exemption that will mainly benefit religious individuals, we have little reason to trust legislative majorities.

A quite different approach to accommodation from one of deference is skepticism about any legislative accommodation. According to the view that sees accommodations as benefits for religion that are a kind of trade-off for various disabilities required by the Establishment Clause, when disabilities shrink (as they have in recent years), permissible accommodations should also shrink to keep matters in balance. For reasons I explain in volume 1, I

---

[51] Kelley, note 15 supra.

[52] This problem may be heightened when the benefiting groups are national and the opposing interests are local, as with zoning regulations that apply to churches.

do not think special protections for religious exercise are mainly a question of offsetting disadvantages required by the Establishment Clause. Rather, the protection of religious liberty is independently valuable. Thus, I do not believe, and the Court has never suggested, that the range of permissible accommodation should expand or contract with expansions and contractions in Establishment Clause limits.

Summary

In drawing the line between permitted accommodation and forbidden establishment, courts must engage a number of inquiries. Sometimes their analysis can be categorical, whether a law is of one kind or another, but often they must assess subtle nuances and matters of degree to determine whether the border between the constitutional and the unconstitutional has been crossed.

CHAPTER 18

Financial Support to Religious Institutions

Many major problems about Establishment Clause law involve public funding of endeavors undertaken by religious organizations—such as hospitals, schools, adoption agencies, and drug rehabilitation centers. This chapter identifies some central issues about funding, before turning to Supreme Court decisions regarding services other than schools, and controversial aspects of President George W. Bush's "faith-based initiative" for social services. The following chapter concentrates on the complex topic of aid to private religious schools.

The modern Supreme Court's decisions about funding have started from the premise that the government should not give financial support to religious organizations to pursue dominantly religious objectives. If the government gave a grant of $20 million to the Presbyterian Church to repair church buildings[1] and offer religious television programs, that would promote and sponsor Presbyterianism and constitute a forbidden establishment of religion. The government cannot directly finance a church's teaching of religious ideas any more than it can teach such ideas itself. Even were such grants given to all religious groups, that would promote religion in comparison with nonreligious activities and with antireligious groups and perspectives.[2] The conclusion that such assistance is impermissible would not be deflected by a claim that the government gives these grants because religious people make good citizens. Although the value of good citizenship might constitute a secular reason to support religion,[3] the government cannot single out religious groups as specially warranting support. One of the major themes of James Madison's "Memorial and Remonstrance," written in opposition to

---

[1] I am assuming here that the money for repair is not to compensate for damage the government has caused or as an offset for restrictions of historical landmark status.

[2] Andrew Koppelman, "Secular Purpose," 88 *Virginia Law Review* 87, 133–39 (2002), has suggested that government may favor religion in general, so long as it treats all groups that address religious questions, including atheist and agnostic groups, equally, but he does not challenge the bar on the funding of religious activities as such. Id. at 144.

[3] People's participation in religious groups can be a fruitful lesson in respect for others and political involvement, and throughout our history, many have claimed, with Washington in his Farewell Address, that religion is a vital bulwark of morality, and that morality is a critical component of good citizenship.

a state bill providing tax assessments for churches, was that tax money should not support churches. That conclusion has been regarded since *Everson* as a guiding principle of the Establishment Clause, and I take it as a starting point.[4]

APPROPRIATE FUNDING FOR PUBLIC SERVICES

The difficult questions about public funding arise when a religious organization provides a service that has a public, or secular benefits, such as a hospital or school. The law has sometimes required that in order to receive funds, religious organizations must set up secular corporations, but three substantial arguments may be made in favor of allowing funds to go directly to religious organizations. The first two of these arguments are made explicitly by those who support President Bush's "faith-based initiative," and the third is implicitly suggested by much of their rhetoric.

Nondiscrimination

So long as the state assists private organizations that provide valuable services, the nondiscrimination argument for aid to private religious providers is very strong. When the state undertakes social services that were previously rendered by private groups, its entry into the market, as it were, is usually meant to supplement, not displace. A city opening a municipal hospital wants private hospitals to continue. As taxes rise and patients may go to state-run alternatives, managing a private hospital without public assistance may become difficult. Some private hospitals may be unwilling to take indigent patients unless the government pays the bill. The government's total financial burden is likely to be less if it assists private hospitals than if it spends all its money on public facilities.[5] Beyond economic considerations, legislators may not want a public monopoly, believing that a mix of public and private facilities will best serve the public and provide a desirable range of choice.[6]

---

[4] As I have noted, some people think the government should be able to promote religion in general, including giving evenhanded financial support to all religions. If one rejects that view, the only substantial questions about financial assistance to religious groups, given just because they are religious groups, are raised by tax exemptions and tax deductions, forms of indirect economic assistance.

[5] It may want to avoid driving most private facilities out of business or causing them to restructure to provide privileged care for the wealthy.

[6] An alternative scenario is legislators' deciding that a service should remain entirely in private hands but that the state should provide public support. Timothy S. Burgett, in "Note, Government

Assuming that the state aids private providers of valuable services, the argument for including religious providers is straightforward. The crucial reason for public support is to provide the secular services effectively; all who provide the service equally well should be treated the same.[7] Were the government to prefer religious providers over all others, it would promote religion, but treating all private hospitals or shelters equally does not do that.

Although treating religious providers worse than others seems unfair in principle and may serve to inhibit religion, three possible concerns about equal assistance remain. By aiding religious providers, the government will assist religious activity; it may support religious discrimination in admissions or employment; and in performing necessary monitoring of the use of government funds, it may unduly entangle itself in the affairs of religious organizations.

Religious activities inevitably benefit as by-products of financial assistance. That assistance helps realize the hopes of consumers and providers who have religious reasons for wanting the service to come from a religious organization. And public funds, even if carefully earmarked for secular purposes, will free up other money that a group can spend for explicitly religious activity. Grantors can almost never assure themselves that in the absence of a grant, not a single penny of a recipient's money would have been spent for the purpose to which the grant goes. Money of the recipient that might have been expended for that purpose can now go elsewhere. However, if a provider affords a valuable public service and public money goes directly for that service, the group's enhanced ability to spend other funds for religious purposes is too indirect and unintended a form of support to justify treating religious providers worse than all others.

A narrower, more troubling possibility of aid to religious activity is that public funds might themselves be employed to promote explicitly religious messages. Suppose a Roman Catholic hospital used a public grant to improve its chapel or to print religious literature for its patients. One might take the view that if public money is being given for the value of services already rendered, a religious organization should be free to decide how to

---

Aid to Religious Social Service Providers: The Supreme Court's 'Pervasively Sectarian' Standard," 75 *Virginia Law Review* 1077, 1081 (1989), suggests, "Existing private organizations usually can provide the desired service more effectively than a comparable government bureaucracy because of a number of factors, including their reliance on unpaid volunteers and familiarity with the communities in which they operate."

[7] The government may reasonably treat nonprofit providers differently in some respects from those who are out for financial gain.

spend it. If the government pays a civil servant a salary, he is free to spend as much as he wishes for a religious purpose. Why should not the same be true of a religious hospital that is rewarded for giving medical services?

Here we need to draw a distinction. If a religious hospital is paid directly for a specific service it has rendered, for example, treatment of patient on Medicare, the payment compensates the hospital's own expenditure for medical care. There is indeed no objection to such money going into the hospital treasury to be mingled with other funds and spent as the hospital chooses. But if the grant is for a future project or work, another conceptualization is more appealing: namely, that the money should go for the secular service that is the reason for the grant, not for any related religious activity. Whether a private hospital is religious or nonreligious, one would expect building and similar grants to be earmarked for a precise purpose. But what is prudent management of the government's money for nonreligious private hospitals is in respect to religious ones a demand of the principle that government may not promote religion.

A conclusion that grants should be earmarked and used for specific public purposes raises the concern that government monitoring of how its funds are used might intrude too deeply into the working of religious organizations. With a construction grant, no extensive oversight is needed to make sure the money goes where it should, but, as we shall see, this problem proves more troubling for some other kinds of funding.

Whether religious providers should be able to discriminate in favor of their own members in employment has proved a highly sensitive issue, perhaps the key controversy over President Bush's faith-based initiative. I reserve discussion of that, and of the related issue of discrimination in choosing people to receive the service, until I turn to consideration of the Bush initiative and of "Charitable Choice" more generally.

Effectiveness

A second argument for funding religious groups is that they are often the most effective providers, or among the most effective providers; it would be counterproductive to direct money elsewhere if the best investment is in church groups. Whatever aspect of public benefit is involved, funding authorities should care who provides a service most effectively. When experienced people claim, as I have heard at conferences, that church groups do better than other groups in helping youngsters in poor urban areas find a sense of meaning and stay away from a life of hard drugs and crime, that constitutes a powerful appeal for assistance. The force of this argument is highly fact dependent—on what is happening with particular kinds of social services, among particular groups, in particular geographic areas. Although governments can finance the most effective providers of services, they cannot single out the religious components of programs to finance or choose providers simply because they are religious—even if officials plausibly believe that a religious component enhances the likelihood of success.[8]

Free Exercise

A third argument for support is somewhat more complicated. If potential consumers want to receive the service from a religious group because of their religious identity, and if dedicated individuals provide a service out of religious commitment, perhaps the state appropriately accommodates to the free exercise of recipients and providers by aiding the providers. This is a free exercise argument that brings us back to the limits of accommodation. We need to ask under what conditions such a free exercise argument might have force, and whether it would entail that the government *must* provide financial support to religious providers, or only that it may do so.

It helps here to imagine a time when a particular service, such as assistance to the poor or hospital care, was provided exclusively or dominantly by religious groups. In that setting, the government was not impairing anyone's free exercise by leaving religious groups unaided and unregulated, on the same footing as many other parts of the private sector.[9] Subsequently, the government undertook to provide such services itself, by, for example, building a public hospital that duplicated the kind of care religious hospitals gave. The mere fact of government "competition" would not itself be enough to trigger a free exercise claim so long as people who wanted to use the religious hospital were free to do so and were not required to pay for the government hospital. Even required tax support of the government agency would not

[8] Thus, aid could be given to a religious group that has proved successful in the past with its programs or has proposed a promising program. A religious group could not be favored over a nonreligious one simply on the basis that it is religious.

[9] It may be doubted whether there was ever a historical period in which churches were the main providers of various social services *and* churches were not connected to government. According to Stephen V. Monsma, "The 'Pervasively Sectarian' Standard in Theory and Practice," 13 *Notre Dame Journal of Law, Ethics and Public Policy* 321, 322 (1999), "[T]hroughout American history there has been a lively, continuing partnership between government and nonprofit service organizations, including faith-based ones."

impair consumers' exercise of religion, unless they had religious grounds to use a religious provider.[10]

In order to render the free exercise claim of hospital users appealing, one would need not only government competition with the religious hospital[11] and required tax support of the state hospital by religious consumers, whether or not they use the hospital, but also among many consumers a sense of religious conscience, or strong religious inclination, to use the religious hospital. The free exercise claim might be strengthened further if government entry into the hospital business led to restrictions that made running a private hospital more expensive than it once was.

I have focused on consumers, but the providers themselves might also advance a free exercise argument. A religious group as an entity, as well as affiliated individuals who directly provide services—doctors, nurses, orderlies, and so on—could have a sense of religious mission to offer medical services. If they became unable to provide the hospital services for financial reasons, they might believe their religious exercise has been impaired. Were the free exercise argument for providers to rest on financial exigency alone, it would be misconceived. People who wish to exercise their religion in various ways may suffer financially. A monastery may find that the demand for its farm products has dropped or that the number of brothers has declined. That a religious group of providers experiences economic hardship is not itself sufficient to justify public aid.

To be plausible, the providers' argument for relief would need to include a claim that from some appropriate baseline, the government has imposed a burden.[12] The idea would be that the government has burdened religious hospitals by creating competing enterprises subsidized by taxes. In this respect, the providers' argument is weaker than that of consumers. If members of the religious group care enough, they can increase their subsidies to its hospitals; and if the group has many hospitals, some, at least, will be able

---

[10] Whether tax support for public hospitals would give rise to a plausible free exercise claim by *religious providers* is a separate issue I address shortly.

[11] Competition could consist of public support of *other* private agencies, rather than direct provision of the service.

[12] As we have seen, free exercise accommodation is relevant mainly when the government is lifting some burden. Otherwise, the principle that government should not promote religion controls. Thus, if all that can be said is that the religious providers of the service would be better able to carry out their mission if they had public support, that alone does not generate a viable free exercise argument. My own response to this possible baseline argument for providers is the same as that I develop shortly in respect to consumers, namely that all government taxes and forms of welfare will affect the economic positions of private individuals and organizations and should not themselves be viewed as burdens on free exercise in a manner that could generate a free exercise obligation to relieve the burden.

to stay in business. Individuals strongly committed from a religious perspective to providing medical services will probably be able to find a hospital of their religious group in which to do so,[13] and they may find they can offer many medical services outside hospitals.

Let us examine the consumers' free exercise argument in the context in which it has most often been raised, on behalf of aid to Roman Catholic parents who want to send their children to Catholic schools. The basic argument is this:

> We believe we have an obligation to send our children to Roman Catholic schools. You (the state) have created free schools, and we pay substantial taxes to support them. If the state had not entered the school business, we would have much more capacity to finance parochial education. What you have done is to force us to choose between our economic viability and what our religious convictions tell us to do.[14] You should give appropriate relief from this dilemma by aiding us, as you aid the parents of children in public schools, to provide the education for our children that our religious commitments tell us they should have.[15]

One important aspect of this argument is that, if it is convincing, it applies particularly to parents sending children to religious schools for religious reasons.[16] A second important aspect of the free exercise argument is its force. Does it entail that the government must finance parochial schools, on pain of having done a serious wrong to Roman Catholic parents and perhaps of having violated their free exercise rights; or does it show only that helping these parents would be an appropriate measure to enhance their free exercise? Relatedly, does the argument stand on its own as a positive reason for aid, or is it mainly a counterweight to various arguments against aiding parochial schools?

---

[13] This analysis is not airtight. One small group desperate for funds, operating only one hospital, might have to go out of the hospital business; but broad government policy cannot be based on such fortuities.

[14] The compulsion resembles that on Ms. Sherbert, the Seventh Day Adventist whose religious conscience did not allow her to work on Saturday. Her successful free exercise claim is discussed in chapter 6 of the free exercise volume.

[15] Were the free exercise argument the major basis for financing religious schools, the state might be able to finance these schools and not finance other nonprofit private schools. However, as with matters discussed in volume 1, it might be that nonestablishment or equal protection principles would require extension of a basic privilege grounded in free exercise.

[16] It does not cover parents who choose a private school because it provides a better learning environment; it does not even cover parents who pick a private school because they adhere to its nonreligious philosophy. As with many of the free exercise problems we examined in volume 1, including the Amish claim to withdraw children from ordinary education, it seems unlikely that many nonre-

One can get a better handle on these questions if one understands the typical response to the free exercise argument:

> Whatever may have been true historically, it is now widely accepted that the government should provide certain services to its citizens, allowing private groups to provide similar services if they wish. Everybody pays for the government services through taxes, however they would otherwise choose to spend their money. People who never use their services pay for state-run adoption agencies. Childless couples and individuals, and parents who regard public education as inadequate, all pay for public schools. Every form of taxes impinges on free exercise to the extent that money otherwise available for religious expenditures is taken by the state. A childless couple might want to use their school tax money to help to rebuild their church. Parents who want to send children to parochial school have no special complaint about paying school taxes; and without such a complaint, their free exercise argument collapses.

We can quickly see that this answer starts from a baseline different from that of the argument to which it responds. It assumes a level of desirable state expenditures paid from tax funds, and asks whether parents who feel that out of religious conscience they should send children to parochial schools suffer any unique deprivation. The answer is no. The free exercise argument builds from a baseline in which education begins in private hands, and the state enters the picture to alter the balance in a manner that discourages parents from "paying twice" and doing what their consciences tell them to do, namely, send their children to parochial schools.

We have no neat way to resolve the appropriate baseline. Although the free exercise argument has some intuitive appeal, I find the answer to it to be substantially more powerful, because all taxes affect the degree to which all taxpayers are able to spend money on what matters to them, including spending money to meet their senses of religious obligation and need.[17] That judgment affects my sense of how the force of the free exercise argument should be understood.

Courts should definitely not declare that the Free Exercise Clause *demands* financing of religiously sponsored schools or of other social services provided by religious groups. Among other problems, it would be impossible

---

ligious parents would have inclinations to choose a particular private school as strong as those that would lead some parents to want their children educated in a school of their own religion.

[17] For what it is worth, my older children were mainly educated at a school operated by an order of Episcopalian nuns, and one other child spent some years at a Roman Catholic school. However, our family's financial condition was such that the burden of paying for such education was not as overwhelming as it would be for many parents who want to send their children to religious schools.

for courts to say how much aid was necessary to satisfy the state's obligation. A failure to fund is not a serious wrong; *at most* a decision to fund would be appropriate assistance that is partly responsive to free exercise concerns. The free exercise argument works better as one counter to arguments against financial assistance than as the main reason for granting that assistance.

CONSTITUTIONALITY

In terms of constitutional principle, there are three possibilities about aid to religious providers in relation to aid for nonreligious providers. It may be that they must be treated as well, or that aid cannot go to religious providers even if nonreligious providers are granted it, or that legislatures and administrative officials may decide whether to treat religious providers equally with nonreligious ones. (I put aside the possible argument that aid may go to religious providers even if it is denied to nonreligious ones.) The Supreme Court has had relatively little occasion to review public aid to religious organizations that are providing social services, except for aid to schools and colleges, which has made up a large part of its Establishment Clause diet. This section concentrates on the one modern case that is not about school aid.

A word of explanation is needed about why this chapter precedes discussion of the constitutionality of school aid. If one simply looked at the language of opinions, one might see aid for education and for other social services as parts of a unified doctrinal structure. Certainly the school aid cases figure prominently when the Supreme Court and other courts address aid to religious organizations that are providing other services. Nevertheless, I believe that aid to religious schools has always been more controversial than aid to religious hospitals and soup kitchens, and one gets occasional glimpses of this in the opinions. The bases for the difference are a tradition of public schools, a historic distrust of Roman Catholic education, and a sense that parochial schools intermix elements of religious and secular education. (I shall say more about this in the next chapter.) For this reason, I treat aid to schools as distinctive, and take up that subject after we have considered aid to religious organizations providing other services. In following this course, I do, however, need to refer to certain school aid decisions that are important doctrinally for all aids to religious organizations.

The Supreme Court's very first case under the Establishment Clause was a challenge to Congress's funding the building of a hospital operated by an order of Roman Catholic Sisters. In the 1899 case of *Bradfield v. Roberts*,[18] the Court rejected the challenge. The act incorporating the hospital did not mention religion. Whatever the religious sympathies of its members, the corporation had a "nonsectarian and public purpose."[19] That was sufficient to meet Establishment Clause objections.

It is worth pausing a moment over what *Bradfield* does not say. It does not say that the hospital will or must be operated in a nonreligious manner. And if we can imagine what a hospital run by Catholic sisters might have been like around 1900, we can realize that the creation of a "nonreligious" corporation is no guarantee that the service the corporation provides will be free of the marks of a religious entity and its beliefs and practices. This is an important point when we get to "Charitable Choice" and President Bush's faith-based initiative. Much is made of the fact that under many earlier federal and state laws, religious organizations created secular arms to receive public assistance; but, apart from occasional anecdotes about unreasonable demands that religious elements be scrapped, we have little sense just how much difference the secular corporations made to how services were provided. To take just one example, nonprofit subsidiaries of Catholic Charities USA receive a large amount of federal money. According to one author, the programs they deliver "do not proselytize, engage in worship, or provide religious education, nor do they generally discriminate in whom they serve or hire."[20] But the particular programs that Catholic Charities supports are mainly (or exclusively) run by Catholic groups, presumably in accord with doctrines of the Catholic Church. We would need to have a clear sense of how much these programs on the ground convey a Catholic identity to assess *how much* difference it makes that funds are given to corporations that are formally nonreligious.

A crucial question for modern constitutional law is how far the government must go to assure that it does not promote religious activity, either by having its money used directly for religious purposes or by supporting activities in which religious proselytizing is effectively intermingled with the provision of secular services.[21] Related to these questions is an issue about judicial oversight. If a program in its conception seems to present significant risks,

---

[18] 175 U.S. 291 (1899). Congress also conveyed property to the hospital.

[19] Id. at 298.

[20] David Saperstein, "Public Accountability and Faith-Based Organizations: A Problem Best Avoided," 116 *Harvard Law Review* 1353, 1359 (2003).

[21] Whether the government may allow religious discrimination in programs using its funds is another difficult question.

should a court hold it invalid "on its face" or wait to see if it is actually administered in an unacceptable way? The most important Supreme Court case on these subjects was *Bowen v. Kendrick*,[22] a case that lies somewhere on the border between aid to ordinary services, such as hospitals and adoption agencies, and aid to education.

The Adolescent Family Life Act offered aid to public and nonprofit private organizations for services involving premarital adolescent sexual relations and pregnancy. Among the purposes of the grants were promoting "self-discipline" and other prudent approaches to sexual relations and promoting adoption as an alternative for adolescent parents.[23] No grants could go to programs that provided abortions or abortion counseling or referral.[24] One funded activity was "educational services relating to family life and problems associated with adolescent premarital sexual relations."[25] The act explicitly directed the inclusion of religious organizations. Those challenging benefits given to religious groups not only tried to show a potentiality for religious instruction, they produced substantial evidence that it had been taking place.

Chief Justice Rehnquist, for the Court, upheld the act as valid on its face. Assisting a variety of organizations, including religious ones, was appropriate, as was requiring grant applicants to show how they would involve religious organizations in funded programs.[26] Approaches such as promoting self-discipline and adoption were not "inherently religious," although they "may coincide" with approaches "taken by certain religions."[27] The coincidence of views between Congress and some religious grantees did not itself warrant a conclusion that the statute advanced religion, nor did it create an impermissible symbolic link between government and religion, any more than aid to a religious hospital creates an impermissible symbolic link.[28] The absence of a statutory prohibition against the use of federal funds for religious purposes was not a fatal flaw; the secretary of Health and Human

[22] 487 U.S. 589 (1988).

[23] Id. at 593.

[24] Id. at 597. A program could provide referral for an abortion if an adolescent or her parent requested it.

[25] Id. at 594.

[26] Congress could decide that religious organizations could play a part in resolving secular problems. Id. at 607. The First Amendment does not disable religious institutions from participating in social welfare programs. Id. at 609. Ira C. Lupu and Robert W. Tuttle have defended a requirement to "mix" secular and religious providers as designed to reach different target groups of potential beneficiaries. "The Faith-Based Initiative and the Constitution" 55 *DePaul Law Review* 1, 41–42 (2005).

[27] *Bowen*, note 22 supra, at 605.

[28] Id. at 609.

Services could assure that grants were not used for improper purposes.[29] Since there was no reason to assume that recipient organizations were "pervasively sectarian," intensive monitoring was not needed to see that the grants were used for secular purposes; the statute, thus, did not create an excessive entanglement.[30]

Recognizing that using "religious organizations to advance the secular goals of [the federal act], without thereby permitting religious indoctrination, is inevitably more difficult than in other projects, such as ministering to the poor and sick," Justice O'Connor nevertheless agreed with the Court that the partnership "need not result in constitutional violations."[31]

Four justices dissented. Providing examples from the record, Justice Blackmun argued that religious teachings were likely to be intertwined with advice about sexuality and pregnancy.[32] For example, one home for unmarried pregnant teenagers used federal funds to purchase books containing Catholic doctrine on chastity, abortion, and homosexuality, and distributed the books to participants.[33] The potential for an impermissible fostering of religion, Blackmun wrote, does not depend completely on whether an organization is "pervasively sectarian."[34] The program should be declared invalid because "[g]overnment funds are paying for religious organizations to teach and counsel impressionable adolescents on a highly sensitive subject of considerable religious significance, often on the premises of a church or parochial school, and without any effort to remove religious symbols from the sites."[35] Counseling pregnant teenagers is different from running a soup kitchen or hospital.[36] The difficulties were amplified by the absence of any statutory restrictions against use of funds to promote religion.[37]

---

[29] Id. at 614–15.

[30] Id. at 615–17. The Court remanded the case to the district court to determine whether the grant was being improperly administered, including the question whether grantees were pervasively sectarian. Justice Kennedy, joined by Justice Scalia, made clear that he did not regard it as dispositive to the permissibility of aid whether an organization was pervasively sectarian. How "it spends its grant" is what matters. Id. at 625.

[31] Id. at 633.

[32] Rather than sharply distinguishing a challenge on the face of the statute from one "as applied," Justice Blackmun said that "the Court should not blind itself to the facts revealed by the undisputed record," which was designed to show that the government was implementing the program in an unconstitutional way, not merely that some grants were invalid. Id. at 628–29.

[33] Id. at 635 n. 7.

[34] Id. at 633.

[35] Id. at 635.

[36] Id. at 641.

[37] Id. at 642.

One of the lessons of *Bowen v. Kendrick* is that the Court was (and is) divided over funds being used for educational functions that are highly susceptible of being performed according to a religious perspective. Two other lessons are that grants to religious organizations to provide more ordinary social services are less controversial and that government funding should not go directly for religious teaching.

CHARITABLE CHOICE AND THE FAITH-BASED INITIATIVE

In this section, we will continue to review issues of constitutionality and policy in light of developments in the statutory and administrative law in the decade up to 2006. Part of the effort here is to clarify what exactly is involved in the ideas of "Charitable Choice" and President George W. Bush's faith-based initiative, but this section has a more enduring ambition. Legislative and constitutional issues about financial aid to religious organizations are bound to recur over time. The issues will take different hues, but we should expect that much of what divides our polity now will continue to do so in the years to come. This discussion is framed to help readers grasp proposals and controversies that lie in an uncertain future.

Charitable Choice: Basic Provisions and Controversial Issues

Although the rhetoric of a "faith-based initiative" has belonged to George W. Bush, and controversy over the details of desirable assistance have characterized his legislative proposals and executive acts, the main aspects of what he has urged were already contained in so-called "Charitable Choice" legislation adopted in 1996 while William Clinton was president.

Prior to that year, the ground rules for government assistance generally were that a religious provider, operating through a secular arm, could receive federal and state money but was not allowed to use money for religious purposes or to discriminate in choosing the persons it hired.[38] To take one simple example, the federal government would grant money for hospital construction and medical research, and it would reimburse hospitals for treating patients eligible for Medicare and other federally funded medical

---

[38] See generally Stephen W. Monsma, *When Sacred and Secular Mix: Religious Nonprofit Organizations and Public Money* (Lanham, Md.: Rowman and Littlefield, 1996). Monsma, note 9 supra, at 325–27, writes that the vast majority of faith-based groups he surveyed received public support; in 1993, 65 percent of Catholic Charities revenues came from government sources (Monsma, *When Sacred and Secular Mix*, at 1).

treatment. When payment was for a specific service for a patient that had already been rendered, a hospital was free to spend the money as it wished; but more general grants were available only for nonreligious purposes.

In 1996, Senator John Ashcroft, later to become attorney general under George W. Bush, introduced Charitable Choice into the Personal Responsibility and Work Opportunity Reconciliation Act (the Welfare Reform Act) of 1996.[39] The aim was to allow greater participation by religious organizations in certain federally funded social service programs, such as assistance to needy families, job training, and guidance to end out-of-wedlock pregnancies.[40] Charitable Choice allows states participating in federally funded programs to contract directly with religious organizations (which do not need to set up secular subsidiaries and which can accept vouchers on the same basis as other providers). The law forbids discrimination against religious organizations. The religious organizations remain independent in their religious practices, and they need not alter internal governance or remove religious texts and art. The organizations cannot use government funds for worship, proselytizing, or religious education, and they must not discriminate against recipients because of their religion or their refusal to participate in religious practices. Religious organizations maintain their exemption from federal laws against employment discrimination (but the federal act does not assure their protection against state antidiscrimination laws). If a beneficiary objects to the religious character of a provider, a state must assure the availability of an alternate provider.[41]

We can roughly divide the concerns such legislation raises into four related questions: (1) is the government too closely implicated in religious practices? (2) are beneficiaries coerced or pressured into participation in religious programs? (3) are religious organizations actually being favored over other private nonprofit providers? (4) are these organizations engaged in unacceptable discrimination? Cross-cutting these various questions are two others: (1) does it matter whether government support takes the form of grants (which might come directly from a government agency or from an intermediary that receives government funds and distributes them to particular programs) or takes the form of vouchers that go to recipients of a service who choose to

---

[39] 42 U.S.C. § 604a (Supp. V 1999).

[40] The specific provisions of Charitable Choice with citations to relevant sections may be found in Brian Craig Kimball, "Comment, The Federal Faith-Based and Community Initiative: A Guide for Future Legislation," 71 *Mississippi Law Journal* 241, 257–60 (2001).

[41] The act further provides that if a religious organization segregates federal funds into a separate account, the government can audit only the federal funds. An organization cannot participate if its social service program violates the Establishment Clause.

spend it with a particular provider? (2) if a legislative approach is acceptable in conception, is it seriously flawed in the risks that it presents or in its actual application? Finally, we should think of these various concerns and questions as involving legislative and executive policy as well as constitutional law. The outer boundaries of what is constitutionally permissible, according to what the Supreme Court will say, or according to one's judgment about sound constitutional principles, or both, is not necessarily what one will think is a wise (or politically acceptable) approach to support of religious organizations. If the constitutional rule turns out to be that the political branches may in particular circumstances decide whether or not to extend financial aid to religious providers or to attach various conditions to its assistance, it falls on legislators and executive officials to make the delicate judgments about desirable connections between government and religious organizations.

It can help put some of these questions in a specific context to consider a major challenge to Wisconsin's funding of a faith-based alcohol and drug addiction treatment program called Faith Works. Wisconsin's funding was itself supported by federal funds under the Charitable Choice legislation. In an initial decision, a federal district judge in Wisconsin held direct funding of Faith Works unconstitutional.[42] Subsequently she upheld indirect funding, and that decision was affirmed by the Seventh Circuit Court of Appeals.[43] The name of both cases was *Freedom from Religion Foundation, Inc. v. McCallum.*

Faith Works is a residential treatment center that describes itself as a " 'faith-based program designed to meet the needs of individuals recovering from addiction to alcohol and other drugs.' "[44] According to its Statement of Faith, " 'The essence of this ministry is to develop a community of believers that would foster religious honesty; first with God, second with oneself and third with the Body of Christ.' "[45] Staff members "counsel participants to develop a personal relationship with God."[46] The Faith Works version of a twelve-step program is more explicitly and intensely religious than the standard program of Alcoholics Anonymous.[47] During mandatory meetings,

---

[42] *Freedom from Religion Foundation, Inc. v. McCallum,* 179 F.Supp. 2d 950 (W.D. Wis. 2002).

[43] *Freedom from Religion Foundation, Inc. v. McCallum,* 214 F.Supp. 2d 905 (W.D. Wis. 2002), aff'd, 324 F.3d 880 (7th Cir. 2003).

[44] 179 F.Supp. 2d at 955.

[45] Id. at 983.

[46] Id. at 955.

[47] The crucial question about religiosity for AA and Narcotics Anonymous is the "surrender to a higher power" involved in the twelve steps through which recovering alcoholics and addicts must go. No doubt the exact nuances of various small groups and meetings differ, but based on limited reading

participants are encouraged, but not required, to discuss faith. A former executive director said that most clients do not practice a faith before they enter the program but develop a relationship with God by the time they leave.[48] Although "Faith Works does not impose religious restrictions on staff appointments," a "[c]ommitment to Christian beliefs and values is a hiring consideration," and according to the organization's Standards of Practice, staff members are required to grow in their " 'faith life by regular church attendance, prayer, Bible study and seeking Spiritual direction from a Pastor/Shepherd in our faith community.' "[49]

With money from a federal grant, the state Department of Workforce Development made block grants to Faith Works (not dependent on the number of individual participants) from the governor's discretionary fund.[50] These state funds were not kept separate from funds from private sources.

Applying the *Lemon* test, as refined by the *Agostini* case, Judge Crabb determined that Faith Works, a "pervasively sectarian" institution,[51] engaged in religious indoctrination and that the indoctrination was attributable to the government.[52] "[D]irect state funding of persons who actively inculcate religious beliefs crosses the line between permissible and impermissible government action under the First Amendment."[53] Because the Charitable Choice statute provided that a program violating the Establishment Clause was ineligible for a grant, Judge Crabb found it unnecessary to pass on the validity of the federal law.

---

and conversations, and attendance at two meetings, my sense is this. In its origins, Alcoholics Anonymous was definitely understood as religious and the "higher power" the founders had in mind was God (according to the individual's own beliefs about God); the official organization policy is that the "higher power" need not be anything transcendent or religious—it *could* be the memory of a beloved friend—and this policy is conveyed to newcomers at meetings; most individuals who are testifying to their own experience talk of a "higher power" as if it is a transcendent spirit, leaving the impression that the standard expressed sense of participants, as well as the ordinary implications of the phrase "higher power," is religious in a fairly traditional sense; and the overarching measure of success in the programs has not to do with any standard of belief, but with the conduct of staying "clean" and with having worked one's way through the various steps. For one analysis suggesting that AA is "religious" for Establishment Clause purposes, see Michael G. Honeymar, Jr., "Alcoholics Anonymous as a Condition of Drunk Driving Probation: When Does It Amount to Establishment of Religion?" 97 *Columbia Law Review* 437 (1997).

[48] 179 F.Supp. 2d at 957.

[49] Id. at 955, 957.

[50] Id. at 962–64.

[51] Id. at 969.

[52] In *Agostini*, one of the three main criteria for what has a primary effect of advancing religion was whether a statute or program results in governmental indoctrination. Id. at 966.

[53] Id. at 968.

The issues over indirect funding arose in connection with Wisconsin's Department of Corrections contracting with Faith Works to pay for the treatment of offenders on parole and probation.[54] The offenders were required to participate in a rehabilitation program as an alternative to being in jail, but none were required to go to Faith Works. Department of Corrections agents might recommend Faith Works, which had a substantially longer residential program (nine months) than other providers, but they would tell offenders that the program was religious and that they could not be ordered to participate in it.[55] According to the most recent administrative directive, agents had to offer a specific secular alternative.[56] All offenders referred to Faith Works said they had no objection to its religious components.[57]

Judge Crabb concluded that this state funding reached Faith Works only as a consequence of a private choice that was independent. The choice to support religion was made by individual participants, not the state. The individual choice broke the circuit between the government and religion, and the Establishment Clause was not violated.[58]

Richard Posner wrote the opinion for the Seventh Circuit, affirming the decision. Although the state's money does not actually go through the hands of the offenders, its funding scheme in effect gives offenders "vouchers" to decide whether to go to a secular or religious halfway house.[59] To insulate the government from religion, the choice to participate had to be that of the offenders. Paying little attention to the subjective experience of the offenders who were choosing Faith Works, Judge Posner determined that the choice was, in fact, theirs.[60] Plainly, government officials are not barred from recommending religious providers, as the example of high school guidance counselors recommending Catholic colleges shows, and there was no evidence that corrections agents were influenced by their own religious preferences. In answer to the argument that offenders have no real choice because Faith Works may provide a better program than the secular alternatives, Posner responded that quality is not coercion, that a choice may be free even though the options are not equally attractive.[61] (My appraisal of this comes later.)

---

[54] 214 F.Supp. 2d at 908–9.

[55] Id. at 912.

[56] Id.

[57] Id. at 910.

[58] Id. at 915.

[59] 324 F.3d at 882.

[60] Id. Lupu and Tuttle, note 26 supra, at 73, comment that the facts raised serious questions about the experience of drug offenders controlled by the Department of Corrections, which was regularly recommending Faith Works.

[61] 324 F.3d at 884.

The Ambitions and Programs of the Bush Administration

If we could put the aspirations of George W. Bush in regard to private providers of public services into a brief compass, it would be to see the basic approach of Charitable Choice extended to a much wider range of federal programs. His proposals have not yet met with legislative success, but he has been able to achieve much of what he has wanted by executive order.

One could easily get the impression that President Bush is interested in more than an equal place for religious providers, that he believes they have a distinctive ability to run successful programs that should be acknowledged and supported. During his first campaign for the presidency, he talked of a faith-based initiative and upon taking office he established a White House Office of Faith-Based and Community Initiatives. In his State of the Union address of 2003, urging Congress to adopt his faith-based initiation, Bush remarked that "there is power, wonder-working power, in the goodness and idealism and faith of the American people." And, "God does miracles in people's lives."[62] On other occasions, he has urged a focus on results, not process.[63] "If faith is the integral part of a program being successful, the government ought to say hallelujah."[64] "Faith-based programs are only effective because they do practice faith. . . . We want to fund programs that save Americans, one soul at a time."[65] "[T]he cornerstone of any good recovery program is the understanding there is a Higher Being."[66] Whether his comments flowed from a deep-seated belief in the efficacy of faith-based programs or from attention to his political base, or (as seems likely) both, President Bush's words seem not to put faith-based providers on an equal plane with other providers but at a higher level. Although one could argue that special attention is needed for religious groups that suffered past discrimination in the allocation of funds, that clearly is not the full explanation for Bush's emphasis on faith-based groups.

Whether or not administrators responsive to sentiments they discern from the White House have shown an actual favoritism for religious groups, the President, in his executive orders and legislative recommendations has been

---

[62] 149 *Cong. Rec.* H212–01, H213 (Jan. 28, 2003).

[63] Remarks by the President at Habitat for Humanity Event, Waco, Texas, August 8, 2001, Weekly Compilation of Presidential Documents, Week of August 13, 2001, 1145.

[64] Remarks by the President at So Others Might Eat, November 20, 2001, Weekly Compilation of Presidential Documents, Week of November 26, 2001, 1694.

[65] Remarks by the President to Faith-Based and Community Leaders in New Orleans, January 15, 2004, Weekly Compilation of Presidential Documents, Week of January 19, 2004, 71.

[66] Remarks by the President at White House National Conference on Faith-Based and Community Initiative, June 1, 2004, Weekly Compilation of Presidential Documents, Week of June 7, 2004, 979.

wise enough or prudent enough not to go that far. But whenever officials with discretion to choose among groups believe that religious involvement is particularly effective in helping people pull themselves up, they will have some inclination to prefer religious providers over others, an inclination that runs squarely against the Establishment Clause as it has been interpreted.

In 2001 the House of Representatives passed a bill called the Charitable Choice Act of 2001. In its basic provisions, it closely resembled the 1996 act we have just examined. It explicitly affirmed the religious freedom of beneficiaries to receive services from religious organizations they choose;[67] it required that beneficiaries have available an equivalent secular alternative and that they be notified of their right to that alternative;[68] it drew a distinction between direct and indirect funding, with the prohibition that no public funds be spent for "sectarian worship, instruction, or proselytization" applying only to direct funding;[69] it protected the right of religious providers to discriminate on religious grounds in employment under Title VII of the Civil Rights Act of 1964, as amended, and declared that any program provisions to the contrary imposed by states would be invalid.[70] (Because the Title VII exemption for religious organizations protects only discrimination based on religious grounds, providers could not discriminate on other grounds covered by Title VII, and the bill gave them no federal right to discriminate on grounds such as sexual orientation and marital status that federal law does not reach but some state and local laws cover.) Most important, the House bill extended the coverage of Charitable Choice to a wide range of federal programs, including those directed at juvenile delinquency, crime prevention and assistance to crime victims, housing assistance, aid to the elderly, the prevention of domestic violence, job access, hunger relief, and education outside of school hours.[71]

The House bill faced opposition in the Senate, most significantly because of its provision on employment discrimination. Senators troubled in principle by the idea that religious organizations using federal funds to provide social services could discriminate on the basis of religion have been bolstered by a Pew Forum poll in which 78 percent of those asked said that religious organizations getting government dollars should not "be allowed to only

---

[67] See H.R. 7, in the Senate of the United States, July 19, 2001, 107th Cong., 1st Sess., § 1991(b)(5). A good account of what the bill provides is Robert W. Carter, Jr., "Faith-Based Initiatives: Expanding Government Collaboration with Faith-Based Social Service Providers," 27 *Seton Hall Legislative Journal* 305 (2003).

[68] § 1991(g)(1)(2).

[69] See Carter, note 67 supra, at 352.

[70] § 1991(e).

[71] § 1991(c)(4).

hire people who share their religious beliefs."[72] A Senate alternative was proposed by Senators Lieberman and Santorum.[73] It omitted the crucial language about employment discrimination, but also failed passage. In succeeding sessions of Congress up to 2007, no charitable choice legislation has been adopted.

President Bush has accomplished much of what he has sought by executive orders. He issued the most sweeping of them in December 2002.[74] This included many of the provisions of the defeated House bill, providing that faith-based organizations cannot be discriminated against in the allocation of federal funds and that they are exempt from the prohibition on hiring discrimination based on religion contained in another executive order. (Because the executive cannot contravene what Congress has adopted in a statute, the executive order cannot permit discrimination that various federal statutes may forbid.)[75] On one occasion, and apparently contrary to what the Salvation Army was expecting, the Bush administration declined a request by it to be exempted from local laws barring discrimination against homosexuals.[76] Because executive orders can be superseded by subsequent presidents with different views, Bush has continued to urge Congress to adopt a broad Charitable Choice statute.

Fundamental Considerations Regarding Government Aid to Religious Organizations

We now have enough detail about possibilities to tackle the fundamental and enduring issues about government aid for religious providers of social services. At one end of the spectrum of approaches is what we can call a

[72] See Peter Steinfels, "Beliefs; Hiring for Faith-Based Programs: Issues May Be Complicated, but the Public Has an Emphatic View," *New York Times*, June 9, 2001, B6. A substantial majority still opposed religious discrimination when the question put to them did not suggest exclusive hiring of co-believers.

[73] The Charity Aid, Recovery, and Empowerment Act of 2002, § 1924, 107th Cong. 2d Sess., February 8, 2002. See Carter, note 67 supra, at 371–74.

[74] Executive Order 13, 279, December 12, 2002. See Carter, note 67 supra, at 376–79.

[75] The Workforce Investment Act, for example, does not exempt religious providers from its prohibition on employment discrimination. The crucial exemption in Title VII (allowing discrimination on religious grounds) does not specifically address religious organizations that are running programs with government funds. Although one might argue that the exemption does not reach that far, the more natural reading of the language is that a religious organization does not lose the exemption in that context. Insofar as one argues that such an extensive exemption is unconstitutional, the argument does not vary much whether the exemption comes from Congress or the executive. (Courts might, however, give more deference to the judgment of Congress than to that of the executive.)

[76] Frank Bruni and Elizabeth Becker, "Charity Is Told It Must Abide by Antidiscrimination Law," *New York Times*, July 11, 2001, A15.

combined neutrality and free exercise position, well set out by Carl Esbeck in a 1997 article that defends direct aid to religious providers.[77] In contrast to the position he ascribes to separationists, Professor Esbeck argues that the activities of faith-based providers cannot be neatly separated into spiritual and temporal, and that religion is not a private matter that people should avoid involving in public affairs.[78]

According to a principle of neutrality, religious providers should have benefits equal to those given other providers. Equality, here, is not an end in itself but a means to the higher goal of "minimization of the government's influence over personal choices concerning religious beliefs and practices."[79] In Esbeck's view, the Establishment Clause is a check on government interference with religion, not on religious activities themselves;[80] and religious groups should not be required to strip themselves of their religious identity in order to receive funds. (A practical consideration some have raised is that for many individual churches, synagogues, etc., it may too onerous to set up independent secular subsidiaries for services they provide.) The government need not assure that funds are used exclusively for nonreligious purposes; religious groups should not be disabled from receiving funds because they are "pervasively sectarian"; and religious groups should not lose exemptions they would otherwise have.[81] About the categorization of "pervasively sectarian" providers, Esbeck writes that use of that criterion violates the principle that government should not discriminate among religions, and it requires courts to probe too deeply into the significance of religious activities.[82] Esbeck acknowledges that allowing religious groups to receive funds and to be exempted from antidiscrimination provisions permits them to get "the best of both worlds," but that is desirable to maximize religious liberty and limit the power of the regulatory state.[83] Someone who took argument about liberty

---

[77] Carl N. Esbeck, "A Constitutional Case for Governmental Cooperation with Faith-Based Social Service Providers," 46 *Emory Law Journal* 1 (1997).

[78] Id. at 9.

[79] Id. at 8. See also Monsma, note 9 supra, at 334–37, objecting that inquiries about whether a provider is pervasively sectarian are unfair and interfere with religious liberty.

[80] Esbeck, note 77 supra, at n. 73. Esbeck says that the clause was not designed to protect minority religion from majority religion. Given that those who opposed establishment worried that a majority religion might be linked to government, I doubt that one can draw the distinction so sharply between protection from government and protection from majority religion.

[81] Id. at 12.

[82] Id. at 5. Esbeck suggests that groups that are more conservative theologically will seem more sectarian, id. at n. 60, and that there are many ways to measure religiousness, id. at n. 62. See also Monsma, note 9 supra, at 337–38, who draws the conclusion that a neutrality approach should be used for direct as well as indirect funding.

[83] Esbeck, note 77 supra, at 8.

for religious groups to the limit might contend that religious providers should be allowed to discriminate among recipients of their services on the basis of religion—thereby creating an ideal religious community of co-believers providing and receiving services—but Esbeck does not address that question.

At the pole opposite from the neutrality-free exercise position stands a separationist view, developed by, among others, David Saperstein.[84] According to this view, the traditional technique of using secular corporations to distribute government funds is the proper approach. Under the Establishment Clause government should not promote religious activities. When religious components are an integral part of the way a group provides services, it is impossible to aid the nonreligious components and not to aid the religious ones. Assuring that government funds will not be directly spent to promote religion is difficult; and, even if that objective is achieved, government support will allow an organization to free other funds for religious purposes. A further problem is that government funding can undermine the religious missions of religious providers. It can encourage organizations to develop programs that will receive public funding rather than ones they would design independent of that consideration—in Massachusetts, Catholic Services shifted its efforts substantially from soup kitchens and child protective services to drug and alcohol treatment centers when funding became available[85]—and the regulation that ensues from funding may interfere with an organization's judgment about what is best from its own religious point of view. If organizations are to run programs that are substantially supported by public funds, they should run them in accord with public objectives, including, very importantly, laws against discrimination in the provision of services and in employment.

Before we engage the troublesome problems in more depth, it helps to say a word about the direction of constitutional law and about what, at least for now, appears to be a measure of common ground. Because most of the crucial Supreme Court decisions concern aid to parochial schools, the next chapter provides a much fuller sense of how the law of aid to sectarian providers is developing. But what one can say with some confidence is that over the near future, the Court is likely to be accepting of most forms of aid. A case involving computers and other material supplies for parochial schools, *Mitchell v. Helms*,[86] is particularly notable. A plurality opinion by Justice Thomas treated aid given on a per capita student basis as like a voucher

---

[84] Saperstein, note 20 supra.

[85] Id. at 1367–68. By 1995, Catholic Charities in Massachusetts spent 80 percent of its funds on substance abuse programs.

[86] 530 U.S. 793 (2000).

program (although parents of children attending religious schools did not actually decide to allocate government assistance to the schools). In contrast to earlier cases, he treated neutrality in the criteria for aid as sufficient to withstand an Establishment Clause attack, so long as aid was not given for religious purposes. It would not be unconstitutional for a recipient quickly to divert the aid it was given to religious use, because that use could not be attributed to the government. Near the end of his opinion, Thomas mounted a sharp attack on the Court's past consideration of whether religious educational institutions were "pervasively sectarian," a categorization born of (anti-Catholic) bigotry that should be abandoned.[87]

Justices O'Connor and Breyer, concurring in the result, resisted the plurality's claim that divertibility and actual diversion were not issues.[88] As of now, this concurring opinion, with its narrower grounds, represents the holding of the case, but should Chief Justice Roberts and Justice Alito accept the plurality's approach, that will be transformed into the majority view.[89]

In its major voucher case, upholding substantial funding, through parental choice, of religious schools in Cleveland, the Court put great emphasis on the availability of other educational options.[90] When we put the Court's decision in this case together with the plurality approach in *Mitchell*, we can predict a permissive approach to aid that is indirect, based on individual choice or a per capita measure of recipients. Thus far, in upholding programs of aid, the Court has distinguished its earlier separationist decisions as involving direct aid; but we can probably expect a more permissive attitude than those older cases represent when the present Court resolves issues of direct aid. Of course, what the Supreme Court may decide does not necessarily represent sound constitutional law, and my own view is that the basic approach of the *Mitchell* plurality is decidedly unsound. If the Court does adopt a highly permissive approach to the outer boundaries of aid, Congress and state legislatures will be left to determine the parameters of actual assistance.

[87] Id. at 828.

[88] Justices O'Connor and Breyer did not join the attack on the "pervasively sectarian" standard, but neither did they defend it. Professors Lupu and Tuttle, note 26 supra, at 24–25, take their silence, combined with the inclusion of some intensely religious schools among the beneficiaries, as indicating their agreement with the abandonment of the inquiry whether schools are pervasively sectarian.

[89] It is probably not coincidental that three of the four members of the *Mitchell* plurality criticizing the inquiry about whether organizations are pervasively sectarian are themselves Roman Catholic. One might surmise that subsequently appointed Chief Justice Roberts and Justice Alito, also Roman Catholic, may wish to see an end to a form of categorization used historically to deny aid to Roman Catholic schools.

[90] *Zelman v. Simmons-Harris*, 536 U.S. 639 (2002).

We can identify a broad common ground about a number of legislative issues, a consensus no doubt formed partly in response to earlier Supreme Court decisions. Although one can construct a free exercise argument for allowing religious providers to prefer their own members in giving services, the rule that religious organizations should not discriminate on the basis of religion in admitting applicants to funded programs (whether aid is direct or nondirect) is now uncontroversial, and is extensively embodied in federal regulations. It also is agreed (at least in formal legislative proposals and executive orders) that religious providers should not be selected over others simply *because* they are religious; rather a level playing field is the most that proponents of neutrality seek. Further, however difficult it may be to divide various functions, in order to foreclose government funds from going to religious components of programs, the government should not pay directly for the core religious activities of worship, religious instruction, and proselytizing. When religious providers are to be funded, directly or indirectly, potential recipients should be able to choose an alternative secular provider. Finally, everyone now seems to agree that *if* religious groups do set up secular corporations and administer programs in a manner that lacks a substantial religious component, it is perfectly acceptable for governments to fund their social service programs directly or indirectly. (Among those who are in favor of the secular corporation approach, one might find disagreement over when religious components of service to beneficiaries become too great, though, surprisingly, one finds this little discussed in the literature.) Neutralists object to the injustice of requiring religious organizations to set up secular corporations, but many of them would grant that that choice is at least open to legislatures.

As attitudes about funding religious providers shift over time, some of these uncontroversial assumptions may be thrown into doubt, but it makes sense to concentrate our attention on the questions that now divide politicians, judges, and scholars.

A relatively minor question in my view is whether legislative proposals that purport to give equal treatment to religious providers actually discriminate in their favor. I am not referring here to administration of the laws; one can well imagine that administrators, or officers of intermediary private organizations, who are deciding what programs to fund, will be influenced by their inclinations for or against religion, or particular religions.[91] But does

[91] On such claims about discrimination in application, see Lupu and Tuttle, note 26 supra, at 42–45; Ira C. Lupu and Robert W. Tuttle, "The State of the Law 2005: Legal Developments Affecting

the very structure of proposed laws favor religious groups? They are protected against official discrimination, nonreligious groups are not; they alone
are allowed to engage in religious discrimination in employment; and they
are subject to less comprehensive review of their financial arrangements.[92]
Since the premise of such legislation is that religious groups have been discriminated against in the past, and it is widely assumed that discrimination
in favor of religious providers is barred by the Establishment Clause, the
fact that a bill does not specifically protect nonreligious providers against
discrimination does not loom very large. The intensity of auditing reflects a
sense that government scrutiny of religious activities should be kept to the
minimum needed to assure that government money is properly spent. I shall
return to the issue of discrimination in employment, but it is enough to say
here that if religious providers are allowed to discriminate in favor of those
who adhere to their religious views, that does not work a serious discrimination against nonreligious providers, who have little reason to discriminate
on religious grounds.[93]

Another probable form of discrimination is more troubling—that the end
result of direct aid to religious providers will be to favor majority religious
groups over minorities. Officials choosing what groups to fund are unlikely
to look kindly on the applications of the Nation of Islam or the Unification
Church. What *should* happen is that officials will not make judgments on
the basis of theological views—though they can consider whether the social
views that will be expressed in a program will conflict with the government's
legitimate objections. (Thus, a religious group taking the view that "property
is theft" or that obedience to God requires perpetual revolution against the
state could be rejected for prison rehabilitation programs.) But what should
happen and what does happen often do not coincide. The concern about
bias in favor of dominant religious groups is serious enough to give legisla-

---

Partnerships between Government and Faith-Based Organizations" 61–68 (Roundtable on Religion
and Social Welfare Policy, December 2005). See also Ira C. Lupu and Robert W. Tuttle, "The State of
the Law 2006: Legal Developments Affecting Government Partnerships with Faith-Based Organizations" (Roundtable on Religion and Social Welfare Policy, December 2006). They describe a report
of the Government Accounting Office that stresses the need for better notice to grantees of their
obligations and better monitoring to assure compliance, pp. 1–2, and they summarize a guidance
from the Department of Health and Human Services, issued after settlement of a lawsuit, on what is
needed to segregate secular government-funded portions of programs from religious aspects,
pp. 2–18.

[92] See Scott M. Michelman, "Faith-Based Initiatives," 39 *Harvard Journal on Legislation* 475, 490
(2002).

[93] Because federal law does not forbid ideological discrimination, nonreligious groups may discriminate on nonreligious ideological grounds. Thus, a feminist organization providing aid to battered
women could favor feminists in hiring (though not women over men).

tors pause about adopting direct funding when choices among programs involve considerable discretion, rather than accepted objective criteria of effectiveness.[94] A related worry about discretionary choice is the anger and resentment that may be generated in groups that find themselves frequently rejected. People's estimates of the dangers of divisiveness along religious lines vary widely, but I believe that the past few decades are sufficient to show that, though violent domestic religious conflict is, one hopes, largely behind us,[95] we are far from reaching the peaceful shores of religious harmony. Competition among religious groups for limited public funds could easily become a potent cause of disharmony.

We come now to what I take to be the three major issues: the government's implication in religious activity, pressure on potential beneficiaries, and employment discrimination. The first two of these issues are interwoven in the sense that the greater the coercion or pressure on beneficiaries to participate in religious activities, the more their involvement in these activities is attributable to the government.

In what is the most thoughtful broad look at the subject of aid for religious providers of social services, Ira C. Lupu and Robert Tuttle make the absolutely crucial point that there are great differences among the kinds of programs.[96] Suppose a number of Brazilian families move into a small community, and the town government believes it would be desirable if more citizens had some grasp of Portuguese. It offers to finance education in the Portuguese language for any group willing to undertake that task and admit all comers. The only group that steps forward to run such a program is a local evangelical church. It announces that its meetings will begin with a prayer and that its instruction will devote an equal amount of time to secular readings and a Portuguese translation of the Bible. No town resident has to learn Portuguese, and any could pursue the various methods for learning a language on one's own. Those who do learn Portuguese at the church will not be pushed at these meetings to adopt the church's religious perspective. If the only funded program turns out to be religious, that does not seem to be the city's fault; it has said it will finance any group willing to operate such a

---

[94] However, the United States Court of Appeals for the District of Columbia has indicated that the discretionary nature of criteria is irrelevant constitutionally. *American Jewish Congress v. Corporation for National and Community Service*, 399 F.3d 351, 357 (2005).

[95] For this purpose, I am not counting the violence directed at Western countries by some Islamic fundamentalists as internal religious conflict, and I am not counting our invasions of Afghanistan and Iraq as significantly religious.

[96] Ira C. Lupu and Robert Tuttle, "Sites of Redemption: A Wide Angle Look at Government Vouchers and Sectarian Service Providers," 18 *Journal of Law and Politics* 537 (2002).

program. Someone looking at this set of facts might fairly conclude that the religious elements of the program should not be attributed to the city.

By contrast, consider a city that has chosen to fund only one drug rehabilitation program for offenders, one run by a religious group like Faith Works. Offenders have a choice of entering the program or going to jail. The program's aim is to transform the spiritual lives of its participants, attacking addiction to alcohol and drugs by religious transformation. It will accept non-Christians, but it regards leading participants to accept Christ as an indispensable element of its mission. Although participants are not forced to express religious sentiments, they must attend meetings at which accepting Christ and testifying to one's faith are strongly encouraged. In this context, the government uses the threat of severe legal compulsion to engage participants in a program that compels exposure to powerful religious persuasion. The government can hardly divorce its funding from the religious components of the program, since those components are such a central part of what the program aims to do.

We saw that, despite secular alternatives, the District Court ruled invalid the direct funding of Faith Works. Indirect funding was upheld because offenders had a choice between it and secular alternatives. Recall that corrections officials might have recommended Faith Works to offenders because it involved a nine-month residency, much longer than the three-month residency of the alternatives. That difference was not thought to impair a free choice among the offenders. But suppose the stays in residence had been reversed—three months at Faith Works, nine months at a secular alternative, or one year in jail. Since most addicted offenders will initially prefer a short stay to a long stay in residence, the degree of compulsion for them to join Faith Works would then be substantial.

Considering the radically different circumstances between voluntarily learning Portuguese without pressure to change one's life and being coerced into a program that aims for a personal transformation along religious lines, we can draw two easy conclusions. The first is that it is a grave mistake to think of the provision of social services by religious groups as all of one cloth. There are radical differences in degrees of pressure to participate and in the nature of a program's religious components. An undiscriminating approach that fails to draw distinctions is bound to be misguided. The second conclusion is a corollary of the first. Whatever the explanation for the development of the category of the "pervasively sectarian," and whether that exact categorization of organizations that might receive funds is explicitly abandoned by a majority of the modern Supreme Court, any thoughtful approach to religious providers must consider how religious components figure in their programs.

Professors Lupu and Tuttle consider three relationships: between recipients and the state; between providers and the state; and between providers and recipients.[97] The central issues about recipients and the state are the degree of freedom recipients have to choose a program for themselves and the extent to which the government's purposes can be distinguished from religious transformation. In respect to the state's relationship to providers, the government can set levels of funding in a way that will or will not attract nonreligious providers as well as religious ones. If the government is steering recipients toward religious providers, it matters whether recipients can refuse to participate in a provider's religious activities. Putting these and other elements together, the authors claim that it matters (1) whether there is legal or factual compulsion of recipients, (2) whether a program has transformative goals, (3) what is the number and mix of providers, (4) what are the ways in which government policies and market characteristics affect the mix of providers, (5) what is the nature of government monitoring, (6) whether the service is separable into religious and nonreligious components.[98]

As the Lupu-Tuttle analysis of voucher programs indicates, one must, for both legislative policy and constitutional analysis, attend to the precise role of religious components in the provision of social services. Faith Works is at a far remove from a soup kitchen set up by a church that provides food to all comers and offers a religious service after the meal for those who wish to stay. When thinking about coercion or pressure on recipients, we can distinguish: (1) pressure to enter some program of a particular type; (2) pressure to choose a religious provider over a secular provider; (3) pressure to participate in or submit to religious components, if one is using a religious provider. Pressure of the first two kinds can be legal or factual. To take the Faith Works example, pressure on offenders to enter a program of drug rehabilitation involved legal compulsion; time in jail was their alternative. According to the district court and court of appeals, corrections agents adequately informed offenders that they could use one of a number of secular options. There was no direct legal compulsion to choose Faith Works. (I pass over the point here that a vulnerable addicted offender might think that refusing a strong recommendation from an agent could sow seeds of further difficulty with legal officials.) However, if an offender understood that the

---

[97] Id. at 560–75.
[98] Id. at 575–84.

basis of a recommendation for Faith Works was that it alone offered a nine-month residential stay and, further, believed that his problems of addiction were serious enough so that a nine-month stay promised a much greater chance of success than a three-month stay, then he would be under considerable pressure of circumstance to choose Faith Works although he would have preferred an otherwise similar secular provider.[99] Judge Posner correctly resisted the idea that a choice to go to Faith Works was unfree if its program was superior to the alternatives, but he should have acknowledged the government's responsibility to assure recipients roughly comparable choices when they are subject to legal compulsion or strong circumstantial pressure to participate in a program, and the government is supplying significant funding for the religious provider.

The third form of pressure concerns participants in a faith-based program. If secular and religious components are definitely separable, the issue is whether the religious provider allows a free choice about participation in religious activities, as in the soup kitchen example I suggested. If the components are inseparable—if the aim of a drug rehabilitation program is to draw addicts toward a Christian commitment—one who participates in the program at all will be inevitably exposed to strong religious elements.

An extreme example of a lack of free choice in selecting a program and in the degree of one's participation in religious elements was involved in a case we examined in chapter 13, holding invalid an InnerChange prisoner rehabilitation program in Iowa.[100] According to the federal district court, Inner-Change was the only contender for a thorough value-centered rehabilitation program,[101] and its transformative aims flowed from a powerful Evangelical Christian perspective. Its Christian language and practice effectively precluded all but Evangelical Christians from participating.[102] All participants had to take part in the Christian-based program,[103] as to which it was impossible to distinguish secular from sectarian aspects.[104] Participants had significantly more congenial living arrangements in their unit than other prisoners. With the power to punish and to dismiss participants from the program,[105]

---

[99] One might regard this pressure as involving considerations of future legal compulsion, insofar as an offender realized that if he could not shake his addiction, he would continue to be in trouble with the law.

[100] *Americans United for Separation of Church and State v. Prison Fellowship Ministries*, 432 F.Supp. 2d 862 (S.D. Iowa, 2006).

[101] Id. at 932. There was an objective lack of a secular alternative.

[102] Id. at 905.

[103] Id. at 900.

[104] Id. at 927.

[105] Id. at 912, 920.

the staff of InnerChange was able to impose serious negative consequences on participants who were not making adequate spiritual progress. I suggested in chapter 13 that one might view this as an example of a religious organization performing a government function. The court emphasized a different, though not inconsistent, approach. Considering InnerChange as pervasively sectarian, it concluded that in the circumstances the state was too deeply implicated in sponsoring a religious view; its use of the program had the impermissible effect of promoting religion.[106]

It may help at this point to note some alternatives to the label "pervasively sectarian" that allow greater refinement about types of programs, and focus more directly on the programs themselves than the organizations that operate them. According to one breakdown, "faith-saturated" providers have "explicit, extensive, and mandatory" religious content in their programs.[107] "Faith-centered" providers have programs that include religious messages and activities, but may allow participants to opt out of them and do not assume that a positive outcome depends on involvement in the religious aspects.[108] "Faith-related" providers may display religious symbols and offer opportunities for religious dialogue, but their programs do not contain explicit religious messages or activities.[109] "Faith-background" providers have historical religious ties, but their programs lack explicit religious aspects.[110] "Faith-secular partnerships" do not refer to religion.[111] Perhaps this terminology, or something like it, will allow courts to pay attention to the religious components of faith-based programs without getting hung up on the now highly controversial label of "pervasively sectarian."

We have already looked at the decision that direct funding of Faith Works implicated the government impermissibly in religious indoctrination. A recent case in which a district court found that a program stepped over the border but the court of appeals disagreed was *American Jewish Congress v. Corporation for National and Community Service*.[112] The Corporation

---

[106] Id. at 921–39.

[107] Search for Common Ground, "Finding Common Ground: 29 Recommendations of the Working Group on Human Needs and Faith-Based and Community Initiatives," 32 (2002), http://www.sfcg.org/Programmes/us/report.pdf (visited October 3, 2007). One might subdivide this category into programs that are exclusively faith-based and those that mix in techniques from the medical and social services. Ronald J. Sider and Heidi Rolland Unrab, "No Aid to Religion? Charitable Choice and the First Amendment," *Brookings Review*, Spring 1999, at 46, 48.

[108] See Working Group, note 107 supra.

[109] Id.

[110] Id.

[111] Id.

[112] 323 F.Supp. 2d 44 (U.S. D.C. 2004), rev'd, 399 F.3d 351 (D.C. Cir. 2005). The case is discussed in Lupu and Tuttle, note 26 supra, at 67–70.

sponsored an AmeriCorps Education Program under which participants contracted with various groups, including faith-based groups, to administer the program. Among them was the Alliance for Catholic Education (ACE). Participants in the ACE program attended a heavily Catholic summer training program; many taught religious courses and engaged in other religious activities in the religious schools to which they were assigned; ACE emphasized its spiritual and Catholic mission; no effective record-keeping or monitoring distinguished participation in religious and nonreligious activities. The Corporation chose ACE and other grantees on the basis of highly discretionary judgments, not neutral criteria. People could participate in AmeriCorps only by enrolling in preapproved programs, and grantees actively recruited and selected participants. Some programs required that participants be of a particular faith. Considering these various factors, the court concluded that the government's involvement with the religious teaching and other activities of ACE participants was so great that the religious indoctrination was reasonably attributed to it and was unconstitutional under the Establishment Clause.

For the court of appeals, what was crucial was that the government's financing of programs was indirect.[113] Individuals awarded grants could participate in secular or religious programs, and there was no evidence of an unavailability of secular programs. Any programs that required participants to be of a particular faith had violated the statute, but these violations had already been corrected. That the Corporation employed discretionary criteria in choosing grantees was irrelevant constitutionally. The court of appeals decision well illustrates the importance of the distinction between direct aid and the indirect aid of voucher programs. It also illustrates the tendency to accept indirect aid even in circumstances that present disturbing opportunities for favoritism toward religious groups.

I turn now to the issue of employment discrimination. Under Title VII of the 1964 Civil Rights Act, religious employers are allowed to discriminate on grounds of religion;[114] and the Supreme Court has upheld that provision against an Establishment Clause challenge, even for positions other than those of leadership.[115] The statute itself says nothing about whether organizations entitled to such an exemption might lose it for activities that are funded by the government, and it would be a stretch to read in any such qualification. This leaves two questions. Should Congress permit discrimination in

---

[113] The case also involved modest grants to organizations themselves to defray some of the costs of complying with federal requirements. The court treated these as direct aid that was allowable.

[114] 42 U.S.C. § 2000e-1(a).

[115] *Corporation of the Presiding Bishop v. Amos*, 483 U.S. 327 (1987).

favor of co-believers for programs receiving government funding? Does funding make such discrimination unconstitutional?

It is not hard to see the arguments on each side. From the perspective of those whose view of Charitable Choice resembles that of President Bush: faith-based organizations should be able to participate equally in providing social services; it would be unfair to strip them of their fundamental identity, and because the religious components of programs may be positively beneficial, they should not be required to eliminate their religious character; one crucial aspect of retaining that character is hiring people who share their religious sense of mission. The opposing view is that when a program is funded substantially by the government, the standards of employment should be public, and that means following basic principles of nondiscrimination in hiring and firing. As I have mentioned, most people in the country apparently accept the latter view, and the issue about employment discrimination has been the major stumbling block for adoption of an extensive Charitable Choice statute by Congress.

Two analytical points can help clarify one's thinking about this subject. The first is an obvious connection between the discrimination issue and what programs should be funded. Consider Faith Works again. If the program seeks Christian conversions, it would be odd to say that Faith Works should not take religious perspectives into account when it hires staff to deal with the program's participants. On the other hand, if a program's secular and religious components are comfortably separable, the argument is strong that religious views should not determine hiring of those who are running the secular, funded, aspects. A person who strongly thinks that providers should not discriminate in employment should recognize that this view loosely implies a limit to the kinds of programs government should fund.

My second point concerns the question what counts as religious discrimination. More particularly, is discrimination against gays based on a religious view that homosexual relations are sinful a form of religious discrimination? One concern is that if Congress authorizes religious discrimination in funded programs, that may support discrimination against gays that might otherwise violate a state or local antidiscrimination law. (Federal law does not bar such discrimination.) This issue is a piece of a larger, complicated topic, whether an employment decision based on a moral judgment that is rooted in the employer's religious view but does not refer to the *religious* perspective of the potential worker counts as religious discrimination covered by Title VII. In chapter 18 of volume 1, I addressed that question and concluded that such a basis for judgment does not count as religious discrimination *if* some others would make the same moral judgment on nonreligious grounds. One court that has concluded that this kind of discrimination against gays is not religious adopts a simpler analysis than my own, treating as fully dispositive the employer's disregard of the religion of the worker.[116] I believe the decision is sound (though I do not accept the exact theory of the court). If the decision is correct, an authorization to engage in religious discrimination would not undermine whatever protection state and local laws provide against discrimination based on sexual preference.

On the constitutional status of discrimination that *is* religious, one court, considering the Salvation Army's firing of a victims' assistance coordinator who reproduced Wiccan materials on its copiers, held that the Title VII exemption to engage in religious discrimination is invalid as it applies to a program mainly funded by the government.[117] More recently a different court sustained the use of religious criteria by the Salvation Army in selecting employees for such programs.[118] Yet another court held that a religious college could employ religious criteria in hiring despite receiving government funding.[119] Perhaps for constitutional purposes, the degree of government involvement should be determinative. If government is the main source of funding or is actively involved in the running of a program, religious discrimination in employment by the faith-based provider for that program should be held unconstitutional.

---

[116] *Pedreira v. Kentucky Baptist Homes for Children, Inc.*, 186 F.Supp. 2d 757 (W.D. Ky. 2001).

[117] *Dodge v. Salvation Army*, 1989 WL 53857 (S.D. Miss. 1989).

[118] *Lown v. Salvation Army*, 393 F.Supp. 2d 223, 250 (S.D. N.Y. 2005).

[119] *Siegel v. Truett-McConnell College, Inc.*, 13 F.Supp. 2d 1335 (N.D. Ga. 1994).

CHAPTER 19

Aid to Religious Schools

The controversial, important subject of aid to religious schools has given rise to far more Supreme Court cases than any other establishment issue. Many citizens have been upset by the Court's rulings against prayer and Bible reading in public schools, but national life would not be greatly affected if those schools started the day with a prayer. By contrast, a great deal of money is potentially at stake over aid to private schools, and were states to provide generous aid, that could significantly affect the education a large portion of our nation's children receive.

For *some* conceptual purposes, aid to private education differs little from aid to private hospitals, adoption agencies, soup kitchens, and drug rehabilitation programs we covered in the last chapter. In that chapter, I used an illustration involving schooling to exemplify free exercise arguments for aid. The reason is that more people feel strongly that they should send their children to religious schools than that they should use religious hospitals or welfare agencies.

Ordinary people, and most modern Supreme Court justices, have looked on aid to schools differently from aid to other religious providers. Although the number of evangelical Protestant schools has risen substantially over the last few decades,[1] the history of the subject has overwhelmingly involved Roman Catholic parochial schools, and perceptions of how they differ from public schools.

---

[1] According to the Private School Universe Survey (PSS) data from 1989–90 to 2003–4, the number of Conservative Christian schools increased from 4,063 to 5,060 and enrollment increased from 528,236 to 773,847 (their share of total private school enrollment increased from 10.9 percent to 15.1 percent). Elizabeth Gerald, National Center for Education Statistics, U.S. Department of Education, Private School Universe Survey, 1989–1990 (NCES 93–122) (1992), available at http://nces.ed.gov/pubsearch/ pubsinfo.asp?pubid=93122 (visited September 22, 2007). Stephen P. Broughman and Nancy L. Swaim, National Center for Education Statistics, U.S. Department of Education, Characteristics of Private Schools in the United States: Results From the 2003–2004 Private School Universe Survey (NCES 2006–319) (2006), available at http://nces.ed.gov/pubsearch/pubsinfo.asp?pubid=2006319 (visited October 3, 2007).

A few years ago a friend from the Midwest who was strongly opposed to aid to religious education remarked (approximately), "We could deal with the Roman Catholics; it's the evangelicals who worry us."

Public Assistance and Schools

The vast majority of elementary and secondary schools in the United States are public schools. The vast majority of private schools are religious schools. Roman Catholic schools flourished during the nineteenth century when public schools had a distinctly Protestant character, and most religious private schools are still Catholic.[2] The composition of colleges and universities is different; many universities are private, and many of these, including some of the most prestigious, are not religious. Among religious institutions of higher education, Roman Catholic ones do not predominate to quite the degree of Roman Catholic schools.[3] Until recently, the problem of aid to primary and secondary religious schools has seemed mainly to concern aid to Roman Catholic schools. Although anti-Catholic prejudice should play no part in an evaluation of political and constitutional choices, one cannot understand the history of aid without paying attention to Roman Catholic schools—their strengths, weaknesses, and social effects—and to the ways in which these schools have been viewed by non-Catholics. Were extensive government assistance given to all private, nonprofit schools, the development of new private schools would alter the distribution between Roman Catholic and other schools. Nevertheless, for the foreseeable future, a substantial percentage of private schools will remain Roman Catholic.

The public school movement in the United States has relied upon and spread an attitude about schools that differs greatly from people's attitudes toward hospitals. The ethos about public schools in the United States is that they are a vital, perhaps the central, means for teaching social equality and toleration. People of different economic classes, cultures, ethnic and religious backgrounds, and parental attainments gather together and learn what it is to be an American. Public schools exemplify the cultural ideal of the melting pot. Most citizens who accept this ethos would not wish to forbid attendance at private schools, but they think it would be unfortunate were a large segment of American students to attend private schools. It would be especially unfortunate if these schools propounded anti-American values.

In the past, people with this perspective typically viewed Roman Catholic schools with suspicion. No doubt undiluted anti-Catholic prejudice played its part; but the church's own teachings could give pause to fair-minded

---

[2] Religious elementary and secondary schools are 58 percent Catholic. Broughman and Swaim, note 1 supra.

[3] Catholic schools account for half of all students enrolled at religious institutions of higher education. Association of Catholic Colleges and Universities, Membership Statistics, http://www.accunet .org/display.asp?Category=6 (visited July 25, 2006).

outsiders. The message that Roman Catholicism was the only true faith was less than welcome for people who sought mutual toleration.[4] And until 1965, with the Second Vatican Council, the church's official position was that, ideally, a state should cooperate closely with the Roman Catholic Church, that liberal democratic ideals of full religious liberty and church-state separation were a poor second-best. Reasonable citizens could conclude that the state should not support teachings antithetical in these respects to the American ethos.

Another basis for concern was the Roman Catholic aspiration that all aspects of Catholic education should be guided by religious understanding, that teachers should teach religious ideas in all facets of the curriculum. Outsiders could doubt that public assistance should go for secular educational benefits, if those benefits were closely intermingled with religious indoctrination.

Matters have now shifted in three crucial respects. First, during Vatican II, the Roman Catholic Church embraced the principles of religious liberty and liberal democracy (separation of church and state along American lines is still not favored). And the American church is now very American. Worries non-Catholics may once may have had about intolerant, undemocratic influences on the political process now seem mostly ill conceived, although disturbing involvements occasionally rear their heads,[5] and a more subtle concern remains that a religious organization that itself is strongly hierarchical and that reserves its most important positions for men sends regrettable signals about social relations. (Although the church does not now assume that its own assignment of internal roles should be replicated in the external world, internal allocation may influence people's views of themselves and of authority.)

Second, Catholic education has become less pervasively religious. This is partly by design and is partly the consequence of the much higher percentage

---

[4] Historically, if one can generalize, Catholic views that Protestantism was not true Christianity were matched by Protestant views that Roman Catholicism was a perversion of Christianity; but Protestants did tend to accept the authenticity of Protestant denominations other than their own.

[5] I have in mind here particularly the well-publicized position of a minority of American bishops in 2004, that politicians who support permissive laws about abortion should be denied communion, and the further position taken by Archbishop Raymond Burke of St. Louis and Bishop Michael J. Sheridan of Colorado Springs that ordinary Catholics who vote for such politicians should not receive communion. Tim Townsend, "Bishops This Week May Wrestle with Fellows' Statements on Politics," *St. Louis Post-Dispatch*, June 13, 2004. According to my outsider's understanding of Roman Catholic tradition, such political choices fall within the realm of prudence. See Mario Cuomo, "Religious Belief and Public Morality: A Catholic Governor's Perspective," 1 *Notre Dame Journal of Law, Ethics and Public Policy* 13 (1984). But whatever one might say within the tradition, such efforts strike many outsiders as an unhealthy attempt to control votes.

of laity and non-Catholics now teaching in Catholic schools, itself largely the result of the decline in vocations of priests, brothers, and nuns.[6] Third, a crisis of confidence has developed about the public schools, accompanied by a sense that private endeavors may improve educational quality, directly by dint of the options they offer, and indirectly by stimulating public schools to greater achievement. Almost everyone agrees that public schools within the inner cities are doing very poorly, and these schools are often compared unfavorably with Roman Catholic ones, which now educate a considerable number of youngsters, including non-Catholics, within our country's worst slums.[7]

Giving broad support to nonreligious private schools without giving similar support to religious private schools is not politically feasible, and it would seem grossly unfair to parents whose children attend religious schools. My discussion thus assumes that any substantial support of primary and secondary private education will include religious education.[8]

To develop a sense of a desirable relationship between public and private schools, one must make difficult judgments about educational excellence, social influences, and religious teaching. One educational prospect is that new, imaginative programs begun in private schools, and the increased competition these schools can provide with greater aid, will invigorate and improve public schools. A drearier outlook is that private schools will draw away better students, that with funding for the private schools that they prefer many parents will have little (selfish) incentive to vote adequate budgets for their public schools, that bereft of their best students and with diminished financial resources, public schools will languish. People, experts and nonexperts, disagree strongly about the overall effect on educational quality of funding private education. Although my own children have mainly attended private school, I, as a nonexpert, am troubled enough about the likely effect on public schools, which I and my siblings attended, to be against any

---

[6] Gerard V. Bradley, "An Unconstitutional Stereotype: Catholic Schools as 'Pervasively Sectarian,' " 7 *Texas Review of Law and Politics* 1 (2002), explains why Catholic schools are not pervasively sectarian in the sense of having religious perspectives strongly influence the teaching of secular subjects.

[7] See Bradley, id. at 8, who points to the large enrollment of non-Catholics as one indication that the schools do not indoctrinate students in the Roman Catholic faith. Non-Catholic enrollment in Catholic elementary and secondary schools has increased from 2.7 percent in 1970 to 13.5 percent today. Dale McDonald, National Catholic Educational Association, United States Catholic Elementary and Secondary Schools 2005–2006: The Annual Statistical Report on Schools, Enrollment and Staffing (2006), available at http://www.ncea.org/news/AnnualDataReport.asp (visited October 3, 2007).

[8] Although a few radical plans may call for the dismantling of public education, I am assuming that that will continue for the foreseeable future.

extensive general support of private schools. However, the dangers of support may be much less for programs focused on particular geographical areas and groups of students, most especially students from the poorest economic backgrounds. Increasing their opportunities by funding their chance to go to private schools may not have any substantial negative impact on public education.

A major concern about social influences is diversity. One might hope that substantial support of private schools would not undermine the democratic effects of our educational institutions, but the risk exists that if private schools receive heavy support, students might be sorted out on lines of religion, ethnicity, and class more than they now are. Although the neighborhood character of public schools typically keeps them from resembling a slice of a diverse national population, wider support of private schools might further reduce interactions of children with variant backgrounds. This concern is serious, although, again, the social effects of extensive general support would not be the same in all regions,[9] and one would expect few negative effects on diversity from programs focused on the poorest part of the population.

Finally, how should we regard religious teaching? Most private schools are religious, and some teach doctrines that are narrow and inhospitable to other faiths. We may be virtually certain that if widespread generous public support was extended to private schools, many new religious schools would spring up. Whether the state should be financing public benefits that are accompanied by extensive and strong religious teaching is a troubling question, one we have already touched upon in the previous chapter. Let us assume that 60 percent of the newly created private schools would be religious, and that half of them would give significant emphasis to particular religious views that most people in the country would not accept.[10] The idea of public money going to schools that teach religious doctrines, especially doctrines that are highly exclusive, is disquieting, *even if* the money is supplied on a neutral basis and does not exceed the secular benefit of what the school is doing.

Should it matter how the money is supplied to a school? Money may come indirectly to schools though parents. The basic idea is that each private

[9] The private Episcopalian school in New York City, to which my three older children went, was far more diverse economically, ethnically, and racially, and was probably more diverse even religiously, than the public schools I attended in an affluent suburb.

[10] I mean to draw a contrast here with vague references to God or to a generalized Christianity that now characterizes some religious schools. The school my elder sons attended did not teach Episcopalianism, although that form of worship was the basis for some aspects of the chapel service. My impression is that the Roman Catholic school, not a parish parochial school, that my daughter attended taught little, if any, specifically Roman Catholic Christianity, but it did refer to Christian understandings.

school receives an amount of money each year according to parents' choices to have that school educate their children. (The state could give the money directly to the school, or it could give money, or vouchers, to parents who would then transfer the money to the school.)[11] A program that ties funds to parental choice and student enrollment is far preferable to the state's allocating money on the basis of official judgments about who should receive funds. The latter scheme creates too great a possibility that schools teaching religious ideas with which most citizens, or educational officials, are sympathetic will receive the lion's share of money.[12]

Another significant difference in techniques of funding is the contrast between earmarking and general grants. General grants, whether or not in the form of payments per pupil, open themselves up to the use of money received from the state in support of religious endeavors. Earmarking aims to avoid this feature, although, of course, use of state money for a needed secular, aspect of education may indirectly free up other money for a religious aspect. Earmarking also creates difficulties regarding supervision. All states already monitor religious schools to some degree, since educational officials must satisfy themselves that the schools meet state educational standards. If a state supporting broad educational programs wants to avoid having its money go for religious purposes, it needs to ensure that teachers, many of whom were devoted to the religious objectives of the school, do not include religious ideas in their teaching of "secular" subjects. Such supervision can be difficult and intrusive. For general support of private education, earmarking seems less promising than grants on a per student basis. People can reasonably differ about whether such grants are objectionable because they involve state aid to religious teaching. I believe they are. Neither neutrality in grantees, nor funding that does not exceed secular benefit, nor both together is enough to wipe out the undesirability of using tax funds to provide broad support that includes the religious practices of religious institutions.[13]

Two other features amplify the worry about aid to religious schools. In geographical areas with small populations, only two schools may be viable; a public school and one private religious school. A government program of support will end up offering parents only two practical options. Some parents

[11] In practical effect, a program that allocates money on the basis of enrolled students differs extremely little from a program in which parents allocate money to schools. But there is a difference in principle. A very few parents may wish to send children to religious schools but *not* receive public funds. They should be able to decline that support, if they wish.

[12] Whatever may be true of hospitals and adoption agencies, educational officials should not give grants based on the overall quality of religious schools.

[13] We shall see the significance of the qualification about broad support when we turn to constitutional principles, and to the G.I. Bill and more extensive Pell grants.

who are persuaded that private education is preferable will send their children to the private school, though they are not attracted, or are even disturbed, by its religious teaching. Other parents who stick to the public school will resent that those of a dominant faith have an opportunity for publicly funded education that they lack. These (unintended) elements of effective favoritism and of pressure to attend the school of one faith are undesirable.

Legislative decisions over educational funding are also worrisome. Groups that have many religious schools may push hard for more money for private education; minority religious groups with few or no schools and many nonreligious groups may be in opposition. The prospect is of religious groups fighting over how much public money is going to go to religious institutions. As we have seen, one reason to separate church and state is to eliminate, or reduce as much as possible, sectarian struggles over who will benefit from the apparatus of government. Extensive private school funding could well induce such struggles.

We may achieve an added perspective on general aid to religious schools by considering a yet more radical proposal. Thus far, we have assumed that whatever else it may do, the state should not, cannot, support the religious endeavors of churches, synagogues, and so on, with public funds. But what of the following possibility?

Robert Putnam and some other scholars have emphasized the importance for decent government of citizens participating actively in organizations of civil society.[14] Suppose that Congress, worried about the decline of such participation, decides to give grants to participatory organizations on a per member basis.[15] Recognizing that active membership in religious bodies can contribute to good citizenship, that a high percentage of the participation in American civil organizations is in religious groups,[16] and that funding only nonreligious groups would create a problem of unfair discrimination, Congress decides to give general grants to all participatory bodies, including religious ones, based on membership. Each organization can spend its grant as it wishes. Religious groups can repair churches, hire new clergy, and so forth.

---

[14] Robert D. Putnam, *Bowling Alone: The Collapse and Revival of American Community* (New York: Simon and Schuster, 2000); Robert D. Putnam with Robert Leonardi and Raffaella Y. Nanetti, *Making Democracy Work: Civic Traditions in Modern Italy* (Princeton: Princeton University Press, 1994).

[15] It would somehow have to distinguish organizations with active member participation from those in which membership means only signing up and making a donation each year.

[16] Religious organizations represent 34.8 percent of total volunteer participation in the country. Bureau of Labor Statistics, U.S. Department of Labor, Volunteering in the United States 2005, table 4 (2005), available at http://www.bls.gov/news.release/pdf/volun.pdf (visited September 12, 2007).

If block grants to schools based on numbers of pupils are all right, does it follow that this program would also be all right? Two possible major differences are that public money given directly to religious bodies could be spent for their core activities, and that the "secular benefit" of funding is much more amorphous than it is with schools. On the latter point, participation in bigoted churches may make bad citizens rather than good ones, but the state cannot measure benefits to citizenship of participation in individual churches, as it can measure whether schools meet minimal education standards. As for core activities, worship and ministry are certainly central for most religious bodies; but teaching the religion to young people, a function many religious schools perform, is also commonly regarded as extremely important.

I continue to assume that the state should definitely not give direct grants to religious bodies that can be used for core religious activities, even if the grants further an amorphous secular benefit such as good citizenship, and even if the state treats all private nonprofit organizations similarly. This program resembles general grants to private schools closely enough to generate doubt about the wisdom and acceptability of the school grants.[17]

Constitutional Decisions

Much of the major shift in Establishment Clause doctrine over the past sixty years has played itself out in cases involving forms of aid to religious schools. To understand various directions in which a future Supreme Court might go, and to evaluate sharply disparate views about how nonestablishment should be understood in this context, we need to have a sense of the Court's approaches during those six decades, but without involving ourselves in numbing detail.

The modern story begins with *Everson v. Board of Education*,[18] but I should say an initial word here about a relation between state and federal constitutional provisions that I believe is unique. A substantial majority of states have constitutional provisions with similar language that is much more

---

[17] People who find neutrality and secular benefit sufficient to justify school grants may see the differences between those and grants to churches and similar religious bodies as more important than I do, or they may be led by the comparison to conclude that, after all, the general grants to churches, etc., would be appropriate. One argument along those lines is that such benefits would not be unlike tax exemptions for church property and tax deductions for church contributions, which do benefit churches generally, and indeed have an economic effect indistinguishable from funding. Chapter 15 has claimed that one can sensibly distinguish these tax benefits from funding.

[18] 330 U.S. 1 (1947).

detailed about aid than is the federal Establishment Clause.[19] Very briefly, the historical explanation is this. In the late nineteenth century, at a time of strong opposition to public aid to Catholic schools, James G. Blaine proposed an amendment to the federal Constitution that would have barred aid to sectarian schools by the federal government or the states.[20] A version of the proposed amendment barely failed to pass the Senate; but many states subsequently included such language in their state constitutions.[21] Thus, most states have specific language in their state constitutions that forbids aid to sectarian education. As we shall see near the end of the chapter, these provisions raise a federal constitutional issue whether a state that is more restrictive about aid than the federal Establishment Clause requires is thereby violating the federal Free Exercise, Free Speech, or Equal Protection Clause.

Everson v. Board of Education

Debate over how the Establishment Clause applies to aid to parochial education has been substantially structured by the Supreme Court's first modern encounter with that problem in *Everson v. Board of Education*. In two earlier cases, the Court had held that Indian (Native American) trust funds could be spent on religious education,[22] and that aid to private religious schools constituted a public purpose,[23] but in neither opinion was there any serious examination of Establishment Clause limits. When that came in *Everson*, the Court, as we saw in chapter 2, announced a highly separationist account of the clause's significance, while barely upholding reimbursements to parents for bus fares to Catholic schools.[24] According to Justice Black's

---

[19] See Kyle Duncan, "Secularism's Laws: State Blaine Amendments and Religious Persecution," 72 *Fordham Law Review* 493, 515–28 (2003).

[20] The Blaine Amendment was proposed at a time when legislators did not suppose that the Fourteenth Amendment made the Bill of Rights applicable against state governments. This supposition is somewhat weakened as evidence of "the original understanding" at the time the Fourteenth Amendment was adopted, because the Slaughter-House Cases, 83 U.S. (16 Wall) 36 (1873), had interpreted Section 1 of that amendment very narrowly.

[21] Most state constitutions are much easier to amend than the federal one.

[22] *Quick Bear v. Leupp*, 210 U.S. 50 (1908).

[23] *Cochran v. Louisiana State Board of Educ.*, 281 U.S. 370 (1930).

[24] A New Jersey law required districts that provided bus transportation for schoolchildren to include those attending nonprofit private schools. The justices disagreed about how the actions of the state and district should be understood. The dissenters treated the case as one in which children of public and Catholic schools were treated one way and other children another way. See *Everson*, note 18 supra, at 20–21 (opinion of Jackson, J.); id. at 62 (opinion of Rutledge, J.). However, given the clear general language of the New Jersey statute and the absence of evidence that Ewing Township had any children attending nonprofit non-Catholic private schools, it was sensible to treat the district as specifying Catholic schools because those were the only nonprofit private schools, not because it favored Catholic over other nonprofit schools. Two dissenters drew conclusions from the statutory

opinion for the Court, religious liberty was a crucial motivation for colonists settling this country. Nevertheless, many of the colonies had their own forms of establishment. In Virginia, the struggles for religious freedom and nonestablishment received eloquent articulation in Madison's "Memorial and Remonstrance" and statutory expression in the Virginia Statute for Religious Freedom, drafted by Jefferson. Citing *Watson v. Jones*[25] and *Reynolds v. United States*,[26] Black wrote, "This Court has previously recognized that the provisions of the First Amendment ... had the same objective and were intended to provide the same protection against governmental intrusion on religious liberty as the Virginia statute."[27] As Jefferson's letter to the Danbury Baptists put it, the Establishment Clause was designed "to erect 'a wall of separation between church and state.' "

All nine justices in *Everson* accepted this historical understanding of the religion clauses, one that relies heavily on Jefferson and Madison and developments within Virginia. More recently, various justices have challenged this account, and if the Court shifts sharply toward accommodationist rulings, it will probably reject this historical version.

Passages from Justice Black's opinion can be used to support a variety of views about school aid. Language that emphasizes that benefits helped parents, not schools,[28] can support other programs that aid parents or children rather than schools. The proposition that individuals cannot be excluded *"because of their faith, or lack of it,* from receiving the benefits of public welfare legislation"[29] suggests that aid to schools given on a nondiscriminatory basis is acceptable. But the general thrust of the opinion[30] is that financing bus transportation is all right because it is marginal to a school's educational endeavors. Black draws an analogy to police and fire protection, available to churches and parochial schools, as well as to other enterprises.[31] When he wrote of "benefits of public welfare legislation," he had in mind legislation not directed at the educational function of schools.[32]

---

exclusion of schools for profit, arguing that it would not make sense unless the aim was to help schools rather than children. Id. at 20–21 (Jackson, J., dissenting). (See also id. at 61–62, Rutledge, J., dissenting.) Justice Black's opinion for the Court put that issue aside, professing uncertainty about whether New Jersey's Supreme Court would construe the statute to benefit children attending profit-making schools. Id. at 4–5.

[25] 13 Wall. 679.

[26] 98 U.S. 145.

[27] *Everson*, note 18 supra, at 13.

[28] "The State contributes no money to the schools." Id. at 18.

[29] Id. at 16.

[30] One borne out by Justice Black's subsequent opinions.

[31] *Everson*, note 18 supra, at 17.

[32] He acknowledged that even the aid for bus transportation could make it easier for some parents to send children to parochial schools, but that is true of all the state services that are uncontroversially

Justice Rutledge wrote a lengthy opinion for the four dissenters. He argued that the historical purpose of the First Amendment "was to create a complete and permanent separation of the sphere of religious activity and civil authority by comprehensively forbidding every form of public aid or support for religion."[33] He argued that New Jersey was requiring its taxpayers to pay for the propagation of religious opinions in which they do not believe, a primary concern of Madison's "Memorial and Remonstrance."[34] In another dissent, Justice Jackson drew on Roman Catholic writing to emphasize the religious aims of Catholic parochial schools and the subjection of religious teaching to the authority and inspection of the church.[35] He wrote that the First Amendment removed every form of propagation of religion from "the realm of things which could be supported at taxpayer's expense."[36] As for the majority's approach, Justice Jackson remarked, in a famous phrase, that the most fitting precedent was Byron's Julia, who "whispering 'I will ne'er consent,'—consented.' "[37]

Up through *Lemon*

In its next aid case, *Board of Education v. Allen*,[38] the Supreme Court approved New York's local school boards lending textbooks to children enrolled in private schools. The texts had to be designated for use in public schools or approved by a board of education regulating public schools. Justice White's opinion for the Court had a tone very different from *Everson*.

---

extended to parochial schools. He intimated that the program "is within the State's constitutional power even though it approaches the verge of that power." Id. at 16.

[33] Id. at 31–32. He said that for Madison "religion was a wholly private matter beyond the scope of civil power either to restrain or to support." Id. at 40.

[34] Id. at 44–45. The importance of Madison's "Memorial and Remembrance" for Rutledge's view is reflected in his printing its text as an appendix.

Rutledge noted that state cases have divided on the issue. Id. at 55. Reflecting a rather individualistic view of religion, he wrote, "The realm of religious training and belief remains, as the Amendment made it, the kingdom of the individual man and his God." Id. at 57–58. Remarking that the transportation provided was by ordinary public buses, Rutledge rejected the argument that the measure was one about safety. Id. at 60.

[35] Id. at 22–23. Jackson said that the premise of secular education is that that "can be isolated from all religious teaching" on the assumption that "after the individual has been instructed in worldly wisdom he will be better fitted to choose his religion." Id. at 24. This is an interesting vision of the nature of secular and religious understanding and of how religious understanding should develop, a view that emphasizes individual rationality and conviction over corporate life. Jackson did go on to say he would not try to answer whether such a disjunction is possible or wise.

[36] Jackson construed the district's assistance as limited to Catholics, as establishing a religious test by which beneficiaries were selected. On that view, the aid certainly was impermissible. But see note 24 supra.

[37] Id. at 19.

[38] 392 U.S. 236 (1968).

Eschewing any retelling of history, White emphasized that the financial benefit from the state's lending textbooks goes to parents and children, not
schools.[39] Unlike bus fares, textbooks may be critical to the educational process, but the state may assist sectarian schools to perform the valuable public
purpose of secular education.[40] If *Everson* left doubts on this score, it became
clear with *Allen* that state assistance would not be held invalid simply because state aid for a secular educational purpose could leave private money
available to be spent for some religious purpose. In 1971, the Court considered more ambitious programs of aid to parochial schools, as well as construction grants to private sectarian universities. Refining the standard for
judging establishment cases and adopting strikingly differential treatment of
grants to sectarian schools and sectarian universities, these cases also marked
the beginning of a threefold division on the Court among justices who disapproved of any aid, justices willing to accept virtually all forms of aid that
the Court reviewed, and justices in the middle whose votes determined the
outcomes of cases.

The two school cases, decided under the name of *Lemon v. Kurtzman*,[41]
were from Rhode Island and Pennsylvania. Statutes in both states authorized
payments for part of the salaries of teachers of secular subjects in nonpublic
schools;[42] Pennsylvania also provided payments for textbooks and instruc-

---

[39] Id. at 244. Referring to *Abington School Dist. v. Schempp*, 374 U.S. 203, 222 (1963), White
noted that the law had a secular purpose and "'a primary effect that neither advances nor inhibits
religion.'" Id. at 243.

[40] Justice Harlan concurred. The state must be neutral toward religion, but what neutrality requires
is not simple. The test should be one drawn from Justice Goldberg's concurring opinion in *Schempp*
(joined by Harlan): whether the activity involves the state "'so significantly and directly in the realm
of the sectarian as to give rise to . . . divisive influences and inhibitions of freedom.'" Id. at 249.
Three justices dissented. Talking of a "flat, flagrant, open violation of the Establishment Clause,"
Justice Black, the author of the *Everson* opinion, distinguished books, "which are the heart of any
school, from bus fares, which provide a conventional and helpful general public transportation service." Id. at 253. Justice Douglas, who had written strongly accommodationist language in *Zorach
v. Clauson*, emphasized that, with parochial schools deciding what textbooks they want loaned and
local school boards deciding if these are secular or religious, the school board will be under "religious-
political pressures . . . to provide the books that are desired." Id. at 244–45. If the result were that
nonsectarian books were put into religious schools, that would tend toward state domination of the
church, another consequence the Establishment Clause was designed to prevent. Id. at 266.

[41] 403 U.S. 602 (1971).

[42] The courses had to be ones in mathematics, physical sciences, foreign languages, and physical
education and could not contain "'any subject matter expressing religious teaching, or the morals or
forms of worship of any sect.'" Rhode Island limited the salary supplement to 15 percent of the
teachers' salaries. Other conditions were that the supplemented salary not exceed the maximum paid
to public school teachers, that the school employing the teacher have an average per-pupil expenditure
on secular education less than that of the public school average, that the subjects taught be offered in
public schools, and that the teachers use teaching materials used in public schools.

tional materials. In Rhode Island, about 95 percent of the pupils attending nonpublic schools went to Roman Catholic schools, in Pennsylvania about 96 percent went to church-related schools, most of which were Roman Catholic.[43]

Chief Justice Burger wrote for the Court that three tests "may be gleaned from our cases. First, the statute must have a secular legislative purpose; second its principal or primary effect must be one that neither advances nor inhibits religion; finally, the statute must not foster 'an excessive entanglement with religion.' "[44] Before applying these tests, Burger threw out two cautions that have been drawn upon by those inclined to downgrade the significance of the *Lemon* formulation. Burger remarked that "we can only dimly perceive the lines of demarcation in this extraordinarily sensitive area of constitutional law,"[45] that "the line of separation, far from being a 'wall,' is a blurred, indistinct, and variable barrier depending on all the circumstances of a particular relationship."[46]

As in subsequent school aid cases, the Court had no difficulty finding a secular purpose—the enhancement of secular education. Treating effect and entanglement as analytically separable, the opinion does not actually determine whether either law had a forbidden effect, but there can be no doubt that the justices' sense of effects strongly influenced their conclusions about entanglement.

In considering Rhode Island's law, Burger noted connections of the Catholic elementary schools to the Catholic Church, including their closeness to parish churches, their religious symbols, their use of nuns as two-thirds of their teachers, and their efforts to make religious instruction a natural part of school life. Religious authority, Burger wrote, pervades the Catholic school system, and parochial school teachers, advised that religious formation is not confined to formal courses, may find it hard to separate secular teaching from religious doctrine.[47] In contrast to the content of a text, a teacher's handling of a topic is not ascertainable. In order to ensure that subsidized teachers do not inculcate religion, the state has conditioned aid on "pervasive restrictions." "A comprehensive, discriminating, and continuing state surveillance will inevitably be required to ensure that these restrictions are obeyed," involving "excessive and enduring entanglement between state and

[43] In Rhode Island about 25 percent of all students attended private schools, in Pennsylvania 20 percent.

[44] *Lemon*, note 41 supra, at 612–13. The third test was taken from *Walz v. Tax Commission*, 397 U.S. 664, the 1970 tax exemption case.

[45] Id. at 612.

[46] Id. at 614.

[47] See Bradley, note 6 supra, at 11–15, for the view that neither church authority nor the personal religious vocations of teachers undermine the autonomy of secular subjects within Catholic schools.

church."[48] The Pennsylvania program, which included direct aid to the schools themselves,[49] was subject to similar objections.[50]

Although the Court was less than precise about what makes supervision excessive[51] and about how excessive supervision relates to the necessary (accepted) supervision accompanying accreditation, its view of entanglement was powerfully influenced by its concern over the danger of government financing of religious instruction.

The opinion then turned to what it called "entanglement of yet a different character"—"the divisive political potential of these state programs."[52] It commented:

> [M]any people confronted with issues [about aid] will find their votes aligned with their faith. . . . Ordinarily political debate and division, however vigorous or even partisan, are normal and healthy manifestations of our democratic system of government, but political division along religious lines was one of the principal evils against which the First Amendment was intended to protect.[53]

The problem would be "particularly acute because the appropriations benefit relatively few religious groups."[54]

As I noted in chapter 10, political divisiveness is quite separate from administrative entanglement,[55] and its place in constitutional analysis has been controversial. No doubt one strong reason for nonestablishment, a reason that influenced many founders, is avoidance of political conflict along religious lines. But whether in individual cases courts should assess the likely extent of political conflict is questionable.[56] Although political divisiveness seems in *Lemon* to be a nearly independent element of a complex entangle-

---

[48] *Lemon*, note 41 supra, at 619. Another unacceptable area of entanglement is when the state must determine how much of parochial education expenditures are going for secular education.

[49] Continuing cash subsidies "have almost always been accompanied by varying measures of control and surveillance." Id. at 621.

[50] The scrutiny necessary to see that funds did not support religious education condemned expenditures for books and instructional materials, as well as teachers' salaries. Id. at 622.

[51] This was especially true about reimbursement for books and instructional materials. Burger mentioned in particular the accounting procedures and auditing required under the Pennsylvania law, and the state's power to inspect a school's financial records to determine what expenditures are religious. Id. at 621–22.

[52] Id. at 622.

[53] Id. at 622–23.

[54] Id. at 623.

[55] One might have a high degree of the latter for some uncontroversial program that is not seriously divisive, and one may certainly have political conflict over programs that involve little administrative supervision. To include both concerns under the single label of entanglement is confusing.

[56] Not only is assessment difficult, having it as an element of a constitutional test might encourage opponents of programs to create divisive conflict in order to bolster their constitutional arguments.

ment test, its significance in opinions for the Court as a whole subsequently diminishes.

In his concurrence, Justice Douglas emphasized how pervasive the teaching of religion is in Catholic schools.[57] Close surveillance to prevent any religious teaching could intrude on the teacher's free exercise of religion.[58] In another concurrence, Justice Brennan wrote that the subsidies impermissibly served "the essentially religious activities of religious institutions," and "used essentially religious means to serve government ends, where secular means would suffice."[59] Noting that fewer than six states do not have a constitutional ban against the use of tax funds to support sectarian schools,[60] Justice Brennan claimed a consensus that states should not subsidize sectarian schools.[61] For Justice White, dissenting, the government's purpose of supporting an important separable secular function was sufficient to sustain the state programs.[62]

On the same day it decided *Lemon*, the Court ruled five to four, in *Tilton v. Richardson*,[63] that the federal government could make construction grants to church-related colleges and universities. Under the challenged statute, grants could not go to facilities to be used for sectarian instruction or religious worship. Writing for a plurality, Chief Justice Burger found no evidence that religion had seeped into the use of any of the funded facilities,[64] or that "religion so permeates the secular education provided by church-

---

[57] He quoted a Jesuit sociologist for the proposition that religion "permeates the whole curriculum. . . ." *Lemon*, note 41 supra, at 636. Douglas also drew at length from the Handbook of School Regulations for the Diocese of Providence to show "how pervasive is the religious control over the school and how remote this type of school is from the secular school." Id. at 640. According to Douglas, "It is well known that everything taught in most parochial schools is taught with the ultimate good of religious education in mind." Id. at 636. Religious hospitals may be aided, provided they are open to people of all creeds, but "the hospital is not indulging in religious instruction or guidance or indoctrination." Id. at 633. For a contrary view about Catholic schools, see Bradley, note 6 supra.

[58] Id. at 636. Many historical events, such as the Reformation or the Inquisition, can be taught with the gloss of a particular religion, and the state's policing teaching of them "would be insufferable to religious partisans."

[59] Id. at 643, 658. Brennan had proposed these standards in his concurring opinion in *Abington School District v. Schempp*, the school prayer case.

[60] Id. at 647.

[61] Id. at 648. Near the end of his discussion of the school subsidies, Brennan remarked, "This Nation long ago committed itself to primary reliance upon publicly supported public education to serve its important goals in secular education." Id. at 658.

[62] Id. at 664. He also remarked that the Free Exercise Clause should be considered relevant in cases like these. White talked of an "insoluble paradox" the Court had created: the government cannot finance religious instruction, but if it seeks to ensure that that does not happen, it becomes excessively entangled in religion. Justice White was undoubtedly correct that the Court's approach had just this effect; it flowed from the judgment that state aid to religious schools presents a danger of promoting religion that should be avoided.

[63] 403 U.S. 672 (1971).

[64] Id. at 681.

related colleges and universities that their religious and secular educational functions are in fact inseparable."[65] In contrast to the cases involving schools, in which it assumed that Catholic education in general was pervasively sectarian,[66] the Court in *Tilton* and in subsequent challenges to aid to higher education inquired about the nature of particular institutions. The chief justice did conclude that the statute's provision that after twenty years facilities would go to the colleges without restriction was unconstitutional; restrictions cannot expire so long as a building has substantial value.[67] On the crucial issue of entanglement, Burger wrote that, because college students are less impressionable and less susceptible to religious indoctrination than students in lower schools, and because the internal discipline of college courses tends to limit opportunities for sectarian influences, there is less need for intensive surveillance.[68]

The 1970s

During the next decade, legislatures attempting to provide aid to religious schools (in New York, Pennsylvania, and Ohio) sparred with a majority of the Supreme Court. Although the Court continued to allow assistance to religious colleges and universities—in the form of construction bonds[69] and

---

[65] Id. at 680.

[66] See Timothy S. Burgett, "Government Aid to Religious Social Service Providers: The Supreme Court's 'Pervasively Sectarian' Standard," 75 *Virginia Law Review* 1077, 1089 (1989).

[67] *Tilton*, note 63 supra, at 683.

[68] "Many church-related colleges and universities are characterized by a high degree of academic freedom and seek to create free and critical responses from their students." Id. at 686.

"Such inspection as may be necessary to ascertain that the facilities are devoted to secular education is minimal and indeed hardly more than the inspections that States impose over all private schools within the reach of compulsory education laws." Id. at 687. Entanglement was also reduced because the aid was nonideological in character, id., and was a one-time, single-purpose grant, id. at 688.

Justice Brennan, dissenting, and Justice White, the necessary fifth vote to uphold the construction grants, both challenged Burger's treatment of entanglement. As they pointed out, assuring that no courses with any religious content are taught in a building does call for continuing and substantial surveillance, very similar to what is needed to assure that Roman Catholic school teachers do not teach religion in their courses. Id. at 660–61 (Brennan), 668–69 (White). Blunting this critique requires one to believe that surveillance of colleges can be less severe because college teachers are more to be trusted not to mix religion with secular education or that occasional mixing is much less significant with college-age students. The plurality apparently indulges both these assumptions, without quite saying so.

The main theme of Justice Brennan's dissent was that construction grants to sectarian institutions are impermissible. Id. at 659. He would have remanded for a determination whether the aided colleges were "sectarian." He assumed that if a sectarian institution accepts public financial aid, it may not, under the Equal Protection Clause, discriminate in admissions and faculty selection. Id. at 651.

[69] *Hunt v. McNair*, 413 U.S. 734 (1973).

grants based on the number of students[70]—providing in the second case a sense of how religious a college might be without being "pervasively sectarian,"[71] the Court declared invalid most schemes of aid to relieve the burdens of primary and secondary schools.

The Supreme Court, finding impermissible aid to religion or entanglement, did not allow (1) an annual grant to schools (based on number of pupils) for the maintenance and repair of facilities;[72] (2) reimbursement of schools

[70] *Roemer v. Board of Public Works*, 426 U.S. 736 (1976).

[71] Justice Blackmun, writing the plurality opinion, accepted the district court's finding that the church-related colleges whose grants were challenged were not so pervasively sectarian "that their secular activities cannot be separated from sectarian ones." Blackmun summarized the factors that supported the district court's conclusion:

   (a) Despite their formal affiliation with the Roman Catholic Church, the colleges are "characterized by a high degree of institutional autonomy." None of the four receives funds from, or makes reports to, the Catholic Church. The Church is represented on their governing boards, but, as with Mount Saint Mary's, "no instance of entry of Church considerations into college decisions was shown."

   (b) The colleges employ Roman Catholic chaplains and hold Roman Catholic religious exercises on campus. Attendance at such is not required; the encouragement of spiritual development is only "one secondary objective" of each college; and "at none of these institutions does this encouragement go beyond providing the opportunities or occasions for religious experience." . . .

   (c) Mandatory religion or theology courses are taught at each of the colleges, primarily by Roman Catholic clerics, but these only supplement a curriculum covering "the spectrum of a liberal arts program." Nontheology courses are taught in an "atmosphere of intellectual freedom" and without "religious pressures." . . .

   (d) Some classes are begun with prayer. The percentage of classes in which this is done varies with the college, from a "minuscule" percentage at Loyola and Mount Saint Mary's, to a majority at Saint Joseph. There is no "actual college policy" of encouraging the practice. "It is treated as a facet of the instructor's academic freedom." Classroom prayers were therefore regarded by the District Court as "peripheral to the subject of religious permeation," as were the facts that some instructors wear clerical garb and some classrooms have religious symbols. . . .

   (e) The District Court found that, apart from the theology departments, faculty hiring decisions are not made on a religious basis. At two of the colleges, Notre Dame and Mount Saint Mary's, no inquiry at all is made into an applicant's religion. Religious preference is to be noted on Loyola's application form, but the purpose is to allow full appreciation of the applicant's background. . . . Budgetary considerations lead the colleges generally to favor members of religious orders, who often receive less than full salary. Still, the District Court found that "academic quality" was the principal hiring criterion, and that any . . . "effort by any defendant to stack its faculty with members of a particular religious group," would have been noticed by other faculty members who had never been heard to complain. . . .

   (f) The great majority of students at each of the colleges are Roman Catholic, but the District Court concluded from a "thorough analysis of the student admission and recruiting criteria" that the student bodies "are chosen without regard to religion." Id. at 755–58.

[72] *Committee for Public Education and Religious Liberty v. Nyquist*, 413 U.S. 756 (1973). Relying on past decisions, Justice Powell rejected the claim that the grants are acceptable because they do not

for the expenses of exams, most of which were prepared by teachers, and might contain religious ideas;[73] (3) lending of instructional materials, including periodicals, maps, charts, and films, whether formally to schools[74] or to pupils or parents;[75] (4) expenditures for transportation on field trips;[76] (5) the provision of auxiliary services—counseling, psychological testing, speech and hearing therapy, teaching for exceptional students and remedial students—by public school personnel within private schools;[77] (6) tuition reimbursement for low-income parents;[78] and (7) a variable tax deduction for tuition that decreased as parental income increased.[79]

The Supreme Court did permit (1) lending of textbooks approved for use in public schools;[80] (2) supplying of standardized tests and scoring services used in public schools;[81] (3) reimbursement for pupil evaluation and other expenses connected with state-prepared examinations and procedures;[82] and (4) the provision of diagnostic services within private schools and of therapeutic and remedial services within public schools for private school students.[83]

As we shall see, the Supreme Court's position has definitely shifted about a number of issues decided in this period. Other results holding aid invalid

---

exceed the monetary value of the maintenance that would be attributed to secular use of the facilities. Id. at 777. On that rationale, teachers could be reimbursed for the secular value of their teaching, a position that the Court was unwilling to adopt when it held invalid payment of a percentage of teachers' salaries.

[73] *Levitt v. Committee for Public Education and Religious Liberty*, 413 U.S. 472 (1973).

[74] *Meek v. Pittenger*, 421 U.S. 349 (1975).

[75] *Wolman v. Walter*, 433 U.S. 229 (1977). Justice Blackmun wrote that making the legal bailee the parents would not alter how the instructional materials were used or stored. Id. at 250.

[76] Id. at 253. The parties had stipulated that the trips would be to places designed to enrich secular studies; but schools would choose the destinations, and individual teachers would make the trips meaningful, with an accompanying risk that they would foster religion. Public school authorities would be unable to ensure that use of field trip funds was secular without intensive supervision that would create an excessive entanglement. Id. at 254. Justice Powell would have sustained support of transportation for field trips as not distinguishable from the bus transportation allowed in *Everson*. Id. at 264. Chief Justice Burger also would have accepted financing of bus transport for field trips. Id. at 255.

[77] *Meek*, note 74 supra. Justice Stewart wrote that when teaching takes place in an atmosphere dedicated to advancing religious beliefs, the danger persists that "religious doctrine will become intertwined with secular instruction." Id. at 370. To prevent that, the state would have to undertake continuing surveillance that would constitute excessive entanglement. Id. at 372.

[78] *Nyquist*, note 72 supra.

[79] Id.

[80] *Meek*, note 74 supra; *Wolman*, note 75 supra.

[81] *Wolman*, note 75 supra.

[82] *Committee for Public Education and Religious Liberty v. Regan*, 444 U.S. 646 (1980).

[83] *Wolman*, note 75 supra. According to Justice Blackmun, communication between diagnosticians and pupils raised little danger of religious influence. Therapeutic and remedial services offered by

may continue to have significance or may represent for a new Court only minor obstacles to be distinguished or rejected outright. Two broader aspects of decisions during the decade up to 1980 are worth remarking. The first concerns understanding of the *Lemon* test; the second the arbitrariness of results reached under that test.

The Court's most general comments about the criteria of the *Lemon* test were that they were "no more than helpful signposts,"[84] serving "only as guidelines with which to identify instances in which the objectives of the Establishment Clause have been impaired."[85] As I have intimated in chapter 10, what exactly such comments mean is murky. One possibility is that, for some circumstances, the Court will decide in a way not indicated by "the test." That did prove true in a later case permitting legislative chaplains, but it had not yet occurred in any school aid case up to the time the Court offered these cautions. The comments might mean that the *Lemon* test is vague, requires fact-centered appraisals, and often does not yield predictable outcomes. Other constitutional tests, such as "clear and present danger," have a similar character, yet we do not find the Court repeating that they are only guidelines. The reference to "guidelines" might be a kind of tip-off that the test's language does not reveal all the factors relevant to decision, and their weight for particular cases.[86] And, it is quite likely that the apparently innocuous language about guidelines had a different significance for different justices.

On a more specific point, an opinion for the Court by Justice Powell explained what is required for a "primary effect" of advancing religion.[87] Answering a dissent that criticized the Court for failing to decide what was a statute's dominant purpose, Powell responded that a law with "the direct and immediate effect of advancing religion" is invalid even if it has a primary effect to promote a legitimate secular end. Contrasted with what are only "remote and incidental" effects,[88] "primary effect," on this understanding, is not necessarily "the main" effect.

The Court's invalidation of New York's program for tuition reimbursement and tax deductions holds some special interest in light of theories that

---

public personnel away from the premises of the nonpublic schools presented less risk of religious instruction than when similar services are given within pervasively sectarian schools.

[84] *Hunt*, note 69 supra, at 741.

[85] *Meek*, note 74 supra, at 359.

[86] Thus, as I have suggested, what is tolerable administrative entanglement may depend partly on how serious the threat of aiding religion seems to be, a consideration that the language of the *Lemon* test obscures.

[87] *Nyquist*, note 72 supra.

[88] Id. at 783–84 n. 39.

benefits to parents and children should be accepted and in light of the Court's approval of property tax exemptions for churches.[89] For Justice Powell, that reimbursement went to parents rather than schools was "only one among many factors to be considered."[90] In practical terms the tax deduction (or credit) was distinguishable from a property tax exemption: it enjoyed no long historical precedent, did not minimize involvement between church and state, and was limited to a class composed predominantly of religious institutions.[91]

Opinions of dissenting justices and scholarly writings have expressed dismay over the arbitrariness of distinctions between what the Court upheld and what it struck down in these cases. That, in turn, has been taken as powerful evidence of the impoverishment of the *Lemon* test. We need to look at these appraisals carefully. The most important point is one I have made earlier. When one speaks of what the Court has decided, one is concentrating on what five justices at that time have ruled. Even apart from changes in the composition of the Court, which can explain shifts in direction, a distinction that controls two outcomes may be accepted by only a minority of justices. To take a simple abstract illustration (actually realized in the 2005 cases about displays of the Ten Commandments discussed in chapter 5): if four justices think laws A and B are similar and invalid, four justices think laws A and B are similar and valid, and one justice thinks the laws are different in a way that renders A valid and B invalid, the Court's outcomes will depend on a distinction that only one justice discerns. In these aid cases, one group of justices was ready to strike down almost any form of aid, another group was ready to accept a great deal of aid. The distinction one finds between loans of texts and loans of other instructional materials, undoubtedly hard to rationalize, is one that appealed only to a minority of justices.

A second point is that a *part* of what governed various outcomes was the decisions of earlier cases, which justices were hesitant to overrule. Finally, one can see from my brief summary that there is a nearly infinite number of nuances in how states can aid schools. Relatively easy cases tend not to arise at all or to get resolved in lower courts. When the Supreme Court regularly reviews cases in an area—as it did with school aid challenges—it takes on

---

[89] Id. at 781.

[90] Id. at 781.

[91] Chief Justice Burger, joined in this part of a dissenting opinion by Justices White and Rehnquist, argued that the tuition grant and tax relief programs were permissible, because the benefits went to private individuals, not schools. He objected to "the unsupportable approach" of examining the percentage of recipients who use money for religious education. Id. at 804. Justice Rehnquist asserted that the tax benefits could not be distinguished from other tax deductions and from the property tax exemption that the Court had approved in *Walz*. Id. at 808–9.

an almost steady diet of borderline situations, about which even justices employing the same conceptual approach may disagree. A court that sets out to treat as invalid forms of assistance that aid religion too directly or require unacceptable state supervision of religious endeavors, while allowing other forms of aid, will not find it simple to draw lines. People can disagree strongly over where exactly the lines should be drawn, but under almost any approach, some distinctions between the allowed and the disallowed may look embarrassingly arbitrary.

In contrast to most observers, I do not take the 1970s cases as abject failures, but (especially given the vagaries of decision by majority and the weight given to earlier rulings) as a reasonable effort to work out an approach that would allow some aid, but only aid that would not significantly advance the religious efforts of religious schools.

Moving toward a Permissive Approach

The 1983 case of *Mueller v. Allen*[92] marked a substantial advance in aid the Supreme Court was willing to permit. A Minnesota statute allowed parents to deduct from their state income tax payments for tuition, textbooks, and transportation for children attending school. By far the most important item financially was tuition; the only public school students paying ordinary tuition were a handful who attended schools outside their districts. Of the students attending private schools, about 95 percent attended sectarian schools. Thus, a high percent of savings under the act went to parents of children in sectarian schools.

Justice Rehnquist, who had been dissenting regularly in cases denying aid, wrote the Court's opinion. He emphasized that the deduction for tuition was only one of many available deductions,[93] that it was available to all parents,[94] and that any aid to parochial schools came indirectly through the choices of individual parents, thus avoiding a state's imprimatur of approval for any religion. Against the contention that the statute primarily benefited religious institutions, Rehnquist proclaimed a more formal approach: "We would be loath to adopt a rule grounding the constitutionality of a facially neutral law on annual reports reciting the extent to which various classes of private citizens claimed benefits under the law."[95]

---

[92] 463 U.S. 388 (1983).

[93] Id. at 396.

[94] Id. at 397.

[95] Id. at 401. Whatever unequal effect may result "can fairly be regarded as a rough return for the benefits" to the state of parents sending children to parochial schools. Id. at 402.

Justice Marshall's dissenting opinion argued that this tax benefit was not distinguishable from the tuition grant and tax deduction the Court had struck down earlier.[96] He urged that a tax deduction has a primary effect of advancing religion if it offsets expenditures that are not restricted to a school's secular activities.[97]

After *Mueller v. Allen*, many observers believed the Court was ready to undertake a radical shift, sustaining forms of aid that had previously been held invalid. Their hopes, or fears, were unrealized in two 1985 cases, when Justice Powell (in the *Mueller* majority) voted with the separationist group of justices.

In one of the two cases, *School District of Grand Rapids v. Ball*,[98] a substantial majority of the Court struck down a school district's community education program, under which teachers at private, mostly religious, schools were hired part time to teach after-school courses at those schools. *Ball* also involved a Shared Time program that provided public school teachers to teach courses such as "remedial" and "enrichment" mathematics, reading, and art in nonpublic schools. In the companion case, *Aguilar v. Felton*,[99] New York City administered a similar federal program to assist educationally deprived children from low-income families. The city used federal funds to pay public school teachers to offer courses in remedial reading, reading skills, remedial mathematics, and English as a second language, and guidance services. The teaching took place within classrooms of parochial schools cleared of all religious symbols.

Justice Brennan, who had consistently opposed programs of aid, wrote for the Court in both cases. Starting from the premise that the Establishment Clause "absolutely prohibits government-financed or government-sponsored indoctrination into the beliefs of a particular religious faith,"[100] he concluded that the Shared Time program of Grand Rapids presented a danger that public school teachers might subtly conform their instruction to the religious environment,[101] entailed a "symbolic union of church and state,"[102] and provided a direct aid to a religious school's educational function that is indistinguishable from a cash subsidy.[103] New York had adopted a system of

---

[96] Id. at 404–13.

[97] Id. at 414.

[98] 473 U.S. 373 (1985).

[99] 473 U.S. 402 (1985).

[100] *Ball*, note 98 supra, at 385.

[101] Id. at 388.

[102] Id. at 390.

[103] Brennan said that it did not matter whether the courses had been previously offered in the religious schools, and that any principle that made that critical would allow the state to subsidize more and more of the curriculum of religious schools. Id. at 396–97.

monitoring to prevent religious instruction in the funded classes, but that resulted in an excessive entanglement of church and state.[104]

Dissenting about the Shared Time and New York City programs, Justice O'Connor proved prophetic about the Court's future direction.[105] Because federal funds could be used only for services that would otherwise not be available to participating students,[106] they would not subsidize religious functions. Because a dedicated public school teacher would not be likely to proselytize students,[107] the need for supervision was much less than the Court supposed.[108]

The contrast between *Mueller v. Allen* and the decisions about public school teachers using classrooms in religious schools well illustrates a point about swing votes. *Mueller* approved fairly significant tuition aid to parents, which might allow more parents to afford tuition and allow schools to raise tuition. *Aguilar v. Felton* and *Grand Rapids School Dist. v. Ball* disapproved public school teachers using classrooms of sectarian schools, although not many of these teachers would undertake religious indoctrination, the indirect aid to religious education seemed no greater than in *Mueller*, and any symbolic union of state and sectarian school seemed modest. The same justices who decided *Mueller* decided *Aguilar* and *Ball* two years later. Only Justice Powell was in both majorities. The authors of the three opinions for the Court wrote in a way designed to garner his acceptance. The *Mueller* opinion emphasized the indirectness of any aid to schools; the opinions in *Aguilar* and *Ball* emphasized the troubling connection of having public school personnel teaching in religious schools. But, again, only one of nine justices thought these distinctions between the two kinds of circumstances were enough to tip the balance.

In the decade after *Aguilar* and *Ball*, the Court decided two cases that initially seemed of marginal significance but subsequently were employed to justify a powerful shift in the Court's approach to aid. In *Witters v. Washing-*

---

[104] Because aid was provided in a pervasively sectarian environment and provided in the form of teachers, ongoing inspection was required; but that inspection infringed values underlying the rule against excessive entanglements. Id. at 412–13. In a concurring opinion, Justice Powell remarked on the risk of political divisiveness. He acknowledged the "extremely narrow line" created by the interrelation of the "primary effect" and "entanglement" tests.

[105] She initially expressed doubt in *Aguilar* about treating entanglement as a separate standard. Note 99 supra, at 422. In her view, "Pervasive institutional involvement of church and state may remain relevant in deciding the *effect* of a statute which is alleged to violate the Establishment Clause . . . but state efforts to ensure that public resources are used only for nonsectarian ends should not in themselves serve to invalidate an otherwise valid statute." Id. at 430.

[106] Id. at 422. The worry about supplanting secular course offerings in parochial schools did not depend on where the classes were held. Id. at 426.

[107] Id. at 427.

[108] Id. at 428. Justice O'Connor pointed out that within public schools themselves, there is also a chance that a teacher "will bring religion into the classroom."

ton Department of Services for the Blind,[109] a unanimous Court held that under a program for vocational rehabilitation of the blind, a claimant could use state aid to study at a private Christian college, seeking to become a pastor or do other religious work.[110] The decision confirmed indirectly what many commentators had assumed about funding of higher education for veterans.[111] Justice Marshall, a strong separationist, wrote for the Court that only a minuscule amount of aid would flow to religious education, that money was paid directly to the student, that the program created no incentive to undertake sectarian education.

The Court reached a similar conclusion in *Zobrest v. Catalina Foothills School District*[112] about public funding for a sign language interpreter assisting a deaf child who was attending a Roman Catholic high school.[113] Justice Rehnquist's opinion for the Court emphasized that the program distributed aid neutrally, that no aid went to the school itself, and that the interpreter would do no more than "accurately interpret whatever material is presented to the class as a whole."[114]

Between 1985 (the year *Aguilar* was decided) and 1997, the Court had undergone a very significant change in its composition. Of the majority in *Aguilar*, Justices Brennan, Marshall, Blackmun, and Powell were no longer on the Court. Among the new Justices were Scalia, Kennedy, and Thomas, a group one would rightly have expected to be much more accepting of aid.[115] In 1997 the Court followed a very unusual procedure and reexamined its decision in *Aguilar*. The district court had complied with that decision by issuing a permanent injunction against public school employees teaching in sectarian schools. The city had responded by providing assistance for students from those schools in mobile units off school property, a practice that was substantially more expensive (according to one estimate the number of private school children aided declined 35 percent). The suit in *Agostini v. Felton*[116] was to obtain relief from the injunction.

---

[109] 474 U.S. 481 (1986).

[110] The Washington Supreme Court had upheld the commission's denial of aid, on the ground that that would violate the Establishment Clause.

[111] It was widely assumed that veterans using money under the G.I. Bill to study at religious colleges was constitutionally permissible.

[112] 509 U.S. 1 (1993).

[113] Money for sign language interpreters was provided under the Individuals with Disabilities Education Act.

[114] *Zobrest*, note 112 supra, at 13. In a dissent, Justice Blackmun, joined by Justice Souter, urged that the Court's decision mistakenly "has authorized a public employee to participate directly in religious indoctrination." Id. at 18.

[115] Justices Souter, Ginsburg, and Breyer were also on the Court; Chief Justice Burger and Justice White had left.

[116] 521 U.S. 203 (1997).

Justice O'Connor, a dissenter in *Aguilar*, wrote for the Court. She concluded that relief was appropriate because the controlling law had altered since the injunction.[117] Relying mainly on *Zobrest* and *Witters*, O'Connor wrote that the Court had abandoned the ideas that placing of public employees in parochial schools would result in state-sponsored indoctrination, would constitute a symbolic union between government and religion,[118] or would impermissibly aid the school's educational functions.[119] Justice O'Connor used intervening decisions to bolster her dissenting position in *Aguilar* that public school employees would not be inclined to religious teaching just because they are in sectarian schools, and therefore did not require pervasive monitoring.[120]

Justice O'Connor's opinion readjusted the relationship between entanglement and effect. Because the examination of entanglement involved many of the same factors as an inquiry about effect, entanglement would henceforth be treated as one aspect of effect—not an independent strand in a three-part test. Gauging the practical significance of this formal shift is difficult, but folding entanglement into effect could diminish its significance.

Justice Souter, dissenting, objected to the state's subsidizing religion.[121] Given the wide range of subjects covered in the program, he wrote, public school teachers would undertake kinds of teaching that the schools themselves would otherwise provide.[122] No line between "supplemental" and general education could be drawn.[123] In contrast to *Zobrest*[124] and *Witters*, aid was given directly to the religious schools.[125]

---

[117] All four dissenters joined Justice Ginsburg's opinion contending that under the Court's rules, the justices should have deferred reconsideration of *Aguilar* until they were presented with the issue in a different case. Id. at 255.

[118] Id. at 223.

[119] Id. at 225.

[120] Id. at 233–34.

[121] Id. at 242.

[122] Id. at 244.

[123] In answer to the majority's response that this argument applied with equal force to services rendered off the school premises, Justice Souter suggested that schools may be less likely to dispense with subjects given in outside instruction and that "the difference in degree of reasonably perceptible endorsement is substantial." Id. at 247.

[124] Souter argued that *Zobrest* rested on the limited role of the sign language interpreter. Id. at 248. Whereas Justice O'Connor took *Zobrest* as a basis to expand, Justice Souter noted its limits. Neither opinion is uniquely right about the earlier case, except in the sense that one or the other may develop a sounder approach to school aid. The use of precedent cases broadly or narrowly to support one's position is among the most common techniques in lawyers' briefs and judges' opinions.

[125] Both of the earlier cases involved single beneficiaries; New York City's Title I program served "about 22,000 private school students, all but 52 of whom attended religious schools." Id. at 257. Finally, Justice Souter criticized the Court's failure to follow precedent. When *Aguilar* was decided everyone knew that compliance would be costly; so there were no unexpected facts to undermine the conclusion of the earlier case. Id. at 254.

'In *Mitchell v. Helms*,[126] a 2000 case, the Court continued its march toward upholding aid. Six justices sustained the use of federal funds for local agencies to lend educational materials and equipment to private schools; they rejected the contrary conclusion of earlier cases. Justice Thomas's plurality opinion, for himself, Chief Justice Rehnquist, and Justices Scalia and Kennedy, undertook a sweeping reconceptualization that would open the door to virtually all aid. What Thomas said fell one vote short of representing a majority, but were Chief Justice Roberts and Justice Alito to embrace his position, it would control future cases. Thomas's dominant theme was "neutrality," in the sense of equal treatment. If aid is offered to a broad range of groups without respect to their religious affiliation, and the aid itself is not religious in content, the aid is permissible even if the main beneficiaries are religious groups and the aid is actually diverted by them to religious purposes. Any indoctrination cannot be attributed to the government *if* aid is subsequently used for religious purposes.[127] Thomas wrote that recent cases emphasize the principle of private choice—namely, that when private choices determine how aid is given, that makes it less susceptible to invalidation—but he stretches the principle considerably in suggesting that it applies to aid that goes directly to schools on the basis of enrollment.[128]

Although *Mitchell v. Helms* involved the provision of instructional materials such as computer software, one supposes that Justice Thomas would reach the same conclusion about direct financial assistance.[129] Money is no more religious in content than is computer software, and its diversion to religious use by a recipient would presumably not be attributed to the government.

In the course of his opinion, Justice Thomas addressed the focus of many earlier cases on whether schools are pervasively sectarian. He called such an approach "not only unnecessary but also offensive."[130] Courts should not

---

[126] 530 U.S. 793.

[127] Id. at 809–10, 821–25. Were Justice Thomas's position to become the law, it would alter radically the ground rules for aid. All earlier cases had treated divertibility of assistance as a serious issue; programs had to assure that aid would not be put to religious use. Neutral criteria for aid was one, but only one, requirement for permissible aid. For example, in 1988 in *Bowen v. Kendrick*, 487 U.S. 589, reviewing federal aid to private organizations providing services for premarital sexual relations and pregnancy, Chief Justice Rehnquist wrote for the Court that the funding of religiously affiliated organizations that were giving advice to adolescents about sex and family planning was valid on its face, but the opinion assumed that the government's assistance could not be used for religious purposes.

[128] According to Justice Thomas, the aid "first passes through the hands (literally or figuratively) of numerous private citizens who are free to direct the aid elsewhere. . . ." *Mitchell*, note 126 supra, at 816.

[129] See id. at 821, 819 n. 8.

[130] Id. at 828.

be "trolling through a person's or institution's religious beliefs."[131] The doctrine that pervasively sectarian schools should be excluded from otherwise permissible aid, "born of bigotry, should be buried now."[132]

Justice O'Connor's concurrence, joined by Justice Breyer, rejected the broad theory of the plurality.[133] Government can supply instructional materials for religious schools, but an *actual* diversion for religious use would not be consistent with the Establishment Clause. Adhering to the principle of earlier decisions that aid should not advance the religious missions of sectarian schools, O'Connor argued that a significant difference exists between programs that rely directly on private choices and those that provide direct assistance on a per capita basis.[134] She pointed that the plurality's reasoning would allow governments to provide direct money payments for churches, which churches could use for religious purposes, so long as the money was provided on some neutral basis to nonreligious organizations as well.[135]

Justice Souter's dissent defended the premise that public funds cannot be used for religious aid, on the basis that compelling an individual to support religion violates freedom of conscience, that government aid corrupts religion, and that government establishment of religion is linked with conflict.[136] Souter pointed out that, although neutrality as evenhandedness has been one relevant factor in establishment cases, it has never been sufficient by itself to qualify aid as constitutional. Rather, it has mattered whether recipients are pervasively religious primary and secondary religious schools, whether aid is direct or indirect, and what are the characteristics of the aid itself—its religious content; its cash form; its divertibility or actually diversion to religious support; its supplantation of traditional items of religious school expense; and its substantiality.[137]

Souter's defense of the criterion of "pervasiveness" raises the question whether the plurality's attack on it is justified. It is unlikely coincidental that three of the four justices charging that the standard was based on anti-Catholic bigotry are Roman Catholic. Although the prevalence of anti-Catholic prejudice some decades ago, including prejudice among many intellectual leaders, makes plausible some causal connection between prejudice and the "pervasively sectarian" criterion, bigotry is hardly needed to explain the

---

[131] Id., relying on *Employment Division v. Smith*, 494 U.S. 872, 887 (1990).

[132] Id. at 829.

[133] Id. at 837–38.

[134] Id. at 842–44.

[135] Id. at 843–44.

[136] Id. at 870–72. Souter did not defend this third concern as a criterion for individual decisions, but regarded it as a motivating concern behind the Establishment Clause. Id. at 872 n. 2.

[137] Id. at 885.

criterion's appeal. Justices relied primarily on Roman Catholic sources explaining an ideal of pervasive religious education. The justices were not as clear as they might have been about what exactly makes religious instruction pervasive. In particular, did nearly all courses have themselves to be suffused with religious messages, or was it enough that the (or an) overarching purpose of the entire education was to increase religious understanding? One might take the latter view about a religious school without supposing that all, or most, subjects should themselves reflect a religious viewpoint.[138] But judicial lack of clarity is not decisive evidence of bigotry.

It is arguable whether courts should be in the business of evaluating whether any school or set of schools is "pervasively sectarian." That difficult judgment is troublesome from the standpoint of religion clause values and is anathema to believers in clear lines, such as Justices Scalia and Thomas. Apart from the line-drawing problem, however, it makes sense to think that the more a school is suffused with religious teaching, the harder it is to aid secular functions alone, a problem we identified in the last chapter regarding aid to religious organizations engaged in forms of social welfare. Perhaps Roman Catholic schools were never as pervasively sectarian as justices assumed. Almost certainly, they are now less sectarian than they were in the years prior to the Second Vatican Council, due in part to changing church perspectives (particularly about human freedom and religious liberty) and to the steep decline in numbers of priests and nuns. But some schools of the Christian Right, as well as a smaller number of Orthodox Jewish and conservative Islamic schools, may be pervasively religious in the way that concerned the earlier Court.[139]

It will be highly unfortunate if debate over continued use of that criterion, or some comparable substitute, gets tangled up with unresolvable claims and counterclaims about whether its origins are tainted by bigotry.

Whatever one concludes about the origins of the "pervasively sectarian" standard does not settle whether it, or something like it, should remain an aspect of Establishment Clause doctrine. I shall consider three challenges—that it is irrelevant, unduly restrictive of religious liberty, and inadministrable. The perceived merits of the irrelevancy challenge depend largely on how one responds to the hypothetical program I suggested in the last chapter of

---

[138] Bradley, note 6 supra, claims strongly that within Catholic schools, most subjects do not reflect a religious viewpoint.

[139] Interestingly, Bradley does not doubt that some schools could be vehicles for indoctrination, even though Catholic schools are not. Id. at 7–8. He suggests the teaching of creation science as an illustration of religious indoctrination in a science course.

giving unrestricted money to all voluntary private organizations, including churches. If one believes, as I do, that the government should not be directly financing core religious activities, even as part of a neutral program of aid, one will also be troubled by the idea of the government's financing schools whose overarching mission, carried forward in virtually all courses, is to propound a particular religious faith. At least for direct aid, the degree of religiosity of a school could be relevant under the Establishment Clause.

The free exercise–fairness objection is that government should not be discouraging individuals and institutions from practicing their religion as they see fit.[140] I confess I had twinges of discomfort assisting Walter Gellhorn, who was asked many years ago by Fordham University, a Catholic institution, what changes it needed to make in order to be eligible for New York state funds that could not go to sectarian institutions.[141] Nonetheless, *if* the government should not be assisting dominantly religious practices, it is a reasonable condition on the availability of funds that recipients not be dominantly religious in their supported activities. The free exercise of religion does not entail that one's support or nonsupport by public funding be completely independent of whether the practices that might receive support are overarchingly religious.

The problem of administration of the standard of "pervasively sectarion" is severe.[142] It may not be hard to distinguish Faith Works (the drug rehabilitation program that aims to lead addicts to a Christian commitment) from a soup kitchen of the Salvation Army, but distinguishing among religious schools on the basis of which are so religious as to be "pervasively" so is no easy task. One would need, to begin, a more precise account of what makes a school pervasively religious, and one would still face perplexing problems of classification. In light of these difficulties, it might make more sense to say that qualification under a neutral standard is sufficient, even though that means that some pervasively religious schools will receive aid (the direction in which the Court is probably moving) or to restrict aid to religious schools to specific secular aspects, whether the schools are or are not pervasively religious. Opposed as I am to substantial aid that can go to religious aspects

[140] See Stephen V. Monsma, "The 'Pervasively Sectarian' Standard in Theory and Practice," 13 *Notre Dame Journal of Law, Ethics, and Public Policy* 321, 337 (1999); Burgett, note 66 supra, at 1096–1100 (but see also id. at 1113, considering that primary and secondary education may be recognized as a distinctly religious function).

[141] The conclusions were published in Walter Gellhorn and R. Kent Greenawalt, *The Sectarian College and the Public Purse* (Dobbs Ferry, N.Y.: Oceana Publications, 1970).

[142] Monsma, note 140 supra, at 334, remarks, "The pervasively sectarian standard is neither well-defined nor consistently applied."

of education, I would favor the latter course.[143] Under either of these strategies, courts would not have to decide exactly which school educational programs are "pervasively sectarian."

Approval of Substantial Voucher Programs

The most important Establishment Clause decision of recent decades was
handed down in 2002. In *Zelman v. Simmons-Harris*, the Supreme Court
sustained a voucher program designed for low-income families in Cleveland,
a city in which the free public schools had been performing extremely
poorly.[144] Parents received vouchers from the state in the form of a check,
covering as much as 90 percent of tuition up to $2,250, that they made
payable to a private school their child was attending. (Public schools outside
Cleveland were eligible to receive vouchers for Cleveland students,[145] but
none of them had chosen to participate.) In order to be eligible, schools could
not discriminate on the basis of race, religion, or ethnic background, and
they could not teach hatred of groups classifiable on any of these bases.[146]
Of the participating schools in the 1999--2000 school year, 82 percent had a
religious affiliation, and more than 96 percent of the 3,700 students involved
attended those schools.[147]

Asking whether the Ohio program had a forbidden effect of advancing
religion, Chief Justice Rehnquist for the Court emphasized that the program
provided aid indirectly and reached the schools only as a result of parents'
choices. The standards for aid were neutral, and it was irrelevant that religious schools would receive most of the aid. Relying on *Mueller* and *Agostini*
(and in contrast to some of the earlier cases), Rehnquist wrote that the constitutionality of programs depended on the criteria for assistance, not whether
recipients overwhelmingly sent their children to religious schools.[148] Claiming a jurisprudence that "remained consistent and unbroken," Rehnquist asserted that the Court had rejected each challenge to a program "of true private choice, in which government aid reaches religious schools only as a

---

[143] This was, in fact, the approach the Court has taken when it has assumed that parochial schools
are pervasively sectarian.

[144] 536 U.S. 639, 644 (2002).

[145] Id. at 645.

[146] Id. The prohibition on discrimination clearly covered admissions and clearly did not prohibit
teaching religious ideas. The status of employment was not clear. See text accompanying note 156,
infra.

[147] Id. at 647.

[148] Id. at 658.

result of genuine and independent choice of private individuals."[149] Because aid is given according to neutral criteria and goes to individual recipients, any incidental advancement of religion or perceived endorsement of a religious message would be attributed to individual recipients, not the government.[150]

Dissenting for himself and three other justices, Justice Souter argued that extensive public funding of religious education was unconstitutional. Earlier cases had rightly paid attention to whether public aid could be diverted to religious education; whether aid was disbursed to parents rather than directly to schools was only one factor to be considered.[151] *Mueller* had started down the road to formalism from a desirable realism about whether aid assists religion, but not until this case had the Court treated the amount of aid as irrelevant or held that purely formal criteria determine constitutionality.[152] Souter argued that the way the Cleveland program operated was hardly neutral. Because private schools were sharply restricted in the tuition they could charge poorer parents who received state vouchers (those with incomes up to twice the poverty line), religious schools, which operated on lower budgets than other private schools were able to do, were bound to enroll a high proportion of participating students.[153] Given the small number of available secular private schools, parents lacked a free and genuine choice about how to spend their voucher money.[154]

Justice Souter developed the theme that public funding was bound to bring more state control, already evidenced by the rule that no school receiving vouchers could discriminate on religious grounds or teach hatred of a religious group.[155] Souter noted that the discrimination provision by its terms may well cover hiring as well as admissions.[156] Perhaps a religious school

---

[149] Id. at 649. Rehnquist discussed *Mueller*, *Witters*, and *Zobrest* in this connection. The tuition reimbursement and tax deduction the Court had held invalid in 1973, *Nyquist*, note 72 supra, seem to fit his definition of a program of private choice, but Rehnquist distinguished that program as giving benefits to private schools and being designed to assist sectarian institutions. Id. at 661–62. For a challenge to the view that individual choice sharply alters the degree of government responsibility for religious aspects of education that its funding may assist, see Laura S. Underkuffler, "Vouchers and Beyond: The Individual as Causative Agent in Establishment Clause Jurisprudence," 75 *Indiana Law Journal* 167 (2000).

[150] *Zelman*, note 144 supra, at 652.

[151] Id. at 692–93.

[152] Id. at 693, 695.

[153] Id. at 704–6. Souter took the fact that two-thirds of parents using vouchers did not embrace the religions of the schools they chose as showing an absence of genuine choice. Id. at 649, col. 2. (One might take that to show that Roman Catholic schools (and maybe others) are providing especially effective education.)

[154] Id. at 698–700.

[155] Id. at 712–13.

[156] Id. at 712.

could not choose for its head a member of the clergy of its faith over an otherwise better qualified layperson of a different religion. And the hatred provision might be interpreted to cover teaching articles of faith about the error and ignorance of others.[157] Souter quoted passages from scripture;[158] but did not mention the long-standing (however ill-informed) belief among many Christians that modern Jews are somehow to be blamed for the death of Jesus, or the common assumption among Protestants of the pre-Revolutionary era that the pope was the Antichrist and that in the cosmic struggle between good and evil, the Roman Catholic Church represented evil.[159] Suppose a Protestant school taught these, or similar, ideas. Whether they would amount to teaching hatred of a group would be hard to say; but one can certainly see how official enforcement of the provision of the law forbidding teaching of such hatred could generate controversial administrative decisions and impinge on the expression of religious beliefs.[160]

Justice Breyer's dissent developed at length another concern found in the Souter opinion, the divisiveness of a scramble for public money. Underscoring the concern of the founders of the United States over religious conflict in Europe, and surveying examples of Protestant oppression of Catholics and Jews in American history,[161] Breyer argued that school voucher programs differ from other public assistance to religious organizations that the Court had previously upheld, both in supporting "a core function of the church: the teaching of religious truths to young children,"[162] and in providing aid that is very substantial.[163] According to Breyer, history shows that when government gets involved in religious primary education, that is far more divisive than other aids that go to religious institutions. The inevitable consequence of programs of substantial aid, even ones that rely on parental choice, will be conflict among religious groups.[164]

Zelman presents an issue that is difficult as well as important. Among the major interrelated objections to voucher assistance of the kind there provided are that (1) it involves substantial aid to religious schools, with no

---

[157] Id. at 713.

[158] Id. at 713–14 n. 24.

[159] See George M. Marsden, *Jonathan Edwards: A Life* (New Haven: Yale University Press, 2003).

[160] See *Zelman*, note 144 supra, at 724 (Breyer, J., dissenting). Were this the only difficulty with the law, a court might interpret teaching group hatred in a very narrow way, or it might declare this aspect of the law unconstitutional, or it might recognize that such interference with religious expression could be justified by a compelling state interest.

[161] Id. at 718–20.

[162] Id. at 726.

[163] Id. at 727.

[164] Id. at 728.

restriction to secular aspects of their education; (2) it dominantly benefits religious institutions; (3) it is accompanied by disturbing regulation of religious endeavors; (4) it is bound to generate divisive conflict among religious lines; (5) it is not really neutral; and (6) it does not offer parents an adequately free choice between secular and religious alternatives. Much of the complaint of the four dissenters concerns the way the majority treats neutrality and private choice, but for none of the dissenters does this issue turn out to be crucial. Each of them would have considered the Ohio program to be invalid even if their own standards for neutrality and choice had been met. Thus, I reserve discussion of neutrality and choice until I have considered the other issues.

In considering all the objections to voucher programs, it helps to keep in mind three different perspectives: appropriate uses of government money, judicially administrable standards, and relations between aid to education and aid to other functions performed by religious institutions—discussed in the last chapter. The first perspective asks whether, taking everything relevant into account, a program goes too far in the direction of assisting religion. This is obviously a relevant question for legislators, and it may bear on what judges should decide as a matter of constitutional law. The second perspective focuses on what courts should do. One might believe, as do a number of Supreme Court justices, that courts are ill suited to evaluate many factors that would bear on wise legislation. Perhaps courts need relatively formal, easily applicable, standards that do not require evaluation of complex consequences and matters of degree. If so, the standards for what judges should declare to be violations of the Establishment Clause will lead to acceptance of some programs that, all things considered, go too far toward establishing religion, and to rejection of some programs that do not go too far. The third perspective provides a point of comparison. Whether the concern is wise legislation or judicial evaluation of constitutionality, the standards used to evaluate aid to religious education should be the same as those used to evaluate aid to other endeavors undertaken by religious groups *unless* one can point to reasons of relevance to desirable legislation or constitutionality for treating education differently.

I think we can initially put aside potential divisiveness as, at most, of subsidiary concern. Were a program otherwise unobjectionable, we might not expect sharp divisions along religious lines, and even if we did, we would not suppose that that alone would make unconstitutional what would otherwise be plainly constitutional. Still, apprehension over religious conflict was one reason the federal government and states adopted antiestablishment programs for their constitutions, and I think Justice Breyer is right that the potential for debilitating conflict has not disappeared. Potential for divisiveness should count as one relevant element in an appraisal of constitutionality as well as legislative wisdom. To be clear, that potential should be judged in terms of broad categories, such as aid to education, not in terms of the degree of conflict over one particular program.

The worry about creeping regulation and a close relative, responsiveness to financial incentives, is serious. By regulation, I mean such constraints as nondiscriminatory admissions and hiring and not teaching hatred of religious, racial, or ethnic groups. By financial incentives, I mean support for kinds of programs that may skew what a religious group would otherwise do. We saw in the last chapter that Catholic Charities in Massachusetts had shifted its programs toward substance abuse after public money was made available to support that. We can imagine similar incentives affecting educational programs.[165]

There can be little doubt that nondiscriminatory hiring—in particular, not taking religious convictions and affiliations into account—could greatly affect the quality of a religious school; so also can nondiscrimination in admissions, though to a lesser extent. And Justice Souter amply demonstrates that the rule against teaching hatred of groups is fuzzy enough at the edges, so that it might be understood to cover teaching of various ideas that are embraced by many religious groups.[166] Further, as public aid increases, so also may regulation to ensure that government money is spent to promote the welfare of the whole society.

Two possible responses to the concern about regulation are that religious groups can avoid regulation if they choose, by refusing public money, and that extensive regulation already accompanies public aid to hospitals, adoption agencies, and other religious endeavors serving public needs. The ability of religious groups to avoid regulation by refusing money does not eliminate the worry about religious liberty. The society as a whole has an interest in religious groups being free of government control, even of the groups themselves are willing to surrender their freedom to a significant degree. Perhaps even more to the point in terms of practical realities is the effect of progressive amounts of aid accompanied by progressive regulation. A religious school may initially accept substantial financial support on the basis of a deliberate choice that forms of regulation are perfectly acceptable. Years

---

[165] This is less obvious with indirect aid (which supports entire school programs) than targeted direct aid, but a legislature *might* limit voucher availability to private schools that provide certain specified kinds of courses.

[166] Id. at 713–14.

later, its educational program may be heavily dependent on public funds. If regulations objectionable to it are then introduced, it may be unwilling to pay the price of severe cutbacks in its educational program in order to avoid the regulations.

The comparison with regulation of other forms of religious undertaking is largely misconceived. Close regulation of hospital practices does not touch the core aspects of what religious groups do to nearly the same degree as regulation of the education religious groups provide.[167]

The concern abut regulation ties to the issue about substantial aid. It is when aid becomes substantial, not fringe, that one can imagine religious groups being steered from their own sense of how best to educate children in their schools.

In relation to how substantial aid is, we can think of the total amount of aid to religious schools, the percentage of total aid to private schools that goes to religious schools, the degree to which aid is likely to support religious activities, the percentage of a school's budget that is supplied by public aid, and the percentage of any individual's participation that is supplied by public aid. As Justice O'Connor points out in her concurrence, the total amount of aid going to religious schools is dwarfed by the public funding of religious hospitals and by the benefits churches realize from tax exemptions and deductions.[168] An individual's stay at a religious hospital may be supported heavily or exclusively by public funds. The three measures of real concern are the percentage of all aid to private schools that goes to religious schools, the percentage of a religious school's budget that is supplied by public aid, and the likelihood that aid will go to religious activities.

Let us start with the last point. If aid is in the form of vouchers, schools are free to spend them as they wish. If the school's religious teaching and other religious activities are significant, some of the income supplied by vouchers will almost certainly support religious aspects of a school's program. Is this a problem? Only if one thinks education is special or one takes a highly restrictive view of all aid to religiously sponsored activities. If public money goes to hospitals, adoption agencies, or drug rehabilitation centers on the basis of clients served, without strings attached, the money is also likely to provide some support for the religious aspects of programs. These consequences are relatively uncontroversial. But one may think that public support of the religious education of young people is particularly troublesome, that

[167] See id. at 726–27 (Breyer, J., dissenting).
[168] Id. at 666–68.

it falls close to public support of core religious activities. (One might take a similar view of proselytizing within a drug rehabilitation program.)

It is not easy to say just why public support of religious teaching may be wrong. One account, urged by Justice Souter, draws on Madison's "Memorial and Remonstrance" to claim that it violates the conscience of taxpayers to use tax money for religious purposes.[169] Madison was focusing, at least primarily, on taxes directed specifically to support religion. Even if he also had in mind, or would have had in mind if he had thought about it, money provided according to more general, nonreligious criteria, we face the problem that in modern times tax money goes to all sorts of projects to which various taxpayers object in conscience, not least of which is support of wars that some taxpayers regard as gravely unjust. Perhaps one can regard religion as different because religion should be specially beyond the government's concern, but then the conscience argument becomes largely dependent on some other kind of claim about how religion and government should relate to each other.

The percentage of money going to religious schools among all schools seems important because a program that dominantly serves religious schools seems to be an aid to religion, whatever secular services these schools provide. Here is one place where a formalist approach to constitutional law differs from an approach that is more "realistic" and contextual. A formalist will say, "We can't get into actual percentages. We must rely on criteria for assistance." A contextual realist regards percentages as highly relevant.

The percentage of a school's budget that comes from public sources is relevant in general terms as to whether the government seems to be supporting religion. It is also relevant, as we have seen, in relation to whether a school's religious mission is likely to be diverted because of regulations or other criteria for assistance.

One commonsense response to the legislative issue posed by vouchers might be this. They do trespass to a degree on desirable relations between state and church, but what might otherwise be unwise can be justifiable if the situation to which vouchers respond is desperate. In poor urban areas the school situation is desperate enough to warrant measures that would be unacceptable where public schools are functioning reasonably well. None of the justices explicitly takes this approach to the constitutional issue; each writes as if the Establishment Clause analysis is not a matter of balancing, as if the result would be the same if the voucher program had covered middle-

---

[169] Id. at 711–12.

income parents in districts with good public schools.[170] In declining to give weight to the need for a voucher program, and in opposing any substantial aid to religious schools, the dissenters display a kind of formalism of their own, a refusal to look at all the factors that might warrant vouchers that go to religious schools.

Much of the opinions is taken up with neutrality and parental choice. One might think the dissenters' complaints about the majority's approach are substantially irrelevant, since the dissenters would have disapproved a program that satisfied their own contentions about neutrality and choice. But this concern about irrelevance would be misconceived for two reasons. For the dissenters, neutrality and choice could make a difference for *some programs* devoted to social services and education. So a sound view about those subjects could make a difference for their votes in other cases. More important, assuming that a majority of the Court follows the approach of *Zelman* (which seems likely with Chief Justice Roberts and Justice Alito replacing Chief Justice Rehnquist and Justice O'Connor, who constituted two-fifths of that majority), the Court must develop a thoughtful approach to neutrality and choice in a range of situations. We cannot suppose that the last word has been spoken on those topics.

The question of neutrality concerns the actions of the government. Has the government been neutral with respect to religious and nonreligious alternatives? The question of choice seems mainly to concern what choices are actually available to the recipients of vouchers: are their choices sufficiently free? But in respect to choice, one could also focus on what the government has done to assure freedom of choice; if it has done all one could fairly expect, perhaps it is not so important what range of choice recipients of vouchers actually have. Let us begin with neutrality. Here all the justices agree that a voucher program that reaches religious organizations must be neutral between religious and nonreligious providers of a service. It would definitely not be sufficient for the government to restrict voucher funding to religious providers on the theory that state schools constitute an adequate secular provider. The government cannot favor religious schools over nonprofit nonreligious schools.

The disagreement between the majority and the dissenters is over what one can discern in this instance and (apparently) about how enterprising the investigation of unequal effect should be. Justice Souter in dissent argues

---

[170] However, Justice Stevens, id. at 684, did suggest that since most students will remain in public schools, the voucher program will do relatively little to cure the basic problem of inadequate education.

that the program is not really neutral between religious and nonreligious schools because the voucher amount is set at a level that is mainly attractive to religious schools.[171] For a variety of reasons, not the least of which has been teaching staff with religious vocations, religious schools have spent less per pupil than the great majority of nonreligious schools. In the Cleveland context, the average tuition charged by Roman Catholic schools in 1999–2000 was $1,592.[172] If such a school receives the full voucher amount allowed to it and charges the permissible copayment, it gets as much per voucher pupil as it charges other students. But imagine a private school charging $4,500 in tuition. If it receives the voucher amount for a student from a poor family ($2,250) and charges the $250 it is allowed to charge such a family in addition to the voucher,[173] it receives less than it would get for a student paying full tuition. In other words, it will have to decide it is willing to offer a $2,000 scholarship to the poor students it accepts under the voucher program. Although the voucher program may be formally neutral, Souter claims, the amount of the vouchers effectively ensures that the main recipients among private schools will be religious schools.

Chief Justice Rehnquist contends in response that no evidence supports the notion that nonreligious private schools have been discouraged from participating, and also points out that the percentages of religious schools among schools participating in the voucher program is not significantly different from the percentage of religious schools among private schools in the state and country.[174] One is not quite sure what the chief justice believed he was demonstrating. For this reader, he has certainly not overcome the plausibility of the Souter's claim that the voucher amount will not operate neutrally in fact. But it is highly doubtful if Rehnquist really supposed that is relevant. At least if the legislature has acted in good faith, not setting the amount in order to favor religious schools (which would amount to an impermissible purpose),[175] probably it is sufficient for the majority that there is no formal favoritism of religious schools. If religious schools happen to be better situated to take advantage of the voucher program because of the level at which the voucher is set, so be it.

Assuming that this is how the majority understands neutrality, it not only disagrees with the dissenters about the probable facts, it demands less to satisfy the constitutional demand of neutrality. If we take this question as a

[171] Id. at 704–5.
[172] Id. at 705.
[173] See id. at 646.
[174] Id, at 656–58.
[175] Rehnquist, himself, was, of course, consistently skeptical about purpose analysis.

general one and put aside how clear it is that this particular program is nonneutral in effect, I think Souter has the better of the argument. The government should be required to set up programs that will not in inevitable effect encourage religious providers to the near exclusion of nonreligious providers.[176]

The issues about choice are closely interrelated with those about neutrality, but they differ in some important respects. One question is what degree of absence of free choice renders a program unacceptable, but the more important issue concerns what can be taken into account in evaluating choices. We shall see that, ironically, the less the need for a voucher program, the freer choices may seem.

Chief Justice Rehnquist puts the question about choice as "whether Ohio is coercing parents into sending their children to religious schools."[177] "Coercion" is too strong a word for the relevant question. If the state sets up a system in which most parents feel that for their children's welfare, they need to send the children to religious schools, that should violate a requirement of free choice even if one would hesitate to say that the parents were "coerced."

More important than the degree of pressure is what range of alternatives count. The majority includes public school options, particularly community schools (governed by independent boards) and magnet schools with special programs,[178] and this approach is vigorously defended in Justice O'Connor's concurrence.[179] Justice Souter claims that the relevant comparison should be in terms of possible uses of the vouchers; if no nonreligious options are available, choice is not adequately free, whatever programs public schools may offer.[180] Here, Justice Souter's conceptual argument is too broad, but his final conclusion may be right about the Cleveland program.

Imagine that a public school in a small community is good enough so that few parents, except those who want a religious education for their children, have any inclination to opt for a private school. With a statewide voucher program in place, the only private school in the community is a religious school. Parents must choose between it and the public school. If almost everyone would prefer the public education unless they seek religious education for their children, their choice would be adequately free between religious and secular education. (One might wonder about the adequacy of

---

[176] See Ira C. Lupu and Robert Tuttle, "Sites of Redemption: A Wide Angle Look at Government Vouchers and Sectarian Service Providers," 18 *Journal of Law and Politics* 537, 560–84 (2002).

[177] Zelman, note 144 supra, at 655–56.

[178] Id. at 664, 672–76.

[179] Id. at 664, 672–76.

[180] Id. at 698–99, 707.

choice for those who want a different kind of religious education, but perhaps the answer is that no program can assure everybody the kind of religious education they want, because there will always be many groups that are too small to support a school.)

The majority's decision to consider public school offerings thus seems defensible. But the fact that two-thirds of the voucher students attend schools of denominations other than their own is disturbing. Although parents who are not Catholic may reasonably value Catholic education,[181] the percentages suggest that many parents who do not trust the public school system do not have a range of choice they would like in respect to alternatives. Whether this renders choice unfree enough to matter is debatable. Not only is there the issue about how much lack of freedom is sufficient to fail the standard of choice, there is also the question of what proportion of parents must exhibit that degree of feeling unfree. Suppose, to simplify, that 80 percent of parents are reasonably satisfied with various public school options, but that 20 percent strongly find all those options unacceptable; and that 60 percent of the 20 percent (i.e., 12 percent of all parents) feel pushed against their strong inclinations toward sending their children to religious schools. My own sense is that this alone should probably *not* be enough to render a program unconstitutional, but when it is combined with the absence of neutrality in effect of the Cleveland program, it should push the program over the line of unconstitutionality, even if one rejects the broader theories of the dissenters about Establishment Clause limits.

Were legislators widely to pick up on the shift in the law of the Establishment Clause that *Zelman* represents, the funding of private education would be drastically altered in this country. Thus far, legislatures have hesitated to enact voucher programs except to benefit lower-income families or students with disabilities, although the Bush administration has proposed a broader federal voucher program. It remains to be seen whether legislative reluctance to enact programs covering most students will diminish over time with the removal of a potential constitutional bar.

The Content and Constitutional Status of More Restrictive State Provisions

The rise of neutrality as evenhandedness and the Court's reliance on formal standards have made it clear that in most situations the government *need not*, as far as federal constitutional law is concerned, treat religious endeav-

---

[181] See Bradley, note 6 supra, at 9.

ors worse than comparable nonreligious ones. Combined with the free speech rule against viewpoint discrimination (as broadly understood by the Court) and the free exercise rule against discrimination aimed at religion, the neutrality approach has raised a further question: May individual states restrict aid to religion and to religious education, in particular, in an effort to further principles of nonestablishment?

I noted in an early part of this chapter that most state constitutions forbid the use of public money for sectarian education. If a state, in observance of such a restriction, allows assistance to private education but not to private religious education, does this violate the federal constitution—the Free Exercise Clause or the Free Speech Clause, or both?

After the earlier Supreme Court decision allowing state funds to go to a blind person for his use at a religious institution to prepare to become a pastor or do other religious work, the Washington Supreme Court decided that such a use of funds would violate the state constitution.[182] The U.S. Supreme Court's first engagement with such a state restriction occurred in 2004, in *Locke v. Davey*.[183]

The State of Washington offered Promise Scholarships to students attending college within the state, for their first two years of study, but these were unavailable to those pursuing a "degree in theology," understood as a degree that is "devotional in nature or designed to induce religious faith."[184] Although someone could certainly become a minister without pursuing such an undergraduate degree, and someone could pursue such a degree without intending to become a minister, the Supreme Court reasonably regarded the restriction as aimed at avoiding the financing of education for the ministry.

The outcome of the case was unexpected, at least in the division of the justices. Seven voted to uphold the state's program, with Chief Justice Rehnquist writing a fairly narrow opinion that states could, within "the play of joints" of the federal religion clauses, choose not to finance ministerial education.[185] Justices Scalia and Thomas, dissenting, concluded that Wash-

[182] Witters v. Washington Comm'n for the Blind, 771 P.2d 1119 (Wash. 1989).

[183] 540 U.S. 712 (2004).

[184] The Supreme Court's construal of exactly which programs of study were ineligible was more precise in content than what one could fairly glean from administrative practices and any state court opinions on the topic. Because the scholarships covered the first two years of study, a student willing to lie about his plans could easily designate another kind of degree, take some devotional theology courses in his first years, and then switch to devotional theology as a major. In fact, Davey specified a double major in pastoral ministries and business. Id. at 717.

[185] Id. at 718–19. Rehnquist's surprising vote showed that he deemed respect for state authority or legislative choice, or both, as more important than any idea that the key to the religion clauses is evenhandedness. The result in the case is defended in Laura S. Unterkuffler, "*Davey* and the Limits of Equality," 40 *Tulsa Law Review* 267 (2004).

ington's restriction discriminated against religion and, therefore, violated the Free Exercise Clause.[186]

Because the opinion was written specifically in regard to financing ministerial education, it is difficult to predict whether the Court will also accede to state restrictions on aid to sectarian education as they operate more broadly. This issue could arise in one of two ways. A state legislature might provide assistance to private education but without including sectarian institutions, however those might be defined.[187] Or a state legislature's decision to assist religious and nonreligious education alike could be challenged as violating the state's constitution. In either event, a religious educational institution, or someone who wanted support for attendance at such an institution, would urge that any exclusion of religious or sectarian education would violate the federal Constitution.

Chief Justice Rehnquist obscured the difficulties of such future inquiries in two related respects. He provided little guidance about how a court is to decide whether a program that treats religious education less favorably than nonreligious education presumptively violates the Free Exercise Clause or is fully within "the play of the joints" of the two religion clauses. And he dismissed free speech concerns in an unconvincing manner, disposing of the Court's cases on that subject on the ground that the Promise Scholarship Program is not a forum for speech.[188]

The problem with the opinion's treatment of free speech is not difficult to discern. Davey was (relevantly) a consumer of speech, not a speaker, so, as the opinion notes, he was not situated as was the student newspaper *Wide Awake* in the *Rosenberger* case.[189] But suppose (to draw loosely from a painful dispute at Columbia University in 2004–5), a state provided financial assistance for students taking courses in Middle Eastern politics if, and only if, they were taught from a point of view sympathetic to Israel, thus refusing assistance for enrollment in any courses deemed biased in favor of a Palestinian perspective. Quite apart from difficulties in applying this standard to various courses, the approach would involve clear "viewpoint discrimination," even though the state's direct involvement was with those mainly receiving speech rather than speakers. Although I will not make the argument

[186] *Davey*, note 183 supra, at 1315–20. For one academic critique of the Court's conclusion that Washington's restriction did not violate the Free Exercise Clause, see Thomas S. Berg and Douglas Laycock, "The Mistakes in *Locke v. Davey* and the Future of State Payments for Services Provided by Religious Institutions," 40 *Tulsa Law Review* 227 (2004).

[187] Walter Gellhorn's study for Fordham University, in which I assisted, note 141 supra, undertook to discern what was then needed in New York to be not sectarian.

[188] *Davey*, note 183 supra, at 720 n. 3.

[189] See chapter 11.

here, I think such discrimination in terms of teacher perspectives would be a violation of the Free Speech Clause. Certainly one cannot comfortably dispose of free speech worries, as Rehnquist's opinion does, on the basis that financial aid programs are not forums for speech.

Were the Court to approach state limits on aid to religious education as presumptively violating the Free Exercise Clause or the Free Speech Clause, those limits could be sustained only if supported by a compelling state interest. That could be a very hard showing for a state to make, especially in instances when the federal Establishment Clause definitely would permit a state to include religious education in its program of aid. (It was common ground that Washington was not required by federal constitutional law to exclude religious studies from its Promise Scholarships.)

The preferable approach is for a court to examine carefully considerations relating to free exercise and nonestablishment in order to decide whether religious education can be excluded from a program of aid, without a prejudgment that such an approach is presumptively unconstitutional.[190] Under that approach, states would be permitted to create some limits on funding beyond those that a shifting Supreme Court has decided that the Establishment Clause imposes. In other words, states would be allowed to undertake some exclusions that the Court does not require. That, indeed, is the approach of the Supreme Court in *Locke v. Davey*; what is missing is serious development of the way in which courts should deal with future cases in which the contest is over a state's ability to promote its own view of nonestablishment by refusing to aid religious education.

A determination that in most circumstances, a state must treat nonreligious and religious private education similarly would not *necessarily* help advocates of aid.

We can imagine at least three possibilities in that respect. The first is that the state provision in question suffers from a malign purpose, an anti-Catholic bias. Here the idea is that such bias explained the proposal of the federal Blaine Amendment, and infected most of the state provisions that followed. The *Davey* Court says that Washington's constitutional provision is not a Blaine Amendment, and perhaps it means by this that evidence of such bias is lacking.[191] If a court determined that such bias did explain enactment of a

---

[190] See Kent Greenawalt, "Is It Davey's Locker for the No-Funding Principle," 46 *Journal of Church and State* 25 (2004); Ira C. Lupu and Robert W. Tuttle, "*Zelman*'s Future: Vouchers, Sectarian Providers and the Next Round of Constitutional Battles," 78 *Notre Dame Law Review* 917 (2003).

[191] *Davey*, note 183 supra, at 723–24 n. 7. In terms of context, the Washington provision is not so different from various state provisions usually called Blaine amendments. A clearer approach to categorization is one that treats as a "Blaine amendment" any "state constitutional provision that

prohibition on aid to sectarian education *and* it concluded that that bias continues to bear on the modern provision, it would hold the provision invalid as based on an unconstitutional purpose.[192] In that event, a legislative program of general aid to nonprofit schools would go forward.

Suppose, instead, a court did not find the purpose behind a restriction on aid to sectarian education as itself unacceptable. It might, for example, think that such a restriction was a reasonable attempt to see that public funds went for education the state could control. (Perhaps nonreligious, nonprofit private schools were then so rare that disregard of them was understandable,[193] or perhaps those who adopted the provisions reasonably thought state control of education in those schools would be much easier to accomplish than state control of what then went on in religious schools, or perhaps the state acted in response to a condition Congress set on its admission to statehood.)[194] Nevertheless, a court might decide that the line between religious and nonreligious schools is now constitutionally unacceptable. It might then declare the whole provision invalid (the same result as if the purpose was malign), or it might ask whether those who adopted the provision would prefer permitted aid to all private nonprofit schools or no aid to such schools. Recall that Justice Harlan suggested such a strategy for Congress's attempt to limit conscientious objector status to religious claimants; he asked if Congress would rather include nonreligious objectors or exempt no one, concluding that it would have preferred to expand the exemption, not eliminate it.[195] If sectarian schools dominate the field of nonprofit private

---

bars persons' and organizations' access to public benefits explicitly because they are religious persons or organizations." Duncan, note 19 supra, at 515.

[192] A court might conclude that time has altered the rationale of the provision, in something like the way the Supreme Court said time has altered the purpose of Sunday closing laws.

[193] A few state constitutions do forbid aid to all private education. E.g., Alaska Constitution, Art. VII, § 1. And see the Florida Supreme Court's construal of a provision requiring the state to provide high quality public school education. *Bush v. Holmes*, 919 So. 2d 392 (2006).

[194] The 1889 Enabling Act, which allowed North Dakota, South Dakota, Montana, and Washington to join the union as states, required that their constitutions provide for "systems of public schools . . . free of sectarian control." See Duncan, note 19 supra, at 513–14. Some scholars have regarded such acts as requiring Blaine amendments. See, e.g., Mark Edward DeForrest, "An Overview and Evaluation of State Blaine Amendments: Origins, Scope, and First Amendment Concerns," 26 *Harvard Journal of Law and Public Policy* 551, 574 (2003); Joseph P. Vitteriti, "Blaine's Wake: School Choice, the First Amendment, and State Constitutional Law," 21 *Harvard Journal of Law and Public Policy* 657, 673 (1998). Unless Congress somehow conveyed a requirement beyond the language it used, this view is mistaken, at least as to the aspect of Blaine amendments that is now controversial. A state could consistently have a public school system free of sectarian control and provide aid to religious schools. By its terms the 1889 Enabling Act did not require a bar on assistance to sectarian education.

[195] *Welsh v. United States*, 398 U.S. 333, 361 (concurring opinion) (1970).

education, one might reasonably think that those who adopted restraints on aid to sectarian education would have preferred no aid to nonprofit education rather than aid to all nonprofit education, the vast majority of which is sectarian. According to such an analysis, a state could retain its restriction on aid to sectarian education *and* meet federal free speech and free exercise requirements, by treating all private nonprofit education equally, that is, equally unfavorably.

The exact fate of programs challenged as violating the thirty-seven state Blaine amendments[196] will depend on the texts of the amendments,[197] on how state court judges choose to interpret them, and on whether any particular application of a state constitutional text is deemed to violate the federal Free Exercise Clause or Free Speech Clause. A court's view of federal constitutional requirements is likely to affect its interpretation of what a state constitution entails; among available options, it may prefer an interpretation that does not offend the federal restraints.

Perhaps the most important state voucher case up through 2005 is *Bush v. Holmes*, decided first by the intermediate appellate court and then by the Supreme Court in Florida.[198] The court was reviewing a statewide Opportunity Scholarship Program that provided state financial assistance to students who were attending failing public schools to go to private schools, sectarian or not. The intermediate court interpreted a provision of the Florida constitution that says that no public revenue shall be taken "directly or indirectly in aid of any . . . sectarian institution."[199] This language is broadly restrictive in covering all sectarian institutions, not just schools, and in its specification that aid cannot go either "directly or indirectly." Sitting en banc, the court divided eight to five, with one other judge concurring in part and dissenting in part. The majority read the constitutional language straightforwardly to forbid the kind of indirect aid to sectarian schools that was sustained by the U.S. Supreme Court in *Zelman*.[200] It distinguished various cases decided by the Florida Supreme Court as not significantly relevant because they did not involve the spending of public funds. These cases involved a church easement in a public park, revenue bonds, a property tax exemption, and church use of public school buildings.[201] The court did not resolve precisely what makes

---

[196] See Duncan, note 19 supra, at 493.

[197] By one classification, the state constitutional provisions may be divided into less restrictive, moderate, and most restrictive. DeForrest, note 194 supra, at 576–601.

[198] Bush v. Holmes, 767 So. 2d 668 (Dist. Ct. App., 1st Dist. Fla. 2004); aff'd, 919 So. 2d 392 (Fla. 2006).

[199] Florida Constitution, Art. I, § 3.

[200] 886 So.2d at 358–60.

[201] Id. at 354–56.

a school sectarian, but it took the record as showing that most schools receiving state funds teach the religious and sectarian values of the groups operating them, and it remarked on the religious mission of "forming youth in the Catholic faith" of schools operated under a diocese whose schools were enrolling 90 percent of those receiving vouchers in one county.[202] Without explaining in any detail what the relevant differences might be, the court declared that its holding did not reach all the social programs under which money might go to groups affiliated with religious organizations.[203] Finally, the court relied on the "play in the joints" language of *Locke v. Davey* to conclude that its interpretation of Florida's restriction did not violate the federal Free Exercise Clause.

The dissenters disagreed with the majority on many scores. Arguing that the state constitutional provision draws no distinction between schools and other social services and that the state supreme court cases have adopted a limiting construction of the provision,[204] the dissenters contended that the voucher program was constitutional because it was neutral and parents had a choice.[205] In their view, the Florida provision tracks the demands of the federal Establishment Clause; it does not exceed them.[206] The dissenters take *Locke v. Davey* as creating a very limited "play in the joints" regarding the training of ministers. When religious institutions are treated less favorably than nonreligious ones as broadly as under the majority's ruling, that violates the federal Free Exercise Clause.[207]

The Florida Supreme Court affirmed the lower court's decision, but it relied on a different state constitutional provision requiring the state to provide high-quality public schools.[208] By implication, this provision barred the transfer of funds from school districts to private schools. This ingenious and strained construction allowed the court to avoid deciding whether a bar that covered sectarian education but not other private education was permissible.

The range of latitude that state court interpretation may provide is well illustrated by earlier cases from Alaska and Wisconsin.[209] The Alaska constitution prescribes, "No money shall be paid from public funds for the direct

---

[202] Id. at 354.

[203] Id. at 362.

[204] Id. at 376–83. The dissenters were assuming that the aid to other social services is so well established, it is evidently permissible.

[205] Id. at 384–85.

[206] Id. at 385–88.

[207] Id. at 387–91.

[208] 919 So. 2d 392 (Fla. 2006).

[209] For broader surveys of state cases, see Duncan, note 19 supra, at 523–28; DeForrest, note 194 supra, at 577–601; Vitteriti, note 194 supra, at 680–99.

benefit of any religions or other private educational institution."[210] (Unlike typical Blaine amendments, the Alaska provision treats other private institutions like religious ones, and thus does not single out religious education for a special prohibition.) Reviewing a tuition grant program that awarded residents money to be spent on tuition at private colleges, the state supreme court, in 1979, concluded that the substantial aid provided private institutions was "direct" within the meaning of the constitution.[211]

In 1998, the Wisconsin Supreme Court sustained a voucher program, the Milwaukee Parental Choice Program, against claims that it violated the state constitution.[212] The constitutional language forbids public money going "for the benefit of religious societies, or religious or theological seminaries."[213] The court said that this language should be interpreted like the federal Establishment Clause, and that an indirect benefit to religious schools did not constitute a "primary effect" to advance religion within the meaning of the *Lemon* test.[214]

We have seen that in *Witters v. State Commission for the Blind*, the Washington Supreme Court declared that the state constitution did not permit Witters to receive money to study for the ministry,[215] thus destroying the practical benefit for him of his victory in the U.S. Supreme Court. The state constitution did not allow public money to be "appropriated for or applied to any religious . . . instruction."[216] The same court upheld a tuition grant program for college juniors and seniors that allowed the grants to be used at religious colleges, among others.[217] That program was acceptable because it, like the Promise Scholarships in *Locke v. Davey*, did not allow enrollment in programs that included religious instruction. Three dissenters complained that money was going to religious colleges that required all students to take courses in religion.[218]

Interpreting a provision like that of Washington,[219] and a separate provision forbidding appropriation of public money for a sectarian school,[220] the Arizona Supreme Court sustained a tax credit given to parents of children

---

[210] Alaska Constitution, Art. VII, § 1.
[211] *Sheldon Jackson College v. State*, 599 P.2d 127.
[212] *Jackson v. Benson*, 578 N.W.2d 602 (Wis. 1998).
[213] Wisconsin Constitution, Art. I, § 18.
[214] *Jackson v. Benson*, note 212 supra, at 620–21.
[215] *Witters*, note 182 supra.
[216] Washington Constitution, Art. I, § 11.
[217] 48 P.3d 274 (Sup. Ct. Wash. 2002).
[218] Id. at 296–300. DeForest, note 194 supra, at 590–601, reviews other Washington cases.
[219] Arizona Constitution, Art. II, § 12.
[220] Id., Art. IX, § 10.

in private schools.[221] The court reasoned that a tax credit did not involve spending public money.[222]

Just how far so-called Blaine amendments will restrict voucher programs that include religious schools depends partly on whether construals of state provisions that bar funding are deemed to violate the federal Free Exercise and Free Speech clauses. I have suggested that states should be able to bar substantial public funds from going to religious schools if they choose,[223] that the play in the joints between the federal religion clauses should be great enough to allow such policies. Other scholars disagree.[224] We know from their dissents in *Locke v. Davey* that Justices Scalia and Thomas think that such a singling out of religion for unfavorable treatment is unconstitutional. It remains to be seen how many other justices will agree when the exclusion of religious programs or institutions extends beyond preparation for the ministry. Chief Justice Rehnquist's opinion in *Davey* was drawn narrowly enough to include justices who would accept Blaine amendments more broadly and those who thought preparation for the ministry was special. If we look at the Court of 2007, we can guess that Justices Stevens, Souter, Ginsburg, and Breyer will probably vote to extend the holding of *Davey* more broadly. They, after all, thought the Cleveland voucher program violated the Establishment Clause; they are not likely to think a state's condemnation of such a program violates the Free Exercise Clause. That leaves Justices Kennedy and Alito and Chief Justice Roberts, only one of whom actually participated in *Davey*.

Apart from the federal constitutional issues, we must revert to the texts of the various state provisions and how state courts choose to interpret them. We have seen that five members of an intermediate appellate court (in dissent) were willing to treat Florida's provision as allowing voucher aid although the natural language, including "indirect" aid, was hardly propitious. State court judges inclined to approve forms of aid may find ways of interpreting their state constitutions to allow it. For many of the state provisions, it is easier to argue for the indirect aid that vouchers supply than for direct public grants to religious schools. Thus some state interpretations of Blaine amendments may reinforce the direction of the Supreme Court's recent Establishment Clause decisions, by accepting substantial indirect assistance based on parental choice, but not substantial direct aid.

---

[221] *Kotterman v. Killian*, 972 P.2d 606 (1999).

[222] Id. at 616–25.

[223] See Greenawalt, note 190 supra.

[224] See, e.g., Duncan, note 19 supra, at 533–93; DeForrest, note 194 supra, at 606–25.

CHAPTER 20

Religion Clause Skepticism

This chapter and the next four differ from their predecessors. Rather than concentrating on specific topics about free exercise and nonestablishment, they consider more general, theoretical questions. Here, we shall focus on three kinds of skeptical responses to how courts determine the coverage of the Free Exercise and Establishment clauses. My ambition in this chapter is a modest one, to suggest that certain skeptical views about religious clause adjudication are not convincing. Although I make various comments about positive approaches to decisions about free exercise and nonestablishment, I do not present a comprehensive theory that I claim is immune from all challenges. There is, in fact, no such theory. Rather, my method in these two volumes has been to develop a sensible, nuanced approach to the religion clauses, one that involves a number of debatable choices and does not reduce to any simple formula.

A skeptical position, in the sense I employ here, goes beyond an assertion that a case or set of cases is wrongly decided; it claims that the whole endeavor of judges deciding religion cases is undermined in some more sweeping fashion.[1]

I distinguish roughly among three forms of skepticism. The first proposes that the Supreme Court's actual performance is deeply flawed across the wide range of cases under the religion clauses, despite the possible availability of more sound alternatives to its approaches; the second, that some fundamental impediment precludes sound, coherent judicial development of religion clause law; the third, that any aspiration to achieve relations between governments and individuals in regard to religion that are legitimate and sound is itself inevitably fated to failure. Saying more about each variety of skepticism as we proceed, my analysis concentrates on three critical essays

---

[1] One might distinguish skepticism about how courts can decide constitutional cases from skepticism about what constitutional standards "really mean," or how other officials should regard them. Some of the forms of skepticism we will examine refer specially to judicial performance, but most also reach questions about what the religion clauses "really mean" and how officials other than judges should construe them.

about church-state issues: books by Frederick Gedicks[2] and Steven Smith[3] and a long article by Stanley Fish.[4] Among them, these authors suggest most of the various complaints I discuss, but my focus is on relevant possibilities,[5] rather than fixing exactly what a particular author believes.[6] Agreeing with certain of the skeptics' claims, I reject their far-reaching negative conclusions about what judges and citizens might reasonably aspire to achieve.

Skepticism About Judicial Performance

The most modest of the three kinds of skepticism concerns the Supreme Court's actual performance. Urging that not only are particular cases mistakenly decided, or even that the Supreme Court has systemically relied on mistaken criteria to decide cases about religion, a critic may mount one or more of the following challenges: (1) the results and opinions of the cases, taken together, are incoherent or inconsistent; (2) the Supreme Court's reasons to support its decisions fail to explain the results; (3) the bases of the decisions, even if faithfully followed, cannot yield adequately determinate results; (4) no coherent theory or principle can explain most of the Court's decisions.

I shall devote less attention to this narrow skepticism about actual judicial performance than the other two forms of skepticism because the volume on free exercise and this volume examine at length how the Supreme Court has addressed religion cases, and various chapters in the two books indicate wide-ranging challenges to the shape of the Court's religion jurisprudence. In this volume, for example, I have suggested that the *Lemon* test's inquiry into purpose, effect, and entanglement is more coherent and can yield more guidance than many scholars of the religion clauses believe.

A critique of judicial performance is the main subject of Gedicks's book, *The Rhetoric of Church and State*.[7] Differing from authors who urge their own preferred theories to replace the Supreme Court's misguided efforts, Gedicks claims that no fix is feasible for the mess we are in.

---

[2] Frederick Mark Gedicks, *The Rhetoric of Church and State: A Critical Analysis of Religion Clause Jurisprudence* (Durham, N.C.: Duke University Press, 1995).

[3] Steven D. Smith, *Foreordained Failure* (New York: Oxford University Press, 1995).

[4] Stanley Fish, "Mission Impossible: Settling the Just Bounds between Church and State," 97 *Columbia Law Review* 2255 (1997).

[5] Although some positions the authors advance are limited in scope to religion clause cases and church-state relations, many are obviously relevant for other areas of law and political and moral philosophy. Much of what I write in this chapter also has broader significance, but I do not pause to develop that.

[6] Thus, although I try not to misstate anyone's position, I do not attempt to settle what an author may mean if his essay is not clear or different passages appear to point in different directions.

[7] Gedicks, note 2 supra.

Professor Gedicks's main thesis is that the Supreme Court's dominant "discourse" has been "secular" and "individualist," but that many of its decisions can be adequately explained only by an older "religious communitarian" discourse that allows governments to exercise their power to encourage people to accept the foundational morality of conservative religion.[8] Gedicks concludes that were the Supreme Court to make the doctrinal changes that would render the law of the religion clauses "a coherent expression of secular individualism," that would be highly unpopular.[9] And, at this stage in the country's history, "[r]eligious communitarian discourse is not a viable alternative to secular individualism."[10] The Court cannot develop a compromise position because the two discourses are "mutually exclusive."[11]

According to Gedicks, decisions upholding "released time" programs and Sunday closing laws and allowing publicly sponsored religious symbols, notably crèches, cannot be adequately supported by the "secular" and "individualist" rationales that the justices typically employ. Rather, they can best be explained as an accommodation to religion, a moderate support of religion by the government. Insofar as the Court's rhetoric is explicitly accommodationist, as it was in *Zorach v. Clauson*[12] (upholding released time for public school students for religious instruction off the premises), it fits poorly with the secular, individualist approach of other cases. When the Court employs a secular, individualist rhetoric to disclaim the religious significance of Sunday closing laws and indisputably religious symbols, its stated justifications are unpersuasive and diverge from what might be plausible bases for decision.

Gedicks claims that the Court's major doctrinal tests are subject to manipulation. In particular, the notion of neutrality can be manipulated; and Gedicks thinks, as do many other critics, that the threefold test of *Lemon v. Kurtzman* is so vague, one must look beyond it to explain results. Not only are the "secular, individualist" and "religious, communitarian" approaches unable to explain the sweep of the Court's decisions; no alternative theory can accomplish the job. Thus, on any viable theory, many results do not fit.[13]

---

[8] Id. at 11.

[9] Id. at 21.

[10] Id. at 123.

[11] Id. Thus, we must await the passage of time to see what the replacement of secular individualism may be. Id. at 125. As Andrew Koppelman has pointed out to me, Gedicks's disregard of a religious view (dating back at least to Roger Williams) that supports separation of church and state as necessary for healthy religion omits one possible bridge or intermediary between the two positions he emphasizes.

[12] 343 U.S. 206 (1952).

[13] Gedicks also argues that in more circumscribed areas, results are incompatible with each other. (We need to remember, of course, as chapter 19, among others, emphasizes, that a shift of one or two votes can change outcomes. *Results* can be incompatible even though seven or eight justices vote for compatible results.) Prior to 2002, the Court largely denied financial aid to sectarian schools while allowing it to sectarian colleges, relying heavily on an assumption that the former, but not the latter,

Given *most* of what Gedicks says about the religion clause jurisprudence, we might hope that matters could be rectified, but his account moves from critique of what the Court has done to skepticism about what it could do. His skepticism is as sweeping as it is because he denies that the Court can choose a religious communitarianism approach or a secular, individualist approach and apply it consistently, or achieve a compromise between the two approaches. Gedicks also denies that we can now identify a tenable third theory. Thus, for the foreseeable future, but not necessarily forever, we will lack a coherent theory, consistently applied, for religion cases.

Gedicks is right that no single-featured, or simple, theory or principle could explain all the results that would make good sense under the religion clauses. As this volume and its predecessor show, multiple values are at stake, and they often conflict with one another. Judges and other officials are reduced to trade-offs among these values that are not comfortably captured by any clear formula. But if one is willing to accept an "approach" or "discourse" in which a court enumerates relevant values and affords some idea about how it makes trade-offs, then a viable theory may well be available.[14]

To draw from the discussion in chapter 7, I have suggested that classroom moments of silence to start the school day do give some weak encouragement to prayer. Thus, they should be held invalid under a rigorous secular, individualist theory that would bar any government encouragement of religion. But many people believe that significant life activities should begin with prayer, and a moment of silence does not impinge in any significant way on students who choose not to pray. Thus, moments of silence can be an appropriate way to accommodate the felt religious needs of a large group of citizens. Were the Supreme Court candidly to advance such an analysis, it would be engaged in the kind of explicit compromise between absolute nonencouragement of religion and government support of religion that I have in mind.

If such enumerations of conflicting values and resolutions of trade-offs between them represent a feasible approach, we should not accept Gedicks's discouraging prognosis about the Court's religion clause jurisprudence in the past and in the foreseeable future, unless we are persuaded by some deeper form of skepticism that reveals inherent limits on what the Court can accomplish in this domain.

---

are pervasively sectarian. According to Gedicks, modest examination reveals that the degree of sectarianism of many schools does not differ much from that of religious universities such as Notre Dame. Further, if the government is not allowed to provide financial aid to religious schools, when it finances the education of most young people, that hardly represents neutrality between religion and nonreligion, which the Court has announced as a guiding principle.

[14] I suspect that Gedicks does not think either that this approach counts as a discourse *or* that it would be a satisfactory way to proceed.

Intrinsic Barriers to Courts Developing Sound
Doctrines for the Religion Clauses?

A second form of skepticism about judicial interpretation of the religion clauses discerns some fundamental impediment to development of a body of religion clause law that is sound and coherent in the manner to which judicial opinions and scholarly writings aspire. A critic in this vein may assert that (1) standard legal sources and techniques of reason cannot provide persuasive answers to religion clause issues; (2) otherwise acceptable doctrinal formulations are inevitably broadly indeterminate in application, and central principles such as neutrality and fairness turn out to be empty or at least seriously misleading; (3) courts cannot formulate coherent principles of decision that yield acceptable results; (4) no principles of decision for religion cases can stand free of underlying assumptions about the nature of human beings and religious truth, or (5) some of these defects combine.

Although Gedicks's main basis for his skepticism rests on the sorry state to which actual judicial performance has brought us, rather than intrinsic impediments to sound adjudication, he does intimate another basis for skepticism that, if sound, would sharply reduce any expectations about what a future Supreme Court could achieve. He offers a sweeping observation about linguistic and legal indeterminacy: "Any use of language, no matter how specific and constrained, can always be made to appear sufficiently ambiguous to permit plausible arguments leading to mutually inconsistent interpretations. Constitutional interpretation exemplifies this thesis of linguistic indeterminacy, and no amount of doctrinal refinement is likely to reduce the indeterminacy of any constitutional test."[15]

Lifting this passage for scrutiny may be unfair to Gedicks's overall argument, but, taken literally, it overstates any defensible thesis about indeterminacy. Gedicks is certainly right that both every linguistic formulation leaves some situations on the edge of what the formulation covers and that context plays a significant role in how language is understood; but he also seems to deny that words of rules ever preclude plausible arguments for conflicting interpretations. That thesis is mistaken, as I try to show elsewhere.[16] Briefly, and by way of example, given our legal culture's present understanding of "ordinary income," I cannot reasonably argue that my university salary is other than ordinary income for tax purposes.

If statutory and administrative rules can constrain plausible arguments, so also can judicial doctrines. Some doctrinal tests are indeterminate across

---

[15] Id. at 45.
[16] Kent Greenawalt, *Law and Objectivity* (New York: Oxford University Press, 1990).

a broad range of cases; other tests are more determinate. In the area of church-state law, the rule of *Employment Division v. Smith* that claims of free exercise confer no special rights for those who violate ordinary laws does more to constrict plausible arguments for conflicting results than the compelling interest test that *Smith* displaced.[17]

We cannot generalize about whether doctrinal refinements increase or decrease the range of determinacy, understood as yielding fairly clear results for concrete circumstances (i.e., precluding plausible arguments for contrary results). But we definitely cannot assume that the degree of determinacy will remain exactly the same for church-state law regardless of the doctrinal tests that the Court employs. This, of course, is not to say that reductions in determinacy are always desirable. Greater range for judicial appraisal of multiple factors may be thought good in itself, and, as I have contended about the *Smith* case, the price of an increase in determinacy can be an unwise sacrifice of fundamental values.

Steven Smith has devoted a book to showing the impossibility of the court's developing adequate legal principles regarding religious freedom.[18] He presents a twofold argument that ordinary legal sources fail to give guidance and that no overarching theory of religious freedom is satisfactory in the right way. Along the way, he tackles the concept of neutrality, suggesting that it can never be a helpful guide to preferring one approach over another. Smith thinks that the aspiration to a principle or principles of religious liberty is doomed to failure, that we should settle for what he calls a prudential approach[19] and should ask ourselves whether the courts might profitably play less of a role than they do now in circumscribing church-state relations.

The more narrowly legal aspect of Smith's skepticism peculiarly concerns the federal religion clauses; in its exact form, it does not apply to most federal constitutional issues or to the religion clauses of states. As we have seen in chapter 2, Smith suggests that the enactors of the religion clauses aimed *only* to assign the subject of religion to the states.[20] The clauses had *nothing* to say about how the federal government conducted itself within federal

---

[17] *Employment Division v. Smith*, 494 U.S. 872 (1990). The case increases determinacy despite considerable indeterminacy about just when the rule of the case applies.

To take another example, the very simple test Justice Thomas proposes for the plurality in *Mitchell v. Helms*, 530 U.S. 793 (2000), would reduce indeterminacy about when public aid to religious schools and charities is permissible.

[18] Smith, note 3 supra.

[19] Although I am not sure whether Smith would regard my suggested approach as principled or prudential, probably it falls on the prudential side of the line, despite analyses of particular problems that carry heavier doses of principle than Smith thinks wise.

[20] Id. at 18.

domains. Chapter 2 challenges that thesis: the language of the First Amendment and the surrounding history indicate that both religion clauses restricted the federal government within federal domains. Even if Smith were correct about the original understanding of the religion clauses, by the time of the Fourteenth Amendment, when most states' constitutions had both free exercise and nonestablishment provisions, people viewed the federal religion clauses as embodying substantive rights; these could be carried forward against the states.

Two other legal sources are available for a modern Supreme Court deciding religion cases. State court decisions about the meaning of state constitutional provisions regarding religion can yield insight about how the federal clauses were understood when the Bill of Rights and Fourteenth Amendment were adopted. Another, more obvious, source is the Supreme Court's own precedents. Smith might respond to the last point that if the Court has made up principles of religious freedom without justifying them in existing legal sources, that can hardly produce a satisfactory claim to legitimacy. But in a system in which constitutional precedents, even when misguided, count for the future, this kind of self-generation of principles in the Court's past could underlie a justifiable reliance on them in the present.

I hope that my discussion of a range of free exercise and establishment issues has shown that various legal sources, understood in a suitably complex way, provide greater potential than Smith acknowledges for discerning adequate constitutional principles for religion cases. To take one example, the Court's own cases have settled the principle that the government may not teach particular religious doctrines as true. Were present legal standards and case decisions as confused and as incompatible with one another as Gedicks and Smith both suppose, existing legal sources might be a poor guide to clear, coherent, defensible principles. But part of my burden in these two volumes has been to suggest that the Court's decisions and doctrines, though many are subject to sharp criticism, are more coherent than many critics concede.

Can Recognizably Sound Relations Between Church and State Be Realized?

We now turn to a still deeper, third variety of skepticism, one that challenges any aspiration to realize sound relations between government and individuals and organizations as respects religion. A critic may argue (1) no principles of moral and political philosophy that stand free of particular views about religion, human nature, and the role of the state can resolve issues of church and state; (2) claims about neutrality or fairness are empty or misleading; whether a person sees one principle as more neutral or fair than another depends on initial premises that the person cannot expect all other citizens to accept; (3) broad principles are no real help in resolving church-state issues because, in this domain, the best way to proceed is by a series of ad hoc judgments, adjustments, and compromises; (4) principles are no real help in resolving these issues because, on analysis, principles are employed instrumentally in light of predetermined objectives; and reasoned analysis, as distinguished from rhetoric, gives us no basis to adopt one set of resolutions of church-state issues in preference to another.

My response to these claims is that although relevant principles of moral and political philosophy do depend partly on views about religion, human nature, and the state, claims about neutrality and fairness need not be empty or misleading; principles often are not employed instrumentally for predetermined objectives, and the question about the role of principles for resolving church-state issues needs to be addressed in light of particular topics, not resolved wholesale by some skeptical solvent.

In distinguishing this third form of skepticism from claims about other impediments to sound judicial doctrine, I am drawing a line between skepticism about standard legal sources and forms of reasoning that are particularly legal and skepticism about conclusions of political and moral theory.[21] If political and moral theory can provide a guide to desirable relations of church and state, judges will have one potential basis to reach good constitutional decisions.[22] If political and moral theory is unavailing, *either* because it provides no guidance that is helpful *or* because whatever guidance it might provide in general is not appropriately relied on by judges, then this avenue of sound judicial decision is foreclosed.

Smith suggests that one basis for establishing principles for the religion clauses could be a political theory about just and desirable relations between

[21] One *might* think legal sources provide answers to questions that are not determined by political philosophy, or that political philosophy provides answers that (for some reason) judges do not appropriately take into account.

[22] Within the domain of legal philosophy, there is an argument whether reliance on sound moral and political philosophy is an intrinsic aspect of ordinary legal reasoning or is analytically separable from initial determination of what the law requires. Very crudely, the latter theory is that in difficult cases the law runs out, and that judges "fill gaps," resolving issues in terms of what is a just or good result or rule of law. The former theory is that reliance on one's best judgment about principles of moral and political philosophy is an inextricable aspect of interpreting relevant legal materials. For my purposes, this jurisprudential dispute is not crucial. All that is crucial is that some skeptics are critical of our ability to arrive at sound principles of church-state relations, quite apart from what our present law provides, and that that skepticism bears on the possibility of sound judicial conclusions.

church and state, but he claims that no theory can be arrived at that does not itself depend on premises about human nature and true religion, that neutrality is an impossible ideal, and that we have no coherent secular theory of religious freedom. Much of Stanley Fish's critique is similarly directed, although his skepticism is more thoroughgoing than Smith's and obviously goes beyond church-state relations to other efforts to ground moral and po-litical principles.[23]

Recognizing that political theory may be one (but only one) source of sound constitutional decisions, we may begin with the assertion of Smith and Fish that no theory of religious freedom can stand on its own, somehow independent of assumptions about human nature, political organization, and the truth in matters of religion. Both writers discuss John Locke,[24] and we can understand their claims easily in respect to his theory.

In his 1689 Letter Concerning Toleration,[25] Locke argued that people can-not be coerced into believing things, that Christian belief can be religiously efficacious only if it arises voluntarily, that many subjects that have divided Christians are really matters of indifference, and that government should concern itself only with protecting life, liberty, health, and outward posses-sions, not with the "care of souls."[26] Accordingly, people should be free to believe what they choose, to express those beliefs, and to practice religion as they see fit.[27] Laws cannot be *aimed* against religious practices, such as animal sacrifice, but religious practices that happen to violate laws adopted for independent reasons can be stopped. Thus, if a law forbidding the killing of calves is adopted because "some extraordinary murrain" (pestilence or disease) has destroyed the stock of cattle, officials rightly enforce the law against members of a religious group that sacrifices animals.

As Fish and Smith point out, Locke's theory depends on highly debatable premises: about the effectiveness of coercion to affect belief;[28] about the need

---

[23] Fish, note 4 supra, at 2324–32. Although he concentrates on liberal theorists who focus on just political arrangements rather than legal doctrines, Fish's skepticism about just principles for church-state relations reaches the law of church and state, insofar as that law relies on theories of religious freedom.

[24] See Smith, note 3 supra, at 64–68; Fish, note 4 supra, at 2258–69.

[25] Reprinted in John Locke: *A Letter Concerning Toleration, in Focus* 12, John Horton and Susan Mendus, eds. (London: Routledge, 1991).

[26] However, Locke suggests that though the magistrate may not coerce about religion, he can persuade.

[27] There are certain apparent limits to freedom—atheists cannot be trusted to keep promises, and perhaps Roman Catholics need not be tolerated because they owe allegiance to a foreign power—but the general stance is liberty of religious exercise.

[28] Most obviously, if adults are effectively coerced not to express a particular belief, children are not likely to arrive at that belief.

for voluntary acceptance of religious truth; about the unimportance of precise nuances of doctrines and forms of worship; about the state's responsibility to protect natural rights rather than seeing that people lead good lives; and perhaps on an implicit assumption that external actions are not central for true religion.[29]

Fish and Smith argue that Locke's general approach to religious liberty depends on numerous background beliefs with which other people disagree, and that Locke can mount no convincing set of arguments to lead opponents to surrender their background beliefs in favor of his. What is true for Locke, say Fish and Smith, is true for any theory of religious freedom. Their outlook is well captured by Fish's response to a passage of Jeremy Waldron's, suggesting that insofar as Locke's position is developed on the basis of Christian premises, it is "insufficiently general to be philosophically interesting."[30] Fish answers that one cannot "devise principles of such generality that they speak to the intuitions of all persons however situated . . . and are therefore acceptable to all persons, even those whose interests might be disadvantaged by their realization in public life."[31]

Fish and Smith are right that no theory of religious freedom can satisfy everyone, regardless of background belief. A person who is convinced (1) that only true believers will be saved, with others condemned to everlasting fire, (2) that coercion can induce true, saving belief, and (3) that governments are well situated to identify religious truth, will be unlikely to endorse as ideal anything like American notions of free exercise and nonestablishment.[32] A person who believes that the most fruitful religious experience is within a unified national community in which almost everyone worships in

---

[29] Let me pause a moment over this last point. Fish claims that Locke's conclusion about the law protecting calves shows that he does not value highly forms of worship that might run up against prohibitions adopted for reasons not related to religion. "Not only does Locke . . . equate" the harms of economic disadvantage for the ordinary farmer and inability to engage in the religious ritual, he "denies the severity of the religious harm by identifying true and essential religious practice with the internal notions of mind and heart." Note 4 supra, at 2266–67. If Locke saw external actions as a vital aspect of religious practice, Fish implies that he would have considered whether an exemption should be given for practitioners of animal sacrifice. I am not so certain. Locke may have thought that the law could not tolerate a regime of exemptions or that no appropriate religious practices would ever raise this problem. Or, concentrating on laws directed against religious practices themselves, he may have conceded the example involving a general law that is not directed at religion without carefully considering whether an exemption would be preferable.

[30] Jeremy Waldron, "Locke: Toleration and the Rationality of Persecution," in Horton and Mendus, note 25 supra, at 98, 99, discussed in Fish, note 4 supra, at 2270–71.

[31] Fish, note 4 supra. at 2271.

[32] However, persons with these convictions, recognizing they are in a small minority, might accept religious liberty and nonestablishment as the best they can hope for in a society in which their religious opinions are not widely shared.

the same way will also find liberal notions of religious freedom uncongenial. The relevance of background beliefs is one obvious lesson of the revulsion extreme Islamic fundamentalists have to the values of our society.

These illustrations might be challenged as not involving people who believe in religious freedom, but someone might believe that *true* religious freedom lies in having the opportunity to adopt the correct religious understanding, which a government can identify and promote, even by coercive means. In any event, if we depart from such extreme examples, we may well find differences in background beliefs between those who think public schools should be able to engage students in voluntary prayer and those who believe the Supreme Court rightly declared such prayer unconstitutional, competing views that lie within the broad range of modern American society.

What follows from the impossibility of satisfying everyone, regardless of background belief? May a society nonetheless have a justified approach to religious liberty, based on legal and political tradition, or on a consensus, or on sound principles? Certainly, legal and political tradition, including constitutional decisions, rule out some possibilities as far as judges are concerned. In respect to the justice of arrangements, many societies may enjoy very broad agreement among people with widely different background beliefs about basic relations of church and state. If, let us say, 98 percent of the population happen to agree that their government should not suppress claims about religious truth, perhaps they may proceed accordingly, even if no one can present a convincing argument to persuade the other two percent.[33]

Fish and Smith, though for somewhat different reasons, would regard agreement among the 98 percent as failing to provide a just resolution for many issues. The agreement is irrelevant to Fish's fundamental point, which is that the 2 percent end up as losers for reasons that cannot be expected to persuade them.[34] In respect to American society (and other Western societies), Smith would say that any such broad agreement will be abstract, too

---

[33] A crucial question in this regard is whether people can agree not only on some basic approaches, such as not establishing a state church and not restricting advocacy of religious ideas, but can also agree that resolutions of debated issues can be reached without people repairing to their own background beliefs, relying instead on shared common grounds (i.e., shared by the 98 percent). I think that in the United States there is an overlapping consensus about many fundamental matters regarding government and religion, but I am skeptical that people can resolve debated issues without reference to their particular background beliefs. Thus, I am not persuaded by John Rawls's idea that an overlapping consensus will support decisions made only by reference to principles of liberal democracy. See Kent Greenawalt, *Private Consciences and Public Reasons* 106–20 (New York: Oxford University Press, 1995); Greenawalt, "Some Problems with Public Reason in John Rawls's Political Liberalism," 28 *Loyola Los Angeles Law Review* 1303–17 (1995). See also chapter 21, infra.

[34] However, even if the 2 percent want a theocratic state, they may well prefer modern religious freedom to a theocracy of a majority religion sharply opposed to their own. See note 32 supra.

circumscribed in substantive content, to provide a cogent theory of religious freedom for resolving constitutional cases. Judges facing actual cases, and left with a shared public understanding that is too thin to yield coherent principles, will need to refer to their own background beliefs or to other criteria, such as the original intent of those who adopted the Constitution or doctrines settled by judicial precedents.

Theories of religious freedom depend on background beliefs. What follows? Some of what Smith says and much of what Fish says follows does not. Smith correctly asserts that there is no univocal principle of religious freedom.[35] Smith is right that we cannot expect everyone to agree on the same full principle of religious freedom. People may disagree about how far religious freedom should be sacrificed for other values, such as security; about whether one kind of freedom (say in church government) matters more than another (wide choice for individual members); about the comparative importance of freedom for different individuals; and even about whether a particular measure, such as forced exposure of children to a range of religions, increases or decreases freedom to make decisions about religion.[36] We cannot expect citizens actually to adopt uniform theories about religious freedom or about all the particular practices in which governments might or might not engage.

Perhaps more important than what Smith says about a theory of religious freedom is what he and Fish say about neutrality and fairness. They are right in claiming that "neutrality," a key concept in the Supreme Court's religion jurisprudence, cannot be self-defining. One must determine neutrality of what kind for whom in respect to what aspects of which subjects; and the path one chooses will depend on background beliefs. Thus, one person might urge that neutrality as to religion would exclude creationism from public schools, if religious conviction is the underlying basis for belief in creationism. Another might object that neutrality requires that students be exposed to creationism if they are exposed to the competing theory of evolution, a theory that rejects

---

[35] Smith, note 3 supra, at 11. He subsequently suggests that a theory that depends on a preferred set of background beliefs may only be a theory of tolerance, not a true theory of religious freedom. Id. at 73. Smith's doubt about whether a theory relying on background beliefs could be a genuine theory of religious freedom is not well founded. Suppose a modern Baptist conception about church-state relations is that legally and politically Baptists should receive no advantage over any other religion or over nonreligious and antireligious positions, further that officials should not rely on any specifically Baptist conception when they make decisions, and further that in ordinary social life, people (including Baptists) should afford no advantage to Baptists. Although based on a Baptist conception, the theory calls on government and society not merely to tolerate other religions but to give them all the respect and liberties that Baptists enjoy.

[36] Even here, one might distinguish among *aspects* of a freedom to choose, some of which are undeniably promoted or set back.

the religious understandings of many citizens.[37] Of course, one might claim, as I have in chapter 8, that the legal status of teaching creationism is determined by the principle that government cannot teach religion; but if one sticks to neutrality in the abstract, one cannot say which approach is more neutral. Judgment on that score requires filling in a number of assumptions.[38] Fish says that "neutrality, like any other abstraction, has meaning only with some set of background conditions; as a rule or measure it will always reflect decisions and distinctions it cannot recognize because it unfolds and has applications within them."[39] Smith remarks that "the ideal of religious neutrality is simply not coherent."[40] On the closely related topic of fairness, Fish tells us that the hope of liberals—"to establish a form of political organization that is fair to all parties—cannot possibly be realized."[41]

Let us grant right away that no schema can be established that all citizens will actually perceive to be neutral or even that they *should* find acceptable, consonant with their own background beliefs. It neither follows that "neutrality" is empty nor that no schema is fairer or more importantly neutral than any other.

Once one specifies a subject matter, "neutrality" has some minimum content. Neutral treatment of individuals or groups implies not taking some characteristic into account; it involves some form of equal treatment.[42] The idea that a government should be "neutral as to religion" has a fair amount of descriptive content. Not every conceivable approach to how the state should treat religion is well cast as filling in the "empty" content of neutrality; some positions self-consciously reject neutrality in favor of other values. Thus, two people might agree that one government is more "neutral" toward religions than another, yet disagree sharply over which approach is preferable. Philosophically inclined members of the Taliban might well acknowledge that the American government is more neutral about religion than was

---

[37] Smith, note 3 supra, at 82–83, criticizes the assumption in *Epperson v. Arkansas*, 39 U.S, 97 (1968) (a decision holding invalid a law forbidding the teaching of evolution) that teaching of a secular theory about the creation of life is neutral.

[38] See chapter 9, supra. A more general approach to conceptions of neutrality for the religion clauses is developed by Douglas Laycock in "Formal, Substantive, and Disaggregated Neutrality toward Religion," 39 *DePaul Law Review* (1990). For comment on the proliferation of possible types of neutrality, see Andrew Koppelman, "The Fluidity of Neutrality," 66 *Review of Politics* 633 (2004).

[39] Fish, note 4 supra, at 2226. I am more hopeful than Fish that if people engage in close examination of their own ideas, they will be able to "recognize" crucial "decisions and distinctions."

[40] Smith, note 3 supra, at 94.

[41] Fish, note 4 supra, at 2256.

[42] On the subject of whether "equality" is empty, my views are in Kent Greenawalt, "How Empty Is the Idea of Equality?" 83 *Columbia Law Review* 1167 (1983); " 'Prescriptive Equality: Two Steps Forward," 110 *Harvard Law Review* 1265 (1997).

their regime, but they would reject neutrality as an ideal in favor of adherence to the true faith.[43] Similarly, defenders of special privileges for national Orthodox Christian churches in Eastern Europe might grant that they are choosing an approach that is less neutral than some alternatives. A defender of Justice Scalia's position that the government properly conveys messages in support of the idea of a single Deity, *should* recognize that this approach is less neutral toward religions that do not contain that idea, and to atheism and agnosticism, than is a principle that the government should refrain from supporting any religious idea.

Another point is still more important. *If* one set of background beliefs is best, then the ideal church-state relations for any particular society would be what the best set of beliefs recommends for a society constituted as is that society.[44] If that ideal were implemented, if a society had the best form of church-state relations possible for it, and that form achieved neutrality in some sense, then everyone in the society could be treated fairly, and the best form of neutrality would be realized, although not all citizens could be expected to recognize that.

Were liberal political philosophy, or some version of that philosophy, to require that everyone perceive that they are being treated fairly, or that they be presented with arguments that should convince them on that score (with the background beliefs they have), we should recognize that that aspiration of fairness *is* impossible to achieve. But if that particular aspiration of fairness is impossible to achieve, should we not also conclude that genuine fairness does not require that everyone recognize that they are fairly treated?[45] Norms of nondiscrimination on the basis of gender may be fair even if one cannot expect assent from people who believe God has ordained special roles for men and women and expects societies to enforce these roles. To shift to a more controversial issue, I understand that many people have background beliefs according to which various forms of affirmative action are unfair; I also understand that no argument may be available that should convince them to the contrary (given their background beliefs); yet I believe nonethe-

---

[43] Of course, they *could* say that the ideal is to treat every true religion neutrally and every false religion neutrally, but to treat these two categories differently.

[44] Some background beliefs may suggest that the government's treatment of religion should not depend on the particular culture and prevailing religious beliefs within a society; other background beliefs would treat those as relevant, either because the ideal government for a society would depend substantially on its culture and religion *or* because a tiny religious minority could not expect in fact to rule a country, even if its rule would otherwise be desirable. As the next chapter reflects, I think culture and religious beliefs may matter for what relations should be between government and religion.

[45] This is not the occasion to explore the history of liberal political philosophy, but that history is rich, and many liberal theorists have not subscribed to the version Fish attacks.

less that affirmative action is fair. If it is impossible for people to agree on what is fair, we should not make such an agreement a requisite for what actual fairness entails, as Fish may do.[46]

What I have said about neutrality and fairness, of course, hinges on the assumption that some sets of background beliefs really are better than others. These background beliefs might be what Rawls calls comprehensive views, but they could also include ideas of political philosophy that are detached from specific comprehensive views. Fish suggests powerful doubt that any set of background beliefs is really better, or identifiably better, than any other. In a revealing, if elusive, footnote he tells us, "I shall several times deny the availability of any mechanism or calculus for determining the truth about a matter. This does not mean that I believe there to be no such truth, only that I believe there to be no way of flushing it out so that everyone, however situated, will assent to it."[47]

According to the least sweeping version of this passage, relevant truth cannot be flushed out so that *everyone* will assent to it. That seems right, at least in regard to many claims of truth.[48] However, people certainly do not give up talking about truth if this condition cannot be met. Most of us are highly certain about some scientific and historical facts (such as the killing of millions of Jews and other civilians in Nazi death camps during World War II), although we acknowledge that not everyone can be expected to assent to those truths.[49] We lower our sights and accept that many strong arguments about what is true and not true may be valid although these arguments will not (and even hypothetically could not, under varied conditions) convince everyone, regardless of their background beliefs.

This brings us back to the possibility that one set of background beliefs might be better than any other *and* that human beings may have a degree of capacity to identify sound background beliefs. Someone might answer that political, moral, and religious positions are somehow different from science and history, not susceptible to discovery, not true or false, even according to a less ambitious criterion than an ability to win universal agreement. I once offered as a position that admits of a judgment of truth that is accessible to common human understanding: "unrestricted governance by sadists is unde-

---

[46] Possibly he means only that this particular liberal aspiration to fairness is impossible to attain.

[47] Fish, note 4 supra, at 2257 n. 4.

[48] There are many truths that everyone does take for granted: e.g., that 2 + 2 = 4, and that outdoors it is brighter when the sun shines than in the middle of the night.

[49] Perhaps my example is ill chosen. One might think that given a minimal level of intelligence and access to information, no one could reasonably deny the truth of the death camps. But what are we to say of someone who confidently asserts that Holocaust history is the product of conspiratorial control of media outlets?

sirable."[50] The idea was that if governing sadists used their own citizenry to satisfy their sadistic inclinations, that would be bad even for sadists (except those few in power). Fish calls this observation "as safe as it is unhelpful."[51] What I think it establishes in the realm of political and moral philosophy is that there is at least some room for reasoned consideration of what is right and wrong that rises above particular cultural presuppositions and personal beliefs. And if that is possible for "safe" conclusions, it *may* be possible for less safe ones, although I have not established here that it *is* possible.

What are we to make of Fish's own thesis in his essay? It contains a set of claims about what is impossible. These are about what is true philosophically, although Fish cannot expect everyone to assent,[52] given the background beliefs many people have that are fundamentally at odds with his claims.

Once we understand the crucial question as whether, and how far, human beings can grasp religious, moral, and political truth, we quickly see that the answer cannot be yanked out of a hat of conceptual deconstruction. It requires serious analysis of various assertions about truth or validity in these domains.

Where does all this leave us with respect to church-state relations? Fish suggests that principles are inevitably tools of rhetoric, not devices to discern truth.[53] In discussing the views of David Smolin, who acknowledges that he would like to convert others to his Christian views but wants to do so "fairly," Fish admires his candor but expresses puzzlement at his failure to take the final step of dispensing with illusory constraints of fairness.[54]

Fish's treatment of Smolin reveals strikingly how unpersuasive is his dismissal of ideas of fairness. Smolin may believe that God wants true religion

---

[50] Greenawalt, *Private Consciences*, note 33 supra, at 26–27.

[51] Note 4 supra, at 2262.

[52] I am offering here a variation of the common argument made against claims that truth is subjective or relative. One could respond that the claim "truth is subjective" is the one truth claim that is not subjective, and perhaps Fish can develop a similar rejoinder.

[53] See id. at 2319–22. He also suggests that recognition of this fact will not change our behavior. Id. at 2325–33. But if we are persuaded by Fish, we will understand that what really count are our objectives, the ones that we use principles to try to achieve. If we think other people are also persuaded to this understanding, might we not self-consciously calculate that contentions about principle will be less (or conceivably more) effective in achieving our objectives than we believed when we, and others, thought principles had intrinsic power? Even if we are the only ones persuaded by Fish, we might come to view principles in a different way, deciding to talk more directly about objectives, or perhaps being more self-consciously manipulative. There is no conceptual reason to suppose our behavior would be completely unaffected by the insight Fish gives us; whether we would be affected is an empirical question, and Fish offers no empirical basis for his skeptical answer about that.

[54] Id. at 2330–32, discussing David M. Smolin, "Regulating Religious and Cultural Conflict in a Postmodern America: A Response to Professor Perry," 76 *Iowa Law Review* 1067 (1991) (book review).

to flourish in an atmosphere of freedom. A government fully responsive to Smolin's concerns would support religion in ways that secular liberals reject; but Smolin does not want the law to silence dissenting religious voices. Smolin wants to spread his beliefs but to do so according to principles of government that he deems fair to opposing views. Fish regards this as peculiar, showing a kind of failure by Smolin to carry out his full convictions. But notions of fairness comprise part of Smolin's overall background beliefs.[55] Ideas of fairness are part of many people's background beliefs, and principles of fairness might well comprise part of the best set of beliefs, perhaps connecting to religious ideas about human freedom. We would be foolish to simply throw out ideas of fairness and neutrality or to suppose they are only rhetorical tools in people's pursuit of more concrete or substantive objectives. What is true for principles of fairness may well be true for other principles people perceive as restricting their pursuit of various objectives. Thus, Fish's arguments fail to sustain his extremely skeptical conclusions about developing sound principles of moral and political philosophy, principles that could in turn partially support the development of constitutional law.

The implications of my analysis for Smith's positions are more interesting and less clear. Smith might concede every one of my points and conclude that, given pervasive disagreements over background beliefs and our inability to go very far in resolving them, a judge will not find at hand any coherent theory of religious freedom to interpret the Constitution. Smith, in fact, does argue that secular approaches to religious freedom raise too many factual and normative problems to yield a coherent theory. And I agree with Smith that any theory that judges and other officials are directly to employ cannot be based on an assumption that any particular religious view is correct. Smith might even suppose that the very best set of background beliefs, if universally accepted, would not produce coherent principles of the sort he has in mind. This best view might recognize that the notion of religious freedom involves many values, that these frequently are in competition with one another and with other values such as security, that one can find no neat formula (except a formula too vague to be helpful) for resolving the conflicts, that desirable resolutions depend heavily on specific context, on the stage of

---

[55] Imagine a tennis player who is playing in the finals of a tournament she desperately wants to win. Her opponent hits a ball that the linesman calls out, but she sees clearly that the ball is in. According to her beliefs, winning is important but one should do so fairly, and she thinks (as many others do not) that taking advantage of an obviously mistaken call is unfair. She asks the umpire to have the point played over (or she loses the next point on purpose to counterbalance the unfair advantage). There is nothing irrational or peculiar in her behavior. Similarly, many people think their pursuit of political and moral objectives should be constrained by notions of fairness. If all this is so, why should we assume principles of fairness are merely manipulative to other objectives?

a country's historical development, and on its religious and cultural composition. Were this to be the reality, courts might better pursue what Smith calls a prudential approach than one aiming for large principles, and conceivably they would be wise to defer to legislatures more than they do now.

Thus, Smith's most important practical conclusions could be maintained in the face of doubts about many of his conceptual claims. But then the persuasiveness of his conclusions would depend on a careful examination of constitutional standards and legal traditions in the United States, as well as competing political theories about religious freedom. Those conclusions cannot depend on the more general conceptual skepticism that he and Fish offer to us.

In these two volumes, we have looked at the country's constitutional standards and legal traditions. Although I agree with Smith that many problems of church and state are too complex to be susceptible of resolution by simple formulas, I have assumed that the legal sources and theories that support them provide considerably more guidance than Smith believes, yielding such important principles as the legitimacy of accommodating to some claims of free exercise, the bar on discrimination among religions, and the rule against governments adopting positions about what religious propositions are true.

CHAPTER 21

Alternative Approaches

We have reviewed and rejected various skeptical approaches to the law of the religion clauses. In this chapter, we appraise three comprehensive positive approaches: (1) that governments should avoid influencing choices about religion insofar as possible; (2) that governments should be relatively free to engage in symbolic displays but should observe a strict institutional separation from religious organizations; and (3) that governments should respect "equal liberty," comprised of principles of nondiscrimination, nonpreferentialism, and broad liberty. Each of these approaches has been proposed by one or more prominent scholars of the religion clauses; each reflects to some degree past or recent developments in Establishment Clause jurisprudence and overlaps partially with my own suggestions. Identifying some strengths and weaknesses of these approaches can help us evaluate the efforts, sometimes stumbling, of the Supreme Court over the years. I shall reserve most of my discussion for the third approach, defended in a recent book by Christopher Eisgruber and Larry Sager,[1] because it seems to me the most appealing outright competitor to the more eclectic approach I have supported in these two volumes.

No Influence or Substantive Neutrality

One approach to the religion clauses is that the government should aim to influence choices about religion as little as possible. Judge Michael McConnell has written that the government should aim for a "hypothetical world in which individuals make decisions about religion on the basis of their own religious conscience, without the influence of government."[2] Douglas Laycock has urged that "religion is to be left as wholly to private choices as anything can be. It should proceed as unaffected by government as

---

[1] Christopher C. Eisgruber and Lawrence G. Sager, *Religious Freedom and the Constitution* (Cambridge: Harvard University Press, 2007).

[2] Michael W. McConnell, "Religious Freedom at a Crossroads," 59 *University of Chicago Law Review* 115, 169 (1992). In a different article, McConnell says that "the ultimate purposes of the Religion Clauses [are] to ensure that religion, as nearly as possible, is free from government control

possible."[3] The basic idea that government should not interfere with religious choices is attractive, and it could, depending on context, justify both particular exemptions and particular disabilities for religion. The exemptions would counter what would otherwise be negative effects on religious choices. The disabilities would counter what might amount to an undue preference for some religious perspectives or for religion in general. Thus, a state might be able to single out other educational fields, such as medicine or social work, for special financial aid, but it could not decide to fund education for the ministry alone. That would push people toward choices in favor of organized religion and would inevitably favor some forms of ministry over others. For similar reasons, a state could not teach particular religious doctrines as true in its schools, though it could teach the truth of particular views in virtually every other domain of human concern.

This approach treats religion as special. Depending on just how it is developed, it could correspond well or poorly with present or past Supreme Court doctrine, and with most of the recommendations of these two volumes. For example, in respect to free exercise, were an advocate of "no government influence" to place on legislatures the main burden of determining what exemptions to grant, his view could fit the Court's jurisprudence after *Employment Division v. Smith*. Were someone to follow McConnell and Laycock in regarding many exemptions as matters of constitutional right, to be enforced by courts, his approach would resonate much better with pre-*Smith* law and with the positions in my first volume.

Eisgruber and Sager criticize this approach as providing no genuine guidance—in light of all government does, "[W]hat could it mean for religion 'to proceed as unaffected by government as possible?' "[4]—and as seeming to condemn desirable government policies, such as discouraging racism, that will influence religious understanding. This "no guidance" critique is overstated, but it does require us to look carefully at alternatives that the general formulation of "no influence" tends to obscure.

Some years ago, a faculty colleague told me that parents should expose their children to the widest spectrum of views about religion so that the children could make their own choices what to believe. Parents would not regularly take their children to their own houses of worship if they have one; rather they would treat all perspectives equally. I regarded this view as

---

or influence, whether favorable or unfavorable." "The Problem of Singling Out Religion," 50 *DePaul Law Review* 1, 3 (2000).

[3] Douglas Laycock, "Formal, Substantive, and Disaggregated Neutrality toward Religion," 39 *DePaul Law Review* 993, 1002 (1990).

[4] Eisgruber and Sager, note 1 supra, at 28.

reflecting a naive conception about how children develop their senses of reality and their identities within families, and may now be stating it less sympathetically than would its proponent, but it was a proposal that parents should aim to have their children as unaffected by their own religious convictions and as free to make independent choices about religion as possible.

Of course, complete success in this endeavor would be unimaginable. Parents' behavior in many respects is related to their religious convictions, and even choices they may perceive as nonreligious, such as whether to treat sons and daughters equally, could affect the attractiveness of various religions for their children. Further, the very fact of growing up in a nuclear family with two parents could well influence a child's choice of religion. Nevertheless, the suggestion that parents should be neutral is starkly at odds with how most parents act, and we can see how acceptance of that view could affect parental behavior. In a roughly similar way, I think that the suggestion of "no influence" can *to a degree* guide government actions.

Clearly the basic notion cannot be attempting to create conditions of choice like those people would have were there no government whatsoever, any more than the guide to parents could be to attempt to create conditions like those that would exist were the children to have no parents.[5] Rather, the idea must be that basic functions of government would be taken for granted and that within that context the aspiration would be freedom of choice. Such an approach does require a degree of judgment about what is to be taken for granted, but that does not necessarily render the approach useless.

A general formulation about "no influence on religious choices" contains three ambiguities, at least two of which are important for our purposes. The first, least complicated, ambiguity concerns what count as religious choices—basic choices about what religion to practice or all choices motivated by religion. The answer of McConnell and Laycock, who discuss discrete religious acts as well as basic commitments, is that both are covered; people should be uninfluenced so far as possible in what religion to practice *and* they should be able, so far as possible, to carry out the actions their religious consciences call for.

The second ambiguity is whether the state should avoid aiming to influence or should aim to minimize influence. The political branches of a government could adopt as one realistic aspiration not to *aim* to influence people's religious views and actions. And fulfillment of this aspiration might be enforced by judicial review. Were only this required, a government, operating

---

[5] Laycock, note 3 supra, at 1005, writes that treating religion as if government did not exist would be a "conceivable mechanical standard" with nothing to recommend it other than "intellectual purity."

on objectives that had nothing to do with influencing religious choices, could proceed without worrying about unintended effects on those choices. Alternatively, governments could make an effort to avoid or counter unintended effects.[6] On this view, it should sometimes grant religious exemptions, such as allowing worshipers to use peyote, even though the restrictions for which the exemptions are needed were not adopted with an aim to affect religious choice. Laycock and McConnell definitely assume that governments should sometimes counter unintended effects.

But how does one decide whether in the circumstances, it is sufficient for a government not to aim to influence religious choice or whether it needs to counter unintended effects? Laycock draws an analogy to affirmative action and comments that Americans agree that whether equal opportunity and equal treatment, on the one hand, or equal impact and equal outcomes, on the other, are appropriate depends on context, but often disagree over which is the relevant measure.[7] He acknowledges that his position, which he labels "substantive neutrality," requires "judgments about the relative significance of various encouragements and discouragements to religion."[8] Thus, since few will join a religion for an occasional sip of wine, and sacramental use of wine is very important for some Jews and Christians, a ban on drinking alcohol should include an exemption.[9] On the other hand, the encouragement to religion of a religious exemption from paying taxes would be great; for that equal treatment in the sense of no exemption is the right approach.[10]

The third ambiguity involves the relation between the "no influence" standard and political and legal decisions about the relevance of the religion clauses. That standard could be the key to what decision to make; it could at least be a total account of religion clause values; it could be one side of a balance for final decision; it could be only one important consideration suggested by the religion clauses.

Were *avoiding aiming* to influence religious choices the only "no influence" requirement for the state, one could claim that this standard should always be followed. Decisions about laws and policies would be made on various grounds, but an aim to influence religion should never be among them. At least if one could divide concrete choices like whether to forbid

---

[6] I discuss this option in respect to public school education in *Does God Belong in Public Schools?* 32–33 (Princeton: Princeton University Press, 2005).

[7] Laycock, note 3 supra, at 997.

[8] Id. at 1004.

[9] Id. at 1003–4.

[10] Id. at 1016–17.

snake-handling, which is practiced in certain Protestant services, into permitted reduction of physical risk and not-permitted aims to discourage a religion, one could think that "no influence" (in this limited sense) provides a full answer to whether the state's involvement offends the religion clauses.

Once one suggests that the state should also avoid unintended influence, the matter becomes much more complicated. Consider a law against handling snakes. The state says it doesn't want to interfere with religious choices, it just wants to protect people from dying. But the law (if enforced) will influence both what actions people undertake on religious grounds and what religions they accept. The same is true about laws that require parents to take very ill children to doctors and authorize punishment of parents whose children die because they fail to seek medical help, even if religious conviction is what led the parents to oppose ordinary medical care. Laws supporting military endeavors and challenging racial discrimination also affect religious choices. (With respect to support of the military and laws against racial discrimination, it might be said that a failure to act would favor pacifist and segregationist religions; but, given the incentives people have not to handle poisonous snakes and to seek medical care for their children, religiously based privileges to handle snakes and to decline medical care would not provide much positive encouragement to join the religions they benefit.)

For these subjects, the caution about "no effect of influence" can only be one side of the balance, telling us whether or not something is being sacrificed in terms of the government's relation to religion, but not whether a law overall is justified. Once we understand that "no influence" in this sense is often only one side of a balance, we will see that it alone cannot resolve many controversies, which will turn on the strength of government justifications for restrictions that undeniably will have some influence on religious choices, and more of such influence than would removal of the restrictions.

Judge McConnell has at times proposed fairly libertarian answers to such issues—education ideally would be in private schools chosen by parents,[11] protecting adults from themselves would not be a legitimate basis to interfere with religiously motivated behavior,[12] economic considerations typically should not outweigh claims of religious freedom[13]—but the "no influence"

---

[11] Michael McConnell, "Education Disestablishment: Why Democratic Values Are Ill-Served by Democratic Control of Schooling," in Stephen Macedo and Yael Tamir, eds., *Moral and Political Education* 87–97 (New York: New York University Press, 2002). For an analogy with a market that is undistorted by government interference, see Michael W. McConnell and Richard A. Posner, "An Economic Approach to Issues of Religious Freedom," 56 *University of Chicago Law Review* 1 (1989).

[12] Michael McConnell, "Taking Religion Seriously," *First Things*, May 1990, 30, 34.

[13] See Michael W. McConnell, "Accommodation of Religion," 1995 *Supreme Court Review* 1, 37, 54.

standard alone does not get us there. And Laycock has a more expansive understanding of government's proper role.

Even if the "no influence" view does not purport to say when its injunction may be overridden by other considerations unrelated to religion, it might be thought to encapsulate relevant religion clause values. This, as Professor Laycock has recognized, would be a mistaken approach.[14] There are concerns about government interference with religion and religious intrusion on government that are not reducible to the desirability of avoiding influences on religious choice. The problem with churches making final decisions about liquor licenses in *Larkin v. Grendel's Den*,[15] discussed in chapter 13, was not mainly about government influencing religious choice. And government drawing political lines on religious criteria[16] is troubling even if it arguably promotes rather than retards religious choice. Finally, although protecting free religious choice is one reason that courts should refrain from deciding cases on the basis of determinations of religious doctrine, many other reasons, as chapter 16 of volume 1 reflects, also support the courts not entering into this particular thicket.

In summary, the notion of "no influence" is often an uncertain guide, partly because officials must decide whether in context they should aim for equal treatment or equal result. Further, the criterion often captures only one side of a delicate balance of relevant considerations. Even more significant, although it does loosely mark one significant factor, that standard, if taken alone or given overarching importance, slights other factors that should be relevant to interpretation of the religion clauses.

SYMBOLIC FEAST AND INSTITUTIONAL FAMINE

With a rich sense of early American history and with practical experience trying to help Iraq develop a constitution that would give special recognition to Islam, Noah Feldman has proposed a regime for the law of the Establishment Clause that is decidedly contrarian in light of recent developments.[17]

---

[14] See Laycock, note 3 supra, at 998–99. In an address at an April 2007 conference at the University of West Virginia School of Law, Laycock remarked, "I have never claimed or intended that substantive neutrality should be the single explanation or only value of the Religion Clauses." "Substantive Neutrality Revisited," to be published in the *West Virginia Law Review*.

[15] 459 U.S. 116 (1982).

[16] *Board of Education of Kiryas Joel Village School District v. Grumet*, 512 U.S. 687 (1994), discussed in chapter 13. I should note that McConnell thinks the case was wrongly decided.

[17] Noah Feldman, *Divided by God: America's Church-State Problem—and What We Should Do about It* 9, 211–12, 237–38 (New York: Farrar, Straus and Giroux, 2005).

As we have seen, the Court has moved toward acceptance of substantial public money flowing to religious institutions so long as the rationale for funding is a nonreligious secular benefit, such as education or hospital care, and the criteria for funding do not make reference to religion. Over the same period, the Court has been fairly strict in not allowing devotional practices in schools and government-sponsored displays of religious symbols. Feldman's proposal is to reverse these directions. He would permit more religious expressions by government, eliminating both a secular purpose and a no endorsement standard for Establishment Clause adjudication,[18] and he would require strict institutional separation. He defends his proposal as consonant with the history of the Establishment Clause and as a healthy compromise given the split in our society between what he calls legal secularists and values evangelicals.

According to Feldman, liberty of conscience was the dominating concept underlying the religion clauses,[19] and people at the time of the founding regarded coercion to contribute money to religious endeavors as a serious violation of conscience.[20] With their overriding concern about direct coercion, they were not disturbed by the government's employment of religious imagery.[21] And when public schools developed in the early nineteenth century, no one supposed that "nonsectarian" devotional practices and teaching, which were effectively nonsectarian Protestant, offended some principle of nonestablishment.[22] Like many historical studies of the religion clauses, Feldman's is comparatively neglectful of attitudes about establishment when the Fourteenth Amendment was adopted, but his treatment of views about public schools and of opposition to financing parochial schools strongly suggest that he does not think attitudes about public expressions and financial aid had changed.

The more serious question about his historical argument is about the nature of the funding that members of the founding generation believed would violate conscience. The funding to which they objected was aid given to support clergy and other religious purposes. Contrary to what Justice

---

[18] Id. at 237.

[19] Id. at 12, 20, 27–33, 36, 42.

[20] Feldman writes at one point of the protection of religious dissenters "against compelled taxation to support teachings with which they disagreed." Id. at 12. But some influential objections were broader than that, covering all compelled taxation to support religion. Id. at 32–37.

[21] Id. at 50–51.

[22] Id. at 61–65. The issue, of course, was not whether practices within state schools, such as Bible reading from the King James Bible and teaching history from a Protestant perspective, violated the federal Establishment Clause, which at that stage did not apply against the states, but whether these practices were or were not regarded as establishments of religion.

Thomas claimed in the modern case requiring that the University of Virginia fund the printing of an evangelical Christian publication,[23] it is hardly apparent from James Madison's "Memorial and Remonstrance" that his concern was restricted to taxation and funding that was directed specifically to religious endeavors, but that is what he and others were thinking about. One cannot be entirely confident what principles the early opponents of funding of religion would have embraced had they conceived a welfare state in which religious and nonreligious private organizations provide vital social services that might or might not be assisted by government.

In any event, Feldman's primary reliance is on the desirability of his approach in the modern context. Here we may distinguish an argument about political prudence from one about intrinsic wisdom. The country is now sharply split, he writes, between legal secularists and values evangelicals. The former do not, like early secularists, condemn the practice of religion itself,[24] but they do want to remove it from legal and political life.[25] The values evangelicals do not, in the main, want public reliance on any particular religion, but they do want recognition of traditional values resting on a broad religious base.[26] Both groups are seeking a kind of unity in the religious diversity of modern society.[27] Allowing greater expressions of religion would grant the values evangelicals what they most care about, that is, cultural recognition of religion, whereas strong institutional separation would give the legal secularists what they most care about, avoiding a mixture of public authorities and religious groups.[28] Feldman presents his proposal as one that members of both competing factions might recognize as a reasonable compromise and that might find its way into constitutional doctrine.[29]

Feldman also provides reasons for his proposal that one can divorce from the present competition between legal secularists and values evangelicals. Funding of religious endeavors is particularly likely to be divisive in society.[30] Moderate religious expressions by government, such as crèches in public squares, are relatively innocuous.[31] While Feldman was growing up as a Jew,

---

[23] *Rosenberger v. Rector and Visitors of the University of Virginia*, 515 U.S. 819, 853–56 (1995) (concurring opinion). Feldman comments that the Court in *Rosenberger* adopted "a position almost squarely the opposite of the original intent of the Establishment Clause." Feldman, note 17 supra, at 209.

[24] Id. at 113–30.

[25] Id. at 8.

[26] Id. at 6–7, 13–14, 188, 194, 229.

[27] Id. at 8, 220.

[28] Id. at 218.

[29] Id. at 236–37.

[30] Id. at 15, 238.

[31] Id. at 16–17.

reminders that he lived in a Christian country did not make him feel uncomfortable;[32] and the manner in which members of minority religions regard expressions of a majority faith is a question of their "interpretive choice" whether to feel excluded.[33]

Perhaps the omission is defensible in a broad proposal, as compared with a comprehensive plan, but Feldman is not very precise about *which* religious expressions by government he would allow and which he would not allow.[34] And, focusing mainly on the circumstance of religious schools, he sounds as if he would not permit any substantial funding of such schools, yet in a highly compressed treatment he draws back from such a conclusion about most religiously sponsored charities, suggesting rather that aid should not go to those "that rely on faith to accomplish their goals."[35] Certainly some religious schools could argue that they do not rely on faith to accomplish their goals. A stricter restriction on aid to schools than to other charities could be defended on the bases that the government needs to be especially careful about instruction in religion and that public schools have been such a unifying force in American life, but Feldman does not explain why he would be stricter about aid to schools than other social services (if, indeed, that is his position).

Another blemish in Feldman's account is his suggestion that a voucher plan must (to be constitutional) allow the teaching of unacceptable values, such as racism and sexism. Although Feldman is right that certain judgments about good and bad values would be constitutionally foreclosed as criteria for a state providing aid, he exaggerates the scope of those limits. Courts will permit states to set some conditions on the ideas that schools receiving aid may teach, as Ohio required that schools receiving voucher money in Cleveland not teach hatred of groups classified by race, religion, or ethnic background.[36]

A more substantial flaw in Feldman's analysis is his conjoining of the question of public religious expressions *by government* with the question whether citizens and officials may employ religious premises in deciding what laws to enact.[37] He overstates considerably when he generalizes that "legal secularists *are* in favor of a constitutional rule under which the fact that support-

---

[32] Id. at 16–17.

[33] Id.

[34] He would "allow public religion where it is inclusive, not exclusive, and . . . religious displays and prayers so long as they accommodate and honor religious diversity." Id. at 15–16.

[35] Id. at 247.

[36] See chapter 19, supra.

[37] Feldman, note 17 supra, at 221–23.

ers have invoked religion in support of a bill in Congress could arguably disqualify that bill from taking effect as law."[38] Feldman correctly says that *some* secularists have suggested that laws based dominantly on religious premises violate the Establishment Clause, and he points to the religious purpose strand of the *Lemon* test. What he does not say is that few scholars think that a moderate degree of expressed support in religious premises would make a law invalid, that the courts have been very hesitant to find religious purposes when nonreligious purposes are also present, *and* that the Supreme Court has never declared that every kind of reliance on religious premises constitutes a religious purpose. I shall argue in chapters 23 and 24 that it makes a great deal of difference just *how* a religious conviction figures in the approval of a law or policy—that some crucial reliances on religious convictions should not be regarded as religious purposes, even were there no doubt that every legislator voting for a law relied on just the same religious conviction in just the same way. In any event, because religious premises mix with nonreligious ones for individuals, and among individuals, who support proposed laws, the likelihood is slim that courts will declare laws unconstitutional simply because people relied on religious convictions and expressed that reliance in public discourse.

To be clear, insofar as Feldman takes the view that reliance on religious convictions in political discourse and judgments is often appropriate, he and I are in agreement.[39] We are also in agreement that the Establishment Clause has little direct relevance to this problem, especially if one is thinking about judicial enforcement. What is confusing is his linking of this problem with expressions that are by the government as such. This linkage confuses in two respects. First, it obscures the possibility that someone who thinks constitutional law should lie close to the secularist end of the spectrum as far as *government expressions* about religion are concerned may also embrace a view that is far from that end of the spectrum in respect to reliance of religious presuppositions by individual officials and citizens in support of proposed laws. (That has been my position for two decades.)[40]

The second confusion lies in the apparent benefits to each side of the compromise Feldman proposes. He would "give" to the values evangelicals constitutional acceptance of government expressions about religion and political use of religious premises, in return for concessions to the legal secularists

---

[38] Id. at 223.

[39] However, it does not appear that he accepts the modest limits I propose in chapters 23 and 24 as a matter of political philosophy and constitutional law.

[40] *Religious Convictions and Political Choice* (New York: Oxford University Press, 1988); *Private Consciences and Public Reasons* (New York: Oxford University Press, 1995).

about funding and institutional separation. He does not explain that although the present law about government expressions is not to the liking of the values evangelicals, they already have most of what they want (as far as constitutional law is concerned) about political use of religious convictions. In the main, when officials ask themselves whether to rely upon and express religious premises,[41] the primary reasons why they might hesitate involve their prudential judgments that a broader nonreligious appeal will be more effective and their sense of what the political culture deems appropriate,[42] *not* a worry that a court might declare a resulting law invalid. Especially if the kinds of religious expressions in which governments could engage would be limited ones that are fairly bland or widely inclusive (or bland *and* inclusive), the "values evangelicals" would be getting less out of the compromise than the legal secularists, who would be assured of serious limits on funding that the Supreme Court has now approved.

Once one cuts through these various complications, the wisdom of Feldman's proposal comes down to these three inquiries. Is there a plausible constitutional theory to support greater permissiveness about religious expressions by government and greater restrictions on funding, even when the aid is supplied according to neutral criteria? Does funding promise to be as divisive as Feldman suggests, and would the denial of funding to religious endeavors constitute an unjust discrimination? Are government expressions of religious views as unthreatening as Feldman asserts?

Feldman has provided us a plausible constitutional theory that is more than an ad hoc compromise between competing armies in a culture war. My views about funding have been developed in chapters 18 and 19. The dangers of discord are real in respect to schools. For other social services (which lack an analogue to pervasive public schools), religious organizations have a substantial claim of justice to be treated like other private organizations, and the very significant funding they have already received has not been highly divisive. At least if these organizations do not discriminate in admissions or employment and secular alternatives are available, I would not expect their continued funding to be *very* divisive in the future. As chapters 5 and 6 reflect, I do not think religious expressions by government are as innocuous as Feldman claims, a point we can examine more fully as we turn to the approach of Professors Eisgruber and Sager.

---

[41] Of course, *if* the expressed purpose of a law is to declare the government's support of a religious point of view, that purpose would now be invalid, but could be all right under Feldman's proposal.

[42] I believe the main constraint is on *expressed* relevance.

Equal Liberty

Christopher Eisgruber and Larry Sager have proposed a basic approach to both religion clauses that they call "equal liberty." They reject (in principle at least) the "dominant view" that religion should be privileged in some respects and disfavored in others, and they also reject as misleading and unhelpful the dominant metaphor of "separation of church and state."[43] The two guiding principles of their own approach are that (1) "no members of our political community ought to be devalued on account of the spiritual foundations of their important commitments and projects" and (2) "all members . . . ought to enjoy rights of free speech, personal autonomy, associative freedom and private property that, while neither uniquely relevant to religion nor defined in terms of religion, will allow a broad range of religious beliefs and practices to flourish."[44] A crucial aspect of this approach is that the only basis to give religion special benefits or disabilities is a concern about inequality and discrimination.[45] "Equal Liberty . . . denies that religion is a constitutional anomaly, a category of human experience that demands special benefits and/or necessitates special restrictions."[46]

Eisgruber and Sager, with important qualifications, thus approve the Court's movement toward neutrality, in the sense of same treatment, as the key to both the free exercise and establishment clauses. As the Supreme Court held in *Employment Division v. Smith*,[47] people with religious reasons to engage in forbidden behavior should, in general, have no special right to violate laws of general application. For Eisgruber and Sager, statutes that provide such rights across a wide range of subjects, such as the Religious Freedom Restoration Act (RFRA)[48] and the Religious Land Use and Institutionalized Persons Act (RLUIPA)[49] are seriously misguided, and indeed unconstitutional in whole or part.[50] When it comes to financial aid, religious groups may benefit if they fall within a larger category of beneficiaries, and the legislature is not aiming particularly to assist some religious endeavors

---

[43] Eisgruber and Sager, note 1 supra, at 5–7.

[44] Id. at 4.

[45] Id. at 6–9.

[46] Id. at 6.

[47] 494 U.S. 872 (1990).

[48] 42 U.S.C. § 2000 bb–2000 bb-4 (2004).

[49] 42 U.S.C. § 2000 cc to § 2000 cc-5 (2004).

[50] RFRA was fundamentally flawed in relieving religious organizations and individuals of burdens others must share. Eisgruber and Sager, note 1 supra, at 264. In its application to local zoning regulations, RLUIPA suffers from the same defect, id. at 270–71, but its treatment of prisoners' claims may be justified as a response to discrimination by prison officials. Id. at 269–70.

over others or religious endeavors over nonreligious ones.[51] Thus, the Supreme Court correctly accepted the principle that a state may grant substantial vouchers for parochial schools among others.[52] And, whatever may be true of education for the ministry in isolation, *Locke v. Davey*'s approval of a state's refusal to fund religious education for the ministry should not be extended to broader constraints on aid to sectarian education.[53] The upshot would be that, across most of their coverage, state Blaine amendments should be treated as unconstitutional because they discriminate against religion.

In their fundamental concern that members of the political community not be devalued on account of their spiritual foundations and commitments, Eisgruber and Sager echo Justice O'Connor's rationale for her endorsement test. They would be even less accepting than she was of government sponsorship of religious messages.[54] In respect both to religious expressions by government and financial aid to religious entities, Eisgruber and Sager sharply oppose Noah Feldman's positions. We need to consider who is right, or whether each view captures a part of the truth.

Answering critics who have claimed that their view is inconsistent with the historical understanding of the religion clauses, Eisgruber and Sager note that members of the founding generation often spoke of equal liberty, and that "one purpose of the religion clauses was to protect religions from discrimination."[55] "Equal Liberty's historical pedigree is pretty good," they say.[56] Well, that depends on what one demands of a pedigree. The concern about discrimination against minority religions was one aspect of free exercise clauses in state constitutions and of the federal religion clauses, but that concern accompanied a view that religion was distinctive and specially important, just what Eisgruber and Sager deny. To take just two illustrations, some state constitutions, as well as Madison's "Memorial and Remonstrance," spoke of a duty to worship God,[57] and although the idea of excusing religious pacifists from military duty had a wide appeal, few would have extended this privilege to

---

[51] Id. at 200–16.

[52] *Zelman v. Simmons-Harris*, 536 U.S. 639 (2002).

[53] Eisgruber and Sager, note 1 supra, at 227–32, consider and reject the appropriateness in this context of judicial reliance on a prophylactic theory that would allow a state to forbid all aid to religious education in order to prevent favoritism toward religion.

[54] Id. at 134, 147–52.

[55] Id. at 72.

[56] Id. at 71.

[57] See volume 1 at 17–18, for the provisions in Maryland and Massachusetts. The "Memorial and Remonstrance Against Religious Assessment" § 1 (1785) is reprinted in Philip Kurland and Ralph Lerner, eds., 5 *The Founders' Constitution* 82 (Chicago: University of Chicago Press, 1987).

those whose pacifism was based on nonreligious conscience.[58] The best that can be said for the historical pedigree of equal liberty is that it draws upon one historical strand and disregards others. Such an exercise can be justified only if the result well fits modern conditions and understandings, and that indeed is the authors' overarching claim of support.

Eisgruber and Sager claim that the dominant view, which recommends special privileges and special disabilities for religion, is "a surefire recipe for inconsistency."[59] The "distinction between removing a burden and conferring a benefit is vanishingly thin, if not purely semantic."[60] When it comes to privileges, courts must engage in an impossible balancing act. Equal liberty, by contrast, provides a clear principle of decision, they assert. They recognize that some cases will be difficult and arguable under equal liberty, but they are far from retracting their claims that it is far more coherent and manageable than the "no hindrance—no aid" approach.[61]

In regard to coherence and difficulty of application, volume 1 of this study gives a sense of the "no hindrance" approach, and this volume explores the parameters of "no aid." Here, I inquire whether Eisgruber and Sager manage to stick faithfully to their own claimed principles and whether these principles actually permit of more straightforward judgments than does the dominant view. The difficulties I identify cast strong doubt on whether equal liberty is a viable approach, as *the* one controlling standard for adjudication under the religion clauses.

We begin by considering equal liberty, as it relates to religious expressions by government in the form of public displays and teaching in public schools. Crucial questions are whether public displays of majority religious ideas and traditions do convey a "message of exclusion" and make members of minorities feel devalued, and whether Eisgruber and Sager can explain either why religion is distinctive in respect to government expression or what other subjects besides religion should receive similar treatment. Without doubt, Eisgruber and Sager's position follows more closely from the modern drift toward concern for disadvantaged members of society than does Feldman's.

Feldman is on to an important truth when he claims that non-Christians may have very different attitudes toward Christian symbolism. Some, like himself, raised as an Orthodox Jew, may not find the occasional Christian

---

[58] McConnell, "Singling Out Religion," note 2 supra, at 12–13, remarks that some members of Congress considering the possibility of a constitutional exemption did not want it to go to "those who are of no religion." Probably, many people did not even imagine nonreligious pacifists.

[59] Eisgruber and Sager, note 1 supra, at 29.

[60] Id. at 25.

[61] Id. at 87, 93, 119.

symbol troubling. And, one might add that when non-Christians choose to immigrate to a country they know is dominantly Christian, they can hardly be surprised or dismayed about occasional public recognition of that fact. Similarly, immigrants who believe in no God or many gods should not be surprised at symbolic recognitions of a single God. But different people react differently. Some, perhaps less self-confident and secure than Feldman, will feel more like outsiders when they come across government expressions of monotheism and Christianity. When Feldman asserts that it is an "interpretive choice" to feel excluded, he makes this attitude more voluntary and more trivial than it is for many people, *especially children*. Eisgruber and Sager call the strategy of telling offended parties to react differently "naive. People do feel excluded when the government endorses one or another religion, whether they ought to or not."[62] And the idea that people shouldn't complain if they get what they expect can carry us only so far. If I were working for an oil company and were sent to Saudi Arabia, I would not expect to be permitted to engage in Christian worship in public, but I would certainly feel like an outsider and I would not think that country's approach to religious liberty was warranted. For as long as our country has existed, immigrants of diverse backgrounds could expect, as a matter of fact, government discrimination according to race, gender, religion, ethnic origin, and sexual preference; but constitutional principles about equality should more nearly reflect the country's aspirations than its actual performance. If a dominant principle now is that people should be considered as equal regardless of race, gender, ethnic origin, sexual preference, or religious identity, the sense of exclusion engendered by government expressions of religious ideas is a cause for serious concern, whatever the intensity of the feelings of most outsiders.

The problem of whether and why religion might receive special treatment in regard to public displays and teaching in public school is raised by Eisgruber and Sager's claim that only concerns about discrimination can justify such treatment. The authors accept the prevailing view that public schools cannot teach that religious ideas such as the divinity of Jesus or the existence of benign omnipotent God are true or false. They square this position with their general thesis by pointing to characteristic features of religion and by suggesting other ideas that government would be barred from teaching, but this twofold strategy is less than fully successful.

In their chapter on religious symbols, Eisgruber and Sager suggest that Americans are highly sensitive to their religious identities and that "public

---

[62] Id. at 156.

endorsements of religion carry a special charge or valence."[63] At the end of their chapter on public schools, they write that equal liberty does not deny that a ground may exist for treating religion specially; that ground is "the vulnerability of conscience to discrimination, mistreatment, and neglect."[64] In the same chapter they indicate other ideas that public schools could not teach, such as partisan political ideas. They generalize that "the Constitution protects children from the imposition of orthodoxy, religious or not,"[65] and comment that "the restrictions on religion in the schools are not so unusual as people sometimes suppose."[66]

Although the Supreme Court has not decided such a case, were a public school teacher to continually express explicitly racist or sexist ideas, that would be one form of a violation of equal protection, and were such a teacher to praise the Republican Party as evidently superior to the Democrats, that might violate a principle of freedom of speech, or of our Constitution taken more broadly in its assurance of free voting. But public schools are at liberty to take positions on many controversial issues: that the war in Iraq is justified or not justified, that our early settlers, by and large, did or did not treat Native Americans fairly, that immigrants do or do not contribute to the overall vitality of the country, that all citizens should or should not have to learn to speak English, that abstinence from sex is or is not desirable for teenagers, that the national government should or should not be making much more strenuous efforts to protect the environment. In brief, various organs of government, including public school teachers, may express positions on many issues in ways that would involve forbidden viewpoint discrimination were the same government to include and exclude private speakers from a public forum based on their positions about such issues.[67]

How are we to square such freedom in respect to other subjects with much more severe restrictions on teaching religious ideas? One possibility is to deny that teaching on any of these other subjects is as likely to involve discrimination or to touch the core identities of students and their families. That strikes me as implausible, and Eisgruber and Sager do not quite claim otherwise. A second possibility is that our notions of what public schools may teach as true and sound need to be much more restrictive than they are now. Perhaps across a wide range of topics, schools should have to teach *about* various understandings as they may teach *about* religious understand-

[63] Id. at 126.
[64] Id. at 197.
[65] Id. at 171.
[66] Id. at 197.
[67] See McConnell, "Singling Out Religion," note 2 supra, at 9–10.

ings, eschewing claims of truth in favor of one position or its competitors. Such "neutral" teaching may often be desirable pedagogically, but it would be a huge stride to conclude that it is constitutionally required across the range of topics that touch important personal identities and generate serious concerns about discrimination. Eisgruber and Sager do not explicitly assert that position. Finally, one might conclude that the public schools should be able to do more teaching about religious truth, bringing their ability in respect to that subject in line with what they may say on other sensitive topics. Eisgruber and Sager do not hint at recommending such a shift concerning religion.

Exactly how they mean to deal with this issue is less important than the more straightforward inference one might draw from the widely assumed asymmetry about a government's role in regard to controversial topics. It is this: There are important reasons for the government to stay out of the realm of religious truth apart from a concern about discrimination. Notably, governments are woefully incompetent judges of truth in religion.[68] This provides strong evidence that equal liberty should not be, cannot be, *all* there is to the religion clauses.

The Eisgruber-Sager approach to financial aid is, in its main outlines, much simpler, but it presents its own difficulties. The basic notion is that organizations need not be denied assistance, available to others, because they are religious. Thus, if aid is being given to schools, hospitals, and addiction programs, religious groups may be treated like other private organizations. (The authors do indicate that a state *may* choose to prefer secular private schools, in the sense of schools not based on a religious or other exclusionary perspective, over schools that privilege religious, ideological, cultural, or ethnic subgroups.)[69]

The perplexities with what Eisgruber and Sager say about financial aid concern the following issues: (1) Could aid go to religious groups explicitly for religious purposes? (2) Must the state supply a secular alternative if only religious groups come forward to qualify for aid? (3) What constraints, if any, may states place on the content of religious teaching in private schools receiving public funds?

The authors focus on aid for secular purposes such as education or health care. Suppose, instead, legislatures made a judgment that people's involvement in religious groups is particularly good for their personal and civic lives. Grants are made directly to religious groups to be used as parts of

---

[68] Id. at 23–24.
[69] Eisgruber and Sager, note 1 supra, at 219.

their general budgets. If the *only* worry about financial aid to religion is discrimination, and the program is well designed to treat all religious groups equally, say by keying assistance to the number of active members, it would create no substantial problem about discrimination among religions.[70] In answer to a concern about discrimination against nonreligious views, the grants might extend to atheist and agnostic groups and other groups dedicated to carrying out philosophies of life.[71] According to the present understanding of the Establishment Clause (and according to McConnell, Laycock, and Feldman), such aid definitely would not be all right, but its status would seem much more doubtful under equal liberty.[72] That Eisgruber and Sager omit treatment of this possibility may be further evidence that concerns about discrimination are not all that underlies the religion clauses. At the least, the omission obscures a potential objection to the proposal that equal liberty stands alone.

Eisgruber and Sager suggest that the *Zelman* Court case rightly focused on whether the voucher plan treated "parents and children with different religious convictions equally,"[73] and, drawing on the work of Ira Lupu and Robert Tuttle, which we looked at in chapters 18 and 19, they conclude that the issue of an adequate secular alternative was more difficult than the Supreme Court justices admitted.[74] Recall that the general public schools in Cleveland were of poor quality; parents had an adequate secular alternative only if the nonreligious private schools receiving vouchers, plus special programs in the public schools, sufficed. Eisgruber and Sager comment that for equal liberty, "the existence of a genuine secular alternative is the heart of the issue."[75] Why they insist that there must be an adequate secular alternative is not entirely clear.

Let us assume that, as in the Ohio program, the government's criteria for assistance to private endeavors are nonpreferential, that none of the religious groups receiving assistance use discriminatory standards of admission to their programs, that the state is also providing the service in question, however poorly. Initially, the state has a drug rehabilitation program that is not

[70] Of course any formula will have the effect of helping some religions more than others, and there could be divisive struggles over the right formula, but this would not mean that every formula raises a serious concern about discrimination.

[71] Insofar as the concern about discrimination were connected back to the founding generation, most of its members were not worried about unfavorable treatment for atheists and agnostics.

[72] One *might* think any favoritism of organized efforts to promote philosophies of life would discriminate against more informal, individual, approaches.

[73] Note 1 supra, at 213.

[74] Id. at 215.

[75] Id.

very effective and has too many participants; it offers to provide a substantial subsidy for any private group that proposes an effective program. Only two groups make proposals: one is evangelical Christian and the other is nondenominational liberal Christian. Both groups propose to make religion a significant feature of their programs. The state funds both programs, which are quickly recognized to be much more effective than the state-run one. Drug users who choose not to participate in a religious program are no worse off than they would have been if those programs had not received funding. They can still use the (now somewhat less overburdened) state program. *If* the only concern is about likely discrimination in regard to religion, why is it not enough that the state has offered, and continues to offer, the funds according to nonpreferential criteria?[76] Of course, one might say, as Eisgruber and Sager do, that the absence of an adequate secular program will push some people toward religious programs whose ideas they do not embrace;[77] but that is not directly a matter of discrimination.[78] Eisgruber and Sager may believe that an adequate secular alternative is needed as a prophylactic against covert attempts to promote religion, or in order to avoid the impression that the state is promoting religion,[79] but they do not develop either of those points against possible challenges.[80] Chapters 18 and 19 of this book agree with Lupu and Tuttle that the reasons for an adequate secular alternative are not wholly encompassed by concerns about discrimination, that, in particular, the government should not (even inadvertently and without apparent sponsorship) push people toward religious programs with its financial resources.

My final point in regard to financial aid involves what restrictions states may put on what funded schools teach. As we have seen, Feldman suggests that if states fund religious schools, they must do so on an even basis and cannot refuse, according to the law as it has developed, to aid a school because it teaches "racism, or anti-Americanism, or sexism."[81] Recall that Ohio's voucher plan did preclude teaching of hostility based on religion or

---

[76] If the only group coming forward had a particular view about how recovering addicts should live—say telephoning a counselor and a family member every day after they leave the program—a program with an alternative approach would not be required.

[77] Id. at 207–8.

[78] If the government had never directly provided a certain kind of service and decided it should license private providers, the fact that in some areas they only private providers were religious would not make the government licensing discriminatory. Why should funding be different?

[79] See id. at 214–16.

[80] One assumes they would allow tax exemptions for churches even if these allow churches to put on attractive social events that would be more expensive when hosted by organizations paying taxes.

[81] Feldman, note 17 supra, at 246.

race. Although a state cannot discriminate on the basis of the theological propositions of a religion, it may be able to require that a school's ethical and political teachings be not wholly at odds with premises of our liberal democracy. Eisgruber and Sager do not discuss this issue. If the only concern is about discrimination, the inquiry should be whether state restrictions on forms of teaching constitute some kind of discrimination. Presumably more would need to be shown than that some religious groups actually do want to engage in the kind of teaching that is disallowed. As the discussion in chapter 19 suggests, however, the concern here goes beyond discrimination to whether the government impedes religious liberty by setting up standards for instruction about morals and politics with which religious groups wanting state assistance for their schools must comply.

The most significant test for equal liberty may be the question of accommodations to religious exercise, the subject of chapters 16 and 17 of this book and of much of volume 1. Eisgruber and Sager squarely acknowledge that their approach will introduce difficult questions of evaluation; nevertheless, by initially comparing their own basic principle against the complexities of the dominant alternative and then introducing nuances one by one, mainly as responses to actual and possible critiques, they tend to overstate the comparative clarity in application of their approach. Their neglect of some of the hardest cases for their perspective has a similar effect.

Readers of volume 1, and of chapter 17 of this volume, will remember that the crucial issues about accommodation to religion come in three forms. (1) When, if ever, is accommodation constitutionally required? (2) When may legislatures choose to afford an accommodation for people with religious reasons not to comply with laws? (3) When, if an accommodation is supplied for religious exercise, must it also be extended to other reasons not to comply, and what other reasons must enjoy similar treatment? Thus, to take the central facts of *Employment Division v. Smith*,[82] must governments with laws prohibiting the use of peyote permit its use by members of a church for whom that is the central aspect of their worship service? The Supreme Court answered no. May states choose to create an exemption for members of a single church or for all religious groups engaging in similar use? The Court's opinion in *Smith* clearly indicated that was constitutionally permissible. However, if a legislative accommodation imposes too severely on others, as did Connecticut's requirement that employers give all their employees a day off on their Sabbath, the law becomes an impermissible establishment

---

[82] Note 47 supra.

of religion.[83] If religious use is protected directly by the Free Exercise Clause (contrary to what the *Smith* Court held) or may be protected by legislative action (in accord with what the *Smith* Court said), what other uses, if any, must also be protected? Such a privilege cannot go to one church and be denied to otherwise similar churches.[84] Whether it could be denied to nonreligious groups that claim that peyote provides unique insights about life and to people who use peyote to reduce acute physical pain is less certain, but the Supreme Court's opinions suggest that such distinctions are generally permissible. The most important of these opinions are in *Wisconsin v. Yoder*, which indicted that the constitutional privilege of the Amish to withdraw children from school did not extend to the Henry Thoreaus of the world,[85] and in cases upholding the favored treatment of religious exercise by federal statutes that cover religious claims in general and do not cover analogous nonreligious ones.[86]

A fourth question about accommodation that lies in the background of many cases and has occasionally been addressed by the Supreme Court is what distinguishes an accommodation to religious exercise (permitted if it does not impose too severely on others) from forbidden promotion or advancement of religion. In *Texas Monthly, Inc. v. Bullock*, for example, the Court held that special tax privileges for religious periodicals were unjustified favoritism, not accommodation.[87]

As we saw in volume 1, the determination in *Employment Division v. Smith* to deny constitutional protection to strong claims of religious exercise was highly controversial, and I believe it was misguided. Without endorsing the Court's ruling, Eisgruber and Sager strongly disagree with its scholarly critics. They claim that the only basis to exempt exercises of religion from generally valid laws is the concern about discrimination, a matter of "protection." They believe that scholars and others who suppose that religion should enjoy a special "privilege" are mistaken.[88] For this reason, they also

---

[83] *Estate of Thornton v. Caldor, Inc.*, 472 U.S. 703 (1985).

[84] I pass over here what should count as otherwise similar churches, whether for example, long continuity and a high retention of members could play a role as it seemed to do in *Wisconsin v. Yoder*, 406 U.S. 205 (1972).

[85] Id. at 215–16.

[86] *Cutter v. Wilkinson*, 544 U.S. 709 (2005); *Gonzales v. O Centro Espirita Beneficente União do Vegetal*, 546 U.S. 418 (2006).

[87] 489 U.S. 1 (1989).

[88] The distinction between "privilege" and "protection" is central in an earlier article of theirs, "The Vulnerability of Conscience: The Constitutional Basis for Protecting Religious Conduct," 61 *University of Chicago Law Review* 1245 (1994).

sharply oppose legislative choices to create privileges for religious exercise in general, in the manner that RFRA, RLUIPA, and state RFRAs do.

In addition to this "in principle" objection, they argue that the privilege-balancing approach is defective, because it requires courts to assess the degree of impairment of religious exercise and the strength of state interests, and to decide whether the interests are strong enough to warrant the impairments. If courts really required that a state, in order to restrict religiously motivated behavior, must have an interest that is compelling, much too much religious action would be protected; instead, constitutional standards should, for example, allow local governments to be able to subject churches to ordinary zoning regulations without having to show that the government's need to do so is genuinely compelling.[89] To be plausible, a balancing formula would have to contain a proportionality standard "sensitive to the nature and weight of the burden imposed on religious exercise as well as to the gravity of the state's interest," but as one moves away from a strict compelling interest test, "a good deal of indeterminacy and ad hockery enters the picture."[90] Without a clear standard, judges and other officials will be likely to favor familiar claims of conscience over nonfamiliar ones. "These problems are symptoms of a deeper pathology: the balancing approach lacks a coherent normative foundation."[91]

Eisgruber and Sager offer an alternative that they believe is cleaner conceptually and more manageable judicially. Everything comes down to the concern about discrimination. Claims of religious exercise should enjoy constitutional protection if there is a serious risk that the claimants are suffering discrimination. Legislatures properly grant exemptions when they are attempting to treat particular religious claims fairly in relation to other behavior that society allows, thus avoiding discrimination. The central focus on discrimination both for problems typically classed as "aid" and for those conceived as "accommodation" would obviate the need for courts to use any independent criteria of when purported accommodation slides into impermissible promotion. Fair treatment and avoidance of discrimination would also determine what analogous behavior must be treated like religiously motivated behavior that is exempted from ordinary standards of behavior.

Whatever attractive simplicity this approach may appear to possess largely unravels when one comes to many practical applications. To their credit, Eisgruber and Sager try hard to face up to the difficult issues, but they do

---

[89] Eisgruber and Sager, note 1 supra, at 84–85.

[90] Id. at 85.

[91] Id.

not always succeed. They do recognize that many religious activities are elective, not compulsory, and that some practices may be seen as substitutable for others.[92] But they tend to neglect these insights when they undertake most of their comparisons between religious and nonreligious reasons for action.

Although in fundamental sympathy with Justice Scalia's attack on the balancing approach of pre-*Smith* free-exercise jurisprudence, Eisgruber and Sager adopt a position toward free exercise claims that is both more generous and more complex than *Smith*'s. In their view, for the legal prohibition of peyote to be validly applied against use in worship, it is not enough that the law has a rational purpose, and is general and applies neutrally—the *Smith* standard. If the law would not have been adopted except for the insensitivity of legislators to their religious use of peyote, members of the Native American Church could succeed on a claim that they have been victims of a kind of discrimination. A crucial comparison would be with Prohibition laws that provide exemptions for use of wine for sacramental purposes.[93] The authors recognize that peyote might reasonably be regarded as more dangerous than alcohol,[94] and its use thereby more damaging to state interests, but the Constitution, they say, requires accommodation if the "failure to accommodate bespeaks a failure of equal regard."[95] It sounds as if the peyote users should succeed if they can show that the quantum of danger from the two substances is about equal, and at one point Eisgruber and Sager write that in the absence of a nonreligious analogue, a court can ask "the counterfactual question of whether more mainstream concerns would have been treated more favorably."[96]

What are we to make, from the standpoint of equal liberty, of failures to forbid firmly entrenched practices that are dangerous? Let us consider first a prohibition without exemption. All use of cocaine is forbidden. Someone says the law reflects a discrimination against cocaine users as compared with cigarette smokers, because tobacco cigarettes are more dangerous than cocaine. The comparison here is far from perfect, because the kinds of dangers are not comparable, but suppose the implicit answer from the legislators is, "Yes, we agree cigarettes are worse. If we were starting from scratch, we would outlaw all smoking of cigarettes, but largely ignorant of their danger, people in vast numbers started smoking. Even aware of the danger, many

---

[92] Id. at 103.

[93] Id. at 92.

[94] Id. at 92–93. More precisely, alcohol might be less dangerous in the amounts typically used for sacramental purposes.

[95] Id. at 93.

[96] Id. at 106.

find it extremely hard to stop. Were we to prohibit all cigarette smoking, we would make a large proportion of our citizens into criminals, and enforcement problems like those during Prohibition would be severe. We are hoping that few enough people now use cocaine that a prohibition may work reasonably effectively." This is a plausible rationale for treating cocaine less favorably than cigarettes that does not depend on the comparative damage the two products will cause.

Legislators could adopt a similar rationale about exemptions. "We can't succeed with any prohibition that bars use of a substance called for by religions to which a high proportion of our citizens belong. If we could stamp out use of alcohol in worship services we would; we believe we can succeed in respect to peyote." What matters here is not the factual plausibility of this argument, but its structure. Some acts are legally accepted just because they have been a part of our culture for so long. A legislature might reasonably choose to forbid other acts that are no more dangerous, because they think the prohibition may work.

Does this show a failure of equal regard to those who want to engage in the forbidden acts? If it is a failure, it is one that may be justified in terms of effective laws. There is room in what Eisgruber and Sager say to conclude that it would not count as a failure of equal regard. The legislators are not treating those who worship with peyote worse because they are unfamiliar or unsympathetic with their commitments, or because they devalue those "commitments on the basis of their spiritual foundations."[97]

Whether or not one characterizes the legislative approach here as failing in equal regard, the crucial point of the example is that the relevant constitutional comparison cannot be exclusively in terms of relative danger. One possible way for judges to be faithful to an equal liberty approach would be for them to estimate whether legislators did honestly adopt the rationale I have suggested (or would have if it had occurred to them). At one point Eisgruber and Sager say, "The question is whether a government that was alert and sympathetic in principle to the religiously inspired interests of a particular minority faith could have fashioned the contested disparity in accommodation."[98] That sounds less like a guess about what actual legislators did think about why to treat the uncommon religious practice less favorably than the common practice—a difficult surmise at best—than an inquiry about what reasonably legislators might have thought. But how can we know why reasonable legislators might have decided against an exemption

[97] Id. at 89.
[98] Id. at 102.

if comparative danger is not the exclusive key? The obvious way would be to assess the infringement on religious exercise against the strength of the government's reasons to prohibit. That might tell us whether reasonable legislators would have been unsympathetic to the minority or prudently trying to stamp out a harmful practice despite sympathy for its practitioners. The problem is that this inquiry looks like very much like the very kind of balancing against which Eisgruber and Sager rail, a "benighted quest" that "Equal Liberty forsakes."[99]

Responding to a possible challenge that there are no secular analogues to religiously based noncompliance with dress codes, the authors agree that secular moral commitments will rarely be comparable to such religious duties, but equal liberty "will call for exemptions in most dress code cases" because the "burdens imposed are especially likely to result from neglect."[100] If legislatures or administrators fairly considered the imposition on members of minority religions of a uniform dress code, they would have made exceptions. Here we run into two significant complexities to which Eisgruber and Sager do not advert. It might be that the reason *not* to make a particular exception—say for girls in school wearing head scarves—is that usage reflects and conveys (for some people) a prescribed role for women that does not correspond to liberal democratic values.[101] Does that constitute a failure of equal regard? The more powerful is the state's reason not grant an exemption, the less its unwillingness to do so will appear to deny equal regard; but this inquiry throws us back into the uncomfortable assessment of religious need against state interest.

The second complexity in regard to dress codes is that one needs to consider forms of dress that are motivated but not required by one's religion. Chapter 13 of volume 1 discusses a case in which a prisoner wished to wear a cross despite a ban on all wearing of jewelry; he did not think he had to wear a cross but he regarded doing so as a valuable expression of his faith.[102] For many individuals who wish to deviate from prescribed dress, their chosen form of dress may reflect a strong sense of their personal identity (e.g., a "nonconformist") and perhaps a political position (as long hair once upon a time reflected a rejection of militarism). When one reflects on these comparisons, it becomes difficult to say which failures to exempt religious claims to

---

[99] Id. at 87.

[100] Id. at 97.

[101] That the "meaning" of head scarves is highly variable and controversial is eloquently illustrated in Orhan Pamuk's novel *Snow* (New York: Alfred A. Knopf, 2004).

[102] *Sasnett v. Sullivan*, 908 F.Supp. 1429 (W.D. Wis. 1995), aff'd, 91 F.3d 1018 (7th Cir. 1996), vacated and remanded, 521 U.S. 1114 (1997).

be excepted from dress codes should be matters of constitutional right. One might conclude that only forms of dress that are required by one's religion should receive constitutional protection, but that would require courts to discern whether individuals regarded standards of dress, such as wearing a beard, as mandatory or merely desirable.

The crucial comparison between religious and nonreligious reasons for exemptions comes up again when the issue is whether a nonreligious claim should receive the same treatment as a religious one. Here the question is not whether some religious claims are neglected; rather it is whether a claim is favored because it is religious, something the principle of equal regard does not allow.[103] Eisgruber and Sager propose that nonreligious moral claims must be treated similarly to religious claims.[104] Thus, a nonreligious pacifist who objects to military service or work on armaments must be treated like a religious pacifist. However, according to Sager and Eisgruber's views, a hypothetical Mother Sherbert, unwilling to work on Saturday because she cannot find adequate child care, would not be entitled to unemployment compensation that went to the actual Ms. Sherbert, a Seventh-day Adventist who could not work on Saturday as a matter of religious conscience.[105] The hypothetical Mother Sherbert does not experience an inflexible obligation, and the state may permissibly judge that parents who try hard enough will find adequate child care.[106]

I have argued in the free exercise volume that one crucial consideration when courts decide whether analogous nonreligious claims should receive an exemption that tracks the one given to religious claims is whether a standard for decision is administrable. For dress code issues, it is usually simpler to trace a religious basis than to weigh the connection to personal identity and political conviction of an individual who wishes to violate the rules. Eisgruber and Sager appear to give little weight to this factor, although they do say that what counts is a rule maker's "stance or attitude,"[107] and, as I have already suggested, legislators who vary their responses to different

---

[103] Although their theory would seem to authorize it, Eisgruber and Sager do not discuss this possible argument for a nonreligious claim for exemption: "There is a certain kind of religious claim that has not received a legislative exemption because of neglect. It must, therefore, receive an exemption (though no such claim has actually been made) and our analogous claim must be treated similarly."

[104] Note 1 supra, at 112–18.

[105] Id. at 116–17 (comparing their hypothetical woman with the successful claimant in *Sherbert v. Verner*, 374 U.S. 398 (1963)).

[106] Id. at 116–17. The authors say that a state's determination "does not . . . involve any imposition on religious freedom," id. at 117, but the issue here is whether the state is unfairly favoring religious freedom over moral freedom.

[107] Id. at 300 n. 37.

claims based on whether an exemption is reasonably workable might be thought to be acting with equal regard.

In respect to a person's unwillingness to work on Saturday, Eisgruber and Sager might profitably have considered the following variations. Religious Mother Sherbert (R) and secular Mother Sherbert (S) deem it fundamentally important that they spend weekend days with their children.[108] Eisgruber and Sager write in footnotes comparing religious and secular moral requirements that some persons recognize "their duties to care for their children" are "binding moral strictures,"[109] and that "caring for loved ones" may well be a secular interest and commitment that is "serious" and "identity-defining."[110] For many of these people, paying someone else to do the job will not meet their perceived obligation. Eisgruber and Sager apparently acknowledge that Mother Sherbert (S) might feel an obligation not to work on Saturday that compares in strength and sense of compulsion with that of the Seventh-day Adventist.[111]

In thinking about which of the women should have a constitutional right to be given unemployment compensation despite an unwillingness to meet the general requirement of being available to work on Saturday, we begin with the assumption that the Seventh-day Adventist has such a right. For Eisgruber and Sager, that is not because she wins according to a balancing approach, it is because, when one considers the status of workers unwilling to work on Sunday and the force of other reasons legislators recognize as excusing one from ordinary requirements, the failure to treat the Seventh-day Adventist similarly shows a neglect of her (minority) religious commitments.

Once those situated like the real Ms. Sherbert are to be protected, who else must be similarly protected? We can assume with Eisgruber and Sager that no one has a secular compulsion not to work on a particular day just because it is that day of the week. That leaves us with Mother Sherbert (R) and Mother Sherbert (S). Both feel very strongly that they should spend

---

[108] Against a possible critique that parents will not have this attitude, I can report that in the years after my wife Sanja died, I thought the most important responsibility in my life was being available for my children during evenings and at various school events. I was immensely fortunate to have a job that allowed this.

[109] Id. at 301 n. 39.

[110] Id. at 300 n. 37.

[111] Their treatment of two women who feel a responsibility to operate soup kitchens is relevant here. One is "impelled by her religious commitments," the other by "what she describes as 'a deep and abiding concern for those who suffer the misfortunes of poverty and hunger . . .' " Id. at 54. The authors suppose that the two women could have a similar sincerity and depth of commitment, and should be treated similarly, that their treatment should not turn on "the moral or religious content" of their commitments. Id. at 55.

Saturday with their children, R because of a religious sense of family obligations, S because of a nonreligious sense that nothing in life is more important
than personally caring for one's children. I shall oversimplify a bit and assume that neither thinks she has an absolute obligation to avoid work on
Saturday—each would rather work than suffer the alternatives of dying,
languishing in prison, or having her children taken away.[112] If the law exempted everyone who felt any responsibility to be with children on Saturday,
it would punch a huge hole in any requirement that a person must be willing
to work on Saturday to receive unemployment compensation.[113] One might
draw the line by requiring an absolute commitment (thus excluding both
Mother Sherberts) by requiring a religious commitment (thus excluding S),
by requiring a commitment of a certain strength (thus treating R and S according to the degree of compulsion they feel to be with their children),
or by requiring a commitment that is both religious and very strong (thus
excluding S and leaving R's fate to the degree of compulsion she feels).

Eisgruber and Sager write as if the one line that should not be drawn is
between similar religious and nonreligious commitments,[114] but that line
might be supported by the argument that sincerity and depth of commitment
to be with children are much easier to measure when there is a claimed
religious base. And how should a court view the claim of Mother Sherbert
(R) if legislators and administrators fail to grant her the exemption that goes
to the actual Ms. Sherbert? One might think that requiring that the perceived
obligation be unconditional and absolute (like Ms. Sherbert's) does not show
disrespect for those whose idea of what they can do is more flexible; but an
equally plausible perspective would be that officials who do not grant R
similar treatment are yielding to claims strongly supported by organized religious groups and are not treating with equal regard more nuanced, individual views of religious responsibilities.

It is not my aim to figure out just how equal liberty solves the puzzle of
the various Sherberts, but two things are apparent. When Eisgruber and
Sager write that from the secular perspective that courts must adopt, "the

---

[112] The basic idea here is that the aim of being with one's children would be defeated by certain
consequences. One *might* conceivably believe one should never voluntarily give up Saturdays with
children—as one might believe one should never kill an innocent person—no matter what, but it
would be a peculiar attitude.

[113] I am not defending the view that a legislature should impose such a requirement.

[114] In an earlier article, they suggested that the state could second-guess the "reasonability" of
secular claims for special treatment. Eisgruber and Sager, note 88 supra, at 1293. Responding to a
critique of Michael McConnell, "Singling Out Religion," note 2 supra, at 33–35, that uses the example of religious and nonreligious strikebreakers, Eisgruber and Sager abandon that position, grounded
as it was on different epistemic bases for religious and nonreligious judgments.

comparative force of religious and secular convictions is a matter for empirical, scientific inquiry"[115] and that "implausibly fine-grained comparisons are
not required by equal regard,"[116] they fail to acknowledge how little may
separate *some applications* of equal liberty from the balancing they reject.

To judge the comparative complexity of equal liberty and the dominant
approach, one would need to survey the wide range of potential applications.
I have certainly not proved that, overall, equal liberty is as at least as complex
in application as its rival. The two volumes of this study give a fair sense of
how complex it is to apply the dominant approach in various contexts. What
I have shown in this chapter is sufficient to suggest that simplicity of application should not be the main reason to select equal liberty. And various of
the nuances we have explored go some distance to show that equal liberty
disregards or downplays various considerations that should be relevant to
decision under the religion clauses. My overall conclusion is that the factors
Eisgruber and Sager make critical are indeed relevant for understanding the
scope of both clauses, and they have enriched the ways in which judges and
others may discern forms of explicit and implicit discrimination; but it would
be a mistake for their proposal to replace all other criteria for what government actions violate the Free Exercise and Establishment clauses.

[115] Note 1 supra, at 103.
[116] Id. at 300 n. 37.

CHAPTER 22

Justifications for the Religion Clauses

In this volume and its companion on free exercise we have explored questions about how free exercise and nonestablishment of religion should be understood, in respect to a range of specific problems, considering values that underlie the religion clauses, but without fitting these values into an overarching theory. In the next three chapters we will engage more fully with the underlying issue of what problems, if any, arise when citizens and officials justify their actions on the grounds of religion. This chapter addresses the specific inquiry whether religious justifications have any place when citizens and officials explain and defend the basic principles of religious liberty themselves. The possible use by officials of religious justifications for religious liberty raises an important issue about the establishment of religion. The following two chapters explore more broadly the use of religious premises in our liberal democracy to justify laws and policies, such as statutes against cruelty to animals, restrictions on embryonic stem cell research, aid to the poor, and prohibitions of various sexual practices.

In respect to the possible use of religious justifications for political and legal arrangements, we can quickly identify competing claims of equality and fairness. People who are not religious, or are members of minority religions, may believe they are being treated unequally and unfairly if those who make and interpret laws rely on justifications they cannot be expected to accept. On the other hand, believers who regard religious understandings as being at the center of moral and political judgment may feel they are suffering unfair discrimination if they are told that religious justifications they find most compelling are, in some sense, inadmissible.

Members of our society disagree sharply about sound justifications for the free exercise and establishment clauses of federal and state constitutions. Are the best justifications themselves religious? Do they, instead, rest on another perspective about how life should be lived? Or do they rest on reasons that can be detached from competing visions—religious and nonreligious—about how people should live? Do public officials and citizens need to decide which justifications are most powerful, or may they support and interpret the religion clauses without resolving questions of comparative strength among justifications? The answer to whether it is practically necessary to resolve which justifications are most sound depends largely on whether competing justifications have what I call "differential carry-through" for interpretations and applications of the religion clauses.

The chapter's treatment of underlying justifications begins with a clarification of why various justifications for legal norms often "carry through" in different ways. I then briefly describe some justifications for the religion clauses, and analyze what makes a justification sound. I suggest that the requisites of soundness are different for private citizens and for officials acting for the government. We will explore the possible paradox that public officials might not be able to rely on what are intrinsically the most powerful justifications, concluding that this paradox does not have disturbing practical implications because of the overriding nonestablishment principle that government should not sponsor religion.

The chapter makes the following six major claims. First, given our country's history and dominant present beliefs, religious justifications for the religion clauses cannot be dismissed as unconvincing, inappropriate, or unimportant. Second, so long as many citizens are religious believers, most religious justifications can be transposed into nonreligious justifications.[1] Third, because many competing justifications yield the principle that government should not sponsor religion, these justifications have little "differential carry-through" for how the clauses should be applied. Fourth, the principle of nonsponsorship, defended in chapter 4, bars religious justifications from being offered in official government communications. Fifth, because of nonsponsorship and its implications, the paradox of officials possibly being denied the strongest justifications for the religion clauses is not troubling. Sixth, judges and other officials need not resolve what exactly is the best set of justifications for constitutional standards regarding free exercise and establishment.

JUSTIFICATIONS AND APPLICATIONS: THE TYPICAL CARRY-THROUGH

A familiar illustration involving the Free Speech and Free Press Clauses shows how beliefs about justifications often affect the application of constitutional norms. If a person believes that the fundamental reason for free expression is that speech and writing contribute to the search for truth, she

---

[1] Thus, no one can reasonably believe that some widely accepted religious justification is very strong and that *every* nonreligious justification is very weak.

may conclude that the Constitution protects commercial speech that provides consumers useful information about products and prices. If another person thinks free speech is justified as the personal expression of individual sentiments, he will believe such commercial speech should enjoy no protection.[2] The implications of these two justifications for free speech may be reversed for harsh personal invective. Because such "hate speech" powerfully expresses feelings, but contributes little to society's search for understanding, it fares better under a "personal expression" approach than a "contribution to truth" approach.

The basic point that particular justifications can carry through to how constitutional norms are interpreted and applied survives variations in the source and number of justifications. As to source: suppose a legislator or a Supreme Court justice relies on justifications as perceived by the founders, or as now understood by most citizens, rather than on justifications she finds intrinsically most forceful. The justifications with which she begins will affect her views about desirable applications.[3] As to greater complexity: if someone thinks free speech is supported by multiple valid justifications, she will assess how far, and with what strength, those justifications apply to various categories of expression.[4]

Some Basic Justifications for Religious Liberty

A crucial claim in this chapter is that justifications for the religion clauses are substantially atypical in respect to carry through. By this I mean that certain sharp differences people have in their fundamental starting points for considering why our society should embrace religious liberty do not produce large variations in the more concrete constitutional doctrines that seem appropriate. We begin our inquiry by looking at some common justifications for the religion clauses.

---

[2] See, e.g., Edwin Baker, "Scope of the First Amendment Freedom of Speech," 25 *U.C.L.A. Law Review* 964 (1978).

[3] That is, the relation between justification and implementation is similar whether the inquiry about justification is broadly normative (what really are the best reasons?), historical (what did legislators or people *then* believe?), sociological (what do people now believe?), or some combination of these. I believe all these matters appropriately may count in interpretation. One can perhaps imagine a "specific practice" originalism that focuses only on practices that were once accepted and does not give any weight to perceived underlying justifications. If such a position is not incomprehensible, it is very foolish. In this essay, I mainly discuss the connection between "best reasons" justifications and applications of norms, but I assume that the connection between historically and sociologically derived justifications of norms and the applications of those norms is similar.

[4] I make this effort in *Speech, Crime, and the Uses of Language* (New York: Oxford University Press, 1989), and *Fighting Words* (Princeton: Princeton University Press, 1995).

Members of a society have various reasons to be committed to principles of religious free exercise and nonestablishment. We may divide these reasons into three categories: those that flow from religious perspectives, those that flow from overarching nonreligious views about a good life, and those that do not rest on any particular religious or other overarching view. (Although some reasons for free religious exercise might be thought to permit some form of established religion, I simplify to a degree by speaking of justifications for "religious liberty" that cover values protected by both clauses.)

Justifications That Flow from Religious Belief

Many religious persons conceive religious understanding, practice, and experience to be the crown of human existence. For those who believe that eternal salvation depends on acceptance in this life of religious truth, the preeminent importance of that truth is obvious. But even those who doubt a correlation of such simplicity may think religion lies at the center of a well-lived life. Throughout history, many believers have thought that their government should support what they take to be religious truth, and some believers still take that view. But strong religious belief need not entail a conviction in favor of state support. As John Garvey has suggested,[5] a believer may think that valid religious faith must be voluntary, not coerced. With confidence in the strength of religious truth, and perhaps with faith that God's revelation is progressive, she may favor open discourse and free practice concerning religion. She may take obligations to God as overriding any conflicting duties to the state or fellow citizens. She may worry that the religious realm will be sullied by the heavy hand of secular government, and that religious involvement in running governments will corrupt the religious spirit. A person with these fundamental religious convictions could embrace constitutional norms of free exercise and no establishment as the best approach for relations between religious institutions and the state.

Justifications from Nonreligious Overarching Views

Someone might support religious liberty because he accepts a nonreligious overarching view of life,[6] such as the idea that human happiness or freedom of choice is the most important human value. If a person genuinely believes

---

[5] This brief summary draws substantially from John H. Garvey, "An Anti-Liberal Argument for Religious Freedom," 7 *Journal of Contemporary Legal Issues* 275, 283–86 (1996).

[6] One kind of nonreligious view is explicitly antireligious. Someone who regards religion as foolish superstition and believes that freedom is the best way for people to learn this crucial truth of human life might also support religious liberty, including a rule of nonestablishment.

that happiness or free choice (in the sense of unconstrained choice) is really the most valuable aspect of human life, the highest good, her perspective opposes most religious conceptions,[7] yet she might well be led to a conclusion that choices about religion should not be constrained by government.

Justifications That Do Not Rest on Religious or Other Overarching Views

Rather than depending on religious or nonreligious overarching views about human good, some justifications for protecting religious liberty rest on factors that seem relevant from almost any perspective. The most notable exemplar, a justification based on political analysis and history, is that destructive conflict, suffering, and resentment follow religious competition for political favor and government interference into a society's religious life. Also, insofar as citizens' participation in religious life builds civic virtues, and religious institutions forestall or combat tyrannical government, religious organizations may best perform these functions when they are free of government.[8]

Many justifications for religious liberty that are based on religious (or other overarching) views can be transformed or transposed into parallel justifications that do not rest on such views.[9] If many people in society conceive of religion as highly important, if they take religious obligations as superior to secular duties, if they suppose that political influence will corrupt the purity of their religions, building political structures that are responsive to these sentiments may show respect for religious believers and contribute to

[7] Religious convictions typically make the quality of choices important, not just the freedom with which they are made. Ordinary happiness on earth is not the ultimate good for most religions. Religious believers often think that true happiness lies in leading a life that is good or right from the best religious perspective. On this view, a final compatibility exists between true religion and true happiness; but this happiness is not achieved by being sought for its own sake.

A justification for religious liberty based on happiness or autonomy might be understood in a somewhat modest way. A proponent might say, "I am not talking about ultimate human good. I am concerned with the relations between a state and its citizens, and what the state should understand as the good of its citizens. The state should aim for happiness (or autonomy)." Such a view could plausibly arise out of religious beliefs themselves; that is, a full theory from a religious perspective might assign secular government this role. Even if secular political theory were the basis to conclude that the state should aim for happiness or autonomy, that view could be compatible in its practical implications with a religious view that assigned the government no responsibility for religious truth.

[8] See generally Garvey, note 5 supra, at 281–82; Douglas Laycock, "Religious Liberty as Liberty," 7 *Journal of Contemporary Legal Issues* 313, 316–24 (1996); Suzanne Sherry, "Enlightening the Religion Clauses," 7 *Journal of Contemporary Legal Issues* 473, 485 (1996).

[9] See Laycock, note 8 supra, at 324–26; Ira C. Lupu, "To Control Faction and Protect Liberty: A General Theory of the Religion Clauses," 7 *Journal of Contemporary Legal Issues* 357, 359–60 (1996).

social stability. One can reach these conclusions without making a judgment about the intrinsic merit of the religious convictions themselves.[10]

Not every conceivable religious justification for religious liberty can be transformed in this way, and transformation need not yield a new reason of the same strength as the religious one.[11] The force of a transposed justification depends on how many people hold a religious view and on the intensity of their feelings. If only a few citizens share the view, accommodating their understandings may be relatively unimportant for social stability. And people's personal feelings about the realization of an ideal may be weaker than the basic reasons supporting the ideal. Thus, someone who believes that God wants all people to have religious liberty, may not care very much if people of other faiths actually enjoy such liberty. Nevertheless, when all the qualifications are in, it remains highly significant that in a society in which a great many citizens care deeply about religion, those designing or running a government have a strong nonreligious reason to respect their religious perspectives.

SOUNDNESS IN JUSTIFICATIONS

What makes a justification for a constitutional provision sound or unsound? Normative soundness and a capacity to explain the provision are crucial; as I shall explain, cultural resonance, accessibility, and assertibility sometimes matter as well. We will see how these requisites can drive a wedge between justifications that may be sound for private citizens and those on which officials may rely.

Normative Soundness

A sound justification in moral and political discourse rests on an accurate factual appraisal and good judgment about normative and metaphysical questions. A justification based on autonomy, in the sense of unconstrained

---

[10] It does not follow that government should accommodate every widely held sentiment. The appropriate response to some pernicious sentiments (such as racial prejudice) is to combat them. But, given the history of the United States, as well as its constitutional law, one cannot reasonably argue that the government should treat common religious convictions as pernicious excrescences on acceptable thoughts and feelings.

[11] Further, it is not necessarily true that a religious reason that is transposed into a nonreligious form will have the same practical implications as the underlying religious reason or as other nonreligious reasons. If one accommodates to people's strongly held sentiments as a form of respect, one might do something different from what one would do if one accepted their sentiments as true.

choice, is not sound if autonomy is neither the ultimate human good nor a very important good that government should recognize and promote. A justification for religious liberty based on its avoidance of civil strife may now be unsound if at this stage of our history civil peace could comfortably survive establishments of religion and serious inroads on free exercise.[12]

If one focuses on legal rather than political or moral justification, the criteria of normative soundness may shift. For legal purposes, the civil strife justification might count if many people once believed it, or now believe it, however realistic such views are in present circumstances.[13]

A central thesis of this chapter is that the soundness of a justification of the religion clauses depends significantly on someone's political role.[14]

Capacity to Justify a Provision

A justification for a constitutional norm must successfully cover the content of the norm. An otherwise sound justification fails if it justifies little of what a constitutional norm provides. A justification offered on behalf of *both* religion clauses is at least a partial failure if it justifies free exercise but fails to support nonestablishment.[15] More generally, no justification can be the primary justification for a constitutional provision if it is radically underinclusive in its coverage of that provision.

Overinclusiveness, that is, much broader coverage than the constitutional norm, need not be similarly fatal. John Garvey has pointed out that claims about autonomy, standing alone, hardly explain why religion should receive special treatment,[16] because any principle of maximizing autonomy would cover many areas of choice that do not receive similar constitutional protection. However, we can identify two reasons why this overinclusiveness does not necessarily undermine autonomy as a justification for the religion clauses.

---

[12] An advocate of this justification might counter that more subtle forms of strife remain very much with us, and that were legal protections of religious freedom to be disappear, outright violence might follow.

[13] An "originalist" might say that judges should accept as sound those justifications accepted by people when a constitutional provision was adopted.

[14] Whether a much broader thesis along these lines is true depends, as the following chapter reflects, on analysis of the nature of liberal democracy in modern social conditions. See, e.g., Kent Greenawalt, *Private Consciences and Public Reasons* (New York: Oxford University Press, 1995).

[15] A norm of nonestablishment does not follow automatically from a norm of free exercise, as can be seen from the many countries that provide freedom of religious exercise and have some form of established religion. International human rights documents that protect religious freedom do not bar establishments of religion. See Michael Perry, "Religion, Politics, and the Constitution," 7 *Journal of Contemporary Legal Issues* 407, 417 (1996).

[16] Garvey, note 5 supra, at 278.

Suppose we grant that an emphasis on autonomy would lead to a wide range of constitutional liberties, including, for example, sexual freedom. Nevertheless, religion was singled out for protection when the Bill of Rights was adopted. On this account, the Constitution would have been better if it protected more freedoms than it does, but the entire treatment of religion might be justified in terms of autonomy.[17]

Another telling response—one made by Douglas Laycock—is that autonomy must be considered along with other reasons for the religion clauses.[18] This observation has more general relevance, and it reaches some failures of underinclusiveness as well as overinclusiveness. Because justifications for important legal norms are typically multiple, not single, a failure of coverage of any one justification need not destroy its relevance. A legal norm could fit perfectly the force of the entire range of sound justifications, even though it fits no single justification perfectly.

My assumption thus far that a justification does or does not fit a constitutional provision is much too simple. As we saw in respect to free speech, people disagree about the parameters of any broad constitutional norm. A justification may fit one version of a provision but not other versions. An appealing justification that fits the dominant understanding of a provision poorly may be the basis for shifting how people conceive of the provision.[19] If two competing justifications yield different understandings of a provision's content, convictions about the force of justifications will influence judgments about coverage.

General Persuasiveness of Justifications: Cultural Resonance and Accessibility

Some disagreements about justifications of constitutional norms concern the criteria a good constitutional justification should satisfy. Should a justification fit dominant patterns of cultural understanding—that is, have cultural resonance? Should it be framed in reasons that will have force for most peo-

---

[17] On the other hand, if a justification indicates that constitutional protection wrongfully discriminates, that does present a serious problem. To illustrate, if the religion clauses unambiguously treated choices for religion more favorably than choices against religion, and this differentiation is unjust according to the principle of autonomy itself, that principle could not justify all of what the religion clauses do.

[18] Laycock, note 8 supra, at 323–24.

[19] Suppose, for example, that the strongest justification for the free exercise of religion warrants a weak version of the Establishment Clause, one that bars only a formally established church and extreme forms of government sponsorship of religion. People accepting the justification would begin to understand the Establishment Clause in this minimal way.

ple (or would have force if they considered the problem in a fair and detached manner)—that is, be accessible according to public or generally shared reasons? Without engaging this immense topic in depth,[20] I shall suggest that standards of cultural resonance and accessibility of reasons do sometimes matter for political and legal justifications; much depends on the role of the person who is making and defending a judgment. Most notably, some justifications that ordinary citizens properly rely upon may not be available for officials.

For many choices, the intrinsic soundness of a justification is all that counts. Suppose, at the age of twenty, I consider whether living as an ascetic hermit is the best life for me. I recognize quickly that almost everyone I know regards such a life as extremely odd, and I doubt that I can produce reasons that would persuade any of my family and friends that such a choice is sensible. Yet I believe, based on wide reading, meditation, and other personal experience, that I have good reasons for living that way. I think I have a valid justification, although it will not convince others.[21]

For many other subjects, a sound justification requires some cultural resonance. We do not ordinarily speak of a person as having a "moral duty" unless the duty fits with presuppositions about moral behavior within the society.[22] Arguments about political duties and responsibilities, including official duties, often rest on shared assumptions. Even when claims about moral and political duty reach beyond what most people presently assume, they build on cultural assumptions, gaining strength from their reliance on premises that are very widely accepted.[23]

Some theorists have argued that claims of political justification should be broadly accessible within a society, or accessible to all people who are judging reasonably. Accessibility in either of these versions differs from a standard of cultural resonance.[24] We can see how by supposing that most members of a society embrace closely similar religions that are based heavily on faith. These believers grant that their religious convictions cannot be supported by reasons that would persuade people who are not yet the subject of God's

[20] I discuss many aspects of the topic in Greenawalt, note 14 supra.

[21] The idea of having "reasons" involves having bases that other people could recognize as having force; but one may believe people will recognize that force only if they have some personal experience (such as a religious conversion) that they cannot be persuaded to have on the basis of ordinary reasons.

[22] However, the phrase "moral duty" is sometimes used in respect to how people ideally should regard their responsibilities. Thus, a vegetarian may say, "We all have a moral duty not to eat meat."

[23] When I say "they gain strength," I mean they really are stronger, not just that they have more appeal.

[24] Perhaps not everyone agrees about this. Some people, including many postmodernists, believe that all starting points for argument are nonrational assumptions; either no perspectives are especially reasonable, or ideas of what is reasonable do no more than reflect cultural assumptions.

special grace. A justification cast in terms of these religious convictions would have cultural resonance, but it might not be accessible in the sense that matters. Conversely, some defenders of "animal rights" may think their arguments are rationally compelling, though so far only few people accept them.

When people offer justifications for legal norms that are to count for interpretation of those norms, they usually assume that the justifications have cultural resonance and are accessible, that they hold out persuasive power for any reasonable judge. Political arguments about what laws legislatures should enact usually have cultural resonance, or they claim grounds that should have force for everyone, or both. Standards of cultural resonance and accessibility involve more than effective advocacy; having justifications that meet one or both of those standards may constitute a condition of what one can fairly expect others to do and of morally legitimate government coercion.[25]

Assertibility

A justification should usually be publicly assertible by the people who rely upon it. In law and politics particularly, a valid justification should not be concealed. Although closely related to cultural resonance and accessibility, assertibility differs from each. In private decisions, such as the choice to become an ascetic, people rightly assert justifications that they realize have neither cultural resonance nor force for most reasonable listeners. For other decisions, some particular justification that has both cultural resonance and reasonable force may not be one that should be asserted. The rule against viewpoint discrimination in free speech law provides an example. Neither executive officials nor judges can justify prohibiting one publication and allowing another because the second represents a sounder point of view, even if cultural assumptions and all reasonable people would support the judgment about comparative soundness. A similar conclusion about religion lies at the heart of this chapter.

RELIGIOUS JUSTIFICATIONS OF CONSTITUTIONAL NORMS—ARE THEY APPROPRIATE?

Our inquiry now turns to whether religious reasons are inherently flawed as justifications for constitutional norms of a liberal democracy. Can one dismiss these justifications without sustained argument that they are unpersuasive?

---

[25] The assertion that more than effective advocacy is involved in achieving resonance and accessibility comes down to this: if enough individuals to make up a majority happen to embrace a variety of

Liberal democratic societies are pluralistic in respect to religion. The reality that people do not agree about religious premises may suggest limits to the use of religious justifications; but it does not follow that people should never rely on such justifications for political institutions and constitutional norms.

That religious justifications may have a place can be seen clearly if we imagine a new government being created by diverse but deeply religious people. All of them agree that valid religious faith is voluntary and that religious understanding should influence every aspect of life, including the kind of government under which people should live. Realizing the religious pluralism of their political community, people, reasoning from their own religious points of view, agree that a liberal democracy is best. Conceiving religious reasons to provide their most powerful justifications, these people create a liberal democracy.[26] If during a subsequent period, a candidate for the presidency has promised to introduce a different form of government if he is elected, deeply religious citizens may take religious reasons as their strongest ones for maintaining liberal democracy. In sum, when people decide what government to have or keep, they do nothing improper in relying upon and stating religious justifications for liberal democracy.

Apart from the question whether any particular religious justification actually holds up, the serious issues about religious justifications concern the levels at which they operate and the persons who employ them. Because people within a pluralist society may disagree about the most fundamental reasons why liberal democracy is justified, perhaps they properly rely on religious justifications for liberal democracy itself, but should then seek generally accessible justifications for more specific subjects, such as the content of particular constitutional norms. This broad idea has been made familiar by John Rawls, who has suggested that support for the most basic political premises may be achieved by an overlapping consensus, grounded partly on religious and other overarching views, but that citizens should employ a common, public reason about constitutional norms and basic issues of justice.[27] People may have diverse views supporting a political order that is "a system of fair social cooperation between free and equal persons";[28] within

---

idiosyncratic reasons for adopting a law, none of the reasons having *either* cultural resonance or general rational force, the majority would be wrong to coerce the entire population.

[26] I provide a more elaborate illustration along these lines in Greenawalt, note 14 supra, chap. 2, pp. 12–22.

[27] See John Rawls, *Political Liberalism* 133–68, 212–27 (New York: Columbia University Press, 1993).

[28] John Rawls, "Justice as Fairness: Political not Metaphysical," 14 *Philosophy and Public Affairs* 223, 230 (1985).

that order, people should resolve constitutional issues according to common reasons based on shared premises.

Can we expect people's diverse underlying justifications for liberal democracy to "bow out," once these justifications coalesce on some abstract principle of liberal democracy of the sort that Rawls had in mind? I have argued elsewhere that that is not a reasonable expectation,[29] because overarching views will influence how one perceives the content of some constitutional norms and issues of justice. The next section focuses on this problem in the context of the religion clauses.

The Paradox about Religious Justifications for the Religion Clauses, and Its Implications

Religious Justifications and the Religion Clauses

A two-level approach, according to which religious and other overarching views figure in people's arriving at fundamental shared principles of democracy, but acceptance of the religion clauses is determined by shared premises of liberal democracy, is not tenable. We can see the artificiality of this approach if we focus on the historical and analytical relationship between religious pluralism and fundamental liberal democratic notions of justice. What it means to treat people as free and deserving of equal respect is largely informed by ideas of how members of diverse religions should regard each other. Commentators often use notions of religious freedom and equality by analogy when they discuss how other problems of liberal democracies should be resolved. One can hardly think about liberal democracy, about treating people as political equals, without having a clear sense about many aspects of religious liberty. In short, one is hard put to conceive of religious perspectives influencing basic notions of political justice without their bearing directly on the treatment of religious diversity.

A related reason supports the conclusion that the people should not restrict themselves to using religious justifications at some meta-level that stands above all specific constitutional norms. People committed to a religious perspective will be disinclined to leave the state's treatment of religion to be decided on grounds removed from that perspective. One can imagine people agreeing to certain political dispositions that fit uncomfortably with

---

[29] See Greenawalt, note 14 supra, and Kent Greenawalt, *Religious Convictions and Political Choice* (New York: Oxford University Press, 1988).

their specific religious views, on the basis that achieving a consensus in a diverse society warrants reliance on shared nonreligious grounds.[30] But they are unlikely to agree to a treatment of religious matters that fails to correspond with their fundamental religious perspectives. In summary, were individuals asked whether and why the religion clauses are justified, we should expect those for whom religion has overriding significance to ask whether the norms established by those clauses fit with their religious perspectives.

If we ask what *really* are the most powerful reasons for having religious liberty, we cannot expect agreement. A devout religious person who takes her religious commitments as overriding will not suppose that other justifications, however forceful, are more significant than her religious reasons. She can, of course, as John Garvey has done,[31] evaluate the strength of other justifications; but even if she finds them to be plausible, she will not regard them as more compelling than her religious justifications. A person who rejects religious premises will believe religious justifications are irremediably flawed by mistaken belief. Similarly, a person who accepts one set of religious premises will not think radically competing religious premises are sound.

Most religious justifications for free exercise and nonestablishment are not accessible to all citizens, because the religious premises themselves are not accessible in the way that counts. But many of these justifications have cultural resonance, dating back to a time long before the Constitution was adopted. Groups that we might now categorize as evangelical Protestants were highly instrumental in the movement toward greater religious freedom and disestablishment, and John Locke's influential argument for religious toleration was itself rooted firmly in a perspective about religious truth. A large proportion of the American people remain seriously religious, and their religious perspectives bear on their views about relations between government and religion.

Limits on Official Justifications

A special problem exists about official justifications for the religion clauses, a problem that bears more broadly on other constitutional and legal justifications. Most modern justifications for the religion clauses, including religious justifications, conceive a religious liberty that is more extensive than freedom from coercion of religious practice and from a formally established church. The justifications suggest that government should not promote and sponsor particular religious ideas.[32] For a devout religious believer, say a Bap-

---

[30] I am assuming, of course, that their religious perspective leads them to accept such an approach.
[31] See Garvey, note 5 supra, at 278–82.
[32] I assume that official government organs must also not invoke an explicitly atheist justification.

tist, it may follow from the nature of religious truth and human understanding of that truth, that nonsponsorship by government is a desirable principle for every society. Thus, the Baptist perspective itself yields the conclusion that the government should not promote a Baptist understanding, or any other religious understanding. An individual Baptist may accept free exercise and nonestablishment mainly because she accepts a Baptist understanding; but a central principle of the religion clauses is that the government should not sponsor that point of view. This creates a paradox about justification.

The principle of nonsponsorship affects what official government organs can say about justifications. If Supreme Court justices explicitly relied on a Baptist justification for the religion clauses, as they might rely on the truth discovery justification for free speech, they would be endorsing and promoting the Baptist religious view, just what the religion clauses forbid. Official organs, thus, must rely on justifications, such as avoidance of civil strife, that do not take a stand on religious issues, or they must avoid the question of justification altogether, or they must say something vague, such as "The religion clauses are justified because most citizens believe they are justified, for diverse reasons." Government may not assert a direct religious justification.[33]

Just what count as official justifications is itself a complicated question. Persons sometimes speak as officials but not in a formal way, as when legislators make arguments before legislative assemblies or address public school graduations. Precisely what justifications various officials[34] should employ in various contexts is debatable;[35] the critical point here is that direct religious justifications may not be asserted by government officers in many contexts, including statutes, administrative regulations, and judicial opinions.

The exclusion of religious justifications by government creates the paradox that if the best justifications for the religion clauses happen to be religious, these are nevertheless not available for official documents. This paradox would generate a grave practical problem if *no* nonreligious justifications were very persuasive. Officials would have to rely publicly on nonreligious justifications, but none of these would give powerful support to the norms of the religion clauses. Abandoning the clauses, or sharply curtailing their scope, would be mistaken because they are backed by intrinsically sound religious justifications that most citizens, and most officials

---

[33] This exclusion of official religious justifications reaches other constitutional norms. A court can no more invoke "the Baptist understanding" to justify a ban on cruel and unusual punishment than to justify the religion clauses. Official justifications in religious terms are out.

[34] Some private persons, such as presidents of major corporations and universities, have great visibility and may address a broad public about subjects such as whether the religion clauses should be amended to allow public school prayer.

[35] See Greenawalt, note 14 supra.

in their private capacities, accept. Should the officials silently rely on these religious justifications while announcing nonreligious justifications they recognize as inadequate? Or should they disregard the intrinsically sound justifications they cannot use publicly? This would be a troubling dilemma.

A more subtle, second practical problem could arise if nonreligious justifications can adequately explain the basic features of the religion clauses, but, as to certain subjects, different justifications would yield different interpretations and applications of the two clauses. If the religious justifications are really strongest and they yield somewhat different applications from nonreligious justifications, should public officials who recognize the power of the religious justifications silently rely on them, or should they try to rely only on the justifications they can openly state? Again, public officials would face a dilemma in deciding how to interpret and apply the clauses.

The Paradox of Official Assertibility Does Not Raise Serious Practical Problems

The Plurality of Sound Justifications If Typical Religious Justifications Are Sound

Our more extreme dilemma, which would arise if *only* religious justifications strongly supported the religion clauses, does not now exist in our society, because widely shared religious justifications are not uniquely sound. The reason is the phenomenon of transformation I have already sketched. Let us suppose that a set of religious reasons—including the intrinsic truth of some religious beliefs—such as belief in a benevolent God who wants human beings to make religious choices freely—provides the most powerful justification for religious liberty. In a society that has many citizens who accept this set of reasons based on religious perspectives, the desirability of respecting their attitudes toward religious liberty produces justifications that have force for people who reject (or are agnostic about) the underlying religious premises. Reference to typical attitudes of citizens toward religion gives officials some strong nonreligious justifications, whatever may be the strength of still other nonreligious justifications, such as the one based on avoiding civil strife.

Why Differential Carry-Through Is Not a Serious Problem

The worry that religious justifications might have a different carry-through from other justifications may appear more troubling; but it is met if different justifications coalesce behind a common principle that itself can be employed to reach decisions. In fact, very different underlying justifications for the religion clauses support the principle of nonsponsorship. If an issue arises over sponsorship in one form or another, officials can employ the principle of non-sponsorship to resolve the issue. They do not need to decide which particular justification for nonsponsorship is strongest if they are confident that the range of justifications that support nonsponsorship is stronger than justifications that support some very different approach to religious liberty. The principle of nonsponsorship yields more discrete doctrines and applications. Insofar as each justification merges with competitors in supporting a similar version of nonsponsorship, each ceases to yield distinctive doctrines and results.[36]

Of course, religion clause interpretation is not limited to issues of sponsor-ship. One crucial issue we have examined in both volumes is whether exemp-tions from otherwise valid laws should be afforded to religious claimants. Perhaps for that question, the comparative strength of religious and other justifications of the religion clauses might matter; and the power of various justifications could affect just whom is to receive an exemption if some reli-gious exemptions are called for. Different justifications might have distinc-tive carry-through on this set of issues, if not about sponsorship. Thus, a justification that rests on the real value of religion might conceivably support granting exemptions, and also support limiting exemptions to religious be-lievers, rather than extending them to other claimants of conscience. Other justifications might suggest different results.

We should notice, however, that the principle of nonsponsorship undoubt-edly affects the problem of exemptions in two important ways. Even for religion clause issues that are not directly about sponsorship, courts cannot offer explicitly religious arguments. Thus, official nonassertibility requires that religious justifications not be "carried through" as the publicly stated reasons for a court's position about exemptions.[37] If courts should not rely openly on a religious justification for the clauses in order to support exemp-tions limited to believers, that is a reason to conclude that they should not rely covertly. Although they can take account of the importance of religion in people's lives, courts should try to settle issues about exemptions without relying on the truth or falsity, value or disvalue, of religion.

A second effect of nonsponsorship would be to bar a classification for exemptions that implicitly involves endorsement. Such an endorsement might be claimed if religious believers are favored. Thus, the principle of nonsponsorship itself constitutes one reason not to favor religious claimants over all others.

---

[36] I am assuming here that the particular version of nonsponsorship does not vary with the underly-ing justification.

[37] A court might, however, say that wide acceptance of the religious justification by citizens affects how the issue should be viewed.

Conclusion about Justifications

I have argued that for most purposes we need not resolve which justifications of the religion clauses are really the strongest, and we should not expect, or even seek, agreement about that. Justifications that are diametrically opposed in basic premises may prove to be complementary in practical implication. I have definitely not shown that the issue of the comparative soundness of various justifications will never have a practical importance connected to their differential carry-through. Therefore, I have not shown that officials will never face the dilemma of whether they should silently rely on nonassertible justifications. However, many religious justifications for religious liberty will coalesce with other justifications to support a principle of nonsponsorship for the religion clauses; and this fundamental principle drastically reduces any differential carry-through of the various justifications for the religion clauses that support nonsponsorship. If nonsponsorship is rightly viewed as a fundamental principle of nonestablishment, we can see that it affects not only what measures government can adopt, but what justifications judges and other officials may give for what they do.

CHAPTER 23

Religiously Based Judgments and Religious Discourse in Political Life

This chapter and the next explore related subjects that lie at the outer boundaries of the restraints the Establishment Clause imposes on governments or concern issues of political philosophy that reach beyond constitutional limitations. In the following chapter we will consider a constitutional question we have not yet directly addressed: when the law enforces a moral judgment that is grounded squarely on religious sentiments, does that violate the Establishment Clause? No one doubts that laws against killing and stealing are all right, although *one reason* that some people think these acts are wrong is because the Ten Commandments forbid them. But what of laws that lack a plausible secular justification or would not have been adopted except for religious sentiments? Some think one or both of these characterizations are true about laws limiting marriage of persons of different genders, laws restricting sexual acts among consenting adults, laws (or administrative decisions) forbidding government assistance for embryonic stem cell research, and laws prohibiting abortions. Occasional judicial opinions and more extensive writings by scholars have suggested that certain exercises in the enforcement of a morality that is grounded in religious premises are unconstitutional. The next chapter undertakes to explain to what extent this thesis has support in the existing law and to what extent it represents a wise understanding of the Establishment Clause. In that endeavor, we will look carefully at exactly which kinds of laws and government policies might be singled out as depending on religious sentiments.

The controversy over legal enforcement of morality is one aspect of a wider discussion about the role of religion in our political life, and in the political life of liberal democracies more generally. This discussion, which is often cast as one about "public reasons," definitely reaches beyond *constitutional law*, but one can, as I shall explain, think of it as concerning concepts of nonestablishment and free exercise in the realm of political philosophy. It thus merits our consideration for its own sake, but it is also a needed backdrop for the specifically legal discussion in the chapter that follows. Because

I have written on this subject extensively,[1] my treatment here will be highly summary, but it does sketch the basic positions and competing claims.

Before we begin, a caution about the relation between the competing claims in political philosophy and their relevance for constitutional law may help. For the most part in these two volumes, we have assumed that when a government violates the Free Exercise Clause or the Establishment Clause, a court presented with a case involving a violation will say so. That, I have noted, is an oversimplification, one that is particularly relevant for these two chapters. One might believe that a fair amount of legislation enforcing morality violates the Establishment Clause, but not in a way a court can declare. One might believe that individual legislators violate the Establishment Clause, or some spirit of the Establishment Clause, even though the official action to which they contribute does not do so. I shall say more about these nuances in what follows, but readers need to recognize that the conceivable options about the status of various claims are more complex than (merely) political philosophy or (judicially enforceable) constitutional law.

"Public Reasons" and the Status of Religious Judgments

Influenced by the writings of John Rawls,[2] political philosophers in recent decades have debated whether political decisions in liberal democracies should be based on public reasons, reasons accessible in the right way to all citizens. It is generally assumed that reasons grounded in religious premises fall outside the domain of public reasons. If citizens and officials improperly rely heavily on religious premises in advocating and adopting laws, we could think of that as a misguided "establishment" of religion, although not one necessarily covered by the Establishment Clause.

People who challenge the injection of religion in politics adopt what we may call an "exclusivist" position. Religion should be excluded from politics. In the politics of pluralist liberal democracies, decisions (they claim) should be made on grounds that are shared premises of that form of government and on forms of justification and ways of determining facts that are accessible to all citizens. Whatever is the exact mix of the rational, nonrational, and irrational in religious understandings, no religious perspective is shared by all citizens, no perspective rests on methods of justification and

---

[1] *Religious Convictions and Political Choice* (New York: Oxford University Press, 1988); *Private Consciences and Public Reasons* (New York: Oxford University Press, 1995).

[2] The most relevant passages for this subject are in *Political Liberalism* 212–54 (New York: Columbia University Press, 1993).

determining facts that are accessible in the required way. To some extent, religious belief depends on faith, personal experience, and distinctive tradition; adherents of one religion cannot present "logical" arguments that alone will persuade outsiders to their basic religious presuppositions and the conclusions they draw from those presuppositions. Religious belief and practice is fine for individuals and communities of faith; and religious perspectives may enrich our cultural understandings. But at least when citizens are coerced, the state acts unfairly unless it has reasons that have force *for all citizens*. Religious reasons do not fall into this category. They do not belong in democratic politics. This is a matter of fairness, and also of political stability. Neither citizens nor officials should present religious reasons in public debate; neither group should rely on such reasons.

Some brief clarifications about this "exclusivist" position can help avoid confusion. First, it concerns politics, not broader public culture. It need not assert that religion belongs in a private, wholly nonpublic sphere; it need assert only that religion should be kept out of politics. Second, no one claims that people *will be wholly uninfluenced* by religious understandings. Any claim of that sort would be absurdly naive. The assertion is that people should discuss political issues in public without reliance on religious premises and they should *try* to make up their minds accordingly. Third, the claim is not that religion is foolish superstition and *therefore* deserves no place in our political life. Of course, all arguments based on foolish superstition should be avoided, but if *that* were the basis for excluding religion, the exclusion would have to rest on persuasive argument that religion is foolish superstition. Whatever they may think about religion, the leading proponents of exclusion base their position on premises of democratic government, not on the intrinsic foolishness of religion. More to the point, more than 90 percent of our citizens identify themselves as religious; one cannot reasonably suppose they should avoid religion in politics because religion is foolish. Finally, we have to be careful about what the "exclusivist" position entails. What is mainly being urged is "self-exclusion." No one proposes that anyone can be punished or silenced for making religious arguments; indeed, guarantees of free speech and free exercise protect such arguments. The proposal is that people should refrain from making religious arguments because they do not fit with how liberal democracies should work. Whether a misguided reliance on religious grounds could make a law invalid is left for our next chapter.

The competing "inclusivist" position is that citizens and officials should be able to rely on whatever sources of understanding seem to them most reliable and illuminating. If a respected religious authority like the pope, or a divinely inspired text, or one's personal sense of how God relates to human beings, suggests that we should help those who are less fortunate, why should that not count for our position on welfare reform and medical insurance? People do not feel whole if they try to divorce their deepest sources of insight from their political stances. Moreover, shared premises and methods of justification are too thin to resolve many political issues; they just do not settle enough in a society as diverse and divided as our own. Fairness consists not in exclusion, even self-exclusion, but in everyone relying on what they think is most convincing. Indeed, the ability to rely on one's religious convictions is part of the free exercise of religion. A full airing of all those views will enrich everyone's understanding. People can often learn from others who do not share their fundamental religious beliefs.[3] A healthy democracy will not be unstable if religious arguments are part of political discourse.

For the inclusivist position, only one clarification is required. A defender of that position need not claim that *every ground* for a political position is appropriate. Some grounds may be contrary to premises of liberal democracy. We now suppose that racism and other denials of equal worth fall into this category. But religion has never been so regarded in our country. From the beginning, religious belief and practice have been thought fully compatible with the underpinnings of our political order.

As I have put it so far, the controversy about religious grounds seems fairly straightforward, if not easy to resolve; but matters are in fact much more complicated. No one claims that it is *only* religious reasons that are excluded by public reasons, and it becomes evident on examination that deciding which reasons count as public is not simple. Perhaps we might do better to think of reasons which are more or less public. And I shall argue that it should make a crucial difference for whether one should rely on nonpublic reasons that he or she is an ordinary citizen or an official and, if an official, engaging in public discourse or silently employing grounds of judgment.

Some of the difficulties with deciding what count as "public reasons" may be illustrated with reference to natural law theory, a theory that is powerfully associated with Roman Catholic tradition, but is not limited to that tradition and in modern times has typically been defended as not resting on religious premises.[4] According to my understanding, the standard, full-bodied,[5] natural law position rests on the following premises.

---

[3] See Jeffrey Stout, *Democracy and Tradition* (Princeton: Princeton University Press, 2004).

[4] The leading treatment in Anglo-American legal philosophy is that of John Finnis, *Natural Law and Natural Rights* (Oxford: Clarendon Press, 1980).

[5] Readers of legal philosophy will be familiar with Lon Fuller's idea of a procedural natural law, *The Morality of Law* (rev. ed., New Haven: Yale University Press, 1969), and Ronald Dworkin's "naturalism," *Law's Empire* (Cambridge: Belknap Press of Harvard University Press, 1986); "Natural Law Revisited," 34 *University of Florida Law Review* 165 (1982). These are much more modest in their claims.

1. Human life is integrally related to all of existence.
2. Human nature is universal.
3. The defining characteristic of human beings is their reason or rationality.
4. Human beings have inherent purposes (the teleological approach associated with St. Thomas Acquinas) or self-evident goods (the approach some modern proponents of natural law defend).
5. These purposes, or goods, are discoverable by reason, reason being understood in a broad sense to include the light of experience.
6. Morality is objective, universal, and discoverable by reason.
7. People's moral obligations are consonant with their own true purposes, or their realization of self-evident goods, and with their true happiness.
8. At the deepest levels, no conflict arises between individual good and the common good.
9. Human laws appropriately reflect the natural law (though not every dictate of natural law should be subject to state coercion). Human laws appropriately determine details left open by natural law, such as the precise punishments for various crimes, and they settle matters of indifference.
10. Human laws that are not in accord with natural law are not "really" law in some sense. A failure to accord with natural law may occur if a human law requires behavior that natural law forbids, or if a law forbids behavior that natural law values, or if the burdens and benefits of a law are highly unjust.

AN ILLUSTRATION: THE STEM CELL DEBATE

To grasp the complexities of a concept of public reasons and the place of natural law, it helps to start with an illustration drawn from a contentious political issue during the presidency of George W. Bush—the question whether the federal government should fund research with embryonic stem cells. Before the president's decision to allow funding only to existing lines of stem cells, the *Wall Street Journal* carried a debate between David Baltimore, Nobel laureate scientist and president of the California Institute of Technology, and Robert George, a political and legal philosopher who teaches at Princeton.[6]

Dr. Baltimore argued strongly in favor of federal funding. Adult stem cells are not now a viable alternative to embryonic stem cells, which have "the potential to become every part of the human body" and "could be used to

[6] Compare David Baltimore, "Stem Cell Research: A Debate—Don't Impede Medical Progress," *Wall Street Journal*, July 30, 2001, at A18, with Robert P. George, "Stem Cell Research: A Debate—Don't Destroy Human Life," *Wall Street Journal*, July 30, 2001, at A18.

make up for the deficits in brain and pancreas cells that cause Parkinson's disease or diabetes."[7] For these stem cells to become practically effective in curing human diseases, scientists must carry forward work of many types. The "publicly funded American research effort is the most effective . . . in the world. To refuse to allow it to participate in this exciting research would be an affront to the American people, especially those who suffer from diseases that could one day be reversed by these miraculous cells."[8]

About the concern that the embryos deserve protection, Baltimore had this to say: "To me, a tiny mass of cells that has never been in a uterus is hardly a human being. . . . By treating the use of stem cells as akin to murder, we would lose a great deal."[9]

That is the issue to which Professor George devoted his full attention. He did not discuss the likely medical benefits of stem cell research because these are irrelevant, in his view. It is wrong to harvest organs from human beings without their consent. "[K]illing for the purpose of harvesting body parts . . . is inconsistent with the inherent dignity of all human beings."[10] A human being, George claimed, is a whole, living member of the species *Homo sapiens*. Unlike a sperm cell or an ovum, or skin cells, human embryos, "[m]odern science shows[,] . . . are whole living members of the human species, who are capable of directing from within their own integral organic functioning and development into and through the fetal, infant, child, and adolescent stages of life and ultimately into adulthood."[11] It is not that a human embryo has the potential to be a human being; he or she "is already a living human being."[12] George eschewed relying on controversial religious premises such as "ensoulment"; he said "the science will do just fine" and he would be pleased if opponents would agree that "the scientific facts about when new human beings begin" should be determinative.[13] Given the status of embryos as human beings, compromises, such as using stem cells from embryos created by in vitro fertilization that would be discarded in any event, are unacceptable.[14]

Do Baltimore's and George's arguments count as ones of public reason, and should that matter? To answer those questions we need to relate the

---

[7] See Baltimore, note 6 supra, at A18.

[8] Id.

[9] Id.

[10] George, note 6 supra, at A18.

[11] Id.

[12] Id.

[13] Id. Professor George notes in passing that the Catholic Church has no official position on the "eternal destiny" of embryos. Id.

[14] Id. Professor George does not comment on President Bush's actual compromise of allowing federal funding of research on lines from embryos already destroyed. Id.

basis of philosophies of public reasons to the possible scope of those reasons. We need to ask both what count as public reasons and when people should be constrained to rely on them.

A typical public reason is that citizens' opportunities should not depend on their race, gender, or religion. This is a central tenet of the modern political theory of liberal democracy; to embrace it, one need not reach to controversial moral theories or religious perspectives. David Baltimore's contention that use of stem cells can produce important medical benefits is a public reason; everyone agrees that cure of disease and disability is good. On the other hand, the claim that biblical passages tell us that God abhors homosexual acts is not a public reason; it relies on a text that does not carry authority for all reasonable citizens.

Whatever the exact range of public reasons, they do not include reasons drawn from biblical revelation or church authority. Within a liberal society, people will disagree about such fundamental matters as the existence and nature of God and the quality of a good life. The idea is that when citizens adhere to public reasons, they respect each other as free and equal citizens, they take intractable moral and religious questions off the political agenda. *If* Robert George's argument against embryonic stem cell research depended on a belief about ensoulment, derived from church doctrine, it would not be a public reason.

Theorists disagree not only about who should constrain themselves to rely on public reasons but also when. Does the constraint apply in the same way to officials and ordinary citizens? Should public reasons underlie all laws and policies, or all coercive laws,[15] or, as John Rawls proposed, constitutional essentials and basic matters of justice?[16] Does a constraint of public reasons concern the underlying grounds on which people decide, the explanations and arguments they put forward on behalf of their positions, or both of these?

Theorists also disagree over exactly what makes reasons nonpublic. Among the candidates that have been suggested are ideas of the good (or controversial ideas of the good), nonrational grounds, reasons that are not widely accepted, and comprehensive views (roughly, overarching philosophies of life).

The notion that coercive laws, in particular, should be based on public reasons is that governments should not compel people on the basis of reasons that are not persuasive for them. If the government is not coercing people, its reasons matter less. Our stem cell example presses hard on that distinc-

---

[15] I am putting aside for purposes of this analysis those situations in which it is perfectly appropriate to vote on the basis of self-interest.

[16] See generally Rawls, note 2 supra.

tion. We know that the government would fund this research were it not for concern about embryos. If it refuses to fund, many scientists will not do embryonic stem cell research and, much more important, sufferers of diseases like Parkinson's and Alzheimer's may not receive critical medical benefits that might otherwise have been available. Can it be that the government needs public reasons if it is to *coerce* people not to hunt endangered species, but that it can curtail potential lifesaving medical assistance on the basis of nonpublic reasons? That would be paradoxical.

The stem cell illustration also helps to show why we should not draw a sharp distinction between ordinary political issues and constitutional essentials and basic questions of justice. As Rawls once applied these terms, a right to abortion falls within constitutional essentials;[17] funding of stem cell research is an ordinary issue. For both abortion and embryonic stem cell research, the central question is whether conception gives rise to a human being (or potential human being) who deserves society's protection. Can it be that we should rely only on public reasons to determine the legal treatment of abortion but may rely on nonpublic reasons in respect to stem cell research? Not only is this conclusion odd from a theoretical point of view, convincing people that the status of an embryo may be determined in one way for one political issue and must be determined in another way for a related issue would be very hard. I conclude that, insofar as public reasons are concerned, no sharp line should be drawn between coercive and noncoercive laws or between ordinary issues, on the one hand, and constitutional essentials and questions of basic justice on the other.[18]

WHEN SHOULD PEOPLE FEEL CONSTRAINED BY PUBLIC REASONS, NOT RELYING ON SPECIFICALLY RELIGIOUS GROUNDS? PRELIMINARY CONCLUSIONS

Most proponents of public reasons have assumed that any constraint applies in the same manner to officials and citizens, and in the same manner to grounds of judgment and public discourse.[19] My position differs. It relies

[17] See id., at 243 n. 32 (discussing balance of political values concerning human life, reproduction, and equality of women).

[18] One might think, however, that a constraint to follow public reasons is especially important as laws and policies impinge on members of society in more important ways.

[19] For a discussion of various arguments about how public reasons apply to citizens, see Paul J. Weithman, "Citizenship and Public Reason," in Robert P. George and Christopher Wolfe, eds., *Natural Law and Public Reason* 125 (Washington, D.C.: Georgetown University Press, 2000).

heavily on distinctions between advocacy and justification, on the one hand, and grounds of judgment, on the other, and between officials and ordinary citizens.

When we think about how we make up our minds and how we discuss issues, we realize that monitoring our discourse is a lot easier than restricting our bases for decision. Moreover, while other people hear our discourse, they cannot know our full grounds of decision. These truths matter.

Most people would be hard put to *try* to carry out a program of excluding their deepest religious convictions from their political judgments. They could not disentangle what they believe because of underlying religious convictions from what they would believe if they relied only on premises of liberal democracy and shared techniques of understanding.

Speaking without reference to religious convictions is not difficult. Members of our law faculty share an assumption that school problems are to be resolved in terms of values that are not explicitly connected to particular comprehensive views. I have yet to hear a specifically Jewish, Christian, atheist, or Benthamite argument for a faculty decision. Yet, when decisions involve the point of legal education, I doubt that colleagues try rigorously to remove the threads of their religious understandings about the nature of society and education for a profession.

If it is working, a constraint of public reasons is reciprocal. People can tell easily whether arguments are being made from explicit religious premises; they will know if restraint on their part is matched. If they try to purge their silent deliberations of religious influence, they cannot be sure if others are similarly motivated. And once someone realizes just how arduous this purging exercise is, he will question the success of others, even if he thinks they are trying. Such uncertainties are a poor basis for reciprocity.

Consider some differences between officials and ordinary citizens. Officials have a lot more to do with the law that gets made and applied than do citizens; there are a lot more citizens than officials. Officials are used to making judgments and offering reasons that do not include all that is relevant in their personal lives. Citizens are less used to practicing such restraint. Perhaps a highly educated, participating citizenry could learn to draw distinctions between what matters for most aspects of life and what matters for politics. But that is not our citizenry. When officials practice restraint, that impinges much less on a population's religious liberty than when citizens do so. Official restraint more greatly affects the quality of political life. These basic distinctions—between advocacy and judgment and between officials and citizens—suggest that if any self-exclusion is justified, it is mainly self-exclusion for officials in their public statements.

Among officials we can divide roughly between those who apply law and those who make law or exercise ordinary discretionary judgment. Among those who apply law, judges and quasi-judicial officials often provide reasoned justifications for their decisions. At this stage of American history, one does not often find explicitly religious grounding in opinions, even when courts reach beyond standard legal sources to comment on the social benefits or harms of a possible ruling. By an explicitly religious grounding, I mean reasoning in this form: "Given a true religious proposition, these conclusions about social good follow." Some examination of religious sources might be acceptable to show the community's attitudes toward a practice or its deep moral assumptions, and judges might employ familiar religious stories to illustrate a point; but none of these is a reliance on religious grounds in the sense that I mean. Although judicial opinions are rarely completely candid about the strength of competing arguments, one expects judges to rely on arguments they believe should have force for all judges. In our culture, this excludes arguments based on particular religious premises.

When we turn to legislators, we may start with the proposition that if an explicit religious grounding were placed in the preamble to a statute, that should be viewed as a promotion of religion that would violate the Establishment Clause. Although the use of religious language has increased among legislators and executive officials during the second Bush administration, it is still true that members of Congress typically do not make religious arguments on the floor of Congress or before their constituents. There is, however, no accepted understanding that they should avoid giving any weight to their own religious convictions, and to those of constituents, in the formulation of their positions. I believe legislators should give greater weight to reasons that are generally available than to those they understand are not; but some reliance on religious and similar reasons is appropriate, especially since the generally available reasons are radically indecisive about some crucial social problems.

If legislators rely on religious understandings more than their public advocacy reflects, are they not lacking in candor? Does restraint impoverish discourse and leave voters less well informed than they might be? Realism counsels that much legislators say is far from fully candid, so self-restraint about religious grounds is hardly a *major* contributor to lack of candor. In any event the value of self-restraint overrides this drawback and whatever reduction in information voters suffer. Legislators should not deny religious bases that motivate them, but they should not develop public arguments in these terms.

Because citizens are not used to practicing self-restraint of this kind, and because most citizens have little involvement in the political process, I do not think they should regard themselves as constrained to avoid relying on religious grounds *or* to avoid stating those grounds. Some citizens, however, such as university and corporation presidents, and individuals consistently engaged in political life, have a much more public role. For them, something like the constraints for legislators are appropriate.

Religious leaders and organizations have a special place. They properly develop religious grounds as these relate to political problems, and they also properly take part in direct efforts to win support for particular positions, although it is usually unfortunate when religious leaders endorse parties or candidates.

Much of the theorizing about public reasons and religious reasons has been cast in terms of liberal democracies in general, or as what the Establishment Clause of our Constitution actually requires. Neither of these approaches answers the most central practical questions. The Establishment Clause, in its direct force, has modest implications. It is mainly about what laws do, not why they are enacted. What of liberal democracies and theories of legitimacy? Democratic theorists argue persuasively that in a liberal society people will adopt many different comprehensive views. This condition will not change. The history of Western liberal democracies, forged out of religious division, shows that differences in religious views can be a source of intense conflict; but we can imagine people of various religious views who seek to learn from one another and who trust each other's social judgments. These people might welcome religious perspectives in political discourse. On the other hand, one might not recommend an explicitly religious politics as the most fruitful approach for a newly constituted Northern Ireland or for the fledgling, fragile union that may emerge in Bosnia. Much depends on history, culture, the religious and other broad views that people hold, and their degree of mutual tolerance and respect. Specific principles of self-restraint should be offered for particular political orders, not in gross. If this is true about religious discourse and public reason, it is also true about many other practical issues to which political philosophers speak.[20]

The United States is a country of great diversity in culture and religion. The percentage of our people that is neither Christian nor Jewish increases

---

[20] One may analyze the problem of public reason and the closely related problem of religion and politics from a particular religious or other "comprehensive" view, say Roman Catholicism, Orthodox Judaism, liberal Protestantism, or Kantianism, and see what implications follow, or one may try to do "detached" political philosophy, not relying on any particular comprehensive view. Both exercises are valuable. What I do summarily in this chapter is the latter, "detached" political philosophy, although readers will not be surprised that my conclusions fit my own comprehensive view, a variety of liberal Protestantism. The hope is that the analysis will appeal to those who hold different comprehensive views.

steadily, with immigration policies that no longer discriminate egregiously against Asians. Outright religious conflict is rare, but religious differences remain a source of distrust and tension. Religious convictions are intense and widespread enough to influence politics and to disturb people with their influence. That is partly why some restraint may be needed.

What Count as Public Reasons?

A general degree of acceptance cannot alone be the test of what reasons are public. Were that the only standard, Christians could rely on the New Testament in a country that was mainly Christian; Muslims could rely on the Koran in a Muslim society. This evident inequality for what happen to be minority perspectives conflicts with the ideals of liberal democracy. General acceptance might play some role in whether reasons are relevantly public, but it cannot be the exclusive or primary standard.[21]

Sometimes it is suggested that particular ideas of the good, or controversial ideas of the good, are what are excluded by public reasons.[22] People have various convictions about what makes life good, and they should be able to pursue them within a framework of just social relations and mutual respect.[23] This position, to be clear, is not that the government should avoid all moral questions, but that it should limit itself to moral questions that concern justice and mutual respect, not resolving moral questions about the kinds of activities people should value in their lives.[24]

This constraint alone leaves untouched much that proponents of public reasons believe should be excluded. Most notably, it does not exclude much that religions have to say about just social relations.[25] Here, our stem cell illustration is illuminating. Whether embryonic stem cells should be used for medical purposes is *not* an issue about the good life; it is an issue of justice and respect for the embryo that may be a human being. If the only public-

---

[21] For one claim about general acceptance, see Mario M. Cuomo, "Religious Belief and Public Morality: A Catholic Governor's Perspective," 1 *Notre Dame Journal of Law Ethics and Public Policy* 13, 18 (1984).

[22] See generally Charles E. Larmore, *Patterns of Moral Complexity* (New York: Cambridge University Press, 1987).

[23] See id. at 118–35.

[24] See id. at 133 (stating that "the ideal of neutrality must always take precedence over disputed ideals of the good life").

[25] More precisely, it does not exclude religious conclusions about just relations that do not depend on claims about what is a good life.

reasons constraint concerned claims about the good life, an argument that a papal encyclical condemns stem cell research would be within the realm of public reasons. But that sort of argument is just the kind that the public-reasons filter is designed to exclude. So a constraint of public reasons cannot be limited to questions of the good life.

Should it at least include all such questions, whatever else it may also contain? The answer is no. We expect public schools to educate children about desirable ways to live, about the importance of physical and mental health, about the dangers of addictions, about the benefits of culture, and about the value of activity as contrasted with indolence. All these aspects of what schools do cannot be summarized fully as helping to make children into good citizens and aiding them to realize whatever goals they set for themselves; they encourage students to live well according to our society's ideas of what a good life contains. State support of arts and literature and high taxes on alcohol and cigarettes show that the government's involvement in questions of the good life extends to adults. Laws against the use of drugs are controversial, but few object to laws that forbid human beings from having sex with animals. These cannot be defended as consistent with neutrality about the good life, unless one (implausibly) regards them as mainly protecting animals who would be potential sexual partners.

It is at least a defensible position that the state should not coerce people in respect to *controversial* judgments about the good life;[26] but the basis for such a position seems to be more a judgment that individuals should have autonomy in this realm than a judgment that the reasons for coercion could never be sufficiently public.

Another possibility for grounds that do not qualify as public is reasons that do not rest on rational grounds. Here, roughly, the idea is that people should be able to rely on reasoned arguments that other people can understand and accept, not on faith or intuition that others do not share.[27] Remember how careful Professor George was to say that his argument against stem cell research did not depend on controversial religious premises but on "the scientific facts." One difficulty with the "rational grounds" approach is

[26] See Jeffrey Reiman, "Abortion, Natural Law, and Liberal Discourse: A Response to John Finnis," in George and Wolfe, supra note 19, at 107, 109–10 ("What is ruled out is forcing people to live this way or that, beyond what is needed to protect every sane adult's chances of living as he or she sees fit").

[27] See Thomas Nagel, "Moral Conflict and Political Legitimacy," 16 *Philosophy and Public Affairs* 215, 230 (1987) (referring to grounds of decision that "can be shown to be justifiable from a more impersonal standpoint").

drawing the line between rational grounds and nonrational bases for judgment. In much of what we believe, rational understanding, however that is conceived, intertwines with other assumptions.

Insofar as a constraint conceived in terms of rational grounds privileges one particular way of understanding, some people object that it unfairly discriminates against other modes of apprehension; but a more troubling practical worry arises out of divergent opinions about what can be established rationally. A good many people believe that the existence of a beneficent God can be established rationally. Years ago, one of my sons had me read a book that claimed that by proof of miracles and accurate prophecies, the Bible established itself as the infallible word of God and showed that Jesus was the Son of God. Any constraint of public reasons is to operate as a self-restraint. If people agreed that they should rely only on rational grounds, they would still disagree vigorously about what rational grounds could establish. The author who thought that he could rationally establish the infallibility of the Bible would feel free to rely on biblical passages; others who believed that recognition of biblical truth depends on faith could not rely on the same passages, though they might be no less certain the passages represent God's true word.

The most appealing single category of claims that do not count as ones of public reason are those based on comprehensive views, overarching philosophies of life.[28] According to Rawls, people resolving constitutional essentials and basic questions of justice should rely neither on religious perspectives nor on secular philosophies, such as utilitarianism or the view that human autonomy is the most fundamental good.[29]

We need to recognize that what people will sacrifice if they forgo reliance on comprehensive views will be uneven. A utilitarian will give up less than a Christian fundamentalist, because the specific arguments a utilitarian makes do not depend on his utilitarian premises in the way that would be

---

[28] See Rawls, supra note 2, at 62 ("There is no reason . . . why any citizen, or association of citizens, should have the right to use the state's police power to decide constitutional essentials or basic questions of justice as that person's, or that association's, comprehensive doctrine directs").

[29] If someone's comprehensive view reflects his overarching approach to life, how can he possibly be expected not to rely on it? Rawls's answer to this question is a two-level approach. People with a variety of comprehensive views will coalesce around the premise that liberal democracy is a desirable form of government. A feature of liberal democracy is resolving political questions in a way that is detached from people's comprehensive view. Thus, a person's comprehensive view calls on him to accept a political arrangement in which issues are resolved without direct reference to comprehensive views. There is nothing illogical about this arrangement, as we can see clearly if we imagine people of different religious convictions who agree upon principles of religious liberty and separation of church and state, including a principle that officials will not resolve issues based on their own understanding of religious truth.

true for the fundamentalist. Thus, David Baltimore's argument about the great potential medical benefits of stem cell research lies within premises that are shared in the society. It is also the kind of argument a utilitarian makes. Granted, a utilitarian has a particular device for weighing reasons—the greatest happiness principle (or some similar principle)—and he has a basis for excluding some possible grounds; but all the reasons a utilitarian will be likely to suggest for or against a policy are likely to fall within the domain of arguments that people accept independent of their comprehensive views. That certainly is not true for much a religious fundamentalist holds true. This inequality of sacrifice is troubling, but it may be acceptable if we have good reasons to exclude comprehensive views from the domain of politics.

To recapitulate, what are not public reasons? We have looked at grounds that are not widely accepted, conceptions of the good, grounds that are not rational, and comprehensive views. Although the most plausible single criterion for what reasons are public is that they do not rest on comprehensive views, we should be open to the possibility that more than one of these criteria may count for whether a reason is public. We should also be open to the possibility that some reasons may be more or less public, rather than public or not.

DIFFICULTIES IN CLASSIFYING NATURAL LAW ARGUMENTS

Recognizing that the very concept of public reasons is far from unproblematic, we turn now to some perplexities in discerning what should count as reasons that are public, focusing particularly on natural law arguments such as Professor George's argument that the embryo is a human being.

We may start with this thought by Robert George and Christopher Wolfe: "On the one hand, if 'public reason' is interpreted broadly . . . , then natural law theorists believe that natural law theory is nothing more or less than the philosophy of public reason. . . . On the other hand, if 'public reason' is interpreted in the narrower sense . . . [which] generally excludes reliance on 'comprehensive' moral, philosophical, and religious doctrines, then natural law theorists reject the idea."[30] Although this sentence captures a large measure of truth, I think we can delve more deeply into which aspects of natural law reasoning might qualify as public reasons, under various approaches to public reason.

[30] Robert P. George and Christopher Wolfe, "Introduction," in George and Wolfe, supra note 19, at 1, 2.

John Courtney Murray, the most widely read American theorist of natural law in the twentieth century, and a drafter of the Second Vatican Council's statement on religious liberty, claimed in his book *We Hold These Truths*[31] that American traditions and natural law understanding coalesce. He urged that the American political community is based on a tradition of natural law and natural rights, resting on a belief that "the people as a whole are inwardly governed by the recognized imperatives of the universal moral law."[32] The American consensus implies "that there are truths that we hold in common, and a natural law that makes known to all of us the structure of the moral universe."[33] Natural law reasoning best articulates the principles of this consensus, although they can be fully understood only by the wise. According to Murray, therefore, a natural law approach provides the best reasoned foundation for the public philosophy of our society, and its government. Rather than analyzing how Murray's understanding would look in light of more recent theorizing about public reason, I shall suggest a number of distinctions regarding natural law theories, trying to discern how far claims of natural law might fall within a domain of public reason. For this exercise, I am assuming that claims *might* be disqualified as public reasons because they do not rest on rational grounds, because they are based on controversial ideas of the good, or because they are aspects of comprehensive views.[34]

The distinctions regarding natural law that seem important are these: (1) nonreligious understandings of natural law principles contrasted with religious understandings; (2) the theoretical premises of natural law approaches contrasted with practical ways to resolve moral problems; (3) teleological understandings of morality contrasted with the idea that basic moral premises are self-evident; (4) rational derivation of moral conclusions contrasted with judgments based on the fruits of experience; (5) moral claims that are dependent on ideas of a good life contrasted with those that are independent of those ideas; (6) conclusions susceptible to universal understanding contrasted with those that only the wise can grasp; (7) understanding that is independent of time and place contrasted with understanding that develops according to time and culture. These distinctions can contribute to analytical

---

[31] John Courtney Murray, *We Hold These Truths: Catholic Reflections on the American Proposition* (New York: Sheed and Ward, 1960).

[32] Id. at 36 (contrasting this belief with highly voluntaristic accounts of natural rights).

[33] Id. at 40.

[34] We need to remember that if important natural law claims are "disqualified," that does not necessarily mean that they do not belong in politics given the controversial status of any theory that citizens or officials should constrain themselves to rely on public reasons.

clarity, but I definitely do not mean to suggest that every version of natural law theory or every particular moral claim comes down neatly on one side or the other of the dichotomies.[35]

Religious Understanding or Not

The close association between Roman Catholicism and the natural law tradition leads some outsiders to suppose that natural law is an essentially religious view about law and morality, but that is contrary to what most modern natural law theorists claim. They contend that, in some sense, morality is universal and that fundamental moral norms can be grasped by people whatever their religious traditions and opinions.[36]

Natural lawyers within the Christian tradition have believed that scripture and church teachings complement what we can discern by natural reason, and some believe that a relatively few moral duties are discoverable only from religious sources; but these views alone do not disqualify natural law arguments from being ones of public reason.[37] Various Protestant theologians and a few Roman Catholic ones have challenged this universalist natural law view as failing to be distinctly Christian; for them, a Christian ethic should depend on Christian sources and a Christian worldview.[38] Jean Porter's study of scholastic philosophers and theologians shows that they drew a less sharp distinction between natural reason and religious sources of in-

---

[35] For example, insofar as we can differentiate between rational derivation from basic premises and reliance on the fruits of experience, a theorist might believe both are highly relevant to drawing sound moral conclusions.

[36] See Jean Porter, *Natural and Divine Law: Reclaiming the Tradition for Christian Ethics* 29–30 (Grand Rapids, Mich.: Eerdmans, 1999) (describing Catholic version of natural law: "Because moral norms are grounded in human nature, which is the same everywhere, they are accessible to all reasonable men and women without the necessity of revelation"); Yves R. Simon, *The Tradition of Natural Law: A Philosopher's Reflections*, Vukan Kuic, ed. 125–36 (New York: Fordham University Press, 1965) (explaining that natural laws are premises that all societies grasp, but from which they may draw different moral conclusions); George and Wolfe, supra note 19, at 56 (describing view held by natural law theorists: "basic moral norms are widely known, though in some cases they or their more specific applications may be obscured by wayward passions or corrupt customs or habits").

[37] A full analysis needs to take account of people whose certainty about resolution of a moral issue is increased because of religious sources or whose sense of the validity of a natural law conclusion is based on religious sources, but I leave these nuances aside here.

[38] See Porter, note 36 supra, at 30–34 (reviewing criticisms of natural law raised by Reinhold Niebuhr, Stanley Hauerwas, Karl Rahner, Bernard Lonergan, and James Gustafson, among others); id. at 168–72 (discussing criticisms of natural law raised by Karl Barth, who is described as believing that "an adequate account of morality must be not only theological but specifically and distinctively Christological").

sight than modern natural lawyers tend to do.[39] She suggests that the scholastic approach has much to teach us about ethical understanding.[40] Whatever the intrinsic soundness of the approach Porter reports and recommends, reasoning and conclusions that depend on specifically Christian sources do not satisfy requirements of public reason, as elaborated by modern theorists of liberal democracy.

Overall Theory or Ways of Reasoning about Moral and Political Problems

Most natural law theorists have provided accounts of human good and moral duty within an overall perspective about fundamental reality.[41] Typically, the theorists have connected human existence to the rest of the physical universe, in which all objects, or all living objects, have a natural inclination to fulfill their essential purposes.[42] In this teleological view of life, human beings share some purposes with animals, and perhaps some even with plants and stones, but they have a higher purpose than all other earthly beings. That purpose is to realize their rational nature. In many versions, God is a crucial element in this structure of being. When natural law claims rest directly upon assertions about God, or upon a complete theory of natural reality, they are based on a comprehensive view in Rawls's sense. But that need not disqualify every moral and political argument made by natural lawyers from being consonant with public reason.

The complete relation between full natural law theories and their bases of moral reasoning is complex, but here is how moral claims might escape depending on a comprehensive view. Most natural-law accounts assert that people do (descriptively) reach common judgments about basic moral issues and that these judgments are sound.[43] So long as a theorist believes that

[39] The scholastics used scripture to determine which aspects of nature to treat as normative, and they used their understanding of nature and reason to interpret scripture. Rather than forming two complementary tracks to moral understanding, religious interpretation and natural reason interpenetrated each other. See id. at 129–40.

[40] See id. at 303–17 (suggesting that moral reflection is theological yet "remains open to the best insights of the natural and social sciences").

[41] See generally Lloyd L. Weinreb, *Natural Law and Justice* 55–60 (Cambridge: Harvard University Press, 1987).

[42] See Porter, supra note 36, at 70 (quoting a "highly influential definition" of natural law made by Ulpian, a Roman jurist: "The law of nature is that which nature teaches all animals. For that law is not proper to the human race, but it is common to all animals which are born on the earth and in the sea, and to the birds also").

[43] There is substantial variation in how much common reason reaches. Compare Porter, supra note 36, at 29–30 (describing Catholic version of natural law, which holds that the same moral norms are

people can reason to sound moral judgments *without* understanding or accepting any overall theory that explains how these judgments fit with physical reality or God's purposes, then the moral arguments the theorist presents might qualify as public reasons, even though his complete theory definitely does not.[44]

Notice, in this respect, that George made his appeal without explicitly relying on any comprehensive natural law theory. If his contention about the status of an embryo can be detached from such a theory, it could be a public reason not to engage in embryonic stem cell research.[45]

Teleology or Self-Evidence

The traditional understanding of natural law is built on a purposive sense of nature; as an acorn develops into an oak, things have a tendency to fulfill their essential purposes. Human beings live good lives if they fulfill their true purposes; the norms that they should observe help them realize their essential nature. To take a practical example, we might discern that the essential purpose of human sexuality is procreation. We could proceed to condemn masturbation, homosexual relations, and the use of artificial contraceptives as unnatural deviations from appropriate sexual acts. This theoretical approach has been challenged by Germain Grisez and John Finnis,[46] and by Robert George, although their own conclusions about practical moral issues differ little from those whose teleological approach they reject. Their account unties moral understanding from any theory of physical reality. Rather, human beings are capable of identifying certain goods as self-evidently valuable. From this identification of basic goods and from recognition that none has priority over others, we can ascertain what actions are morally right or morally wrong.

Our question is whether either of these approaches is intrinsically more susceptible of providing public reasons than the other. Insofar as the teleolog-

---

accessible to all persons), with Simon, supra note 36, at 3–5, 23–26, 66, 146–48 (expressing skeptical view about how much is really shared in common).

[44] See Simon, supra note 36, at 62 (speaking of acquaintance with natural law as being logically antecedent to knowledge of God's existence, although understanding of natural law is preserved only by recognizing God as its ultimate foundation).

[45] However, when a natural law theorist advances a moral claim, it may be very difficult to decide just how far the claim can fairly be detached from his overall theory.

[46] The explication with which I am most conversant is John Finnis, *Natural Law and Natural Rights*, note 4 supra, which I reviewed in 10 *Political Theory* 133 (1981). In a book that is critical of this approach, Russell Hittinger examines its major claims in detail and refers to many writings of its defenders. See generally Russell Hittinger, *A Critique of the New Natural Law Theory* (Notre Dame, Ind.: University of Notre Dame Press, 1987).

ical theory rests on broad claims about purpose in nature, it certainly amounts to a comprehensive view in Rawls's sense.[47] No doubt, the Grisez-Finnis-George approach is also a comprehensive view, but it does not follow that every moral claim made from that perspective must rest on the comprehensive view. George, for example, might argue that his particular claim about the embryos is self-evidently correct, and can be seen to be so by people who need not accept the idea that self-evident truths lie at the core of moral understanding.[48]

Rational Derivations or the Fruits of Experience

How are we to draw correct moral conclusions? Various natural law theorists have emphasized rational derivations from first principles or insights from human experience. I do not want to overstate the dichotomy. Everyone agrees that reflection on experience is a vital aspect of understanding moral truth, and no one rejects rational analysis that moves from general truths to particulars. But, nevertheless, some theorists rely much more heavily on rational derivations than do others. Many modern proponents of natural law, both those who maintain a teleological perspective and those who start from self-evidence, draw highly controversial conclusions from supposedly irresistible first principles. To take just one example, the natural purposes or self-evident values of human sexuality are said to lead to a conclusion that persons who are powerfully inclined from birth to homosexual rather than heterosexual relations should refrain from sexual acts altogether, rather than engage in the only sexual acts that attract them.[49]

In the abstract, rational derivation is fully consonant with public reason. After all, if one begins with a valid first principle and draws from it by rigor-

---

[47] See Rawls, supra note 2, at 175 (stating that "[a] doctrine is fully comprehensive when it covers all recognized values and virtues within one rather precisely articulated scheme of thought, whereas a doctrine is only partially comprehensive when it comprises certain (but not all) nonpolitical values and is rather loosely articulated").

[48] Rawls has talked about people relying on practices of common sense and science. See John Rawls, "Kantian Constructivism in Moral Theory," 77 *Journal of Philosophy* 515, 539 (1980). Such a reliance does not stray from public reason. George talks about his conclusion as based on science, but the scientific evidence alone does not tell us how the embryo should be valued. If George conceded as much, he might still contend that his conclusion that an entity capable of development through internal organic functioning into a human being *is* a human being is a conclusion of common sense (albeit a kind of rarified common sense). Conceivably, a teleological theorist could advance similar arguments that some claims about basic human purposes, such as preserving life, rest on a shared common sense; but, in general, claims within a teleological perspective seem to rest more directly on a comprehensive view than claims asserted as self-evident.

[49] I have criticized this position. See Kent Greenawalt, "How Persuasive Is Natural Law Theory?" 75 *Notre Dame Law Review* 1647, 1666–71 (2000).

ous analysis, one's conclusions are rationally compelling. Regrettably, what for some natural law thinkers are unassailable first principles and irrefutable derivations strike many outsiders as uncongenial abstractions that have lost sight of the human condition. If we were focusing exclusively on this feature of claimed rational derivation, the proponent of a norm about sexual behavior might think his view falls within the domain of public reasons; an outsider might find that the norm is not only unpersuasive on balance but that it appeals to an esoteric set of assumptions rather than any common reason.

The more modest approach of reliance on human experience may fall more indisputably within the range of public reason, at least if the reliance on experience is of a certain kind.[50] Someone who examines the morality of incest by surveying the norms of various cultures and psychological studies of family relations begins with the evidence of social science. If he concludes that, even apart from genetic hazards and the unacceptability of sexual relations with minors, incestuous sexual relations carry very serious risks to family life, and are therefore rightly regarded as immoral, that judgment falls more easily within the domain of public reasons than the top-down reasoning one finds in some natural law approaches.

Dependent on Ideas of the Good or Not

Natural law theory has developed notions of morality out of judgments about what are fulfilling lives for human beings.[51] Were "public reason" to exclude all ideas of the good, it would disqualify most claims of natural law.[52] Undoubtedly, the natural lawyer's best response is that no sensible version of public reasons should exclude claims about the good life. The natural lawyer *might* acknowledge that controversial claims of the good may be excluded, but say that his claims about the good life are uncontroversial. Faced with the indisputable fact that many natural law claims about good lives *are* controversial, he might claim that he *begins* with uncontroversial claims about the good life and derives his controversial conclusions by a

---

[50] A reliance on one's own personal experience, in the sense of subjective reactions, is not clearly in the domain of public reason, unless one has a basis to suppose that other people react similarly.

[51] See Mark C. Murphy, *Natural Law and Practical Rationality* 46 (New York: Cambridge University Press, 2001) (noting that natural law theorists claim that individuals act to increase their well-being). This characterization fits both teleological and self-evidence approaches.

[52] Interestingly, George's particular argument about stem cell research does not rest on a controversial notion of a good life, or perhaps on any notion of a good life. George's main argument, based on science and what we should reasonably conclude about an entity that can develop into an adult person, is about who counts as a human being. That argument is more about right or justice, the required respect for persons, than it is about what constitutes a good life.

chain of rationally persuasive arguments. In form, this argument has considerable appeal, but if we look at most practical examples, we find either that the initial premises are controversial or that the derivation of conclusions does not seem rationally compelling to outsiders, even ones who are fair and open-minded.[53]

Universal Understanding or Understanding of the Wise

Although natural law theorists have claimed that fundamental moral understanding is universal, it has not followed that ordinary people can resolve complex moral questions on their own. How to resolve some difficult problems, they believe, can be grasped only by the wise.[54] This role for the wise is not a serious difficulty for "public reason" if the wise can explain their initial conclusions in a way that all the rest of us will understand is convincing, or if the wise are a group conveniently identified by public reason. If all of us understand the conclusions the wise reach, their reasoning is what convinces us, even if we lacked the insight to reach those conclusions by ourselves. But our understanding might not be essential. For many matters, notably scientific ones, most people depend on the judgments of experts, and they are not able to evaluate why the experts are right. So long as the experts can be identified in some objective way, relying on what they say is consonant with a reliance on public reason.

If reliance on scientific experts fits with public reason, why should not the same be true for reliance on "the wise" for moral and political judgments? We can see two related possible objections. One is that in deciding what is right morally and politically (insofar as that does not depend on scientific understanding about what is true descriptively), people should rely on their own judgments, not those of experts. On this account, a moral argument that is so complicated that only the wise can understand it falls outside the domain of public reasons.[55] A second objection is that we have no confident

---

[53] This very disagreement about what can be persuasively derived from uncontroversial premises might be used to bolster the contention that only uncontroversial conclusions about the good life qualify as public reasons, not controversial conclusions purportedly derived from uncontroversial premises.

[54] We can imagine a view that ordinary people resolve moral issues just as well as anyone else, but that they are incapable of rationalizing and theorizing their insights as well as the most intelligent and highly trained among us. But the role of the wise in much natural law theory goes beyond this. That view, which fits well within the notion that reason is the distinctive human characteristic, is that the wise are better capable of resolving moral issues than the less wise.

[55] For a suggestion that arguments should be discounted if they are extremely difficult to assess and are subject to reasonable disagreement, see Stephen Macedo, "In Defense of Liberal Public Reason: Are Slavery and Abortion Hard Cases?" in George and Wolfe, note 19 supra, at 23.

way to identify the morally wise. This objection seems to me crucial to deciding that conclusions that only the wise may perceive are not within the domain of public reasons.[56]

Understanding Independent of Time and Place or Understanding Dependent on Time and Place

To draw a stark contrast, one can imagine a moral understanding that is more or less constant across times and cultures or a moral understanding that develops and recedes in context.[57] On the second view, explaining how anyone could ever have thought that slavery was consonant with natural law becomes easier; but that view renders one less confident that conclusions reached now have any permanent validity. This distinction, by itself, has little bearing on the issue of natural law and public reason within a particular society,[58] although the developing view fits more comfortably with a sense that the wise have a special role.

If this quick survey of natural law perspectives and arguments and their relation to ideas of public reason suggests a great deal of complexity, that indeed is the point. With a particular argument by a natural lawyer on some political issue, we (and he) might doubt how much the argument depended on religious premises, how closely it was tied to an overall theory that would amount to a comprehensive view, whether it was self-evident in a way that would make it part of the stock of common reasons, whether any claimed derivations from higher premises followed in the way the argument asserted, whether it rests on a controversial idea of the good, and whether it could be understood by ordinary people or only the wise. We can imagine that even if a speaker and listener agreed on the standards for determining if reasons are public, they might disagree over whether a particular argument by the speaker qualified. We can also imagine that many arguments might not seem to be sharply public or sharply nonpublic, but to fall into some gray area of arguably public or more or less public. Finally, we can imagine that the problem of classification is still more difficult because there is uncertainty about what the criteria are for reasons being public. As difficult as it may be to say whether any particular argument is "in" or "out" of the domain of public

---

[56] If almost everyone could agree on who was "wise," and the basis for that agreement was itself a matter of public reason, then we would have a good public reason to accept a consensus of the wise.

[57] Simon adopts a strong version of the second view. See Simon, note 36 supra, at 161–63 (arguing that our knowledge of natural law develops gradually with progression of human nature).

[58] That is, one could believe that natural law arguments are ones of public reason within a culture even if they are substantially conditioned by time and place.

reasons, generalizing across the wide range of natural law arguments is virtually impossible.

If natural law arguments are this hard to classify, we can expect the same to be true of many other approaches to moral and political questions that do not depend on explicit religious perspectives. We might find that many reasons and arguments seem to be more or less "public" rather than public or not. We might also wonder if the appropriate degree of publicness of arguments depends on the circumstances. What might be insufficiently public for the preamble of a statute may be sufficiently public in a speech by a senator to her constituents.

Law as an Illustration of Public Reasons

We might be drawn to an even more skeptical conclusion: namely, that whatever other virtues it may have, a theory of public reasons founders completely on the impossibility of specifying just what reasons are public. But standing against this skeptical rejection of any ideal of public reasons is the law. Is not the law, and I mean here assessment of what the law provides, a domain in which a theory of public reasons is realized? If so, does not that raise the possibility that politics could be a domain of public reason? Rawls talks about the Supreme Court's work as an exemplar of the use of public reason,[59] and it is certainly true that some reasons that count outside the law count for less or do not count at all inside the law. I initially supposed that what Rawls said about the law was uncontroversial, that law is an area in which a theory of public reasons applies, and that the difficult question is whether the limited stock of reasons within the law has any bearing on the broader realm of politics. But I have found surprising resistance to the idea that law is a domain of public reasons.

Everyone seems to agree that some reasons that might carry weight outside the law do not count when judges interpret statutes or constitutions or develop the common law. Thus, a Roman Catholic judge would not render a decision on the basis that it accords with the stance taken in a papal encyclical.[60] Within the law, judges are supposed to rely on reasons that have force for other judges, and the reasons need to be accessible, both in the sense of being comprehensible and in the sense of being capable of being grasped on

---

[59] See Rawls, note 2 supra, at 235.

[60] However, reference to the encyclical might be made as evidence that all major religious traditions unite in taking a certain view.

the basis of rational thought, not faith or intuition. So the law limits relevant reasons; it requires that reasons be understood by rational analysis and have a force that is generally understood. These seem to be strong credentials for the law's being a regime of public reasons.

Just how many reasons lie wholly outside the law for various kinds of legal issues is debatable. But even if the discrepancy between reasons that count in politics and reasons that count in law is not large, particular reasons have different weight within and without the law. An argument that a particular result will be more just or will make people happier *may* have some weight when judges interpret statutes, but it will not carry the day if the language of a statute clearly requires a contrary conclusion. Perhaps the most significant difference between reasoning within the law and reasoning in politics has to do with the special weight that certain reasons have in law, especially reasons concerning textual meaning, legislative intent, and the force of precedents, and the diminished weight accorded other reasons. In any event, we may say that in some imprecise way, leaving room for debate over many specific examples, that some reasons that can carry force outside the law do not carry force for legal interpretation, and that the weight of many other reasons is sharply affected by whether one is talking about personal judgment or legislative policy, as contrasted with legal interpretation.

What might be said against the proposition that the law is a system of public reasons, a system in which people are supposed to rely on reasons that have a general or public force and in which many reasons are disqualified or diminished? Skeptics have put the point something like this: "The law allows all reasons to count that are made relevant by the law. One need ask not about what reasons are public reasons but what reasons the law makes relevant."[61] So put, the challenge seems a matter of conceptual labeling,[62] but I believe a deeper question lies beneath it. The deeper question is the manner in which one resolves what reasons the law allows. My response is that the manner in which one determines whether the law allows some reasons is very similar to how one might decide what reasons count as public for political life.

We might imagine two contrasting ways in which to resolve which reasons the law admits. One way would be to see the law as a distinctive endeavor that has its own peculiar strategy to identify what reasons count. It is as if we said that the reasons that are relevant to settle disputes in tennis are the

[61] This is my paraphrase of a position taken by some participants during a May 2001 conference at Catholic University on public reason.

[62] My response to the formal distinction between reasons the law allows and public reasons is that the distinction itself is indecisive about every important normative issue.

reasons supplied by the rule book of tennis. Then we would have a limited stock of reasons, comprehensible reasons of force for every decision maker, but all this would be a consequence of the narrow coverage of the rule book.[63] That tennis has a limited stock of comprehensible reasons with force for all decision makers would tell us hardly anything about public reason in politics, about why people might eschew otherwise persuasive reasons for justifying laws and policies.

An alternative way that one might resolve whether the law admits reasons is to ask whether otherwise persuasive reasons for reaching decisions are (or should be) excluded because they do not meet some requisite degree of publicness. If the answer were yes, if this were how we decided what reasons the law excludes, we would have an example of "public reasons" that could be relevant for politics. In that event, the assertion that the law makes some reasons relevant and other reasons irrelevant would be quite consistent with the conclusion that the law is a regime of public reasons.

Without doubt, the distinctive character of law, and the authoritative sources of law, lead to some reasons counting within the law and others counting little or not at all in many contexts. For example, the practice that misguided precedents are deemed to have force is an aspect of common-law jurisprudence. To this extent, the law is not so unlike tennis governed largely according to the rule book. But lawyers may usually argue to judges that, in an otherwise close case, one interpretation of a precedent or a reading of a statute will promote justice or human welfare better than another. In fact, the domain of *relevant* arguments in law is not much narrower than the domain of relevant arguments in politics, although, as I have said, differences in weight are critical.[64] The considerations that determine whether reasons are excluded resemble those that have been suggested for political life by proponents of public reason.

The point is easiest to illustrate for determinations that judges must make that do not depend much on authoritative statutes or precedents. In virtually all states, the main standard for determinations of child custody is "the best interests of the child."[65] Suppose a judge must decide whether to place a child with her father or with her mother, who is living with another woman in an

---

[63] In fact, I doubt if tennis or any similar game (I put aside board games) could be completely self-contained in this way; general notions of fairness, for example, would be bound to affect interpretation; but *most* of the reasons that count in tennis might be derived from the rule book.

[64] It is sufficient for my argument that it is correct for common law, even if, contrary to what I believe, reasons of justice and desirability are properly excluded in statutory or constitutional interpretation, or both.

[65] See 24A Am. Jur. 2D Divorce and Separation § 931 (West Group, 2006).

intimate relationship. The judge should not refuse custody to the mother because the Bible condemns homosexual relations as sinful. Nor should the judge announce the truth of greatest happiness utilitarianism as the basis for resolving what is in the child's best interest. The basis for excluding these possible reasons is very similar to the arguments put forward by public-reasons theorists in respect to politics: the reasons do not have appropriately general force and they rely too heavily on controversial overarching views.

All this is sufficient to suggest that the law is not only a domain of limited reasons,[66] but that part of the basis for deciding what reasons are included and excluded has to do with determining which reasons are public.

If the law *is* a domain of public reasons, then it is at least possible that in politics, people do have, or should have, a sense that their reasons should be public, and it is possible that that sense could strengthen and sharpen over time, *or* that it could dissipate in the face of challenges that God should not be removed from the public square. As I have said, my own sense is that the constraint of public reason applies primarily to the public expressions of officials, and that saying just what count as public reasons in various contexts is no simple matter.

CONCLUSION

Our treatment of public reasons may seem to have wandered far from the constitutional principle that no law should be adopted that establishes religion. The crucial connection is that whatever other reasons may be *non*public, it is widely assumed that religious reasons fall within that amorphous category. According to a theory of public reasons, if laws are adopted based mainly on the religious convictions of citizens and officials, something has

---

[66] If we ask just what reasons count in law and how much they count, we face difficulties like those that troubled the examination of natural law and public reason. Notably, Supreme Court justices disagree about the relevance of legislative history in statutory cases, and related to this is an apparent disagreement whether the subjective intentions of legislators matter. One theory of common-law development is that judges should very heavily rely on community norms. See generally Melvin Eisenberg, *The Nature of the Common Law* (Cambridge: Harvard University Press, 1988). Another theory is that they should forthrightly interpret in light of their own judgments about justice. See generally Ronald Dworkin, *Law's Empire*, note 5 supra. People who agree that certain arguments are relevant may disagree greatly about how much weight these should carry in relation to other arguments. Thus, our law is hardly a model of a regime in which telling arguments are neatly lined up with their appropriate weight. But all this does not deprive it of being a domain of public reasons, in which some arguments are acknowledged not to be valid because these arguments fail to exhibit sufficient publicness, and the force of other arguments may be diminished because they seem less public than alternative arguments.

gone wrong from the standpoint of liberal political philosophy, and that impropriety may well be considered a kind of establishment of religion. No one thinks that because *some* citizens and officials have relied upon religious convictions, resulting laws actually violate the Establishment Clause as a matter of law. But conceivably if enough officials rely mainly on their religious convictions or those of the constituents, laws are invalid, and should be so declared by courts.

The part of this chapter devoted to the uncertain boundaries of public reasons does not directly touch the status of reliance on the Bible or on church authority—those are unpublic in the relevant sense—but if affects that reliance in a more complicated way. Any minimally fair theory of public reasons cannot include religious reasons and no other reasons. If religious reasons are to be "excluded," then other reasons that are similarly not rational or based on comprehensive views must also be excluded. If one is hard put to explain just what other reasons are nonpublic, that casts doubt on whether it is fair to insist that good citizens and officials not rely on religious reasons.

The earlier part of the chapter summarizing my own limited, "intermediate," account of the constraints of public reasons provides a more decisive response to extravagant claims about the relevance of the Establishment Clause for this subject. It has never been widely assumed in the course of the country's history that people should refrain from relying on their religious convictions when they consider the wisdom of proposed legislation. Among other movements, arguments for abolition of slavery, for Prohibition, and for civil rights were substantially religious. Neither widespread reliance on religious premises nor the active involvement of religious groups should, alone, be regarded as marking laws that violate the Establishment Clause, much less as marking laws that courts should declare to violate the Establishment Clause.

What remains for our next chapter is consideration whether certain narrower connections of religion to laws that are adopted—connections different from ones we have considered in earlier chapters—might render the laws unconstitutional.

CHAPTER 24

Legal Enforcement of Religion-Based Morality

This chapter explores the implications for constitutional law of the broader subject we considered in the previous chapter—legislative and executive policies that are grounded in religious premises. At the end of the day, these implications are very slight if one is interested in what measures courts should hold invalid, or so I shall argue. But the analysis leading to this conclusion can help dispel confusions about the relation between political rhetoric and judicially enforceable constitutional law. It can also enable those who would like the courts to play a more active role to see exactly how they differ from those who reject such a role.

The overarching question for us in this chapter is which laws and policies violate the Establishment Clause *because* they rest on religious premises. The question mainly has cogency in respect to legally enforced morality; but to understand why this is so, we need to clear away various matters that are not at issue.

Most of this volume has been about tangible assistance to religious groups and about government sponsorship of religious ideas. We have examined a number of topics and the major constitutional approaches for dealing with them. Government assistance can be open, as with financial aid to religious charities, or covert, as with the hypothetical example of a highway route chosen because it will benefit a particular church. Government sponsorship of religion can be undeniable, as with devotional Bible reading in public schools and the hiring of army chaplains, or it can be more subtle or debatable, as with moments of silence and "under God" in the Pledge of Allegiance. If the obvious and dominant purpose or a "primary" effect is to aid religion, legislation is invalid under the Establishment Clause.

As far as purpose is concerned, the Supreme Court has declared invalid only those laws whose overriding objective was to promote religion. One can certainly imagine stricter approaches, ones under which more legislation would fail a purpose test. A court might ask whether a religious aim was influential or whether a statute would have been adopted in the absence of religious objectives. Our highway board example involved secret deliberations, but let us suppose instead that the proceedings were open, that two of the five-member board voted for Route C, which would have gone thirty miles from the Baptist church (thus inconveniencing churchgoers), that one member who voted for Route A said she would have voted for Route C except that she wanted to aid the church and its members, and that two other members said they preferred A on a number of grounds, one of which was that it would aid the Baptists. In these circumstances, we could say that the religious aim was influential *and* that the decision would (almost certainly) have been different without it. In deciding whether a worker had been improperly fired because of his race or religion, a court might employ such an approach, not allowing the firing to stand if it probably was a consequence of discrimination.[1] And I have suggested that if an individual legislator votes for a bill only for a religious reason that would render a statute invalid if it was the reason of every legislator, the individual legislator has violated the Establishment Clause.[2] But the Supreme Court has been very clear that it will not engage in such nuanced inquiries. On the understanding that courts should accord deference to legislatures, it has required that promoting religion be the evident dominant purpose if legislation is to fail the purpose test.

The legislative measures we are considering in this chapter do not mainly promote religious groups or religious perspectives. They do not give religions tangible aid and they do not encourage people to adopt any particular view about religion. What most do, to put it starkly, is to force nonadherents to behave in ways that those with particular religious views think they should behave. Thus, laws that forbade people from engaging in sexual acts with others of the same gender were not intended to convert to a religious view; rather, they were aimed at making people comply with a moral standard, or, to put it differently, at preventing people from falling into sin.

For analytical purposes, it helps initially to assume that every legislator has the same attitude about a law and that this shared attitude is spread on the record for all to see. What attitudes run counter to the Establishment Clause? Religious convictions that underlie reasons to vote might function in one of at least five different ways. (1) Among entities that undoubtedly deserve the protection of the state, religious convictions are the basis for determining what is a just distribution of resources, privileges, and penalties. Into this category could fall laws regarding welfare for the poor and authorizing, or not authorizing, capital punishment. (2) The crucial question is

---

[1] Emmel v. Coca-Cola Bottling Co., 95 F.3d 627, 629 (7th Cir. 1996); *Venters v. City of Delphi*, 123 F.3d 956, 972 (7th Cir. 1996).

[2] One might fairly resist this conclusion and say the legislator has violated only the spirit of the clause.

whether entities of some kind deserve serious protection, and religious convictions determine the answer. Arguments based on religious authority for a law against use of embryonic stem calls (because embryos are human beings) or against scientific experimentation with animals fall into this category. (3) Religious convictions determine judgments whether actions will harm persons other than consenting adults who are most directly involved. One argument against incestuous marriage is that the knowledge that such marriage is possible among adults will have a detrimental effect on family relations while children are still minors (e.g., a brother and sister may relate differently to each other, and in a less healthy way, if they realize they can marry each other when they are old enough). A person might believe this argument is persuasive *only* because a sacred text condemns incest. (4) Religious convictions are the basis to decide that actions will harm the adults who choose to perform them. A person's religious beliefs might lead him to think that homosexual relations are bound to be psychologically damaging to participants, damaging according to ordinary assessments of psychological health. (5) Religious convictions are a basis to judge acts as wrongful, though without any harm as conceived by nonreligious standards. A person might oppose homosexual acts in the face of powerful evidence that they do not cause ordinary physical and psychological damage, on the basis that they constitute sins in the eyes of God (perhaps to be punished in some form of afterlife).

We should not be surprised that argument about this topic tends to focus mainly on my last two categories, usually without a distinction being drawn between them. I shall concentrate on these as well, but I first explain why the first three categories are also important and are different. Normative questions about what entities deserve protection and about what justice requires for these entities are not matters of simple fact. In a liberal democratic society, there will be wide agreement about some of these questions. All or virtually all human beings who have been born and are now alive warrant protection, and justice for people within a society requires some form of equal treatment. At the edges of which entities deserve protection and to what degree, there is controversy. What protection, if any, should be given to animals, to the environment (for its own sake), and to embryos and fetuses? How far should the state assist the less fortunate? Should capital punishment be available as a penalty? As to these matters, disagreements hardly fall out with religious opinions lined up neatly on one side and secular opinions on the opposite one. Various religious people have different views. It would be hard to trace any particular position a legislature might adopt directly to religious convictions. It is true that most people in the United States now who want to protect embryos are people of religious faith, but, as we have seen with Robert George's argument against stem cell research, many of these people also believe that one need not rely on religious premises to justify that protection.

Two other aspects about issues of justice and the borders of protection strike me as very important. For many of these issues, rational analysis is highly indecisive.[3] In making up their minds about whether to protect higher mammals, everybody will rely to an extent on nonrational (I do not say irrational) intuitions. Were citizens and officials permitted to rely on nonreligious intuitions but not to rely on religious convictions, that would constitute a form of implicit discrimination against religious perspectives. Moreover, any religious individual would have a hard time saying where his religious convictions leave off and what his intuitions would tell him apart from these convictions.

The other crucial aspect of our first two categories concerns the rationale for regulating behavior. Suppose it were true that only those with particular religious convictions believed that the state should protect dolphins, and they managed to get a law adopted that prohibited the killing of dolphins. Their *aim* would not be to promote a religion or even to prevent sin, but to protect entities that deserve protection. It would be odd to think that it should be impermissible for society to protect dolphins, even if the great majority of its members holds the religious view that they deserve that protection.[4] When the issue is the distribution of benefits and burdens, the analysis of legislative aims is typically similar. It is not that those adopting a law particularly want to control behavior to make sure it is moral; rather they want to see that people (and other protected entities) get the benefits they deserve and share burdens fairly.

Although arguments against restrictive abortion laws are often cast as ones about immoral behavior, and thus not so different from arguments about laws restricting sexual behavior, in fact the most powerful argument *for* a restrictive law is quite different. It involves, first, a claim that at the moment of conception, or at some later stage, the embryo, or fetus, deserves protection. (Often this point is put in terms that the fetus is a human being, implying that the fetus deserves as much protection as a full human being,

---

[3] In *Religious Convictions and Political Choice* (New York: Oxford University Press, 1988), I make an extended argument along these lines about animals, the environment, the status of a fetus, and some issues of just distribution.

[4] One *might* take a different view if the reasons for protection are actually *at odds* with what rational, secular morality might indicate—if, for example, the species that received special protection had much lower capacities than some other species but was thought by some to be favored by God. I discuss this possibility in id. at 204–7.

but someone might believe a fetus deserves significant protection from the state though less than does a full human being.) The protection afforded it by a restrictive law is of the kind that would benefit the fetus from any point of view. It concerns physical survival. The second part of the argument against abortion is one about justice, about burdens and benefits. The innocent fetus should be protected even if the cost is that the pregnant woman must carry the fetus against her wishes and give birth to a baby she would rather not have. Because the basic issues about abortion concern disagreements about entities deserving protection and about the degree to which fetuses should be protected if that impinges severely on the liberty of persons who undoubtedly deserve protection (i.e., pregnant women), any assertion that restrictive laws about abortion violate the Establishment Clause is less promising than similar assertions about laws more easily classifiable as aimed at sin.

Our third category (like the fourth and fifth categories) mainly involves laws that are directly addressed at people who together wish to perform a forbidden act. There is no immediate innocent victim, in the way that the fetus is an innocent victim in the eyes of those who want restrictions on abortions. Often with respect to such laws, people disagree about indirect harms. I have used the example of incest. If we put aside the concern about the genetic effects of inbreeding, which rest on a solid scientific base but would not apply to incestuous marriages of couples unable to conceive children together, we face a concern about the effect on minor children within families who knew that they might someday be eligible to marry a parent or sibling. Perhaps legal permission would have extremely little effect, especially if social taboos about incest remained strong. Were social scientists to study the effect of the repeal of laws against incest on typical family life, changes in attitudes would take time, and claimed causal relations would be disputable. And, of course, all anyone could do in advance of such a legal change would be to make an educated guess. A person might respond to this inevitable uncertainty from the standpoint of social science by reasoning as follows: "My religion firmly condemns incest. That is a strong basis to conclude that legal acceptance of incest would harm family life more broadly."

As I have put the point so far, the exact chain of inference from religious basis to harm for families is inexact. Here are two oversimple stark alternatives. (1) "My religion condemns incest. So also, I believe, do most other religions. Whatever the theological truth of my religion, the rejection of incest probably reflects a sound moral sense that it is destructive of family life." (2) "My religion condemns incest. I believe my religion accurately understands God's will. Since God forbids incest, that probably means it is destructive of family life." Were someone to rely on the first chain of inference, that could hardly present a problem for liberal political philosophy or the Establishment Clause. If one looks to past societies to provide *some evidence* of what kinds of restrictions promote healthy social life, one could hardly disregard what religious traditions have to say.[5] The second chain of inference, relying on the truth of a particular religion, is more questionable, but, *if* social science evidence is substantially indeterminate, people should be able to rely on religious convictions as well as nonreligious intuitions to fill in their sense of the broad effects of proposed laws.[6] *If* one believed, contrary to my view, that in some way the Establishment Clause *was* at odds with officials' relying on the second kind of inference, that would still not provide a workable principle for courts to invalidate laws under the Establishment Clause.

This leaves us with our last two categories, involving laws that restrict behavior just because it is immoral or because it is thought to harm the very people who choose to engage in it. In moving to these last two categories, we already are practicing deceptive oversimplification, because those who want to restrict behavior as immoral almost always believe that behavior does have corrosive effects on the broader society. But for clarity of analysis, we can put claims about those effects aside.

Laws restricting sexual conduct among consenting adults provide the main examples for these last two categories. We can focus on laws against homosexual acts, against fornication, and against bestiality, and on restrictions on marriage between persons of the same gender. The Establishment Clause argument against such laws is that they would not be adopted were it not for people's religious convictions and that they, therefore, amount to an establishment of religion. At least so long as the proponents of the restrictions do not rely heavily on claimed harm to innocent third parties, these laws differ from ones we have yet considered. They are not about borderlines of status or about distributive justice;[7] they *are* efforts to control behavior because that behavior is regarded as intrinsically wrongful.

Before engaging the main discussion, I need to defend my inclusion of bestiality on this list and to note alternative routes to constitutional protec-

---

[5] However, were one to rely only on that first approach, one would need to be open to moral assumptions of other religions, to evidence not from religious traditions, *and* to the possibility that various restrictions have reflected indefensible oppression or outright ignorance.

[6] As a matter of liberal political philosophy, I am inclined to think they should not rely in politics on factual judgments (grounded in religion) that are strongly opposed to what the evidence of science and social science establishes. Thus, people who believe the world will end five years from now should not press for government policies based on that assumption. Note 3 supra, at 204–11.

[7] I am here assuming that the argument that the majority should be protected against behavior that affronts it is not an appropriate claim of justice in a liberal society.

tion of much of the behavior involved. When the establishment claim is presented with respect to bestiality, it is often answered that laws prohibiting sex between humans and animals protect the animals from cruelty.[8] I find that implausible, whether it is offered as a causal explanation of why such laws are adopted or as a justification for them. If a society were mainly concerned with the welfare of animals, it would be very odd to allow humans to kill them for almost any reason and to confine them in small spaces on factory farms where they lead incredibly impoverished lives, but to impose a serious penalty to protect them from infrequent sexual relations with humans.[9] And if inducing male animals to orgasm to obtain sperm for breeding purposes is regarded as perfectly all right, why are actual sexual relations qualitatively much worse?[10] The overwhelming reason why sex with animals is forbidden is that it is regarded as utterly degrading for the human beings who choose to engage in it.

Two alternative constitutional arguments against restrictive laws about sexual behavior are ones of substantive due process (or constitutional privacy) and equal protection. The minimal notion of substantive due process[11] is that a law must have a "rational basis," but for most kinds of laws courts have stretched to find rational grounds for their enactment.[12] A heightened review has been exercised for laws regulating sexual behavior and abortion, but the main emphasis has been on the underlying right that is curtailed, not on the basis for restriction. The Establishment Clause argument concerns reasons for enactment rather than the nature of the behavior that is restricted.[13] Were the due process argument similarly to focus mainly on the reasons for enactment, it would differ from the Establishment Clause argument in disqualifying certain grounds for enactment, whether they were religious or not. For example, suppose it were determined that a mere wish to prevent immoral behavior (absent any plausible theory of harm to entities deserving protections) was an invalid basis for legislation. If a court then

---

[8] DeBartolomeo v. State, 486 A.2d 256, 260 (Md. 1984); *Dronenurg v. Zech*, 741 F.2d 1388, 1397 (D.C. Cir. 1984).

[9] In South Dakota, for example, engaging in a sexual act with an animal is a Class 6 felony, punishable by up to two years in prison. S.D. Codified Laws §§ 22–22–42, 22–6–1 (2007).

[10] Perhaps the comedy show *Ali G* is a poor authority, but in one episode Borat explains that in Kazakhstan his job was to bring animals to orgasm for breeding.

[11] "Due process" is mainly a matter of fair procedure. How far the Due Process clauses of the Fifth and Fourteenth Amendments *should* be used to review the substantive bases for legislation is controversial among scholars and justices.

[12] See, e.g., *Williamson v. Lee Optical Co.*, 348 U.S. 483 (1955).

[13] One can imagine some sort of weighing process in which the quality of the actions restricted would influence evaluation of the reasons for restriction.

decided that a prohibition on bestiality was grounded on such a wish, it would not matter whether the moral opinion was religious or not.

This illustration shows why, for practical purposes, the due process approach has advantages over the establishment approach. Whatever may have been the origins of feelings about human beings having sexual relations with other species, most people now would react that they are seriously degrading without reference to specific religious views. For many subjects, people might be hard put to say how far their feelings of revulsion depend on religious premises and how far they rest on nonreligious intuitions or cultural sentiments. Yet the Establishment Clause approach requires such distinctions.[14]

The second alternative constitutional argument is cast in terms of oppressed groups. The idea is that regulation violates equal protection of the law. Laws against interracial marriage violate equal protection;[15] laws against intragender marriage could be similarly viewed, since homosexuals as a group have long suffered discrimination by the majority. For this alternative argument, one needs to find a group that has suffered historical discrimination, something easier to do with abortion laws and limits on the privileges of gay couples than with fornication and bestiality. In any event, these last few paragraphs are a caution that Establishment Clause challenges to laws in our last two categories are only one kind of constitutional claim against their validity, and perhaps far from the most promising.

Our two crucial inquiries for Establishment Clause analysis are (1) whether laws that are directed against behavior just because it is immoral promote or endorse religion; and (2) what the connection would need to be between religious premises and a law's enactment to generate an invalid establishment of religion. On the question of promotion or endorsement, we need to assume that the reason legislators prohibit behavior is not because it bears a close relation to what they consider to be distinctive and desirable religious practices. Arnold Loewy has hypothesized a law requiring attendance at Methodist church on Sunday because it is immoral not to go to that church[16] and a law forbidding all members of society from driving vehicles during the Jewish Sabbath.[17] The first of these is obviously unconstitutional because it requires attendance at particular worship services; the connection

---

[14] The strength of that approach is that it fits comfortably with notions of improper religious purposes. It is harder to say that the Due Process clauses do not allow prohibitions that reflect the moral sentiments of society.

[15] Loving v. Virginia, 388 U.S. 1 (1967).

[16] Arnold H. Loewy, "Morals Legislation and the Establishment Clause," 55 *Alabama Law Review* 159, 166 (2003).

[17] Id. at 164.

of the second law to Sabbath observance is also probably strong enough to make it a promotion of that religious practice.[18] Laws against homosexual acts and bestiality are not quite like this. The legislators regard the behavior as wrongful whenever it is engaged in, and refraining from the behavior does not, in itself, involve any strong connection to anyone's religious practices.[19]

The two contrasting positions about laws that forbid behavior just because it is immoral, according to a religious view, are that (1) to enforce the morality of a religion *is* to promote and endorse that religion[20] and (2) to enforce morality is different from promoting religion, and it has always been assumed that legislatures can enforce the dominant morality in society.[21] I think a more discriminating analysis is needed.[22] Let us suppose that the overwhelming basis for a restriction is a religious view that behavior is wrong. So long as it is clear that all legislators want to do is to stop the behavior, their aim is not to promote the religious practices of a particular religion. Whether citizens will take the law as expressing approval of a particular religion may depend on circumstances, and particularly whether the religious perspective about morality that wins enforcement is sharply at odds with the moral views of others. Whether a particular religion is or is not implicitly approved, I believe that requiring people to comply with the moral code of a religion, absent any belief about ordinary harm to entities deserving protection, is a kind of imposition of that religious view on others. Thus, as a matter of theoretical principle, I think enactment of a religious morality could violate the Establishment Clause, even if the religion, as a set of beliefs and religious practices, is not promoted or endorsed in the more straightforward sense.

This comparatively modest view of when enforcement of a religiously based morality might be regarded as violating the Establishment Clause does not take us very far in a practical sense, because we have yet to examine possible differences between our fourth and fifth categories and to consider the appropriate role of courts reviewing legislation. Were a legislator to con-

---

[18] Loewy thinks that the strongest permissible argument for the ordinance would be to protect the safety of the larger than usual number of pedestrians.

[19] Of course, one *might* view refraining from sinful acts as parts of religious practice.

[20] Loewy, note 16 supra, at 161, concludes that a law should be held to violate the Establishment Clause if it "simply condemns the activity because it is immoral."

[21] See Michael Perry, "Why Political Reliance on Religiously Grounded Morality Does Not Violate the Establishment Clause," 42 *William and Mary Law Review* 663 (2001); Scott L. Idleman, "Religious Premises, Legislative Judgments, and the Establishment Clause," 12 *Cornell Journal of Law and Public Policy* 1 (2002). Professor Idleman provides an extensive review of relevant cases and competing scholarly opinions.

[22] See Greenawalt, note 3 supra, at 87–95.

sider bestiality to be a grave sin even though he does not believe it typically causes any damage in this life to voluntary human participants and causes only a very slight impairment of the interests of the animals, his rationale for prohibiting it would fall into our fifth category. A law adopted by all legislators for just this reason would violate the Establishment Clause, and, according to my earlier analysis, a single legislator who voted for just this reason would either himself violate the Establishment Clause, or would violate the spirit of the Establishment Clause, by engaging in a course of action that would, if replicated by his fellows, violate the Establishment Clause.

But suppose our legislator, instead, reasons as follows. My religion condemns sexual relations with animals. This is substantial evidence that such relations probably do harm human participants in this life, giving them a degraded sense of themselves and impairing their possibilities of healthy sexual relations with other people. (We can understand a similar argument about why frequent sexual relations with prostitutes have a detrimental effect on committed relationships.) As we have seen in respect to harm to third persons (and a future human sexual partner might be regarded as a relevant third person here), such a factual conclusion might or might not be grounded on the theological truth of the religion. Even if it is grounded on the truth of the religion, I have suggested that people should be as free to rely on their religious convictions as on nonreligious intuitions in respect to factual questions about which science or social science provide no convincing answers. If the evidence is scanty on what happens to otherwise healthy individuals who happen to engage in sexual relations with animals[23]—we might imagine shepherds left alone with flocks of sheep for many months—one would expect citizens and legislators to rely on their own senses about likely consequences. Many of them would not easily distinguish their religiously informed sense from the intuitions they would have otherwise. Once we acknowledge that religion may properly play a role in influencing judgment about harms to voluntary actors, we can see just how narrow is our last category—prohibition because an act is morally wrong, but without a belief in ordinary harmful consequences.

A further clarification narrows that category even further. We have touched in other chapters on arguments that a liberal society should not make judgments about the good life. These arguments are closely similar to J. S. Mill's principle in *On Liberty* that the government has no business

---

[23] The evidence could not be drawn from a random selection of those who engage in bestiality in a modern society, because, very likely, those who do so in a culture in which it is so condemned may be psychologically unhealthy to begin with.

constraining self-regarding acts. That principle rules out paternalistic legislation designed to protect actors against their own misguided choices. Neither neutrality about the good life nor antipaternalism has ever been an accepted premise of actual liberal democracies or of our constitutional law. Further, were either of these principles to be adopted as part of our constitutional law, the logical vehicle would be some form of substantive due process, *not* the Establishment Clause. The reason is simple. Paternalism and judgments about the good life can flow from nonreligious as well as religious sources. Neither of these proposed restraints on legislative action would be limited to religious visions about the good life or about the need to protect actors from themselves. If it continues to be true that neither of these controversial principles becomes part of our constitutional law, then the factual reasons that our fourth category embraces would include factual claims that relate to "the good life" and to the need for paternalism. People could rely on religious convictions that inform their factual judgments about healthy forms of life and desirable protections against bad choices.

The division between our last two categories—is a practice thought to cause ordinary harm to participants or not?—has implications for government officials. Suppose a legislator thinks that bestiality is definitely a sin and probably has adverse psychological consequences for human participants. In deciding whether to vote for criminalization, the legislator should not count his simple judgment about sin; rather he should ask if the likely adverse consequences are sufficient to justify making the behavior a crime. It is possible that if he performs this exercise conscientiously, he will see that the legitimate reasons for voting to criminalize are weaker than he initially thought, that if he discounts his "pure" judgment of sin, he does not believe the probable consequences are damaging enough to warrant a prohibition.

But what is a court to do? We can roughly sketch out three possible standards for judicial application of the Establishment Clause.[24] (1) A law violates the Establishment Clause if religious convictions were influential in its adoption. (2) A law violates the Establishment Clause if "a substantial number of religious skeptics" would not have supported it.[25] (3) A law violates the Establishment Clause if the ascertainable dominant reason for its passage was a view that acts are immoral, based on a religious point of view and detached from any perspective about harm in this life that would be sufficient to justify a prohibition or regulation. The third position is my own. Given

---

[24] I put aside here fact-sensitive appraisals that a particular law strongly, if indirectly, endorses some religion.

[25] Loewy, note 16, supra.

all the other ways religious judgments can figure in legislative choice, given the mixture of religious and nonreligious reasons individuals may have, given the mixture of reasons different legislators bring to bear, and given the deference courts do and should show to legislative decisions, this approach will rarely, if ever, lead a court to invalidate a law.

The first approach is much too broad. Religious convictions figure in many appropriate ways in the judgments of citizens and legislators. For that reason and because of considerations of deference, much too much legislation would be held invalid were religious influence sufficient to render laws invalid.

The second approach may seem more promising. If a court asks whether a substantial number of skeptics would support the legislation, that seems reasonably deferential to the legislature. The court is not applying a fine-tooth comb to the legislative process or trying to pry apart mixed motives. If few skeptics would support legislation, is not that a sure indication that religious convictions underlie it? This approach, however, founders on three objections. The first objection is that it will not be easy to decide whether the number of skeptics would be substantial, and to decide what number counts as "substantial." The second objection involves the connection between religious grounds and nonreligious ones. Suppose it were determined that the number of skeptics who would restrict embryonic stem cell research is not substantial. Suppose it were also determined that many serious Roman Catholics believe with Robert George that the wrongness of such stem cell research can be established on nonreligious "scientific" or natural law grounds. A substantial number of citizens do believe the wrongness of research need not depend on religious convictions. Are we to label these citizens as dishonest or deluded, to say that their self-consciously nonreligious understanding doesn't count because they have a religious understanding with the same import for legal regulation and *we know* that the latter drives the former? That is not an approach that is very respectful of fellow citizens, and it is not the kind of judgment a court should be essaying.

The third objection takes us back to the various ways religious convictions can figure. Professor Loewy puts forward his test as an application of a principle that the legislature cannot simply condemn an activity because it is immoral. That sounds like our fifth category. But it is possible that many people with religious convictions will believe, reasonably or not, that an activity (such as marriages of people of the same gender) will have harmful enough consequences to justify a prohibition, although few skeptics will agree. In their minds, these religious people would not be forbidding the activity simply because it is immoral; they think they would be protecting people from harm.

Having argued that many reliances on religious convictions are appropriate, I do not accept a standard that would render laws invalid if few skeptics would support them. I have resisted the idea that all legislation of religious morality is constitutional, but, as far as courts are concerned, and apart from situations in which a religion or a specific religious outlook is promoted or endorsed, the limits on appropriate grounds for laws are too narrow to have much practical significance.

CHAPTER 25

Conclusion

In our final five chapters, we have moved from discrete topics of legal significance to more general theories about the scope of the Free Exercise and Establishment clauses and about how far religious convictions should figure in the politics of liberal democracies. These chapters may serve partly as a reminder that no sharp boundary line separates constitutional law from related ideas in political philosophy that do not generate legal constraints. The chapters also raise an implicit question about how much theorizing may be done about liberal democracies in gross, and how far persuasive resolutions depend on the history, culture, and makeup of particular societies. This is a question that is particularly sharp in respect to degrees of establishment of religion, because liberal democracies vary so greatly in their treatment of that broad topic.

That citizens should enjoy the free exercise of religion is a foundational principle for all liberal democracies, enshrined in various international treatises. There are differences among countries about exactly what counts as *the practice* of religion and over how far forms of religious practice are protected against neutral laws of general application; but all agree that people cannot be penalized because of their religious convictions or discouraged from religious practices because the government is hostile to their religious understanding.

Things are different with establishment. Most Western European countries continue to have established religions, although both as a consequence of legal change and the diminishing religiosity of the populations, these establishments have grown increasingly less influential in the life of their societies. Great differences exist among liberal democracies in the extent to which religious education figures in state schools and to which governments help finance private religious education. Some of the variations among countries may provoke second thoughts about how the U.S. Constitution should be understood or about whether the resolution of our constitutional issues represents a desirable approach for any liberal democracy. This volume has concentrated on the basic law and historical setting of our country, but in reviewing the broad topics we have considered, I will comment briefly on how conclusions reached in various chapters are ones I would generalize as desirable approaches for liberal democracies in general.

A number of chapters have dealt with expressions by government regarding religion. We have seen that the Establishment Clause precludes federal and state governments from endorsing the truth of particular religious positions (though in asserting the soundness of various scientific, historical, and ethical claims, government officers, including teachers, may implicitly indicate that opposing religious views are false). In public schools, and in other domains, governments may teach *about* religion, providing information and insights that do not depend on contested claims about theological truth. Public schools may not themselves sponsor devotional practices, though they may allow voluntary religious clubs to use school facilities. States may not endorse particular religious views through symbolic representations such as crèches in courthouses.

All these conclusions implicate a broader principle, namely that government should keep itself out of the business of promoting religious ideas. According to this principle, religion is distinctive, in the sense that governments are subject to an incapacity in respect to religion that does not apply to the broad range of subjects of human concern. That religion is special in this way is based on the importance of religious liberty for citizens, the incompetence of government officials with respect to religion, and the dangers both to religion and to government if public officials intrude into the spiritual domain.

Subject to certain qualifications, I believe the principle that government should not promote religious ideas is a sound one for liberal democracies in general. The qualifications are these. Governments properly involve themselves directly in religious practice when a failure to do so would inhibit the free exercise of religion of persons who do not have access to the ordinary resources of civil society. This qualification justifies the government providing religious resources to military personnel and prisoners. A second qualification is that the government may indirectly and unintentionally promote a religious view to some degree when it celebrates certain historic events. Recounting the landing of the Pilgrims on the shores of Massachusetts or the settlement of the Salt Lake region, or representing those events in paintings in government buildings, may convey something favorable about Pilgrim or Mormon religion. Making Martin Luther King, Jr.'s birthday a holiday may convey an implicitly favorable view about his religious understanding. Some such connections are inevitable in a country whose history is suffused with influential religious movements and with crucial actions motivated (at least partly) by religious convictions. In my view, this second qualification definitely does not cover school systems having their students reciting "under God" in the Pledge of Allegiance.

A third qualification concerns the hold of traditional culture. In a country in which religious ideas or symbolism, or both, have long been associated with the government, one cannot expect a complete break once the principle of "no sponsorship of religion" begins to take hold, whether as a political principle or a doctrine of constitutional law. In my mind, this is the real explanation for acceptance of what I have called "mild endorsements," not the implausible claim that such practices as Thanksgiving Day and "under God" no longer carry any religious significance. This qualification differs from the previous two in that ideally, over time, these milder endorsements will get weaker and weaker and will eventually disappear within liberal democracies.

A fourth qualification concerns only some liberal democracies. A country *may* understand its present identity as very closely related to a particular religion. That is undoubtedly true of Israel, though most of its citizens are not religious, and is probably true of Saudi Arabia. A country can, overall, be a liberal democracy even if the government to some degree reflects and reinforces a particular religion, and Israel qualifies as a liberal democracy in this way. Such a country may regard continued confirmation of its religious identity as more important than the reasons for detaching government from religion. I believe such a choice does involve a degree of sacrifice of liberal democratic principles. In respect to religion, such a country fulfills a model of liberal democracy less well than an otherwise similar democratic country that is not promoting religion; but to say that a choice involves some sacrifice of liberal democratic principles is not necessarily to conclude that the choice is wrong.

When we turn to financial aid going from government to religion, we have distinguished aid based on criteria other than religion from aid given to religious groups as such. In respect to endeavors such as hospitals, adoption agencies, and drug rehabilitation programs, religious groups should be treated as similar to other private, nonprofit providers; but a state needs to make sure there is some available nonreligious provider, so that people are not forced to participate in a religious program if they do not wish. In the United States, the government should require both that a religious provider offer the service to all comers regardless of their own religion and that employment for providing the funding service typically not be based on religious criteria. (However, selection for some positions should be allowed according to religious criteria if the aim of the program is to generate religious transformation—as with some drug rehabilitation programs.) In regard to direct aid at least, government should not finance the religious aspects of programs with secular benefits.

For many years, the Supreme Court has treated schools as special, and, given the vital role of public schools in this country, and the sense that religious education is not far from the core of religious activity, I have concluded that the strong shift toward permitting substantial state aid to flow to private religious schools, so long as the aid is in the form of indirect voucher payments, is regrettable. I have taken this position despite the appeal of the arguments that the state should be able to aid all nonprofit schools equally and that parents who want a religious education for their religion should not have to bear a heavy extra burden in addition to paying ordinary taxes for public schools.

For ordinary services, such as hospitals and adoption agencies, treating religious providers equally with all other nonprofit providers is an appropriate resolution for all liberal democracies, but one can imagine variations in the precise conditions that should be set for public aid. Suppose a country was about equally divided among adherents of religion A, adherents of religion B, and nonreligious citizens, and that the area of the country was small enough in relation to its population so that otherwise comparable hospitals run by groups A and B as well as secular hospitals were conveniently available for all citizens. In that setting (quite different from the United States), it *might* make sense to allow the religious hospitals to discriminate by religion in admissions (for nonemergency cases) and (if the potential employees were divided in roughly the same percentage as the population) to be free to choose employees by religion. On these matters, one could not generalize across the entire spectrum of liberal democracies.

That caution is even more true about religious education. Countries have different traditions about the place of public and religious schools, and despite the long-term trend toward movement of workers among countries, most countries remain ethnically and religiously more homogeneous than the United States. For those countries, creating a common citizenry out of highly diverse elements may be somewhat less important than it is here. Different attitudes about public support of private education, including religious education, are consistent with full acceptance of principles of liberal democracy, although, whatever a country's historical tradition in this respect, it should now move toward treating other nonprofit private schools on the same basis as it treats religious schools.

The American approach is that principles of nonestablishment preclude aid to religion as such. The government cannot spend money in order to help religions perform their religious functions. This is far from a uniform view among existing liberal democracies, many of which do provide forms of assistance to established churches or to a broader array of religious entities;

but it is my view that such aid does not fit well with the fundamental idea of nonsponsorship that should be drawn from the basic conception of liberal democracy.

I have treated tax exemptions as different from aid, as does our law. Because exemptions are one way to detach religious institutions from government, they may be granted specifically to religious groups; but the appropriateness, and possibly the constitutionality, of most such exemptions depends on their being granted to a broad category of charitable and educational activities within which religious activities fall, rather than being restricted to religion alone.

This brings us to other kinds of exemptions, permissions to engage in practices, such as using peyote, that are forbidden to other citizens, or to refrain from satisfying general obligations, such as military duty and jury service. These kinds of exemptions have taken up a large portion of volume 1 as well as chapters in this volume. I strongly believe that such exemptions are often appropriate, and I would extend this conclusion to all liberal democracies. They should all accord respect to religious conscience, and religious exercise, and that respect should include allowing certain actions that are generally prohibited, if the public need to compel people against religious conscience and inclination is not strong.

This conclusion itself leaves open three fundamental, if subsidiary, questions. Should such concessions to conscience be matters of constitutional right or decided by legislative choice? Should such concessions also be extended to those with powerful nonreligious reasons to engage in similar behavior? Should a right to some concessions of this sort be viewed as a fundamental human right recognized in international law? I have contended that in the United States, contrary to the Supreme Court's present free exercise jurisprudence, more than a few accommodations against neutral laws should be regarded as included in the constitutional protection of free exercise. *In general*, persons with similarly compelling nonreligious reasons (the nonreligious conscientious objector to military service is a leading example) should be treated similarly, but, both because some religious claims are never or rarely replicated by nonreligious ones and because the feasibility of excluding fraudulent claims is an important consideration, sometimes legislatures and courts appropriately limit exemptions to those whose basis is religious. Principles of liberal democracy leave open a great deal of latitude in the assignment of responsibilities to legislatures and courts, and in the degree to which a written constitution will restrict choices made by a legislature. The exact allocation for which I have argued may not be best for all liberal democracies, even for all of them with written constitutions that include religious exercise or conscience among their protected rights. I have not addressed at all what should count as an international human right in this respect, but I do believe that some exemptions—including one from compelled military service—should be recognized in this way.

The final two chapters of this book well illustrate my conviction that in political philosophy, as well as constitutional law, much depends on a country's history and culture and on the identities and activities of its citizens. Whether, and how far, citizens and officials should try to stick "to public reasons" in their political judgments and discourse depends a good deal on a country's religious makeup and the level of mutual tolerance and respect that it enjoys. My conclusions about what now makes most sense in the United States are not intended to be generalizations for all liberal democratic political orders.

Principles of free exercise and nonestablishment are fundamental aspects of our country's legal and political orders. We understand that avoiding establishment of religion can sometimes seem to be in conflict with promoting free exercise, but that across most of the coverage of the two clauses, the free exercise of religion is fully compatible with nonestablishment; and that nonestablishment is strongly conducive to religious liberty. People differ sharply over the proper boundaries of constitutional rights under the religion clauses. I have both defended the broad strokes of the Supreme Court's "no hindrance—no aid" approach to the clauses against proposals that would radically shift the constitutional focus, and have sharply criticized some recent Court decisions as insensitive to the basic values underlying the conceptions of free exercise and nonestablishment.

It is in the nature of fundamental constitutional principles that their full content is never settled once and for all. One aspect of our culture, in which religious liberty greatly matters, is that scholars, lawyers, and laypersons ask themselves from time to time just how the religion clauses of our Constitution should best be understood. Asking questions about that understanding, not in the abstract but by focusing on concrete issues in context, has been the burden of these two volumes.

INDEX